Infinite Greed

....

INSURRECTIONS: CRITICAL STUDIES IN RELIGION,
POLITICS, AND CULTURE

INSURRECTIONS: CRITICAL STUDIES IN RELIGION, POLITICS, AND CULTURE

Slavoj Žižek, Clayton Crockett, Creston Davis, Jeffrey W. Robbins, Editors

The intersection of religion, politics, and culture is one of the most discussed areas in theory today. It also has the deepest and most wide-ranging impact on the world. Insurrections: Critical Studies in Religion, Politics, and Culture will bring the tools of philosophy and critical theory to the political implications of the religious turn. The series will address a range of religious traditions and political viewpoints in the United States, Europe, and other parts of the world. Without advocating any specific religious or theological stance, the series aims nonetheless to be faithful to the radical emancipatory potential of religion.

What Does Europe Want? The Union and Its Discontents, Slavoj Žižek and Srećko Horvat

Harmattan: A Philosophical Fiction, Michael Jackson

Nietzsche Versus Paul, Abed Azzam

Christo-Fiction: The Ruins of Athens and Jerusalem, François Laruelle

Paul's Summons to Messianic Life: Political Theology and the Coming Awakening, L. L. Welborn

Reimagining the Sacred: Richard Kearney Debates God with James Wood, Catherine Keller, Charles Taylor, Julia Kristeva, Gianni Vattimo, Simon Critchley, Jean-Luc Marion, John Caputo, David Tracy, Jens Zimmermann, and Merold Westphal, edited by Richard Kearney and Jens Zimmermann

A Hedonist Manifesto: The Power to Exist, Michel Onfray

An Insurrectionist Manifesto: Four New Gospels for a Radical Politics, Ward Blanton, Clayton Crockett, Jeffrey W. Robbins, and Noëlle Vahanian

The Intimate Universal: The Hidden Porosity Among Religion, Art, Philosophy, and Politics, William Desmond

Heidegger: His Life and His Philosophy, Alain Badiou and Barbara Cassin, translated by Susan Spitzer

The Work of Art: Rethinking the Elementary Forms of Religious Life, Michael Jackson

Sociophobia: Political Change in the Digital Utopia, César Rendueles, translated by Heather Cleary

There's No Such Thing as a Sexual Relationship: Two Lessons on Lacan, Alain Badiou and Barbara Cassin, translated by Susan Spitzer and Kenneth Reinhard

Unbearable Life: A Genealogy of Political Erasure, Arthur Bradley

Accidental Agents: Ecological Politics Beyond the Human, Martin Crowley

Energy and Change: A New Materialist Cosmotheology, Clayton Crockett

For a complete list of titles, see the Columbia University Press website

Infinite Greed

The Inhuman Selfishness of Capital

Adrian Johnston

Columbia University Press

New York

Columbia University Press
Publishers Since 1893
New York   Chichester, West Sussex
cup.columbia.edu

Copyright © 2024 Columbia University Press
All rights reserved

Library of Congress Cataloging-in-Publication Data

Names: Johnston, Adrian, 1983– author.
Title: Infinite greed : the inhuman selfishness of capital / Adrian Johnston.
Description: New York : Columbia University Press, [2024] | Series: Insurrections: critical studies in religion, politics, and culture | Includes bibliographical references and index.
Identifiers: LCCN 2023049507 (print) | LCCN 2023049508 (ebook) | ISBN 9780231214728 (hardback) | ISBN 9780231214735 (trade paperback) | ISBN 9780231560436 (ebook)
Subjects: LCSH: Economics—Psychological aspects. | Capitalism—Psychological aspects. | Profit—Psychological aspects. | Self-sacrifice. | Self-interest.
Classification: LCC HB74.P8 J646 2024 (print) | LCC HB74.P8 (ebook) | DDC 330.1—dc23/eng/20240126
LC record available at https://lccn.loc.gov/2023049507
LC ebook record available at https://lccn.loc.gov/2023049508

Cover design: Milenda Nan Ok Lee
Cover art: Chronicle / Alamy

For Jeremi and Mike—a lifetime of friendship

For capitalism is already essentially abolished once we assume that it is enjoyment that is the driving motive and not enrichment itself.

—Karl Marx

It is only the phallus that is happy—not the bearer of said.

—Jacques Lacan

Contents

Preface. Self-Destructive Selfishness: Devouring Its Own Children   xi

Acknowledgments   xxiii

Introduction. Infrastructural Analysis:
Remarrying Marxism and Psychoanalysis   1

1. The Conflicted Political Animal:
The Psychoanalytic Body and the Body Politic   8

2. From Closed Need to Infinite Greed: Marxian Drives   90

3. The Self-Cleaning Fetish:
Repression Under the Shadow of Fictitious Capital   158

4. The Triumph of Theological Economics:
God Goes Underground   201

Conclusion. Real Reduction: It's the Stupid Economy!   243

......

Notes   289

Bibliography   333

Index   353

Preface

Self-Destructive Selfishness: Devouring Its Own Children

Selfishness is supposed to be essential to capitalism. If there is one thing that capitalism's critics and defenders alike agree upon, this would be it. Critics lament the capitalistic valorization of personal self-enrichment. They bemoan the privileging of the acquisitive individual above all else, usually in finger-wagging moralistic terms. These anticapitalists see conscious intentions preoccupied with zero-sum competition and amassed wealth as malicious. Correspondingly, they denounce the actions flowing from such intentions as socially corrosive, if not also environmentally detrimental.

Capitalism's defenders typically do not deny that the system they champion is arranged around the monetarily steered greed of private persons. Instead, they tend to employ a two-pronged rebuttal in responding to complaints about the selfishness at the heart of capitalism. According to the first prong of this well-worn rebuttal, they maintain that humans are, by eternal nature, incorrigibly selfish. Given this, leftist dreams of a body politic in which individuals voluntarily prioritize the collective good over their own good(s) are just that, namely, hopelessly unrealistic utopian fantasies. Considering this assessment of what is hypothesized to form an inherent part of "human nature," any attempts to create a selfless, public-spirited "New Man" through either reform or revolution are, at best, doomed to be ineffective. At worst, these attempts bottom out in the horrific brutality of totalitarianism, terror, and the gulag.

Then, as the second prong of this rebuttal, such advocates and apologists for capitalism go on to insist that humanity's incurable natural selfishness is to be embraced and celebrated rather than regretted and curbed. Classically liberal defenses of capitalism along these lines often cite a certain remark from Adam

Smith's *The Wealth of Nations*—"It is not from the benevolence of the butcher, the brewer, or the baker that we expect our dinner, but from their regard to their own interest. We address ourselves, not to their humanity but to their self-love, and never talk to them of our own necessities but of their advantages."[1] Such more traditional defenses are likely also to invoke Bernard Mandeville's *The Fable of the Bees*, with its refrain about private vices being public virtues.

Less historically informed versions of this procapitalist transubstantiation of selfishness from vice into virtue might appeal instead to the popular-culture figure of Gordon Gekko, the cinematic financier played by Michael Douglas in the 1987 Oliver Stone film *Wall Street*. In a famous speech in this film, Gekko declares, "Greed, for lack of a better word, is good." The fictional Gekko's speech about greed in capitalism is based on an actual speech by the all-too-real stockbroker Ivan Boesky, who was convicted in 1987 of insider trading.

Whether in its classical liberal (referring to the likes of Mandeville and Smith) or contemporary neoliberal (referring to the likes of Boesky and Gekko, not to mention Milton Friedman et al.) guises, this line of argumentation proposes that individuals' ruthless pursuit of their own self-interests does not undermine any greater good. Quite the opposite—this pursuit is said to contribute to a rising tide of materialistic quality of life, a tide raised up by a benevolent invisible hand, which allegedly lifts all boats (thanks to technological innovation, consumer price competition, trickle-down effects, philanthropy, and so on). What is more, with the proper combination of a minimum number of regulatory sticks and carrots wisely legislated by a light-touch laissez-faire state, the potent, ineradicable natural forces of human greed and selfishness can be harnessed by society, can be socially tamed and domesticated, so as to create a viable and enduring collective order of peaceful economic and political agonism (rather than violent antagonism).

Anticapitalists, often but not always coming from the left, generally focus on contesting the procapitalists' claims about the beneficial collective effects of harnessing selfishness (as self-interest, greed, acquisitiveness, etc. specifically oriented toward money and commodities). But such anticapitalists do not contest the assumption, one they share with procapitalists, that capitalism panders to human selfishness, whether for better (as per the procapitalist right) or worse (as per the anticapitalist left). One of my primary aims in this book is to refute this assumption common to critics and defenders of capitalism past and present. As I will argue, the logic of capital both demands multiple sorts of self-sacrifice from its subjects and is antithetical to the most foundational self-interests of all those caught up in it (regardless of whatever they might think).

PREFACE   xiii

Admittedly, the just-mentioned standard leftist questioning of the purported beneficial effects of capitalism's socially harnessed greed, selfishness, and the like is not without its merits. However, this questioning needs to be taken further. More precisely, the various failures of capitalism to serve and satisfy the material self-interests and psychical well-being of the overwhelming majority of people living under it (whether this majority be labeled the "99 percent," à la Occupy Wall Street, or otherwise identified) should not be taken merely as a defective translation or actualization (at the level of generated effects) of an underlying sociosystemic purpose (as itself a generative cause) to gratify the human selfishness presumably animating the logic of capital. Instead, these failures ought to be interpreted as indicating that capital's fundamental logic in and of itself, as generative cause in capitalist systems, is not oriented toward selfishness. In other words, capitalism's indifference or even hostility to the concerns, interests, needs, wants, and so on of its masses is no accident, mistake, or contingent mistranslation with respect to an imagined abiding intention to foster physical and mental flourishing among a plurality of its people. What, exactly, do I mean?

Forty-plus years of triumphant neoliberal capitalism have produced an array of misfortunes and disasters, ones arguably culminating in the multifaceted misery of today's socioeconomic and geopolitical status quo. The litany of these historically recent setbacks and catastrophes, at both international and country-by-country levels, would be much too long to recite here. For my present prefatory line of thought, I need not try in vain to compose a comprehensive list of the woes of neoliberalism. But one particular effect attributable directly to such capitalism is crucial for my reasoning: the indisputable fact of there being drastically widening gaps of wealth inequality within individual nations as well as across the world as a whole.

According to an October 2020 Credit Suisse Global Wealth Report, the world's richest 1 percent of people own 43.4 percent of total global wealth, while those with less than $10,000 in monetary or other resources, constituting 53.6 percent of the world's overall population, own just over 1.4 percent of total global wealth. Moreover, the top 0.002 percent of the world's wealthiest individuals possesses 6.2 percent of total global wealth.[2] In other words, nowadays roughly half of humanity owns nothing or next to nothing while, correspondingly, a tiny sliver of humanity controls almost half the world's aggregate assets. Succinctly put, half have nothing, and a handful have half.

There is no uncertainty or dispute about the glaringly evident reality that today's material inequality either already has surpassed or is in the process of surpassing the wealth gaps of over a century ago, those associated with the era of the Robber Barons. Today's capitalism is even on the cusp of producing its first trillionaires, whose very existence will be an appalling affront to any idea of social justice. After nearly half a century of running amok thanks to aggressive deregulation and related neoliberal policies, the turbulent flows of multinational capital have deposited humanity on the shores of a socioeconomic and geopolitical environment prompting observers of various political stripes to draw ominous comparisons between today and the Gilded Age, the Belle Époque, and the eve of World War I. A few commentators go so far as to characterize our present circumstances as even more regressive, as "neofeudal." We still are flailing about to find ways adequately to capture in words and concepts the rapidly emerging unprecedented extremes of twenty-first-century capitalism.

I remain doubtful that the combination of shockingly grotesque wealth inequality and a prominent minority of rentiers (from the old real-world landlords of the landed aristocracy to the new online landlords of Big Tech) warrants claiming that contemporary capitalism has morphed into neofeudalism, that we have left behind the capitalist mode of production. Rents, whether extracted from parcels of land and concrete buildings or internet pages and cloud storage space, remain only a portion of the surplus value generated out of the unpaid working time of commodified labor power as exploited within industrial (rather than financial or virtual) capitalist activity. Industrial capitalists use this appropriated surplus value to pay not only profits to themselves and rents to the internet's landlords but also rents to traditional terra firma, bricks-and-mortar landlords as well as interest to financiers and taxes to governments. Karl Marx himself, throughout his historical-materialist critique of political economy, already registers the continued existence of various types of rentiers and foresees the rise of monopolies (whether in the guise of Standard Oil or of Google) within the specifically capitalist mode of production. Indeed, and as I will illustrate throughout much of this book, Marx's economic analyses of capitalism remain incredibly timely, perhaps never more so than now. This is thanks to us in the twenty-first century having collectively slid back into the Dickensian-style rapacious capitalism of Marx's nineteenth century.

Certain commentators' recourse to the notion of neofeudalism is understandable. This recourse charitably can be interpreted as a justifiable attempt to register in theory the unique awfulness of cutting-edge ongoing trends in present-day capitalism. Alain Badiou, likewise responding to this same awfulness, feels compelled to recast Marx's "history hitherto"[3] (i.e., the history of unequal class-based societies, up to and including the current moment of capitalist social history) as, in its entirety, an extremely extended version of "the

Neolithic era."[4] Despite—or maybe partly because of—the techno-scientific achievements surrounding us, we remain, as we have for approximately five thousand years now, stuck within the vicious barbarism of societies still predicated on structurally inherent material inequality. The strongest of language is called for so as to begin conveying, however inadequately, the depressing truth that thousands of years of historical "progress" have eventuated in a twenty-first-century here-and-now in which the wealth gaps between classes are widening rather than narrowing—indeed, in which a minuscule fraction of the human race controls the vast bulk of the world's riches and resources.

A dizzying array of myriad harms can and should be traced to today's staggering wealth inequalities, themselves the outcome of capitalism's business as usual. I will not try to catalogue these harms here. Many others have enumerated them better than I could.

But one truth above all others about today's material inequalities within global capitalism deserves stressing in relation to my preceding claims: a system that leaves 90-plus percent of humanity with little to no material wealth or sociopolitical power, that condemns the massive majority of human beings to abject poverty and mute impotence, is really quite lousy at aligning with the self-interests or gratifying the selfishness of members of the species *Homo sapiens*. In relation to this truth, one must never forget how proponents of capitalism tirelessly insist that their preferred socioeconomic order is designed to materially benefit the general populations living under it, not just a privileged elite.

Yet the verdict of recent and not-so-recent economic history regarding this capital-justifying insistence is damning. Capitalism repeatedly fails to meet its own criteria for success by failing to foster the comfort and thriving of a large plurality of its subjects.[5] And these repeated failures are too frequent and persistent to be dismissed as nothing more than aberrant misfirings of an underlying sincere intention to succeed. They should be read instead as bungled actions (i.e., "parapraxes") à la the Freudian psychopathology of everyday life.

One does not even have to be a psychoanalyst to appreciate that if a person continually behaves contrary to their professed aims, ends, or goals, then they probably are not actually animated by these unconvincingly professed *teloi*. The same arguably holds for entire societies. In this case, if capitalist societies fail again and again to yield mass-scale physical and psychological flourishing despite declaring that they intend to succeed at yielding such results, then should one not be, at a minimum, highly skeptical about whether these societies really are organized around such a (merely) declared purpose? How convincing ought one to find protests by capitalism personified along the lines of "I keep meaning to achieve a Gini coefficient close to zero, but I keep arriving at a Gini coefficient close to one"? Especially after several centuries, one would be a fool to be convinced by this type of defensive, self-justifying protest, however worded. "Methinks thou doth protest too much" is the only fitting response here (aside from the cliché "actions speak louder than words").

Admittedly, the very title of this book, *Infinite Greed*, seems to suggest my overt adherence to the thesis according to which capitalism's distinctiveness involves its channeling rather than constraining or combating people's selfishness. Would not the phrase "infinite greed" connote greediness raised to its highest power? Would not the infinitization of selfishness maximally elevate it in intensity or enhance it in extension? The explanation I am about to give of this title and why it does not signal my agreement that selfishness is essential to capitalism brings to light another sense in which the capitalist mode of production is antithetical to people's centering concern on themselves. This sense is more subtle and less obvious than my arguments basing themselves on the majority-harming effects of capitalism.

As I will scrutinize in detail subsequently, Marx characterizes singular people as "bearers" or "personifications" of economic categories (such as class identities with their defining features). At times, this appears to be a strictly methodological feature of Marx's investigations into the capitalist mode of production and its historical genesis. As an exclusively methodological stipulation, saying that individuals are bearers/personifications of economic categories is also implicitly to concede that individuals are always more than just such categories, are richer in attributes and facets than allowed for within the theoretical parameters of the historical-materialist critique of political economy.

Marx's stipulation about the irreducibility of people to economic categories is just one of myriad pieces of evidence rebutting the commonplace accusation according to which his historical materialism is a crude determinism reducing everyone in their entirety to being nothing more than the passive objects of the iron laws of economic history. Yet as the past hundred-plus years of Marxism-after-Marx reveals, this sort of rebuttal of non- or anti-Marxist complaints about Marx's reductive, deterministic "economic essentialism" comes at a high price. It opens the door to supposed Marxists and leftist post-Marxists, in the name of opposing "economism" (i.e., economic reductionism and determinism), latching onto certain of Marx's caveats and qualifications in order to revise Marxism such as to eliminate any privileging of the economy whatsoever. I eventually will bring this book to a close by delineating the theoretical and practical problems with Western Marxist and post-Marxist revisionist defangings and abandonments of classical historical materialism in the name of antieconomism.

It must be acknowledged that reductions and determinations happen not only in theory but also in practice. That is to say, the very being of the social in itself actually can be truly reductive, in addition to our thinking of the social as potentially being falsely reductive. Moreover, from the perspective of the sort of historical consciousness significantly nurtured by Marx's own work, one would have to grant that the degrees of real reductiveness operative within societies vary within and between these societies as well as across the wide expanse of social history—with capitalism à la Marx intrinsically involving especially intense and extensive economic (over)determinations of everyone and everything under the sun.

Marx's countless statements about "alienation" and related phenomena within capitalism indicate that, at least for the capitalist mode of production, people really are reduced to being (almost) wholly just bearers/personifications of roles assigned to them by this particular socioeconomic system, with its peculiar means and relations of production. This holds not only for capitalism's expropriated and exploited, who both are alienated (objective alienation) and tend to feel alienated (subjective alienation) but also for its expropriators and exploiters, who might not feel alienated but who nonetheless effectively are alienated in reality (with capitalists being governed, often unconsciously or against their isolated wills, by the transindividual forces and factors of the economy and attendant social constellations). Because of capitalism's intrinsic and objectively real tendencies toward reducing all entities, people included, to nothing but components of economic relations and operations, Marx's claim about bearing/personifying ought not to be construed from an exclusively methodological or epistemological angle.

Instead, this claim by Marx should be interpreted as part of a social ontology of life under the capitalist mode of production. For capitalism's subjects, their capitalist masks are not just masks, having become their irremovable visages. As I will maintain throughout this book, psychoanalysis offers indispensable assistance to Marxism in theorizing why and how such face transplants succeed in taking among a critical mass of those subjected to capitalism.

Even if one concedes that selfishness is inherent to an invariant, ineradicable human nature, the fashions in which it manifests and operates are inflected by varying sociohistorical contexts. Within the capitalist mode of production, the socially dominant form of selfishness is the greed specific to capitalists. Consumers' cupidity, aroused and stimulated by advertising, branding, planned obsolescence, and so on, is a secondary effect reflecting and serving capitalists' insatiable pursuit of surplus value. Capitalist-specific greediness is a selfishness configured according to the fundamental logic Marx spells out as M-C-M' (money-commodity-more money). Stated with greater precision, this logic expresses this sequence: capital for investment → invested capital as constant capital (land, buildings, machines, tools, materials, etc.) + variable capital (human labor power purchased with wages or salaries) → money equal to the initial outlay of invested capital + surplus value as additional money over and above this outlay (with this surplus, arising out of variable capital as bought and exploited human labor power, to be divided into profit for the capitalist, interest for the financier, rent for the landlord and other rentiers, and taxes for the state).

Human selfishness might be natural, but capitalist greed definitely is not. The motivating structural dynamic of M-C-M' presupposes the historical inventions of money and commodities (including, especially, commodified labor power as the sole source of surplus value) as well as the socially constituted spheres of production, distribution, exchange, and consumption (with these infrastructural spheres also relying on an ensemble of superstructural institutions and beliefs, including cultural, ethical, legal, moral, philosophical, political, and religious frameworks). In fact, capitalism's greed, as M-C-M', is a political-economic apparatus directly grafted onto the libidinal economies of capitalists and indirectly grafted onto the libidinal economies of consumers. Through this grafting, capital's subjects do not so much bear or personify as embody and live the impersonal, faceless logic of capital.

What is more, selfishness specifically as capitalist greed qua M-C-M' is "infinite" (as per my title *Infinite Greed*) by virtue of the mathematization of this selfishness through its monetary mediation. A standard purposive telos has an end in both senses of the word "end," namely, an aim or goal that also is a stopping point once reached (with the quotidian notion of greed assuming it to be finite greed insofar as it would have an end as per a traditional teleological conception of human agents' intentions and actions). However, "more money" (M') would be, from this perspective, a nonstandard telos insofar as the accumulation of additional quantities of currency, precisely as quantitative, has no finite end.

Just as the counting of numbers on a number line can go on ceaselessly, so too is there no stopping point, no unsurpassable limit or ultimate apex, for the accumulation of surplus value. One always can have more money. And, according to the very logic of capital, no capitalist ever has enough money. The end-that-is-not-an-end of M' simply sends the capitalist back to the beginning of the sequence M-C-M', with him/her being compelled to repeat the movement again (and again and again . . .). The buck never stops. Money never sleeps. And this leaves everyone under capitalism perpetually prostrate.

M-C-M′ is not a finite linear teleology with beginning, middle, and end but an endlessly repeating loop. It is a perpetual-motion merry-go-round. If the concept of "repetition compulsion" (*Wiederholungszwang*) from psychoanalytic drive theory has any sociopolitical application, this is it. Indeed, M-C-M′ is the drive (*Trieb*), albeit one relying on largely exogenous rather than purely endogenous elements, of capitalists and capitalism as a whole. This is so according not only to an apparently anachronistic psychoanalytic interpretation of Marx's critique of political economy but also, as will be seen later, literally according to Marx.

The infinitude of the supposed "end" of capitalist greed means that no capitalist can gratify their greed insofar as gratification entails reaching a determinate resting state, arriving at the placid repose of satiety. Likewise, the capitalist's consumers, interpellated by the capitalist's greed, also cannot attain, despite marketing's false promises to the contrary, enough of one or more commodity to thoroughly and enduringly slake the thirst of their capital-stoked covetousness. A fully and finally satisfied capitalist would step off the hamster wheel of M-C-M′ and thereby cease to be a capitalist. Correlatively, a fully and finally satisfied customer, withdrawing from the noisy marketplace into serene contentment, would cease to be a customer (which obviously would interfere with the further accumulation of surplus value for capital). Capitalism is fueled exclusively by sustained dissatisfactions, whether those of the capitalist who never has enough surplus value or those of the consumer who correspondingly never has enough commodities. Satisfaction is antithetical to the reproduction and maintenance of this peculiar socioeconomic system. Only by reproducing perturbing lack, rather than calming fullness, can capitalism reproduce itself. It parasitically feeds on our malaise.

Arguably, gratification, satiety, satisfaction, and similar states physically or mentally register the fulfillment of first-person self-interests for the individuals thus fulfilled. One defensibly could say that such states, even when arising from altruistic concerns and conduct, inevitably involve at least a margin of selfishness broadly construed—if only as the satisfaction of the self-interest motivating one to live up to one's own other-directed ethical principles and moral values. Procapitalists tend quite explicitly to link satisfaction and selfishness, claiming that capitalism is natural and unsurpassable because it delivers a maximum of first-person individual happiness conceived as a mixture of self-involved titillation and creaturely comfort (although this claim looks to be false in the harsh light of, among other considerations, glaringly visible empirical economic evidence).

Yet capitalism is not about selfishness. Its fundamental driving force, the unquenchable thirst for surplus value (i.e., M-C-M′ as the core logic of capital), is a strange selfless greed. This motivating structural dynamic is an acephalous and anonymous prosthetic drive, an impersonal template implanted into those subjected to capitalism. Moreover, this *Gier-als-Trieb*, this depsychologized but animating greed as socially quantified and thereby infinitized, produces dissatisfaction instead of satisfaction, discontent instead of contentment, in those who must bear its burdens and carry out its imperatives.

Capitalism's subjects, rather than selfishly heeding their interests in their own pleasures and well-being, are compelled repeatedly to deliver themselves up to the icy inhumanity, the asubjective indifference, of capital's cold calculations. In myriad ways, everyone living under the thumb of the rule of capital submits themselves or is submitted to the enigmatic, unpredictable authority of the deified invisible hand of the market. This hand really does pull the strings of us as its puppets. Only it enjoys the spectacles it orchestrates, not us as its playthings. Instead, we invariably end up suffering the harmful consequences of its reckless, anarchic games.

Furthermore, capitalism's characteristic infinite greed is a terrible both-are-worse convergence of opposites. It manages to combine religious-like renunciations with libertine excesses. On the renunciative side, capitalists must continually reinvest profits and move where directed by the lashes of intracapitalist competition. Consumers must mortgage their futures via credit and debt as well as endure an abiding, gnawing feeling of emptiness despite or, really, because of their continual acquisition of ever more commodities.

On the excessive side, capitalists wallow in opulent lifestyles and also amass, well beyond their own private consumptive capacities, scandalously large quantities of surplus value. Consumers burn through goods and devour services, leaving behind veritable oceans of detritus and mountains of garbage as if there were no tomorrow. Indeed, there very well might not be a tomorrow, considering how pollution now threatens to bring about multiple environmental disasters and even total ecological collapse.

What is worse, for everyone within capitalism (capitalists, consumers, laborers, rentiers, etc.), libertine excesses, paid for with religious-like renunciations, prove to be profoundly and inevitably unsatisfying. The title of Mary Trump's 2020 book about her uncle and their family, *Too Much and Never Enough*, applies equally well to all capitalists and the rentiers accompanying them (as well as to all others in capitalism and to capitalism as a systemic whole). Each and every obtained M′ or C′ sooner or later generates a disappointment morphing into the expectation of M″ (and then on to M‴, and on again and again, without gratifying closure) or C″ (and C‴ . . .). For all subjects of capital, the augmentation of satisfactions (whether as the accumulation of capital or of commodities) in itself produces the depletion of sacrifices (as the futile chasing of various dragons, alienations objective as well as subjective, effects at odds with actors' purposes and interests, consequences menacing people's livelihoods and even lives, and so on).

My guiding agenda throughout *Infinite Greed* is to develop a psychoanalytic Marxism that illuminates why and how capitalism necessarily does not grant the wishes it nonetheless constantly elicits from those it addresses, sustaining itself through this very process of elicitation. This necessity is caused not only by capitalism's manifest empirical outcomes but also by its latent underlying essence. Additionally, even the most privileged upper-decimal portions of the wealthiest 1 percent of today's capitalism do not escape being seized, manipulated, and left with unscratched (and unscratchable) itches by the invisible hand they faithfully serve.

For several centuries now, those on both the right and left sides of the political spectrum have persistently associated capitalism with selfishness (as involving narcissism, satisfaction, gratification, etc.) and socialism/communism with selflessness (as involving altruism, renunciation, sacrifice, etc.). In the preceding, I have provided a succinct preview of my case against the capitalism-selfishness association. I will be making this case at length in what follows.

Relatedly—this is to combat the association of socialism/communism with selflessness paralleling the one between capitalism and selfishness—would not putting a stop to the reign of capital and its logic via rational collective planning and radically redistributive measures be more compatible with most humans' concerns with their own survival and prospering than the highly unequal socioeconomic status quo and the violent, class-riven history leading up to it? Would not ameliorating the countless agonies of the wretched impoverishment to which the sizable majority of humanity remains condemned be more conducive to "the greatest good for the greatest number" than the present order with its astounding wealth inequality and minute minority of elites? Would not straining to avert a profit-driven ecological apocalypse be more in line with the enlightened self-interest of both individuals and the entire human race than letting a tight-knit cabal of corporations and the ultrarich drive the whole world, themselves included, off a cliff in their blinkered chase after nothing more than higher earnings next fiscal quarter?

If human beings inevitably must be selfish, preoccupied with their self-interests and well-being, then there is only one true choice: communism or inhumanity. Moving beyond capitalism, especially nowadays, is not about a socialist transition to an ideal utopian fantasy of a giant commune of selfless martyrs, a fantasy dreamt up in the coziness of moralizers' armchairs. Such a transition, however far off or unlikely, will be, if ever it comes to pass, about brute survival, about the *conatus* of the species *Homo sapiens*, as the most elementary and basic of all self-interests. It will express the inversion of an old anticommunist slogan: Better red than dead!

Albuquerque, January 2022

Acknowledgments

Over the past several years, I was fortunate to have multiple opportunities to work through the ideas and arguments in this book with both students and audiences at various venues. In terms of students, I especially would like to thank those who participated in courses with me on Marxism, psychoanalysis, and the interrelations between these two fields. I learned a lot from exchanges with these students. They certainly helped me refine and clarify the lines of thought running throughout the present book.

Likewise, participants at talks I gave in recent years based on the contents of this book provided me with insightful and productive feedback. Their questions, comments, and criticisms enabled me to improve and strengthen a number of aspects of this project. I greatly appreciate the following institutions and organizations for having invited me to share my work on Marxism and psychoanalysis: DePaul University, Emory University, the Institute of Philosophy of the Scientific Research Centre of the Slovenian Academy of Sciences and Arts in Ljubljana, the Mahindra Humanities Center at Harvard University, the Psychology and the Other annual conference (hosted by Boston College), the University of Essex, the University of New Mexico, and Villanova University.

Also, early-draft versions of portions of this book have appeared in print. I would like to thank the editors of these book volumes and journal issues for their critical input on this material. I also would like to thank them for allowing revised versions of this content to be included here.

Portions of chapter 1 appeared as "Communism and Ambivalence: Freud, Marxism, and Aggression," in *Critical Theory and Psychoanalysis: From the Frankfurt School to Contemporary Critique*, ed. Jon Mills and Daniel Burston (New York: Routledge, 2022), 26–65; and as "The Drive of Capital: Freudo-Marxism's

Dialectical Materialism," *Filozofski Vestnik* (2023), forthcoming. Portions of chapter 2 appeared as "From Closed Need to Infinite Greed: Marx's Drive Theory," *Continental Thought and Theory: A Journal of Intellectual Freedom* 1, no. 4, special issue, "Reading Marx's *Capital* 150 Years On," ed. Mike Grimshaw and Cindy Zeiher (October 2017): 270–346; and as "The Plumbing of Political Economy: Marxism and Psychoanalysis Down the Toilet," in *Psychoanalysis and the Mind-Body Problem*, ed. Jon Mills (New York: Routledge, 2022), 270–303. Portions of chapter 3 appeared as "Shades of Green: Lacan and Capitalism's Veils," in *Objective Fictions: Philosophy, Psychoanalysis, Marxism*, ed. Adrian Johnston, Boštjan Nedoh, and Alenka Zupančič (Edinburgh: Edinburgh University Press, 2022), 45–63; and as "The Mother of Every Insane Form: Fetishistic Interest and Capitalistic Perversion," *Journal for Cultural Research* (2023), forthcoming. Finally, portions of chapter 4 appeared as "The Triumph of Theological Economics: God Goes Underground," *Philosophy Today* 64, no. 1, special issue "Marxism and New Materialisms" (Winter 2020): 3–50.

This published version of *Infinite Greed* is significantly shorter than the manuscript I initially submitted to Columbia University Press in January 2022. For those interested in what the fuller scope of the original manuscript looked like, several portions I decided to cut because of concerns about length can be found elsewhere. These include: "Capitalism's Implants: A Hegelian Theory of Failed Revolutions," *Crisis and Critique* 8, no. 2, special issue: "The Two-Hundredth Anniversary of Hegel's *Philosophy of Right*," ed. Agon Hamza and Frank Ruda (2021): 122–81 (my original chapter 1); "Humanity, That Sickness: Louis Althusser and the Helplessness of Psychoanalysis," *Crisis and Critique* 2, no. 2, special issue: "*Reading Capital* and *For Marx*: 50 Years Later," ed. Frank Ruda and Agon Hamza (2015): 217–61 (my original chapter 3, coming between the present book's first and second chapters); "'I Am Nothing, but I Make Everything': Marx, Lacan, and the Labor Theory of Suture," in *Parallax: The Dependence of Reality on Its Subjective Constitution*, ed. Dominik Finkelde, Christoph Menke, and Slavoj Žižek (London: Bloomsbury, 2021), 173–84 (also part of my original chapter 3); and, "'A Mass of Fools and Knaves': Psychoanalysis and the World's Many Asininities," in *Psychoanalytic Reflections on Stupidity and Stupor*, ed. Cindy Zeiher (Lanham, MD: Rowman & Littlefield, 2023) (originally part of a much longer version of what here serves as the book's conclusion).

Finally, I am deeply grateful to Agon Hamza, Todd McGowan, and Slavoj Žižek for having closely read the original, full-length manuscript of *Infinite Greed*. The thoughtful assessments of this work each of them generously provided were invaluable to me in thinking about how to revise the manuscript for publication. I am very fortunate to have such friends and interlocutors.

Introduction

Infrastructural Analysis: Remarrying Marxism and Psychoanalysis

Efforts to wed Marxism and psychoanalysis are almost a century old now. In the early 1920s, certain thinkers in V. I. Lenin's Soviet Union, such as Alexander Luria and Lev Vygotsky, sketch paths toward a rapprochement between Marxian materialism and Freudian metapsychology (with Stalinism soon squelching any such efforts through its condemnation of analysis as nothing more than imported Western bourgeois ideology). During the 1920s and 1930s, such leftist analysts as Wilhelm Reich and Otto Fenichel, rooted in the non-Soviet European context (although both of them eventually end up in the United States), begin exploring convergences between Marx and Sigmund Freud. Soon after, the first generation of the Frankfurt School develops what comes to be labeled "Freudo-Marxism."

Then, starting in the 1960s, Jacques Lacan's version of Freudian psychoanalysis attracts the attention of new generations of radical leftists. Whereas Freud pours cold water on early attempts to marry his ideas to revolutionary politics, Lacan openly flirts with, even sometimes encourages, the utilization of his concepts by those of Marxist bents; Lacan himself elaborates his own set of sophisticated interpretations of Marxian claims and arguments. Both in France and beyond, the later decades of the twentieth century see the emergence of what could be called "Lacano-Marxism." This tradition is alive and well today, with a plethora of contemporary theorists, including Slavoj Žižek and an entire school inspired by his work, committed to a Marx-*avec*-Lacan coupling.

Given the Stalinist stigmatization of psychoanalysis, which abruptly aborts early Soviet strivings in the direction of an Eastern Freudo-Marxism, the project of interfacing historical and dialectical materialisms with analytic metapsychologies is relegated almost entirely to investigators in the West. From the 1930s to

INTRODUCTION

the present, these Western fusions of Marx's and Freud's (if not also Lacan's) frameworks persistently have focused on superstructural (including ideological) dimensions. Of course, classical Marxism, as epitomized by Marx's historical-materialist critique of political economy (especially as per *Das Kapital*), is preoccupied with analyzing the infrastructural bases of societies and their histories. The mature Marx foregrounds modes of production, with their entangled means and relations of production, as foundational for all sociohistorical structures and dynamics. Correspondingly, he devoted most of his intellectual energies during his later years to wrestling with economics and economic phenomena.

Western moves to broker a marriage between Marx and Freud (or to establish a politburo headed by a triumvirate consisting of Marx, Freud, and Lacan) unfold alongside primarily European revisions of nineteenth-century Marxist orthodoxy. Initiated by such nonclassical Marxist figures as Georg Lukács, Karl Korsch, Antonio Gramsci, and Ernst Bloch, the tradition Maurice Merleau-Ponty comes to dub "Western Marxism" counters a classical Marxist emphasis on matters economic with stresses on more-than-economic cultural forces and social formations as irreducible to, and even shaping of, societies' economies. Western Marxism's antieconomistic privileging of the superstructural over the infrastructural is foundational for both yesterday's Freudo-Marxism and today's Lacano-Marxism alike. Nearly all combinations of Marxism and psychoanalysis hitherto have relied, whether avowedly or not, on Western revisions of Marxist historical materialism in which the critique of political economy is downplayed and sidelined in favor of the critique of ideologies and other superstructural variables.

Western Marxism in general as well as the Freudo- and Lacano-Marxisms bound up with it have tended largely to neglect the economic dimensions of social history so crucial for Marx himself. One of my agendas in *Infinite Greed* is to remedy this neglect. I seek to do so by laying the foundations of a psychoanalytic Marxism in which Marxism's critique of political economy in particular (and not its critical reflections on mainly extraeconomic cultural and ideological phenomena) is the key portion of historical materialism to be paired with Freudian and Lacanian analytic metapsychology. The investigations undertaken in this book's chapters are situated precisely at the intersection of political economics and libidinal economics.

Prior Freudo- and Lacano-Marxisms typically privilege superstructural analysis in their marrying of Marxism and psychoanalysis. I wish to try remarrying these two theoretical traditions on the basis of privileging infrastructural analysis instead. In so doing, I also indicate how this infrastructure-based remarriage of Marxism and psychoanalysis contributes to problematizing Europe-centered Marxists' century-old antieconomism, which is on display in everything from Gramsci's "philosophy of *praxis*" to Ernesto Laclau's "radical democracy" and beyond.

The first chapter, "The Conflicted Political Animal: The Psychoanalytic Body and the Body Politic," turns directly to the crossroads between Marxism and psychoanalysis. It critically assesses, on the one hand, Freud's extreme pessimism about Marxist revolutionary theory and practice and, on the other hand, someone like Herbert Marcuse's extreme optimism about the prospects for libidinal as well as political liberation. This chapter does so by offering both Marxist pushback against Freud's criticisms of Bolshevism in particular as well as psychoanalytic pushback against Marxist criticisms of psychoanalysis (including complaints that analysis is insufficiently sensitive to the social and historical dimensions foregrounded by Marxian materialism).

Surprisingly, despite there now being a century's worth of efforts at integrating Marxism and psychoanalysis, there still remains no sustained sympathetic Marxist reckoning with the later Freud's various objections to the ideas and ambitions of the likes of Marx and Lenin. One of the first chapter's contributions is to make up for this deficit by passing through, rather than bypassing, these Freudian objections on the way to a psychoanalytic Marxism that takes into account (instead of ignoring) what Freud has to say about historical materialism and its revolutionary aspirations. Another of this chapter's contributions is its identification of conceptual components of lasting value in the earliest Eastern and Western attempts at fusing Marxism with psychoanalysis. I argue here that Luria, Vygotsky, Reich, Fenichel, and Marcuse share in common a fundamentally correct insight according to which the theory of drive (*Trieb*) is a load-bearing pillar for any psychoanalytic Marxism.

Chapter 1 closes with an exploration of some of Lacan's hints for what a viable synthesis of Marxism and psychoanalysis might look like, albeit one concerned with accurately describing the capitalist blending of political and libidinal economies rather than with prognostications about capitalism's downfall. My Lacan-inspired synthesis of Marxism and psychoanalysis here strives to preserve the virtues of these two orientations (including elements to be carried forward from early permutations of Freudo-Marxism) while avoiding the vices of the mutual misunderstandings between them (misunderstandings worked through in the prior portions of this same chapter).

Chapter 2, "From Closed Need to Infinite Greed: Marxian Drives," is, in a way, the keystone of this entire book. In it, I examine how Marx himself, before Freud, already delineates a theory of *Trieb* strikingly foreshadowing properly psychoanalytic drive theory. Lacan famously credits Marx with inventing the Freudian concept of the symptom *avant la lettre*. As I see it, Marx also should be credited with doing the same apropos the Freudian concept of *Trieb*.

Thanks to human beings' malleable natures (including their libidinal economies), social systems and the modes of production upon which they rest are able to hijack and reconfigure, or even outright replace, the drives of their psychical subjects.[1] Marx himself identifies the logic of capital, M-C-M', and its characteristic manner of arranging the economic domains of production, distribution, exchange, and consumption as the drive(s) of capitalism and, hence, of all those living within this specific socioeconomic system. Those thrown by birth into capitalist societies, initially stranded in the uniquely human state of prolonged prematurational helplessness, are abandoned and susceptible to the tender mercies of their societies' ruling invisible hands. These hands promptly insert into these young subjects-to-be libidinal circuits (consisting of drives, demands, desires, fantasies, fetishes, addictions, and so on) crafted by capital's logic and its ideological accompaniments. The Marx of *Das Kapital* and related texts, particularly through his well-known recourse to the notion of fetishism to characterize capitalist subjects' relations to commodities as well as to capital itself, emphasizes the libidinal-economic ramifications of capitalism's political-economic foundations.

This second chapter is the one in which, on the basis of a close reading of the mature Marx's critique of political economy, I elaborate the concept of "infinite greed" as characteristic of capitalism's drive(s). Part of this elaboration involves an extended version of my argument against the association of capitalism with selfishness, an argument I provide a short synopsis of in the preface. Moreover, I delineate in this chapter just how much of Freud's metapsychological conceptualization of *Triebe* really is anticipated by Marx.

Yet despite this Marxian foreshadowing of the Freudian drive, I maintain in the later portions of chapter 2 that Lacan's own metapsychology of the libidinal economy is the most fitting psychoanalytic partner for Marx's historical-materialist drive theory *avant la lettre*. In particular, I show why and how Lacan's interlinked concepts of *jouissance*, *désir*, and *objet petit a*—all of these operate "beyond the pleasure principle," according to Lacan—are crucial for, in Hegelian terms, raising Marx's hybrid political-and-libidinal economics (grounded on the infinite greed of M-C-M') to the dignity of its Notion. This Lacanian perspective brings out most effectively, among other things, how capitalism is sustained through all its subjects sacrificing themselves, under a death-drive-like compulsion, to the inhuman "dark god" of Capital and its mechanical repetition of accumulations producing far more actual pain than pleasure for all concerned.

Informed by the immediately preceding, the third chapter, "The Self-Cleaning Fetish: Repression Under the Shadow of Fictitious Capital," examines money as it features in both Marxism and psychoanalysis. Of course, money is the epitome of Marx's fetishized commodity. And in Marxist discussions of the connected topics of currency and commodity fetishism (as reliant mainly on *Capital*, volume 1), it often is left underappreciated that such fetishism reaches its apotheosis only with the development of interest-bearing money-as-capital (i.e., with the emergence of fictitious finance capital in the guises of credit, banking, etc. as dealt with in *Capital*, volume 3).

In psychoanalytic treatments of money from Freud onward, monetary means usually are tied to libidinal sources and stages in the subject's ontogenetic life history (in line with Freud's tight tethering of psychical investments in money to anal erotism). Furthermore, the term "fetishism" features in the Freudian field too in ways that partially cross-resonate with Marxian commodity fetishism. This third chapter makes two gestures, one as regards Marxism and another with respect to psychoanalysis. Apropos Marxism, I counterbalance the usual, long-standing (over)emphasis on commodity fetishism as per the first volume of *Das Kapital* with a foregrounding of this fetishism as per the third volume.

Apropos psychoanalysis, I shift away from its traditional fixation on reducing financial matters to libidinal contents. I explore instead the implications of the forms of capitalist fetishism for reconsidering the forms of intrasubjective defense mechanisms. This leads me to posit a complementary inversion of Lacan's dictum according to which "repression is always the return of the repressed": The return of the repressed sometimes is the most effective repression.

To pose a rhetorical question paraphrasing Bertolt Brecht: What is the laundering of money compared with the laundering that is money? Appreciating this question is important for the Marxist account of the unconscious sides of socio-economic ideologies. It also promises to be transformative for the psychoanalytic account of the unconscious of psychical defensive dynamics.

The fourth chapter, "The Triumph of Theological Economics: God Goes Underground," puts the Marxist and psychoanalytic critical assessments of religion in dialogue with each other. Both Marx and Freud are very much children of the Enlightenment. As such, they each sometimes display a qualified but firm optimism about history inevitably making progress in specific desirable directions. For instance, Freud predicts that continuing scientific and technological advances eventually will drive religiosity from human societies once and for all.

Marx likewise forecasts the withering away of religions. Additionally, he treats this predicted process as symptomatic of even more fundamental socioeconomic developments, namely, his (in)famous anticipations of subsequent transitions to socialism and communism.

However, the past century-plus of human history obviously has not been kind to any sort of Enlightenment-style progress narratives, Marx's and Freud's included. Chapter 4 takes inspiration especially from the later Lacan's honest reckoning with a "triumph of religion." This victory flagrantly defies Freud's expectations of relentlessly broadening and deepening secularization.

In the fourth chapter, I argue that sociopolitical phenomena of the past several decades bear witness to religious superstructures having infused themselves into economic infrastructures. I claim this dynamic has gone so far that contemporary humanity is now largely secular where it believes itself to be religious and religious where it believes itself to be secular. To do justice to this, I plead for a reactivation and updating of Marx's critique of political economy. Nonetheless, I propose modifying the infrastructure-superstructure distinction of classical Marxian historical materialism, particularly in light of more recent shifts in the relations between the economic and the religious. This modification perhaps helps explain why many of Marx's prognostications regarding the futures of capitalist societies have not (yet) come to pass.

The conclusion, "Real Reduction: It's the Stupid Economy!," brings *Infinite Greed* to a close by critically examining the antieconomism of the Western Marxist tradition dominating extant permutations of psychoanalytic Marxisms. Western Marxists and their offspring, from those of the 1920s up to a number of contemporary European and European-inspired (post-)Marxists, consistently have been worried about the ostensible dangers of traditional and/or crude forms of historical materialism indulging in economism, namely, in economically based determinism and reductionism. Such (post-)Marxists, in straining to avoid at all costs anything resembling economistic vulgarities, valorize the superstructural (i.e., the extra- or more-than-economic) over the infrastructural (i.e., the economic). Sometimes this valorization goes so far that little or nothing of Marx's original historical-materialist critique of political economy is recognizably retained in their post-Marx theoretical "innovations."

Infinite Greed concludes with my advocating against the excessiveness of Europe-centered Marxisms' antieconomism and correlatively pleading for a return to the classical Marxist focusing on capitalism's economic forms and movements. In so doing, I draw on Lacan's ideas about interpretation, materiality, reductionism, and stupidity (as per my handling of these ideas elsewhere).[2] To cut a long story short, I argue here that the (mis)perceived stupidity of reductive economism is not a distorting vice of theoretical thinking but an accurate reflection of the actually reductive being of capitalist reality in all its rotten objectivity.

With exhausting ceaselessness, the capitalist mode of production, the societies resting upon it, and the persons subjected to it all dance to the monotonous tune of the meaningless, mindless, idiotic repetitive looping of M-C-M′, the restless perpetual chase after ever-more surplus value as a valueless end-that-is-no-end. When all is said and done, the truth of capitalism, a truth still ruling our world, is incredibly, almost unbelievably, stupid. This is so despite however much theoretical complexity and sophistication is required to achieve sober (and sobering) insight into its really reductive stupidity.

I

The Conflicted Political Animal

The Psychoanalytic Body and the Body Politic

§1. WHO THINKS IDEOLOGICALLY? MARX, FREUD, AND THE PARTISANSHIP OF TRUTH

In this chapter, I will critically assess, and sometimes rebut, the later Freud's reservations and objections vis-à-vis Marxism. Freud's skepticism about socialism and communism is well known. But despite the tradition of psychoanalytic Marxisms being almost a century old, Freud's reservations and objections apropos the Marxist tradition strangely have been left more or less unanswered in any serious detail by Marxism-sympathetic readers of the founder of psychoanalysis. I will be making up for this deficit here.

While doing so, I additionally bring out the manners in which Freud vacillates between two images of humanity lying at the heart of Western sociopolitical thinking: human beings as social animals qua the Aristotelian *zoon politikon* versus human beings as antisocial animals qua the Hobbesian lone wolf. The older Freud exhibits a tendency to favor Hobbesianism's stories about the violent state of nature and the pacifying social contract. Yet, as I will argue, much of Freud's metapsychological apparatus points in the opposite direction, namely, toward a further validation of the Aristotelian picture of human nature shared by both Hegel and Marx (a picture fundamentally at odds with the atomistic individualism of early-modern British liberalist thinking).

This chapter's focus on Freud also enables me to initiate an engagement with the earliest attempts at interfacing Marxism and psychoanalysis. I look at both Eastern (Soviet) and Western (European) efforts along these lines primarily during the 1920s through the 1950s (with Russian labors in this vein being brutally cut short under J. V. Stalin's reign).[1] These earlier-twentieth-century permutations of what has come to be known as "Freudo-Marxism" help bring out those aspects of Freud's theoretical edifice compatible with Marxist ideas and at odds with the bourgeois individualist ideology to which Freud intermittently succumbs. At the same time, I correlatively but conversely illustrate why and how certain key facets of Freudian (as well as Lacanian) metapsychology problematize some of the pioneering Freudo-Marxists' notions about psychoanalysis and its implications for Marxism.

Of course, two major historical developments run parallel to each other during the late 1910s and early 1920s: the Bolshevik Revolution of October 1917, with its protracted aftermath, and an interlinked set of fundamental shifts in Freud's ideas, involving both his topography of the psychical apparatus as well as his account of drives (*Triebe*). Moreover, Freud, during this pivotal period in the evolution of his psychoanalytic thinking, sees fit to reflect upon these contemporaneous political events transpiring in Russia. Although obviously no communist—as Russell Jacoby observes, "Freud's subversiveness is derived from his concepts and not from his stated political opinions"[2]—Freud's manners of bringing analytic concepts to bear on the Soviets' project during this time provide openings not only for exploring the intersections between Marxism and psychoanalysis but also for reworking each of these theoretical orientations.

However, taking advantage of these openings afforded by Freud's glosses on Marxism requires first addressing some of the mutual misunderstandings between Freud and the Marxists. In this first section ("Who Thinks Ideologically?: Marx, Freud, and the Partisanship of Truth") as well as the third ("Communism and Ambivalence: Freud, Marxism, and Aggression"), I will unpack Freud's comments on socialism, communism, and Bolshevism. The second section, in between ("Not of This World: A Lacanian Excursus on the *Weltanschauung* Question"), examines some of Lacan's interventions apropos this same Freud. As already indicated, I will be offering pushback against many of Freud's criticisms of Marxism.

Then, I shift from what Freud says about the Soviets to what the Soviets say about Freud. The fourth section ("The Drive of Marxism: Freud and Dialectical Materialism") will examine points made about Freudian psychoanalysis by the Soviet psychologists Lev Vygotsky and Alexander Romanovich Luria, as well as by Western psychoanalytic thinkers influenced by Marxism, such as Wilhelm Reich, Otto Fenichel, and Herbert Marcuse. Just as I temper Freud's criticisms of Marxism in the first and third sections, I undermine some of the Soviet and Western-Marxist objections to Freudian psychoanalysis in the fourth section. The corrections of the mutual misunderstandings between Freudian psychoanalysis and Marxian historical materialism in the first four sections here clear the way for the fifth section ("The Plumbing of Political Economy: Marxism and Psychoanalysis Down the Toilet"). This last section rethinks how best to interface Marxism with psychoanalysis both Freudian and Lacanian, thereby paving the way for this book's subsequent chapters.

The first and most famous of Freud's remarks upon Bolshevism occur in 1930's *Civilization and Its Discontents*. This widely read book by the later Freud centrally involves redeploying the relatively new theory of the death drive (*Todestrieb*) first introduced a decade earlier in *Beyond the Pleasure Principle* (1920). *Civilization and Its Discontents* focuses on those dimensions of the *Todestrieb* associated with aggression, with destructiveness as directed by human beings against one another. For this Freud, the death drive as aggression poses the greatest permanent threat to the very existence of civilization (*Kultur*) qua cohesive human social groupings enjoying historical endurance. In this vein, he signals his sympathy with one of the most un-Marxist of worldviews, namely, Thomas Hobbes's political philosophy, according to which human beings are naturally (in the supposed "state of nature") isolated selfish predators preying on each other. Freud joins Hobbes in repeating Plautus's "*homo homini lupus.*"[3]

In *Civilization and Its Discontents*, immediately after endorsing man being a wolf to man via the hypothesis of a naturalized aggression (i.e., an innate *Todestrieb*), Freud turns his attention to revolutionary Russia. He begins by attributing to "communists" a crude Rousseauian vision having it that "man is wholly good and is well-disposed to his neighbour; but the institution of private property has corrupted his nature."[4] Ironically, Antonio Gramsci, in a letter roughly contemporaneous with *Civilization and Its Discontents*, accuses Freudian psychoanalysis of promoting a new version of the Rousseauian myth of the "'noble savage' corrupted by society, that is to say, by history."[5] That noted, whether Marx's own conception of human nature (*als Gattungswesen*) as essentially linked to social laboring requires disavowing aggression, evil, viciousness, selfishness, and the like, as Freud charges, is highly debatable. What is more, Marx emphatically rejects all forms of the "state of nature" myth, whether Hobbesian, Rousseauian, or any other permutation. Freud appears to be relying more on Soviet propaganda for his image of communism than on a careful consideration of the actual textual basis of Marxism (just as Gramsci appears to be relying on popular misperceptions of Freud in hurling at psychoanalysis the same accusation of Rousseauian romanticism that Freud, with equal unfairness, hurls at "communists").

Freud promptly proceeds to attack what he takes to be communists' beliefs in a lost-but-recoverable original goodness purportedly lying at the historically eclipsed basis of human nature. After admitting his lack of qualifications for assessing the economic feasibility and desirability of implementing a Marxist approach to political economy,[6] he asserts apropos Marxism that "the psychological premisses [*Voraussetzung*] on which the system is based are an untenable [*haltlose*] illusion."[7] He then warns: "In abolishing private property [*Privateigentums*] we deprive the human love of aggression [*menschlichen Aggressionslust*] of one of its instruments, certainly a strong one, though certainly not the strongest."[8] One should note in passing Freud's admission that property is neither the unique nor the most important conduit for channeling aggression. That noted, Freud goes on to argue that aggression, both phylogenetically and ontogenetically, precedes the emergence of the institution of private property.[9] He even worries about an imagined communist "free love" ethos stoking explosively violent rivalries in the field of human sexual relationships.[10]

One obvious Marxist rebuttal of Freud's line of criticism in this context is to draw attention to the crucial distinction between private property and personal possessions. When Marx speaks of "private property" (*Privateigentum*), he does not thereby designate the transhistorical category of any object of ownership and this ownership's attendant claims or rights. By "private property," Marx instead designates means of production intended to serve as surplus value–generating capital and held by individual capitalists as members of one class among several within specifically capitalist societies.

Marx does not envision depriving individuals of their personal possessions. Socialism and communism would not require whole groups to share the same communal toothbrush, for example. Hence, the Marxist abolition of private property is not equivalent to the abolition of personal possessions. Rather, it amounts to the abolition of property as capital specifically. This already takes some of the sting out of Freud's objections to "the communists." Although sizable inequalities between personal possessions indeed would be problematic for socialism/communism—these would be inequalities sufficient to recreate class-like social stratifications—differences in possessions, and the very having of personal possessions as not capital qua private property strictly speaking, are not of real concern for socialist/communist political economics.

In the context of these reflections on Bolshevism in *Civilization and Its Discontents*, Freud makes another observation that packs greater critical punch thanks to its resonance with the tragic realities of Stalinism. He remarks: "It is intelligible that the attempt to establish a new, communist civilization in Russia should find its psychological support in the persecution of the bourgeois. One only wonders, with concern, what the Soviets will do after they have wiped out their bourgeois."[11] The Stalinist purges of Kulaks (and "sub-Kulaks"), old-guard Bolsheviks (including former members of Lenin's Politburo), and numerous others seem sadly and amply to justify Freud's concern. Yet, this Freud's naturalistic eternalization of the death drive as aggression implies that Stalin's reign of terror, with its show trials, gulags, executions, and assassinations, was an inevitable, preordained outcome of the October Revolution. Obviously, whether Stalinism was or was not a necessary consequence of Leninism remains one of the biggest unsettled questions left by the history of the Soviet experience. And, whether the viciousness of a naturalized *Todestrieb* settles the matter is open to vigorous debate.

Several chapters later in *Civilization and Its Discontents*, Freud briefly picks back up the thread of his discussion of Bolshevism. Intentionally or not, he accentuates an ambivalent tone already detectable in his prior remarks regarding this subject. Apropos dealing with "aggressiveness" as "a potent obstacle to civilization,"[12] Freud states: "I too think it quite certain [*unzweifelhaft*] that a real change in the relations of human beings to possessions [*Besitz*] would be of more help in this direction than any ethical commands; but the recognition of this fact among socialists has been obscured and made useless for practical purposes by a fresh idealistic misconception of human nature."[13] It seems that Freud, in this passage, softens and qualifies his critique of Marxism (as socialism, communism, and/or Bolshevism). Earlier in *Civilization and Its Discontents*, he appeared, as seen, to assert that Marxist-type changes of wealth distribution either would fail to defuse or even further aggravate aggression between people. Now, Freud instead concedes that economically egalitarian redistributions of possessions (*als Besitz*) or property (*als Eigentum*) indeed are "quite certain" (*unzweifelhaft*) to result in some genuine progress in the history of societies' struggles to temper and control the destructive side of the death drive—and this by contrast with mere ethical admonishments of a "Love thy neighbor as thyself" sort.[14]

Within the pages of *Civilization and Its Discontents*, Freud's stance regarding Marxist political economics abruptly shifts from denying it will be of any assistance against aggression to admitting that it promises real help on this front. His reservation becomes one concerning the management (or lack thereof) of expectations. Instead of denying the antiaggression efficacy of combating material inequality, Freud simply warns against expecting too much progress along these lines from socialist or communist economic changes.

Lacan's ambivalent engagements with Marx—the later Lacan teases his audience by saying that they cannot tell whether his Marx-related remarks are "ringing on the left or on the right" (*vient de droite ou de gauche*) of their ears[15]—sometimes convey the same Freudian message. Lacan cautions that crushing disappointment and traumatizing disillusionment await those overoptimistic leftists

THE CONFLICTED POLITICAL ANIMAL   13

anticipating paradise on the other side of a political-economic revolution, should one come to pass,[16] with the later Lacan expressing his pessimism about such an eventuality[17] (although at one point, in 1972, he describes consumer capitalism as in overt crisis and doomed soon to implode).[18] Already in *Seminar VI* (*Desire and Its Interpretation* [1958–1959]), Lacan puts forward his metapsychological category of impossible-to-satisfy desire (*désir*) as the key "discontent in civilization" (*malaise dans la culture*) to be managed by all societies, postrevolutionary Marxist ones included.[19] The twenty-first seminar (*Les non-dupes errent* [1973–1974]) features a Lacanian neologism signaling a problematic tendency for revolutionaries to be excessively hopeful utopians: "*rêve-olution*," in which "*révolution*" is made to contain the word "*rêve*" (dream).[20] Similarly, Lacan did not think that the Soviet Union had gotten very far along truly revolutionary lines.[21]

After *Civilization and Its Discontents*, on two occasions published in 1933, Freud returns to the topic of Marxism. He addresses it both in the *New Introductory Lectures on Psycho-Analysis* (primarily in his lecture on "The Question of a *Weltanschauung*") and in the exchange with Albert Einstein entitled "Why War?" Both of these texts from 1933 contain reiterations of Freud's 1930 objection to Marxism according to which socialist/communist economic policies are powerless to tamp down the *Todestrieb* as an aggression inherent to an incorrigible human nature.[22] The myth of a future Soviet "New Man" is fated to remain just that, namely, a mere fiction of hopelessly utopian propaganda.

However, in 1933, Freud adds further points and nuances to his considerations of Marxism not to be found in *Civilization and Its Discontents*. To begin with, in the *New Introductory Lectures on Psycho-Analysis*, he proffers an ambivalent assessment of what he takes to be the essence of historical materialism as a conceptual framework. Therein, Freud praises Marx for discovering the previously un- or underappreciated influences of economic forces and factors on societies and the human beings shaped by them.[23]

Yet Freud qualifies this praise of Marxian historical materialism with two caveats. First, he argues against the idea that the entirety of more-than-economic superstructure can be reduced wholly and completely to a mere reflection of whatever constitutes the current infrastructure (i.e., the economic base established by a society's given mode of production). With the concept of the superego in view, Freud comments:

> A child's super-ego is in fact constructed on the model not of its parents but of its parents' super-ego; the contents which fill it are the same and it becomes the vehicle [*Träger*] of tradition and of all the time-resisting [*zeitbeständigen*] judgements of value which have propagated themselves in this manner from

generation to generation. . . . It seems likely that what are known as materialistic views of history sin in under-estimating this factor. They brush it aside with the remark that human "ideologies" are nothing other than the product and superstructure of their contemporary economic conditions. That is true, but very probably not the whole truth. The past, the tradition of the race and of the people, lives on in the ideologies of the super-ego, and yields only slowly to the influences of the present and to new changes; and so long as it operates through the super-ego it plays a powerful part in human life, independently of economic conditions.[24]

Already in *Civilization and Its Discontents*, Freud speaks of a "cultural super-ego" (*das Kultur-Über-Ich*).[25] However, this passage from the *New Introductory Lectures on Psycho-Analysis* indicates that this phrase is a pleonasm. The superego is by metapsychological definition inherently cultural qua an internalization of socio-historical forms and contents transmitted primarily via the family unit.

Faced with this just-quoted Freud, the very first thing that any Marxist worth their salt ought to do is point out the oversimplification of historical materialism relied upon in this quotation. Perhaps taking certain more vulgar Marxists as accurately representing the core commitments of Marxism, Freud's remarks reveal that, as he understands it, historical materialism posits that the entirety of a given society's superstructure springs wholly out of that same society's infrastructure (qua mode of production). This sort of superstructure therefore would contain no surviving traces of earlier historical periods tied to different modes of production.

Such classical Marxist moments as Friedrich Engels's October 27, 1890, letter to Conrad Schmidt, in which Engels clarifies that historical materialism insists on economic determination as a matter of "in the last instance," warn that neither Marx nor Engels espouse a crudely simplistic doctrine according to which a single economic base generates each and every more-than-economic dimension and detail of society contemporaneous with this base.[26] (Luria, citing this same Engels, points out a sad parallel between the unjustified charge of economic reductionism against Marx and the equally unjustified charge of sexual reductionism against Freud.)[27] Hence, Freud is wrong to assume that historical materialism presupposes or posits a one-and-only linear causal relationship between a particular infrastructure as cause and a corresponding superstructure, in its entirety, as effect of this, and exclusively this, particular infrastructure. Incidentally, Freud belatedly, in 1937, comes to concede that his pre-1937 criticisms of Marx and Engels involving recourse to the analytic theory of the superego were ill-informed and invalid.[28]

Furthermore, Marxist questions can and should be raised about whether and how much "the ideologies of the super-ego" really are "independent of economic conditions." If Freud is willing to concede that "contemporary economic conditions" influence "human 'ideologies,'" then why would past economic conditions not have influenced "the tradition of the race and of the people" that "lives on in the ideologies of the super-ego?" If so, then the Freudian superego would reflect a lag between the influences of at least two modes of production, one current and one or more preceding ones[29] (with Bertell Ollman maintaining that such time lags still need to be better theorized by and integrated into Marxist thinking).[30] But in this case, the superego would not be independent of economic conditioning.

There is another Marxist line of response which this Freud would need to take into account. Specifically, how would he respond to the Marxist who, on the one hand, admits that contemporary society contains vestiges of prior social formations while, on the other hand, maintaining that these carryovers from the past are able to persist in the present only if and when they are amenable to being pressed into the service of the present socioeconomic system? Would this not indicate an infrastructural mediation, if only an indirect one, by the present mode of production of even those superstructural ghosts originating out of earlier modes of production?

Also, in the 1933 block quotation above, Freud employs the German word *Träger* ("vehicle") to characterize the superego. This is the same word Marx uses to depict individuals as vehicles (or bearers) of class identities and functions (with, for example, the individual capitalist as a bearer for the logic of capital as M-C-M').[31] In this vein, is there not ample evidence in capitalist societies of persons' superegos operating, at least in part, as vehicles for the productive and/or consumptive demands of capital? Is not one of the appealing aspects of Lacan's linking of the superego to the imperative to "Enjoy!" its ability to capture the injunctions and pressures bearing down upon, and introjected within, psyches immersed in (consumerist) capitalism?[32]

Even if the cultural superego contains residues of the precapitalist past, it also seems to harbor fragments of the capitalist present. It indeed would be a false dilemma to insist on a forced choice between either an entirely precapitalist or an entirely capitalist superego wholly of the past or wholly of the present. Especially for a psyche said by Freud himself to be, at its unconscious base, blithely unconcerned with avoiding contradiction[33] (not to mention indifferent to linear chronological time),[34] such either/or alternatives definitely should be off the table as regards theorizing the superego. Indeed, in the *New Introductory Lectures on Psycho-Analysis*, just six pages after the above quotation concerning communism and the superego, Freud mentions that "the logical laws of thought do not apply in the id, and this is true above all of the law of contradiction."[35]

What is more, the same later Freud who criticizes Marxism along the lines presently under consideration also portrays the type of cultural superego typical of his late-nineteenth- and early-twentieth-century European cultural milieu as essentially Kantian. That is to say, the superego of concern in, for instance, *Civilization and Its Discontents* closely resembles the will and conscience of Immanuel Kant's deontological ethics of pure practical reason, with its categorical imperative and "You can, because you must!" (*Du kannst, denn du sollst*) unconditionality.[36] The *New Introductory Lectures on Psycho-Analysis* continues to associate the superego's severity with Kantian ethical rigorism.[37] And, in 1923's *The Ego and the Id*, Freud is especially explicit about the connection between Kant's conscience and his superego—"The super-ego—the conscience at work in the ego—may ... become harsh, cruel and inexorable against the ego which is in its charge. Kant's Categorical Imperative is thus the direct heir of the Oedipus complex."[38] And the Kantian metaphysics of morals is itself a barely disguised pseudosecularization of a Protestant ethical worldview.

Protestantism is born at roughly the same time as European capitalism. Additionally, as both Marx and, after him, Max Weber stress, Protestant Christianity plays a key role in the rise and persistence of industrial capitalism.[39] And of course, Kant and his work are situated in the German-speaking world of late-eighteenth-century Europe. So, if the Freudian cultural superego is modeled on the subject of Kantian ethics, then, once again, just how "independent" is this superego of its surrounding "economic conditions?"

In addition to Freud's just-criticized qualification of historical materialism involving the theory of the superego, his 1933 pronouncements on the topic of Marxism also put forward a second caveat tempering his concessions to the (partial) validity of this economically centered political perspective. In the context of lecturing on the topic of *Weltanschauungen*, Freud claims that Marxism, in its atheistic fight against religious worldviews, has itself become another religious worldview. One should bear in mind that by 1933 Stalinism is in terrifying full swing. Freud states:

> The newly achieved discovery of the far-reaching importance of economic relations brought with it a temptation not to leave alterations in them to the course of historical development but to put them into effect oneself by revolutionary action. Theoretical Marxism, as realized in Russian Bolshevism, has acquired the energy and the self-contained and exclusive character of a *Weltanschauung*, but at the same time an uncanny likeness to what it is fighting against. Though

THE CONFLICTED POLITICAL ANIMAL   17

originally a portion of science [*Ursprünglich selbst ein Stück Wissenschaft*] and built up, in its implementation, upon science [*Wissenschaft*] and technology, it has created a prohibition of thought [*Denkverbot*] which is just as ruthless as was that of religion in the past. Any critical examination of Marxist theory is forbidden, doubts of its correctness are punished in the same way as heresy was once punished by the Catholic Church. The writings of Marx have taken the place of the Bible and the Koran as a source of revelation, though they would seem to be no more free from contradictions and obscurities than those older sacred books.[40]

At the start of these remarks, Freud again grants a great deal of validity to historical materialism, with its emphasis on the role of economic dimensions in history. The second sentence of this passage then opens with what appears to be an implicit distinction between the intellectual framework of historical materialism (i.e., "Theoretical Marxism") and its concrete sociopolitical implementation (i.e., "revolutionary action" "as realized in Russian Bolshevism").

Apropos this implicit distinction, it remains unclear here whether Freud considers Bolshevik practice to be a high-fidelity extension of Marx's theory. On the one hand, given Freud's other comments about the Soviet experiment I have already examined, it seems he would have to assume that Bolshevism's practices can be taken to be faithful applications of Marx's theories. This assumption is questionable.

Yet on the other hand, the above quotation involves Freud distinguishing between an initially scientific (*als wissenschaftlich*) historical materialism as per Marx himself ("originally a portion of science" [*Ursprünglich selbst ein Stück Wissenschaft*]) and a subsequent loss of this scientificity through Marxism's alleged degeneration into just another religious sect, a cult of Marx with its dogmas, deifications, and *Denkverbote*. This narrative of a decline from science to religion suggests that Freud indeed recognizes substantial differences between Marx's theories and the Bolsheviks' practices. If nothing else, Freud's assessments of the Bolsheviks look to be ambivalent, vacillating, and shot through with inconsistencies. At one point in 1933, Freud basically admits to his indecision and uncertainty apropos Marx's ideas.[41]

Clearly, the central thrust of the preceding passage from the *New Introductory Lectures on Psycho-Analysis* is the unfavorable comparison of Bolshevism with Catholicism and/or Islam. This comparison should come as no surprise in a lecture entitled "The Question of a *Weltanschauung*." As is well known, Freud is at pains in this particular lecture to deny that psychoanalysis constitutes its own worldview. He famously insists that analysis merely participates in the

Weltanschauung of modernity's empirical, experimental sciences of nature. This appeal to the scientific worldview brings with it the familiar contrasts between science and religion, reason and faith.[42]

Marx already warns against his work's being turned into a fixed and inflexible creed. For example, in replying to the criticisms of *Capital* by the Russian Narodnik Nikolay Mikhailovsky, he denies that his historical materialism amounts to "a general historico-philosophical theory"[43] (a denial akin to that of Freud apropos turning psychoanalysis into a worldview). Other letters involve Marx similarly emphasizing the unpredictably contingent character of social history. Addressing the concerns of Mikhailovsky and another Russian, Vera Sassoulitch, he foregrounds historical materialism's admittance of alternate courses of social development (such as a Russian leap from feudal-agrarian tsarism directly to socialism and communism) other than those mapped out in his mature critique of political economy (with its England-centered analyses seeming to suggest that capitalism is a necessary phase of development between feudalism and socialism/communism).[44] All of this is to say that this later Marx presents historical materialism as an intellectual framework that can and should be open to modification, revision, and supplementation in relation to various unforeseeable unknowns, especially those regularly served up by the twists and turns of continually unfolding history. In this light, Marx's materialism would appear to be more like science than religion or philosophy.

Finally, there is a real irony to Freud chastising Marxism for allegedly having become just another religion. Beginning already during Freud's own lifetime and despite his protests against the existence a psychoanalytic *Weltanschauung*, countless others have accused psychoanalysis of exactly the same sins as Freud here accuses Marxism (or, at least, Bolshevism). The psychoanalytic movement has been depicted time and again by many of its critics as a cult of Freud-the-father in which the texts of the Master are worshipped as infallible Holy Writ. Likewise, a plethora of Freud's detractors would say of his writings what Freud says on this occasion of Marx's writings, namely, that they are filled with "contradictions and obscurities." Freud's attempts to parry such attacks by allying analysis with science (and the scientific *Weltanschauung*) have proven unconvincing to his opponents and even are treated by some of his followers as symptomatic of a grave self-misunderstanding on his part. Various analytic types, including the majority of Lacanians, are skeptical of and/or allergic to Freud's appeals to the natural sciences.

The Marxist tradition has available yet another line of counterargument against Freud's 1933 denunciation of (Bolshevik) Marxism as a new religion. This line brings together related aspects of Marxism's theories of both knowledge and ideology. In terms of epistemology, Marxism entails an account of the inherent partisanship of knowledge and truth, at least when it comes to social theory. Insofar as all perspectives on class-based societies (i.e., the societies of Marx's "history hitherto")[45] are themselves tied to and reflective of class positions within these same societies, there is no neutral, nonpartisan perspective on classes and the societies based upon them. Just as there is no sexless view of sexual difference, so too is there no classless view of class difference.

However, one must be careful at this juncture not to lapse into the commonplace conflation of neutrality and objectivity. Recent and contemporary American political journalism is rife with examples of this far-from-innocent conflation. For instance, when reporting on a debate between two opposed politicians in which one of the politicians clearly bests the other, these journalists strain to seem objective by trying to be neutral. They issue statements such as "Both sides had some good points," "Both sides fared badly," or "The debate was too close to call," even though it is glaringly evident that one side won with good points and the other lost with bad points (or that one side at least did less badly than the other). Such fake objectivity insidiously favors types of politics and politicians unable to prevail in the back-and-forth of argument and counterargument, perhaps because they are irrational and/or indefensible.

The assumption behind these sorts of journalistic verbal contortions is that the objective truth is inherently nonpartisan (à la the cliché "The truth always lies in between"). Journalists tying themselves in these knots do so assuming that being objective requires being neutral qua nonpartisan. Yet as the example of the political debate I just mentioned shows, the objective truth (in this case, the reality of one politician besting the other) sometimes *is* partisan (i.e., one political side really did out-argue the other).

What is worse, one only needs to imagine the disastrous, if not also comic, consequences of applying the erroneous conflation of objectivity with neutrality to fields such as mathematics and natural science. The truth most definitely does not lie in between incompatible judgments such as "$2 + 2 = 4$" and "$2 + 2 = 5$" or "Phlogiston is necessary to explain combustion" and "Oxygen is necessary to explain combustion." The partisans of certain sides in these conflicts have objective truth on their side, and the partisans of other sides do not. As Jacoby proposes apropos an overlap between Marxism and Freudianism, those partisans with objective truth on their side (such as Marxists and Freudians) perhaps should pursue a "liberating intolerance" as regards their opponents and these opponents' falsehoods, an intolerance that frees others from such untruths.[46] And Jacoby's liberating intolerance avowedly is the complementary inverse of Marcuse's notion of "repressive tolerance,"[47] itself a correlate of Marcusian "repressive desublimation" and "repressive progress."[48] Moreover, Marcuse, in describing the false nonpartisanship tied to the erroneous and insidious conflation of objectivity with neutrality, observes, "It refrains from taking sides—but in doing so it actually protects the already established machinery of discrimination."[49] He soon adds, "Such objectivity is spurious—more, it offends against humanity and truth by being calm where one should be enraged, by refraining from accusation where accusation is in the facts themselves."[50]

For Marxism, the same holds as concerns class-colored social theories as holds with the obvious nonequivalence between objectivity and neutrality in such fields as mathematics and science. The fact that there is no class-neutral perspective on class societies does not mean that social theorizing is a truthless, relativistic free-for-all lacking in any objectivity (with the objective truth presumed to lie in between clashing class views). Instead, Marxist epistemology wagers on the partisanship of truth, namely, non-neutral objectivity. In capitalist societies, the proletarian perspective, although one class view on capitalism among other capitalist class views, nonetheless uniquely articulates the objective truth of capitalism. Historical materialism is an expression of proletarian class consciousness. But its critique of political economy enjoys a status as objectively true knowledge of the underpinnings of the capitalist mode of production in ways that other partisan perspectives competing with it do not (such as the multiple forms of bourgeois economics, trying to pass themselves off as objectively neutral qua classless/nonpartisan when, in fact, they amount to ideology masquerading as mathematics).

The preceding reflections on Marxist epistemology, with its partisanship of truth, lead into a couple of manners of responding to Freud's critical linking of Marxism with religions. First, and as I noted a short while ago, psychoanalysis likewise often is treated by its critics as not scientific but instead as a dogmatic faith resting on a misguided deification of the figure of Freud. However, are not defenders of psychoanalysis justified in responding to this line of criticism with evidence and arguments about how and why important objective truths about human mindedness and like-mindedness cannot be grasped without the contested hypothesis of the analytic unconscious and related Freudian concepts? Has not psychoanalysis been an embattled partisan perspective from its beginnings right up through the present?

These questions give rise to still others: Why would partisanship on behalf of psychoanalysis be any more or less dogmatic than partisanship on behalf of Marxism? More generally, should any and all passionate commitments to and fierce advocacies of specific intellectual orientations be dismissed as religious-style fanaticism? If so, is not Freud himself vulnerable to this very same dismissal that he has recourse to in response to Marxism? If not, what specific criteria enable Freud to differentiate between his non-neutrality in favor of psychoanalysis from Marxists' non-neutrality in favor of historical materialism?

A second manner of responding to Freud's unfavorable comparison of Marxism with religion made possible by the Marxist idea of the partisanship of truth has to do with the topic of worldviews as ideologies—and, hence, with the Marxist theory of ideology. Given Freud's fashion of contrasting science and religion coupled with his attribution of a worldview to modern science itself, he has to admit that something can be a worldview without, for all that, therefore being a religion too. In the block quotation above, Freud indeed appears to distinguish between Marxism as a scientific *Weltanschauung* (i.e., Marx's original historical materialism) and Bolshevism as a religion departing from this worldview.

Nevertheless, interesting questions remain. How would Freud relate the concept-terms "*Weltanschauung*" and "ideology?" Are all worldviews also ideologies? Or, are some worldviews (such as, perhaps, the scientific one) not ideological? Furthermore, and apropos the Marxist tradition, if Freud grants that historical materialism is (or participates in) a scientific *Weltanschauung* without being a religion, can the translation of this theory into practice through (revolutionary) sociopolitical action be accomplished in a nonreligious way? Or, for Freud, is the alleged morphing of the science of Marxism into the religion of Bolshevism made inevitable by the very nature of the general process of turning ideas into politics? Does the eternal, inescapable innateness of the aggression of the *Todestrieb* cement in place this inevitability? Alas, much of what these questions ask about remains hazy or even unaddressed in Freud's writings.

Certain strains of classical Marxism share in common with Freud an Enlightenment-style inclination to assume or advocate a strict difference in kind between science and religion, with the latter but not the former as ideological. In this vein, both Marxist and psychoanalytic outlooks put forward, among other things, critiques of religions specifically and ideologies generally. The sort of traditional Marxist who adopts this Enlightenment stance along with Freud could respond to the latter's 1933 objections to Marxism-become-religion along lines I already suggested: Regardless of one's interpretation of the historical case of Russian Bolshevism, why should theoretical and/or practical militancy on behalf of historical materialism be any more or less "religious" than such militancy on behalf of psychoanalysis? This question is particularly pressing if both Marxism and Freudianism participate in scientific worldviews while not being themselves religions.

A less traditional form of Marxism would go even further by problematizing Enlightenment presumptions about ideologies as limited, circumscribed, and surpassable phenomena. Various sorts of classical historical materialism predict an "end of ideologies" with the advent of classless societies. From this perspective, ideologies are necessary only in class-based societies requiring such forms of false consciousness in order to secure the acquiescence primarily of the exploited and oppressed classes. With the abolition of classes and, along with them, relations of exploitation and oppression, the need for ideologies vanishes too. They become superfluous and automatically wither away.

This Enlightenment-type Marxist likewise believes that the historical materialist is the one from whose eyes the scales of ideologies have fallen. The critic of political economy simply stands outside of ideology, enjoying a pure, uncompromised externality. Freud's notions of scientificity and "the scientific *Weltanschauung*" similarly flirt with suggesting that the scientist (and the scientifically minded psychoanalyst) not only repudiates religiosity but rationally transcends all ideology whatsoever.

But Louis Althusser's recasting of Marxism, to take a nontraditional variant of this orientation, rejects all visions of any end of ideology, Marxist ones included.[51] According to Althusser, all modes of production, even socialist and communist ones, spontaneously secrete ideologies as the "imaginary" (à la the Lacanian register of the Imaginary) contents (such as beliefs, categories, concepts, customs, faiths, ideas, ideals, mores, norms, notions, rituals, values, etc.) rendering the "real" of an established social system a livable reality for its subjects. Without ideologies conceived thus, societies would not seem livable and, hence, would fail to be produced and reproduced. So long as there are societies, up to and including fully communist ones entirely liberated from and free of classes and private property, there will be ideologies. The latter are like the air that is breathed by all social subjects.

One of many upshots to this Althusserian account of ideology is that Marxist theory, although itself a nonideological science, must work with and through nonscientific ideologies (and not just because it is always surrounded by ideology as an omnipresent, unsurpassable feature of social existence). This is particularly necessary, for Althusser, at the level of Marxist political practice. For Marx himself, the superstructures of ideologies are the terrain on which, speaking of class conflict caused by crises in relations and modes of production, "men become conscious of this conflict and fight it out"[52] (with this statement from the preface to 1859's *A Contribution to the Critique of Political Economy* being crucial to Gramsci,[53] among others). Following this Marx, Althusser too maintains that despite his own strict distinction between science and ideology, the practical-political deployment of the scientific theory of historical materialism inevitably will interact with and need to rely upon certain ideologies in its enveloping *Zeitgeist*.

In Freud's eyes, this inevitable commingling of science and ideology in the translation of theory into practice might very well be tantamount to the degeneration of the scientific into the religious. Yet in line with Althusser, is this commingling not requisite for a scientific theory to enjoy actual transformative efficacy at the practical level of real-world politics? Are not phenomena commonly associated with religiosity, including belief, devotion, faith, fervor, and passion, crucial ingredients of any effective political movement? One who wishes to avoid dirtying their hands with ideologies and anything resembling religious phenomena also wishes to avoid all revolutionary activity. As will be seen in what follows, Freud himself comes to concede that what he disapproves of as the religious aspects of Bolshevism may turn out to be indispensable to its quest to usher in a "new social order."

The just-delineated Althusserian response to Freud's criticisms of Bolshevism as yet another fanatical sect involves a qualified acceptance of associations of Marxism with the worldviews constituted by ideologies generally and religions specifically. In the present context, Lacan offers a sharply contrasting approach both to Freud's indictment of the Bolsheviks as promulgating a religious *Weltanschauung* as well as to what Freud has to say about psychoanalysis's ties to the scientific *Weltanschauung* (with all of this to be found in "The Question of a *Weltanschauung*," the lecture bringing 1933's *New Introductory Lectures on Psycho-Analysis* to a close). Regarding these matters, Lacan takes his distance from Freud.

§2. NOT OF THIS WORLD: A LACANIAN EXCURSUS ON THE *WELTANSCHAUUNG* QUESTION

With respect to the Freud of the *New Introductory Lectures on Psycho-Analysis*, Lacan rejects both Freud's allying of psychoanalysis with any *Weltanschauung*, including a supposed scientific one, as well as Freud's critical treatment of Marxism as a worldview. Lacan makes various remarks, scattered across the years of *le Séminaire*, about the basic idea of a *Weltanschauung* (as "*une conception du monde*" and/or "*un système du monde*"). From Lacan's perspective, worldviews rest on problematic assumptions, ones with which analysis as a "science of the Real" dispenses.[54] Implicitly originating with the illusory microcosm of the unified totality presented by the Imaginary body of the mirror stage (i.e., the *imago-Gestalt*), the "world" of any worldview is fantasized as being a spherical macrocosmic whole, namely, an all-encompassing bubble usually identified as "nature."[55]

Lacan is adamant that psychoanalysis fundamentally breaks with and disrupts any such envisioning of being, nature, and/or the Real as a world qua well-rounded One-All organically harmonizing microcosm and macrocosm.[56] He treats the vision of such worldviews as a "dream" (*rêve*).[57]

In *Seminar XXIV* (*L'insu que sait de l'une-bévue, s'aile à mourre* [1976–1977]), Lacan indicates that the subject qua "speaking being" (*parlêtre*) is positioned as a human being facing a world that has always-already fallen away. This Lacan associates the void of *le monde* with the hole at the center of the torus, a key topological figure for Lacan's metapsychological speculations.[58] To cut a long story short, the torus's hole signifies for Lacan the lack(s) forming the center of gravity for the libidinal economy's repetitive circling around things missing. This means that the nonexistent world is an absence eliciting fantasies in the forms of *Weltanschauungen*.

However, in *Seminar XX* (*Encore* [1972–1973]), Lacan cautions that "what is enclosed in a torus has absolutely nothing to do with what is enclosed in a bubble [*une bulle*]."[59] This warning underscores the difference between, on the one hand, what would be the presence and positivity of a really-existing world qua truly-there unity (i.e., "a bubble") and, on the other hand, what is the absence and negativity of the lack of any such world. This lack provokes the effervescing of fantasies about world-forming bubbles fantasmatically filling in the hole of worldlessness.

Of course, Freud denies that psychoanalysis has its own worldview only to affirm that it tethers itself to the *Weltanschauung* of the (natural) sciences. By contrast, Lacan not only reiterates Freud's denial of there being a distinct analytic worldview—contra Freud, he also denies the existence of a scientific *Weltanschauung*. In the January 9, 1973, session of the twentieth seminar, Lacan observes: "The world, the world is in [a state of] decomposition, thank God. We see that the world no longer stands up [*Le monde, nous le voyons ne plus tenir*], because even in scientific discourse it is clear that there isn't the slightest world. As soon as you can add something called a 'quark' to atoms and have that become the true thread of scientific discourse, you must realize that we are dealing with something other than a world."[60]

Both here and elsewhere,[61] Lacan anticipates and inspires Slavoj Žižek's utilization of quantum physics in forging a new form of dialectical materialism eschewing reliance on anything resembling a "world" qua a solid, homogeneous, undivided completeness. Incidentally, had Lacan lived longer, he certainly would have felt further vindicated by the recent advent of string theory in theoretical physics. This would be not only thanks to string theory's further decomposition of subatomic units but also to its mobilizations of multidimensional topologies as well as speculations replacing a one-and-only universe with the proliferating becomings of multiverses.

In the above quotation from *Seminar XX*, Lacan tacitly takes advantage of the fact that the physics of the smallest bits of the material Real typically is assumed by both scientists and nonscientists alike to reveal the ultimate foundation of the physical universe, the base to which, at least in principle, everything in this universe is reducible. If one grants such reductionism in the context of post-Newtonian physics, then the material Real of the natural sciences is doubly worldless (and, if one does not grant this, then one opts for an antireductionism also entailing worldlessness, now in terms of a vision of nature as fractured into a heterogeneous multitude of irreducible-to-one-another levels and layers). First, as Lacan emphasizes, any core underlying unity vanishes through the atomic qua indivisible, as per the original meaning of the ancient Greek ἄτομος, suddenly succumbing to division and multiplication with the advent of subatomic physics. Second—Lacan does not mention this—post-Newtonian physics, with physics as the ostensibly foundational branch of the sciences of nature, has remained stubbornly split through the present day between the yet-to-be-reconciled dimensions of the microcosm of quantum mechanics and the macrocosm of general relativity theory. There is no world qua indivisible unity to be found at either the micro or macro levels.

These remarks concerning science and the world (or the lack thereof) follow on the heels of Lacan, earlier in the same seminar session (January 9, 1973), having turned his attention to the phrase "worldview" (*conception du monde*), no doubt with Freud's employment of *"Weltanschauung"* in mind. Partitioning psychoanalysis from philosophy, Lacan treats worldviews as the risible products of the latter: "Already, by merely swimming with the tide of analytic discourse, we have made a jump known as a 'world view' [*conception du monde*], which to us must nevertheless be the funniest thing going [*le plus comique*]. The term 'world view' supposes a discourse—that of philosophy—that is entirely different from ours."[62] He continues: "If we leave behind philosophical discourse, nothing is less certain than the existence of a world. One can only laugh [*Il n'y a qu'occasion de sourire*] when one hears people claim that analytic discourse involves something on the order of such a conception."[63]

If psychoanalysis has anything to say in connection with the world of any philosophical *conception du monde*, it would be that such a being or object, as a synthesized, conflict-free whole, does not exist (as per Lacan's ontological extrapolations from his *"il n'y a pas de rapport sexuel"* during the era of *Seminar*

26 ⋙ THE CONFLICTED POLITICAL ANIMAL

XX). Along with modern science, psychoanalysis dissolves such worlds into multiplicities of heterogeneous elements. Hence, there is neither a psychoanalytic nor, implicitly *pace* Freud, a scientific *Weltanschauung*.

Lacan immediately proceeds to deny that Marxism too has or constitutes a worldview. Whereas someone like Reich identifies Marx's materialism as amounting to a *Weltanschauung*,[64] Lacan unambiguously rejects this identification. Again in the same session (January 9, 1973) of the twentieth seminar, he states:

> I would go even further—putting forward such a term to designate Marxism is also a joke [*fait également sourire*]. Marxism does not seem to me to be able to pass for a world view. The statement of what Marx says [*L'énoncé de ce que dit Marx*] runs counter to that in all sorts of striking ways. Marxism is something else, something I will call a gospel [*un évangile*]. It is the announcement that history is instating another dimension of discourse and opening up the possibility of completely subverting the function of discourse as such and of philosophical discourse, strictly speaking, insofar as a world view is based upon the latter.[65]

Interestingly, Lacan's observations counterintuitively suggest that at least some religions, especially Messianic ones, are not actually worldviews per se. His reasoning is that for those religions involving something on the order of "a gospel" (*un évangile*), the current world is incomplete (insofar as it still awaits completion through a coming, redemption, resurrection, etc.) and/or will be transcended with the arrival of a radically new world *à venir*. On the basis of such reasoning, Lacan dissociates Marxism too with any worldview insofar as the historical-materialist critique of political economy prophecies a future rupture breaking history in two, namely, a revolutionary transition from class-based to classless societies (one cannot help but think of Walter Benjamin's association of historical materialism with Messianism[66] as well as Ernst Bloch's work on the topic of utopias—and this despite Bernard Sichère, in the course of an indignant tirade, denouncing Lacan's association of Marxism with the messianism of a gospel).[67] The old world of Marx's "history hitherto" will give way to another sociohistorical logic altogether.

In the block quotation immediately above, Lacan also points to a Marxist "subversion" of established "discourses," including "philosophical discourse." Given Lacan's definition of *discours* as a symbolically structured "social link" (*lien social*),[68] with him also associating such social links with ideologies,[69] an undermining of discourses would be tantamount to a transformation of social links, in other words, to a revolution in the Marxist sense. However, the more specific subversion of philosophical discourse to which Lacan here refers likely has to do with Marx's manners of situating philosophy within social superstructure as treated by ideology critique.[70] A historical-materialist account of the genesis, evolution, and function of philosophy certainly is strikingly at odds with philosophy's more traditional conceptions of itself as a discipline.

So, at this juncture, it can be seen that Lacan denies that psychoanalysis, science, Messianism, and Marxism are, any of them, *conceptions du monde*. All four of these fields are thereby set in contrast against one discursive domain in particular, namely, that of philosophy. Even more precisely, Lacan zeroes in on the philosophical subdiscipline of ontology. During this period of Lacan's teaching (i.e., the early 1970s), he is engaged in a thinly veiled polemic against his former friend, the German philosopher Martin Heidegger.[71]

Of course, Heidegger's main claim to fame in the context of twentieth-century philosophy is to have advocated for a return to and renewal of ontology under the shadow of Kantian and post-Kantian epistemological reservations about ontological speculations in general. Indeed, the entirety of the Heideggerian oeuvre fairly can be characterized as the pursuit of a "fundamental ontology." Tacitly disparaging Heidegger as well as all other aspiring ontologists, the Lacan of the early 1970s coins the neologism *hontologie*, homophonous with *ontologie*, so as to deride ontology as a shame (*honte*).[72] Lacan is subtly echoing Freud's Heinrich Heine–inspired disregard for the theory-of-everything ambitions of systematic metaphysics.[73] Moreover, in the January 9, 1973, session of *Seminar XX*, Lacan posits a chain of equivalence in which philosophy equals worldview equals ontology.[74] For this Lacan, Marxism and psychoanalysis both entail critiques of ontologies as philosophical worldviews.

Yet another detail in the January 9, 1973, session of the twentieth seminar is worth appreciating in the present context. Right after talking about worldviews, Marxism, and philosophy, Lacan adds to his objections to the philosophical discourse of ontology. As brought out by Heidegger's core notion of "ontological difference" (i.e., the distinction between Being as ontological and beings as ontic), ontology is concerned with the fundamental "is" (i.e., Being) underlying and pervading each and every thing that is (i.e., beings). Especially as per Heideggerian ontological difference, there is an irreducibility of ontological Being to ontic beings. Although these dimensions are complexly and intimately entwined with each other, fundamental ontology allegedly can, does, and should separate out Being as distinct from beings.

The Lacan of *Seminar XX* contests ontological difference, with its gesture of distinguishing the ontological from the ontic. One could argue that despite

Lacan evincing no awareness of this fact, this contestation of an isolable onto-logical Being is foreshadowed by the opening moments of Hegel's *Logik*.[75] That said, Lacan begins expressing this line of criticism contra ontology thus: "Ontology is what highlighted in language the use of the copula, isolating it as a signifier [*comme signifiant*]. To dwell on the verb 'to be'—a verb that is not even, in the complete field of the diversity of languages, employed in a way we could qualify as universal—to produce it as such is a highly risky enterprise [*une accentuation pleine de risques*]."[76] Lacan goes on to propose:

> In order to exorcise it, it might perhaps suffice to suggest that when we say about anything whatsoever that it is what it is, nothing in any way obliges us to isolate the verb "to be." That is pronounced "it is what it is" [*c'est ce que c'est*], and it could just as well be written, "idizwadidiz" [*seskecé*]. In this use of the copula, we would see nothing at all. We would see nothing whatsoever if a discourse, the discourse of the master, *m'être*, didn't emphasize [*ne mettait l'accent*] the verb "to be" [*être*].[77]

I strongly suspect that Lacan intends this to operate as an immanent critique of the Heidegger who, at the start of 1946's "Letter on Humanism," famously proposes that "Language is the house of Being."[78] Lacan's critical strategy seems to be to grant this Heidegger's proposal precisely so as to problematize ontological difference à la Heidegger himself (as well as fundamental ontology in general).

If, as Lacan suggests, the multitude of languages does not allow Being, as the verb "to be" (*être*), to be "isolated" and treated as "universal," then the very possibility of (fundamental) ontology, at least as a *logos*, is cast into serious doubt. Along these lines, Lacan's neologism *seskecé* collapses the homophonous *c'est ce que c'est* so as to make audible the lack of differentiation and separability of the *est* as a conjugation of *être*. Instead of the free-standing "is" of "it is what it is," the conjugated "to be" merges with and dissolves into "idizwadidiz." That is to say, the ontological "is" and the ontic "it" become indistinguishable and inseparable, by contrast with the maintenance of any ontological difference.

Lacan also here exploits another homophony, that between *maître* and *m'être*. He clearly equates philosophy in general and ontology in particular with the discourse of the master (*maître*). During a subsequent session of *Seminar XX*, Lacan elaborates further on his wordplay between *maître* and *m'être* (and, in so doing, he subtly refers to and embellishes upon Pierre Corneille's line "Master of the universe but not of myself, I am the only rebel against my absolute power"): "Development is confused with the development of mastery [*maîtrise*]. It is here that one must have a good ear, like in music—I am the master [*m'être*], I progress along the path of mastery [*m'êtrise*], I am the master [*m'être*] of myself [*moi*] as I am of the universe ... The universe is a flower of rhetoric."[79]

One should combine these statements from the February 13, 1973, session with the already-quoted statement from the January 9, 1973, session according to which "we would see nothing whatsoever if a discourse, the discourse of the master, *m'être*, didn't emphasize [*ne mettait l'accent*] the verb 'to be' [*être*]." Doing so enables one better to discern the line of argumentation condensed in Lacan's plays across *maître* and *m'être* as well as *maîtrise* and *m'êtrise*.

The ontological as Being, the isolated "to be" (*être*), would be the "uni-" of the universe of ontic beings. As "uni-," it would be a One as an All or Whole. Such a totality, Lacan maintains, is a macrocosmic projection of the microcosmic fictional unity of the ego (*moi*), as are all worldviews (*Weltanschauungen, conceptions du monde*) for him. Likewise, Lacan bluntly maintains that no "cosmos" qua grand unity actually exists.[80] Therefore, like the ego itself, the world of ontology is a vain, fantasmatic attempt to get a masterful grip (via *der Begriff*) on the fields of existence. This mastery (*maîtrise*) is asserted by bundling these fields together in a uni-verse, which itself is unconsciously modeled, in a process of *m'êtrise*, on the *imago-Gestalt* forming the ego's nucleus as originating in the mirror stage.

Hence, what appears as the seemingly impersonal, anonymous Being of ostensibly universal metaphysics is, in truth, the me-being of the ego deceptively writ large. Ontology thus would be a narcissistic delusion, the ultimate puffing up of the pretentious little master that is the ego. Such worldviews, with their ahistoricism as well as reliance on the atomlike *moi* of the ego, are anathema to psychoanalysis and Marxism alike.

§3. COMMUNISM AND AMBIVALENCE: FREUD, MARXISM, AND AGGRESSION

Returning to Freud again, there are two more sets of lengthy remarks he makes about communism in his 1933 lecture on "The Question of a *Weltanschauung*" I have yet to address. Both of these portions of this lecture evince a pronounced, explicit ambivalence on Freud's part apropos Marxism and its political implementation in the guise of Bolshevism. As I will argue in this section, these two passages from the *New Introductory Lectures on Psycho-Analysis* provide openings for an immanent-critical reworking of Freud's political reflections, a reworking informed by a synthesis of Marxism and psychoanalysis.

30   THE CONFLICTED POLITICAL ANIMAL

Whereas Lacan stresses Marxism's messianic dimension (as "a gospel" [*un évangile*]), Freud downplays this side of it. He dismisses the claims of classical historical materialism to predictive power. However, he values this same historical materialism for its insights into the previously un- or underappreciated importance of economies for human social existence. In this vein, Freud comments:

The strength of Marxism clearly lies, not in its view of history or the prophecies of the future that are based on it, but in its sagacious indication of the decisive influence which the economic circumstances of men have upon their intellectual, ethical and artistic attitudes. A number of connections and implications were thus uncovered, which had previously been almost totally overlooked. But it cannot be assumed that economic motives are the only ones that determine the behaviour of human beings in society [*Gesellschaft*]. The undoubted fact that different individuals, races and nations behave differently under the same economic conditions is alone enough to show that economic motives are not the sole dominating factors. It is altogether incomprehensible how psychological factors can be overlooked where what is in question are the reactions of living human beings; for not only were these reactions concerned in establishing the economic conditions, but even under the domination of those conditions men can only bring their original instinctual impulses [*ursprünglichen Triebregungen*] into play—their self-preservative instinct [*Selbsterhaltungstrieb*], their aggressiveness [*Aggressionslust*], their need to be loved [*Liebesbedürfnis*], their drive [*Drang*] towards obtaining pleasure and avoiding unpleasure. In an earlier enquiry I also pointed out the important claims made by the super-ego, which represents tradition and the ideals of the past and will for a time resist the incentives of a new economic situation. And finally we must not forget that the mass of human beings who are subjected to economic necessities also undergo the process of cultural development [*Kulturentwicklung*]—of civilization [*Zivilisation*] as other people may say—which, though no doubt influenced by all the other factors, is certainly independent of them in its origin, being comparable to an organic process and very well able on its part to exercise an influence on the other factors. It displaced instinctual aims [*Triebziele*] and brings it about that people become antagonistic to what they had previously tolerated. Moreover, the progressive strengthening of the scientific spirit [*wissenschaftlichen Geistes*] seems to form an essential part of it. If anyone were in a position to show in detail the way in which these different factors—the general inherited human disposition [*die allgemeine menschliche Triebanlage*], its racial variations and its cultural [*kulturellen*] transformations—inhibit and promote one another under the conditions of social rank, profession and earning capacity—if anyone were able to do this, he would have supplemented Marxism so that it was made into a genuine social science [*einer wirklichen Gesellschaftskunde*]. For sociology too, dealing as it does with the behaviour of people in society, cannot be anything but applied psychology. Strictly speaking there are only two sciences [*Wissenschaften*]: psychology, pure and applied, and natural science [*Naturkunde*].[81]

A remark by Gramsci is a fitting response to Freud's concerns (ones Freud shares with the likes of Weber)[82]—"Frequently, people attack historical economism in the belief that they are attacking historical materialism."[83] Economistic vulgarizations of historical materialism perpetrated by the likes of both the Second International and Stalinism indeed are vulnerable to the sorts of reservations and objections raised by Freud in this passage. However, Marx and Engels, especially given their concessions apropos the role of human mindedness in sociohistorical processes,[84] are far from guilty of the neglect of "psychology" prompting Freud's criticisms here.[85] And, of course, almost the entirety of the Western Marxist tradition from Lukács, Korsch, and Gramsci onward amounts to a sustained struggle within Marxism against the crudely reductive economism problematized by Freud. If anything, I believe Western Marxism has too excessively deemphasized economics in its antieconomism campaigns.

In the quotation above, Freud also refers back to his employment of the theory of the superego against historical materialism's prioritization of the economy (an employment contained in one of the earlier lectures, "The Dissection of the Psychical Personality," in his *New Introductory Lectures on Psycho-Analysis*). Having already responded to this, I will not repeat myself now. I also will leave aside Freud's highly debatable assertion having it that "strictly speaking there are only two sciences [*Wissenschaften*]: psychology, pure and applied, and natural science [*Naturkunde*]." I will limit myself to suggesting that this is true only on an exceedingly broad construal of "psychology."

Furthermore, the just-quoted passage from "The Question of a *Weltanschauung*" also involves Freud repeating his now-familiar recourse to the notion of an immutable human nature as an obstacle to the perhaps unrealistic aspirations of socialist and communist sociopolitical programs. He speaks of humanity's "original instinctual impulses" (*ursprünglichen Triebregungen*) as constituting this purportedly incorrigible nature. However, the very list Freud then furnishes of these *Triebe* provides openings for Marxist responses to his charging of Marxism with a hopeless, doomed utopianism.

Freud identifies the following as instances of the "original instinctual impulses" he has in mind when warning Marxists about the impossibility of radically reforming human nature: "their self-preservative instinct [*Selbsterhaltungstrieb*], their aggressiveness [*Aggressionslust*], their need to be loved [*Liebesbedürfnis*], their drive [*Drang*] towards obtaining pleasure and avoiding unpleasure." As seen both in *Civilization and Its Discontents* and elsewhere in the *New Introductory Lectures on Psycho-Analysis*, Freud focuses exclusively on aggression as the purportedly natural drive or instinct threatening to derail Marxist revolutions. On these other occasions of making the human-nature objection to Marxism, Freud does not mention self-preservation, love, and the (un)pleasure principle.

Apart from the issue of aggression, which I will address momentarily, the other "original instinctual impulses" Freud mentions in the preceding block quotation from "The Question of a *Weltanschauung*" first, pose no obstacles to socialism/communism; second, readily could be pressed into the willing service of such new social orders; and third, potentially could be encouraged to rebel against really existing capitalism. Apropos the "self-preservative instinct" (*Selbsterhaltungstrieb*), is not today's global capitalism, with its staggering wealth inequality, vulnerable to (and deserving of) being judged an abject failure by the majority of the world's population? Does this capitalism not fail to satisfy even the most basic "self-preservative" needs of the billions of people it abandons to squalid poverty? Does it not turn the bulk of humanity into "the wretched of the earth"? By stark contrast, what about the core promise of socialist and communist political projects to furnish real economic equality and decent material standards of living for everyone? Is not Marxism much more in line with what the enlightened self-interest of most people's "self-preservative" tendencies would and should demand?

As regards Freud's postulated "need to be loved" (*Liebesbedürfnis*), there seems to be no reason whatsoever to presume that this drive-level natural impulse can be satisfied only through nonsocialist/noncommunist social arrangements or that such a need cannot be satisfied through socialist/communist social arrangements. One must recall that this same later Freud ties love to a sweeping vision of "Eros" inspired by the ancient Greeks. Starting in 1920's *Beyond the Pleasure Principle*, Eros's life drives, enjoining the individual organism and its psyche to forge links and unite with others, are portrayed by Freud as pushing back against the *Todestrieb*'s inclinations toward hostility, severance, and withdrawal.[86]

This push and pull between the centrifugal and constructive life drives and the centripetal and destructive death drive(s) is very different from the

THE CONFLICTED POLITICAL ANIMAL   33

uncontested dominance and one-way thrust of virulent, undiluted aggression. Could not the need for love and striving for (social) connectedness be harnessed and bolstered by Marxist revolutionaries? What would prevent them from potentially forging a powerful alliance with Eros? Does Freud, especially when arguing that human aggressiveness will bring to naught all socialist/communist endeavors, simply assume that the *Todestrieb* as aggression always in every instance will win in its conflicts with Eros?

Indeed, elsewhere, including in *Civilization and Its Discontents* when not objecting to Marxism, Freud describes the struggle between Eros and the *Todestrieb* as open-ended and of uncertain outcome. In *The Ego and the Id*, when entertaining the possibility that the id is "under the domination of the mute but powerful death instincts [*unter der Herrschaft der stummen, aber mächtigen Todestriebe stünde*]," he admits, "perhaps that might be to undervalue the part played by Eros [*aber wir besorgen, doch dabei die Rolle des Eros unterschätzen*]."[87] And the concluding paragraph of the sixth chapter of *Civilization and Its Discontents* draws to a close, after emphasizing the threat posed by innate human aggression to organized sociality itself,[88] with a sweeping vision of the war between Eros and the *Todestrieb* as on grand display across the entire arc of human history:

> Now, I think, the meaning of the evolution of civilization [*der Kulturentwicklung*] is no longer obscure to us. It must present the struggle between Eros and Death [*Kampf zwischen Eros und Tod*], between the instinct of life [*Lebenstrieb*] and the instinct of destruction [*Destruktionstrieb*], as it works itself out in the human species. This struggle is what all life essentially consists of, and the evolution of civilization may therefore be simply described as the struggle for life of the human species [*der Lebenskampf der Menschenart*]. And it is this battle of the giants [*diesen Streit der Giganten*] that our nurse-maids [*unsere Kinderfrauen*] try to appease with their lullaby about Heaven.[89]

Two closely related features of this passage are important to note in the present context. First, Freud says nothing about the outcome one way or another of "the struggle between Eros and Death." He is silent regarding the future course of this "struggle for life of the human species" (*Kampf als Lebenskampf der Menschenart*). Thus he by no means forecasts the victory of death over life, of the *Todestrieb* over Eros (nor vice versa).

Second, Freud's last sentence above, with its dismissive reference to "nurse-maids . . . with their lullaby about Heaven," indicates that Freud sees himself as having to labor mightily against the weight of tradition, received wisdom, popular views, and/or persistent illusions serving most of the rest of humanity as defenses against painful truths. Just like other deeply entrenched and widespread defensive prejudices undermined by psychoanalysis, such as those concerning sex, love, and mindedness, faith in the victoriousness and reliability of "the better angels of our nature" cannot but be profoundly shaken by the analytic hypothesis of the *Todestrieb* and its consequences. However, although Freud seeks to bend the stick against rosy or even Pollyannaish pictures of a benevolent human nature (as per any "lullaby about Heaven"), he does not preach a diametrically opposed necessitarian antigospel about Hell. That is to say, the triumph of love over death is not guaranteed in advance (contra nursemaids' lullabies), but neither is the triumph of aggression (*Todestrieb*) over sociality (Eros). Although Freud is no optimist, neither is he a fatalist.[90]

Then, *Civilization and Its Discontent* concludes by circumnavigating back to the Empedoclean strife pitting life against death drives. This book's final paragraph observes regarding the future fate of humanity:

> The fateful question for the human species [*Die Schicksalsfrage der Menschenart*] seems to me to be whether and to what extent their cultural development [*ihrer Kulturentwicklung*] will succeed in mastering the disturbance of their communal life by the human instinct of aggression and self-destruction [*menschlichen Aggressions- und Selbstvernichtungstrieb*]. It may be that in this respect precisely the present time deserves a special interest. Men have gained control over the forces of nature to such an extent that with their help they would have no difficulty in exterminating one another to the last man. They know this, and hence comes a large part of their current unrest, their unhappiness and their mood of anxiety [*ihrer Angststimmung*]. And now it is to be expected that the other of the two "Heavenly Powers" [*himmlischen Mächte*], eternal Eros, will make an effort to assert himself in the struggle with his equally immortal adversary. But who can foresee with what success and with what result?[91]

An editorial footnote points out that the question bringing this book to a close was added in 1931. Again, one should appreciate that even in the face of the rise of antisemitic fascism and species-threatening techno-scientific warfare, Freud insists on the uncertainty as to whether or not the death-drive forces of hatred and annihilation will triumph.[92] This uncertainty is thanks to Eros, namely, what the *New Introductory Lectures on Psycho-Analysis* identifies as both the "self-preservative instinct" (*Selbsterhaltungstrieb*) and the "need to be loved" (*Liebesbedürfnis*) that are, for Freud, just as intrinsic to human nature as "aggressiveness" (*Aggressionslust*). In this vein, the very title of Marcuse's 1955 manifesto of Freudo-Marxism, *Eros and Civilization*, is telling. A Marxist engagement with psychoanalysis indeed ought to emphasize the role of Freud's Eros in relation to the conflicts and dangers worrying the author of *Civilization and Its Discontents*.

As I highlighted earlier, Freud tends to play the Hobbesian when pitting himself against Marxism. At such moments, he risks implying, among other things, that the *Todestrieb* as aggression is the exclusive or overriding tendency at the base of human nature and psychical life.[93] But Freud's flirtations with Hobbes court the peril of his falling prey to a profound self-misunderstanding (and encourage the same misunderstanding of him in some of his readers,[94] as reflected, for instance, by Edwin R. Wallace's claim that "Hobbes . . . was a philosopher after Freud's own heart"[95] and José Brunner's depiction of the Freudian libidinal economy as an intrapsychical version of the Hobbesian state of nature dominated by violence and aggression).[96] Philip Rieff, in his 1959 study *Freud: The Mind of the Moralist*, explains these matters thus:

> *Homo homini lupus*: the Hobbesian words echo through Freud's social psychology. The natural man is rapacious and self-centered. But Freud recognizes as well the natural sociability of man, his permanent emotional need for community. The natural man is instinctually libidinal, a creature born into a hierarchy of love—which goes a long way toward modifying the Hobbesian view. To use Freud's family metaphor, there is not only a sibling rivalry, the model of social divisiveness; there is also a natural love and dependence on the parents. Man is from the beginning a thrall to society, being born into the society of the family. Although so far as Freud stresses the basic component of human aggressiveness he apparently agrees with Hobbes, he complicates the Hobbesian contention that the law of cunning and force is all that obtains in nature. There are force and freedom, Freud agrees. But there are also love and authority. And superior to all is the law of "primal ambivalence," which provides every strong hate with a counterpart of love, and hobbles every act of aggression with a subsequent burden of guilt.[97]

Rieff's "subsequent burden of guilt" is an allusion to the myth of the primal horde in Freud's *Totem and Taboo*.[98] In this myth, although the band of brothers kills the primal father of their horde so as to cast off the yoke of his oppressive tyranny, they afterward are haunted by remorse since, in their "primal ambivalence," they also love and identify with the *Urvater*.[99] In short, the brothers are ambivalent, not purely hostile (and Jean Roy, in his comparative study of Hobbes and Freud, helpfully distinguishes between Hobbes's notion of violence and

Freud's concept of aggression as per the theory of the death drive).[100] Incidentally, Althusser suggests that Lacan concurs with Jean-Jacques Rousseau's critique of Hobbes's state of nature as a distorting projection of present social conditions back into a mythical (and, via such mythicizing retrojection, thereby falsified) presocial past.[101] The Marcuse of *Eros and Civilization*, for his part, basically accuses Freud of lapsing into the Hobbesianism critiqued by Rousseau in Freud's nevertheless justified rubbishing of the Rousseauian romanticized state of nature.[102]

Freud's human is not (wholly) Hobbes's wolf. Instead, he/she is a reluctant, conflicted political animal profoundly ambivalent about his/her inescapable social entanglements with others, but a political animal nonetheless. Perhaps this ambivalence is so profound that a neologism put forward by Lacan to signify the intensity of ambivalence in psychoanalysis, *hainamoration*[103] (loosely translatable as "hate-love"), is more suitable in this context. The ambivalent *zoon politikon* of analysis hate-loves sociality.

Likewise, Kant, in his 1784 "Idea for a Universal History with a Cosmopolitan Intent," speaks of "men's *unsocial sociability* [*die* ungesellige Geselligkeit *der Menschen*], i.e., their tendency to enter into society, combined, however, with a thoroughgoing resistance [*einem durchgängigen Widerstande*] that constantly threatens to sunder [*trennen*] this society."[104] As with what I have described as Freud's reluctant, conflicted political animal, so too with human nature (*menschlichen Natur*) as per Kant's 1784 essay: This nature is split by a profound ambivalence combining "a propensity [*eine Neigung*] for *living in society* [*vergesellschaften*]" (as associable with Freudian Eros in its drive to bring beings together in larger wholes) with "a great tendency [*einen großen Hang*] to isolate [*vereinzelnen (isolieren)*] himself" (as associable with the Freudian *Todestrieb* in its inclination to sever links and destroy connections).[105] In relation to modern political philosophy, Freud is close to this Kant but not so much to Hobbes. And, with justification, Lucio Colletti links Kant's *ungesellige Geselligkeit* with Mandeville's dialectic of vice and virtue.[106]

This same Kant even gestures at what Freud and Lacan subsequently foreground as humans' prolonged prematurational helplessness. Echoing a thematic refrain tracing back to such predecessors as Plato,[107] Giovanni Pico della Mirandola,[108] and Baron Paul-Henri Thiry d'Holbach[109] and continuing on through German idealism (and well beyond),[110] the "Third Thesis" of "Idea for a Universal History with a Cosmopolitan Intent" states:

> *Nature has willed that man, entirely by himself, produce everything that goes beyond the mechanical organization of his animal existence and partake in no*

other happiness or perfection than what he himself, independently of instinct [frei von Instinkt], *can secure through his own reason.* Nature does nothing unnecessary [*überflüssig*] and is not prodigal [*verschwenderisch*] in the use of means to her ends [*Zwecken*]. Since she gave man reason and the freedom of will based on it, this is a clear indication of her objective [*Absicht*] as regards his makeup [*Ausstattung*]. Specifically, he should not be led by instinct, nor be provided for and instructed by ready-made knowledge; instead, he should produce everything from himself. Provision for his diet, his clothing, his bodily safety and defense (for which he was given neither the bull's horns, the lion's claws, nor the dog's teeth, but only hands), all amusements that can make life pleasant, even his insight and prudence, indeed, the goodness of his will—all of these should be entirely of his own making. Nature seems here to have taken delight in the greatest frugality [*ihrer größten Sparsamkeit*] and to have calculated her animal endowments so closely—so precisely to the most pressing needs of a primitive existence—that she seems to have willed that if man should ever work himself up from the grossest barbarity to the highest level of sophistication, to inner perfection in his way of thinking and thereby to happiness (as far as it is possible on earth), he alone would have the entire credit for it and would have only himself to thank; it is as if she aimed more at his rational *self-esteem* [*seine vernünftige* Selbstschätzung] than at his well-being [*Wohlbefinden*]. For along this course of human affairs a whole host of hardships awaits man. But it appears that nature is utterly unconcerned that man live well [*wohl lebe*], only that he bring himself to the point where his conduct makes him worthy of life and well-being [*Wohlbefindens*].[111]

Of course, with the benefits of hindsight afforded by various post-Kantian insights (particularly those stemming from Darwinism in addition to psycho-analysis), the teleological elements of this passage must be discarded. Kant's idea of Nature-with-a-capital-N as a purposive designer caring about the results of her goal-oriented creative activities, even if this idea is only of a regulative "as if" (*als ob*) sort, is at odds with what the advances of the natural sciences, including and especially those of the life sciences, come to reveal after Kant's death in 1804.

The d'Holbach of 1772's *Good Sense* is much closer to grasping the core character of nature as per post-Kantian natural science. At one moment therein, he declares: "If we attempted to consider without prejudice the equivocal conduct of Providence relative to mankind and to all sentient beings, we should find that very far from resembling a tender and careful mother, it rather resembles those unnatural mothers who, forgetting the unfortunate fruits of their illicit amours, abandon their children as soon as they are born; and who, pleased to have conceived them, expose them without mercy to the caprices of fate."[112] Kant describes Nature as not being "prodigal" (*verschwenderisch*), as exhibiting the "greatest frugality" (*größten Sparsamkeit*), and as "utterly unconcerned that man live well" (*wohl lebe*)—with all of this intended as part of a grand plan for humanity's (self-)betterment. By sharp contrast, d'Holbach construes such frugality and unconcern as evidence of nature not planning in the least as regards human beings. Nature à la d'Holbach is a neglectful and coldly uncaring parent, tossing humans at birth into an indifferent and treacherous world ill-equipped to cope with it. Instead of Kantian calculated benign neglect, d'Holbach points to plain out-and-out neglect reflecting no thought, concern, or intention whatsoever. The pre-Kantian French materialist's vision is much more in line with such post-Kantian perspectives as evolutionary theory and Freudian-Lacanian metapsychology than is Kant's hypothesis of a purposive Nature as a benevolent intelligent designer.

So after jettisoning the teleological aspects of Kant's speculations about Nature in "Idea for a Universal History with a Cosmopolitan Intent," what remains from this essay's "Third Thesis" of worth for a post-Darwinian, psychoanalytic perspective? The value of this Kantian passage resides in its recognition of just how crucial uniquely human *Hilflosigkeit* is for multiple distinctive features of humanity.[113] For Kant, this helplessness appears in the guise of humans' natural lack of both instinctual savoir-faire ("he should not be led by instinct, nor be provided for and instructed by ready-made knowledge") as well as the anatomical and physiological advantages enjoyed by other animals ("he was given neither the bull's horns, the lion's claws, nor the dog's teeth, but only hands"). And the distinctive features of humanity to which this *Hilflosigkeit* gives rise include, according to Kant, societies' denaturalized and historically evolving modes of production ("he should produce everything from himself. Provision for his diet, his clothing, his bodily safety and defense . . . all amusements that can make life pleasant") and the socially inclined side of human beings' "*unsocial sociability*" (as bound up with "the goodness of his will," "the highest level of sophistication," and the "inner perfection in his way of thinking"). Hence, both Marxism and psychoanalysis ought to recognize this Kant and his philosophical anthropology as anticipating their own subsequent insights.

As is well known, one of several central fault lines of opposition running through the history of Western political philosophy is that opposing those who conceive of human beings as *zoon politikon* (such as Aristotle, Hegel, and Marx) and those who imagine humans as atomistic individuals (such as Hobbes and others who subscribe to myths about a state of nature preceding any and every social contract). Especially thanks to the introduction of the Eros-versus-*Todestrieb* dual-drive model in *Beyond the Pleasure Principle*, the later Freud's metapsychological speculations, when appreciated in their fullest scope, transform this sociopolitical opposition from a theoretical contradiction into a real one. That is to say, for Freud, human beings and their societies really are split from within by antagonisms between erotic and destructive tendencies. Insofar as humans are internally torn between Eros and the *Todestrieb* right down to their id-level first natures, they are simultaneously both *zoon politikon* (by virtue of Eros) as well as wolves to one another (by virtue of the *Todestrieb*). With this later Freud, what initially appears to be a conflict within the ideality of thinking (i.e., the opposed conceptions of humans as either *zoon politikon* or lone wolves) blocking access to the reality of being (i.e., human nature *an sich*) proves instead to be the key to the latter as the revelation of a conflict internal to the reality of being itself (i.e., human nature really is split from within along Aristotelian-versus-Hobbesian lines). In this way, Freud implicitly repeats Hegel's signature dialectical gesture of transubstantiating various contradictions from epistemological constraints into ontological disclosures.

Rieff, when invoking Eros in the above block quotation, twice refers to birth: "born into a hierarchy of love" and "born into the society of the family." Regardless of Rieff's intentions, the topic of birth is linked, in Freudian psychoanalysis, to Freud's emphasis on human beings' species-specific prolonged prematurational helplessness (*Hilflosigkeit*) into which they are thrown at birth.[114] In 1895's "Project for a Scientific Psychology," Freud posits that "the initial helplessness of human beings is the *primal source* [Urquelle] of all *moral motives* [moralischen Motive]."[115] Much later, in 1926's *Inhibitions, Symptoms and Anxiety*, Freud revisits this postulate and writes:

> The biological factor is the long period of time during which the young of the human species is in a condition of helplessness [*Hilflosigkeit*] and dependence [*Abhängigkeit*]. Its intra-uterine existence seems to be short in comparison with that of most animals, and it is sent into the world in a less finished state. As a result, the influence of the real external world upon it is intensified and an early differentiation between the ego and the id is promoted. Moreover, the dangers of the external world have a greater importance for it, so that the value of the object which can alone protect it against them and take the place of its former intra-uterine life is enormously enhanced. The biological factor, then, establishes the earliest situations of danger and creates the need to be loved [*Bedürfnis, geliebt zu werden*] which will accompany the child through the rest of its life.[116]

The Future of an Illusion (1927) likewise asserts that "the terrifying impression of helplessness in childhood aroused the need for protection [*Schutz*]—for protection through love [*Schutz durch Liebe*]—which was provided by the father"[117] (with this characterization of the father providing a link to the *Urvater* who was loved as well as hated by his sons). Several features of these 1926 and 1927 remarks about uniquely human protracted childhood helplessness deserve attention.

First of all, Freud's reflections bring up the connection between infantile *Hilflosigkeit* and "the need to be loved" (*Bedürfnis, geliebt zu werden*) or "the need for protection (*Schutz*)—for "protection through love" (*Schutz durch Liebe*) (or also, as he puts it in a passage from 1933 quoted by me a while ago, the "*Liebesbedürfnis*"). Taking into account Freud's notions of human nature, particularly during this period of his thinking, it seems that both prematurational helplessness and the need for love are conceived by him as biologically innate features of the species *Homo sapiens*. Yet how are these two natural factors related to each other? It appears that according to both *Inhibitions, Symptoms and Anxiety* and *The Future of an Illusion* (and perhaps also "Project for a Scientific Psychology"), helplessness is responsible for generating the *Liebesbedürfnis* (as Freud says in 1926 in the block quotation immediately above, "The biological factor . . . creates the need to be loved"). However, taking into consideration the later Freud's repeated insistences on the innateness of Eros's life drives without accompanying references to helplessness, it is far from entirely clear whether he would commit to making the need for love dependent on *Hilflosigkeit* or instead would insist on this need's being its own biological factor independent of, although abetted by, prematurational helplessness. Maybe, for Freud, helplessness as cause transfers its naturalness to the need for love as its direct effect.

Despite any partial obscurity in the *Hilflosigkeit-Liebesbedürfnis* relationship, Freud is neither vague nor ambiguous in asserting that humans' lengthy period of helplessness, itself a biologically innate feature of their organic being, renders them social by nature. Starting with the early total and complete dependence on the *Nebenmensch*-as-helper (usually a caretaking parent or parents), the young subject-to-be is fated/destined (in Freud's sense of *Schicksal* as allowing for multiple, but not limitless, possible paths of development) by biology itself to be entangled with and formed by relations with others. One could say that according to the psychoanalytic account of specifically human helplessness, human beings are naturally inclined to the dominance of nurture (i.e., social mediation via relations with conspecifics) over nature.

Furthermore, *Hilflosigkeit* entails a plasticity of human nature. As Freud indicates, for the psyche rooted in an initially helpless body, "the influence of the real external world upon it is intensified and an early differentiation between the ego and the id is promoted." Of course, the most important features of "the real external world" are social ones, namely, emotionally important others as exerting the decisive influences modulating the nascent subject's id and helping sculpt its emerging ego. The Freudian psyche, with its plasticity, is naturally pre-programmed by helplessness to be socially reprogrammed.

So, not only is Eros substantially empowered by the naturally given and onto-genetically primary couple *Hilflosigkeit-Liebesbedürfnis*—this couple also brings with it a psychical plasticity amounting to the susceptibility of the libidinal economy to being tamed and domesticated by its social milieu. Others' imposi-tions of a social reality principle significantly shape the routes and directions of drives and their derivatives. More specifically, these impositions mold the con-tours of sublimations. Indeed, social valuations, as determining the substitutive object choices of libidinal thrusts confronted with social prohibitions, are inher-ent to the very definition of sublimation as a concept in Freudian psychoanaly-sis.[118] As Marcuse comments apropos psychoanalytic drive theory, "The 'plastic-ity' of the instincts which this theory presupposes should suffice to refute the notion that the instincts are essentially unalterable biological substrata."[119]

Hence, the combination of prematurational helplessness and the need for love to which it gives rise renders the psychical-subject-to-be inclined toward socially specified sublimations. Such sublimations, in relation to Freud's 1920-onward dual-drive model, would not be limited exclusively to the side of Eros. Quite the contrary—considering the later Freud's depiction of aggression as much more existentially threatening to societies than sexuality, developing children inevitably are confronted with social regulations demanding sublima-tions of their aggression.

When in 1933 Freud mentions humans' "drive [*Drang*] towards obtaining pleasure and avoiding unpleasure" (alongside "their self-preservative instinct" [*Selbsterhaltungstrieb*], "their aggressiveness" [*Aggressionslust*], and "their need to be loved" [*Liebesbedürfnis*]) in the context of criticizing socialism/commu-nism, he is talking not about an individual drive (*Trieb*) or type of drive. Instead, he is speaking of the pleasure principle influencing the operations of all drives. Although the pleasure principle is no longer supreme for the later Freud begin-ning with 1920's *Jenseits des Lustprinzips*, its influence remains potent and per-vasive throughout the psychical apparatus.

All sublimations amount to the pleasure principle's continuing successfully to chase pleasure and dodge pain in the face of challenges thrown up to it by external social reality. Indeed, the Freudian reality principle could be defined as the pleasure principle (*Lustprinzip*) once modified in response to this external reality. All societies past, present, and future must generate various sublimations in their subjects. And, if the pleasure principle is indeed as powerful as Freud maintains it to be, then no society, including a future communist one, could prevent its pursuit of pleasure (*Lust*) and avoidance of pain (*Unlust*). Moreover, the aggressiveness (*Aggressionslust*) Freud, in the *New Introductory Lectures on Psycho-Analysis*, invokes side by side with the pleasure principle clearly is open to sublimation and other drive-modifying vicissitudes (i.e., Freud's *Triebschicksale*).

According to Freud's own theory, aggression already is a secondary modification of the *Todestrieb*. The latter originally is an intrapsychically directed self-destructiveness. Extrapsychically directed destructiveness, aggression toward objects and others in external reality, already is a life-affirming deflection/displacement of this originally life-annulling suicidal tendency. For instance, in the 1933 lecture "Anxiety and Instinctual Life," Freud observes: "We recognize two basic instincts [*zwei Grundtriebe*] and give each of them its own aim [*sein eigenes Ziel*]. How the two of them are mingled in the process of living, how the death instinct [*der Todestrieb*] is made to serve the purposes of Eros, especially by being turned outwards as aggressiveness—these are tasks which are left to future investigation."[120] In "Why War?" from the same year, he remarks, "there is no question of getting rid entirely of human aggressive impulses [*die menschliche Aggressionsneigung*]; it is enough to try to divert them to such an extent that they need not find expression in war."[121] Several things merit noting here. To begin with, Freud indeed treats exogenous aggression as a secondary modification of the death drive's primary endogenous self-destructiveness, with Eros playing a role in bringing about this modification.

However, Freud, in "Anxiety and Instinctual Life," confesses his uncertainty regarding the details of exactly how Eros comes to influence and steer the *Todestrieb*, deflecting it from being self-directed to becoming other-directed. This is an issue to be "left to future investigation." Interestingly, in the very same context, Freud's not-unrelated discussions of the prospects of Marxist revolutionary endeavors similarly leave much to be decided by the unpredictable future of social history. Parallel to the unfinished business of the Eros-*Todestrieb* relationship in psychoanalysis's metapsychological theory, there are the unforeseeable vicissitudes-to-come of this same relationship at the level of Marxism's political practice.

Incidentally, Freud's hypothesis according to which the death drive's exogenous destructiveness already is a secondary detour for its primary endogenous self-destructiveness raises an interesting question in connection with his reservations regarding Marxism's prospects. As seen, Freud frets that the *Todestrieb* as aggression (i.e., exogenous destructiveness) will be resistant to and disruptive of any socialist or communist sociopolitical project. Yet if this aggression is itself a dilution and redirection of a more primordial undercurrent of endogenous self-destructiveness, then could not a Marxist program extolling and enjoining self-sacrifice for the sake of the revolutionary cause appeal to and tap into the foundational, archaic thrust of the death drive before its channeling into outwardly directed hostility? Would not the sacrificial self-renunciations demanded by the radical reinvention of society facilitate, perhaps once again with some assistance from Eros, a sort of socialist/communist desublimation tapping back into the original incarnation of the *Todestrieb*? Freud, in his criticisms of Marxism, neither asks nor answers the question: Why should one presume, as Freud appears to do, that the psyche's libidinal economy always and inevitably would prefer satisfying the death drive(s) through capitalism's selfish economic competition (i.e., sublimated aggression as itself the exogenous destructiveness already deflecting endogenous self-destructiveness) rather than socialism's or communism's self-sacrificial social renewals (i.e., sublimated self-aggression)?

The very last set of Freud's observations about Marxism from 1933's lecture "The Question of a *Weltanschauung*" again speaks about the uncertain outcomes *à venir* of the then-new socialist experiment in Russia and the Soviet Union. Freud engages in the following imaginary exchange with the Bolsheviks he has been criticizing intermittently in the *New Introductory Lectures on Psycho-Analysis* (and along lines already spelled out a few years prior in *Civilization and Its Discontents*):

> There is no doubt of how Bolshevism will reply to these objections. It will say that so long as men's nature has not yet been transformed it is necessary to make use of the means which affect them to-day. It is impossible to do without compulsions [*Zwang*] in their education, without the prohibition of thought and without the employment of force to the point of bloodshed; and if the illusions were not awakened in them, they could not be brought to acquiesce in this compulsion. And we should be politely asked to say how things could be managed differently. This would defeat us. I could think of no advice to give. I should admit that the conditions of this experiment would have deterred me and those like me from undertaking it; but we are not the only people concerned. There are men of action, unshakeable in their convictions, inaccessible to doubt [*unzugänglich dem Zweifel*], without feeling for the sufferings of others if they stand in the way of their intentions. We have to thank men of this kind for the fact that the tremendous experiment [*großartige Versuch*] of producing a new order of this kind is now actually being carried out in Russia. At a time when the great nations announce that they expect salvation only from the maintenance of

Christian piety, the revolution in Russia—in spite of all its disagreeable details—seems none the less like the message of a better future. Unluckily neither our scepticism [*unserem Zweifel*] nor the fanatical faith [*fanatischen Glauben*] of the other side gives a hint as to how the experiment will turn out. The future will tell us; perhaps it will show that the experiment was undertaken prematurely [*vorzeitig*], that a sweeping alteration of the social order has little prospect of success until new discoveries have increased our control over the forces of Nature and so made easier the satisfaction of our needs [*die Befriedigung unserer Bedürfnisse*]. Only then perhaps may it become possible for a new social order [*eine neue Gesellschaftsordnung*] not only to put an end to the material need of the masses but also to give a hearing to the cultural demands of the individual [*die kulturellen Ansprüche des Einzelnen*]. Even then, to be sure, we shall still have to struggle for an incalculable time with the difficulties which the untamable character of human nature [*die Unbändigkeit der menschlichen Natur*] presents to every kind of social community [*sozialer Gemeinschaft*].[122]

Freud, in his extreme intellectual honesty, reaches this point of admitting that his "scepticism" apropos Bolshevism by no means amounts to any knockdown arguments against it and the Marxist tradition of which it is a part. He grants that the October Revolution "seems . . . like the message of a better future," at least by comparison with bourgeois false promises of "salvation only from the maintenance of Christian piety." As for the eventual outcome of the socialist experiment, "The future will tell us."

Freud obviously has in mind the figure of Lenin as epitomizing the sort of Bolshevik he employs above as an imagined foil for his own doubts about socialism/communism (i.e., "men of action, unshakeable in their convictions, inaccessible to doubt, without feeling for the sufferings of others if they stand in the way of their intentions"). Freud's speculation that the future might reveal the October Revolution to have been "premature" echoes certain criticisms of Lenin's politics voiced even from within non-Leninist currents of Marxism (by contemporaneous representatives of the Second International, German Social Democracy, Menshevism, etc.). Likewise, whether Freud realizes it or not, his related speculation that a viable postcapitalist "new social order" balancing collective and individual goods might require an extremely high degree of scientific and technological development (in particular, higher than that achieved in feudal-agrarian tsarist Russia on the eve of the Bolshevik Revolution) resonates with moments in Marx's writings as well as with the perspectives of certain factions within Marxism. Yet Freud, in the face of what he anticipates by way of the Bolsheviks' self-justification in response to his reservations, concedes that "this would defeat us. I could think of no advice to give." With Freud's many vacillations and hesitations apropos socialism, communism, and Bolshevism, it would be fair to say that he evinces a marked ambivalence vis-à-vis Marxism.

But despite Freud's oscillations and inconsistencies in his reactions to Marxism, the final sentence of the prior block quotation amounts to him reiterating his oft-repeated claim that human nature as per psychoanalysis poses a perhaps insurmountable barrier to Marxism's revolutionary political-economic agenda ("we shall still have to struggle for an incalculable time with the difficulties which the untamable character of human nature [*die Unbändigkeit der menschlichen Natur*] presents to every kind of social community [*sozialer Gemeinschaft*]"). James Strachey chooses to render *Unbändigkeit* as "untamable character" likely because of this German word occurring in an argumentative context in which Freud is suggesting that "*menschlichen Natur*" will resist efforts to significantly reform or transform it. However, *unbändig* could be translated into English as "boisterous" and/or "unrestrained."

As I demonstrated at length in the preceding, the various elements of "human nature" Freud has in mind when criticizing Marxism are not, according to Freud's own psychoanalytic reasoning, "untamable" in the strong sense, namely, utterly impervious to domesticating social influences bringing about sublimations and the like. That is to say, this nature might be boisterous but still not untamable. Analysis indeed provides ample evidence for this boisterousness. Additionally, it also provides ample evidence that this boisterousness can be, and usually is, tamed by external realities, including social ones.

Recall once again the components of human nature Freud lists in the 1933 lecture "The Question of a *Weltanschauung*": human beings' "self-preservative instinct [*Selbsterhaltungstrieb*], their aggressiveness [*Aggressionslust*], their need to be loved [*Liebesbedürfnis*], their drive [*Drang*] towards obtaining pleasure and avoiding unpleasure." As I argued, three out of four of these components— these are self-preservation, the need for love, and the pleasure principle—pose no special resistances specifically to socialism or communism and, at least potentially, could be better served by, and hence be more cooperative with, socialist or communist social orders. Of these four, Freud tends to single out aggression as the key feature of "*die Unbändigkeit der menschlichen Natur*" constituting a major challenge for Marxist politics and its revolutionary socioeconomic ambitions.

Yet, *Aggressionslust* and the *Todestrieb* underlying it are not, by Freud's own lights, untamable. Again, aggression itself already is, for Freud, an Eros-assisted taming of the originally self-destructive death drive. Furthermore, I would observe that aggression can be and indeed is sublimated in myriad manners.

Freud furnishes countless clinical and cultural examples of such sublimations of aggression in the forms of, for instance, sexual practices, ethico-moral stances, professional rivalries, social status aspirations, and so on. Were aggressiveness not so readily tamable (*als bändig*), future socialist and communist societies would not be the only ones to be in trouble—past and present nonsocialist/non-communist societies would not have maintained their basic group coherence, and would not be able to continue maintaining such coherence, in the face of a critical mass of unsublimated individual aggression. Untamed and untamable *Aggressionslust* would be characteristic of the pre/antisocial anarchy of the mythical state of nature, not of any viable social order. The myriad sublimations of aggression testify to its boisterousness but not its untamability.

From a Marxist perspective, I would go even further and assert that capitalist societies foster sublimations of aggression in fashions that help make possible postcapitalist socialist and communist social accommodations of the *Aggressionslust* Freud fears such postcapitalist socioeconomic systems could not accommodate. What I am about to propose is an addition, inspired by a Marxist appreciation of psychoanalysis, to Marxism's inventory of those features of capitalism serving as historical conditions of possibility for the sublation of capitalism via socialism and communism. As with other capitalist phenomena, this is an instance of something that although superficially appearing to be distant from and/or antagonistic to socialism and communism, actually has the potential to be conducive to these types of postcapitalist arrangements.

As is common knowledge, competition is central to capitalism. The early stages of capitalist industrialization involved economic sectors in which multiple isolated small producers (for instance, individual factories and their owners) jostled with one another for advantage in given markets. Although such small-producer competition longed ago ceased to be a dominant essential feature of capitalist economies,[123] a mythic celebration of such competition continues to live on in capitalist ideologies right up through the present day.

What is more, forms of competition historical materialism would identify as originating at the infrastructural level of capitalist societies have spread like wildfire across the expanses and throughout all the nooks and crannies of the superstructural levels of these same societies. Thus, many of the cultural and political diversions and concerns within capitalism clearly are superstructural sublimations of infrastructural competition, with agonistic competition itself arguably being a sublimation of even more antagonistic and violent aggression. Under capitalism, institutions and spectacles having to do with everything from government and education to sports and games come to be organized as zero-sum, winners-versus-losers competitions, or at least as semblances thereof. Even

THE CONFLICTED POLITICAL ANIMAL   47

the sex and love lives of capitalism's subjects are not untouched by sublimated permutations of cutthroat economic competition. Indeed, as the *Communist Manifesto* already proclaimed in 1848, nothing whatsoever is sacred to capital.[124]

Although historical materialism would propose that superstructural forms of competitiveness originate in capitalism's earlier modes of infrastructural competition, I would venture to posit that over the subsequent course of capitalist economic history, economic competition has itself been transformed, at least in significant part, into a kind of not immediately economic competition. Put differently, capitalists' competitiveness about the accumulation of surplus value, itself a sublimation of aggression as per psychoanalysis,[125] has come to be sublimated in turn by the superstructural sublimations this infrastructural competitiveness initially inspired. In still other words, the riches at stake in the race between capitalists to amass surplus value primarily in the guise of money come to be more-than-economic signifiers of social status, cultural prestige, political power, and the like.[126] In a reversal resonating with a psychoanalytic sensibility encapsulated in William Wordsworth's "the child is the father of the man," the infrastructural parent (i.e., economic competition) has become the child of its superstructural children (i.e., more-than-economic competition). Perhaps this dynamic of an earlier sublimation being recast in the guise of the later sublimations to which it gives rise should be baptized "retroactive resublimation."

Taking the preceding points apropos competition into account, Freud's worries about aggression specifically as an insuperable difficulty for socialism and communism can be largely, if not completely, laid to rest. In particular, two related lines of counterargumentation vis-à-vis Freud on Marxism-versus-aggressiveness are available at this juncture. First, capitalism, in fostering the proliferation of superstructural, sociosymbolic sublimations of infrastructural competitiveness (with the latter as already a sublimation of Freud's *Todestrieb-als-Aggressionslust*), provides potential future socialist and communist societies with ample outlets for the aggressive tendencies of these societies' members. Even with the abolition of private property qua capital and, along with it, the wealth disparities of class-stratified social configurations, capitalism leaves behind and bequeaths to its historical successors plenty of more-than-economic opportunities for (competitively) marking differences between people.

However desirable or not, the sublimated aggression of jockeying for sociosymbolic inequality of recognition and superiority likely will remain after the disappearance of directly material-economic inequality. Twentieth-century experiments in really existing socialism, such as that inaugurated by the Bolsheviks' October Revolution, demonstrated as much. Contra the later Freud's expectations, these sociopolitical systems arguably did not fail because of a lack of opportunities for the subliminatory venting of aggression via these systems' subjects jostling with one another for system-acknowledged advantage, influence, and reputation.

Just as socialist and communist societies can and do take over the science, technology, and infrastructural machinery of the capitalist mode of production, with such appropriation being crucial for the viability and success of these postcapitalist orders, so too can such societies take over the noneconomic sublimations of aggression developed by capitalism at its superstructural levels. If, as per Freud, *Aggressionslust* must be satisfied, if only in sublimated manners, then more-than-economic competitiveness ought to do the job effectively enough. By Freud's own criteria, the measure of such sufficiency should be whether these sublimations allow for avoiding the unsublimated/desublimated violence of outright war, including the war of all against all, as per the above-quoted remark from "Why War?" about "human aggressive impulses," according to which "it is enough to try to divert them to such an extent that they need not find expression in war."

I come now to the second line of counterargumentation with respect to Freud on Marxism-versus-aggressiveness. A moment ago, I described a capitalism-immanent process of economic competitiveness, itself a sublimation of aggression, becoming just one among the more-than-economic permutations of competitiveness (as themselves superstructural sublimations of infrastructural competition-as-sublimation-of-aggression). Especially past a certain threshold in the stacking up of massive amounts of surplus value, wealth as quotas of quantifiable exchange value is, for such incredibly affluent capitalists, more about, for example, outranking the others on lists of the most wealthy individuals, garnering greater amounts of media attention, commanding outsize sway over politics, or outdoing one another in socially praised public philanthropy. For such persons as bearers/personifications of capital, money is no longer really about money, if it ever was in the first place.

Hence, the sublimated aggression deep-pocketed capitalists gratify through economic competition, as a competition already about, for these subjects, things different from quantitative wealth alone, is ready-made to be socially retranslated into expressions in terms other than purely monetary ones. Such capitalists' masses of surplus/exchange values are so far in excess of what could be personally consumed by them and their entourages in tangible qualitative use values as to reveal that this amassing is not motivated by the desire to consume material riches. The latter subjective motive must be seen here in contrast with the animating logic of capital, M-C-M', as the self-enhancing, ever-growing spiral of intangible quantitative exchange values via capital's appropriation of labor-produced surplus values.

Capitalists appear, at the intersection of Marxism and psychoanalysis, in two distinct but not unrelated lights. From the Marxist angle, they are primarily, in their role as capital's personifications/bearers (*Personifikationen/Träger*), depsychologized agents of the structural dynamic of M-C-M′. As such, they are concerned, however consciously or not, exclusively with the in-principle infinite accumulation of quantitative surplus and exchange values. But from the psychoanalytic angle, they also are more than just such personifications/bearers.

As Freud himself would emphasize, capital's agents additionally are, among other things, psychical subjects of enjoyments having to do with sociosymbolic secondary gains exuded from the pure accumulation of capital. Insofar as these secondary gains, as superstructural byproducts of capitalism's infrastructural logic, can be generated by strictly superstructural sociosymbolic pursuits, they can be had without the economic category of capitalist private property (i.e., individually owned means of production). Again, the psyches of capital's *Personifikationen/Träger* should be able to satisfy their aggression-tinged libidinal investments in inter- and trans-subjectively recognized prestige, renown, status, etc. through subliminatory means other than the strictly economic competition associated with the capitalist mode of production. Realizing this goes a long way toward a Marxism that has passed through, rather than simply bypassed, Freud's psychoanalytic reservations about its feasibility.

§4. THE DRIVE OF MARXISM: FREUD AND DIALECTICAL MATERIALISM

Having critically assessed what Freud has to say about Marxists, what do Marxists have to say about Freud? Obviously, surveying the entirety of Marxists' responses to Freudian psychoanalysis here is neither possible nor desirable. Selectivity will be necessary. To begin with, it would be uninteresting and unproductive to linger over, for instance, shrill Stalinist denunciations of Freudianism as repackaged capitalist ideology and, à la Lysenkoism's agitprop rhetoric, "bourgeois science." In fact, any such crude condemnations of psychoanalysis ought not to be dignified with serious engagement. They deserve only to be left to continue moldering in the dustbin of intellectual history.[127]

However, especially during the brief postrevolutionary period before the rise of Stalinism, certain thinkers in the Soviet milieu offer some attention-worthy reflections regarding Freud's body of work. In particular, Luria and Vygotsky put forward thoughtful Marxism-informed assessments of the metapsychology and methodology of psychoanalysis. And strong cross-resonances are audible between these Soviet thinkers' reflections and the early stages of Western Marxism's rapprochement with Freud, starting in texts by Reich and Fenichel and continuing with the Frankfurt School,[128] of whose members Marcuse arguably furnishes the most sophisticated and sustained engagement with analysis (incidentally, Reich claims that Freud's criticisms of communism in *Civilization and Its Discontents* were responses to his [Reich's] Marxism).[129] This is the ground I will cover in the present section.

Martin A. Miller, at one point in his 1998 study *Freud and the Bolsheviks: Psychoanalysis in Imperial Russia and the Soviet Union*, pivots from doing history to engaging in theory. He interjects into his historical narrative an argument according to which all efforts to marry Marxism and psychoanalysis, including those attempted in the Russian and Soviet settings, are doomed to inevitable failure. On Miller's assessment, Freudianism's purported focus on clinically treating individual psychosexual pathologies, allegedly ineliminable by any sociopolitical changes, renders it fundamentally incompatible with Marxist and Bolshevik positions.[130]

Needless to say, I disagree with Miller's assessment of the (lack of) prospects for productively interfacing Marxism and psychoanalysis. Moreover, such Soviet figures as Luria and Vygotsky themselves furnish powerful counterarguments against this sort of assessment. Luria and Vygotsky, in a coauthored introduction to the 1925 Russian translation of Freud's 1920 *Beyond the Pleasure Principle*, write optimistically of how "a new and original trend in psychoanalysis is beginning to form in Russia," one that "attempts to synthesize Freudian psychology and Marxism . . . in the spirit of dialectical materialism."[131] What might have resulted from this 1920s Russian analytic trend if it had not been snuffed out by the effects of Stalinism in the immediately following years? I now will turn to the details of Luria's and Vygotsky's Marxist reflections on Freudian psychoanalysis, with particular attention to be devoted to the former's extended 1925 essay "Psychoanalysis as a System of Monistic Psychology."

Luria begins his thorough 1925 Marxist examination of psychoanalysis by asserting the transdisciplinary validity of dialectical materialism.[132] By "dialectical materialism," he clearly has in mind the Engels of *Anti-Dühring*, *Dialectics of Nature*, and *Ludwig Feuerbach and the Outcome of Classical German Philosophy*. More precisely, Luria, in line with and appealing to this Engels, characterizes dialectical materialism as a "materialist monism" of an always-in-process inextricable intertwining of all things, an ever-fluctuating organic whole of cross-resonating parts.[133] Vygotsky likewise associates dialectical materialism with an emphasis on "development" as change, process, transformation, etc.[134] This development also is said by him to exhibit irregular staccato rhythms, unevenness between its various unfolding levels, complex reciprocal interconnections between its constituents, and revolutionary abruptness as well as evolutionary gradualness.[135]

Whether knowingly or not, Althusser later echoes Luria. In particular, Althusser repeatedly subsumes psychoanalysis under the overarching intellectual authority of historical and/or dialectical materialism. He asserts that *"no theory of psychoanalysis can be produced without basing it in historical materialism."*[136] Additionally, Althusser anticipates historical materialism, in conjunction with advances in biology, playing a key role in making possible future "discoveries that will one day allow the elaboration of the scientific theory of the unconscious."[137] He also avows that "Freud, exactly, like Marx, offers us the example of a *materialist and dialectical* thought."[138] Hence, Freudian psychoanalysis would be ready-made for absorption into the enveloping framework of Marxist materialism.[139]

Althusser's most emphatic and elaborate version of the gesture of situating psychoanalysis within the wider jurisdiction of historical/dialectical materialism is laid out in his 1966 "Three Notes on the Theory of Discourses." Therein, Althusser rather uncontroversially defines psychoanalysis as a theory of the unconscious. But more controversially, he then maintains that psychoanalysis defined thus is a "regional theory" in need of a "general theory," with the latter as a ground establishing the scientificity of the former.[140]

Bringing Lacan into the picture along with Freud, Althusser sketches a hierarchy of theories. Within this hierarchy, the regional theory of psychoanalysis is subsumed under the general theory of the signifier (as per Lacanianism). Then, the general theory of the signifier is in turn itself subsumed under the even more general theory of historical materialism.[141]

Thereby, historical materialism once again is put forward by Althusser as grounding the Freudian field.[142] One of the justifications for all this in "Three Notes on the Theory of Discourses" is Althusser's contention that the analytic unconscious is, in part, a "subject-effect" of ideologies, with their discourses and practices, turning individuals into (heteronomous) subjects (qua subjected) via interpellations.[143] Hence, for this Althusser, historical materialism's critical analyses of ideologies, appropriately informed by a structuralism-inspired general-semiological account of signifiers, would offer access to the preconditions and underpinnings of the unconscious and, with it, of psychoanalysis as the "science of the unconscious."

Well before Althusser, and without Althusser's reliance on structuralism, Lacan, etc., Luria already could be said, like the French Marxist, also to situate psychoanalysis as a regional theory within the general theory of Marxist materialism. Luria insists that the psy- disciplines, including psychoanalysis, need dialectical materialism in order to be truly scientific.[144] (Reich similarly insists that psychoanalysis can supplement but not replace "sociology" qua the explanatory jurisdiction of Marxist materialism.)[145] Such scientificity would involve synthesizing elements from both biology and historical materialism.[146]

For Luria, the anchoring of a regional theory of the psyche to the general theory of dialectical materialism should be especially easy to achieve in the case of psychoanalysis. Why? According to him, this would be because Marxism and psychoanalysis could be described as meeting each other halfway.[147] On the one hand, Luria, like others after him including Althusser, portrays psychoanalysis as implicitly sharing the sensibilities and core commitments of dialectical materialism, including the latter's materialist monism and organicist holism.[148] On the other hand, Luria emphasizes that Marxist materialism, as vehemently antireductive despite its indebtedness to the eighteenth-century French materialists and Feuerbach, acknowledges the relative autonomy of individual personalities and correspondingly refuses to dissolve without remainder singular psyches into anonymous material bases.[149] As Jacoby notes, Reich similarly adheres to the insistence of Marx's first thesis on Feuerbach upon a materialism that retains, rather than dissolves, subjectivities.[150]

Vygotsky also underscores that dialectical materialism likewise refuses to dissolve the human into the animal.[151] Relatedly, Vygotsky, appealing to Engels, contrasts reductive naturalistic with antireductive dialectical approaches to the detriment of the former.[152] For him as for Luria, the dialectical materialism to which psychoanalysis can and should be joined is anything but atomistic, mechanical, etc.

Despite the ancient Greek etymology of "psyche" tethering it to what the word "soul" connotes, Luria is adamant that the Freudian psyche is no soul in any idealist sense whatsoever. For him, analysis is not an idealism. As such, its psyche is not an immaterial mind independent of everything bodily.[153]

So if the Freudian psychical apparatus is not disembodied as per antimaterialist idealisms and/or Cartesian-style ontological dualisms, how does Luria conceive of the soma-psyche relationship in analytic metapsychology? At one moment in "Psychoanalysis as a System of Monistic Psychology," he suggests that unconscious dynamics are "on a level with other processes in the organism from which they are functionally, but not fundamentally, distinct."[154] He immediately specifies that this more subtle difference amounts to psyche being soma insofar as the latter is socially mediated, namely, suffused with and reshaped by "social stimuli" registered thanks to the body's "complex system of receptors and effectors" attuned and receptive to surrounding social environments.[155]

Luria, for whatever reason(s), does not invoke Freud's *Hilflosigkeit* in connection with this asserted receptivity. However, the young human organism's underlying inclination to be profoundly affected in its motivations, emotions, and cognitions by the "social stimuli" it registers is symptomatic of the biological fact of its prolonged prematurational helplessness. From a Marxist standpoint sympathetic to psychoanalysis, this *Hilflosigkeit* arguably plays a crucial role in establishing a crossroads between, on the one hand, both nature and society as understood by dialectical materialism and, on the other hand, the analytic psychical apparatus.[156] This renders Luria's omission apropos helplessness somewhat strange.

That said, Luria's above-noted notion of a functional-but-not-fundamental distinction between soma and psyche appears to entail, as it does for Vygotsky too,[157] that the psychical is a modification of the somatic resulting from social mediation (albeit with the origins of social mediation itself left unspecified). Yet Luria promptly proceeds to muddy these waters. He quickly shifts from characterizing psychoanalysis as a materialism in which the mental is a modification of the physical to depicting analysis as implicitly a Spinozistic dual-aspect monism in which the soma-psyche distinction arises out of an underlying, undifferentiated "energy."[158] (Both Antonio Damasio and Mark Solms embrace Spinozistic dual-aspect monism as the most fitting philosophical framework for neuropsychoanalysis,[159] with Solms also being a great admirer of Luria.)[160] Even if these two renditions of Freudianism by Luria both qualify as monisms, they are two very different forms of monism arguably incompatible with each other.

The biomaterialism Luria attributes to Freud with ample justification has no need for (nay, would repudiate) Spinozism's metaphysical positing of a God-like *natura naturans* as the productive power underlying the physical universe as the congealed materiality of *natura naturata*. Freud's science-shaped materialist sensibilities are such that, in relation to the Spinozistic distinction between the constituting activity of *natura naturans* and the constituted entities of *natura naturata*, he would insist on accounting for human mindedness strictly on the basis of *natura naturata* alone (first and foremost as the biology of the organisms belonging to the species *Homo sapiens*), without recourse to anything beyond, behind, or beneath nature as the physical universe. Instead of Spinoza's *Deus sive natura*, there is simply Freud's lone *natura*. As regards the hypothetical *natura naturans* (or Luria's hypothetical "energy"), Freud would protest *hypotheses non fingo*. Despite both Luria's avowed fidelity to Marxist materialism and the Soviet interest in Spinoza as a forerunner of Marx via Marx's debts to Hegel, I would suggest that the same would hold for Marx as for Freud here.[161]

Luria considers the psychoanalytic concept of drive (*Trieb*) to be the basis and epitome of Freud's monism. Although Luria construes drives as endogenous stimuli—this is at least true of the drive source (*Quelle*) and its attendant pressure (*Drang*) as a "demand for work"—he also recognizes that exogenous stimuli shape drives too (particularly at the level of the drive's object [*Objekt*]).[162] Speaking of "the psychoanalytic system," Luria states:

> Its concept of drive is rigorously monistic, as is its view of the individual in general. Indeed, a drive is not a psychological phenomenon in the strict sense, since it includes the effects of somatic and nervous stimuli and of the endocrine system and its chemistry, and often has no clear-cut psychological cast at all. We should be more inclined to consider drive a concept at the "borderline between the mental and the somatic." The dualism of the old psychology is thus completely discarded. Whether or not the particular person is or can be conscious of drive is entirely of secondary importance, depending on a number of minor details in the development of drive. Moreover, all the hypotheses about the relationship between soul and body, their psychophysical parallelism or interaction (so necessary to the old psychology), are also left by the wayside. Psychoanalysis has shifted the problem to an entirely new plane—a monistic approach to the mind.[163]

A couple of pages later in "Psychoanalysis as a System of Monistic Psychology," he embellishes further on this line of reflection—"for psychoanalysis, drives are not a purely psychological concept, but have a much broader sense, lying at 'the borderline between the mental and the somatic,' and are more of a biological nature."[164] He continues:

> Thus, psychoanalysis attaches special importance to the dependence of mental functions on organic stimuli. It makes mind an integral part of the organism's system; it can hence no longer be studied in isolation. This is what sets psychoanalysis apart from the old scholastic psychology, which attempted to depict the mind as something with no connection at all with the overall life of the organism and studied the brain quite apart from any influence other organs of the body might have on it (e.g., the endocrine glands) and the general dynamics of the organism as a whole. Indeed, the outstanding merit of psychoanalysis has been that it situates the mind within a general system of inter-relations of organs, views the brain and its activity not in isolation, but on a level with the

other organs of the body, and attempts to give psychology a solid biological foundation and to effect a decisive break with the metaphysical approach to the study of the mind. I should not be wide of the mark if I said that in doing this, psychoanalysis took an important step toward creating a system of monistic psychology.[165]

Luria, through his focus on the metapsychological concept of drive, appears to move toward conflating monism with holism. This holism, regardless of Luria's own views, would not require endorsement of any sort of reductionism or epiphenomenalism, including the epiphenomenalist implications of Spinozistic monism.

As just seen, Luria accepts the distinction between soma and psyche relied upon by Freud's drive theory as well as his metapsychology in general. By contrast, a reductive materialism or naturalism would seek to collapse psyche into soma. And a dual-aspect monism would treat this distinction as merely apparent in relation to an undifferentiated underlying ontological substrate (paradigmatically, Spinoza's substance as the hidden ground of the attributes of thinking and extension). If and when Luria has such reductionism or Spinozism in mind when speaking of "monism" in connection with Freudian psychoanalysis, he is wrong to attribute such monism to Freud. But when he attributes holistic tendencies to Freud's drive theory, including complex entanglements of soma (as material body) and psyche (as more-than-material mind), he is amply justified in doing so.

When discussing Freudian drives in "Psychoanalysis as a System of Monistic Psychology," Luria indeed highlights the holistic sensibilities informing Freud's metapsychological conception of *Triebe*. In so doing, Luria enriches the holism of Freudian drive theory and the entire analytic metapsychology for which this theory is so central. Freud himself gestures at the holistic entanglement of soma and psyche, with drives as hybrid constructs sandwiching together somatic and psychical components. Luria's remarks indicate that in addition to this, there are, as regards various phenomena of interest to psychoanalysis (especially an analysis aligned with dialectical materialism), further holistic distributions across multiple components within the internally differentiated central nervous system; between the highly complex brain and the rest of the body with its numerous anatomical and physiological aspects; among the various functions and dimensions of mental/psychical life; and in interactions between the intrasomatic, the intrapsychical, and both the extrasomatic and the extrapsychical natural and social circumstances surrounding the minded and embodied person.[166]

Seen from Luria's Marxist and scientific perspectives, Freudian analysis, in its holism, is nothing if not antilocalizationist about the phenomena with which it concerns itself. Freud already warns against attempts at anatomical localizations of such metapsychological models as his topographies of the psychical apparatus.[167] Likewise, Solms, avowedly taking inspiration from both Freud and Luria, vehemently distances his version of neuropsychoanalysis from any localizationist agenda.[168]

Like Luria in particular, Solms stresses the sprawling extent of the neuroanatomical distribution of most mental functions in human psychical life. Freud can be read as leaving open the possibility of future neuroanatomical localizations of aspects of psychoanalytic metapsychological models based on the assumption that the limits of (then-)present neuroscientific knowledge permit continuing to entertain the viability of this possibility. However, Luria and Solms both argue that the neurosciences already know enough to rule out the legitimacy of anatomical localizations as forming the key links between psychoanalysis and neurobiology. Scientific knowledge (rather than ignorance) of neuroanatomy, with its insights into the high degree of anatomical distribution of mental functions across the regions and subregions of the central nervous system, already rules out reliance on localizations as the load-bearing bridges connecting analysis's psyche with science's brain.

Despite Luria's just-mentioned antilocalizationism, Luria and Vygotsky, in their coauthored introduction to the Russian translation of *Beyond the Pleasure Principle*, echo Freud's hopes for eventual natural scientific vindications of psychoanalytic hypotheses[169] (as does Luria in "Psychoanalysis as a System of Monistic Psychology").[170] These coauthors and collaborators signal their approval of *Beyond the Pleasure Principle*'s science-inspired (and Empedoclean) speculations having it that the conflict between Eros and the *Todestrieb* operative within the human psyche is itself just one expression among countless others of a natural strife between forces of unification and destruction on display across the entire cosmos from top to bottom.[171] Whatever Luria's distributionist reservations about neuroanatomical localizations, he nonetheless does not hesitate to side with Freud's more biologistic moments and argue that psychoanalysis globally grounds the psychical in the somatic, the human subject in the human organism.[172] For the Luria of "Psychoanalysis as a System of Monistic Psychology," Freudian drive theory, with the role played therein by anatomical drive sources, anchors the libidinal economy and, with it, the psyche as a whole in the biological body.[173] Luria's stance combines a denial of discrete neuroanatomical localizations with an affirmation of global organic localization (i.e., the rooting of the entire psyche in soma).

Luria's "Psychoanalysis as a System of Monistic Psychology" and the introduction to the Russian translation of Freud's *Beyond the Pleasure Principle* coauthored by Luria and Vygotsky both date from the same year (1925). Yet there is a strange tension between these two texts' assessments of Freud and the soma-psyche relationship in psychoanalysis. "Psychoanalysis as a System of Monistic Psychology," after lauding Freud's labors for moving psychology toward being founded upon a "materialist monism" compatible with dialectical materialism,[174] inserts the following critical remark as this essay's penultimate paragraph: "If the system of psychoanalysis is to measure up better to the requirements of dialectical materialism, however, it must develop fully the dynamic dialectic of mental life and take a third step toward a holistic approach to the organism: it must now integrate the organism into a system of social influences."[175] An endnote specifies that this integration would be tantamount to a psychoanalytic "advance from mechanical materialism to dialectical materialism."[176] Luria therefore appears to conclude that Freud's corpus does not amply acknowledge "social influences" in its account of human mindedness.[177] In *Thought and Language*, Vygotsky similarly indicts Freud for putting forward "the untenable conception of a pleasure principle preceding a reality principle"[178] (an indictment contested by Reich).[179]

This faulting of Freudian analysis for neglecting the interactions between the somatic-psychical organism and its surrounding social milieus should be contrasted with the concluding paragraphs of Luria and Vygotsky's preface to the Russian edition of *Beyond the Pleasure Principle* (contemporaneous with Luria's "Psychoanalysis as a System of Monistic Psychology"). Therein, Luria and Vygotsky observe:

> If the biological conservative tendency to preserve the inorganic equilibrium is concealed in the deeper layers of psychical life, how can humanity's development from lower to higher forms be explained? Where are we to look for the root of the stormy progression of the historical process? Freud provides us with a highly interesting and deeply materialistic answer, i.e. if in the deep recesses of the human psyche there still remain conservative tendencies of primordial biology and if, in the final analysis, even Eros is consigned to it, then the only forces which make it possible for us to escape from this state of biological conservatism and which may propel us toward progress and activity, are external forces, in our terms, the external conditions of the material environment in which the individual exists. It is they that represent the true basis of progress, it is they that create the real personality and make it adapt and work out new forms of psychic life; finally they are the ones that suppress and transfer the vestiges of

58   ✤   THE CONFLICTED POLITICAL ANIMAL

the old conservative biology. In this respect Freud's psychology is thoroughly sociological and it is up to other materialistic psychologists who find themselves in better circumstances than Freud to reveal and validate the subject of the materialistic foundations of this theory.[180]

They continue:

So, according to Freud, the history of the human psyche embodies two tendencies, the conservative-biological and the progressive-sociological. It is from these factors that the whole *dialectic of the organism* is composed and they are responsible for the distinctive "spiral" development of a human being. This book represents a step forwards and not backwards along the path to the construction of a whole, monistic system, and after having read this book a dialectician cannot fail to perceive its enormous potential for a monistic understanding of the world.[181]

Soon after this, Luria and Vygotsky conclude their introduction to *Beyond the Pleasure Principle* (i.e., "this book" in the preceding quotation) thus: "Bourgeois science is giving birth to materialism: such labour is often difficult and prolonged, but we only have to find where in its bowels materialistic buds are showing, to find them, to rescue them and to make good use of them."[182] By contrast with Luria on his own in 1925, Luria with Vygotsky in the same year grants that Freud puts forward a "*dialectic of the organism*" in which society (as Freud's *Kultur* [civilization]) significantly configures the reality principle embedded in and modulating the psychical apparatus with its driving pleasure principle. Luria and Vygotsky together acknowledge that the Freudian psyche is shot through with and sculpted by the sorts of social mediators of concern to Marxist materialism. Hence, worries about Freud as not socially minded appear to be put to rest in this coauthored introduction to *Beyond the Pleasure Principle*, with Freudian psychoanalysis, according to this introduction, being "thoroughly sociological." I would claim that this putting to rest is fair and appropriate—and this unlike Luria's and Vygotsky's solo indictments of Freud for allegedly ignoring social factors.[183]

Reich, in his 1929 article "Psychoanalysis in the Soviet Union" written shortly after a visit by him to Russia, rightly rebuts Bolshevik condemnations of Freudian psychoanalysis for insufficient sensitivity to social forces.[184] (Oddly, in an essay on Reich, Ollman repeats these same criticisms of Freud rejected by Reich himself).[185] Marcuse likewise problematizes efforts to lump Freud together with bourgeois individualists.[186] In the introduction to *Eros and Civilization*, he insists that "Freud's theory is in its very substance 'sociological,' and . . . no new cultural or sociological orientation is needed to reveal this substance."[187] Marcuse soon proceeds to assert, "Freud's individual psychology is in its very essence social psychology."[188] Jacoby, citing Theodor Adorno,[189] lends his support to Reich's and Marcuse's defense of Freud as himself already a thoroughly social thinker, with the Freudian psychical creature as a *zoon politikon*.[190]

Luria on his own concludes that Freud, as a materialist, has yet to take the step from a mechanistic neglect of social mediation to a dialectical inclusion of such mediation in "the distinctive 'spiral' development of a human being." But in his joint statements with Vygotsky apropos 1920's *Beyond the Pleasure Principle*, he drastically tempers if not abandons altogether this critical conclusion. The judgment shifts from Freud being a nondialectical mechanical materialist to him being, even if only despite himself, a spontaneous dialectical materialist. According to this latter verdict (one echoed outside the Soviet Union by Reich and Fenichel),[191] all that is needed for Marxism to embrace psychoanalysis is the performance with respect to Freud's oeuvre of the classical Marxian-Engelsian operation of extracting (or "rescuing") the "rational kernel" (i.e., "materialistic buds") from the "mystical shell" (i.e., "bourgeois science"). Vygotsky's *Thought and Language* again suggests the need for such a rescue operation of extraction with respect to Freud.[192] (Incidentally, Lacan expresses great admiration for Vygotsky and his *Thought and Language* especially.)[193]

The "*dialectic of the organism*" with its "distinctive 'spiral' development of a human being" referred to by Luria and Vygotsky in their joint presentation (and echoed by Vygotsky in another piece)[194] of Freud arguably alludes to Engels, especially Engels's 1876 essay "The Part Played by Labour in the Transition from Ape to Man" (contained in *Dialectics of Nature*).[195] Vygotsky elsewhere invokes this Engels, along with the Hegel and Marx channeled by Engels. In particular, Vygotsky appeals to Hegel's, Marx's, and Engels's observations about the making and using of tools in the *praxes* of social laboring as responsible for the peculiar dialectics of human nature and history.[196] Luria begins an essay of his entitled "The Problem of the Cultural Behaviour of the Child" highlighting tools along the exact same lines as Vygotsky.[197] Luria and Vygotsky's joint attribution to Freud of a dialectical conception of the human being renders the founder of psychoanalysis particularly proximate to the Marxist materialism they uphold.

Starting with Reich in the 1930s, the Soviets' more positive evaluations of Freudian psychoanalysis are echoed in some of the earliest Western efforts to wed Marx and Freud. Later, I will address what arguably are the two most sophisticated initial attempts in the non-Soviet European context to marry psychoanalysis and Marxist materialism: Reich's 1929/1934 *Dialectical Materialism and Psychoanalysis* (which Paul Robinson describes as "the most tightly argued piece he ever wrote")[198] and Fenichel's 1934 "Psychoanalysis as the Nucleus of a Future Dialectical-Materialist Psychology." In my subsequent treatment of Reich and Fenichel, the cross-resonances with Luria and Vygotsky as summarized above will be audible. In the meantime, and before initially broaching the topic of a Lacanian rapprochement with Marxism in the next section, I want to address the best-known classic articulation of Freudo-Marxism, namely, Marcuse's 1955 *Eros and Civilization*.

Whereas such Western Marxist works as Reich's *The Mass Psychology of Fascism* and the Frankfurt School's collaborative effort *The Authoritarian Personality* arguably mishandle psychoanalysis in the heat of urgent antifascist struggle, Marcuse's 1955 manifesto of Freudo-Marxism is much more faithful to and careful with Freudian theory. In what follows, I will not be reconstructing the contents of *Eros and Civilization* in their entirety. In the wake both of my earlier critical reassessment of Freud's reservations apropos Marxism and of my ensuing examinations of Luria's and Vygotsky's Bolshevik engagements with psychoanalysis, I will be selectively underscoring certain manners in which Marcuse contributes to the issues presently under discussion through his handling of Freud vis-à-vis Marxism in *Eros and Civilization*.

Marcuse rejects the Luria-type Soviet charge against Freudian psychoanalysis of failing to pay attention to sociohistorical dimensions of human existence. However, he develops a different line of criticism with regard to Freud, one foreshadowed by Reich.[199] Specifically, Marcuse, as a historical materialist, warns against Freud's wholesale equation of any and every "civilization" (i.e., all human societies in all times and places) with the inevitable imposition of neurosis-inducing repression *als Verdrängung* (most notably and famously in *Civilization and Its Discontents*).[200]

Freud's "reality principle," especially in the context of *Civilization and Its Discontents*, is in no small part a reflection of specifically social, as distinct from natural, external reality. It can and does dictate certain intrapsychical repressions. However, *Eros and Civilization*, drawing on Marxist sensibilities, maintains that the Freudian reality principle, as reflective of the externalities of different societies, must be historicized in ways Freud fails to carry out despite this being imperative insofar as societies consist of historically variable structures and dynamics[201] (with Jürgen Habermas subsequently carrying forward this Marcusian line of critical reflection on Freudian metapsychology).[202] Relatedly, and latching onto things Freud says in connection with "Ananke" (the ancient Greek personification of unavoidable necessity and compulsion),[203] Marcuse accuses Freud of falsely eternalizing socially created and historically transient material scarcity as dictating discontent-inducing "instinctual renunciation."[204]

Another Marxist line of criticism Marcuse brings to bear on Freud in *Eros and Civilization* has to do with the distinction between work and play. Marx, in connection with his long-running concern with the alienated status of labor under capitalism, observes that the very notion of an antithesis between labor and leisure is symptomatic of capitalistic alienation. That is to say, only when labor is alienated does it appear as the necessity of dull, unrewarding drudgery as opposed to leisure as the freedom of enjoyable, gratifying recreation.[205] A socialist or communist supersession of capitalism presumably would dealienate labor, thereby transforming work (back) into play (or, in a hybrid Schillerian-Freudian manner, overcoming the antagonism between drive and necessity).[206]

Marcuse accuses Freud of uncritically taking for granted the bourgeois ideological eternalization-via-naturalization of capitalism's work-versus-play zero-sum dichotomy symptomatic of the specifically capitalist alienation of labor[207] (and this in addition to perhaps not foreseeing the economic and ideological colonization of the "happiness" of workers' "free time" by capitalism and its forms of commodified repressive desublimation).[208] This accusation forms part of the larger argument in *Eros and Civilization* about Freud's insufficiently historical account of external social reality. In other words, the instinctual renunciations demanded by the social side of the Freudian reality principle are, by Marcuse's Marxist lights, the gratuitous impositions of socially alienating labor conditions, not the unavoidable consequences of naturally dictated toil to which the entirety of humanity is hopelessly condemned forever.

Implicitly linked to the immediately preceding by the tie between labor and time (including subjects' experiences of lived temporality) as conceptualized in Marxism, *Eros and Civilization* also discusses time at the intersection of historical materialism and psychoanalysis. In this vein, Marcuse states: "The fatal enemy of lasting gratification is *time*, the inner finiteness, the brevity of all conditions. The idea of integral human liberation therefore necessarily contains the vision of the struggle against time."[209] Later, in the final chapter of *Eros and Civilization*, he expands on this:

> "Joy wants eternity." Timelessness is the ideal of pleasure. Time has no power over the id, the original domain of the pleasure principle. But the ego, through which alone pleasure becomes real, is in its entirety subject to time. The mere anticipation of the inevitable end, present in every instant, introduces a repressive element into all libidinal relations and renders pleasure itself painful. This primary frustration in the instinctual structure of man becomes the

inexhaustible source of all other frustrations—and of their social effectiveness. Man learns that "it cannot last anyway," that every pleasure is short, that for all finite things the hour of their birth is the hour of their death—that it couldn't be otherwise. He is resigned before society forces him to practice resignation methodically. The flux of time is society's most natural ally in maintaining law and order, conformity, and the institutions that relegate freedom to a perpetual utopia; the flux of time helps men to forget what was and what can be: it makes them oblivious to the better past and the better future.[210]

Marcuse considers the psychoanalytic account of temporality to play into the hands of capitalism's undue burdens of "surplus repression"[211] and ideological rationalizations (via eternalizing naturalization) of these burdens. He here sides with Marxism against Freudianism.

For both Marx and Marcuse following him, a future realization of something along the lines of a communist "realm of freedom" would be inseparably bound up with changes in how people spend the time of their lives on a day-to-day basis. More precisely, the end of the reign of capital ends its logic of M-C-M', in which surplus value is the overriding socially efficacious telos. With the termination of this logic also would come the elimination of the socioeconomic compulsion to condemn the vast bulk of humanity to the tedious lost time of ever more surplus labor (as ever more gratuitous thanks to the material abundance made possible by capitalism's enhancements of social productive power). In other words, with the postcapitalist reduction of labor time to that necessary for the satisfactory production and reproduction of the laborers—this is distinct from the surplus labor time "necessary" for producing surplus value appropriated by the minority formed by nonlaboring capitalists—the day-by-day balance of laboring people's lifetimes between the necessity of work and the freedom of play would tilt substantially in the direction of the latter.[212]

Additionally, given Marcuse's Heidegger-acquired phenomenological sensibilities combined with his appreciation for the young (circa 1844) Marx's vivid descriptions of the laborer's lived experience of "alienation,"[213] the later Marcuse of *Eros and Civilization* probably assumes that a subjective change at the level of phenomenal temporality will be induced as a consequence of an objective transformation at the level of socially structured time. Put differently, Marcuse likely believes (and believes Marx also to assume) that once the external objectivity of the collective organization of individuals' daily scheduled rhythms and routines is radically reconfigured, a dramatic mutation will ensue in the internal subjectivity of people's awareness of the ebbs and flows of past, present, and future. This Marcusian belief perhaps is knowingly reinforced by the early Lukács's more phenomenological musings about the experience of time under the influence of capitalist reification.[214] Similarly, in *Eros and Civilization* Marcuse, in line with his Freudo-Marxism, makes a connection between time and sex, hypothesizing that increased amounts of regular leisure will result in people liberating themselves through resexualizing their bodies in "polymorphously perverse" fashions, as instances of nonrepressive desublimation[215] (with Göran Therborn noting that "Unlike Reich, sexual liberation in the genital sense is not the psycho-analytical aim of Frankfurt theory so much as the investment of all human activity with libidinal energy").[216]

Yet much of what Marcuse has to say about time in *Eros and Civilization* arguably hints, contrary to Marcuse's own intentions, that he might not be so justified in favoring Marxism over Freudianism on this particular issue. Marcuse indeed is correct that psychoanalytic accounts of temporality, starting with those advanced by Freud himself, propose an antagonism between time and pleasure. Marcuse's previously quoted remarks about temporality further indicate that he sees psychoanalytic metapsychology as situating time both on the side of external natural (rather than social) reality as well as on the side of the ego's registration of this external reality in the form of the intrapsychical reality principle regulating the pleasure principle. The supposed inner depths of the id, in line with Freud's repeated depictions of it and the unconscious as "timeless" (*Zeitlos*), are manifestly contrasted by Marcuse with the time-sensitive ego sensitized by the brute given fact of the transience of all things. I now succinctly will contest Marcuse's reading of temporality in Freudian analysis. In so doing, I additionally will challenge how *Eros and Civilization* in particular interfaces psychoanalysis with Marxism.

My 2005 book *Time Driven: Metapsychology and the Splitting of the Drive* amounts, in its entirety, to a sustained rebuttal of Marcuse's manner of handling psychoanalytic temporality in *Eros and Civilization*.[217] *Time Driven*, relying heavily on Lacan as well as Freud, proposes that the unconscious is timeless only in the sense of not conforming to the iron rule of the chronological time so prominent at the level of conscious experience. Relatedly, I maintain that other forms of temporality different from linear chronology can and should be recognized as informing the configurations and operations of unconscious dimensions of psychical life—and this even by Freud's own lights, in addition to Lacan's suggestions to the same effect.[218]

Furthermore, insofar as the id is the seat of the drives, *Time Driven* temporalizes the id in analyzing all drives (*Triebe*) as split, in their inherent metapsychological makeup, between two discrepant, conflicting temporal dimensions. The source (*Quelle*) and pressure (*Drang*) of drive are caught up in the cyclical, recurring temporality of what I designate as the psychoanalytic drive's "axis of iteration." By contrast, the aim (*Ziel*) and object (*Objekt*) of drive are situated within a temporal dimension I call the drive's "axis of alteration." This second dimension consists of complex interactions between projective (from past, through present, to future) and retroactive (from present to past) movements of/in time. While the somatic axis of iteration involves attempted repetition, with its stubbornly relentless seeking after the eternal return of an unaltered past, the psychical axis of alteration involves repetition-thwarting difference, with its perpetual retranscriptions and modifications of its mutable, shifting ideational contents both phenomenal and structural.[219]

These features of *Time Driven* raise several objections to the Marcuse of *Eros and Civilization*. First of all, they indicate that Marcuse is wrong to restrict the place of time in psychoanalytic metapsychology to external natural reality and the ego's inscription of this externality within its secondary-process reality principle. Marcuse's mistake is to treat both the unconscious and the id, with their primary-process pleasure principle, as internal psychical depths untouched by time/temporality.

Moreover, with the temporalization of the drives (along the lines argued in *Time Driven*) going hand in hand with a temporalization of the unconscious and the id, I make a detailed metapsychological case for the insurmountability of the psychoanalytic time-versus-pleasure antagonism as described by Marcuse in the above quotations from *Eros and Civilization*. The "splitting of the drive" of *Time Driven*'s subtitle refers to each and every *Trieb* being internally divided along the fault line between its axis of iteration (source and pressure) and its axis of alteration (aim and object). These two axes are permanently and by their very natures out of synch and at odds with each other. This inner antagonism between incompatible temporal axes renders all drives inherently unable to attain the satisfactions they nonetheless, and in vain, demand again and again.

Therefore, *pace* the Marcuse of *Eros and Civilization*, time's interference with pleasure is not just an issue of an exogenous factor affecting the secondary processes of the ego. Temporality's thwarting of gratification and enjoyment is also a matter of an endogenous arrangement bound up with and inseparable from the primary processes of the unconscious- and id-level libidinal economy in and of itself at the level of this economy's own components (i.e., drives) and their inner workings. In terms of Marcuse's above-quoted playing off of Marxism against Freudianism apropos the topic of temporality, my preceding summary of *Time Driven* and its consequences for *Eros and Civilization* indicates that psychoanalytic insights into the antagonism between time and pleasure are even weightier and harder to offset with appeals to sociohistorical variables than Marcuse realizes.

Even if a socialism and/or communism arrives in which socially necessary labor time is substantially reduced for all persons, this will not usher them into a libidinal paradise in which dissatisfactions disappear with the lifting of capitalism's needlessly excessive surplus repressions.[220] If and when such liberated people get to, for instance, experience the nonrepressive desublimation of resexualizing their polymorphously perverse bodies, they will discover that certain stains of discontent, displeasure, malaise, pain, suffering, and unease appear to be well-nigh indelible—including (and especially) within the field of their very sexualities. Although the lived experience of temporalities may well change, perhaps even quite significantly, on the other side of the rule of capital's clocks, time will not cease and will not cease to function as an ineliminable impediment to the machinations of the drives. To assume otherwise is utopian in a bad sense that ought to be rejected by Marxism itself in line with its sober-minded rejections of other unrealistic utopias.

Nevertheless, psychoanalysis does not and should not commit the error of making the perfect into the enemy of the good. Both Freud and Lacan rightly avoid doing this with respect to Marxism. Freud, in his critical reflections on the Bolsheviks in *Civilization and Its Discontents*, acknowledges that Marxist-type economic programs would be a real boon for humanity, an instance of major historical progress to be welcomed and applauded. He merely appends to this a reasonable cautionary note to the effect that revolutionaries should not project onto such sweeping material-economic changes overly inflated "idealistic" (*idealistiches*) hopes for a total transubstantiation of "human nature" (*menschlichen Natur*) from top to bottom.[221] Alas, Marcuse seems to indulge in precisely such utopian projections. Maybe the better stance here, compromising between the authors of *Civilization and Its Discontents* and *Eros and Civilization*, would be to say: Do not count on revolutionary economic, political, and social transformations replacing a bad old human nature with a good new one, but if such a replacement unexpectedly does happen, one will be free to be pleasantly surprised.

Lacan, like Freud, warns that radical leftists would be wise to manage their revolutionary expectations, to rein in their paradisial anticipations. Without doing so, such political actors, if and when they pass to the revolutionary act and find themselves in this act's aftermath, are in grave peril of succumbing to brutally crushing disappointment. In Lacan's own terms, the unavoidable discrepancy between the "*jouissance* expected" versus the "*jouissance* obtained," a discrepancy insurmountable even via any Marxist revolution, risks provoking a devastating anticlimactic, postpartum-style depression ravaging at least those revolutionary subjects who were unable or unwilling to see this discrepancy coming while in the grip of their fevered prerevolutionary utopian dreams.[222]

The inevitable dashing of these dreams threatens to make the dreamers and those they oversold on their dreams into embittered reactionaries undoing whatever real revolutionary gains are made either from within (a leftist Thermidor) or from without (a right-wing counter-revolution). From this Lacanian vantage point, prerevolutionary fantasies driving revolutionaries to undertake their revolution are some of the greatest dangers to actual postrevolutionary progress if and when it comes to pass—and this despite these fantasies' roles in helping catalyze revolutionary activity. As Lacan observes in his 1965 text "Science and Truth" regarding such risky but indispensable supports to radical political projects: "An economic science inspired by *Capital* does not necessarily lead to its utilization as a revolutionary power, and history seems to require help from something other than a predictive dialectic."[223] This "something other," at least in the case of revolutionaries' prerevolutionary fantasies of the *jouissance* expected on the other side of the revolutionary *passage à l'acte*, both assists in making revolution more likely (however slightly) while simultaneously also jeopardizing the revolution's postrevolutionary longer-term survival if and when the revolution indeed transpires.

In the absence of a prerevolutionary psychoanalytic working-through of revolution as a fantasy in the strict analytic sense—the *rêve* in *rêve-olution*, like all dreams for an analyst, must be interpreted—any revolution that might in fact arrive one fine day cannot but end up appearing even (and especially) to the revolutionaries themselves to be the proverbial "God that failed." The worry is that such revolutionaries would themselves respond to the shortcomings of their first-imagined-but-now-arrived savior with a version of making the perfect into the enemy of the good. They thereby would fail to value and preserve the postrevolutionary *jouissance* obtained (as tangible economic, political, and/or social gains) because it does not measure up to the prerevolutionary *jouissance* expected (i.e., aspirations for such things as the transubstantiation of human nature and the complete elimination of discontent and suffering). Any revolution inspired specifically by Marcuse-type hopes—this also would apply, mutatis mutandis, to the mirage of the "New Man" deceptively upheld as a reality by really existing socialism, including in the sort of Soviet propaganda surrounding the likes of Luria and Vygotsky—would face such dangerous disillusionment. Down the path of disappointment, regression to the prerevolutionary past, or worse, beckons.[224]

I now leave behind this line of psychoanalytic criticism of Marcuse's brand of Freudo-Marxism in bringing this section on the more sophisticated and thoughtful Marxist assessments of psychoanalysis to a close. In these concluding moments, I wish to place a spotlight on certain shared commitments common to Luria, Vygotsky, Reich, Fenichel, and Marcuse as Marxists engaging critically yet charitably with the Freudian field. This will serve as a transition to outlining the fundaments of a Marxism engaging with Lacanianism in addition to Freudianism.

The three analytically inclined Western Marxists dealt with here (i.e., Reich, Fenichel, and Marcuse) all assert that Freud's version of the soma-psyche distinction (most prominently on display at the level of his metapsychological drive theory) is a microcosmic, intrasubjective reflection of the dialectical logic of the macrocosmic, inter/trans-subjective infrastructure-superstructure distinction (as proposed by historical materialism's account of social history).[225] According to this parallel, Freudian soma mirrors Marxian infrastructure and Freudian psyche mirrors Marxian superstructure. However, Reich, Fenichel, and Marcuse subscribe to a version of historical materialism in which the superstructural can and does reciprocally react back on the infrastructural base upon which it rests and from which it arises. That is to say, for Reich, Fenichel, and Marcuse alike, there is a dialectical interaction between infrastructure and superstructure. Theirs is thus a dialectical historical materialism (as opposed to an economistically reductive and mechanical one). Hence, in drawing a parallel with Freud's soma-psyche couple, they urge a sympathetic Marxist construal of Freud as a spontaneous dialectical materialist of sorts (as do Luria and Vygotsky too in places I reference above).

In a related vein, Luria, Vygotsky, Reich, Fenichel, and Marcuse all agree on the central role of psychoanalytic drive theory in a synthesis of psychoanalysis and dialectical/historical materialism.[226] They interpret the interplay of somatic and psychical dimensions and components within each and every analytic *Trieb* as permitting the attribution to Freudian metapsychology of a materialist dialectics bringing Freud the psychoanalyst into proximity with Marx the historical materialist. For them, Freud's *Trieb* is the Cartesian-style pineal gland between psychoanalysis and Marxism.

However, Marx and Freud can be brought together along these lines coming from the other direction too, namely, through reinterpreting pivotal portions of Marx's corpus such as to close the gap with Freud's oeuvre. Specifically, and as I will go on to show in the next chapter, rereading Marx with the benefit of psychoanalytic hindsight reveals the presence in Marx's writings of an already highly sophisticated conceptualization of *Triebe* strikingly foreshadowing the Freudian account of drives. Maybe Marx ought to be credited not only with inventing the psychoanalytic concept of the symptom *avant la lettre*, as Lacan

68 · THE CONFLICTED POLITICAL ANIMAL

proposes,[227] but also with inventing the analytic idea of the drive before Freud. This has multiple ramifications that I will explore throughout much of the rest of this book.

§5. THE PLUMBING OF POLITICAL ECONOMY: MARXISM AND PSYCHOANALYSIS DOWN THE TOILET

Having spent time rectifying the mutual misunderstandings between Freud and his psychoanalytically minded Marxist critics, I turn once again to Lacan. What, if any, kind of marriage between Marxism and psychoanalysis does he consider feasible? Although Lacan is not a Marxist, do his own engagements with Marxism at least open up further possibilities for Marxism and psychoanalysis reciprocally informing each other? Since much of what follows in the rest of this book's chapters will involve scrutinizing Lacan's complex ambivalence vis-à-vis the Marxist tradition, I will limit myself in the present section to introducing only certain basic features of Lacan *avec* Marx.

In a recent essay entitled "An American Utopia," Fredric Jameson makes a straightforward case for prioritizing the specifically Lacanian version of psychoanalysis as a partner for Marxism in any rapprochement between the two fields. Jameson's reading of Lacan situates him as a thinker of the *zoon politikon* in a lineage starting with Aristotle and continuing with both Hegel and Marx.[228] Jameson explains:

> The primacy of desire in Freud remained essentially personal, and included the "otherness" of the family in a merely causal fashion. Lacan was able to insert otherness into the heart of Freud's pathbreaking conception of desire, and to offer a picture of desire from which the presence of the Other—big or small—is never absent, so that in a sense, or rather in all possible senses, individual desire is the desire of the Other, is the Other's desire. This socialization of desire itself now at one stroke renders the attempts to build a bridge between Freud and Marx, between the two great scientific discoveries which characterize modernity, unnecessary. For now the psyche is already essentially social, and the existence of the Other is at the very heart of the libidinal, just as all our social passions are already drenched in the psychic.[229]

He continues: "The fundamental superiority of Lacanian doctrine over the multitude of other psychoanalyses on offer, including Freud's original one, lies in the way it grasps the Other as being structurally internal to subjectivity itself."[230] Finally, Jameson adds:

> Here the stereotypical (and ideological) opposition between "the individual" and "society" cannot obtain, since the two are inseparable in an inextricable dialectic of identity and difference. To put it methodologically, where in other systems the operation of transcoding is unavoidable—we must pass from a language of subjective or psychological individuality to a very different terminology governing the social or the collective (a passage involving a mediation I tend to describe in terms of a translation process)—here transcoding is unnecessary and the same code can apply to either reality. Thus where for Freud, in *Group Dynamics and the Analysis of the Ego*, the superego is somehow outside the self, in the form of the dictator and object of fascination he constitutes, here the Lacanian big Other is within subjectivity, constituting it fully as much as it might be seen to influence it; nor is it some projection of my private desires, as when the Leader somehow symbolically resolves my own oedipal traumas (as for Erickson).[231]

There are three reservations I have about these passages. First, I worry about reading Lacan as radically liquidating any distinction between the individual and social dimensions by dissolving the former into the latter. This renders him difficult to distinguish from, for instance, Jungians hypothesizing a collective mind/unconscious (a hypothesis Lacan rejects).

Second, apropos the Freudian superego specifically, what about Freud's repeated characterizations of the ego-ideal and the superego as each a "differentiated grade within the ego"?[232] Rather than the ego-ideal and/or superego being "somehow outside the self" as per 1921's *Group Psychology and the Analysis of the Ego*—even here, the external leader figure gets internalized via identification, with the eleventh and final chapter of this book being entitled by Freud "A Differentiating Grade in the Ego"[233]—are not the ego-ideal and/or superego qua differentiated grade(s) within the ego arguably "within subjectivity" just as much as are the Lacanian *petits autres* and *grand Autre*? Is Freud not sufficiently emphatic about this?

Third and relatedly, much of my treatment of Freud earlier in this chapter indicates that Jameson's extremely sharp contrast between Freud and Lacan on exogenous sociality/alterity is exaggerated. For instance, the ontogenetic zero-level prematurational helplessness (*Hilflosigkeit*) of the Freudian neonate, as per 1895's "Project for a Scientific Psychology," renders the human psyche naturally compelled to be socially related to others from the very get-go.[234] Moreover, and as I put it earlier, Freud is not Hobbes; namely, he does not posit a purely and thoroughly pre/nonsocial individual at the core of his theoretical framework. Instead, the Freudian psyche is fundamentally ambivalent about others, torn between Eros's relational inclinations toward others and the *Todestrieb*'s antisocial negativities. Freud's human being can be characterized by Kant's internally conflicted "unsocial sociability" (*die ungesellige Geselligkeit der Menschen*) rather than any unequivocal unsociability. Freud has at least one foot planted squarely within the *zoon politikon* intellectual tradition (along with Hegel, Marx, and Lacan).

Incidentally, my preceding examination of Freud on aggression as a social problem goes at least some way toward addressing Jameson's Lacano-Marxist observations, made in the same piece, about the issue of envy (specifically as the Lacanian "theft of *jouissance*") in any possible future postcapitalist society.[235] (Shlomo Avineri, in his 1968 study of Marx, already worries about jealousy compromising and undermining the early stages of socialist and communist social transformations.)[236] I concur with Jameson that the pervasive human tendency to resent others for supposedly stealing one's (always-already lost and forever impossible) enjoyment qua *jouissance* likely will persist within any socialist or communist social order *à venir*. However, I suspect that his fears concerning a sociopolitically unmanageable explosion of envious rage among those members of an economically egalitarian collectivity who fail to flourish are somewhat overblown.

The basis of these Jamesonian fears is that dissatisfied people who still struggle even under the reign of material (and not just formal) equality no longer will have the old alibis afforded by inegalitarian social orders. These alibis enable them to attribute their miseries to the unfairness of society and the machinations of their malicious superiors, namely, the Other or others allegedly responsible for stealing the satisfactions the sufferer purportedly would get to enjoy if it were not for this gratuitous theft. Jameson reasons that in a society without such inequalities, the wretched would have to confront their malaise with no such excuses; they would be left with nobody to blame but themselves for their unhappy lives. Jameson's feared result is an irruption of resentful fury wrecking any socialist or communist social experiment.

But on the same Lacanian grounds appealed to by Jameson, I would maintain that he underestimates the inventiveness and resourcefulness of the fantasizing, projecting, and excuse making that goes along with Lacan's ideas about presumably stolen *jouissance*. I doubt that any realistically feasible form of socialist or communist society would be so absolutely perfect, such a flawlessly realized utopia, that it would not contain various friction-generating imperfections in its intersubjective and trans-subjective structures and dynamics. However

THE CONFLICTED POLITICAL ANIMAL   71

small or slight, these imperfections still could be opportunistically latched onto and exaggerated by future civilizations' discontents as alibis for their persisting *Unbehagen*.

So, on the one hand, I agree with Jameson that, contra certain sorts of leftist utopianism, the "discontent in civilization" foregrounded by psychoanalysis will persist beyond capitalism. But on the other hand, I disagree with him that this unhappiness is quite likely to be significantly worse, especially to the point of being socially unmanageable. One of the many lessons of psychoanalysis is that humans can be extremely creative in concocting convenient counterfactual narratives, as conscious and unconscious fantasies, thanks to which they let themselves off the hook for their own misery through blaming Others/others for any lack of enjoyment. This sad, self-defeating creativity probably would enable the discontents of socialism and communism to continue bearing the burdens of their own misery with nothing more than the continuation of their same age-old grumblings—*plus ça change* . . .

Despite my reservations about Jameson's contrasting of Freud and Lacan, there nonetheless is something to his insistence on Lacan as the best psychoanalytic partner for a Marxism motivated to ally itself with psychoanalysis. The Hegelian-Kojèvian sensibilities Lacan brings to his "return to Freud" indeed render Lacanian psychoanalysis much easier to blend with Marxism. This is thanks in no small part to the facts that Marx is heavily influenced by Hegel and that Alexandre Kojève interprets Hegel's 1807 Jena *Phenomenology of Spirit* partly through the lenses of Marxism.[237] Nevertheless, a general socialization of the unconscious does not make Lacan (or anyone else) a Marxist. Fortunately, Lacan himself helpfully specifies multiple precise points of convergence between his rendition of psychoanalysis and Marxist materialisms.

Some readers might be surprised to learn of the later Lacan's pronounced shifting of his attention to political economy in the context of the period of his most detailed and sustained dialogue with Marxism. Specifically, in his sixteenth (*From an Other to the other* [1968–1969]) and seventeenth (*The Other Side of Psychoanalysis* [1969–1970]) seminars, he advocates replacing Freud's reliance on the natural-scientific discipline of physics for metapsychological metaphors and models with the social/human-scientific discipline of economics instead.[238] This replacement would seem to entail a leap from the natural (of the *Naturwissenschaften*) to the non/more-than-natural (of the *Geisteswissenschaften*), even from the material to the spiritual (*als geistig*). Yet in *Seminar XVI* Lacan warns that this shift from a libidinal-psychical economy pictured on the basis of Freud's naturalist energetics to this same economy recast on the basis of sociohistorical political economy involves no lessening or loss of materialist credentials, no backsliding into idealism.[239] This warning, along with lots of surrounding textual evidence, indicates that the political economy Lacan elects as a disciplinary partner for analytic metapsychology is none other than that of the historical-materialist critique of political economy established by Marx.

Seminar XVII offers additional elaborations apropos the combination of psychoanalysis with political economy. During the February 11, 1970, session of this academic year, right after talking about Marx and "surplus *jouissance*," Lacan states: "From time to time I stick my nose into a stack of authors who are economists. And we can see the extent to which this is of interest for us analysts, because if there is something that remains to be done in analysis, it is to institute this other field of energetics [*cet autre champ énergétique*], which would demand other structures than those of physics, and which is the field of *jouissance*."[240] In the following week's session of the seventeenth seminar, he invokes one of Freud's own references to capitalist economics, in which Freud links this field to libidinal economics. Specifically, Lacan refers to Freud's analogy between the capitalist-entrepreneur relationship and, in terms of the analytic theory of dreams, the rapport between the unconscious infantile wish (analogous to the capitalist) and the day residues (analogous to the entrepreneur) triggering the production of a dream with its manifest content.[241] For Freud, just as the entrepreneur's productive powers are on loan from the capitalist funding the enterprise, so too are the day residues' powers to set in motion the production of a dream funded and fueled by archaic repressed impulses and ideas (i.e., unconscious infantile wishes).[242]

Lacan draws certain consequences from Freud's dream-theoretic analogy involving the capitalist and the entrepreneur. In particular, Lacan links this analogy to his account of *jouissance*:

> Freud . . . tells us that one must not forget that a dream stands on two feet, and that it is not sufficient that it represent a decision, a lively desire [*un vif désir du sujet*], by the subject as to the present. There must be something that gives it support in a desire from childhood [*un désir de l'enfance*]. And here, he takes as his reference—this is usually taken as a display of elegance—the entrepreneur, the entrepreneur of decisions, in his relationship to the capitalist whose accumulated resources, the capital of libido, will enable this decision to pass into action [*passer en acte*].[243]

He continues:

> These are things that look like they are a metaphor. Isn't it amusing to see how this takes on a different value after what I have been telling you concerning the

relationship between capitalism and the function of the master—concerning the altogether distinct nature of what can be done with the process of accumulation in the presence of surplus *jouissance* [*plus-de-jouir*]—in the very presence of this surplus *jouissance*, to the exclusion of the big fat *jouissance*, plain *jouissance*, *jouissance* that is realized in copulation in the raw [*bon gros jouir, le jouir simple, le jouir qui se réalise dans la copulation toute nue*]? Isn't this precisely where infantile desire gets its force from, its force of accumulation with respect to this object that constitutes the cause of desire [*cet objet qui fait la cause du désir*], namely that which is accumulated as libido capital by virtue, precisely, of infantile non-maturity, the exclusion of *jouissance* that others will call normal? There you have what suddenly gives Freud's metaphor its proper connotation when he refers to the capitalist.[244]

I suspect that Lacan is tacitly tapping into capitalist ideology's myths about the origins of capital. More precisely, this would be the moralizing fiction, flattering to capitalists themselves, according to which the (primitive) accumulation of capital originates in abstinence, namely, the virtuous self-renunciations and ethico-pragmatic frugality through which the righteous chosen few elevate themselves to their well-deserved class position as masters of the economy. What is more, given that, as Freud observes, anal personalities often are parsimonious, even capitalist ideology itself (inadvertently) confesses that capitalism is tied to anality, that it comes out of the anus. It really is shit, even by its own (unintended) admission.[245] Althusser's claim that ideology is as much allusion as illusion is perfectly apt here.[246]

With Freud's analogy linking the figure of the capitalist to repressed infantile wishes (as the latent dream thoughts involved in the dream work), Lacan proposes that such "desire from childhood" (*désir de l'enfance*) funding the production of dreams is itself a result of a process of accumulation. However, such saving or storing up is not the result of an inaugural decision or choice on the part of the (dreaming) subject (with "the entrepreneur of decisions" coming on the scene only with the day residues of adulthood, that is, long after the period of childhood to which the latent dream thoughts are tied). Rather, "infantile non-maturity," as the prolonged prematurational helplessness into which birth hurls the human being, forces abstinence and, hence, the accumulation of "libido capital" upon the infant and prepubescent child. This abstinence is a necessity, not a virtue. And, with the capitalist, it becomes a vice bound up with yet other vices.

Lacan here draws attention to a facet of Freudian *Hilflosigkeit*, namely, the child's inability, its impotence, to engage in genital sexual relations with its adult

74   ❦   THE CONFLICTED POLITICAL ANIMAL

significant others.[247] Such sexual helplessness brings with it, as Lacan puts it, "the exclusion of the big fat *jouissance*, plain *jouissance*, *jouissance* that is realized in copulation in the raw [*bon gros jouir, le jouir simple, le jouir qui se réalise dans la copulation toute nue*]" and "the exclusion of *jouissance* that others will call normal." By Lacan's lights, "the capital of libido" is the product of a period of primitive accumulation imposed upon the psychical subject(-to-be) by the brute biological facticity of its specifically sexual prematuration. This prematuration, lasting until puberty, is especially prolonged in human animals (as is the dependence on others for bare survival, this being another crucial aspect of human *Hilflosigkeit*). For Lacan, a libidinal-economic primitive accumulation generates desire (*désir*) as surplus *jouissance* (*plus-de-jouir*) with its corresponding object, namely, *objet petit a* qua object-cause of desire (i.e., "this object that constitutes the cause of desire" [*cet objet qui fait la cause du désir*]).

As Lacan points out the following year in *Seminar XVIII* (*D'un discours qui ne serait pas du semblant* [1971]), the accumulation of *jouissance* in the form of the surplus of *plus-de-jouir* renders enjoyment "impossible."[248] On this occasion, Lacan contends that all economies, including the psyche's libidinal economy, are "a fact of discourse" (*un fait de discours*).[249] As soon as the neonate's psyche begins primitively accumulating undischarged *jouissance*, it also, given the "throw" (*als werfen*) of birth, already is caught within the webs of intersubjective and trans-subjective relations, entangled in networks involving languages, institutions, interests, practices, fantasies, ideologies, and so on.

According to Lacan, the sociosymbolic mediation brought about in and through the signifiers and social links of *discours* renders "big fat *jouissance*, plain *jouissance*, *jouissance* that is realized in copulation in the raw" impossible (à la such Lacanian pronouncements as "jouissance is prohibited [*interdite*] to whoever speaks, as such").[250] That is to say, even when the child in (post)pubescent maturity comes to engage in what others then deem the "normal *jouissance*" of genital copulation, there inevitably will be an unbridgeable discrepancy between the "*jouissance* expected," crystallized in the childhood-in-origin fantasies ($ ◊ a$) funded by the "libido capital" of accumulated *plus-de-jouir*, and the "*jouissance* obtained" in frustratingly unfulfilling fulfillment of these fantasies via an adult copulation that never can measure up to the pregenital anticipatory fantasies orchestrating these later genital encounters. What is more, even if the child improbably were to go to the Sadean libertine extreme of transgressing the prohibition on incest, he/she still would confront the disappointing gap between fantasmatic expectation and actual obtainment.[251] Considering Lacan's emphasis on "infantile non-maturity" as the sexual side of *Hilflosigkeit*, the incest prohibition interestingly is superfluous, forbidding what is anyway impossible, for the child him/herself.

But what, if any, are the upshots of the later Lacan's linking of his libidinal economics (as centered on *jouissance*, desire, object *a*, etc.) to political economics generally and the historical-materialist critique of political economy specifically? Likewise, how should one construe Lacan's glosses on Freud's capitalist-entrepreneur analogy as regards interfacing psychoanalysis with Marxism? Samo Tomšič, in his 2015 study *The Capitalist Unconscious: Marx and Lacan*, addresses this second question thus: "Freud does not say what the Freudo-Marxists will claim later, that the unconscious explains capitalism; he states precisely the opposite: it is capitalism that elucidates the unconscious. The unconscious discovered in the *Interpretation of Dreams* is nothing other than the capitalist unconscious, the intertwining of unconscious satisfaction with the structure and the logic of the capitalist mode of production."[252] I have two hesitations about Tomšič's reading. First, from a Lacanian perspective at least, I am concerned that he runs the risk of excessively historicizing the psychoanalytic unconscious. Lacan would not disagree that the structures and dynamics of the unconscious are significantly inflected by sociohistorical forces and factors, including those of capitalism. However, I believe Lacan would maintain that capitalist modernity's contributions to the discovery and theorization of the Freudian unconscious are an instance of Marx's "Human anatomy contains a key to the anatomy of the ape."[253] Put differently, the explicit surfacing of the analytic unconscious within modern capitalism reveals a metapsychology already implicitly operative within the species *Homo sapiens* long before the rise of the capitalist mode of production.

But if Tomšič means by "the capitalist unconscious" the "intertwining" of a transhistorical unconscious with capitalism as a mediating historical social formation, then this first reservation of mine is mild or even moot. Lacan himself, again in *Seminar XVII*, provides an example of his openness to this intertwining approach when, once more appealing to Marx, he acknowledges that under capitalism "the interests of the subject" (i.e., the subject's drives, desires, etc.) are "entirely commercial" (*entièrement marchands*).[254] That is to say, there is an intertwining of libidinal and political economies such that within a capitalist socioeconomic (and symbolic) order, the subject's libidinal interests are mediated and inflected by the demands and dictates of the mode of production characterizing this trans-subjective enveloping order. Similarly, Lacan, already in *Seminar XIV* (*The Logic of Fantasy* [1966–1967]), suggests that under capitalism, humans' love lives are themselves commodified through sexual and amorous encounters being arranged by the commerce of the "meat market"[255] (a point Lacan would see being even more relevant nowadays considering the roles of the internet, social media, and dating apps in orchestrating libidinally charged couplings).

My second hesitation regarding Tomšič is not so easily allayed. On the one hand, I concur with him that pre/non-Lacanian variants of Freudo-Marxism (including and especially those associated with the Frankfurt School) tend to err in one-sidedly having psychoanalysis explain capitalism but not vice versa.[256] And Tomšič is quite correct that a Lacanian approach, as per what one might label "Lacano-Marxism," tends to offset this Freudo-Marxist one-sidedness by stressing how capitalism explains psychoanalysis. Lacan's above-cited appeals to political economy à la Marxism as indispensable for conceptualizing libidinal economics confirm this aspect of Tomšič's interpretation.

Yet on the other hand, Tomšič appears to favor one sort of one-sidedness (i.e., a Lacano-Marxist elucidation of psychoanalysis through capitalism) against another sort of one-sidedness (i.e., a Freudo-Marxist elucidation of capitalism through psychoanalysis). In my view, what this leaves unaccomplished in its playing off of Lacano- against Freudo-Marxisms is a revisiting of how psycho-analysis illuminates capitalism after passing through Lacan's reflections on how capitalism illuminates psychoanalysis. Failing to do so amounts to forgoing certain insights undiscovered by more traditional Freudo-Marxism. In other words, a Lacano-Marxist illumination of capitalism by psychoanalysis—this illumination is neglected by Tomšič's approach, with its exclusive focus on a Lacano-Marxist illumination of psychoanalysis by capitalism instead—brings certain facets to light left languishing in darkness by the older Freudo-Marxism's more limited and partial illumination of capitalism by psychoanalysis.

Although these various illuminations will be explored throughout much of the rest of the book to follow, I want for now to highlight one key Lacanian insight for an understanding of capitalism. As just seen, Lacan integrates the references Freud makes in his dream theory to the figures of the capitalist and the entrepreneur into the specifically Lacanian account of the libidinal econ-omy. In terms of a Lacano-Marxist explaining of capitalism via psychoanalysis, Lacan's thus-drawn parallels between the capitalist and the accumulator of "libido capital" qua *plus-de-jouir* suggest that even for capitalists themselves, capitalism is not organized around anyone's contentment, fulfillment, gratifica-tion, satisfaction, or the like.

Just as with the Lacanian dynamics of surplus *jouissance*, in which desire ceaselessly chases without end after the infinitely receding fantasmatic *objet petit a*, so too with capital's accumulation of surplus value: The quantitative surplus of surplus value is, as quantitative, an in-principle potential infinity, which, as such, offers no prospect for the closure of completion and satiety to the pursuers of this ever-expanding numerical excess. There is no economic version of the finality of a well-rounded whole of "big fat *jouissance*" waiting for even the most successful of capitalists perfectly obeying the logic of capital. Yet capitalists keep chasing the dragon as though there were some final point to be aimed at and reached. This indicates that the drive of/as capital, the circuit of M-C-M', is nothing if not a death-drive-like painful repetition compulsion (*Wiederholungszwang*) even for the most privileged and pampered bearers/personifications of capital.

Both critics and defenders of capitalism frequently allege that this socioeconomic system is animated by the private narcissistic motivations of acquisitiveness, greed, self-seeking, and the like. But seeing the closed loop of M-C-M' as akin to Lacanian *jouissance* strongly hints that the capitalist drive, the very motor of this mode of production, is something other than personal pleasures pursued through the enlightened cynicism of cold pragmatic calculations of measurable gains and losses. I will come back to all of this subsequently.

Although the bulk of the Lacanian ground I just covered is situated during the period of Lacan's teaching at the end of the 1960s and beginning of the 1970s, his fourteenth seminar, given in the mid-1960s, lays the foundations for much of what he subsequently says about the topic of the economy as per (political) economics. First of all, in the April 12, 1967, session of *Seminar XIV*, Lacan portrays Marxism and psychoanalysis as sharing in common a focus on "economy" in the broad sense of latent structure.[257] Subsequent remarks to the same effect in the sixteenth seminar confirm that the classical (circa 1965) and then-contemporaneous Althusser's quasi-structuralist recasting of Marx is Lacan's source of inspiration in this context.[258]

Another likely source of inspiration in this same vein is Lucien Sebag's 1964 book *Marxisme et structuralisme*. An ethnologist and student of the great structural anthropologist Claude Lévi-Strauss, he was in analysis with Lacan for several years. Moreover, Lacan saw in Sebag someone who could, as Élisabeth Roudinesco puts it, "give his doctrine its second wind"[259] and "lend a new impetus to his own teachings."[260] Additionally, and further severely complicating Sebag's analysis with Lacan, Sebag fell in love with Lacan's daughter Judith, with *Marxisme et structuralisme* being dedicated to her (incidentally, Jacques-Alain Miller, another young leftist upon whom Lacan pinned his hopes for a suitable intellectual successor/heir, went on to marry Judith in 1966). To cut a long story short, Sebag committed suicide on January 9, 1965, at the age of thirty-one. Soon after, the title of the fourth and final chapter of Sebag's *Marxisme et*

78   THE CONFLICTED POLITICAL ANIMAL

structuralisme, "Science et vérité,"[261] also would come to serve as the title of the opening session (December 1, 1965) of Lacan's *Seminar XIII* (*The Object of Psychoanalysis* [1965–1966]), with this session being published on its own in 1966's *Écrits*. It ought to be underlined in passing that Lacan's investment in Sebag circa the early 1960s suggests his interest in Marxism is not simply the result of being forced to address a post–May '68 public caught up in various currents of radical leftism.

Of course, Althusser's structuralist Marxism already draws on psychoanalysis, including of the Lacanian sort, in portraying socioeconomic structures as per the Althusserian version of historical materialism. These structures, according to Althusser, involve various unconscious dimensions and dynamics. Moreover, this same Althusser deploys the interlinked concepts of "structural causality"[262] (blending Spinozism and structuralism) and "overdetermination"[263] (borrowed directly and avowedly from psychoanalysis) to capture how the whole of a given social formation (as infrastructure and superstructure combined) immanently yet invisibly converges upon and configures entities and events situated within such formations. Historical-materialist causation and determining à la Althusser are very much akin to Lacan's portrayals of the influences of the symbolic order qua big Other in shaping speaking subjects subjected to sociolinguistic signifiers.[264]

A week after Lacan's Althusser-inspired identification of overdetermining structure as a common denominator between Marxism and psychoanalysis, in the April 19, 1967, session of *Seminar XIV*, Lacan speaks of the economy of the psychoanalytic unconscious. He declares that "*jouissance*-value . . . is at the source of the economy of the unconscious" (*La valeur de jouissance . . . est au principe de l'économie de l'inconscient*).[265] Then, during the April 26, 1967, session of this seminar, he remarks that "the economy of the unconscious . . . is commonly called primary process" (*l'économie de l'inconscient . . . ce qu'on appelle communément* le processus primaire).[266] Lacan's use, once again, of the phrase "*jouissance*-value" signals that he has Marxist theory in mind when speaking of matters economic in this 1967 context. But what does the thesis that the economy formed by the primary processes of the unconscious is organized around "*la valeur de jouissance*" contribute, especially as regards the implications of psychoanalysis for Marxism?

The April 26, 1967, session of the fourteenth seminar also contains some revealing specifications apropos Lacan's account of *jouissance*, specifications with clear implications for the related concept of *jouissance* value. In particular, Lacan therein makes a reference to Sophocles's *Oedipus Rex* as providing Freud with a founding myth for psychoanalysis. Through implying that Oedipus himself is an Oedipal subject who dares actually to succeed in transgressing the fundamental prohibitions against parricide and maternal incest,[267] Lacan proposes that the tragic conclusion of Sophocles's play reveals the guilt-ridden rottenness, the horrifying putrescence, of the ultimate forbidden fruit if and when it is seized. In being seized, this fruit unexpectedly goes from being tantalizing (when inaccessible) to becoming repulsive (when accessed).[268] The fulfillment of fantasies, as the transformation of *jouissance* expected into *jouissance* obtained, does not provide the ultimate in intensely, purely enjoyable Enjoyment-with-a-capital-E—quite the contrary.[269]

As an aside apropos *Oedipus Rex*, one should note that at its conclusion, Oedipus turns himself into both excretory apparatus and excrement, traumatically expelling himself from Thebes. With the remainder of Sophocles's *Oedipus* trilogy, one has the self-expelled former king miserably floating around before being finally flushed out of the picture for good in *Oedipus at Colonus* (or Colon-anus). And in *Antigone* one of Oedipus's unfortunate sons, Polynices, is pushed out of Thebes by Creon to become excrement through animals eating (and then excreting) his unburied corpse. But this admittedly is a shitty reading of Sophocles.

That said, the economy of the Lacanian unconscious, with its primary processes, is organized as a dynamic of interminably beating around a bush (i.e., *jouissance*) as if there were a desire to accomplish the terminal deed of really hitting the bush. Yet despite the appearance of this "as if," the whole point is precisely not ever to hit the bush. If the bush gets hit, it disappears and, in so doing, reveals that it always marked an absence, namely, what the Lacan of *Seminar VII* (*The Ethics of Psychoanalysis* [1959–1960]) describes as the "vacuole of *das Ding*."[270]

If and when this disappearance and revelation transpire, the whole unconscious economy orbiting around the (absent) center of *jouissance* would grind to a halt and come crashing down. There would be a psychical market collapse, causing the libidinal economy to sink into depression. The primal repression concealing from the libidinal investor the truth that the economy he/she participates in is, in a sense, one giant Ponzi scheme erected on nothing more than empty promises of "big fat *jouissance*, plain *jouissance*, *jouissance* that is realized in copulation in the raw" would be lifted and the jig would be up. A libidinal investor who would go to King Oedipus's bitter end and try to cash out for good would end up empty handed or, perhaps worse still, with a handful of delivered shit in place of promised gold.

Taking the immediately preceding clarifications regarding *jouissance* into account as involved in Lacan's notion of *jouissance* value, what does the above indicate regarding economics not only as per psychoanalysis's libidinal economics but also apropos Marxism's historical-materialist critique of political economy? In *Seminar XIV* and elsewhere, Lacan suggests that his reflections on *jouissance* and *jouissance* value are of direct relevance to a Marxist-type analysis of capitalism. But what exactly is this relevance?

Through the phrases "*jouissance* value" and "surplus *jouissance*" (*plus-de-jouir*), the Lacan of the 1960s and 1970s signals the relevance of his concept of *jouissance* especially for the *telos* around which the capitalist mode of production organizes itself, namely, surplus value (as the "'" in M-C-M'). During a 1972 talk in Milan, Lacan, speaking of capitalism, observes, "There is only this that makes the system work. It's surplus-value"[271] (or, as Tony Smith puts the same point, "The drive to maximize surplus value defines the inner nature of capital").[272] So if surplus value is akin to *jouissance* (as *jouissance* value and/or surplus *jouissance*), then capitalist societies revolve around the unenjoyable incessant pursuit of an elusive, impossible-to-obtain enjoyment. The carnivalesque merry-go-round marketplace is far from all fun and games.

If, as per Lacan, capitalism is ultimately about *jouissance* rather than pleasure, this runs conspicuously contrary to the image of capitalism as straightforwardly and unabashedly hedonistic, as sustained and strengthened by gratifications, happinesses, satisfactions, and titillations of countless sorts. Not only do the exploited noncapitalists under capitalism not get to enjoy the surpluses extorted out of them; not only are capitalism's consumers kept in a constant state of agitated, dissatisfied want so as to keep them ceaselessly moving along the unending chain from purchase to purchase, with no bought commodity ever delivering the fulfillment advertised—even the capitalists, including the biggest of the big bourgeoisie, torment and exhaust themselves in the endless quest after ever-more (infinitely more, in principle) surplus value. In fact, the consumerist chasing of the dragon in the sphere of exchange, with its commodities, is itself an effect, a mere echo, of the capitalist chasing of the dragon in the sphere of production, with its surplus values. For all capitalists and workers as well as producers and consumers alike, what could be called capitalism's Thing (as per Lacan's conception of *das Ding*) sustains everyone caught up in its socioeconomic system in a permanent state of discontented, restless seeking. Capitalism doth make junkies of us all. Everyone ends up impoverished by it in one way or another. I will revisit and unpack at much greater length this Lacanian recasting of capitalism as centered on *jouissance*, rather than on happiness and/or pleasure, later.

I wish to bring the present chapter to a close with one other hint Lacan offers about interfacing Marxism and psychoanalysis. In a 1968 talk given to psychiatrists in training, he unexpectedly broaches the topic of the political economics

THE CONFLICTED POLITICAL ANIMAL   81

of the solid waste disposal business: "Unlike what happens at every level of the animal kingdom—which starts with elephants and hippos and ends with jellyfish—man is naturally characterized by the extraordinary embarrassment [*embarras*] he feels about—what should we call it? By the simplest name we can find, by God—the evacuation of shit."[273] Lacan continues:

> Man is the only animal for whom this is a problem, and it's a prodigious one. You don't realize, because you have little devices that evacuate it. You have no idea where it goes afterwards. It all goes through pipes and is collected in fantastic places you have no idea of, and then there are factories that take it in, transform it and make all sorts of things that go back into circulation [*la circulation*] through the intermediary of human industry, and human industry is a completely circular industry [*une industrie très bouclée*]. It is striking that there is not, to my knowledge, any course on political economy that devotes a lesson or two to it. This is a phenomenon of repression which, like all phenomena of repression, is bound up with the need for decorum [*la bienséance*].[274]

In relation to the traditional philosophical project of identifying those features distinguishing human beings as unique within the full sweep of creation, Lacan, very much as a psychoanalyst, highlights humanity's awkwardness and discomfort in the face of its own excrement. This is by contrast with nonhuman animals' comparatively unperturbed attitude regarding their poops. Unlike all other living beings, humans angst over their own shit. They are troubled by it, by how to dispose of it and what to do with it.

Uniquely for humanity, there is, as per the title of a 1978 book by Dominique Laporte, a "history of shit," namely, an evolution over time of shifting strategies and tactics for how sociosymbolic subjects, both individually and collectively, handle and cope with their excrements. In the above quotations, Lacan indicates that humans' rapport with their own shit is another instance of them being naturally destined for (self-)denaturalization, for (self-)alienation from animality ("man is naturally characterized . . . ," "Man is the only animal for whom this is a problem . . ."). As per a dialectical naturalism also exemplified by the metapsychological significance of biologically determined prolonged prematurational helplessness—this *Hilflosigkeit* is tantamount to a natural determination not to be naturally determined, a natural facilitation of the predominance of social nurture over biological nature[275]—humanity's excremental self-revulsion would be a natural inclination to rebel against nature.

From Lacan's analytic perspective, repression-inducing shame (i.e., "extraordinary embarrassment" [*embarras*], "the need for decorum" [*la bienséance*]) inhibits those interested in economics, whether they be Marxists or not, from looking into such topics as the political economy of shit. Moreover, in the second of the two preceding quotations, Lacan maintains that the treatment of excrement under industrial capitalism reveals essential aspects of capitalism as a whole. He portrays the fecal matter of capitalism's subjects as circulating through looping circuits of pipes and factories. Then, this looping (*boucler*) quality is attributed not only to industrial solid waste processing but also to "human industry" tout court ("human industry is a completely circular industry" [*une industrie très bouclée*]). Lacan could be said to move from the political economy of shit in particular to capitalism's shitty political economy in general.

So, following Lacan's insinuations, the loop of M-C-M′, as the underlying structural dynamic of capitalism *überhaupt*, is a kind of socioeconomic anal-expulsive drive. The figure of the pre/noncapitalist miser, repeatedly compared and contrasted with the bourgeois capitalist by Marx, obeys an anal-retentive drive, since the miser hoards (i.e., retains) wealth. But the capitalist, unlike the miser, spends (i.e., expels into circulation) money in order to make yet more money.

Following the lead of the Freud who sets up the psychoanalytic association of gold/money with feces,[276] capitalism is nothing if not the frenetic perpetual production, circulation, and accumulation of ever more shit. In addition to generating gold/money, it gives rise to mountains of commodities and/as garbage as well as the parasitic recycling industries resembling Lacan's description of the sewage treatment business. With recycling, ecology, and the like in view, it justifiably could be said that the greening of capitalism is also its browning.

In fact, the full circuit of capitalism's shitty looping ad nauseam runs from the capitalist's anal-expulsive drive's (more precisely, M-C-M′ as a sublimation of this *Trieb*) setting in motion production to the consumer's oral-incorporative drive sustained and stimulated by the capitalist's drive. Somewhat relatedly, Laporte observes that both of capitalism's two main classes, capitalists and laborers/consumers, each associate the other class with shit (with the poor person's scorn for the obscene "filthy lucre" of the wealthy and the rich person's scorn for the dirt and grime of the impoverished).[277] The logic of capital is nothing if not scatological.

Taking into account capitalism's extended circuit running through the spheres of production, distribution, exchange, and consumption, capitalism shows itself to be, in the psychoanalytic terms advanced by both Freud and Lacan, one giant loop formed by connecting capitalists' anality with consumers' orality. It composes a disgusting closed coprophagic circle in which shit keeps passing from the productive-expulsive anuses of capitalists into the consumptive-incorporative mouths of consumers . . . and back again, over and over. This is a manic binge-purge oscillation in which, inverting the standard bulimic sequence where binging comes first, purging (as capitalist anal expulsion) precedes and conditions binging (as consumerist oral incorporation).

The capitalist socioeconomic system in its entirety thus resembles a person who shoves his own head up his own ass precisely in order to eat his own shit, or a snake that swallows its own tail specifically so as to consume its own feces. From a Lacanian vantage point especially, this whole vile *boucle* outlines the contours of a central negativity: the black hole of the vacuole of capitalism's Thing, the infinite abyss of the bottomless, self-voiding rectum of absent (unenjoyable) enjoyment. Paraphrasing Leo Bersani, perhaps surplus value is a rectum, a rectum that also is a grave. With reference to a certain punchline ("Rectum? Damn near killed him!"), capitalism is ever nearer to driving all its subjects into early graves (especially its would-be exploited "grave diggers"),[278] wrecking them at a continually accelerating pace (as per Marx's image of "whole hecatombs of workers" as the sacrificial victims of capitalism's ritual-like repeated socioeconomic crises).[279] The ring of the traced rim of the loop M-C-M' is the simultaneously both political- and libidinal-economic sphincter at the heart of capitalism in its totality as a massively shitty political economy.

Hence, for psychoanalysis, particularly in its Lacanian version, literal and figurative sphincters function as Cartesian-style pineal glands stitching together the body and the body politic. As Richard Boothby, engaging with Freud and Lacan, insightfully articulates, "the anal sphincter, despite the socially rehearsed repugnance that attaches to everything excremental—or rather precisely because of that repugnance—must be considered the most profoundly social organ of the body."[280] And in a now-famous set of meditations on national differences in European toilet design, Žižek permits seeing the literal bodily sphincter as a metaphorical pineal gland connecting historical materialism's distinct social levels of economic infrastructure and more-than-economic (including ideological) superstructure. Similarly, for Althusser before Žižek, relations of production constitute the pineal-gland-like switch point, within the economic base, where superstructure and infrastructure converge and interact.[281] Incidentally, this Althusserian thesis enables Marxism to identify Weber's central figure of the Protestant ascetic "man of the calling" (*Berufsmensch*) as a relation of production situated and shaped at the intersection of infrastructure and superstructure—and this rather than the Weberian *Berufsmensch*'s being purely superstructural and, as such, a supposed challenge to historical materialism's purported economic reductionism.[282]

84   THE CONFLICTED POLITICAL ANIMAL

Žižek prefaces his reflections on toilets with a theoretical qualification about appeals to ostensibly no-nonsense, brass-tacks practical usefulness—"in everyday life, ideology is at work especially in the apparently innocent reference to pure utility."[283] With this important caveat about utility in place, Žižek soon proceeds to address the matter of European lavatories. He observes:

> In a traditional German lavatory, the hole in which shit disappears after we flush water is way in front, so that the shit is first laid out for us to sniff at and inspect for traces of some illness; in the typical French lavatory, on the contrary, the hole is in the back—that is, the shit is supposed to disappear as soon as possible; finally, the Anglo-Saxon (English or American) lavatory presents a kind of synthesis, a mediation between these two opposed poles—the basin is full of water, so that the shit floats in it—visible, but not to be inspected.... It is clear that none of these versions can be accounted for in purely utilitarian terms: a certain ideological perception of how the subject should relate to the unpleasant excrement which comes from within our body is clearly discernible.[284]

Since all three types of toilets are equally effective in getting the job of disposing of poop done—they enjoy the same level of the essential use value of being-a-toilet—their differences cannot be explained on the basis of any one design being more utilitarian than the others. This ruling out of a seemingly nonideological utilitarian explanation includes the apparently utilitarian Anglo-Saxon lavatory design.

As Žižek claims, the Anglo-Saxon style of "utilitarian" toilet is itself not a default original design but instead a secondary synthesis, a sort of compromise formation, between German and French lavatory designs. He goes on:

> Hegel was among the first to interpret the geographical triad Germany-France-England as expressing three different existential attitudes: German reflective thoroughness, French revolutionary hastiness, English moderate utilitarian pragmatism; in terms of political stance, this triad can be read as German conservatism, French revolutionary radicalism and English moderate liberalism; in terms of the predominance of one of the spheres of social life, it is German metaphysics and poetry versus French politics and English economy. The reference to lavatories enables us not only to discern the same triad in the most intimate domain of performing the excremental function, but also to generate the underlying mechanism of this triad in the three different attitudes towards excremental excess: ambiguous contemplative fascination; the hasty attempt to get rid of the unpleasant excess as fast as possible; the pragmatic approach to

treat the excess as an ordinary object to be disposed of in an appropriate way. So it is easy for an academic to claim at a round table that we live in a post-ideological universe—the moment he visits the restroom after the heated discussion, he is again knee-deep in ideology. The ideological investment of such references to utility is attested by their *dialogical* character: the Anglo-Saxon lavatory acquires its meaning only through its differential relation to French and German lavatories. We have such a multitude of the lavatory types because there is a traumatic excess which each of them tries to accommodate—according to Lacan, one of the features which distinguishes man from the animals is precisely that with humans the disposal of shit becomes a problem.[285]

Žižek, with this closing reference to Lacan tying off the discussion of toilets, brings things full circle to my earlier deployment of Lacan's 1968 remarks about the political economy of shit. As seen, these remarks push off from Lacan's observation about humanity's embarrassment regarding its own excrement. And as my reflections unfolding in between quoting that Lacan a while ago and quoting this Žižek just now reveal, Lacan's musings about the political economy of shit also turn out to imply the shitty (anal-expulsive, scatological, coprophagic) quality of capitalist political economy as such (i.e., Lacan's "completely circular industry" epitomized by the distinctively "human industry" of the waste disposal business, with capitalism as the "circulation" of both shit and other [by]products).

Furthermore, as Žižek very well knows, the Hegel he invokes here subsequently colors the Marxist tradition. The European spiritual trinity constituted by German, French, and Anglo-Saxon sociocultural formations comes to be referred to by Lenin, among others, as furnishing "The Three Sources and Three Component Parts of Marxism" (as per the title of a 1913 essay by him).[286] On this view, Marx's thought takes shape at the crossroads of German philosophy (as Hegelian speculative dialectics), French politics (as the radical left-wing currents tied to the Revolution of 1789 and its long tail), and British economics (as the classical labor theory of value put forward first and foremost by Adam Smith and David Ricardo). Despite the humorous quality of Žižek's musings about European toilet designs, he is sincere about using the differences between lavatory types to make some quite serious theoretical points at the intersection of Hegelian philosophy, Lacanian psychoanalysis, and Marxist critique. For psychoanalysis, starting with Freud's 1905 *Jokes and Their Relation to the Unconscious*, humor enables normally repressed unconscious truths to reveal themselves, with laughter both inside and outside the analytic consulting room as a not-uncommon sign that such truths have been registered.[287]

For my present purposes, what is most valuable in the Žižekian account of the significance of European toilets are its implications for rethinking both the Marxism-psychoanalysis rapport as well as the infrastructure-superstructure link as per historical materialism. Žižek's hybrid Lacanian-Althusserian conception(s) of the unconscious and/as ideology are pivotal at this juncture. From Lacan, Žižek takes the account of the unconscious as existing primarily in the forms of a manifest material-objective-real exteriority at the sociosymbolic level—albeit with those subjected to this manifest exteriority having eyes not to see it. This Lacanian re-envisioning of the unconscious is diametrically opposed to the commonplace image of the unconscious as a hidden mental-subjective-ideal interiority, as per the picture of psychoanalysis as a hermeneutic depth psychology.

From Althusser, Žižek takes the account of the "materiality of ideology"[288] (an account foreshadowed by Gramsci,[289] among others). This account amounts to Althusser's depsychologization of the ideological, parallel and related to Lacan's depsychologization of the unconscious. According to the distinctively Althusserian theory of ideology, the ideological, despite the etymology of the very word "ideology," is not mainly ideas internal to individual persons' heads in the guises of the misleading thoughts of false consciousness. Rather, ideology exists first and foremost in the extramental guises of external beings, of palpably tangible institutions, practices, rituals, and the like as the incarnate materials of fleshly bodies, concrete buildings, physical objects, and so on. Ideology for Althusser, like the unconscious and its truths for Lacan, is, so to speak, "out there," instantiated in the shared public spaces of sociosymbolic matrices (including public restrooms).

Žižek sees in the diversity of European lavatory styles a condensed quotidian embodiment of unconscious ideology as per a combination of Lacan with Althusser, a condensation with consequences for Marxism, psychoanalysis, and their relationship. In light of Žižek's reflections, bathrooms now can be illuminated as sites of intersection for infrastructural and superstructural dimensions. To begin with, solid waste disposal involves infrastructure in both its technical Marxist sense (as a socially essential economic industry) and its non-technical quotidian sense (as plumbing, sewers, and septic systems, in addition to roads, canals, railways, subways, airports, power grids, communications networks, etc.).

Moreover, as Žižek compellingly demonstrates, toilets also involve, in addition to their infrastructural use and exchange values, nonutilitarian influences and mediations irreducible to purely pragmatic economic considerations and calculations. These influences and mediations are attributed by Žižek to the

THE CONFLICTED POLITICAL ANIMAL 〄 87

superstructural qua ideological, the more-than-economic domain of what Marx and Engels in *The German Ideology* list as "politics, laws, morality, religion, metaphysics, and so on of a people" (*der Politik, der Gesetze, der Moral, der Religion, Metaphysik usw. eines Volkes*) as well as "all the rest of ideology" (*sonstige Ideologie*).[290] Obviously, the German, French, and Anglo-Saxon sociocultural constellations identified by Hegel, influencing Marx, and invoked by Žižek count, for Marxist historical materialism, as superstructures.

Insofar as toilet types reflect these sociocultural constellations in their shiny porcelain, they exhibit how pieces of infrastructure (in both senses, Marxist and non-Marxist) can be and are suffused with superstructure too. Dovetailing with Žižek commenting that here "a certain ideological perception of how the subject should relate to the unpleasant excrement which comes from within our body is clearly discernible," Laporte raises the question, "When considering the history of the senses alongside the history of modes of production and circulation, we must ask, which lights the way for the other?"[291] Between German toilets and German speculative metaphysics, between French toilets and French revolutionary politics, between Anglo-Saxon toilets and Anglo-Saxon utilitarian economics—one is faced in each instance with the same apparent chicken-and-egg dilemma.

When Žižek claims that "we have such a multitude of the lavatory types because there is a traumatic excess which each of them tries to accommodate," he signals his endorsement of a Lacanian psychoanalytic resolution of the chicken-and-egg problem with which Laporte's *histoire de la merde* confronts Marxist historical materialism. Žižek's "traumatic excess" would be the Real of excrement, which the realities of all the different lavatory types are designed to deal with in their distinct, more-than-utilitarian ways. Yet one still could ask of this Žižek whether, through his insightful discussion of toilets, he means to elevate Lacanianism over Marxism. More precisely, is his position that a somatic and/or psychical Real à la psychoanalysis enjoys explanatory priority vis-à-vis the infrastructural (i.e., the economic base qua mode of production) as per traditional historical materialism?

Although I am not entirely certain how Žižek would respond to this question, I am inclined to interpret Žižek's Lacanian Real of excrement as not neatly separate from (and, in its separateness, explanatorily competing with) Marx's Real of modes of production. That is to say, I do not believe and do not believe that Žižek believes that one has to choose between privileging this Lacanianism over historical materialism or vice versa. Why not?

The notion of need connects Lacan on defecation with Marx on the economy. In Lacan's metapsychological theory of the libidinal economy, the primarily somatic sources and pressures of the Freudian drives, the anal drive included, amount to biologically innate human needs that make "demands for work" (as Freud phrases it) on the psyche in terms of clamoring for satisfaction, for the gratifications of discharge, sating, and slaking. As such, need (*besoin*) à la Lacan clearly would be a driving force for the *praxes* of social laboring constituting the economic engine of history as per Marxism, with the "economic" intended by Marx in a broad but carefully defined sense. To be even more exact along Lacanian lines, Žižek's "traumatic excess" would be strictly "extimate" (i.e., intimately foreign and internally excluded) in relation to the infrastructural economic base.[292]

Marx himself has a sophisticated historical-materialist theory of need as underpinning social history. Indeed, need is a pineal gland linking Marxism and psychoanalysis. Even on Lacanian grounds, the Luria, Vygotsky, Reich, Fenichel, and Marcuse examined by me earlier are correct in identifying Freudian drives as pivotal to any interfacing of Marxism and psychoanalysis.

I wish to point out in passing that today's theoretical humanities are blessed or cursed, depending on one's perspective, by a continually proliferating series of "'x' theory" fields. Adding to this proliferation, maybe yet another new intellectual discipline, one sublating the convergences between Marxism and psychoanalysis, needs to be established. This would be "shit theory," a framework that could be said to foreground the bung(hole) in *Aufhebung*.

Shit theory easily could spread everywhere. For instance, a linguistic-semiological variant of it could be developed starting with an analysis of how and why the very word "shit" (like another profanity, "fuck") can signify anything and everything under the sun (as well as places where the sun does not shine). Shit as a signifier in symbolic systems is indeed like gold and money qua "universal equivalents" in economic systems. Both shit and gold/money can stand in for all other things, thus adding an additional buttress to Freud's equation of wealth with feces.

It seems fitting to conclude with a well-known proclamation by Lenin regarding the topic of toilets. This statement provides a surprising and serendipitous link back to the very beginning of the present chapter in its scrutinizing of Freud's reactions to the Bolsheviks. In a November 6–7, 1921, article in *Pravda* marking the occasion of the fourth anniversary of the October 1917 Revolution, Lenin announces, "When we are victorious on a world scale I think we shall use gold for the purpose of building public lavatories in the streets of some of the largest cities in the world."[293] The proposal is that revolutionaries, after both seizing control of the levers of state power as well as grasping the reins of the means of production, must lay their hands on persons' libidinal economies too.

THE CONFLICTED POLITICAL ANIMAL   89

Although this revolutionary storming of bourgeois bathrooms (hopefully) will not be televised, videos of it likely will turn up in unseemly corners of the internet.

In all seriousness, Lenin's declaration indicates the importance of revolutionaries exercising an inverse Midas touch, bringing about a liberatory desublimation (by contrast with Marcusian repressive desublimation) that turns gold back into the feces from whence, according to Freud, it ontogenetically came. Would not one of the best critiques of commodity fetishism be taking a literal shit on its condensed material epitomization? By the combined lights of Marxism and psychoanalysis, a transformative path here comes into view going from the plumbing of the capitalist financial system to the plumbing of the communist sewage system via a restructuring of the plumbing of the libidinal system (with hydraulic metaphors abounding in Freud's characterizations of the libidinal economy). Through this revolutionary restructuring, "new men," unlike the commodity fetishists of old, will come casually to defile gold without a second thought, nonchalantly producing their own, and not someone else's, dirty money on a daily basis. Lenin's toilets concretize a Pascalian-Althusserian anticipation having it that if you free your ass, your mind will follow.[294] To change the psyche with its ideas, one must change the body with its functions. A psychoanalytically minded Leninist might conclude that one knows communism truly has triumphed only if and when shit starts to happen differently.

2

From Closed Need to Infinite Greed

Marxian Drives

§6. REPEATING FREUDO-MARXISM: DRIVES BETWEEN HISTORICAL MATERIALISM AND PSYCHOANALYSIS

The title of this chapter obviously makes reference to Alexandre Koyré's 1957 book *From the Closed World to the Infinite Universe*. Therein, Koyré unfurls a narrative in which modern science is born with Galileo Galilei's insistence that the great book of nature is written in the language of mathematics.[1] On the Koyréan account, the Galilean mathematization of all things natural brings about, as one of its several momentous consequences, a leap "from the closed world to the infinite universe" precisely by rupturing the finite sphere of the qualitative cosmos and replacing it with the centerless expanse of a quantitative limitlessness. Along with the capitalism and Protestantism arising in the sixteenth century, the natural science originating in the early seventeenth century is a foundational component and key catalyst of modernity as such. Hence, by Koyré's lights, the historical transition from the premodern to the modern involves the shift designated by his influential book's title.[2]

Koyré arguably is guilty of an anachronistic reconstruction of the history of the genesis of modern science. Specifically, he retrojects twentieth-century French neorationalist commitments and preferences back onto his chosen historical site of intellectual preoccupation. Koyré's brand of neorationalism leads him both indefensibly to sideline the empiricist epistemology and methodology of Francis Bacon as at all relevant to the founding of scientific modernity as well as correspondingly to (mis)represent Galileo as a Platonic mathematical philosopher little reliant upon empirical observation and experimentation.[3] The Koyréan neglect of Baconian empiricism and downplaying of Galilean empiricism is

FROM CLOSED NEED TO INFINITE GREED   91

unpardonable in what is put forward as an accurate history of the birth of modern science.[4]

That said, Koyré's history and philosophy of science, warts and all, exerts a broad and deep influence on a number of his French contemporaries, including the Marxist Althusser and the psychoanalyst Lacan. This fact of intellectual history brings things close to my concerns in this context, in that what follows will involve a Lacan-inspired engagement with Marx. More precisely, the central thesis of the present chapter is that Marx's historical-materialist critique of political economy (as embodied primarily in the *Grundrisse* and the volumes of *Capital*) contains what could be called a theory of modern drive in the strict psychoanalytic sense of *Trieb*. (Whereas Habermas, apropos superstructural phenomena, claims that "Freud's theory can represent a structure that Marx did not fathom,"[5] I would claim, with respect to drive, that Marx's theory already fathomed a structure that Freud later represented differently but with equal rigor and detail.) To be even more exact, I will argue that Marxian modernity, as ushered in with the advent of capitalism, entails a transition "from closed need to infinite greed" in which the rise of capitalist political economy brings to explicit light features of the human libidinal economy subsequently crucial for psychoanalysis once the latter is founded circa the start of the twentieth century.

Lacan, in identifying the historical possibility conditions for Freudian psychoanalysis, repeatedly relies upon Koyré's story of scientific modernity effectuating a shift "from the closed world to the infinite universe."[6] On Lacan's assessment, Galileo's invention of modern science makes possible Descartes's invention of the modern subject (i.e., the *Cogito*), with the latter in turn making possible Freud's invention of the subject of the unconscious (incidentally, Lacan also associates Marx's thinking with the rise of specifically modern forms of subjectivity).[7] Without retelling this Lacanian tale here—I have done so a number of times elsewhere,[8] as also has, most notably, Jean-Claude Milner[9]—my ensuing psychoanalysis-inflected parsing of Marx's critique of political economy is intended by me as a friendly supplement to Lacan's explanation of the specifically modern conditions of possibility for the Freudian discovery of the unconscious (this friendly supplement is hinted at by Lacan in 1965 but left vague and undeveloped).[10] This small contribution to the psychoanalytic general intellect complements Lacan's emphasis on modern science generating a modern subject pivotal for analysis with a parallel emphasis, via Marxism (especially historical materialism's philosophical anthropology), on modern capitalism generating a modern drive equally pivotal for analysis. That is to say, modernity overall, itself the product of an economic in addition to a scientific revolution (not to

92   FROM CLOSED NEED TO INFINITE GREED

mention, as any Hegelian must, a religious Reformation), renders *an und für sich* libidinal as well as subjective transformations paving the way for Freud's own self-styled "Copernican revolution."[11]

As regards Marx, my focus will be on his mature economic works, namely, the *Grundrisse* and *Das Kapital*. I will show that within these epoch-making volumes one can find historical-materialist anthropological theories tracing a socially mediated mutation in human libidinal economics induced by changing political economics. However, my own interfacing of Marxism with psychoanalysis will not amount to a simple, straightforward historicization of the latter—specifically, a thesis according to which the drives of the libidinal economy are entirely the sociohistorical creations of the political economy of capitalism.

Instead, my thesis, more precisely stated, is that capitalism's distinctive fashions of centering human life around surplus and exchange values (as delineated in Marx's critique of political economy) introduces, so to speak, a difference of degree rather than a difference in kind between premodern and modern libidinal configurations—albeit a difference of degree arguably so great as to approach being a difference in kind.[12] This difference between premodernity and modernity is the referent of my title, "from closed need to infinite greed." For philosophical-anthropological reasons to which Marx himself would not be automatically averse,[13] I accept the assertion of psychoanalytic metapsychology that the structures and dynamics of *Trieb* proper are displayed by psyches distributed across various socioeconomic formations past and present (and likely future too). That is to say, I maintain, following Freud and Lacan, that uniquely human drives are not peculiar to a single historical constellation, such as the capitalist era.

However, I will contend, through an exegesis of select moments in Marx's *Grundrisse* and *Capital*, that capitalism, in terms of the roles of money and commodities therein, renders what psychoanalysis identifies as drives (*als Triebe*) significantly more extensive and prominent as motors of human activity. With reference to the above-mentioned difference of degree (approaching a difference in kind) between premodern (precapitalist) "closed need" and modern (capitalist) "infinite greed," capitalism induces premodern *Trieb* to transition from being more constrained and implicit (in itself [*an sich*]) to becoming more unbound and explicit (for itself [*für sich*]). Although already in antiquity there are to be found clear instances of Marx's driven greed—one need only read Aristotle on certain merchants' insatiable lust for amassing and hoarding currencies[14]—the premodern exception becomes the modern rule under capitalism. Moreover, under capitalism, subjects' relationships to objects, of concern both to Marxian accounts of accumulation and consumption as well as to psychoanalytic accounts of drives, bear the marks of the capitalist commodification of human reality right down to the quotidian intimacies of these subjects' existences (as the young Lukács, among others, brings out very effectively).[15] Along these lines, Lacan suggests there are overlaps between his and Marx's conceptions of object relations (a suggestion to be fleshed out by me in much more detail later).[16] Likewise, my interpretation of political economy à la Marx anticipating libidinal economy à la Freud and Lacan goes against those of a psychoanalytic bent who would fault Marx's philosophical anthropology of human motivation for lacking concepts on the order of analysis's drives, desires, fantasies, etc. (a charge the Lacanian Pierre Martin, for one, levels against Marx in his 1984 study *Argent et psychanalyse*).[17]

My contribution is, in part, a Lacan-informed return to the roots of Freudo-Marxism. Two of the earliest attempts at wedding Marx and Freud are Reich's 1929/1934 *Dialectical Materialism and Psychoanalysis* and Fenichel's 1934 "Psychoanalysis as the Nucleus of a Future Dialectical-Materialist Psychology" (with Reich and Fenichel being arguably the most prominent representatives of a radical leftist faction of European psychoanalysts born around 1900). Reich shares with Hegel and many Marxists (such as Marx himself, Engels, Lenin, Mao, and much of mainly non-Western Marxism) a robustly realist conception of dialectics. Tacitly echoing Engels's interpretations of the natural sciences, he portrays Freudian psychoanalysis as a discipline spontaneously forging an antireductive materialist dialectic entirely compatible with Marxian dialectical materialism.[18]

Fenichel opens "Psychoanalysis as the Nucleus of a Future Dialectical-Materialist Psychology" by stressing, in good Marxist fashion, that the effort "to formulate a dialectical-materialist psychology" must navigate between the Scylla of spiritualist/dualistic idealism and the Charybdis of reductive/eliminative materialism[19] (an emphasis he repeats near the end of the same text).[20] Reich and Fenichel likewise each compare the psychoanalytic depiction of the mind-body relationship to noneconomistic versions of the historical-materialist schema of the infrastructure-superstructure rapport.[21] Additionally, both Reich and Fenichel propose in their own different manners that, to put it in Hegelian terms, Freudian psychoanalysis posits the presuppositions of Marxian materialism. More precisely, for them, Marx's historical-materialist renditions of subjects and societies implicitly assume without explicitly elaborating (at least sufficiently) something along the lines of the sort of dialectical-materialist philosophical anthropology forwarded by Freud's clinically informed metapsychology.[22]

By comparison with Reich, Fenichel goes into much more detail regarding exactly what a synthesis of Marxian dialectical materialism and Freudian psychoanalysis would involve (with the personal and intellectual relationship between Reich and Fenichel rupturing in the mid-1930s).[23] To begin with, he specifies that "a dynamic psychology is always first of all a psychology of drives"[24] (with "dynamic psychology," for Fenichel, ultimately being synonymous with psychoanalysis specifically as "dialectical-materialist psychology"). According to him, *Triebe* are the necessary, albeit not sufficient, conditions of psychical-subjective life; mindedness cannot be reduced to drivenness, although the former arises from and thereafter depends upon the latter.[25] Like Freud, Fenichel, as does Lacan, pinpoints human beings' initial prolonged prematurational helplessness (*Hilflosigkeit*) as making humans, from the ontogenetic get-go, biologically inclined toward the dominance of the social over the biological, namely, naturally predisposed, in terms of internal, intrasubjective immediacy, to denaturalization in terms of external, inter- and trans-subjective mediation.[26] From Marxist perspectives, Marcuse,[27] Althusser,[28] Habermas,[29] and Ernest Mandel[30] all similarly appreciate the profound significance of Freudian *Hilflosigkeit*.

On Fenichel's account, the biological fact of protracted infantile helplessness in human beings is, as it were, the Cartesian-type pineal gland as the pivotal switch point or crossroads between the endogenous libidinal economy of Freudian psychoanalysis and the exogenous political economy of Marxian historical materialism, that is, the site of interactions for these economies. This *Hilflosigkeit* renders id-level beings exposed and vulnerable to modifications and reconfigurations imposed from without by social agents and structures. The actions of infrastructures and superstructures (including ideologies) upon the rudiments of the drives, via "education" in a broad sense as formation (*Bildung*) and/or upbringing (*Erziehung*), effectuate instances of "structural alteration" in the psyches subjected to such education.[31]

Incidentally, Fenichel also is the author of a 1938 article entitled "The Drive to Amass Wealth." Therein, he theorizes the existence of a capitalism-specific libidinal compulsion (or, rather, set of compulsions) in relation to monetary riches.[32] Fenichel also criticizes Sandor Ferenczi's talk, in a 1914 paper on "The Ontogenesis of the Interest in Money," of "the capitalist instinct" as a vicissitude of anal erotism for conducting a dehistoricizing biologization disregarding and occluding the sociohistorical peculiarities of capitalism.[33] Nonetheless, a Marxist committed to the devilish details of Marx's critique of political economy likely would find Fenichel's 1938 article insufficiently engaged with the specifics of historical materialism's economics (for instance, such specifics as its distinction between wealth as money versus wealth as capital proper, its illumination of the strange features of currency as a universal equivalent for all other commodities, and so on).

Lacan had a poor opinion of both Reich and Fenichel. As for Reich, Lacan, in 1953's "The Function and Field of Speech and Language in Psychoanalysis," criticizes him both for reducing sexuality to some sort of natural substance ("an ineffable organic expression beyond speech")[34] and for seeing the ego as simply defensive and nothing more[35] (interrelated criticisms echoed in the 1955 *écrit* "Variations on the Standard Treatment").[36] *Seminar VIII* (*Transference* [1960– 1961]) implies that Reich is nothing more than a sort of sexual gymnastics instructor, rather than a real and true analyst.[37] As pointed out in a session of *Seminar XV* (*L'acte psychanalytique* [1967–1968]), psychoanalysis is not a Reichian-style sexology, with the analyst as an expert in matters of sexuality, a subject supposed to know about sex.[38] Analysis is not about teaching neurotics how to fuck. Lacan is entirely dismissive of what he labels "sexo-leftism" (*sexo-gauchisme*),[39] namely, the sort of Freudo-Marxism with which Reich, Fenichel, and Marcuse are associated.

As for Fenichel, Lacan sometimes uses his name to lament that analytic institutes and training candidates of the mid-twentieth century often prefer the perusal of this sort of second-generation analyst to reading Freud himself,[40] with Fenichel's 1945 classic *The Psychoanalytic Theory of Neurosis* indeed having become a canonical text in the curricula of International Psychoanalytic Association (IPA) training institutes.[41] Fenichel's association with ego psychology and its analysis of defenses unsurprisingly elicits Lacan's disapproval and spite.[42] Moreover, Fenichel is accused by Lacan of turning analytic practice into an unthinking application of oversimplified metapsychological theory.[43] On Lacan's assessment, whereas Freud is a skilled and careful archaeologist, Fenichel carelessly pillages and leaves in disarray whatever sites he stumbles across.[44] Fenichel's ideas about sexuality likewise are found to be seriously wanting.[45]

Especially given my circumscribed purposes here, I am not committed to defending Reich and Fenichel against Lacan's objections, since the latter's low estimation of the two of them is based on references to texts other than the ones that concern me in the present setting. Lacan shows no evidence of having read either Reich's *Dialectical Materialism and Psychoanalysis* or Fenichel's "Psychoanalysis as the Nucleus of a Future Dialectical-Materialist Psychology," both having appeared in print during Lacan's lifetime. Arguably, this is of a piece with Lacan's relative lack of thoroughgoing familiarity with the Marxist tradition (although, as will be on display at the close of this chapter, Lacan exhibits a rather nuanced appreciation of Marx himself).

Nonetheless, I see nothing preventing and a lot recommending[46] a synthesis of Lacanian psychoanalysis with dialectical materialism. The later Lacan even occasionally self-identifies as a dialectical materialist.[47] Along these lines, Lacan's convergences with the Reich of *Dialectical Materialism and Psychoanalysis* and the Fenichel of "Psychoanalysis as the Nucleus of a Future Dialectical-Materialist Psychology" outweigh, in my view, the divergences. Even though Lacan dismisses prior permutations of Freudo-Marxism as hopelessly confused,[48] nothing he says rules out the potential for and viability of a Lacano-Marxism.

Moreover, Lacan's lack of engagement with the psychoanalytic Marxism both of the second-generation analysts (epitomized by Reich and Fenichel) as well as of the Frankfurt School amounts to a lamentable missed encounter. Given Fenichel's self-censorship of his Marxism, especially as an immigrant resettled in the United States, Lacan could not have known about his unpublished but stringent critiques of various post-Freudian trends dovetailing with many of Lacan's own objections to the same analytic phenomena (with Jacoby's 1983 study *The Repression of Psychoanalysis: Otto Fenichel and the Political Freudians* helpfully documenting this obscured side of Fenichel's thinking). However, the same excuse does not hold for Lacan's failure to address the vast bulk of the Freudo-Marxist textual output of the Frankfurt School. This material had been published and was readily available during Lacan's lifetime.

Figures such as Fenichel (in private),[49] Marcuse (in print),[50] and Reich (both in print and in practice)[51] echo many of Lacan's misgivings about the post-Freudian currents that come to dominate the mainstream of the IPA starting in the 1930s. Like Lacan, they complain of the lamentable effects on the Freudian field of the transformation of analysis into a medical specialty as well as the tailoring of its theories and practices to suit mid-twentieth-century American sensibilities. Fenichel, a European immigrant resettled in the United States after fleeing Nazism, is painfully aware of the pressures forcing such refugee analysts to compromise and self-censor in the face of Anglo-American capitalism and its cultural-political ethos (including McCarthyism). Similarly, Marcuse as well as Fenichel, in their shared Marxist commitments, would concur with Lacan's condemnation of ego psychology's emphases on the ego's "adaptation" to "reality" as ideologically insidious, as a reduction of analysis to a technique of social indoctrination "manufacturing consent" in analysands.[52] One aspect of my work here involves filling in the blanks left by Lacan's missed encounter with Freudo-Marxism.

Admittedly, Lacan's 1949 *écrit* on the mirror stage contains a not-unfavorable oblique reference to the Reichian concept of the ego as "character armor."[53]

Additionally, Lacan draws on Max Horkheimer's 1936 study on "Authority and the Family"[54] as inspiration for his own 1938 talk of "the social decline of the paternal *imago*,"[55] a notion also taken up by Adorno[56] and Marcuse,[57] as Juan Pablo Lucchelli establishes.[58] Lucchelli further hypothesizes that Lacan's 1963 *écrit* "Kant with Sade" indeed is profoundly influenced by Horkheimer and Adorno's own linking of Kant and Sade in 1947's *Dialectic of Enlightenment*[59]— and this despite Lacan not mentioning the Frankfurt duo in his 1963 *écrit*.[60] Dany Nobus likewise notes the multiple cross-resonances between *Dialectic of Enlightenment* and "Kant with Sade."[61] But both Lucchelli and Nobus are restricted to educated guesses about this in the absence of any (yet to be discovered) direct, explicit evidence of Lacan's being familiar with and indebted to Horkheimer and Adorno's 1947 book. And, even if Lacan's Kant-Sade coupling, in addition to his "social decline of the paternal *imago*," draws upon the Frankfurt School, it still is the case that much of the rest of what German critical theory has to say about psychoanalysis and the relationship between it and Marxism ends up being ignored by Lacan.[62]

In terms of what I bring to Freudo-Marxism as initiated by the likes of Reich, Fenichel, and Marcuse, there is, to begin with, my rapprochement between Lacan and dialectical materialism I have developed elsewhere in tandem with the substantial contributions of the Slovene School of Lacanian theory.[63] (And I have dealt with the Freudo-Marxism of the Frankfurt School, as paradigmatically represented by Marcuse, on earlier occasions.)[64] Without rehashing that rapprochement on this occasion, one in which Freudo-Marxism is updated as Freudo-Lacano-Marxism, I conceive of my intervention in the current chapter as making four contributions. First, thanks primarily to its Lacanian background, it equips Freudo-Marxism with a more sophisticated and accurate version of Freudian drive theory than versions relied upon by pre/non-Lacanian Freudo-Marxists (such as Reich, Fenichel, and Marcuse). Second, it interfaces this drive theory with the core of the mature Marx's crowning achievements at the level of his critique of political economy. (Like much of the twentieth-century Western Marxism of which it is a component, classical Freudo-Marxism does not really dirty its hands with the nitty-gritty economic details of historical materialism.) Third, this synthesis between Freudian-Lacanian drive theory and Marxian political economy provides both powerful refutations of load-bearing (neo)liberalist assumptions and better understandings of really existing capitalism itself. Fourth and finally, I see this chapter and this book in its entirety as opening out onto avenues for further psychoanalytic research regarding the complex mediations of libidinal by political economies (research some of which I hope to pursue myself in the not-too-distant future).

§7. *DER MEHRWERTSTRIEB*: THE LIBIDINAL ECONOMY OF MODERN SOCIAL HISTORY

At the end of the introduction to the *Grundrisse*, Marx brings up the example of Homer. After referring to the *Iliad*, he famously observes: "The difficulty lies not in understanding that the Greek arts and epic are bound up with certain forms of social development. The difficulty is that they still afford us artistic pleasure and that in a certain respect they count as a norm and as an unattainable model."[65] As Marx is well aware, apart from Homer's *Iliad*, countless other examples drawn from a wide range of fields and contexts manifest the same phenomenon of a striking time-defying endurance. Marx's observation is a warning to the effect that Homeric poetry and similar long-lasting cultural goods pose a serious (nay, insuperable) problem for historical materialism if the latter wrongly reduces itself to a mere historicism mindlessly repeating the gesture of uninformatively pointing out that each and every human historical development indeed arises in a specific social period and place. These kinds of historicist reductionism, to be distinguished from genuine historical materialism, are unable, on their own, to explain instances of phenomena that come to transcend their sites of origin and moments of birth (for instance, the *Iliad*). Such phenomena thereafter laterally cut across, in a temporally stretched-out trajectory, a historical span of different, shifting societal arrangements. Insofar as Marxian historical materialism seeks to be able to register and explain such instances, as Marx himself signals, it includes within itself a theory of the historical and social geneses of the transhistorical and the trans-social.

Of course, the *Grundrisse*'s introduction also contains a certain renowned assertion. A few pages before Marx raises the just-glossed Homer problem, he asserts that "human anatomy contains a key to the anatomy of the ape. The intimations of higher development among the subordinate animal species, however, can be understood only after the higher development is already known."[66] I would suggest that there is a complementarity between these references first to anatomy and then, soon after, to the *Iliad*. That is to say, I view them as designating the two sides of one and the same historical-materialist coin. Whereas Homeric epic poetry epitomizes an irreducible-to-context past-in-the-present, the human-ape relation embodies, correlatively but conversely, an irreducible-to-context present-in-the-past. With Homer, the precapitalist past successfully projects itself forward into the capitalist present. With economics, the capitalist present of "human anatomy" somewhat legitimately (with the appropriate qualifications added to it by the critique of political economy) retrojects itself backward into the precapitalist past of "the anatomy of the ape." As for the

FROM CLOSED NEED TO INFINITE GREED   99

human-ape analogy, the real becoming-abstract of labor under industrial capitalism makes possible the field of economics, with the conceptual abstractions of its theories of economic systems.[67] This in turn helps generate an understanding of the arc of precapitalist social history eventuating in capitalism itself.

Combining Marx's invocations of anatomy and the *Iliad* as I have just recommended, one could say that crucial features of historical materialism, appropriately conceived (as not simply another historicism), are paradigmatically embodied in the odd figure of a Greek primate, Homer as an ape. Such things as great ancient epic poetry (i.e., the *Iliad*) already contain within themselves those facets that lend them such enduring worth in the eyes of subsequent audiences and admirers. However, at least some of these facets (i.e., "the anatomy of the ape") perhaps do not come to light unless and until the historical surfacing of social contexts postdating their social context of origin (i.e., "human anatomy").

Such temporal dialectical dynamics between past and present (as well as future) are central to psychoanalysis in addition to historical materialism.[68] In this chapter, I will be pleading for a historical-materialist metapsychology of *Trieb* in which the anatomy of capitalist drive(s) contains a key to the anatomy of drive as such, of *Trieb an sich* (which itself becomes dramatically more *für sich* in and through capitalism, especially in its recent consumerist permutations). As for the Hegel who identifies Socrates as an ancient precursor and prophet of distinctively modern individualism, so too for me: Another awe-inspiring Greek primate, Aristotle, foregrounds a libidinal economics linked to political economics (i.e., the "love of money") already exhibiting the characteristic peculiarities of drive in the modern psychoanalytic sense—although this libidinal economics does not become the hegemonic, ubiquitous rule (rather than the marginal, compartmentalized exception) until the much later advent of capitalism. Interfacing historical materialism and analytic metapsychology in this way circumvents and renders ill-conceived and obsolete false, zero-sum debates between a reductively historicizing pseudo-Marxism and a transcendentally dehistoricizing pseudo-Freudianism (and/or pseudo-Lacanianism).

So how does the Marx of the *Grundrisse* and *Das Kapital* contribute, at the level of philosophical anthropology, to a historical-materialist metapsychology of the psychoanalytic drive? Where are these alleged contributions to be found in the texts of Marx's mature critique of political economy? In what ensues, I will make my case by proceeding through these works more or less in order, starting with the *Grundrisse* and then turning to the volumes of *Capital* (along with references to *Theories of Surplus-Value*).

Already in the *Grundrisse*'s introduction, a long paragraph on the codependent relationship between production and consumption delineates certain cardinal aspects of Marx's historical-materialist philosophical anthropology of the human libidinal economy (as mediated by political economy). He explains:

> Production . . . (1) furnishes the material and the object [*Gegenstand*] for consumption. Consumption without an object is not consumption; therefore, in this respect, production creates, produces consumption. (2) But the object is not the only thing which production creates for consumption. Production also gives consumption its specificity [*Bestimmtheit*], its character, its finish. Just as consumption gave the product its finish as product, so does production give finish to consumption. *Firstly*, the object is not an object in general [*überhaupt*], but a specific [*bestimmter*] object which must be consumed in a specific manner, to be mediated in its turn by production itself. Hunger is hunger, but the hunger gratified by cooked meat eaten with a knife and fork is a different hunger from that which bolts down raw meat with the aid of hand, nail and tooth. Production thus produces not only the object but also the manner of consumption, not only objectively but also subjectively. Production thus creates the consumer. (3) Production not only supplies a material for the need [*Bedürfnis*], but it also supplies a need for the material. As soon as consumption emerges from its initial state of natural crudity and immediacy [*ersten Naturroheit und Unmittelbarkeit*]—and, if it remained at that stage, this would be because production itself had been arrested there—it becomes itself mediated as a drive by the object [*so ist sie selbst als Trieb vermittelt durch den Gegenstand*]. The need which consumption feels for the object is created by the perception of it. The object of art—like every other product—creates a public which is sensitive to art and enjoys beauty. Production thus not only creates an object for the subject, but also a subject for the object. Thus production produces consumption (1) by creating the material for it; (2) by determining the manner of consumption; and (3) by creating the products, initially posited by it as objects, in the form of a need felt by the consumer. It thus produces the object of consumption, the manner of consumption and the motive of consumption [*Trieb der Konsumtion*]. Consumption likewise produces the producer's *inclination* [*die Anlage des Produzenten*] by beckoning to him as an aim-determining need [*zweckbestimmendes Bedürfnis*].[69]

For a reader familiar with the texts of Freud and Lacan, it is virtually impossible to avoid hearing, at the risk of anachronism, anticipations of psychoanalytic drive theory (as does Fenichel when addressing Marx on needs from an analytic angle).[70] Marx literally refers to a *Trieb* on the side of consumption, with a corresponding *Anlage* on the side of production (an "*inclination*" that itself has a

FROM CLOSED NEED TO INFINITE GREED   101

drive-like character, as will be seen soon enough). Incidentally, although the twentieth-century rises of the advertising industry and consumer capitalism occur after Marx's death, Marx anticipates exactly from whence these post-1883 developments in capitalist social history arise. He discerns what makes possible, both anthropologically and economically, the cultivation and management of ever-proliferating consuming desires.

Additionally, just as the Freudian drive is "objectless" (*objektlos*) qua not innately soldered to the invariant template of a species-universal type of satisfying object of cathectic investment, so too is the Marxian "*Trieb der Konsumtion*" not tethered to "an object in general" (*Gegenstand überhaupt*) as a generic grati-fier of brute primitive need in its "natural crudity and immediacy" (*Naturroheit und Unmittelbarkeit*). For both Marx and Freud, drives are mediated produc-tions instead of immediate givens. More precisely, *Triebe*, for both historical materialism and psychoanalysis, are produced by social mediations (economic and/or familial, among other strata of sociality) involving structural and phe-nomenal dimensions. Even more precisely still, these mediations, as more-than-naturally exogenous rather than naturally endogenous, render all drives' objects (whether as Marx's *Gegenstand* or Freud's *Objekt*) historically specific variables whose determinacy (*als Bestimmtheit*) results from objective externalities intro-jected and metabolized into subjective internalities.[71] The (drive-)object fabri-cates the subject (of drive).

Jumping ahead a bit in the *Grundrisse*, Marx subsequently renders explicit that the producer's drive (i.e., "the producer's *inclination*" [*die Anlage des Pro-duzenten*] as nothing other than *der Trieb des Kapitals*) ultimately is the driver of the consumer's drive (as the "*Trieb der Konsumtion*"). Nonetheless, this producer's drive also remains (co)dependent on the consumer's drive (as the preceding block quotation from the *Grundrisse*'s introduction explicates). Over-all, capital's drive to enhance itself (i.e., to self-valorize) by generating ever more surplus value in and through the processes of production is more driving of con-sumption's clamoring demands than vice versa (in this case, as Sichère observes, the demands of singular subjects subjected to capital can be taken not as idio-syncratic expressions of individual libidinal economies but as demands voiced by the "social reality" of capitalism itself and its political economy).[72] The fourth notebook of the *Grundrisse* states at detailed length:

> The production of *relative surplus value*, i.e. production of surplus value based on the increase and development of the productive forces, requires the production of new consumption; requires that the consuming circle within circulation expands as did the productive circle previously. Firstly

quantitative expansion of existing consumption; secondly: creation of new needs by propagating existing ones in a wide circle; *thirdly*: production of *new* needs and discovery and creation of new use values. In other words, so that the surplus labour gained does not remain a merely quantitative surplus, but rather constantly increases the circle of qualitative differences within labour (hence of surplus labour), makes it more diverse, more internally differentiated. For example, if, through a doubling of productive force, a capital of 50 can now do what a capital of 100 did before, so that a capital of 50 and the necessary labour corresponding to it become free, then, for the capital and labour which have been set free, a new, qualitatively different branch of production must be created, which satisfies and brings forth a new need. The value of the old industry is preserved by the creation of the fund for a new one in which the relation of capital and labour posits itself in a *new* form. Hence exploration of all of nature in order to discover new, useful qualities in things; universal exchange of the products of all alien climates and lands; new (artificial) preparation of natural objects, by which they are given new use values. The exploration of the earth in all directions, to discover new things of use as well as new useful qualities of the old; such as new qualities of them as raw materials, etc.; the development, hence, of the natural sciences to their highest point; likewise the discovery, creation and satisfaction [*Befriedigung*] of new needs arising from society itself; the cultivation of all the qualities of the social human being, production of the same in a form as rich as possible in needs, because rich in qualities and relations—production of this being as the most total and universal possible social product, for, in order to take gratification in a many-sided way, he must be capable of many pleasures [*genussfähig*], hence cultured to a high degree—is likewise a condition of production founded on capital. This creation of new branches of production, i.e. of qualitatively new surplus time, is not merely the division of labour, but is rather the creation, separate from a given production, of labour with a new use value; the development of a constantly expanding and more comprehensive system of different kinds of labour, different kinds of production, to which a constantly expanding and constantly enriched system of needs [*System von Bedürfnissen*] corresponds.[73]

According to Marx, this autoexpanding infernal circle of production and consumption, in which the former is the primary driving impetus, expresses nothing other than the unslakable thirst of capital for surplus value, namely, capital's *Trieb* to enhance itself, to be fruitful and multiply.[74] Much like the Lacanian superego, the (death) drive of capital commands, via its ownership of and

FROM CLOSED NEED TO INFINITE GREED   103

authority over the means of production, consumer enjoyment (*Genuss* as the German equivalent of the French *jouissance*) on the side of capital's legions of servants, its subjected subjects (who come to hear and obey in the guise of polymorphously perverse conspicuous consumption).[75] Capitalism's earth-devouring spiral of frenetic, self-stimulating activity is one that starts with and remains fueled by surplus value–bearing exchange values (tied to quantitative capital) instead of use values (tied to the qualitative facets of commodities).[76] The consumption drives of libidinal economies are symptoms of the production drives of political economies (and, again, not the other way around). Therefore, a historical-materialist comprehension of the cause or origin of the peculiar traits of libidinal economics under capitalism requires grasping *der Trieb des Kapitals* (i.e., "the producer's *inclination*" [*die Anlage des Produzenten*]) as the political-economic root-source of these psychical-subjective characteristics.[77] Or as Hegel puts it already in the 1821 *Elements of the Philosophy of Right*, "A need . . . is created not so much by those who experience it directly as by those who seek to profit from its emergence [*Es wird ein Bedürfnis . . . nicht sowohl von denen, welche es auf unmittelbare Weise haben, als vielmehr durch solche hervorgebracht, welche durch sein Entstehen einen Gewinn suchen*]."[78]

But before undertaking a psychoanalytic reconceptualization of the drives of capital, I feel it worthwhile briefly to remark upon Marx's utilization of the phrase "system of needs" in the just-quoted passage from the *Grundrisse*. One of many things Marx and Hegel share in common is a deep appreciation (albeit, for both, marked by grave reservations and critical objections) of the epoch-making intellectual contributions of Adam Smith. Following the central role played by division of labor in *The Wealth of Nations*,[79] Hegel characterizes labor-dividing socioeconomic apparatuses as systems of needs, namely, frameworks of mutual dependence within which the laboring of a member of society satisfies other members' requirements as well as his/her own (with the same holding in turn for the laboring of these other members too).[80] Moreover, Hegel, with an eye to the modern markets of liberal-bourgeois "civil society" (*bürgerliche Gesellschaft*) and foreshadowing Marx, asserts that divisions of labor as systems of need are effective not only in meeting existing needs but adept at continually creating new needs multiplying into a decadent "luxury" (*der* Luxus).[81] This last Smith-inspired Hegelian observation, one made in light of the socioeconomic apparatus of capitalism, is echoed by Marx when, at the end of the preceding block quotation, he refers to "the development of a constantly expanding and more comprehensive system of different kinds of labour, different kinds of production, to which a constantly expanding and constantly enriched system of needs [*System von Bedürfnissen*] corresponds."[82]

Closely related to the preceding, Marx, in the third volume of *Capital*, speaks of market-mediated "need" (*Bedürfnis*) as "completely elastic and fluctuating" (*durchaus elastisch und schwankend*).[83] In Marx's critique of political economy, this elasticity of needs can and does move in two opposed directions. On the one hand, the flexibility of human beings' requirements is such that they can withstand, and even be pressured into tolerating, deprivations approaching absolute immiseration (as in the paradigmatic Marxian case of the wage-laboring industrial proletariat of nineteenth-century Dickensian England).[84] One could call this downward (or depressive) elasticity.

On the other hand, this same flexibility allows for the stimulation and growth of multiplying impulses and urges in which "needs" are extensively broadened and/or intensively deepened (as in advertising- and branding-fueled consumerist late capitalism, wherein, through capital expanding in time via credit rather than space via colonization, the immiserated, with their stagnant or declining wages, are made to stave off capital's falling rates of profit through consuming their own futures at prices they ultimately cannot afford to pay). One could call this upward (or manic) elasticity. Smith already highlights the boundless upward/manic extendability of needs/wants.[85] Indeed, one does not have to be psychoanalytically educated or inclined in order to discern the bipolar (what used to be labeled "manic-depressive") characteristics of capitalism.

Crucially for my present, psychoanalysis-shaped theoretical purposes, this libidinal flexibility (i.e., Marx's "need" [*Bedürfnis*] as "completely elastic and fluctuating" [*durchaus elastisch und schwankend*]) must not be seen exclusively as a secondary effect or subsequent byproduct of capitalism's circuits of production, distribution, exchange, and consumption.[86] It indeed is this. In fact, capitalism obviously is responsible for inducing increasingly rapid and frenetic transformations drastically amplifying the elasticity and fluctuations of its subjects' libidinal economies. These phenomena would be libidinal flexibility made explicit, *für sich*.

Nevertheless, such explosions of production-driven consumption (i.e., the extensive broadening and/or intensive deepening of Marxian *Bedürfnisse*) are materially-transcendentally enabled by a libidinal elasticity predating capitalism. Put more precisely in psychoanalytic terms, the plasticity of *Triebe*—Marcuse describes this as "the malleability of 'human nature'" through which social mediation "may 'sink down' into the 'biological' dimension" at the base of the psyche's libidinal economy, into "the biology of man,"[87] with Habermas likewise speaking of humanity's "plastic impulse potential [*Antriebspotential*]"[88]—makes possible, at the level of transhistorical *an sich* libidinal structure, the "*durchaus elastisch und schwankend*" profuse multiplication of demands and desires at the level of historical *für sich* libidinal phenomena specific to capitalism. To be even more exact, plastic drive structure, as theorized within a metapsychological qua philosophical/psychoanalytic anthropology, is a necessary condition for capitalism's peculiar libidinal economics as per historical materialism. It becomes a sufficient condition when capitalist production, spurred by the pursuit of surplus value, begins exploiting this plasticity for its gains. Such exploitation, made possible by libidinal elasticity, comes to render this initially latent factor steadily more manifest, aggravating and amplifying it. This chapter's title, "from closed need to infinite greed," thus takes on greater determinacy and concreteness.

§8. ADDICTIONS TO UNENJOYABLE ENJOYMENTS: THE TWIN HEDONISMS OF COMMODITY FETISHISM

Both the *Grundrisse* and volumes of *Capital* have much to say about greed in relation to needs and drives. The *Grundrisse*'s treatment of money highlights the libidinal significance of the historical advent both of currency in general (as universal equivalent) as well as of capitalistic monetary functions in particular (especially when currency operates as self-valorizing capital pursuing its own in-principle limitless accumulation via the accrual of surplus value).[89] In the passage from the *Grundrisse* I am now going to quote (one that resurfaces a year later in slightly modified guise in *A Contribution to the Critique of Political Economy*),[90] Marx suggests a thesis along the lines of my notion of a historical-libidinal mutation "from closed need to infinite greed":

> Money is... not only *an* object [*Gegenstand*], but is *the* object of greed [*Bereicherungssucht*]. It is essentially *auri sacra fames*. Greed as such, as a particular form of the drive [*eine besondre Form des Triebs*], i.e. as distinct from the craving for a particular kind of wealth [*der Sucht nach besondrem Reichtum*], e.g. for clothes, weapons, jewels, women, wine etc., is possible only when general wealth [*allgemeine Reichtum*], wealth as such [*der Reichtum als solcher*], has become individualized in a particular thing [*einem besondren Ding*], i.e. as soon as money is posited in its third quality. Money is therefore not only the object but also the fountainhead of greed [*die Quelle der Bereicherungssucht*]. The mania for possessions [*Habsucht*] is possible without money; but greed itself is the product of a definite social development [*einer bestimmten gesellschaftlichen Entwicklung*], not *natural* [*natürlich*], as opposed to *historical* [*Geschichtlichen*].

Hence the wailing of the ancients about money as the source [*Quellen*] of all evil. Hedonism [*Genussucht*] in its general form and miserliness [*Geiz*] are the two particular forms of monetary greed. Hedonism in the abstract presupposes an object which possesses all pleasures in potentiality. Abstract hedonism realizes that function of money in which it is the *material representative of wealth*; miserliness, in so far as it is only the general form of wealth as against its particular substances, the commodities. In order to maintain it as such, it must sacrifice all relationship to the objects of particular needs [*besondren Bedürfnisse*], must abstain, in order to satisfy the need of greed for money as such [*das Bedürfnis der Geldgier als solche*].[91]

Marx herein elaborates a plethora of details resurfacing again and again throughout the sketches and delineations of what I would call his drive theory in *Das Kapital* itself. To start parsing this key passage, *Bereicherungssucht* literally means addiction (*Sucht*) to enrichment (*Bereicherung*). In addition to Marx's talk here about addictions to enrichment and enjoyment (*Genussucht* [hedonism] being, in German, literal addiction to enjoyment [*Genuss*]), his associations of capitalist speculative activity with gambling further brings capitalism as per the historical-materialist critique of political economy within the orbit of the psychoanalytic clinic of addictions (as themselves, in no small part, libidinal disorders).[92] Furthermore, *"auri sacra fames"* likewise signifies the accursed greed for gold.

Immediately after where the preceding block quotation leaves off, Marx equates "monetary greed" (*die Geldgier*) with "mania for wealth" (*Bereicherungssucht*).[93] Subsequently, the first volume of *Capital*, entirely in line with the *Grundrisse*, identifies the capitalism-specific multiplication of exchange-and-surplus-value-bearing commodities as arousing "the lust for gold" (*die Goldgier*).[94] The historical emergence of commodity production proper awakens and whips up into a frenzy a previously largely dormant libidinal potential, a sleeping monster, slumbering within humanity (an inhumanity in humanity more than humanity itself, as Lacan might say).

Much remains to be unpacked in the passage from the *Grundrisse* just quoted. In fact, the bulk of what immediately follows will be preoccupied with this unpacking in connection with the volumes of *Das Kapital* (with the latter faithfully continuing along these lines laid down already apropos matters libidinal in Marx's notebooks of 1857–1858). The first of several details within the prior quotation I wish to highlight is Marx's historical-materialist insistence on the social specificity of greed *als Bereicherungssucht* in the precise technical sense of his critique of political economy. Marx depicts this peculiar species of lust ("greed as

FROM CLOSED NEED TO INFINITE GREED   107

such" qua *auri sacra fames* or *die Goldgier,* with this greed amounting to the "capitalist soul")[95] as "a particular form of the drive" (*eine besondre Form des Triebs*). Engels, already in his 1845 *The Condition of the Working Class in England,* repeatedly speaks of the bourgeoisie's distinctive "money-greed"[96] (*Geldwuth,*[97] *Geldgier*)[98] and "profit-greed"[99] (*Gewinnsucht*).[100]

Consistent and resonant with this protopsychoanalytic invocation of drive *als Trieb* in the *Grundrisse,* the first volume of *Capital* too repeatedly speaks of "drive," as in, for example, "greed" as a "hoarding drive" (*der Trieb der Schatzbildung*)[101] and "avarice" (*Geiz*) as "the drive for self-enrichment" (*Bereichungstrieb*).[102] Likewise, the third volume of *Capital* refers to "the drive for accumulation" (*Akkumulationstrieb*).[103] Moreover, in *Theories of Surplus-Value,* Marx distinguishes between "accumulation" and "expenditure," stipulating that "accumulation and not expenditure is the immediate object of capitalist production."[104] Ricardo, in *The Principles of Political Economy and Taxation* (1817), already stipulates that increasing production (for production's sake) is the proper *telos* of capital.[105]

In writing of "a particular form of the drive" (*eine besondre Form des Triebs*), the Marx of the *Grundrisse* indicates that greed per se (as *auri sacra fames, die Bereicherungssucht,* and/or *die Goldgier*) is a species of the genus *Trieb als solche.* Thereby, Marx's historical-materialist critique of political economy implies a philosophical-anthropological drive theory. His *Triebtheorie* anticipates that of psychoanalytic metapsychology.

Even more specifically, Marx's claim that money "is . . . not only the object but also the fountainhead of greed [*die Quelle der Bereicherungssucht*]" makes the universal equivalent function as what Jean Laplanche later identifies as the "source-object" (*Quelle-Objekt*) of drive (*Trieb*),[106] with money being the source-object of capitalist greed qua drive. In Marx's drive theory, there is a transhistorical structure of drive or drives (perhaps rooted in humanity's *Gattungswesen* with its natural history)[107] that takes on different precise configurations in its various manifestations across shifting social formations. The infrastructural and superstructural dimensions of social formations at the level of objective political economies mediate the structure of drive(s) at the level of subjective libidinal economies. The previous passage from the *Grundrisse* explicitly suggests, by characterizing capitalism-specific greed as "not *natural* [*natürlich*], as opposed to *historical* [*Geschichtlichen*]," that the drive form in general indeed is natural. By contrast, a socially mediated particular instantiation of this form, such as greed, is historical.

Continuing a bit longer to stick to the details of the same quotation from the *Grundrisse,* Marx identifies money as responsible for bringing into existence the species that is greed out of the genus that is drive. To be more exact, this would be money insofar as it, first, gets embodied in a specific commodity (paradigmatically, gold) coming to function as universal equivalent, namely, as the commodity par excellence that in its universality can be exchanged with all other commodities, and, second, allows for boundless mathematical accumulation (paradigmatically, capitalists' amassing of surplus value via capital's basic circuit of M-C-M'). Related to this, Marx, in the preceding passage, situates a cluster of terms and phrases along the line of a fundamental distinction between those drive forms specific to capitalism and those to be found in pre- and noncapitalist social formations too.

On the one hand, "the craving for a particular kind of wealth [*der Sucht nach besondrem Reichtum*], e.g. for clothes, weapons, jewels, women, wine etc.," is not peculiar to capitalist social formations. As Marx observes, the "mania for possessions [*Habsucht*] is possible without money"—precisely without money as surplus value–producing universal equivalent within systems of commodity relations. On the other hand, "abstract hedonism," as "the need of greed for money as such" (*das Bedürfnis der Geldgier als solche*), becomes prominent and normalized only in and through capitalism as its sociohistorical facilitating condition. Hedonism becomes abstract in and through the becoming-abstract of one particular commodity (i.e., currency-as-capital) vis-à-vis all other commodities (including especially commodified labor power as itself bound up with the real abstraction of labor as such under capitalist economics). This abstracting/abstraction of libidinal economics defensibly can be depicted as a historical transition, facilitated by money turning into "wealth" (*Reichtum*) as "individualized in a particular thing [*einem besondren Ding*]," from concrete-qua-qualitative hedonism to abstract-qua-quantitative hedonism. Concrete-qua-qualitative hedonism would be "the craving for a particular kind of wealth" in the guise of use values to be consumed. Abstract-qua-quantitative hedonism would be the craving for "general wealth [*allgemeine Reichtum*], wealth as such [*der Reichtum als solcher*]" as surplus value–generating exchange values to be assembled into inexhaustible stores of self-valorizing capital. The latter (i.e., abstract-qua-quantitative hedonism) and not the former (i.e., concrete-qua-qualitative hedonism) is peculiar to capitalism.[108]

The well-known distinction I just invoked between qualitative use values and quantitative exchange values also is a deliberate allusion on my part to two connected components of Marx's critique of political economy: more obviously, "commodity fetishism" as per the most famous chapter in all of *Das Kapital*, that of the first volume on "The Fetishism of the Commodity and Its Secret," and, less obviously but nonetheless relatedly, the different socioeconomic and libidinal logics of capitalists and consumers. Apropos this entwined pair of allusions, I propose interpreting the second as a distinction between two varieties of capitalist commodity fetishism. The capitalist as capitalist (and not, as he/she also is, as a consumer) operates according to the law of M-C-M′. The vast bulk of consumers, as not owning any means of production, are not capitalists and hence rarely, if ever, can and do think and act in terms of M-C-M′. Instead, these consumers operate according to the law of C-M-C′.[109] For a worker/employee, his/her only commodity to bring to market is his/her own commodified labor power (C), which is exchanged for money in the guise of wages/salary (M), with this money in turn permitting the purchase of other commodities (C′) as, ultimately, use values to be consumed (and not surplus value–generating exchange values to be accumulated) as the worker's/employee's means of subsistence.

On the basis of the immediately preceding, I contend that commodity fetishism within capitalism comes in two fundamental types: one wholly engendered by capitalism, namely, abstract-qua-quantitative hedonism (i.e., greed as *auri sacra fames*, *die Bereicherungssucht*, and/or *die Goldgier*), and another merely mediated in its specific manifestations by capitalism, namely, concrete-qua-qualitative hedonism (i.e., the "mania for possessions [*Habsucht*]" as "the craving for a particular kind of wealth [*der Sucht nach besondrem Reichtum*], e.g. for clothes, weapons, jewels, women, wine etc."). Abstract-qua-quantitative hedonism fetishizes amassing valorizable exchange values and obeys the logic of M-C-M′. Concrete-qua-qualitative hedonism fetishizes consuming determinate use values and obeys the logic of C-M-C′. All of this is to say that the capitalist and the consumer are seized by different kinds of commodity fetishism. The capitalist fetishizes one commodity above all others (i.e., the universal equivalent as "general wealth [*allgemeine Reichtum*], wealth as such [*der Reichtum als solcher*] . . . individualized in a particular thing [*einem besondren Ding*]"), while the consumer fetishizes commodities other than money (albeit, as commodities, bearing surplus value for the capitalists flogging them).

Connected to this, and to repeat a point I have emphasized several times, Marx's historical-materialist analyses of capitalism insist that capital's quantitative drive toward cumulative self-valorization via exchange values is the core engine generating and propelling various qualitative drives toward the consumption of a proliferating multitude of use values. In other words, consumers' drives to consume are themselves ultimately driven by capitalists' drive to accumulate. Consumerist commodity fetishism (fixated upon C′ as qualitative use values) is itself a symptom whose underlying disease is capitalist commodity fetishism (fixated upon M′ as quantitative exchange and surplus values).

I would argue that both sympathetic commentators on and hostile critics of Marx tend implicitly or explicitly to fixate upon consumerist rather than capitalist commodity fetishism when addressing this renowned portion of the first volume of *Capital*. This is to mistake the symptom as effect for the disease as cause. Capital's drive to produce ever more surplus value, with M' as its *telos*, produces surplus value precisely by spurring, among other things, consumers' drives to consume ever more commodities, with C' as their *teloi*. Within capitalism, the former is primary and the latter is secondary. Likewise, Marx, in the third volume of *Capital*, characterizes consumption as the determined "subjectification [*Versubjektifierung*]" of production qua the producing of surplus value for capital.[110]

Particularly in the wake of the rise of specifically consumerist capitalism starting in the mid-twentieth century, it is quite understandable that many Marxist theorists have trained their critical gazes on the manners in which capital's subjects are interpellated as consumers caught in a constantly accelerating and intensifying looping of the circuit C-M-C'. Advertising, marketing, branding, planned obsolescence, myriad sources of credit, countless purchasing platforms, commodification of the natural and the experiential, big data and the mining of social networks, and so on fuel the steadily increasing rapidity and expansion of this infernal circle of slaving away for shiny trinkets and amusing distractions and, in so doing, selling oneself more and more into the slavery of debt in perpetuity. However, again, this glaringly visible and deafeningly noisy form of commodity fetishism gripping consumers in late capitalism is not the form governing capitalists themselves as proper capitalists.

As is common knowledge, Marx, in his discussion of the fetishism of commodities, distinguishes between the material dimensions of commodities (as qualitative use values) and their social dimensions (as quantitative exchange values).[111] Consumer commodity fetishism arguably involves the category mistake of gauging qualitative use value by quantitative exchange value. The paradigmatic example of this is afforded by the classical miser's near-delusional belief that the power to effect economic transactions (at the social level of exchange value) is a physical property (at the material level of use value) arising from and inhering within the element assigned atomic number 79 on the periodic table— and this in the same way as gold's properties of being metallic, malleable, and yellow (putting aside in this context Kripkean thought experiments about atomic number 79 as a "rigid designator" across possible worlds).[112] Under the influence of the delusion of consumerist commodity fetishism, the miser, in hoarding gold (or whatever commodity is made the universal equivalent), self-subversively and almost comically withdraws from social systems of exchange so as to preserve for him/herself alone gold's (exchange) value. But gold has this fetishized value only in and through the same social systems of exchange from which the miser withdraws it.[113] As Marx observes in the *Grundrisse* regarding money, "it is realized only by being thrown back into circulation, to disappear in exchange.... If I want to cling to it, it evaporates in my hand to become a mere phantom of real wealth [*wirklichen Reichtums*]."[114] If there is no such thing as a private language,[115] there definitely also is no such thing, contra the miser's fantasy, as a private exchange value attached to the commodity par excellence as one of its several thingly qualities. The miser obsessively relates to gold as C rather than M (whereas the capitalist relates to it precisely as M).

Different, but not different in kind, from the miser, late capitalism's consumers, goaded and prodded by capital itself, have their own fashions of fetishistically mistaking quantitative social exchange values for qualitative material use values. Over roughly the past century, capitalism has refined and honed its arts for creating more and more "needs" ex nihilo, implanting in the targets of its ceaseless, relentless publicity efforts multiplying, recurring senses of deprivation, insufficiency, lack, and the like. Whether in the guise of the "Veblen effect" in "conspicuous consumption" or related capitalist socioeconomic phenomena defying naive notions of straightforward supply-and-demand relations, heightened prices and measurable social valuations, at the quantitative level of exchange value, can and do create the illusion that the thus quantitatively (over)valued commodity is, at the qualitative level of use value, intrinsically of greater desirability. In such cases, the consumer feels he/she "needs" the commodity in question because it has been made to appear to him/her to possess consumable material utility on the basis of social exchangeability as an entirely distinct categorial dimension of the commodity. Although the miser fetishizes the metals of currencies and the consumer fetishizes other commodities instead, they both fetishize C rather than M per se as M (again, the capitalist qua neither consumer nor miser indeed fetishizes M per se as M and not C).

So, what about capitalist as distinct from consumerist commodity fetishism? Whereas the latter is structured by C-M-C′, the former, as capitalistic, unsurprisingly is structured by M-C-M′. For capitalists as capitalists, all material, qualitative use values appear useful only insofar as they contribute to and/or are translated into social, quantitative exchange values (as the vehicles bearing and yielding surplus value). Capitalists' commodity fetishism treats use values as exchange values, while, in mirroring reciprocity, consumers' commodity fetishism treats exchange values as use values. Additionally, and to refer back once more to the earlier lengthy block quotation from the *Grundrisse*, fetishistic consumers could be said to be enflamed by the capital-stoked fever of the "mania for possessions [*Habsucht*]" as "the craving for a particular kind of wealth [*der Sucht nach besondrem Reichtum*], e.g. for clothes, weapons, jewels, women, wine etc.," namely, what I earlier labeled "concrete-qua-qualitative hedonism." Fetishistic capitalists, by contrast, suffer from and are in thrall to the malady of greed proper (i.e., *auri sacra fames*, *die Bereicherungssucht*, and/or *die Goldgier*) as "a particular form of the drive [*eine besondre Form des Triebs*]," namely, abstract-qua-quantitative hedonism.

The miser's fetishism would be a transitional, hybrid pathology situated between the parallel fetishisms of capitalist and consumer. Like the capitalist, the miser fixates upon the universal equivalent as the one unique commodity standing in for all other commodities.[116] But unlike the capitalist, the miser, as seen, relates to the universal equivalent in the mode of the consumer, that is, as a material thing (C qua use value) instead of a social relationship (M qua exchange and surplus value). And, as Suzanne de Brunhoff highlights, this creates for the hoarding miser a frustrating contradiction between money in its material form, which always is amassed in necessarily limited quantities because of its qualitative-physical determinacy, and money in its social form, which is in principle limitless because of its purely quantitative-mathematical character.[117] No material hoard hidden away from society, however gargantuan, will, in its insurmountable finitude as tangible matter, approach the infinitude of wealth determined socially in abstract numerical terms. In a sense, the miser remains forever frustrated by the gap between use value and exchange value.

§9. SELFLESS CAPITALISM, SELFISH COMMUNISM: REFUTING LIBERALISM'S FAVORITE OLD CANARD

What is the payoff of my brief revisitation, in the preceding section, of the fetishism of commodities à la Marx? As I see it, there are two primary gains generated by this: first, a line of counterargumentation against a (if not the) standard (neo)liberal objection to Marxism, and, second, further clarification and nuancing of my dual Marxist-psychoanalytic motif of "from closed need to infinite greed." I will deal with the second of these gains in the next section of this chapter. As for the first, both classical and contemporary liberalisms base their objections to Marxism on the all-too-familiar charge, repeated ad nauseam, that human beings are, by nature, fundamentally and incorrigibly self-serving animals, vicious predators especially dangerous to their conspecifics (*Homo hominis lupus est*). From a standpoint of assumed pragmatic realist pessimism, liberals

FROM CLOSED NEED TO INFINITE GREED 113

brandish variations on this bleak, cynical Hobbesian vision of a recalcitrant human nature with an incurable egocentric orientation against Marxists they accuse of hopelessly utopian optimism.

I will not rehearse on this occasion the established, canonical Marxist responses to liberalism's contentions that there is a firmly fixed essence of humanity and that this essence is irredeemably selfish. Starting with Marx, numerous Marxists have raised serious questions and powerful objections as to whether there is a "human nature" in the sense relied upon by liberals and, if this nature exists in some form or other, whether it is refractory to radical transformations and/or forever inherently self-centered. Already before Marx, Hegel aggressively goes on the counterattack again and again against liberalism's myths about nature (especially the so-called state of nature) and "social contracts" (all of this being associated with what Hegel's critiques in these veins label the "natural law" tradition).[118] Needless to say, I am quite sympathetic to these Hegelian and Marxian lines of response to ideological false naturalizations of capitalist (anti)social relations.

That said, what if, at least for the sake of argument, one were to grant to the liberal tradition that there is something to the notion of selfishness being a stubbornly persistent feature of human subjects? Via this argumentative maneuver, I believe I can show why a procapitalism, anti-Marxism conclusion does not follow even if the liberalist thesis about humans' intrinsic self-interestedness is conceded. My demonstration of this will draw and depend on the results of my prior analyses of drive theory and commodity fetishism à la Marx. In good Hegelian fashion, my critique of egocentrism as per liberalism will be immanent rather than external, working from within the liberalist psychology of selfishness so as to arrive at this psychology's (self-)problematization.

As I establish above, the mature Marx's historical-materialist critique of political economy crucially distinguishes between those drives that are peculiar to capitalism as a specific social formation and those that are not. More precisely, capitalism-specific abstract-qua-quantitative hedonism (i.e., "the need of greed for money as such [*das Bedürfnis der Geldgier als solche*]" as *auri sacra fames, die Bereicherungssucht,* and/or *die Goldgier* and whose *telos* is M′) is different in kind from any nonspecific concrete-qua-qualitative hedonism (i.e., the "mania for possessions [*Habsucht*]" as "the craving for a particular kind of wealth [*der Sucht nach besondrem Reichtum*]" and whose *telos* is C′). Marxism carefully differentiates between two categories of inclinations: on the one hand, those oriented toward the production and accumulation of surplus value–bearing exchange values (M′), and, on the other hand, those oriented toward the purchase and consumption of use values (C′).

By contrast, most liberals' images of selfishness tend not to contain or allow for anything along the lines of what could be called Marx's distinction between capitalism-specific and not-capitalism-specific forms of "selfishness," namely, abstract-qua-quantitative and concrete-qua-qualitative hedonisms, respectively. Moreover, I would allege that the egocentrism of liberalism often is envisioned in this tradition and its ideological offshoots more along the lines of the consumerist "mania for possessions" (i.e., concrete-qua-qualitative hedonism) than properly capitalist greed per se in Marx's exact sense (i.e., abstract-qua-quantitative hedonism). When this is the case, the selfishness liberalism appeals to as justifying capitalism in particular is not even the selfishness peculiar to and driving of this very same capitalism. This is a fatal flaw in liberalism's attempted defense of capitalism as the least bad, if not optimally good, socioeconomic arrangement.

Unlike the "selfish" consumer, the "selfish" capitalist, as a proper capitalist, is not driven by a desire to shop until he/she drops, so to speak. However, under the influence of consumerist capitalism in particular, liberals are prone to model selfishness on crowds' manias for consumption. Such modeling constructs a picture of capitalists in which their insatiable public pursuits of profits ultimately aim at private consumptive ends. That is to say, the (neo)liberal image of selfishness, especially within consumerist late capitalism, confusedly collapses the capitalist's abstract-qua-quantitative hedonism fetishizing M' into the consumer's concrete-qua-qualitative hedonism fetishizing C'. In so doing, the capitalist qua capitalist is mischaracterized as being animated at root by "the craving for a particular kind of wealth [*der Sucht nach besondrem Reichtum*], e.g. for clothes, weapons, jewels, women, wine etc."

A mere descriptive phenomenological sketch of the capitalist is enough to illustrate the problems with reducing abstract-qua-quantitative to concrete-qua-qualitative hedonism. If and when a capitalist crosses a certain threshold in the accumulation of surplus value, the further accumulation to which he/she is driven by the very logic of capital and the corresponding framework of capitalism as a socioeconomic system reveals itself to have nothing to do with his/her personal consumption of commodities as material use values (i.e., as "particular kinds of wealth"). In truth, as capitalism-specific greed in Marx's technical sense, it never did have to do with this.

The goal of every capitalist as a capitalist is to accumulate as much surplus value (and not use values [C']) as possible. But once the individual capitalist's quantity of amassed money (M') exceeds a certain amount, he/she would be hard-pressed to spend all of this mass on him/herself in terms of commodities for private enjoyment (a version of this challenge is depicted in the 1985 Richard

Pryor comedy film *Brewster's Millions*). Moreover, were the capitalist somehow to manage to do so, he/she would be out of business, altogether ceasing to be a capitalist by exiting the loop of M-C-M'.[119] He/she would be literally out of the capitalist loop.

Those who embody the aims and aspirations of any and every capitalist as a proper capitalist—nowadays, these avatars of capitalism would be the individuals listed on *Forbes* magazine's annual ranking of the world's billionaires—are not driven by a "mania for possessions" (i.e., concrete-qua-qualitative hedonism as the consumerist drive toward C'). Their accumulated monetary wealth is well beyond both what is necessary for their (and their dependents') extremely high material quality of life and what even would be possible for them to squander on themselves by way of (conspicuous) consumption. Hence, their amassing of money ultimately is not pursued with an eye to consumer-style selfishness. Furthermore, one of the key lessons of historical materialism is that transindividual sociostructural dynamics and not individual psychologies are the real determinants of the conduct of persons as representatives of class positions.

Perhaps Freud is right that sometimes a cigar is just a cigar. But money is never just money. To begin with, there is the Marx-underscored difference between money as currency (i.e., a means of exchange for the procurement of C') and money as capital (i.e., a means of self-valorization for the generation of M'). What is more, there also is, for both Marxism and psychoanalysis, the essentially social status of money (with analysis adding supplementary emphases on the idiosyncratic subjective significances of it too). From the analytic perspective (whether Freudian, Lacanian, Kleinian, etc.), consumers' libidinal-economic relationships to the money-governed marketplace and its commodity-objects are much more individuated, complex, nuanced, and varied than some sort of straightforward universal, natural instinct of the human animal to possess or devour.

Likewise, from the Marxist perspective, capitalists' incessant pursuits of the valorization of their capitals are not at all reducible to the desire to consume commodities as providers of private pleasures. As noted, Marx, particularly when discussing commodity fetishism, associates the distinction between use and exchange values with the material and social dimensions of the commodity, respectively. Hence, and with reference to the (neo)liberal notion of selfishness, one could distinguish between material selfishness (i.e., consumerist fetishism as concrete-qua-qualitative hedonism) and social selfishness (i.e., capitalist fetishism as abstract-qua-quantitative hedonism). To return to the example of *Forbes* magazine's ranking of the world's billionaires—in line with my immanent critique of the (neo)liberal psychology of selfishness, I here run the multiple risks involved with hypothetical descriptions of the psychical-subjective motives of these bourgeois behemoths—if they are "selfish," this is likely almost always a burning thirst for self-aggrandizement as symbolically-collectively recognized status. In this example, money, specifically as the numerical amount of quantified wealth on the basis of which a rank on the *Forbes* list is assigned, is about social rather than material selfishness, about one's fantasized standing in the eyes of an anonymous big Other. In Fenichel's words, money is, for these capitalists, a "narcissistic supply."[120]

On the basis of the preceding, the non sequiturs in the liberal tradition's argumentative wielding of alleged human selfishness against the Marxist tradition now readily can be seen for what they betray, namely, outright sophistry. In apologizing for and speciously justifying capitalism, (neo)liberalism assumes that selfishness in its very nature can be satisfied only by money as itself always merely a means to the end of the egocentric enjoyment of goods and services for private consumption. Were this to be the case, consumerist late capitalism might be the unsurpassably rational culmination of social history.

But really existing capitalism, particularly when viewed through the dual lenses of Marxism and psychoanalysis, shows that the selfishness of the capitalist drive ruling its heart (i.e., Marxian greed as *auri sacra fames, die Bereicherungssucht,* and/or *die Goldgier,* abstract-qua-quantitative hedonism, the circuit of M-C-M′) is something quite different from what liberals have in mind. Liberalism ferociously defends capitalism without understanding its basic logic and phenomena. Liberalism's chain of false equivalences between selfishness, money, and consumption is an emblematic misunderstanding on its part.

If the drives of capitalists (and even of many, if not all, consumers in late capitalism) ultimately are about things social rather than material, then there is no reason why such "selfish" impulses and ambitions cannot be at least symbolically satisfied in a postcapitalist arrangement of a socialist or communist sort. As per my immanent critique of (neo)liberal appeals to selfishness, the psychological narcissism of individual capitalists, such as *Forbes*-ranked billionaires, is largely (if not entirely) about accruing sociosymbolic currency as a means to the end of inter- and trans-subjectively recognized status and standing, not as a means to the end of purchasing and enjoying objects and experiences (although this second end admittedly is a byproduct of the first end under capitalism). Even at the level of the liberalist psychology of selfishness (and this apart from the unconscious structural dimensions of nonpsychological Marxian and psychoanalytic drive theories), capitalism has to be seen, contrary to what is presupposed in liberals' protests against socialism and communism, as driven by something other than literal money as nothing more than the power to purchase goods and services. Moreover, in the new information age, the cutting edge of contemporary consumer capitalism's more affective, socially networked modes of primarily experiential consumption already points in the direction of the growing primacy of social over material selfishness for consumers, too.

Therefore, even if one agrees with liberalism that humans always are fundamentally motivated by some kind of natural self-interestedness, it by no means follows that the unique or best way to accommodate and satisfy such egocentricity is in and through the currency-ruled, commodity-filled economic networks of modern capitalism. Could not postcapitalist forms of cultural-political symbolic recognition provide the same or similar enough gratification as is already the real goal of the biggest of the big bourgeoisie as animated by social rather than material selfishness? And, with such socialist/communist sublimations of both capital's and capitalists' self-valorizations (in several senses of "self-valorization"), what would happen to the material selfishness of consumers (i.e., the "mania for possessions" [C'] as concrete-qua-qualitative hedonism) as a secondary effect driven by and symptomatic of capitalism's primary logic of M-C-M'? What already is happening in terms of the increasing dematerialization (i.e., the becoming social, experiential, and/or affective) of consumption in the internet era?

Before leaving behind this debate with the liberalist tradition, I wish to add a further inflection to my preceding suggestion that the link between capitalism and selfishness is not what (neo)liberals have taken it to be (and, as I will highlight in the subsequent section, Marx makes a suggestion along the same lines via comparing and contrasting the figures of the miser and the capitalist). As seen, I refer as an example to a well-known representative of the capitalist press, namely, *Forbes* magazine. I now will employ reference to another procapitalist magazine, the *Economist*, so as to add the inflection I have in mind. Founded in 1843 and furnishing Marx himself with ample grist for the mill of his historical-materialist critique of political economy, this journalistic bastion of British liberalism remains up through today a tireless cheerleader for global capitalism. As Thomas Picketty observes with acidic accuracy in an endnote to his *Capital in the Twenty-First Century*, the *Economist* manifests a "limitless and often undiscerning zeal to defend the powerful interests of its time."[121] However, not only did Marx consider this weekly magazine well worth consulting and assaulting—it certainly was good enough for his admirable purposes—it remains one of the more sophisticated popular journalistic defenders of (neo)liberal globalization. Defeating one's stronger opponents is always the most productive critical procedure. Additionally, the bourgeoisie is never so honest as when it believes that it is talking only to itself, such as within the pages of the *Economist*.

Like so many other (neo)liberals, the editors of the *Economist* repeatedly rehearse the selfishness objection to Marxism and its branches I rebut above. Yet they fail to register at all the supreme irony that their pleas for the supposedly ideal (although also allegedly feasible and realizable) utopia of frictionless capitalist globalization call for at least as much self-sacrifice as what they imagine both the theory and practice of Marxism unrealistically demand (of course, Marx, in his 1848 speech "On the Question of Free Trade," also pleads on behalf of such globalization, admittedly because he views it as a developmental trajectory inherent to but ultimately destructive of capitalism).[122] To be more exact, the *Economist*, in their frequent hymns to the Schumpeterian "creative destruction" of capitalism (and its more recent computer-age permutation, Christensenian "disruptive innovation"), forget that those who relish the creating (i.e., the tiny minority constituted by capitalists) are not the same as those who suffer the destruction (i.e., the massive majority constituted by everyone else). Of course, creative destruction, despite the deceptive façade of unity presented by this single phrase as single, is internally divided along class lines.

Additionally, the neoliberals who, like the *Economist*'s writers, celebrate creative destruction seem to forget that Joseph Schumpeter forges this concept on the basis of close consideration of Marx's works. Like Marx, he believes that structural dynamics inherent to capitalism are likely sooner or later to bring about capitalism's own self-wrought ruin (albeit in ways different from Marx's account of the details of this process of decline and collapse).[123] Moreover, Schumpeter's phrase is, by virtue of its grammar, more honest about capitalism than Clayton Christensen's apparently similar one. The latter's "disruptive innovation," translated into Schumpeter's words, would be "destructive creation," namely, a 180-degree inversion of the original Schumpeterian phrase. Schumpeter makes "destruction" the substantial noun modified by "creative" as the supplementary adjective, thus suggesting, whether this suggestion is intended or not, that capitalism is primarily ruinous and catastrophic.

By contrast, the Harvard Business School–based Mormon academic Christensen implicitly reverses Schumpeter's grammar. "Innovation" (i.e., creation) is now the substantial noun modified by "disruptive" (i.e., destructive) as the supplementary adjective. Christensen's phrase thereby indicates that capitalism is first and foremost a benign force for bringing about desirable advances and benefits. What is more, "disruptive" arguably is a milder adjective than "destructive," downplaying the true severity of the havoc wreaked and the harms inflicted by capitalism.

The British liberals of the *Economist* and their ilk daydream about a global capitalism in which commodities, including commodified labor power, move unimpeded across borders anywhere in their ceaseless chasing after exchange and surplus values. But these liberals' fantasies have built into them the implicit assumption that particular interests and specific communities selflessly are going to submit to and accept their own destruction, the erosion and liquidation of their forms of life, if and when the creation of gains for capital dictates automation, outsourcing, migration, retraining, impoverishment, unemployment, obsolescence, and so on. The "selfishness" of these particular interests and specific communities is the source of those "frictions" resisting frictionless global capitalism.

If these frictions do not generate the red heat of socialist or communist political pushback against the bourgeoisie, they instead ignite right-wing-populist or fully fascist conflagrations. As Walter Benjamin's deservedly famous insight has it: "Every rise of Fascism bears witness to a failed revolution."[124] Although the Marx of the late 1840s might have been too sanguine about the frenetic dynamics of free-trading globalization inadvertently paving the way for socialism and communism—this is understandable, considering that "the specter of communism" truly was haunting Europe in 1848—these dynamics, if they fail to lead in this radically progressive direction, will pave the way alternately for far-right coups and all their attendant violence and brutality (i.e., radically antiprogressive directions). As Rosa Luxemburg, citing Engels, puts it in her 1915 "Junius Pamphlet"—the geopolitics of the early twenty-first century, with its combustible rivalries between great capitalist powers, frighteningly resembles the circumstances leading up to the First World War—the only two options on the road ahead are "socialism or barbarism."[125]

A "third way" combining liberal parliamentarianism with global capitalism as a new thousand-year Reich continually threading the needle between revolution and counterrevolution is, especially in light of present conditions, the most improbable or impossible scenario for social history à venir. Today's looming specters of right-wing populisms and exponentially accelerating technology-prompted redundancies for white-collar as well as blue-collar workers around the globe—the current prospect of artificial intelligence does not look like its previous false dawns of years past—warn of the stark socialism-or-barbarism-style alternatives already starting to stare humanity in the face. In this light, the *Economist*'s "radical centrism" is the most utopian radicalism of them all. As Marx observes already in 1852 apropos the *Economist* and similar liberal publications, "Verily, there are no greater Utopists in existence than these Bourgeois optimists."[126]

The *Economist* defends capitalism precisely as, by its reckoning, an optimizer of the greater collective good of societies and the world as a whole, a rising tide purportedly lifting all boats. In the name of this greater collective good, its editors insistently urge people to make their peace with and even embrace the (creative) destruction of their modes of existence in the name of the "flexibility" (i.e., precarity, instability, insecurity, and the like) demanded by the flows and fluctuations of the movements of capital around the planet in its tireless questing after always greater surplus value for itself. Hence, what these British (neo) liberal journalists advocate, given their own statements (and not words put in their mouths by me or anyone else), is tantamount to nothing less than forms of self-sacrifice on the part of the vast majority of human beings ostensibly for the abstract sake of maximizing the sum total of quantifiable economic gains distributed, in mathematical theory/ideality, across the numerical aggregates of entire populations.[127] Of course, in the material practice/reality masked by the mathematical theory/ideality, these gains fall disproportionately into the hands of small subportions of these populations. The faceless big Other of the Market, with its stock indices, bond rates, investment grades, and growth statistics, repeatedly demands the selfless offerings of austerity measures and "structural reforms," brandishing weaponized forms of debt so as to reinforce these demands. Belts must be tightened. Capital must eat.

How does the *Economist*'s rallying cry for reconciliation with capitalistic creative destruction not assume a potent, efficacious human capacity for certain sorts of selflessness, for acting against one's own immediate interests in the name of an abstract optimization of overall social well-being? Given this assumption, how can this very same liberal magazine dismiss again and again radical leftists for themselves allegedly assuming an identical potential in humans' natures? If Marxism, for instance, is indefensibly utopian qua unrealistic in supposedly calling for the masses to sacrifice their egocentric self-interests to the transcendent Cause of humanity's greater good in general, is not (neo) liberalism, with its always-just-around-the-corner dream of perfectly frictionless capitalist globalization, at least as (if not more) utopian in the same way and for the same reasons? How and why is serving the invisible hand of the market any less disinterested than serving the invisible hand of history?

As an aside, the *Economist*, like all anticommunists, wrongly equates Marxism with Stalinism. In the *diamat* of the latter, there really is an invisible hand of history. Marx and Marxism(s), at their best moments, reject such views of history.

The editors of the *Economist* continually find themselves, albeit without realizing it, awkwardly in the same position vis-à-vis really existing capitalism as the Marxists they mock *vis-à-vis* really existing socialism. For these (neo)liberals, no empirical evidence of shortcomings in actual, factual capitalism, however serious and severe, ever raises the slightest doubts about the timeless theoretical legitimacy of (neo)liberalism itself. If their procapitalist ideas and ideologies have thus far failed to be confirmed by real facts on the ground, the fault inevitably is found to reside on the side of the "is" of reality and not the "ought" of ideality. Thus, the *Economist*'s narratives continually lapse from journalistic description into editorializing prescription, into exhortations essentially along the Sadean lines of "Gentlemen, one more effort if you wish to be capitalists!" Like the tardy fiancée of a certain joke, capitalism, for the *Economist*, never fails, since, if it fails, it is no longer capitalism.

Both Hegel and Marx insist on negativity (as death, destruction, wars, struggles, etc.) as history's real motor. Hegelian history is a "slaughter-bench,"[128] and Marxian history advances by its "bad side."[129] By contrast, the editorial preaching of the *Economist*, like the mutualist-libertarian socialism of Pierre-Joseph Proudhon as attacked in Marx's 1847 *The Poverty of Philosophy*,[130] makes a convenient unreal abstraction of historically existent capitalism. In this abstraction, one can cherry-pick this hypothetical capitalism's "good" features and quietly leave behind its not-so-good ones that happen to be glaringly on empirical display. The finger-wagging "thou shalt nots" of the *Economist*'s policy recommendations work to sustain the far-from-innocent illusion that capitalism's sins are never deadly, that its grave faults are mere venial sins as isolable and reformable contingent accidents (rather than necessary consequences inseparable from and expressive of capitalism's fundamental structural dimensions and tendencies).

Under the watchful eyes of the priests of the Washington consensus, governments performing the penances of savagely slashing social spending, drastically deregulating all sorts of markets, and artfully striking the right trade deals guarantee the salvation of a heavenly sociohistorical future. With enough political willpower and sufficient cajoling by the prosperity-gospel clerics of capitalist economics, (neo)liberalism will be redeemed in the end. What is the Enlightenment-style narrative of historical movement toward a classless society compared with this pseudosecular theodicy of profit-driven progress toward the raining (or, at least, trickling) down of limitless riches?

Given my immanent critique of the psychological natural selfishness objection brandished over and over against Marxism by (neo)liberalism, Marxists can lay claim to the possibility of sublating/sublimating the social egocentrism of capitalists themselves, with these capitalists' abstract-qua-quantitative hedonism (as different from the material egocentrism of consumers, with their concrete-qua-qualitative hedonism). Additionally, I am tempted to go further and completely turn the tables on such (neo)liberal critics: It is capitalism, in fact, that is vainly fighting an ultimately doomed idealistic war against human selfishness, with socialism and communism being much better suited to satisfying the self-interests of the masses. Not only, *pace* liberalism, is the abstract-qua-quantitative hedonism of capitalists able to be channeled and sated in postcapitalism—considering the relative and absolute immiseration of the vast bulk of humanity under capitalism, the concrete-qua-qualitative hedonism of consumers will be better appeased and soothed once the pursuit of surplus value at all costs (generating everything associated with "creative destruction" as well as gratuitous artificial scarcities, massively unequal distributions of wealth, and so on) is no longer the raison d'être of socioeconomic activity.

In a complete reversal of a standard picture too often accepted by Marxists themselves along with their (neo)liberal enemies, capitalism ruthlessly suppresses individual self-interests in the name of serving an abstract, impersonal big Other, namely, the creatively destructive invisible hand of the market, the Economy as God. By contrast, communism promises the abolition of this self-sacrificial capitalist service and, after it, the free indulgence of everyone in human selfishness, the egalitarian appreciations of both comfortable material quality of life as well as sociosymbolic recognition. If capitalist globalization's utopian overriding of humans' self-interests is not replaced by more realistic radical leftist selfishness, it will be replaced by the nightmarish identitarian delusions of enflamed far-right narcissisms with their hyperaggressive manias. The liberal tradition is right about one thing at least: Human selfishness cannot be effortlessly conjured away by mere ideological fiat.

§10. THE ALL-CONSUMING MISER: CAPITALISM'S HEADLESS SUBJECT

After the preceding excursus on the topic of selfishness, I now return to the task of further specifying and substantiating the motif guiding my synthesis of Marxism and psychoanalysis in the present chapter: the conception of a shift in libidinal economics prompted by a historical mutation in political economics, as per the theme of "from closed need to infinite greed." This theme's reference to Koyré's *From the Closed World to the Infinite Universe*, as I explained at the very beginning of this chapter, is meant to suggest a parallel between scientific modernity's mathematization of the natural world (via Galileo as per Koyré) and economic modernity's mathematization of the social world (via capitalism as per Marx). Both of these mathematizations open out onto infinities, onto certain forms of limitlessness.[131]

As seen, I go on to identify Marx's technical conception of greed strictly speaking (i.e., *auri sacra fames, die Bereicherungssucht,* and/or *die Goldgier*) with abstract-qua-quantitative hedonism. This mode of commodity fetishism peculiar to capitalists alone is the limitlessness of the drive of the capitalist (as per Marx, "a particular form of the drive [*eine besondre Form des Triebs*]") as animated by the structural dynamic of M-C-M'[132] (with capitalistic interest as M-M' being the apogee of this fetishization of limitless accumulation).[133] The M' of surplus value, as the *telos* of this movement, is the indefinite quantitative self-valorization of M functioning as capital proper[134] (rather than as simple currency qua means of exchange, as in C-M-C'). Furthermore, this capitalist drive toward in-principle limitless numerical amassing (i.e., "infinite greed") is the fundamental libidinal-economic motor of capitalism as a general political-economic framework.[135]

In both the *Grundrisse* and volume 1 of *Das Kapital,* Marx repeatedly foregrounds the quantitative infinity of capitalist greed proper.[136] The *Grundrisse,* in connection with the topic of self-valorizing value, speaks of "the constant drive to go beyond its quantitative limit: an endless process [*der beständige Trieb über seine quantitative Schranke fortzugehn: endloser Prozeß*],"[137] the "ceaseless striving towards the general form of wealth [*das rastlose Streben nach der allgemeinen Form des Reichtums*],"[138] "the endless and limitless drive to go beyond its limiting barrier [*der schranken- und maßlose Trieb über seine Schranke hinauszugehen*],"[139] and "the infinite urge to wealth [*unendlicher Trieb der Bereicherung*]."[140] *A Contribution to the Critique of Political Economy* contains echoes of this.[141] Likewise, the first volume of *Capital* refers to a "hoarding drive . . . boundless in its nature [*Trieb der Schatzbildung . . . von Natur maßlos*],"[142] a "boundless drive for enrichment [*absolute Bereicherungstrieb*],"[143] and an "unmeasured drive for self-valorization [*maßlosen Trieb nach Selbstverwertung*]."[144] Here, the drive loop of M-C-M' is an infinite one.[145] It is tempting, from a psychoanalytic perspective, to link this to the matter of repetition compulsion (*Wiederholungszwang*). Just as the mathematization of nature opens up a boundless universe, so too does the quantified accumulation of monetary surplus value open up a boundless greed. Modernity begins by plunging humanity into two bottomless abysses.

The first volume of *Capital,* in close connection with these emphases on the infinitude of the capitalist drive (i.e., abstract-qua-quantitative hedonism), adds another facet to Marx's drive theory, bringing it even closer to the analytic (especially Lacanian) metapsychology of *Trieb.* Apropos value (as exchange and surplus values), Marx characterizes its M-C-M' circuit as "an automatic subject [*ein automatisches Subjekt*]"[146] and "a self-moving substance [*eine prozessierende, sich selbst bewegende Substanz*]."[147] Within capitalism, this quasi-Hegelian

Substanz-als-Subjekt[148] is "the dominant subject [*übergreifendes Subjekt*]."[149] Again, greed per se, the distinctive form of the drive under capitalism, propels along both species of commodity fetishism, namely, the abstract-qua-quantitative hedonism on the side of capitalists with which greed strictly speaking is identical and also, as this greed's secondary effect, concrete-qua-qualitative hedonism on the side of capitalism's consumers. Furthermore, Lacan, in his celebrated eleventh seminar of 1964, likewise describes the drive in general (i.e., *Trieb überhaupt, pulsion tout court*), itself one of "the four fundamental concepts of psychoanalysis" (as per the title of *Seminar XI*), as "a headless subject [*un sujet acéphale*]"[150] and "a headless subjectification without subject [*une subjectivation acéphale, une subjectivation sans sujet*]."[151]

At one point in *Capital*, volume 1, Marx explicitly combines the two just-glossed features of capitalism's fundamental drive: first, infinitude/limitlessness and, second, automaticity/headlessness. He describes the capitalist's abstract-qua-quantitative hedonism as "blind and measureless drive" (*maßlos blinden Trieb*) with its "insatiable appetite" (*Werwolfs-Heißhunger*)[152] (following this Marx, Henryk Grossmann speaks of "a blind, unlimited thirst for surplus value").[153] The individual capitalist can be seen as the "personification" (*Personifikation*) or "bearer" (*Träger*) of this "blind and measureless drive."[154] With respect to the "movement" M-C-M′, Marx explains:

> As the conscious bearer [*Träger*] of this movement, the possessor of money becomes a capitalist. His person, or rather his pocket, is the point from which the money starts, and to which it returns. The objective content of the circulation we have been discussing—the valorization of value—is his subjective purpose, and it is only in so far as the appropriation of ever more wealth in the abstract is the sole driving force behind his operations that he functions as a capitalist, i.e. as capital personified [*personifiziertes*] and endowed with consciousness and a will. Use-values must therefore never be treated as the immediate aim of the capitalist; nor must the profit on any single transaction. His aim is rather the unceasing movement of profit-making. This boundless drive for enrichment, this passionate chase after value, is common to the capitalist and the miser; but while the miser is merely a capitalist gone mad, the capitalist is a rational miser. The ceaseless augmentation of value, which the miser seeks to attain by saving his money from circulation, is achieved by the more acute capitalist by means of throwing his money again and again into circulation.[155]

Marx's comparing and contrasting of the related figures of the capitalist and the miser echoes a passage from the *Grundrisse* I quoted a while ago. In that earlier passage, Marx, on the one hand, compares the capitalist's and the miser's self-sacrificial abstinence vis-à-vis all other commodities besides the universal equivalent (traditionally gold) and, on the other hand, contrasts the miser relating to precious metal as an inert material commodity (C) with the capitalist relating to it as self-valorizing social capital proper (M' as, in the block quotation immediately above, "the valorization of value," "the appropriation of ever more wealth in the abstract," "the unceasing movement of profit-making," etc.). Much later in the first volume of *Das Kapital*, Marx, in line with his distinction between the madness of the miser and the rationality of the capitalist, adds that "what appears in the miser as the mania of an individual is in the capitalist the effect of a social mechanism in which he is merely a cog [*Was ... bei diesem als individuelle Manie erscheint, ist beim Kapitalisten Wirkung des gesellschaftlichen Mechanismus, worin nur ein Triebrad ist*]."[156] Incidentally, *Triebrad* (here translated as "cog") can be rendered literally as "drive-wheel," thus further amplifying the resonances with the Lacanian *pulsion* as restless, interminable looping.

It seems therefore that, in terms of contrasting misers and capitalists, Marx distinguishes between insane idiosyncrasy and sane sociality, respectively. Under capitalism, there is the exception of miserly madness and the rule of capitalistic rationality. However, it would be more faithful to Marx's spirit, if not also his letter, to maintain that capitalistic rationality is, in a way, miserly madness writ large, namely, the sociostructural installation of the (il)logic of an "individual mania" (*individuelle Manie*). Of course, psychopathologies usually are easier to detect in individuals than in collectives; psychopathological symptoms in single persons standing out against social backgrounds are more readily discerned as such, as deviations, abnormalities, or extremes. But one does not have to embrace psychoanalysis in order to have the sense that at least in certain instances, whole societies can and do qualify as "pathological." In capitalism, the miser's mania is normalized by being generalized in the altered guise of the capitalist's greed.[157]

However, I want to focus now on the self-sacrificial conduct Marx identifies as a trait common to both misers and capitalists. This trait flies in the face of the traditional liberal claims that human beings are naturally "selfish" and that capitalism is the unsurpassably most rational qua natural socioeconomic system insofar as it supposedly gives free rein to this selfishness. Marx's historical materialism challenges not only appeals to an ahistorical human nature—its critique of (capitalist) political economy also rebuts liberalism's linking of capitalism and self-interested egocentrism of a consumptive sort.

Well before Weber's 1905 *The Protestant Ethic and the "Spirit" of Capitalism*, Marx's historical-materialist critique of political economy duly recognizes the important part played by Protestantism and related superstructural phenomena in the historical genesis of capitalism.[158] As Roman Rosdolsky notes, "This idea was later written about by bourgeois sociologists and economists as if it was something entirely new."[159] Moreover, Marx himself definitely is not guilty of the economistic reductions of the superstructural to the infrastructural, of the "naive historical materialism," to which Weber objects[160] (with Weber wavering ambivalently in his assessments of historical materialism such as to suggest his awareness that there might be a non-naive version not so objectionable to him).[161] Additionally, David Harvey perspicuously observes that Weber's recourse to Protestantism, unlike Marx's, lends support to the capitalist ideological fiction according to which the capital held by members of the bourgeoisie originates in their virtuous practices of abstinence and deferral of gratifications (rather than the unvirtuous violence of "primitive accumulation").[162]

That said, the *Grundrisse* speaks of "the severe discipline of capital" (*die strenge Disziplin des Kapitals*).[163] Going into more detail, it remarks:

> One sees how the piling-up of gold and silver gained its true stimulus with the conception of it as the material representative and general form of wealth [*allgemeine Form des Reichtums*]. The cult of money [*Das Geldkultus*] has its asceticism, its self-denial [*Entsagung*], its self-sacrifice [*Selbstaufopferung*]—economy and frugality, contempt for mundane, temporal and fleeting pleasures [*Genüsse*]; the chase after the *eternal* treasure. Hence the connection between English Puritanism, or also Dutch Protestantism, and money-making.[164]

Or, as this is put in 1859's *A Contribution to the Critique of Political Economy*: "The hoarder of money scorns the worldly, temporal and ephemeral enjoyments [*Genüsse*] in order to chase after the eternal treasure which can be touched neither by moths nor by rust, and which is wholly celestial and wholly mundane."[165] Marx soon adds that "in so far as the hoarder of money combines asceticism with assiduous diligence he is intrinsically a Protestant by religion and still more a Puritan."[166] In *Theories of Surplus-Value*, he remarks, "Christianity is ... the special religion of capital."[167]

In German-language Lacanian literature, *jouissance* standardly is translated as *Genuss*. However, the *Genüsse* at stake in these just-quoted passages (i.e., "mundane, temporal and fleeting pleasures," "worldly, temporal and ephemeral enjoyments") are matters of pleasure rather than enjoyment, as per Lacan's distinction between *plaisir* (associated with Eros's pleasure principle) and *jouissance* (associated with Thanatos's death drive). Indeed, *Genuss als jouissance* lies on the side of the "asceticism," "self-denial," "self-sacrifice," and "economy and

FROM CLOSED NEED TO INFINITE GREED ⟨⟩⁓ 127

frugality" in the service of the "cult of money" and its "chase after the *eternal treasure*" qua ruthless, single-minded pursuit of "the piling-up of gold and silver" in their function of being "the material representative and general form of wealth" (Serge Viderman's contestable association of the capitalist's drive to accumulate with Eros rather than the *Todestrieb* eclipses the "deathly" features of capitalist accumulation as involving automaticity, destructiveness, anality, compulsiveness, and so on).[168]

After the *Grundrisse*, the three volumes of *Das Kapital* proceed to buttress this emphasis on ascetic self-renunciation as essential to capitalism and as common to both miser and capitalist. The first volume, on the heels of emphasizing the unbound infinitude of the capitalist drive as greed, states:

> In order that gold may be held as money, and made to form a hoard, it must be prevented from circulating, or from dissolving into the means of purchasing enjoyment [*als* Kaufmittel *sich in Genußmittel aufzulösen*]. The hoarder therefore sacrifices the lusts of his flesh to the fetish of gold. He takes the gospel of abstinence very seriously. On the other hand, he cannot withdraw any more from circulation, in the shape of money, than he has thrown into it, in the shape of commodities. The more he produces, the more he can sell. Work, thrift and greed [*Geiz*] are therefore his three cardinal virtues, and to sell much and buy little is the sum of his political economy.[169]

Two features of this passage are worth highlighting. First, it indicates why, according to Marx, the miser is a failed capitalist and the capitalist is a successful miser, so to speak.[170] Earlier, I explained why the miser is a failed capitalist. The miser's commodity fetishism as regards gold fetishizes it as the incarnation of exchange value (assuming this malleable yellow metal to be the paradigmatic embodiment of the universal equivalent). At the same time, this fetishism compels the miser to withdraw his/her gold from circulation—with the social networks of economic circulation being the only spheres within which this element assigned atomic number 79 possesses actual exchange value. Succinctly put, the miser, in hoarding a substance fetishized because it epitomizes value, thereby self-defeatingly nullifies this very value[171] (something Lacan hints at in his sixteenth seminar).[172]

Moreover, Marx pointedly contrasts the miser's failure with the capitalist's success in the endeavor of hoarding gold, namely, accumulating materializations of value. In the case of the miser, greed as the hoarding drive requires not spending in order to save gold (and, in not spending, not generating surplus value for anyone).[173] Miserly avarice relies on mere, sheer withdrawal and hence demands strict asceticism, frugality, renunciation, and the like ("The hoarder ... sacrifices the lusts of his flesh to the fetish of gold. He takes the gospel of abstinence very seriously"—in 1859, Marx writes of "a fantastic Moloch" who "demands all physical wealth [*natürlichen Reichthum*] as a sacrifice").[174] However, the capitalist, precisely in and through spending his/her gold on certain commodities (specifically, labor power as variable capital and both fixed and circulating capitals as constant capital), accumulates value much more effectively than the saving-qua-nonspending miser.[175] Seen in this light, the capitalist is a hybrid of the consumer and the miser. Like the consumer, the capitalist spends M on C. But like the miser, this spending of M on C ultimately is motivated by the desire to hoard M (as M').[176]

If and when the capitalist's investments pay off, his/her hoard grows much larger much faster than the miser's hidden, private stash of metallic bits and pieces.[177] Continual hoarding precisely via perpetuating the cycle of M-C-M' even allows the capitalist to soften (albeit not eliminate) miserly self-sacrificial economizing. The capitalist can spend for consumption some (although far from all) of the profit he/she extracts from the quotas of surplus value generated by the exploitation of labor. Yet the rigid discipline constantly imposed by the merciless whip hand of market competition sets firm limits to this softening of the regime of renunciation.[178]

The second feature of the above-quoted passage from the first volume of *Capital* I wish to underscore has to do with its observation that "work, thrift and greed [*Geiz*] are" the capitalist's "three cardinal virtues." It might seem that the third of these virtues, greed, is at odds with the first two, namely, work and, especially, thrift. However, one must remember that Marx consistently uses "*Geiz*" in his precise technical sense as synonymous with the specifically capitalist drive as abstract-qua-quantitative hedonism (i.e., *auri sacra fames, die Bereicherungssucht*, and/or *die Goldgier*). Instead of being opposed to work and thrift, greed defined thus directly dictates these other two virtues. In fact, the capitalist's greed as his/her peculiar form of hedonism positively commands such other self-sacrificial, self-renunciative characteristics. Recalling that capitalists are consumers too, one could say that each and every properly capitalist subject is split such that his/her abstract-qua-quantitative hedonism (akin to a superegoistic death drive) imposes and impinges upon his/her concrete-qua-qualitative hedonism (akin to an egoistic pleasure principle). As Marx puts this in the first volume of *Capital*, "there develops in the breast of the capitalist a Faustian conflict between the passion for accumulation and the desire for enjoyment [*Akkumulations- und Genußtrieb*],"[179] a conflict also described in *Theories of Surplus-Value*.[180]

In the second and third volumes of *Capital*, Marx accentuates his stress on the importance of appreciating what I have described, against (neo)liberalism, as the selflessness of capitalism. In the second volume, he goes so far as to insist that "capitalism is already essentially abolished once we assume that it is enjoyment that is the driving motive and not enrichment itself [*der Kapitalismus ist schon in der Grundlage aufgehoben durch die Voraussetzung, daß der Genuß als treibendes Motiv wirkt, nicht die Bereicherung selbst*]."[181] As Weber subsequently words this, "Totally unrestrained greed for acquisition cannot in the least be equated with capitalism, less still with its 'spirit.'"[182] Lacan too likewise adds, "The *capitalist* enterprise ... does not put the means of production at the service of pleasure."[183] The third volume of *Capital* expands upon this insistence:

> It should never be forgotten that the production of this surplus-value—and the transformation of a portion of it back into capital, or accumulation, forms an integral part of surplus-value production—is the immediate purpose [*der unmittelbare Zweck*] and the determining motive [*das bestimmende Motiv*] of capitalist production. Capitalist production, therefore, should never be depicted as something that it is not, i.e. as production whose immediate purpose is consumption [*unmittelbaren Zweck den Genuß*], or the production of means of enjoyment for the capitalist [*die Erzeugung von Genußmitteln für den Kapitalisten*]. This would be to ignore completely its specific character, as this is expressed in its basic inner pattern [*ihrer ganzen inneren Kerngestalt*].[184]

A passage in *A Contribution to the Critique of Political Economy*, characterizing the protocapitalist miser/hoarder, already foreshadows this line of argumentation in *Das Kapital*:

> Our hoarder is a martyr to exchange-value, a holy ascetic seated at the top of a metal column. He cares for wealth [*Reichthum*] only in its social form [*gesellschaftlichen Form*], and accordingly he hides it away from society. He wants commodities in a form in which they can always circulate and he therefore withdraws them from circulation. He adores exchange-value and he consequently refrains from exchange. The liquid form of wealth and its petrification, the elixir of life and the philosophers' stone are wildly mixed together like an alchemist's apparitions. His imaginary boundless thirst for enjoyment [*eingebildeten schrankenlosen Genußsucht*] causes him to renounce all enjoyment. Because he desires to satisfy all social requirements, he scarcely satisfies the most urgent physical wants. While clinging to wealth in its metallic corporeality the hoarder reduces it to a mere chimaera [*Hirngespinst*].[185]

These points also are echoed in *Theories of Surplus-Value*.[186] For Marx, the very basis/essence (*Grundlage*) and the "inner pattern" or core shape (*Kerngestalt*) of "capitalist production," its "immediate purpose" (*unmittelbare Zweck*) as "driving" (*treibendes*) and "determining motive" (*bestimmende Motiv*), is "the production of . . . surplus-value" as "enrichment itself" (*Bereicherung selbst*)—in a single symbol, M'. And, this is absolutely different in kind from what would be a defining orientation toward "means of enjoyment for the capitalist" (*die Erzeugung von Genußmitteln für den Kapitalisten*) as "consumption" (*unmittelbaren Zweck den Genuß*) or simply "enjoyment" (*Genuß*)—in a single symbol, C'.[187] To assume, as many liberals do, that selfishness as concrete-qua-qualitative hedonism (in the language of the *Grundrisse*, the "mania for possessions" as "the craving for a particular kind of wealth") is the fundamental driving force of capitalism is to commit a grievous category mistake. By Marx's (as well as Weber's) reckoning, this is to miss the very political- and libidinal-economic nucleus of the capitalist mode of production.[188] As Marx puts it in *Theories of Surplus-Value*, "the industrial capitalist becomes more or less unable to fulfill his function as soon as he personifies the enjoyment of wealth, as soon as he wants the accumulation of pleasures instead of the pleasure of accumulation."[189]

By this juncture, a basic categorial division is glaringly apparent in Marx's historical-materialist critique of political economy. On one side of this divide, there is the abstract-qua-quantitative hedonism of the capitalist drive as greed, *auri sacra fames*, *die Bereicherungssucht*, and *die Goldgier*. On another side of this divide, there is the concrete-qua-qualitative hedonism of the consumerist drive. These twin manifestations of commodity fetishism are closely related yet utterly distinct. In terms of their close relationship, the capitalist drive fuels the consumerist drive, with the former as cause, origin, or source and the latter as effect, result, or symptom. In terms of their utter distinctness, the *telos* of the capitalist drive is M' (i.e., socially produced and recognized quantitative exchange and surplus values), while the *telos* of the consumerist drive is C' (i.e., physically instantiated qualitative use values). The primary product of capitalism is accumulable surplus value,[190] with consumable use value as its secondary byproduct.[191] To fail to understand this is to fail to understand capitalism.

The time has come to finish substantiating my initial thesis according to which the mutations in libidinal economies induced by capitalist political economies are themselves historical conditions for the subsequent advent of psychoanalysis. As I explained, this thesis of mine runs parallel to one of Lacan's having it that the early-seventeenth-century birth of the natural sciences, especially as registered in Descartes's rationalist metaphysics with its *Cogito*, makes possible the later rise of the Freudian field. For Lacan, the modernity-defining shift "from the closed world to the infinite universe" (Koyré) ushered in by science is a historical condition of possibility for the appearance of the analytic subject.

For me, the modernity-defining shift "from closed need to infinite greed" ushered in by capitalism is a historical condition of possibility for the appearance of the analytic drive. For Lacan and me alike, the modern era does not create subjects or drives ex nihilo. Instead, it effectuates a Hegelian-style transition from subject and drive *an sich* to these structural dynamics becoming *an und für sich*. In other words, natural science and capitalist economics introduce differences in degree (albeit ones so intense as to be virtually de facto differences in kind) into the subjective and libidinal dimensions of human beings such that the subjectively and libidinally more latent is rendered significantly more manifest. Such transitions are far from without their real ramifications.

So exactly how and why are the capitalist and consumerist drives peculiar to capitalism as per Marx's historical-materialist critique of political economy possibility conditions for psychoanalysis, with its metapsychology of the libidinal economy? Asked differently, in what fashions does Marxian *Triebtheorie* pave the way for its Freudian successor? Just as Galilean modern science infinitizes nature, so too does the modern capitalist economy infinitize drives. This libidinal infinitization is at work in both capitalist and consumerist drives (with the latter conditioned by the former).

The capitalist drive, as the greed of abstract-qua-quantitative hedonism, is limitless precisely in and through its quantitative nature.[192] This *Trieb des Kapitals* is oriented toward mathematically determined surplus value, namely, the numerically unbounded, open-ended self-valorization of capital. The consumerist drive, *der Trieb der Konsumtion* as the mania for possessions of concrete-qua-qualitative hedonism, echoes the infinitude of the capitalist drive.

Capital-driven production (in pursuit of M′) produces an ever-growing multitude of surplus value–bearing commodities actually generating surplus value only if and when ultimately exchanged for consumption. Indeed, capital requires, in order to reproduce itself, continual consumption-motivated exchanges (in pursuit of C′). Hence, the ceaseless agitation and insatiability of capitalism's consumerist drive is a symptomatic byproduct of capitalist greed (qua M-C-M′) as the primary drive of capitalism.[193] This agitation and insatiability are created and sustained by a variety of mechanisms and manipulations, ones continuing to multiply vertiginously within consumerist late capitalism (to recall a list I presented a while ago: advertising, marketing, branding, planned obsolescence, myriad sources of credit, countless purchasing platforms, commodification of the natural and the experiential, big data and the mining of social networks, etc.).[194]

I will not spend time in this context belaboring the resemblances between, on the one hand, Marx's capitalist drive (i.e., abstract-qua-quantitative hedonism, M-C-M', greed, *auri sacra fames*, *die Bereicherungssucht*, and/or *die Goldgier*) and, on the other hand, Freud's and, especially, Lacan's death drive. Others, particularly Slavoj Žižek and his fellow members of the Slovene School, already have done much invaluable work in this vein. As I will emphasize shortly, the novelty of my contribution, in terms of Lacano-Marxism, pertains more to the link between Marx's consumerist drive and the analytic metapsychology of the libidinal economy as involving sublimation and the like. Nonetheless, I ought to pause briefly to highlight a few of the most important details situated at the conceptual intersection between the Marxian-capitalist and Lacanian-death drives.

As revealed in the preceding, Marx regularly employs the German word *Genuss* in certain places. And as I observed before, German-language Lacanian literature often translates *jouissance* as *Genuss*. However, despite this, Marxian *Genuss* definitely is not synonymous with Lacanian *jouissance*. In fact, Marx's distinction between enrichment (*Bereicherung*) and enjoyment (*Genuss*) instead should be aligned with Lacan's between *jouissance* (enjoyment) and *plaisir* (pleasure) respectively. That is to say, Marxian enjoyment corresponds to Lacanian pleasure, and Marxian enrichment corresponds to Lacanian enjoyment.

Consequently, when Marx insists that capitalism is not about enjoyment *als Genuss*—this insistence beats Weber to the punch and contradicts liberalism's notion that the pleasures of hedonistic selfishness constitute capitalism's core interests—this does not mean that capitalism is not about enjoyment *comme jouissance*. Quite the contrary—Marxian enrichment *als Bereicherung*, as equivalent to the greed of the capitalist drive, is an epitomization of lethal Lacanian *jouissance*. *Pace* Byung-Chul Han's separating and opposing of greed and the death drive,[195] my analyses of Marx, Freud, and Lacan clearly indicate that specifically capitalist greed is itself a socioeconomic instantiation of the psychoanalytic *Todestrieb*. As the production and reproduction of capital, the circuit M-C-M' compels, in its mathematized infinitude/limitlessness, its own interminable repetition. This *Wiederholungszwang* of capital's self-valorization through the boundless accumulation of quantified surplus value is an acephalous kinetic configuration disregarding and overriding all other interests.[196] The latter include even the (self-)interests of those human beings who, as capitalists, are this drive's personifications/bearers.[197]

Even in (hypothetical) instances in which no individual capitalists wish to outsource, automate, pollute, despoil, and so on, the blind structural logic of capital forces them to do so nonetheless. The 2003 documentary film *The*

Corporation nicely illustrates this, showing how individual capitalists, in terms of their psychologies, can be perfectly nonpsychopathic people while, at the same time, participating in transindividual social entities (here, corporations as legal "persons") that themselves are structurally, although not psychologically, psychopathic. Such destructive and self-destructive behavior recurs regardless of whether or not those playing roles in perpetrating and perpetuating it desire to do so. The self-sacrificial renunciations of Marxian *Genuss* (as Lacanian *plaisir*) are dictated directly by the capitalist drive to its representative agents (i.e., Marx's "severe discipline of capital," ascetic "cult of money," and the like à la "English Puritanism" and "Dutch Protestantism").[198]

What is more, this peculiar socioeconomic *Trieb* also commands conduct that can and does sooner or later bring about consequences inimical to the needs and wants of this drive's personifications/bearers. As capitalists, these representatives of the endless loop of M-C-M′ are led again and again by this very loop to generate economic crises undermining their own self-interests specifically as capitalists. Moreover, as subjects not fully identical with or reducible to their roles as capitalists, these persons may also find themselves, however consciously or not, engaged in capitalist activity at odds with those of their inclinations, desires, values, and ideals not directly entangled with the M-C-M′ circuit.

So much for my extremely condensed recapitulation of some of the parallels between Marx's capitalist drive and Lacan's death drive, between greed as per Marx and *jouissance* as per Lacan. Now, what about the connection I have in mind between Marx's consumerist drive and the libidinal economics of psychoanalysis? Although exchange values (and, with them, surplus values) are quantitative and use values are qualitative, the consumption of the latter motivated, at root, by the accumulation of the former (i.e., exchange and surplus values) results in a fluidification of qualities (as qualities under the influence of quantities). As I underlined much earlier, Marx emphasizes how capitalism exploits the flexibility and malleability of human needs. It both pushes hard upon the downward/depressive elasticity of the needs of those forced to endure immiseration and banks on the excitability of the upward/manic elasticity of those called upon to cultivate ever more "needs" in relation to endlessly multiplying commodities. Additionally, each and every commodity-mediated form of consumption, via capital's arsenal of instruments and techniques, is compelled to lust after limitless series of not-so-useful use values (as themselves bearers of exchange and surplus values).[199] Such commodities, in their indefinite and boundless fungibility, lose the sharpness of their qualitative determinacy and distinctness vis-à-vis one another, partially dissolving into rapidly churning currents of compulsively repeated processes of fleeting, incomplete gratifications.

The political economy of capitalism, over the course of its history, steadily has made more and more explicit just how both mediated and plastic is the human libidinal economy. Capital's relentless commodification of anything and everything under the sun transforms the entities and experiences invested in by the drives of consuming subjects, thereby altering these very drives in turn (assuming the fundamental correctness of the Freudian metapsychology of *Trieb*, in which all drives consist of cathected objects, such as invested-in entities and experiences, in addition to sources, pressures, and aims). Both the theory and practice of psychoanalysis rely upon accounts of libidinal economies in which the unconscious is inextricably intertwined with the vicissitudes (*Schicksale*) of drives. Of course, these vicissitudes involve sublimations as well as metaphoric and metonymic displacements (what Lacan describes as the "drifting" of drives, of *Trieb/pulsion* as *dérive*).[200]

My main claim is that the distinctively modern immersion of drives and their drive-objects in flows of capital and the lubricant of currency qua universal equivalent—these are the mathematically infinite expanses of the "icy waters" famously spoken of by the *Communist Manifesto*[201]—renders the mediated, plastic, and drifting features of uniquely human *Triebe* significantly more visible and ubiquitous. As Marx's own drive theory reflects, the capitalist drive, itself a historical mutation of modernity in both political and libidinal economies, depends and parasitizes upon an ever more extended and intensified elasticity and variability of consumerist drives. Is it any accident or coincidence that psychoanalysis is not invented until well after the rise of capitalism? Could Freudian analysis have been created, given its resting upon observations and positions regarding investments that twist, turn, meander, and fluctuate, before the pervasive rule of money makes general fungibility (via exchangeability) a palpably omnipresent component of everyone's daily existences and quotidian motivations? Without the closely paired sociostructural perversions of capitalist and consumerist commodity fetishisms (i.e., abstract-qua-quantitative and concrete-qua-qualitative hedonisms fetishizing M′ and C′ respectively) essential to and ubiquitous within capitalism, would the perversions of psychosexual lives have been sufficiently exhibited and widespread so as to afford Freud the grist for his clinical and metapsychological mill? Not only does Lacan identify money as the fetish par excellence[202]—he indicates that *Das Unbehagen in der Kultur* is nothing other than the later Freud's registration of a *malaise* secreted specifically by monetized, commodified capitalist societies.[203]

For a Lacano-Marxism that itself is, in part, a renewal of the best of the Freudo-Marxist tradition, putting the literal economy back in "libidinal economy" is a long-overdue gesture, one that traditional Freudo-Marxism never adequately performed (largely because of its Western Marxist phobic reactions to economic reductionism). Capitalism brings about the monetization-through-commodification of more and more of subjects' relations to both objects and other subjects. As the universal equivalent, money introduces a general equivalence, an all-pervading substitutability and interchangeability, among and between subject-object and subject-subject relationships.[204] This is what, in Marx's and Engels's eyes, makes bourgeois society, albeit inadvertently and unwittingly, ideologically revolutionary qua profaning and desacralizing.[205]

Obviously, the subject-subject relationship of the analytic clinic, the rapport between analyst and analysand, is itself predicated on a financial pact. Starting with Freud, analysts rightly consider monetary matters, particularly those concerning the analytic fee, important in terms of both techniques and interpretations. Without on this occasion developing a detailed Freudo-Lacano-Marxist treatment of the topic of money, suffice it to say for now that the significances of currency qua universal equivalent go well beyond issues in clinical technique apropos the analytic fee. In addition to the clinic of money (which already has received a certain amount of attention in various bodies of analytic literature), there is a metapsychology of money, too.

I will limit myself here to observing that for any adult subject lying on the couch in a capitalist context, money mediates not only his/her relationship with the analyst but also, in light of Marx's critique of political economy, his/her relations to other subjects as well as virtually all objects (the latter insofar as capital strives to commodify every actual and potential object with a consumable use value). Intrasubjectivity, one's reflexive relation to oneself, even is affected by this monetary mediation. If Marx is right that capitalism continually transforms more and more relations between persons into relations between things, then both the theory and practice of psychoanalysis, at least within capitalism, must take into account this all-pervasive mediation permeating and saturating the very foundations of subjects' libidinal economies. Marx's own drive theory, as I have unpacked it throughout the preceding, indicates both the need for such an account as well as some of the key ingredients required by this *Triebtheorie*.[206] Along with Reich and Fenichel, among others, I see Freud (and then Lacan) as going on to elaborate such a drive theory more fully than Marx, albeit without the accompanying fine-grained clarity apropos the political economy's influences upon drives, desires, needs, wants, and the like.

A hybrid Marxian-psychoanalytic metapsychological anthropology of money-mediated libidinal life must theoretically employ the temporality of "deferred action" (i.e., Freud's *Nachträglichkeit* and/or Lacan's *après-coup*). If the analytic rendition of ontogenetic subject formation and psychosexual development is even basically correct, then at least in the earliest years for the forming psycho-sexual subject-to-be, economic issues of capital and currency are not directly and explicitly thematized as such by and for the very young human being. However, two considerations make it such that this concession to psychoanalysis neither problematizes nor invalidates a Freudo- and/or Lacano-Marxian insistence on the all-pervasiveness of political-economic mediations in relation to libidinal-economic forces and factors.

First of all, as both Marxism and psychoanalysis (particularly the Lacanian version of the latter) highlight, something along the lines of Hegel's transindividual, transgenerational "objective spirit" (whether as Marx's social structure or as Lacan's symbolic order) always precedes the coming into existence of each and every singular, nascent subjectivity. Well before Lacan (not to mention Heidegger, with his concept of *Geworfenheit* [thrownness]), Marx emphasizes the fact that all human beings are hurled at birth into determinate infrastructural and superstructural sets of configurations that are themselves parts of an already-underway social history.[207] As he famously observes at the start of 1852's *The Eighteenth Brumaire of Louis Bonaparte*: "Men make their own history, but not of their own free will; not under circumstances they themselves have chosen but under the given and inherited circumstances with which they are directly confronted. The tradition of the dead generations weighs like a nightmare on the minds of the living [*wie ein Alp auf dem Gehirne der Lebenden*]."[208] The crucial upshot in the present context is that this overlap between Marx and Lacan on thrownness entails there being indirect but efficacious influences of political on libidinal economics from the get-go. In other words, even though, at the ontogenetic beginning, the immature subject-to-be does not immediately register experientially for itself these socioeconomic influences, the latter nonetheless indirectly mediate (via such institutions as the socially constituted family unit) this subjectivity-in-formation. Just as, for Lacan, the incubus (*Alp*) of language acquires the human being before the human being acquires language, so too for Marx (and Freudo-Lacano-Marxism): The economy, hanging over from "the dead generations," participates in drives (pressing down on "the brains [*Gehirne*] of the living") before drives participate in the economy.

Furthermore, ontogenetic subject formation within capitalism makes it such that maturing psyches quickly are marked by very direct and tangible registrations of the interlinked capitalist and consumerist drives. Via media conduits, parental preoccupations and anxieties, errands and outings, schooling and peers, etc., children all too early start to acquire a lifelong intimate familiarity with the various rituals and routines of commodified consumption in capitalism's myriad marketplaces (starting at a time when, as children, they are ill-equipped to fend off critically the effects of capitalist institutions, practices, and ideologies). How can all of this not profoundly impact the wishes, fantasies, and object relations of those exposed as relatively helpless youths to such surroundings and impressions? In a universe of thoroughly corrupted social relations, how can the youth not promptly succumb to corruption?

This is where Freudian-Lacanian *Nachträglichkeit/après-coup* is particularly crucial to appreciate. Why? In addition to the just-noted indirect influences of infrastructural and superstructural dimensions on even the most archaic phases of subject formation and psychosexual development, the subsequent direct metabolizations of socioeconomic structures by libidinal life, as per analytic deferred action, retroactively retranscribe early economic naiveté in terms of later economic worldliness (just as supposed pre-Oedipal stages are reconfigured after the fact in passing through the Oedipus complex). Of course, at the same time, psychoanalysis reciprocally would insist that infrastructures and superstructures (as socioeconomic, political, and related domains) remain themselves marked in turn by sexual, familial, childhood, etc. influences. As, for instance, the older Jean-Paul Sartre already maintains, both Marxism and psychoanalysis can and should acknowledge and delineate the mutual entanglements between their areas of respective focus.[209]

But what, if anything, does Lacan bring to these issues? How are Freudo-Marxism as well as the Marxist critique of political economy altered or enhanced, if at all, by Lacanian theory in particular? I will conclude this chapter by addressing these questions in the next (and last) section.

§11. MANUFACTURING DISCONTENT: LACANO-MARXISM AND THE CRITIQUE OF CAPITALIST ECONOMICS

In the first section of this chapter, I mention Reich and Fenichel as early-twentieth-century pioneers of efforts to marry Marxism and psychoanalysis. It seems fitting to me in this final section to end with one of the latest of these efforts, namely, Samo Tomšič's 2015 study *The Capitalist Unconscious: Marx and Lacan*. Therein, Tomšič furnishes readers with a wide-ranging, thorough exploration of Lacan's references to Marx's ideas and texts. I agree with quite a bit in his survey. But there are crucial differences too, especially in terms of how Tomšič and I each handle the rapport between capitalism and selfishness.

There is much with which I concur in Tomšič's reconstruction of drive theory at the intersection of Marxism and Lacanianism. To begin with, Tomšič acknowledges that "the paradoxes of the drive were not an unknown for Marx, whose manuscripts already contained the connection between the structure of the drive, the abstract nature of the general equivalent and the production of surplus-value."[210] He then quotes the passage from the *Grundrisse* distinguishing between capitalist greed and the not-specifically-capitalist mania for possessions[211] (in the language I have been utilizing, abstract-qua-quantitative versus concrete-qua-qualitative hedonisms). Relying on an asserted equivalence of Marx's greed and mania for possessions with Lacan's drive and desire (*désir*) respectively, Tomšič proceeds to state:

> The desire for the object (wealth) ... accumulates a collection of objects that embody value—it focuses on the *objects of value* and not on *value as object*. The drive, on the other hand, is fixated on *the* object, the general equivalent, which due to its paradoxical status—being both singular and universal, a commodity and a Commodity in which all commodities are reflected—supports the infinitisation of satisfaction, which is to say, its impossibility and endless perpetuation. The capitalist drive for self-valorization is an unsatisfiable demand, to which no labour can live up to.[212]

Here, "*objects of value*" would be C′ and "*value as object*" would be M′, with the consumptive drive (or Lacanian desire as per Tomšič) fetishizing the former and the capitalist drive fetishizing the latter. I should add that what I might call the miserly drive apparently fetishizes the same object as the capitalist drive (i.e., gold as the universal equivalent) but treats this "Commodity in which all commodities are reflected" as a mere "commodity," namely, as an inert substance (a "singular" C as a material thing) rather than a self-valorizing subject (a "universal" M as a social process).

Tomšič concludes above that "the capitalist drive for self-valorization is an unsatisfiable demand, to which no labour can live up to." As I have pointed out several times here with respect to Marx's analyses, the insatiability of the capitalist's infinite greed is a cause, one of whose effects is a corresponding infinitization (and, hence, rendering insatiable too) of the consumer's mania for possessions (another effect being, as Tomšič's wording signals, capital's tendency toward the unlimited exploitation of the ultimate source of surplus value, namely, labor power). Of course, this mania for possessions is the means in and through which capital valorizes itself, since surplus value is realized only if and when

FROM CLOSED NEED TO INFINITE GREED   139

exchange values are realized in purchases of commodities by those intending to consume them (as use values). One consequence of this, given Tomšič's equation of Marx's capitalist and consumerist drives with Lacan's drive and desire, respectively, is that desire (as the mania for possessions, with C′ qua "*objects of value*" as its *telos*) must be viewed as created, and thereafter relied upon, by drive (as greed, with M′ qua "*value as object*" as its *telos*). A Marxist qua historical-materialist perspective would be adamant about contextualizing the Lacanian *pulsion-désir* distinction in relation to capitalist socioeconomic conditions.

I wholeheartedly agree with Tomšič, considering some of the Lacanian ground we share, about what he rightly describes as "the infinitisation of satisfaction" entailing the generation of a particular form of lack or deficit. Adam Smith himself speaks of "those desires which cannot be satisfied, but seem to be altogether endless."[213] Indeed, neither the capitalist, with his/her greed for "*value as object*" qua M′, nor the consumer, with his/her mania for "*objects of value*" qua C′, can reach a sufficient, satisfying end—and this precisely because their *teloi* recede endlessly in being infinitized. The capitalist as capitalist will never have enough infinitely accumulable surplus value.[214]

Correspondingly and consequently, the capitalist consumer will never have enough boundlessly multiplying commodities (whose boundless multiplication is a capitalism-specific byproduct and reflection of the limitless structural push of capital toward ever more surplus value). Capitalism's sociostructural quantification of libidinal economics via the becoming mathematized of political economy makes the infinite into a real abstraction. More precisely, quantitative infinity introduces into social and subjective existences causally efficacious absences and impossibilities (specifically, absences of gratifying ends and impossibilities of satisfying completions). The mathematical mediation of drives, desires, and things closely related to them associated with capitalism creates real voids at the hearts of libidinal economies. With eyes to the interfacing of Marxism and psychoanalysis, Tomšič and I both see these aspects of Marx's critique of political economy as justifying, and able to be done unique justice to by, recourse to Lacanian theory especially.

However, I worry that Tomšič's fashion of mobilizing Lacan's differentiation between *pulsion* and *désir* is not sufficiently sensitive to the distinguishing specificities of capitalism, a sensitivity essential both to Marx and to historical materialism generally. Simply and bluntly put, the Lacanian drive-desire distinction is not, for Lacan, peculiar to properly capitalist socioeconomic systems. Lacan's countless references to ancient and medieval (i.e., premodern, precapitalist) figures, texts, and phenomena, including in connection with the metapsychology of libidinal matters, amply reveal as much. By contrast, the Marxian greed-mania distinction is, in fact, peculiar to properly capitalist socio-economic systems. Immediately identifying, as Tomšič appears to do, manic consumerism with Lacan's *désir* dehistoricizes the former, tearing it out of its capitalist context by decoupling it from its dependence upon and connection with the specifically capitalist drive (i.e., abstract-qua-quantitative hedonism as the circuit M-C-M′). Likewise, greed *als Mehrwertstrieb* comes into effective existence and operation only in and through capitalism.

Resolving the tension between Marx's historicism and Lacan's comparative ahistoricism would require, as a nuancing caveat, hypothesizing that the rise of capitalist modernity brings about an extending and intensification of the con-stellations and kinetics Lacan associates with *pulsion* and/or *désir*. I am not sure whether Tomšič would or would not endorse such a qualification. However, my own position involves precisely this.

As a Lacanian, I would say that the metapsychology of the libidinal economy transcends and is irreducible to merely one or several historical milieus, with capitalism (as one of these milieus) at most generating differences in degree between precapitalist and capitalist libidinal economics. But as a Marxist, I would say that these differences in degree generated by capitalism are so broad and deep as to be tantamount de facto to differences in kind. Moreover, as a Hegelian Marxist, I would say that this tipping over of differences in degree into differences in kind exhibits the dialectical-speculative logic of quantity, quality, and measure.[215] This borrowing from "The Doctrine of Being" of Hegel's *Logik* allows for a Lacano-Marxism in which a metapsychological anthropology of the libidinal economy helps explain some of what facilitates the emergence of capi-talism's political economy as per historical materialism. At the same time, this thus-Hegelianized Lacano-Marxism acknowledges that this thereby-emergent capitalist political economy comes to exert reciprocal modifying influences upon its libidinal-economic catalysts.

Of course, Tomšič is well aware of the importance of historical dimensions for Marx. As he observes regarding Marx's drive theory:

> Marx . . . made an important point when he detached the notion of drive from its biological or physiological connotation. He entirely conditioned it with the social existence of the general equivalent and with historical development. The capitalist drive is therefore not the only possible drive. There is something like a history of the drive, a historical transformation of fixations, which alters the social articulation of the drive together with the function of the general equiva-lent in the predominant mode of production.[216]

FROM CLOSED NEED TO INFINITE GREED ☙ 141

Tomšič continues, making cross-resonate a passage in Marx's *Grundrisse* I quoted a while ago[217] with Lacan's depiction of the Freudian *Trieb* in *Seminar XI*:[218]

> Marx... aims at the historical and the social transformation of the drive, leaving no doubt that the placement of the drive at the intersection of presumably natural need and its cultural articulation can be considered a predecessor of the psychoanalytic notion, for the Freudian notion of the drive is *not* the hunger that swallows raw meat but the hunger that reaches satisfaction through the *montage* of cooked meat, cutlery and table manners. Indeed, Lacan brought this to a crucial point when he compared the drive to a surrealist collage, underlining that the montage of the heterogeneous elements contains a differentiation between the *aim* and the *goal*, so ... between use-value and exchange-value.[219]

It sounds as though there is a slight tension between these two block quotations, with the first striking the ear as more absolutely antinaturalist (with *Trieb* as "detached... from its biological or physiological connotation" and "entirely conditioned" by sociohistorical variables) and the second as more qualified along these lines (with *Trieb* as situated "at the intersection of presumably natural need and its cultural articulation," with its collage-like montages bringing together hodgepodges of somatic and psychical elements). Not only do I consider Tomšič correct to associate this second qualified antinaturalism with Freud's and Lacan's views—despite Marx's views being associated in the first of these block quotations with a thoroughly antinaturalistic, sociohistorical constructionism, I think Marx's own writings, from start to finish, show him to be less of a categorical antinaturalist than he sometimes is taken to be.[220]

That said, Tomšič's first set of remarks quoted above nonetheless signal his appreciation that Marx, like Freud and Lacan, believes drive per se, as a general structural dynamic forming part of a philosophical-metapsychological anthropology, to precede capitalism. That is to say, the capitalist drive and its offshoots are permutations of *Trieb als solche und überhaupt*, with the latter, for proper Marxism as well as for psychoanalysis, exhibiting precapitalist (and, presumably, possible postcapitalist) instantiations too (as seen, Marx speaks of capitalist greed as "a particular form of the drive [*eine besondre Form des Triebs*]").[221] And needless to say at this juncture, I unreservedly concur with Tomšič when he identifies the Marxian drive as "a predecessor of the psychoanalytic notion" of *Trieb*.

But what about, at the end of the second of the two prior block quotations, Tomšič's alignment of Lacan's distinction between a drive's aim and its goal with Marx's (Smithian-Ricardian) distinction between use and exchange values? Lacan, in his eleventh seminar, distinguishes between aim and goal in order to address an apparent contradiction in Freud's theory of sublimation (itself a vicissitude of the drive [*Triebschicksal*]). According to Freud, the aim of each and every drive is its specific variety of satisfaction (*Befriedigung*). Yet Freudian sublimation is nothing other than the achievement of satisfaction in the face of aim-inhibition. So if a drive's aim is inhibited, and this aim is defined as satisfaction, then how can an aim-inhibited drive be said to achieve satisfaction? Lacan's answer, in a nutshell, is that the true aim of *Trieb*—this is its goal of *jouissance* as distinct from its aim of *plaisir*—is repeatedly to circle around its object. This circling includes in its orbit whatever obstacles (i.e., Freudian aim-inhibitions) are placed in its path. The detours imposed by these obstacles simply become part of the larger curved trajectory to be followed. The recurrent enjoyment of the movement of this looping circuit is the real goal qua end-in-itself of *la pulsion*, a goal indifferent to whether or not barriers are raised to aimed-at satisfaction-as-pleasure.

So, what might Tomšič have in mind when he equates Lacanian aim and goal with Marxian use and exchange values respectively? On Marx's account, one of the distinctive peculiarities of capitalism is that it is the first and only socioeconomic system in human history organizing its processes of production around (surplus value–yielding) exchange values rather than use values.[222] In capitalism, consumable goods and services of utility (i.e., use values gratifying needs and wants) are no longer the final causes, the ultimate *teloi*, of economic activity. Instead, commodities, however useful (or not), are mere means to an end different in kind from consumable utility; these objects are the incidental vehicles for transferring and amassing surplus value along networks of exchanges.[223] Capitalism leaves the matter of whether or not enough use values are produced for the needs and wants of populations to the chanciness of the casino-like anarchy of decentralized, headless markets (and, as even a non-Marxist such as John Maynard Keynes has to admit, "When the capital development of a country becomes a by-product of the activities of a casino, the job is likely to be ill-done").[224] The capitalist drive ceaselessly pursues the goal of capital's self-valorization unconcerned with whether other (consumerist) drives are satisfied—with this satisfaction being the aim of those drives other than the capitalist drive, drives concerned with use rather than exchange/surplus values.

Hence, I suspect Tomšič means to underscore that *der Trieb des Kapitals* is indifferent to whether or not aims toward the satisfaction of consuming use values (C′) are inhibited, so long as the goal of repeatedly spinning off surplus value (M′) can be continuously achieved without interruption and ad infinitum. The boundless greed of the capitalist drive (as *auri sacra fames, die Bereicherungssucht, die Goldgier,* abstract-qua-quantitative hedonism, and/or the logic of M-C-M′) can and does reach its goal even when billions gratuitously starve amid plenty and recurrent crises dramatically immiserate multitudes (while fabulously enriching further an already obscenely wealthy few). Capitalism succeeds at meeting its real goal despite, and even because of, failing to reach the aim of social production as producing use values meeting needs and wants (including sometimes the needs and wants of capitalist persons themselves as the mere bearers of the capitalist drive).

However, insofar as Lacan's drive-desire distinction is not historically specific to capitalism, so too is his goal-aim distinction, as internal to his metapsychological conception of drive, not historically specific to capitalism either. I would be loath to deny the virtues of Tomšič's insightful employment of Lacanian aim and goal to illuminate Marx's protopsychoanalytic *Triebtheorie.* But this employment generates the same concerns in me I voiced a short while ago apropos his applications to Marx of Lacan's *pulsion-désir* contrast. Relatedly, I would contend that my above-mentioned, Hegel-inspired manner of finessing the (seeming) tensions between Marxian historical materialism and Lacanian transhistorical metapsychology are called for in order to allay such worries.

At long last, I come now to what I consider to be the most important difference between Tomšič's and my versions of a Lacano-Marxism. This difference is most apparent in relation to the conclusion of *The Capitalist Unconscious.* Tomšič's conclusion, unlike those closing many books, is much more than a summation encapsulating what already came before in his book's main body. Therein, he advances significant new arguments on the basis of preceding elaborations.

Specifically, Tomšič ends his 2015 study with some assertions bearing upon the issue of capitalism's rapport with selfishness. He opens his conclusion with reference to Jean-Claude Milner's reflections on psychoanalysis in relation to the modern sciences of nature. Following Milner, Tomšič portrays Freud, through Freud's self-avowed wounding of humanity's narcissism, as carrying forward from the natural to the human sciences the antinarcissistic implications of modernity's valorization of an anonymous, impersonal, transindividual reason. Whether as the literal revolutionary shift from geocentrism to heliocentrism or Freud's metaphorical "Copernican revolution," Tomšič, in line with Milner, contends that the core of the scientific *Weltanschauung* in which Freudian analysis proudly participates consists of an antihumanist rationality corrosive to human narcissism.[225]

144 FROM CLOSED NEED TO INFINITE GREED

Tomšič links Milner's Lacan-dependent construal of the science-psychoanalysis rapport with Marxism by contrasting the antinarcissistic nature of scientific modernity with the narcissistic character of economic modernity (i.e., capitalism). The latter, according to Tomšič, amounts to "the dictatorship of irrational beliefs and the restoration of human narcissism, the self-love and self-interest that Adam Smith and other political economists took for the foundation of social relations."[226] The politics of capitalism revolves around "a narcissistic subject"[227] (by contrast, "For both Marx and Lacan, the negative, which . . . means the non-narcissistic subject, is the necessary singular point on which political universalism should build").[228] Tomšič adds: "While capitalism considers the subject to be nothing more than a narcissistic animal, Marxism and psychoanalysis reveal that the subject of revolutionary politics is an alienated animal, which, in its most intimate interior, includes its other. This inclusion is the main feature of a non-narcissistic love and consequently of a social link that is not rooted in self-love."[229]

Soon after this, the closing paragraph of Tomšič's book heralds, on the basis of the Lacano-Marxism delineated in this 2015 study, a politics that is properly modern insofar as it finally catches up to the antinarcissistic modernity already achieved in the natural and certain of the human sciences. From this perspective, capitalism and its politics remain stubbornly, aggressively premodern, with slavery and serfdom in the service of capital and worship of the Economy as a pseudosecular transcendent power.[230] Speaking of the rise of a new communism that is as selfless as the reason common to science and psychoanalysis, Tomšič ends his book declaring, "Only then will politics be consistently in synch with modern science and inhabit the same universe."[231] Yet it should be noted that classical British liberalism both philosophical and economic (including such figures as Hobbes and Locke along with Smith and Ricardo) presents itself, with its social atomism and contract theories as well as hypothetical states of nature, as drawing inspiration and justification from seventeenth- and eighteenth-century natural science, particularly Newtonian mechanical physics.

That noted, there is much I find powerful in Tomšič's concluding reflections upon modernity, science, psychoanalysis, and politics. Nonetheless, I have some significant reservations and objections to raise in response to these reflections. To begin with, capitalism's social relations of servitude, domination, exploitation, oppression, etc. ultimately arise from and remain fueled by capitalism-specific greed. Therefore, however much social relations within capitalism appear to reproduce ancient and/or medieval inequalities and hierarchies, this really is an appearance emerging from modern rather than premodern social

FROM CLOSED NEED TO INFINITE GREED   145

structures, a matter of superficial resemblances belying structural differences in kind between incommensurable social orders.

Furthermore, Tomšič, as seen, equates "narcissism" with the selfishness central to the self-conception of classic (Smithian) liberalism and its offspring. He speaks in this vein of "self-love and self-interest." Likewise, Tomšič's closing arguments pivot around a zero-sum binary opposition of the "narcissistic animal" of capitalism versus the "alienated animal" of "revolutionary politics," including a certain Lacanianism. Indeed, Lacanianism's emphasis on "extimate" social mediation "in the subject more than the subject itself"[232] is said to allow for "a non-narcissistic love and consequently... a social link that is not rooted in self-love." By implication, capitalism is supposed to be materially grounded in a social link rooted in self-love.

But this is precisely where there are some serious problems, especially given Tomšič's dual allegiances to both Marx and Lacan. By Marx's and Lacan's lights alike, Tomšič mistakes capitalism's representations of itself for its true real(ity). As Marx warns while delineating the fundaments of historical materialism in the (in)famous preface to 1859's *A Contribution to the Critique of Political Economy*, "Just as one does not judge an individual by what he thinks about himself, so one cannot judge... a period... by its consciousness."[233] Therefore, as a Marxian historical materialist, one cannot judge capitalism by its own ideas about itself. Similarly, psychoanalysis conveys no lesson if not that one cannot trustingly take for granted as accurate the self-awarenesses and self-depictions of both psyches and societies.

Of course, liberal and neoliberal ideologies explicitly assert and rely upon images of capitalism as the social arrangement best suited to accommodate peacefully and sublimate productively an incorrigible human selfishness. In Marx's view, capitalism is split from within by a dialectical-structural discrepancy between what it is for itself (*für sich*) and what it is in itself (*an sich*). For itself, at the superstructural level of the ideological, capitalism seems to be inseparable from selfishness, narcissism, self-love, self-interest, and so on. But at the infrastructural level of the economic, capitalism really is, in itself, a potent accelerator of the socialization of production, a set of material processes transforming means and relations of production such as to bring about a historically unprecedented extension and intensification of social codependence between more and more people and populations. Capitalism does not become synonymous with "globalization" for nothing.

For both Hegel and Marx, when there is a discrepancy between the *für sich* and the *an sich*, the truth resides on the side of the latter. As is well known, one of the principal contradictions at the core of capitalism, in Marx's eyes, is its constitutive juxtaposition of, on the one hand, private property and everything entangled with it politically, legally, and ideologically (i.e., superstructurally) and, on the other hand, a thoroughly socialized mode of production as its real underlying infrastructural base. So, Marx, as already seen here, and Lacan, as will be seen, both object to liberalist and individualist ideologies by arguing that capitalism's conception of itself as serving private persons' egocentrism (i.e., Tomšič's "narcissism") is a misconception, a paradigmatic case of ideological self-consciousness (or *réconnaissance de soi*) as misrecognition (*méconnaissance*, to employ another key term from the Lacanian lexicon).

Although the antagonism Tomšič relies upon between the "narcissistic animal" of capitalism versus the "alienated animal" of "revolutionary politics" has some validity at the level of competing ideologies, of clashing superstructural appearances, it is inaccurate and misleading apropos infrastructural being(s) within the capitalist mode of production. When he says of Marxian and Lacanian subjectivities that "the subject of revolutionary politics is an alienated animal, which, in its most intimate interior, includes its other," this suggests that capitalism's egocentric subject, by contrast, does not harbor within itself any such extimacy (qua public/social mediation within seemingly private/individual immediacy). But one of the load-bearing theses of Marx's historical-materialist critique of capitalist political economy is precisely that, however unconsciously, the subjects of capitalism are caught up and absorbed in a historical trajectory of socialization far exceeding the breadth and depth of such mediation in human history hitherto.

Now, what about Lacan's take on capitalism vis-à-vis selfishness? To begin with, narcissism, in light of the Lacanian accounts of both ego (*moi*) and subject (*sujet*), is vain according to both meanings of this adjective. That is to say, not only is narcissism synonymous with vanity; it also is vain in the sense of futile. For Lacan, the narcissist, corresponding to how Tomšič uses the word "narcissism" (as Freudian secondary narcissism),[234] is stuck in a doomed endeavor to (over)valorize him/herself in and through the alterity of matrices of mediation consisting of words, images, etc. external to his/her "self." Succinctly stated, this vanity of narcissism is tantamount to the impossibility of transubstantiating otherness into otherlessness. It mistakes the outer for the inner.[235]

However, an authentically Lacanian assessment of capitalist selfishness cannot and would not limit itself to such broad brushstrokes of an ahistorical, metapsychological sort. This is especially true considering some of the highly astute glosses on Marx offered by Lacan himself. Indeed, as I will show, Lacan weds Marx's historical-materialist analyses of political economies with his own psychoanalytic account of libidinal economies in ways that further elucidate what I have counterintuitively described as the selflessness of capitalism.

In the context of *le Séminaire*, some of Lacan's earliest references to Marx surface in the fifth and sixth seminars. These hint at a structural resemblance between the ego's self-thwarting (secondary) narcissism and the dynamics of capitalist economics. In *Seminar V* (*Formations of the Unconscious* [1957–1958]), he claims, somewhat enigmatically, that Marx's conception of exchange value anticipates aspects of his own mirror stage.[236] Then, in *Seminar VI* (*Desire and Its Interpretation* [1958–1959]), he maintains, citing Marx's critique of Proudhon in 1847's *The Poverty of Philosophy*, that exchange-valorizing an object is equivalent to devalorizing it.[237] Taking these two 1950s Marx references together, it seems that Lacan is suggesting an isomorphism between his theory of the ego and Marx's theory of value. The Lacanian ego attempts to valorize itself, to validate its narcissistic "selfness," via a detour through mirroring others (and Others). This detour invariably ends up compromising and diluting the (false) self of the ego with alterity, with foreign (i.e., not-self) mediation. Likewise, Marxian use value, on Lacan's reading, enters the economy's networks seeking to be represented as exchange value, only to find that exchange values have no correspondence with use values from the perspective of the latter. For instance, commodities of the greatest utility rarely command notably high prices in the marketplace, while those that are unusually expensive quite often possess little to no practical-material utility.

Lacan's analytic interventions of the 1960s and early 1970s with respect to Marx's theory of value are indispensable for my present purposes. Therein, Lacan develops a hybrid of political and libidinal economics capturing the self-subverting narcissism and ultimate selflessness of capitalism. This will be the focus of my remaining remarks in this chapter.

Admittedly, Lacan is cautious and even ambivalent in his approaches to Marx. He is careful to acknowledge that Marxian historical materialism and Freudian psychoanalysis both deal with specific structures and phenomena distinct from and irreducible to each other.[238] Nevertheless, Lacan's assessment of the Marx-Freud pair clearly counts them as sharing a sizable amount in common: In their wakes, neither thinker can be avoided or surpassed by the intellectually honest;[239] neither thinker "bullshits" (*déconner*), intended as the highest of praise by Lacan;[240] Marx, along with Freud, helps define modernity through contributing to a rigorous conceptualization of the unconscious;[241] and both Marxism and psychoanalysis, by Lacan's reckoning, equally depend on what (post-)Saussurian structuralism comes to delineate in the guise of a general theory of the signifier[242] (Lacan highlights Marx's account of commodity fetishism in particular as depending on "the logic of the signifier,"[243] with currency as the signifying stuff of this fetishism).[244] Additionally, and as I have underscored here as well as elaborated upon elsewhere,[245] Lacan goes so far as to self-identify, from time to time, as a Marxian materialist of a certain sort.[246]

Especially starting during the latter half of the 1960s, Lacan zeroes in on the Marxian theory of value specifically as a scientific qua protostructuralist predecessor of Freudian and Lacanian psychoanalysis. For this Lacan, the complex interactions between use, exchange, and surplus values as delineated in Marx's critique of political economy are largely unconscious for those caught up in capitalism's socioeconomic networks. The acephalous subjectivities of self-valorizing flows of capital, driven on indefinitely by the prospect of ever more surplus value, are inseparable from a signifier-like logic of quantitative real abstractions[247] latently governing the manifest surfaces of social life.[248]

In terms of libidinal economics, Lacan's metapsychological concept of *jouissance* provides him with the basis upon which he constructs his rapprochement of psychoanalysis with Marxism (specifically the latter's value theory as key to its political economics). The later Lacan speaks of *"plus-de-jouir"* in order to bring to the fore certain aspects of *jouissance*. *Plus-de-jouir* can be rendered as both "no more enjoying" and "more enjoying." The latter (i.e., "more enjoying") is rendered by Lacan as "surplus *jouissance*" with an eye to surplus value as the conceptual cornerstone of Marx's decrypting of capitalism.

But before examining the cross-resonances Lacan establishes between Marx's surplus value and his surplus *jouissance*, what about the rendering of *plus-de-jouir* as "no more enjoying"? Several of Lacan's descriptions of surplus *jouissance* reveal that *plus-de-jouir* is another name for Lacanian *désir*. Desire as *plus-de-jouir* is what remains of *jouissance* once and insofar as the latter is mediated by the signifiers of a sociolinguistic big Other. Specifically as regards castration qua the symbolic order's incisions into the singular *parlêtre* (speaking being), the pivotal 1960 *écrit* "The Subversion of the Subject and the Dialectic of Desire in the Freudian Unconscious" famously asserts near its close that "castration means that jouissance has to be refused in order to be attained on the inverse scale of the Law of desire [*La castration veut dire qu'il faut que la jouissance soit refusée, pour qu'elle puisse être atteinte sur l'échelle renversée de la Loi du désir*]."[249] Desire is generated in and through the laws of sociosymbolic mediation. This mediation also generates, along with *désir* as bound and constrained by the structures of Others, the compelling phantasm of an enjoyment-beyond-the-Law, of a noncastrated *jouissance* as pure, undiluted, limitless, and absolute. The incarnations and representations of this impossible-fully-to-obtain (but also impossible-ever-to-exorcise) spectral *jouissance* are manifestations of the Lacanian *objet petit a*. Hence, *plus-de-jouir* is the infinitely receding residue of supposedly lost *jouissance* connected with each and every instance of object *a*.[250] *Plus-de-jouir* is the donkey's carrot, the dragon forever chased but never caught—thus, *plus-de-jouir* as "no more enjoying" (or as "*manque-à-jouir*" [lack of enjoying], as Lacan puts it in 1970's "Radiophonie").[251] Various of Lacan's pronouncements regarding surplus *jouissance* substantiate the highly condensed summary I provide in this paragraph[252] (what is more, my 2005 book *Time Driven: Metapsychology and the Splitting of the Drive* covers much of this ground).

Lacan's *plus-de-jouir* (or, as he translates it into German, *Mehrlust*) is avowedly modeled on Marx's surplus value (*Mehrwert*).[253] The latter is specifically capitalist surplus *jouissance* as orbiting around *objet petit a* in the sociohistorical guise of commodities[254] (as use values bearing exchange values that themselves in turn bear surplus values). Lacan relabels Marx's *Mehrwert* as *Marxlust* qua Marxian *plus-de-jouir*.[255]

The insatiable drives of capitalists and capital-prodded consumers are the embodiments of a *plus-de-jouir* secreted by capitalism as a determinate mode of production.[256] The commodity fetishisms of both abstract-qua-quantitative hedonism (i.e., the capitalist's greed) and concrete-qua-qualitative hedonism[257] (i.e., the consumer's mania for possessions) both vainly chase after, ad infinitum and ad nauseam, schematizations of the metapsychological category of object *a* (with the surplus *jouissance* embodied in *a* incessantly slipping away, metonymically sliding off).[258] Lacan credits Marx, with Marx's fetishism of commodities, as foreshadowing this peculiar object.[259] Likewise, on one occasion, he portrays *objet petit a* as the point of overlap or convergence between Marx's surplus value and surplus *jouissance*.[260] The more (*plus*) commodities capitalism produces, the more discontent (*Unbehagen*, *malaise*, unenjoyable *jouir*) it generates in its various (class) subjects.[261] Capitalism manufactures and markets mountains of objects that quickly and inevitably go from being today's fetishes to tomorrow's garbage.[262]

In *Seminar XVII*, Lacan identifies commodities and associated consumerist spectacles as "imitation surplus *jouissance*" (*plus-de-jouir en toc*), with capitalist "crowds" (*beaucoup de monde*) continually swarming around whatever is advertised as the latest shiny "semblance" (*semblant*) of *plus-de-jouir*.[263] Capitalism, as illuminated by the Marxist critique of political economy, reveals itself to be organized around individual and collective flights toward mirages of never-to-be-attained infinite (and inexistent) enjoyments.[264] *Plus-de-jouir* is a bottomless pit[265] unable to be filled with any amount of profits or products. Or, as Mandel notes in 1972's *Late Capitalism*, "The massive psychological frustrations induced by late capitalism, among other things by the systematic inculcation of consumer dissatisfaction with consumption—without which a durable rise in consumption would be impossible—plays an important role here."[266]

Lacan's sixteenth and seventeenth seminars contain what arguably are his most detailed and significant engagements with Marx. I will return to *Seminar XVII* in a moment. In *Seminar XVI*, Lacan playfully Oedipalizes Marx's *Mehrwert* (surplus value) by associating it with the homophonous *mère verte* (green mother).[267] One indeed fairly could portray surplus value as the mother of capitalism. Capitalism's very raison d'être is the augmentation of *Mehrwert* in perpetuity.

I take the greenness of this *mère* to signal envy. The circuit M-C-M', as movement of capital in pursuit of surplus value, is envious in its extraction of everything else from everyone else. That is to say, *Mehrwert* endlessly demands of others that they sacrifice themselves and their belongings to it, to its boundless self-valorization. Additionally, many might assume that Lacan implicitly conflates *la mère verte* with the figure of the capitalist, thereby making the corresponding figure of the proletarian the addressee of this envious mother's commands. This assumption would align with a cartoon version of Marxism pitting selfish capitalists against victimized proletarians. However, as a perceptive reader of Marx, Lacan does not conflate the capitalist, as bearer or personification of capitalism's greed-as-drive, with the green mother. The depsychologized, structural envy of surplus value (*Mehrwert*) relentlessly extorts sacrifices out of capitalists too as its fungible, disposable bearers/personifications. Although *la mère verte* gives birth to capitalists, she is all too ready to cast them aside or utterly destroy them if they fail to live up to her greedy imperatives. She is an inhuman monster (or, as Han puts it, "Capital is misanthropic").[268]

Several key moments a year later, in *Seminar XVII*, corroborate my immediately preceding assertion that Lacan sees capitalists too as among the green mother's countless potential and actual victims. The first of these moments occurs in the session of November 26, 1969: "In Marx the *a* ... is recognized as functioning at the level that is articulated—on the basis of analytic discourse, not any of the others—as surplus *jouissance* [*plus-de-jouir*]. Here you have what Marx discovered as what actually happens at the level of surplus value [*plus-value*]."[269] After this linkage of Marxian *plus-value* with psychoanalytic *plus-de-jouir* and its *objet petit a*, Lacan continues: "Of course, it wasn't Marx who invented surplus value. It's just that prior to him nobody knew what its place was. It has the same ambiguous place as the one I have just mentioned, that of excess work [*travail en trop*], of surplus work [*plus-de-travail*]. 'What does it pay in?' he says. 'It pays in *jouissance*, precisely, and this has to go somewhere.'"[270] Lacan might have the Althusser of 1965's *Lire le Capital* in mind in the first two sentences here. He perhaps is thinking specifically of Althusser's contention that Marx, in forging the theory of surplus value, did not invent this ex nihilo but, rather, explicitly and systematically posited the implicit and unsystematic presuppositions of such economic predecessors as the Physiocrats, Smith, and Ricardo[271] (economists who blindly bumped up against surplus value without, in Lacan's words, "knowing what its place was"). That noted, Lacan's equation of *plus-value* with *plus-de-travail* is perfectly, orthodoxly Marxist. Marx himself defines surplus value as the value produced by the worker in excess of what the capitalist pays in terms of the worker's wages—an excess arising from surplus laboring time over and above the laboring time necessary for producing value equivalent to the worker's means of subsistence (reflected in wages).[272] Every working day without exception under capitalism contains unpaid overtime, whether this is acknowledged or not.[273]

But what about Lacan's linkage of surplus work with *jouissance*? Although the worker is paid a wage, he/she pays the capitalist back in value exceeding this wage. Despite ideological misrepresentations of labor contracts as fair-and-square deals for the workers "freely" accepting to enter into them—of course, Marx fiercely debunks these insidious, pervasive, and persistent capitalist myths—capitalism is predicated upon the structural injustice of unequal exchange between the bourgeois and the proletarian. Each working day is divided between "necessary labor" (as producing exchange value equal to the entire day's wages paid by the capitalist to the worker) and "surplus labor" (as uncompensated labor producing surplus value accruing to the capitalist at the expense of the worker). In short, surplus labor = unpaid labor = surplus value (= surplus *jouissance*, Lacan adds).

Lacan's psychoanalytic supplement to Marx's meticulous accounts of all this is that the worker "pays in *jouissance*" in exchange for wages that never compensate this loss. There is a libidinal as well as financial imbalance in this socioeconomic relationship between bourgeois and proletarian. Presumably, the "somewhere" to which the worker's *jouissance* goes, to where it is paid, is the capitalist and his/her (deep) pockets. As regards this destination of legally stolen *jouissance*, the worker may well consciously or unconsciously fantasize about something along the lines of an envious parental figure relishing ill-gotten gains with a sadistic smirk.

On the heels of the prior quoted passages from the session of November 26, 1969, Lacan injects a further twist. He states: "What's disturbing is that if one pays in *jouissance*, then one has got it, and then, once one has got it it is very urgent that one squander it. If one does not squander it, there will be all sorts of consequences."[274] *Jouissance* is akin to the proverbial hot potato. As soon as it lands in one's hands, one must quickly toss it to someone else. If one holds on to it for any length, one suffers the painful "consequence" of getting burned (with *jouissance*, if ever attained, proving to be traumatically intense or crushingly anticlimactic). This supposed enjoyment (in)exists in a state of constant circulation, always being passed on to others (and forever being imagined as really enjoyed only by these third parties). Perhaps Lacan is hinting that workers might be, at least in part, libidinally complicit in their exploitation by capital, repeatedly "squandering" the excess/surplus of their lives in payment to capitalists as a means of avoiding what otherwise would be unbearably too much and/or miserably not enough. To paraphrase one of Lacan's glosses on the Oedipus complex,[275] if the exploitation of labor were not a fact, it would have to be invented. But what about the capitalists themselves? What do they do when these payments of *jouissance* land in their laps and start oozing into the lining of their pockets?

Later in *Seminar XVII*, during its March 11, 1970, session, Lacan begins to answer these questions about capitalists. In doing so, he believes himself to be correcting Marx in certain respects: "What is masked at the level of Marx is that the master to whom this surplus *jouissance* is owed has renounced everything, and *jouissance* first up, because he has exposed himself to death, and because he remains firmly fastened to this position whose Hegelian articulation is clear."[276] In the theory of the four discourses developed in the seventeenth seminar and the contemporaneous intervention "Radiophonie," Lacan treats the capitalist as a variant of the figure of the master (*maître*), with "the discourse of the master" being one of the four discourses (along with those of university, hysteric, and analyst). He elsewhere reiterates this subsumption of capitalism under a more general template of mastery.[277] Through this identification of capitalist with master, Lacan then, as he does in the passage just quoted, casts this bourgeois power in the role of the lord as per Hegel's dialectic of "Lordship and Bondage" in the 1807 *Phenomenology of Spirit* (i.e., Hegel's master-slave dialectic, itself the veritable obsession of Lacan's own *maître* in matters Hegelian, namely, Kojève). Already in *Seminar III* (*The Psychoses* [1955–1956]), Lacan treats all historical instances of economic class conflicts as variations on the Hegelian master-slave structure.[278]

To condense a very well-known story, Hegel's lord wins what ends up being a Pyrrhic victory. His apparent triumph turns into, converges or coincides with, his actual defeat. The position of (seeming) mastery is supposed to confirm both the master's transcendence of animality (via defiance of death) and his

FROM CLOSED NEED TO INFINITE GREED   153

authority over others (represented by the slave). Instead, this position proves to be self-subverting, resulting in a regression back into what Aristotle would call the pleasures of a barnyard animal[279] furnished by servants upon whom the lord becomes abjectly dependent. And, of course, these denigrated bondsmen, in their denigration, are unable to confer authority-sustaining recognition (*Anerkennung*) upon the lord, since being recognized by a dehumanized slave counts for nothing. Moreover, as he-who-does-not-work, the Hegelian master unwittingly deprives himself of the only real *praxis* in and through which subjective agents leave lasting traces of themselves within the worked and reworked world. In exchange for risking everything in the initial struggle for dominance, the victor, through his very victory, loses everything. The sacrifice through which he becomes master proves to be self-sacrifice.[280]

In the prior quotation from *Seminar XVII*, Lacan not only alleges that the capitalist, like the Hegelian master, is (however knowingly or not) self-sacrificial—he charges Marx with having failed to learn this lesson from Hegel (with Marx's writings, starting in the early 1840s, exhibiting his familiarity with the *Phenomenology of Spirit*). But I would maintain that this is a rare instance in which Lacan uncharacteristically proves to be a less than stringently rigorous and attentive reader. In fact, Lacan here repeats Weber's mistake of failing to credit Marx with already having alighted upon and done justice to the selflessness of capitalism. As I have shown throughout much of the preceding, Marx's texts reveal him to be acutely conscious of and intellectually responsive to the renunciative character of capitalism for capitalists themselves.

Still in the seventeenth seminar's session of March 11, 1970, promptly after the previous quotation above, Lacan embellishes further upon his misdirected criticism of Marx. He proceeds:

> The master in all this makes a small effort to make everything work, in other words, he gives an order. Simply by fulfilling his function as master he loses something. It's at least through this something lost that something of *jouissance* has to be rendered to him—specifically, surplus *jouissance*.[281]

Lacan continues:

> If, by means of this relentlessness [*acharnement*] to castrate himself that he had, he hadn't computed this surplus *jouissance* [*comptabilisé ce plus-de-jouir*], if he hadn't converted it into surplus value [*fait la plus-value*], in other words if he hadn't founded capitalism, Marx would have realized that surplus value is surplus *jouissance*. None of this, of course, prevents it being the case that capitalism

154 ~❦ FROM CLOSED NEED TO INFINITE GREED

is founded by him, and that the function of surplus value is designated with complete pertinence in its devastating consequences.[282]

When Lacan claims that "simply by fulfilling his function as master he loses something," he likely is relying upon his account of specifically symbolic castration. The very signifiers of mastery (i.e., S_1s as insignias, marks, traits, etc.) are prostheses external to the speaking subject (masquerading) as master. These prostheses always remain irreducible to, not fully identical with, the subjectivity attaching itself to them. A gap stubbornly persists between subject-as-\$ and S_1-as-signifier. This gap is the cut of symbolic castration. Hence, just as the Hegelian master is defeated in and through his very moment of (seeming) triumph, so too is the Lacanian *maître* (symbolically) castrated in and through the very process of being crowned with the emblems of potency-as-noncastration. The signifiers of power simultaneously signify impotence.[283] Put in Lacanian terms, the phallus is the signifier of castration.

Likewise, the Marxian master-as-bourgeois "castrates himself" in and through assuming the very role of capitalist as the ostensible potentate of capitalism, namely, capitalism's subject-supposed-to-enjoy. Lacan almost certainly is well aware of Marx's renditions of the individual capitalist as a mere bearer (*Träger*) or personification (*Personifikation*) of capital. As seen, depsychologized greed as the circuit M-C-M′, the logic of capital itself, is a drive (*Trieb, pulsion*) in the capitalist more than the capitalist him/herself.[284] Abstract-qua-quantitative hedonism is a sociostructural thrust capable of overriding (Lacan might say "overwriting") what would otherwise be the volitions and actions of the person bearing/personifying capital and its drive. This drivenness is, as Lacan indicates in *Seminar XXII* (*R.S.I.* [1974–1975]), the *père-version*, the perversion of the father, for the paternal figure of the capitalist-as-master[285] (in addition to the capitalist's structurally dictated sadism and psychopathy, there is also, for Marx as well as Weber, his/her miserliness and masochism). Therefore, insofar as the "symbolic" in Lacan's "symbolic castration" also refers to the symbolic order as a set of social structures akin to Hegel's objective spirit and/or Marx's infrastructure-superstructure arrangement, Marx's capitalist, seen from a Lacanian perspective, indeed should count as symbolically castrated.

At one point in the seventeenth seminar, Lacan remarks, "it is only the phallus that is happy—not the bearer [*le porteur*] of said."[286] Lacan's French *porteur* is the equivalent of Marx's German *Träger*. And, as noted, the Lacanian phallus is itself the signifier of castration (i.e., the avatar of symbolic castration). So, one must say of the capitalist: It is only capital that is happy—not the bearer of said. Whether Lacan himself, as a somewhat shameless French bourgeois bon vivant, intends for his audience to shed tears on behalf of the poor, castrated capitalists, the mere bearers of M-C-M', is difficult to tell.

In the second of the two preceding block quotations from the seventeenth seminar, Lacan asserts psychoanalytic metapsychology's explanatory priority *vis-à-vis* historical materialism. For him, Marx's surplus value is a species of the genus surplus *jouissance*, with the former being a historically peculiar instantiation of the latter. He evidently assumes that Marx (and Marxists) would have to take this as a critical correction. Lacan maintains that Marx's focus on capitalism-specific surplus value (i.e., the species) blinds him to the transhistorical category of (surplus) *jouissance* (i.e., the genus). Marx purportedly cannot see the forest of *plus-de-jouir* for the tree of *Mehrwert* ("if he hadn't converted it into surplus value [*fait la plus-value*], in other words if he hadn't founded capitalism, Marx would have realized that surplus value is surplus *jouissance*").[287]

As my earlier unpacking and reconstruction of Marx's drive theory indicates, Marx actually is sensitive to such genus-species distinctions. He refers, as underscored previously, to "a particular form of the drive" (*eine besondre Form des Triebs*),[288] thereby signaling a difference between drive as such and its specific instantiations. Hence, it is unclear whether Marx would object, as Lacan presumes he would, to Lacan's analytic insistence on distinguishing between, on the one hand, the socially nonspecific categories of libidinal economics (here, surplus *jouissance*) and, on the other hand, the socially specific manifestations of these categories as mediated by political economics (here, surplus value). Near the start of this chapter, I argued that Marx is not the unreserved, reductive historicizer many view him as being (including Lacan in this context). With Marx's Homer problem and drive theory (with the latter as part of a general philosophical anthropology underpinning historical materialism), he is not automatically averse to the sorts of amendments suggested by Lacan's remarks in the seventeenth seminar.

The second quotation above from *Seminar XVII* also refers to the notion of "computing surplus *jouissance*" (*comptabiliser plus-de-jouir*). This leads into the last of the moments of concern to me in the seventeenth seminar, a moment likewise featuring this idea of *comptabiliser* (*comme compter*). Near the end of the session of June 10, 1970, Lacan observes:

> Something changed in the master's discourse at a certain point in history. We are not going to break our backs finding out if it was because of Luther, or Calvin, or some unknown traffic of ships around Genoa, or in the Mediterranean Sea, or anywhere else, for the important point is that on a certain day surplus

jouissance became calculable, could be counted, totalized [*le plus-de-jouir se compte, se comptabilise, se totalise*]. This is where what is called the accumulation of capital begins.[289]

Lacan's wording indicates his deemphasizing of the historicist sensibilities of three related theoretical perspectives: Hegel's (Luther), Weber's (Calvin), and that of Marxian historical materialism ("some unknown traffic of ships"). Consistent with his maintenance of a level distinction between the dimensions covered by analytic metapsychology and historical materialism, Lacan pinpoints the transition from socioeconomic premodernity to modernity proper ("Something changed in the master's discourse at a certain point in history") at the tipping point of the phase transition wherein transhistorical surplus *jouissance* historically becomes mathematized, mediated by quantification, thereby becoming surplus value ("the important point is that on a certain day surplus *jouissance* became calculable, could be counted, totalized [*le plus-de-jouir se compte, se comptabilise, se totalise*]. This is where what is called the accumulation of capital begins"). Already in *Seminar XIII*, Lacan recognizes that the historical emergence of capitalism induces a fundamental mutation in *jouissance*.[290] And, with this, my own analytic labors here come full circle: This is Lacan's version of "from closed need to infinite greed."

Before concluding, I should note that Lacan's decision to speak of "totalization" in the above quotation is strange and questionable. He proposes that rendering *jouissance* computable, calculable, or countable also renders it totalizable. I assume he means "totalization" as synonymous with the accumulation designated in the phrase "the accumulation of capital." But Marx himself as well as Lacan elsewhere both indicate that the capitalist mathematization of all things (including the seemingly most intimate) infinitizes and, hence, detotalizes *jouissance*, drives, and the like.[291] It is crucial to appreciate that the libidinal unboundedness opened up by quantitative infinitization liquidates any actual or potential totality as final end or ultimate limit.

It now can be anticipated, with the combined lights of Marx and Lacan, that if one ends up at the very top of the *Forbes* billionaires list—God forbid—one will hurl one's enormous mass of accumulated surplus value/*jouissance* into philanthropic endeavors. One thereby not only evades getting burned by *jouissance* attained but, in the process, launders one's past misdeeds, airbrushes one's legacy. Nobody dares be caught dead wallowing in *plus-de-jouir*. Following the Lacan of "Radiophonie," one even can say that capitalism forecloses surplus value by turning it into an infinite void, a never-ending hole, everyone, capitalists included, strains to avoid at all costs.[292] No sooner does the bourgeois (re)obtain it than he/she "squanders" it again. The capitalist repeatedly sends surplus value, and the surplus *jouissance* clinging to it, back into circulation via reinvestment, philanthropy, and/or buying politicians.

As it turns out, capitalism is not good at satisfying selfishness, its supposed primary strength much touted by its defenders and apologists. Agreeing that it at least provides substantial private satisfactions is still to grant it too much credit. Even on the terms capitalism sets for itself, it is wretchedly bankrupt— and this also for Smith's imagined lucky few apart from his admitted unfortunate majority.[293] In actuality, nobody gets truly to enjoy capitalism.[294]

3

The Self-Cleaning Fetish

Repression Under the Shadow of Fictitious Capital

§12. MODES OF THE UNCONSCIOUS: FROM THE IDEOLOGIES OF POLITICAL ECONOMY TO THE DYNAMICS OF LIBIDINAL ECONOMY

Starting with the pioneering efforts of the likes of Reich, Fenichel, and Marcuse, there have been, as I have detailed already, repeated attempts at brokering a satisfying marriage between Marxism and psychoanalysis. Of course, the early decades of the twentieth century throw up discouraging developments flying in the face of Marx's own nineteenth-century hopes and predictions. Understandably, psychoanalysis is seen by the founders of Freudo-Marxism, beginning in the late 1930s, as promising to help explain how and why then-recent events defied the prognostications of classical historical materialism.

Why do saber-rattling nationalisms and antisemitic fascisms arise and unleash mass-scale destructive fury? Why does the Great Depression, that catastrophic global economic crisis of unprecedented proportions, not trigger socialist or communist revolutions in capitalist countries hit especially hard by it? For those twentieth-century Marxists who make the first Marxist turns to Freud and his work, analytic theories about the unconscious, fantasies, family life, the death drive, secondary gain from suffering, and the like appear to be valuable explanatory supplements to an economically based rendition of social history.

Analysis seems to teach, somewhat counterintuitively, that people are disturbingly prone to hug their chains, sing in their cages, and prefer sadistically exploiting and masochistically being exploited to life-enhancing solidarity and cooperation. Perhaps capitalism, fascism, jingoism, and warfare scratch libidinal itches Marx's keen intellect failed to detect. Analysis's psychical subjects certainly look very little like rational socioeconomic actors preordained sooner or later to arrive at an enlightened self-awareness of their true material interests in the guise of (proletarian) class consciousness.

Relatedly, but at a more general theoretical level, projects seeking to interweave Marxism and psychoanalysis involve an appreciation of affinities between Marx's account of ideology and Freud's concept of the unconscious. Indeed, Paul Ricoeur is not without justification in famously identifying Marx and Freud (along with Friedrich Nietzsche) as "great hermeneuts of suspicion,"[1] namely, as suspiciously analyzing occluded dimensions of societies (the ideological as per Marx) and psyches (the unconscious as per Freud). And as the founders of Freudo-Marxism already contend, the social and the psychical are inextricably intertwined with each other as mutual mediators. This has two complementary consequences. On the one hand, Marxism needs supplementation by psychoanalysis so as to register adequately the libidinal economics influencing political economics.[2] On the other hand, psychoanalysis needs supplementation by Marxism so as to register adequately the impact of labor, class, commodities, and capital(ism) on the psyche right down to the levels of drives, dreams, and repressed formations of the unconscious of various sorts.[3]

Furthermore, both the Marxist and psychoanalytic traditions each critically ponder the topic of money in particular. Yet the now almost century-long series of endeavors to synthesize these two traditions has left their parallel reflections on monetary matters underintegrated. Those Marxists interested in psychoanalysis tend to be marked by the Western Marxist tendency to neglect or downplay the centrality of Marx's economics to his sprawling theoretical framework. As a result, they spend most of their time employing the superstructural, rather than the infrastructural, components of Marxism in forging links to analytic metapsychology.

The analysts, for their part, have been preoccupied primarily with money as it features in the analytic clinic of the neuroses. Even on occasions when analytic thinkers consider money's possible metapsychological reverberations, they tend to do so unequipped with anything even remotely resembling Marx's sophisticated historical-materialist critique of political economy. Freud himself is a case in point here. When not discussing the role of cash in treatment in terms of the analyst's fees,[4] he insistently tethers the symbolico-psychical significance of money to anal erotism—with the spending or saving of monetary amounts being a sublimated version of the release or retention of fecal matter.[5] Numerous analysts, from Freud's contemporary Sandor Ferenczi onward, continue in the vein of emphasizing the tight link between wealth and anality (although some argue for connections of money with orality and/or genitality too).[6]

Of course, Marx himself insists on the distinctive status of money as a "universal equivalent," as the peculiar commodity uniquely standing in for all other commodities. Its openness to representing anything and everything under the sun should caution against psychoanalytic attempts to bind the significance of monetary means to just one or several specific psychical-libidinal contents (such as oral, anal, and/or genital sources or stages). Like the Lacanian signifier, money is a type of ultimately meaningless stuff that, in its nonsensical materiality, can and does take on proliferating, shifting ensembles of meanings and referents—without, for all that, money ever being reducible to any of these multiple, changing significations. Along these lines, Lacan, in the *écrit* "Seminar on 'The Purloined Letter,'" characterizes money as "the signifier that most thoroughly annihilates every signification."[7]

Apropos the Marx-Lacan rapport in particular, one could say that what the signifier is for the Lacanian theory of the unconscious money qua universal equivalent is for the Marxian critique of political economy.[8] Moreover, money's roles in ideological phenomena as per Marxism (particularly varieties of "fetishism") reveal it to facilitate repression-like obfuscating processes constitutive of a specifically capitalist socioeconomic unconscious. Indeed, as I will argue, looking at the functions of currency in the formation of ideologies as per historical materialism is at least as, if not more, informative for psychoanalysis than the traditional analytic tendency to perform ontogenetic reductions of money to one or more sexualized organs or phases. In short, analyzing the ideological effects of money perhaps unexpectedly promises to shed further light on the genesis and structure of psychoanalysis's unconscious.

In Marxist discussions of the connected topics of currency and commodity fetishism (as reliant mainly on volume 1 of *Capital*), it often is left underappreciated that such fetishism reaches its apotheosis only with the development of interest-bearing money-as-capital (i.e., with the emergence of fictitious finance capital in the guises of credit, banking, etc. as dealt with in volume 3 of *Capital*). In psychoanalytic treatments of money from Freud himself onward, as I observe above, monetary means typically are tied to libidinal sources and stages in the subject's ontogenetic life history. Moreover, of course, the term "fetishism" features in the Freudian field too in ways that partially cross-resonate with Marxian commodity fetishism.

The present chapter will begin with two gestures apropos, first, Marxism and, second, psychoanalysis. With respect to Marxism, I counterbalance the usual, long-standing (over)emphasis on commodity fetishism as per the first volume of *Das Kapital* with a foregrounding of this fetishism as per the third volume. With respect to psychoanalysis, I shift away from its traditional fixation on reducing financial matters to libidinal contents. I explore instead the implications of the forms of capitalist fetishism for reconsidering the forms of intrasubjective defense mechanisms.

This leads me to posit a complementary twist on Lacan's dictum according to which "repression is always the return of the repressed":[9] The return of the repressed sometimes is the most effective repression. To pose a rhetorical question paraphrasing Bertolt Brecht: What is the laundering of money compared with the laundering that is money? Appreciating this question is important not only for the Marxist account of the unconscious of socioeconomic ideologies but also promises to be transformative for the psychoanalytic account of the unconscious as constituted by psychical defensive dynamics.

§13. MONEY LAUNDERING ITSELF: COMMODITIES, INTEREST, AND CAPITALISM'S QUOTIDIAN OBFUSCATIONS

Section 4 of chapter 1 of the first volume of *Das Kapital*, the section entitled "The Fetishism of the Commodity and Its Secret," is perhaps the most commented-on portion of Marx's best-known book. This section's opening paragraph alone contains immense theoretical riches with far-reaching implications.[10] It is more than understandable why this stretch of volume 1 of *Capital* has seduced and mesmerized so many readers of Marx's 1867 magnum opus.

The brilliance of Marx's discussion of commodity fetishism in the first volume of *Capital* sometimes blinds readers to the fact that such fetishism reaches its highest, purest form only in the third volume of *Capital*. Not until capitalism generates out of itself the entity Marx names "interest-bearing capital" (IBC), that is, not until as late as part 5 of the third volume of *Das Kapital*, does fetishism achieve its culmination. This apogee comes to inflect capitalism in its entirety. IBC, once it emerges, colors vast swaths of capitalism's infrastructural and superstructural features. For the mature Marx of the critique of political economy in its sweeping but unfinished majesty, both the economics and ideology of capitalism cannot be fully understood without appreciating the pivotal position of IBC in the (il)logic of capital.[11]

I will not retraverse here in its entirety the well-trodden ground of "The Fetishism of the Commodity and Its Secret" in *Capital*, volume 1. However, a passage therein crucially foreshadows the treatment of money as IBC in the third volume of *Das Kapital*. This passage reads:

162　　THE SELF-CLEANING FETISH

> Reflection on the forms of human life, hence also scientific analysis [*wissenschaftliche Analyse*] of those forms, takes a course directly opposite to their real development [*der wirklichen Entwicklung*]. Reflection begins *post festum*, and therefore with the results of the process of development ready to hand. The forms which stamp products as commodities and which are therefore the preliminary requirements for the circulation of commodities, already possess the fixed quality of natural forms of social life before man seeks to give an account, not of their historical character, for in his eyes they are immutable, but of their content and meaning. Consequently, it was solely the analysis of the prices of commodities which led to the establishment of their character as values. It is however precisely this finished form of the world of commodities [*der Warenwelt*]—the money form [*die Geldform*]—which conceals the social character of private labour and the social relations between the individual workers, by making those relations appear as relations between material objects, instead of revealing them plainly. If I state that coats or boots stand in a relation to linen because the latter is the universal incarnation of abstract human labour, the absurdity of the statement is self-evident. Nevertheless, when the producers of coats and boots bring these commodities into a relation with linen, or with gold or silver [and this makes no difference here], as the universal equivalent, the relation between their own private labour and the collective labour of society appears to them in exactly this absurd form [*dieser verrückten Form*].[12]

The first two sentences of this quotation echo a simultaneously methodological and metaphysical stipulation stated by Marx in both the 1857 introduction to the *Grundrisse* and the 1873 "Postface to the Second Edition" of the first volume of *Capital*.[13] This stipulation is very much in line with Marx's motif of "inverting" or "turning right side up" Hegel's alleged idealist derivation of material being out of immaterial thinking. It states that theoretical thought and ideas (including the historical-materialist critique of political economy as "*wissenschaftliche Analyse*") are secondary reflections of extramental, real-world entities and events. Thinking is "*post festum*" vis-à-vis being. Moreover, as in a camera obscura and as per the mature Marx's analytic procedure inspired specifically by Hegel's *Science of Logic*, the developmental order of scientific thinking's categories and concepts, moving from the abstract to the concrete, reflects in precisely reversed form the "real development" (*der wirklichen Entwicklung*) of the order of actually existing objects and processes. This latter order, insofar as it generates out of itself thinking generally up to and including scientific thinking, moves in the opposite direction from the concrete to the abstract (or "from

THE SELF-CLEANING FETISH   163

earth to heaven" [*von der Erde zum Himmel*], as Marx and Engels already put it in 1845 in *The German Ideology*).[14]

Much of the rest of the passage quoted above zeroes in on the distinction between the values and prices of commodities as per Marx's labor theory of value (a theory indebted primarily to Smith and Ricardo). For Marx, a commodity, as a specifically capitalist phenomenon (as opposed to a mere product, good, or ware in its bareness as a physical thing), is a material use value bearing a social exchange value, with this exchange value containing a quota of surplus value (i.e., unpaid excess labor time). The values of commodities are created in the spheres of production by the activities of socially divided labor (as per Smith and Ricardo).[15] Their prices are realized in the spheres of exchange by their interactions with other commodities in the marketplace. So, in the real development of the order of being, there is a movement from the production of value to the price of exchange. And, as Marx stresses in the preceding quotation, economic analysis is a backward reflection of this movement. Such analysis starts with prices determined in the exchange of things and derives "*post festum*" the values underlying prices previously generated by social production ("it was solely the analysis of the prices of commodities which led to the establishment of their character as values").

Of course, this passage is situated in *Capital*'s section on "The Fetishism of the Commodity and Its Secret." As is common knowledge, this section famously characterizes commodity fetishism as an inverting, alienating illusion:

> It is nothing but the definite social relation between men themselves which assumes here, for them, the fantastic form of a relation between things [*Es ist nur das bestimmte gesellschaftliche Verhältnis der Menschen selbst, welches hier für sie die phantasmagorische Form eines Verhältnisses von Dingen annimmt*]. In order, therefore, to find an analogy we must take flight into the misty realm of religion [*die Nebelregion der religiösen Welt*]. There the products of the human brain [*Kopfes*] appear as autonomous figures endowed with a life of their own, which enter into relations both with each other and with the human race. So it is in the world of commodities [*der Warenwelt*] with the products of men's hands. I call this the fetishism which attaches itself to the products of labour as soon as they are produced as commodities, and is therefore inseparable from the production of commodities.[16]

A couple of pages later, Marx adds in this vein apropos commodities' exchange values:

These magnitudes vary continually, independently of the will, foreknowledge and actions of the exchangers. Their own movement within society has for them the form of a movement made by things [*Ihre eigene gesellschaftliche Bewegung besitzt für sie die Form einer Bewegung von Sachen*], and these things, far from being under their control, in fact control them.[17]

Just after "The Fetishism of the Commodity and Its Secret," Marx reiterates and underscores these points.[18] In Marx's view, capitalism's fetishistic insanity/ inversion/wrongheadedness (à la the connotations of the German *verkehrt* and its permutations as used by Marx) goes so far as to make relations between socially laboring human producers appear as object-like materiality and to make relations between commodities being exchanged appear as subject-like sociality.[19] And, as Marx makes abundantly clear in both his choice of the word "fetish" and his explicit references to religiosity ("the misty realm of religion" [*die Nebelregion der religiösen Welt*]), the influence of Feuerbach's 1841 *The Essence of Christianity* lingers well beyond both Marx's youthful embrace of Feuerbachianism as well as his 1845 settling of accounts with it.[20]

As in the early-to-mid 1840s, so too in 1867: The alienation Feuerbach discovers within the realms of religion is discerned by Marx as operative within the secular realms of politics and, especially, economics.[21] The essence of "alienation" (*Entfremdung*, *Entäusserung*) here amounts to an inversion in which conditioning, determining subject (humanity, society, producer) and conditioned, determined object (divinity, state, product) change places. The following inversions of the truth are thus arrived at via alienation at the levels of the religious, the political, and the economic, respectively: God makes humans and their world; the state fashions society and its myriad nongovernmental features; capital creates labor and its products. Thereby, tails come to wag dogs.[22]

What is more, these alienations are not just mental inversions but also material ones. They are all-too-real abstractions.[23] This insistence on objective, in addition to subjective, alienation is one of the later Marx's decisive steps beyond Feuerbach.[24] The tail not only appears in thought to wag the dog but actually comes to do so in being itself. Or, to qualify Marx's 1843/1844 declaration according to which "*Man makes religion*, religion does not make man,"[25] after man makes religion, religion reciprocally comes to remake man himself.

Marx's *A Contribution to the Critique of Political Economy* contains a discussion foreshadowing his subsequent explicit introduction, in the first volume of *Capital*, of the concept of commodity fetishism as a real abstraction in which relations between persons really are transformed into relations between things[26] (as I. I. Rubin puts this, "Fetishism is not only a phenomenon of social

THE SELF-CLEANING FETISH   ☙   165

consciousness, but of social being.")[27] This 1859 passage strikingly anticipating 1867's "The Fetishism of the Commodity and Its Secret" reads:

> Money is not a symbol, just as the existence of a use-value in the form of a commodity is no symbol. A social relation of production appears as something existing apart from individual human beings, and the distinctive relations into which they enter in the course of production in society appear as the specific properties of a thing—it is this perverted appearance, this prosaically real, and by no means imaginary, mystification [*diese Verkehrung und nicht eingebildete, sondern prosaisch reelle Mystifikation*] that is characteristic of all social forms of labour positing exchange-value. This perverted appearance manifests itself merely in a more striking manner in money [*Geld*] that it does in commodities.[28]

Marx's talk here of "this perverted appearance, this prosaically real, and by no means imaginary, mystification [*diese Verkehrung und nicht eingebildete, sondern prosaisch reelle Mystifikation*]" indicates the material objectivity, over and above the subjective ideality, of the ideology of commodity fetishism.[29] (Already in "A Contribution to the Critique of Hegel's Philosophy of Right. Introduction" [1843/1844], Marx characterizes status quo states and societies as in and of themselves inverted, as elements of an objectively inverted world [*eine verkehrte Welt*].)[30] For instance, a Marxist theoretician intimately familiar with "The Fetishism of the Commodity and Its Secret" but living surrounded by capitalism might subjectively be under no illusions about the true nature of the commodities confronting him/her in the quotidian consumer marketplaces he/she frequents. Nonetheless, insofar as this enlightened cynic still is compelled to participate in the material reality of purchasing and consuming within capitalism's spheres of exchange, he/she remains objectively in thrall to commodity fetishism qua the inverting of precedence between producing subjects and produced objects.[31] Put differently, under capitalism, relations between persons (as socially laboring producers) really are—they do not merely seem to be—determined by relations between things (as exchange relations between competing commodities).[32] The Marxist critic can read fetishism's "social hieroglyphic" (*gesellschaftliche Hieroglyphe*).[33] But so long as he/she is stuck within capitalism, he/she can only keep reading and rereading this, nothing more.[34]

The last sentence of the preceding quotation from 1859 ("This perverted appearance manifests itself merely in a more striking manner in money [*Geld*] that it does in commodities") points toward Marx's subsequent identification of IBC as the pinnacle of commodity fetishism in the third volume of *Capital*. The "money" this 1859 sentence refers to would be currency specifically in its function as commanding a rate of interest based on its omnipresent potential in capitalism to serve as capital, namely, as potentially generative of surplus value once released into capital's circuit of M-C-M'.[35] Soon after "The Fetishism of the Commodity and Its Secret" in *Capital*, volume 1, Marx identifies the "riddle of the money fetish" (*Rätsel des Geldfetisches*), this shiny and glittering "magic of money" (*die Magie des Geldes*), as the key to "the riddle of the commodity fetish, now become visible and dazzling to our eyes [*Das* Rätsel des Geldfetisches *ist daher nur das sichtbar gewordene, die Augen blendende* Rätsel des Warenfetisches]" through gold and silver currencies.[36] So, what, for the Marx of both *A Contribution to the Critique of Political Economy* and *Das Kapital*, makes money, the commodity par excellence as the universal equivalent, an even more "striking manifestation" of the "perverted appearance" that is capitalistic fetishism?

Even before Marx focuses on IBC (and, along with it, the category of "fictitious capital" as speculative finance and the like),[37] he identifies, also in *Capital*, volume 3, a fashion in which money sustains illusions concealing the true magnitude of oppression and extortion under capitalism. As is well known, Marx distinguishes between surplus value and profit, with the latter as only a portion of the former. In addition to the capitalist's profit, some of which he/she consumes and much of which he/she reinvests, surplus value also is divided into landowner's rent, financier's interest, and government's taxes.

The rates of surplus value and profit are calculated differently. The rate of surplus value is the "'" of M-C-M' measured against only the variable capital (i.e., the labor power purchased by the owner of the means of production) of the capitalist's total capital. This total capital consists of constant capital (i.e., both fixed capital as buildings, machinery, etc. and circulating capital as raw materials, fuels, etc.) in addition to variable capital (as itself also circulating capital). The rate of profit, by contrast, is the "'" of M-C-M' measured against the total capital.

Hence, the rate of profit always will appear lower than the rate of surplus value (so long as any constant capital is involved in the production process). That said, the rate of surplus value is the real measure of the exploitation of labor (as variable capital) by capital.[38] This exploitation thus gets diluted, diminished, and dissimulated by a foregrounding of the rate of profit instead.[39] Moreover, the rate of profit deceptively makes it seem as though the total capital, including constant capital, generates surplus value. Hence, money-as-M' viewed as profit vis-à-vis total capital, rather than as surplus value vis-à-vis variable capital only, whitewashes capital's injustices. One aspect of capital is money as self-laundering.[40] Joan Robinson appears oblivious to the masking of

THE SELF-CLEANING FETISH   167

exploitation by profit when she objects that "there is no reason why the *rate* of exploitation should be treated as either logically or historically prior to the rate of profit."[41]

As Rudolf Hilferding observes in his 1910 study *Finance Capital*, "the direct connection between labour and the yield on capital is already partially obscured in the rate of profit, and completely so in the rate of interest."[42] Hilferding's observation about (the rate of) interest being an even more thorough masking of exploitative surplus value than (the rate of) profit will be important to and clarified by what follows. Moreover, Hilferding makes a related and more general point about how capitalism conceals its injustices by dissolving them in the icy waters of quantification, through lying with its myriad mathematical dishonesties, its statistics, figures, balance sheets, accounting books, etc.[43]

Indeed, in chapter 23 ("Interest and Profit of Enterprise") of part 5 ("The Division of Profit Into Interest and Profit of Enterprise") of *Capital*, volume 3, Marx himself compares interest and profit. Therein, he observes: "The social form of capital devolves on interest, but expressed in a neutral and indifferent form; the economic function of capital devolves on profit of enterprise, but with the specifically capitalist character of this function removed [*aber von dem bestimmten, kapitalistischen Charakter dieser Funktion abstrahiert*]."[44] In this context, profit qua "profit of enterprise" (*Unternehmergewinns*) is associated by Marx with "wages of superintendence" (*Aufsichtslohns*).[45] Both profit of enterprise and wages of superintendence are portions of capital-appropriated surplus value that misleadingly are made to present the capitalist not as a nonlaboring owner of capital but as a laborer earning his/her fair share of income through specific forms of work (such as researching market trends, courting investors, planning business strategies, overseeing and managing his/her employees, and the like).[46]

The capitalist qua capitalist, as the mere bearer or personification of capital's logic of M-C-M',[47] is a nonworking possessor of the means of production and a buyer of the labor power of others. The execution of enterprising and/or superintending labors, even when carried out by the person who also bears/personifies capital, is not performed by the capitalist qua capitalist, namely, insofar as he/she is an owner of the means of production[48] (Smith already, in *The Wealth of Nations*, denies that profit has anything to do with the supposed labor of inspection, oversight, or supervision by persons associated with the functions of capital).[49] In Marx's above-quoted words, through profit of enterprise, "the specifically capitalist character of" the capitalist as representative of M-C-M' is "removed" (or, one could say, repressed). Relatedly, given that profit of enterprise, as profit, still is a portion of surplus value, this profit is derived by the

168   THE SELF-CLEANING FETISH

capitalist from the unpaid labor time of those he/she hires and exploits as variable capital—and not from his/her own labor of whatever sort.[50]

Profit of enterprise and wages of superintendence could be said to repress the fact that capitalists expropriate the fruits of the labor of others. These obfuscating repackagings of surplus labor and the quota of profit it contains do so by passing off capitalists as themselves laborers engaged in different but equally laborious work (planning, overseeing, etc.) alongside the rest of their workers—"The labour of exploiting is just as much labour as the labour that is exploited."[51] Yet as Marx notes at this very same moment in the third volume of *Capital*, the thereby repressed truth of capital's nonlaboring extraction of surplus value from labor returns in the guise of the quantum of interest inevitably accompanying the profit disguised as profit of enterprise and wages of superintendence. Adequately appreciating this point requires the further elaboration of Marx's account of interest (primarily as per *Capital*, volume 3), an elaboration I will proceed to provide momentarily.

For now, before I unpack the significance of IBC in the historical-materialist critical analysis of capitalism, I should make two observations with implications for what ensues below. First, the deceiving division between profit of enterprise and interest is rendered even more deceptive in tending to become manifest as a split between two (seemingly) separate groups of capitalists, namely, financial/money capitalists (who receive interest) and industrial/commercial capitalists (who receive profit).[52] Industrial capitalists easily can appear to be productive themselves through their close connection to processes of producing commodities through industry by laborers. These capitalists therefore look as though they deservedly earn what is presented as their profit of enterprise and/or wages of superintendence.

Financial capitalists, by contrast with industrial capitalists, more glaringly display capital's separateness from labor's productivity in that they reap their rewards without themselves having any direct hand in the productive enterprises to which they lend their money. Bankers, speculators, and their ilk more readily come to enjoy the unsavory reputation of getting something for nothing. But such is the fundamental but inconvenient truth of all capitalists (whether financiers, industrialists, or whatever), of capitalism in general: Capital gets something (i.e., surplus value, from which is generated both the industrialist's profit and the financier's interest) for nothing (with surplus value as unpaid labor, as surplus labor producing an uncompensated excess of exchange value over and above the exchange value of its wages as its means of subsistence, its means of producing/reproducing its own power). The vulture-like speculative investor, scorned for contributing nothing to the "real economy" while

THE SELF-CLEANING FETISH   169

vampirically siphoning off money in the form of interest (as returns on investment, etc.), is the symptom embodying the truth of capital as inherently exploitative (as Engels already indicates in his 1843 "Outlines of a Critique of Political Economy").[53] Yet as G. A. Cohen remarks, "the fetishism of interest reinforces the fetishism of industrial capital."[54]

The second observation I wish to put forward before delving into the details of IBC à la Marx has to do with the parallels I insinuate above between Marx's critique of political economy and psychoanalysis via talk of "repression." More precisely, in what immediately precedes, I deploy a pair of correlations. On the one hand, I associate profit of enterprise, wages of superintendence, and industrial capitalists with repression. This *Verdrängung* conceals the fact that capital, organized around surplus value as the source of all profit, interest, and rent under capitalism, exists solely through getting something for nothing via its unequal (but still perfectly legal) exchange with labor. On the other hand, interest and financial capitalists are associated by me, following Marx's own indications, with the return of this same repressed.

However the Marxian theorization of interest I am about to reconstruct suggests that interest, as the return of the repressed, itself even more potently represses in turn the very fact initially repressed under the veneer of the industrial capitalist's profit of enterprise and wages of superintendence. In this case, it seems that the return of the repressed is not even a practically inefficacious intellectual acceptance of the repressed as per psychoanalysis. Rather, with IBC in relation to other forms of capital, the return of the repressed strangely reinforces the original repression. Or, in the manner of a Hegelian-style convergence of opposites, the moment of clearest revelation (i.e., the return of the repressed) coincides with that of the most obscuring concealment (i.e., a redoubling of the initial repression). Perhaps, as per one of the lessons of Edgar Allan Poe's "The Purloined Letter" dear to Lacan, the best way to hide indeed is in plain sight.

§14. THE MOTHER OF EVERY INSANE FORM: INTEREST-BEARING CAPITAL AND THE ACME OF COMMODITY FETISHISM

When discussing IBC in the third volume of *Capital*, Marx repeatedly emphasizes its status as the very peak and quintessence of the fetishism first delineated in volume 1. In particular, part 5, chapter 24 ("Interest-Bearing Capital as the Superficial Form of the Capital Relation") of volume 3 stresses IBC's

170   THE SELF-CLEANING FETISH

epitomization of capitalistic commodity fetishism. Several passages in this chapter deserve close attention.

Before proceeding any further, I should elucidate how Marx defines IBC in the opening chapter of part 5 of *Capital*, volume 3, namely, chapter 21 ("Interest-Bearing Capital").[55] IBC is money functioning as itself a peculiar type of commodity. With all commodities combining both use value and exchange value, IBC is money that as (potential) capital has the use value of (potentially) producing more exchange value than it itself initially embodies before being employed in the process of M-C-M'. That is to say, IBC is money with the use value of promising to generate exchange value that contains surplus value. The rate of interest paid by the borrower to the lender represents the market price of IBC's distinctive use value of yielding surplus value.[56] This is the essence of IBC as per Marx.[57] It also ought to be noted in passing that IBC's definitional link to the economic category of surplus value renders it a specifically capitalist phenomenon. With all of this clarified, I can shift to focusing on Marx's identification of IBC as the fullest realization of capitalist commodity fetishism.

The opening paragraph of chapter 24 (in part 5 of volume 3) compares and contrasts the elementary formula for capital as industrial/commercial capital, M-C-M', with the formula for financial/money capital as IBC, M-M'. Marx states:

> In interest-bearing capital, the capital relationship reaches its most superficial and fetishized form [*Im zinstragenden Kapital erreicht das Kapitalverhältnis seine äußerlichste und fetischartigste Form*]. Here we have *M-M'*, money that produces more money, self-valorizing value [*sich selbst verwertenden Wert*], without the process that mediates the two extremes. In commercial capital, *M-C-M'*, at least the general form of the capitalist movement is present, even though this takes place only in the circulation sphere, so that profit appears as merely profit upon alienation; but for all that, it presents itself as the product of a social *relation* [*eines gesellschaftlichen* Verhältnisses], not the product of a mere *thing* [*eines bloßen* Dings]. The form of commercial capital still exhibits a process, the unity of opposing phases, a movement that breaks down into two opposite procedures, the purchase and sale of commodities. This is obliterated [*ausgelöscht*] in *M-M'*, the form of interest-bearing capital. . . . It is a *relation* of quantities, a ratio between the principal as a given value, and itself as self-valorizing value, as a principal that has produced a surplus-value. And . . . capital presents itself in this way, as this directly self-valorizing value, for all active capitalists, whether they function with their own capital or with borrowed capital.[58]

THE SELF-CLEANING FETISH   171

This passage warrants careful unpacking. To begin with, its first two sentences resonate with the characterization of IBC as the apex of commodity fetishism offered by Marx in an addendum to part 3 of *Theories of Surplus-Value*. Therein, he comments: "The most complete fetish is *interest-bearing capital*. This is the original starting-point of capital—money—and the formula M-C-M' is reduced to its two extremes—M-M'—money which creates more money. It is the original and general formula of capital reduced to a meaningless [*sinnloses*] résumé."[59] As per *Theories of Surplus-Value*, IBC's fetishistic formula M-M' (i.e., "money that produces more money, self-valorizing value," "money which creates more money") is meaningless, namely, senseless qua *sinnloses*. And, as per *Capital*, volume 3, it is "superficial" (*äußerliche*) too, a word also used in the very title of the third volume's twenty-fourth chapter. Marx's choice of the adjective *äußerlichste* in the quotation above from *Capital*, volume 3, chapter 24, is indeed significant. It condenses within itself a cluster of connotations reinforcing my claims about IBC as a peculiar sort of return of the repressed within capitalism.

The adjective *äußerlichste* indeed can be translated into English as "most superficial." This translation resonates with Marx's use of *sinnloses* in the just-quoted remark from *Theories of Surplus-Value*. This superficiality of M-M' is simplicity to the point of senseless, tautological stupidity, the idiocy of pure identity as a thing's reflexive relating to itself ($A = A$).[60] Much later in volume 3 of *Capital*, in chapter 48 ("The Trinity Formula"), Marx similarly associates the meaninglessness of M-M' with irrationality—"The formula capital-interest is certainly the most irrational [*begriffsloseste*] formula for capital, but it is a formula for it."[61] According to this Marx, then, the culmination of fetishism with IBC is both "*sinnloses*" ("meaningless") and "*begriffsloseste*" ("most irrational"). Hilferding echoes Marx in describing M-M' as "*begriffsloseste*" ("inscrutable").[62]

Additionally, to be superficial qua *äußerliche* is to be manifestly illuminated. It is to be an exposed surface out in the open. In this sense, Marx is indicating, through his choice of this adjective, that finance capital's M-M' makes glaringly explicit the fetishism remaining more implicit in commercial/industrial capital's M-C-M'.[63] As per *Capital*, volume 1, commodity fetishism essentially involves relations between persons being translated into relations between things. Referring to this characterization of the phenomenon, the preceding block quotation from the third volume of *Das Kapital* explains exactly how IBC intensifies and perfects capitalistic fetishism.

Before elucidating how and why IBC epitomizes commodity fetishism, I must note one further dimension of Marx's adjective *äußerlichste*. Enrique Dussel describes varieties of interest as "forms on the surface in which the hidden manifests what is behind: 'surplus value, unpaid labour.' "[64] With *äußerliche* as superficial, the very notion of visible surface brings with it that of invisible depth.[65] It does so such that a surface qua superficial is the site of overlap or intersection for contrasts between the outer and the inner, the manifest and the hidden, and so on. A Hegel-inspired Marx seems to play with these dialectical convergences of opposites apropos IBC as capital's "most superficial and fetishized form" (*seine äußerlichste und fetischartigste Form*). Oddly, interest, as the surface that most reveals surplus value as unpaid labor, simultaneously, with its hypnotizing fetishistic effects, conceals this very same revelation. In the superficiality of the interest fetish, repression and the return of the repressed weirdly coincide.

Now, to come back to the explanation of how IBC intensifies and perfects capitalistic fetishism according to the above-quoted opening paragraph from chapter 24 of *Capital*, volume 3: With M-C-M′, there are, as Marx notes, two separate stages forming the elementary nucleus of the structural dynamic at the heart of capitalism ("the unity of opposing phases, a movement that breaks down into two opposite procedures, the purchase and sale of commodities"). First, there is the sequence M-C (i.e., "the purchase of commodities"), in which the capitalist uses his/her money (M) to buy (or invest in) commodities (C) as both variable capital (i.e., commodified labor power employed for specific lengths of time) and constant capital (i.e., both fixed capital as land, buildings, machinery, tools, etc. and circulating capital as raw materials, fuel, etc.). Second, there is the sequence C-M′ (i.e., "the sale of commodities"), in which the capitalist puts the commodities (C) produced by his/her combined variable and constant capital into circulation on the marketplace. If all goes according to plan, these commodities realize exchange values containing amounts of surplus value (M′) accruing to the capitalist.

Both M-C and C-M′ bring persons into producing and circulating/exchanging relationships with one another. In M-C, capitalist buyers come into contact with sellers of various commodities (i.e., variable capital as sold by laborers qua bearers of labor power as well as constant capital as sold by other capitalists and sometimes also landowners). In C-M′, capitalists, their agents, and middlemen come into contact with buyers of commodities. Thus, with M-C-M′ as combining the two phases of M-C and C-M′, relations between persons remain palpable parts of the movement of capital as industrial/commercial capital (i.e., this capital "presents itself as the product of a social *relation* [*eines gesellschaftlichen* Verhältnisses], not the product of a mere *thing* [*eines bloßen* Dings]"). The fetishism at work within this sort of capital does not completely eclipse the social behind the façade of the thingly. Therefore, it amounts to an incomplete fetishism as per the Marxian definition of commodity fetishism in the first volume of *Das Kapital*.

THE SELF-CLEANING FETISH   ☞   173

But with IBC's abbreviated capitalistic circuit of M-M', commodity fetishism is brought to its perfection and purity though the social being totally and completely "obliterated" (*ausgelöscht*) by the thingly. With IBC, money as the commodity par excellence seems to detach from persons altogether in looking as though it becomes an independent, autoreflexive automaton, an inhuman self-relating mechanism. As Michael Heinrich puts this, with interest's M-M', "money appears to multiply all by itself."[66] Anthony Brewer similarly notes that "interest-bearing capital is the most mysterious and fetishized form of capital. It seems as if a sum of money has the inherent property of producing more money."[67] Duncan Foley associates interest with "the more mystifying illusions of capitalist society."[68] And David Harvey appropriately depicts M-M' as appearing "magical" in the eyes of those beguiled by capitalistic fetishism.[69] As Marx articulates this in the second paragraph of chapter 24 of *Capital*, volume 3:

> $M-M'$. Here we have the original starting-point of capital, money in the formula $M-C-M'$, reduced to the two extremes $M-M'$, where $M' = M + \Delta M$, money that creates more money. This is the original and general formula for capital reduced to a meaningless abbreviation [*ein sinnloses Resumé*]. It is capital in its finished form, the unity of production and circulation processes, and hence capital yielding a definite surplus-value in a specific period of time. In the form of interest-bearing capital, capital appears immediately in this form, unmediated by the production and circulation processes. Capital appears as a mysterious and self-creating source of interest, of its own increase. The *thing* [money, commodity, value] is now already capital simply as a thing [*als bloßes Ding*]; the result of the overall reproduction process appears as a property devolving on a thing in itself [*einem Ding von selbst*]; it is up to the possessor of money, i.e. of commodities in their ever-exchangeable form, whether he wants to spend this money as money or hire it out as capital. In interest-bearing capital, therefore, this automatic fetish is elaborated into its pure form [*dieser automatische Fetisch rein herausgearbeitet*], self-valorizing value, money breeding money, and in this form it no longer bears any marks of its origin [*keine Narben seiner Entstehung mehr*]. The social relation [*Das gesellschaftliche Verhältnis*] is consummated in the relationship of a thing, money, to itself. Instead of the actual transformation of money into capital, we have here only the form of this devoid of content.[70]

Obviously, this passage resonates with the preceding quotation from *Theories of Surplus-Value* ("*ein sinnloses Resumé*," etc.). It also resonates with another passage from the same addendum to *Theories of Surplus-Value*:

> Interest-bearing capital is the consummate *automatic fetish* [*dieser automatische Fetisch vollendet*], the self-expanding value [*sich selbst verwertende Wert*], the money-making money [*das geldmachende Geld*], and in this form it no longer bears any trace of its origin [*keine Narben seiner Entstehung mehr*]. The social relation is consummated as a relation of things (money, commodities) to themselves.[71]

With the transition from industrial/commercial to finance/money capital, the residual relations between persons in M-C and C-M′ are totally obscured behind the appearance of relations between things. More exactly, the eclipsing factor here is the solipsistic self-relation of one thing in particular, namely, money as the commodity standing in for all other commodities.[72] When in both *Capital* and *Theories of Surplus-Value* Marx employs the words *"keine Narben seiner Entstehung mehr,"* what he is referring to is the fact that the marks/ traces (*Narben*) of the origin (*Entstehung*) of IBC's surplus value in social relationships of producing and circulating/exchanging (as all represented by the "C" of M-C-M′) are "obliterated" (*ausgelöscht*) by the purified commodity fetishism of M-M′ (in which "C" drops out of the picture).

Later on in part 5 of *Capital*, volume 3, specifically in chapter 29 ("Banking Capital's Component Parts"), Marx again speaks of IBC. Apropos capitalism's version of the economic category of interest, he maintains that "here the absurdity [*Verrücktheit*] of the capitalist's way of conceiving things reaches its climax [*ihre Spitze*], in so far as instead of deriving the valorization of capital from the exploitation of labour-power, they explain the productivity of labour-power by declaring that labour-power itself is this mystical thing [*dieses mystiche Ding*], interest-bearing capital."[73] A similar observation occurs subsequently in chapter 30 ("Money Capital and Real Capital: I").[74] Marx's language at this moment indicates that he is redeploying his theory of commodity fetishism.

From the summit (*Spitze*) of the capitalist's fetishistic insanity-as-reversal (*Verrücktheit*) of social reality, and as with the Feuerbachian religious believer, a property of subjects qua persons is misattributed to objects qua things. Specifically, the property of producing surplus value is misattributed from labor to capital[75]—even more precisely, from labor power to IBC. According to the Marxist critique of political economy, labor power is the one and only commodity among all other commodities with the strange capacity to produce more exchange values than this labor power itself costs in exchange values (i.e., labor's wages) for its production and reproduction (i.e., maintenance and subsistence). Yet under the distorting influence of capitalistic fetishism, this capacity of laboring persons is ascribed to a thing, money as IBC with its M-M′, instead.

Insofar as IBC is the "pure fetish form" (*reine Fetischform*), this object usurps in appearances the activity for which laboring subjects are really responsible, with "*M-M'* being the subject, a thing for sale [*G-G' als Subjekt, verkaufbares Ding*]"[76] (although, of course, laborers qua bearers of labor power also are commodified things for sale on capitalism's labor markets).

Only labor power is generative of surplus value. But in the guise of interest, money now appears to the subjects of capitalism as the unique commodity enjoying the power to be self-generative of surplus value. Commodity fetishism's inversion between persons and things is here finalized in being brought to its maximum 180-degree point, as Marx himself declares several times.[77] Indeed, if fetishism is, for Marx, a form of inverting alienation (*Entfremdung*), then IBC is "the most estranged and peculiar form" (*entfremdetsten und eigentümlichsten Form*) of the fetishistic commodity of capital.[78]

Marx, earlier in the same paragraph of chapter 29 of *Capital*, volume 3, in which he describes IBC as the "climax" (*Spitze*) of commodity fetishism, speaks of "interest-bearing capital always being the mother of every insane form [*die Mutter aller verrückten Formen*]."[79] Hilferding likewise refers to "the insane character [*verrückten Form*] of fictitious capital."[80] Based on the ground covered above, one sense of Marx's wording here should be obvious: IBC is "the mother of every insane form" qua the ultimate, fullest instance of commodity fetishism.[81]

However, in another sense, Marx's identification of IBC as maternal should provoke puzzlement. Why? Both IBC and the broader economic categories of financial and fictitious capital are later developments in the history of capitalism chronologically subsequent to the commodity form itself and, hence, to commodity fetishism too. Yet the Marx of the third volume of *Das Kapital* depicts IBC as giving birth to this capitalistic fetishism (i.e., as, again, "*die Mutter aller verrückten Formen*"). This looks to be an extremely strange case of a mother who somehow gives birth to her ancestors. An odd retroactive temporality of some sort or another appears to be operative in Marx's theory of interest.

§15. AFTER THE FINANCIAL COUP:
THE RETROACTIVITY OF FETISHISTIC INTEREST

Marx, already in 1844, situates the interest-dealing systems of credit and banking as "consummations" of capitalism's development.[82] That is to say, the institutionalization of interest is a later stage in the evolution of capitalism.[83]

However, as Heinrich contends, there is a historical inevitability to the emergence of IBC once the capitalist mode of production arises and takes hold.[84]

In *Finance Capital*, Hilferding observes, "In capitalist society every sum of money takes on the character of capital."[85] Foley renders this observation more precise in explaining that "once the interest rate emerges as a social fact, every agent in capitalist society is compelled to view money as potentially expanding value."[86] In other words, as soon as IBC surfaces within the temporal unfurling of capitalism, IBC's fashion of making money a commodity (with the distinctive use value of being able to generate surplus value as additional exchange value) comes to color every little bit and piece of the universal equivalent right down to single pennies. All money now shows itself to be potential IBC. Every fraction of currency promises to yield at least the going rate of interest, if nothing else. As Heinrich notes in this connection, "Money is now *potential capital*."[87] Heinrich relatedly insists that IBC becomes a socioeconomically dominant feature of capitalism once it comes into effective existence.[88] Similarly, Henryk Grossmann remarks that "in the language of the banker everything is capital."[89]

Returning once more to *Capital*, volume 3, Marx therein posits the anteriority of the category of surplus value to that of interest. Alluding to the dialectics of quantity and quality in Hegelian *Logik*, he argues that what starts as a purely quantitative division of surplus value (here, into quotas of profit and interest) mutates into a qualitative distinction.[90] This qualitative distinction is that between, on the one hand, directly productive/functioning capital as industrial/commercial capital (associated with profit) and, on the other hand, indirectly productive/functioning capital as financial/money capital (associated with interest).[91] As seen previously, and as emphasized by Marx just one chapter later in the third volume, the quality of the difference between profit and interest is further enhanced by the tendency for two corresponding but distinct groups of capitalists to congeal, namely, the productive capitalists of industry/commerce (with their profit) and the unproductive capitalists of banking/finance (with their interest).[92] Additionally, Ernest Mandel hints that these distinct groups of capitalists come to be at odds with each other, at least implicitly, in ways related to "the law of the tendential fall in the rate of profit" so central to the same (third) volume of *Capital* (and already to be found in Smith's *The Wealth of Nations*)[93] in which IBC is discussed. Apropos interest, Mandel observes, "Since . . . it does not itself participate in the immediate valorization of capital, and this interest must therefore be paid for out of the total social surplus-value, it forces the average rate of profit down even further."[94]

In the wake of the quantitative-become-qualitative splitting up of surplus value, interest seems to autonomize itself.[95] IBC separates itself off from the rest of capital. In so doing, "interest appears as a surplus-value that capital yields in and of itself and which it would therefore yield even without productive application."[96] M-M' comes to look independent of M-C-M'.

But looks are deceiving. IBC's independence is illusory,[97] although this illusion has very real power in capitalism.[98] Money is not a fantastical golden egg that lays additional golden eggs. Marx insists:

> The individual capitalist . . . has the choice between lending his capital out as interest-bearing capital or valorizing it himself as productive capital, no matter whether it exists as money capital right at the start or has first to be transformed into money capital. Taken generally, i.e. when we apply it to the whole social capital, as is done by some vulgar economists and even given out as the basis of profit, this is of course quite absurd. It is utter nonsense to suggest that all capital could be transformed into money capital without the presence of people to buy and valorize the means of production, i.e. the form in which the entire capital exists, apart from the relatively small part existing in money. Concealed in this idea, moreover, is the still greater nonsense that capital could yield interest on the basis of the capitalist mode of production without functioning as productive capital, i.e. without creating surplus-value, of which interest is simply one part; that the capitalist mode of production could proceed on its course without capitalist production. If an appropriately large number of capitalists sought to transform their capital into money capital, the result would be a tremendous devaluation of money capital and a tremendous fall in the rate of interest; many people would immediately find themselves in the position of being unable to live on their interest and thus compelled to turn themselves back into industrial capitalists.[99]

The commodity fetishist's experience of IBC as the magically self-enhancing circuit of M-M', of money as autoproductive of surplus value ex nihilo, is denounced as ridiculous by Marx with straightforward objections. Under capitalism, both profit and interest are portions of surplus value. Hence, profit and interest can exist only if there initially is surplus value.[100]

In Marx's framework, the sole source of surplus value is the exploitation of labor power as variable capital. Surplus value is equivalent to unpaid laboring time producing exchange values in excess of the exchange value cost of labor's wages as representative of its means of subsistence. Exclusively via the variable capital portion of the "C" in productive capital's formula M-C-M' can there come to be produced any surplus value whatsoever. Therefore, since interest is a derivative slice of surplus value, there can be no M-M' without there first being M-C-M'.[101] That is to say, finance/money capital, with its interest as M-M', is parasitic upon industrial/commercial capital, with its surplus value and profit as M-C-M'.[102] Brewer remarks, "Theories of interest cannot explain profits."[103] To be more exact, one cannot defensibly derive the categories of surplus value and profit from that of interest, since interest and profit are, in actuality, both sub-categories (as divisions/parts) of surplus value.[104]

Furthermore, as Marx points out above, the economics of the rate of interest limit the number of capitalists who can retire from productive industrial activity and become financiers, speculators, etc. living off interest payments alone. According to Marx, the supply of and demand for finance capital determines the rate of interest as the price of IBC qua money used to make more money.[105] As he claims in the preceding quotation, if too many capitalists try to be financial/money capitalists, then the glut of IBC on markets so drastically reduces the rate of interest as to push a critical mass of these capitalists back into being industrial/commercial capitalists. This alone makes it impossible for the entirety of the class of capitalists to live as rentiers.[106]

I should take the opportunity to add a nuance apropos the economic category of IBC. Specifically, a distinction needs to be drawn between interest in general and IBC in particular, with the latter but not the former being specific to capitalism. Of course, the institution of interest long predates the capitalist mode of production. However, in precapitalist societies, interest tends to be tied to nonproducers as either merchants or consumers. Merchants buy in order to sell (i.e., exchange), and consumers buy in order to consume.[107] But neither type of economic agent buys in order to produce, so as to make more and other goods.

By contrast, IBC is money lent to those who intend to employ it so as to produce commodities with an eye ultimately to garnering surplus value for themselves (a slice of which is paid back to the lender[s] of IBC). Credit for merchants or consumers, including within noncapitalist socioeconomic contexts, is money for buying and sometimes also consuming goods, but not for producing goods. IBC is credit for industrial/commercial capitalists as those who produce not goods but more precisely commodities as use values to which exchange values containing surplus value are attached. Put differently, IBC is interest precisely as it relates to the productive capitalist version of M-C-M'.

The upshot of this is a supplement to Marx's above-quoted arguments against the possibility of all capitalists transforming themselves into money capitalists. As Marx maintains, the rate of interest itself acts against this. But additionally, the very definition of IBC as peculiar to capitalism in being dependent upon

THE SELF-CLEANING FETISH   179

productive capital's circuit M-C-M' means that without this circuit, there cannot be any IBC strictly speaking. Put differently, if IBC's M-M' is derivative of M-C-M', then all capitalists cannot withdraw from the movement of the latter. If nobody is engaged in capital's M-C-M', then nobody can engage in capitalistic M-M' either.

Yet as Marx acknowledges, the mirage of IBC's self-valorizing autonomy persists. What is more, commodity fetishism, specifically as reaching its most intensive and extensive realization in and through the advent of IBC, thoroughly inverts the truth. This fetishism goes so far as to make it seem as though profit (and, along with it, the entirety of surplus value) is generated from capital's supposedly original self-enhancing power as M-M', money-making money.[108] Not only is interest independent of profit and surplus value—the latter are produced by the former. Marx comments:

> While interest is simply one part of profit, i.e. the surplus-value, extorted from the worker by the functioning capitalist, it now appears conversely as if interest is the specific fruit of capital, the original thing [das Ursprüngliche], while profit, now transformed into the form of profit of enterprise, appears as a mere accessory and trimming added in the reproduction process. The fetish character [die Fetischgestalt] of capital and the reproduction of capital is now complete. In M-M' we have the irrational [begriffslose] form of capital, the misrepresentation and objectification [die Verkehrung und Versachlichung] of the relations of production, in its highest power: the interest-bearing form, the simple form of capital, in which it is taken as logically anterior to its own reproduction process [seinem eigenen Reproduktionsprozeß vorausgesetzt ist]; the ability of money or a commodity to valorize its own value independent of reproduction—the capital mystification in the most flagrant [grellsten] form.[109]

The species appears as the genus and vice versa. The parasite looks to be the host and vice versa. Labor's valorization of capital's materials now seems to be the self-valorization of material capital (up to and including the strange stuff that is money in its various guises). The fetishistic inversion of the paired positions of objective things and subjective persons here arrives at its most extreme endpoint. IBC gaudily (als grellsten) marks this arrival.

IBC also perfects the other major dimension of commodity fetishism as per "The Fetishism of the Commodity and Its Secret" in addition to fetishistic Verdinglichung (i.e., the reifying "thingification" of social relations). This other major dimension is that of fetishism's mistaking of exchange value for use value.

For Marx, a commodity's use value has to do with its material characteristics as an object of consumption. Use values are bound up with the sensible attributes of things as tangible entities. By contrast, a commodity's exchange value has to do with its social status in market relationships between economic actors. Exchange values are determined within inter- and trans-subjective networks according to quantified comparisons and contrasts that disregard the physical qualities distinguishing different commodities qua use values.[110]

However, the capitalistic commodity fetishist is wedded to the category mistake of imagining that social exchange value is some sort of occult property of the commodity as material thing. With varying degrees of awareness, this fetishist envisions exchange value not as an issue of how other economic agents will relate to the commodity in question but, instead, as a hidden, mysterious, nonrelational quality inhering in the commodity qua asocial physical object. This is to misconceive social exchange value as a material use value contained within concrete commodities along with their other material features.

"Exhibit A" of the fetishist's confusion of exchange with use value would have to be gold as the commodity par excellence insofar as it epitomizes money as the universal equivalent of all commodities. Marx, employing instead pearls and diamonds as examples of fetishized commodities, explains in a way that mocks the commodity fetishist (especially the professional capitalist economist):

> So far no chemist has ever discovered exchange-value either in a pearl or a diamond. The economists who have discovered this chemical substance [*Substanz*], and who lay special claim to critical acumen, nevertheless find that the use-value of material objects [*Sachen*] belongs to them independently of their material properties [*sachlichen Eigenschaften*], while their value, on the other hand, forms a part of them as objects. What confirms them in this view is the peculiar circumstance that the use-value of a thing is realized without exchange, i.e. in the direct relation between the thing and man [*im unmittelbaren Verhältnis zwischen Ding und Mensch*], while, inversely [*umgekehrt*], its value is realized only in exchange, i.e. in a social process [*einem* gesellschaftlichen *Prozeß*].[111]

In neither gold, nor pearls, nor diamonds, nor any other commodity qua material entity will anyone ever find the supposed subtle, sublime "substance" responsible for material things' social exchange values. As Marx reiterates this point in *Theories of Surplus-Value*, "No scientist to date has yet discovered what natural qualities make definite proportions of snuff tobacco and paintings 'equivalents' for one another."[112] Even the most powerful electron microscopes will fail to detect the mysterious, magical exchange-value particles woven into the physical makeup of commodities. Any hunt for the economic equivalent of the God particle is forever doomed to failure in advance. Seeing through commodity fetishism, abandoning its futile quest for the very stuff of economic worth, in recognizing the difference in kind between use and exchange values is to (re)invert (*als umkehren*) the fetishistic inversion within which social exchange value is mistaken for being just another material use value.[113] The critique of political economy's inversion of capitalism's fetishistic inversion is akin to a Hegelian negation of negation.

As the commodity par excellence, money is especially susceptible to capitalistic fetishization. Here too, IBC, as per *Capital*, volume 3, amounts to the maximization of commodity fetishism. How so? A less-than-maximal fetishization of money would entail erroneously envisioning the exchange value of currency as having something to do with the currency's embodiment in metallic coins, paper bills, and the like (or to do with the precious metals in the well-guarded vaults of the country's national bank). Such everyday fetishization, common to ordinary consumers, assumes the existence of a spectral exchangeability-stuff hidden within the metal, paper, etc. of cash.

The maximal fetishization of money as IBC goes beyond this more mundane, subdued fetishism of mere currency. As regards commodity fetishism vis-à-vis money specifically, a distinction helpfully can be drawn between the cash fetishism of the consumer versus the interest fetishism of the capitalist. The cash fetishism of the consumer in the marketplace is limited to misclassifying simple exchange value qua social as a species of the genus use value qua material.

By contrast, the interest fetishism of lending and borrowing capitalists, the fetishism of IBC, not only misattributes exchange value to money qua thing—it goes so far as to misattribute the very power to generate surplus value to monetary material. Heinrich labels this "the *fetishism of capital*."[114] M-M′ signifies this more extreme misattribution peculiar to the interest fetishism of capitalists. Money now not only contains magical exchange stuff but also supermagical, self-multiplying stuff.[115] More than merely a special sort of inert object, it is a special sort of spontaneously autoreflexive and self-enhancing subject.

What is more, this interest fetishism comes to entwine itself with the cash fetishism of consumers. These consumers thereby are led to see the money they have to spend on goods for their subsistence as squandered potential capital. The interest fetishism of IBC adds insult to injury: Under the shadow of finance capital's interest-driven regime, capitalism's consumers are made to feel guilty for being forced by their low earnings to spend everything on consumption, rather than to accumulate with an eye to becoming capitalists themselves. It is

182 THE SELF-CLEANING FETISH

their own fault if they fail to rise into the ranks of the bourgeoisie. If only they were abstinent enough to save and invest. Shame on them.

IBC is bound up with financial and fictitious capital as entailing the institutions of banking and the like. Elsewhere in the third volume of *Das Kapital*, Marx identifies the "credit system" composed of these institutions as "a mere phantom of the mind" (*bloßes Hirngespinst*)[116] (with a "*Hirngespinst*" as literally a web [*Gespinst*] spun out of nothing but the brain [*Hirn*]). Nonetheless, as another well-known passage in volume 3 indicates (and as is already indicated in volume 1's section on "The Fetishism of the Commodity and Its Secret"),[117] these phantoms have legs:

> Capital-profit (or better still capital-interest), land-ground-rent, labour-wages, this economic trinity as the connection between the components of value and wealth in general and its sources, completes the mystification of the capitalist mode of production, the reification of social relations [*die Verdinglichung der gesellschaftlichen Verhältnisse*], and the immediate coalescence of the material relations of production with their historical and social specificity: the bewitched, distorted and upside-down world haunted by Monsieur le Capital and Madame la Terre, who are at the same time social characters and mere things [*die verzauberte, verkehrte und auf den Kopf gestellte Welt, wo Monsieur le Capital und Madame la Terre als soziale Charaktere, und zugleich unmittelbar als bloße Dinge ihrem Spuk treiben*]. It is the great merit of classical economics to have dissolved this false appearance and deception, this autonomization and ossification [*diese Verselbständigung und Verknöcherung*] of the different social elements of wealth vis-à-vis one another, this personification of things and reification of the relations of production [*diese Personifizierung der Sachen und Versachlichung der Produktionsverhältnisse*], this religion of everyday life [*diese Religion des Alltagsleben*], by reducing interest to a part of profit and rent to the surplus above the average profit, so that they both coincide in surplus-value; by presenting the circulation process as simply a metamorphosis of forms, and finally in the immediate process of production reducing the value and surplus-value of commodities to labour.[118]

What is translated here as "haunted" (i.e., "*Spuk treiben*") sometimes is rendered into English as "ghost walking." For Marx, history marches, albeit on its feet rather than its head. Marx's real abstractions, including "Monsieur le Capital and Madame la Terre," march too; they also possess legs and walk around; that is, they are causally efficacious[119] (as Russell Jacoby nicely puts this apropos social roles, including the class roles Marx sees individuals bearing/personifying in alienating capitalist conditions, "roles are not only fraudulent, they are also real").[120] And Mr. Capital is most at home wandering about the thoroughly inverted world (*"die verzauberte, verkehrte und auf den Kopf gestellte Welt"*) of capitalism when doing so wearing the form of IBC ("or better still capital-interest"). With this spectral gentleman cloaked thus, commodity fetishism (*"diese Personifizierung der Sachen und Versachlichung der Produktionsverhält-nisse"*) is at its zenith.[121] And this fetishism establishes itself as a concrete com-ponent of quotidian existence, as the very "religion of everyday life" for the denizens of capitalist societies. What is the old "opium of the masses" compared to this new drug? Capital palpably haunts its subjects each and every day and night of their lives.

IBC strictly speaking does not preexist capitalism. Additionally, it comes into its own within capitalism only after the latter has developed historically up to a certain point. However, as Heinrich contends, there is an inevitability to the emergence of IBC once the capitalist mode of production is underway.[122] And, once IBC emerges, it recasts all money and capital and, with them, capital-ist society as a whole in its own peculiar light.[123] Oddly, Robinson complains that, as regards interest, Marx "attaches no importance to its reaction upon other factors in economic life."[124] As much of the preceding shows, this com-plaint is utterly unjustified considering Marx's broad and deep reflections regarding IBC's impact on not only infrastructural (as Robinson's "economic life") but also superstructural (as fetishistic ideologies) dimensions of capitalist society.

Before shifting to a reconsideration of the cross-resonances between the Marxist and psychoanalytic uses of the term "fetishism" (as I will do in the next section), I wish to have brief recourse to the Freudian concept of "screen memo-ries" in connection with IBC as per *Capital*, volume 3.[125] This recourse is moti-vated by the fact that screen memories as per Freud involve two features also crucial to Marx's account of IBC. First, a Freudian screen memory, like interest as the crowning form of commodity fetishism, simultaneously reveals and con-ceals a repressed truth (this combination of revelation with concealment being an essential feature of the distinctively psychoanalytic concept of the symptom). Second, such a memory is shaped by the temporal dynamic Freud labels *"Nachträglichkeit,"* namely, "deferred action" qua retroaction (or, in French, *après-coup*).[126] These two features are essential ingredients of Marx's theory of IBC too. Moreover, Lacan himself treats the fetish object of the analytic fetish-ist as a type of screen memory.[127]

As seen, Marx implies that IBC entails a retroactivity. Although this type of interest is a later development of capitalism as it enters into its financial and fictitious stages, IBC's eventual surfacing sweepingly transforms not only elements of capitalism contemporaneous with this surfacing but features of the historical past too. Perhaps the most famous instance of retroactivity in Marx's corpus is the line from the 1857 introduction to the *Grundrisse*: "Human anatomy contains a key to the anatomy of the ape. The intimations of higher development among the subordinate animal species, however, can be understood only after the higher development is already known."[128] As I argue above, IBC is specific to (financial) capitalism and, thus, different from merchant and consumer credit as well as from precapitalist forms of money lending. Nevertheless, IBC, through its distorting effects on commodity fetishists' perspectives, portrays itself as continuous with non-IBC interest. Under the influence of capitalist commodity fetishism as reaching its apogee with IBC, and paraphrasing a line from the concluding paragraph of Freud's 1899 essay "Screen Memories,"[129] memories *"relating to"* precapitalist economics may be all that capitalism's subjects possess (rather than memories actually *"from"* earlier modes of production).

IBC retroactively renders non-IBC interest as the "ape" anticipating itself, IBC, as the ape-descended "human." Of course, the false eternalization-through-naturalization of what in truth is historically transitory and socially peculiar is the hallmark gesture of ideology as per Marxist materialism. Hence, IBC's just-explained establishment of a misleading continuity between itself and precapitalist varieties of interest, a continuity purportedly traversing all socioeconomic systems, is ideological insofar as it operates so as falsely to eternalize and naturalize various money-lending practices, its own first and foremost.

Obviously, neither money lending nor money itself is natural and eternal, no matter how long-established they have been in the history of human societies. Moreover, interest ought to be extremely difficult for ideology to naturalize. The circuit M-M' appears to amount to a fantastical power of creation ex nihilo on the part of an inorganic product of human artifice. What could be less "natural" in the various senses of this adjective?

Nevertheless, with commodity fetishism as the "religion of everyday life" within capitalism, the "metaphysical subtleties and theological niceties" (*metaphysischer Spitzfindigkeit und theologischer Mucken*) of M-M' are somehow miraculously rendered "extremely obvious" (*selbstverständliches*) and "trivial" (*triviales*).[130] Moreover, these subtleties and niceties are very real abstractions, namely, "misty creations" (*Nebelbildungen*) produced by and forming integral parts of the "earthly kernel" (*irdischen Kern*) of the capitalist mode of production and the social structures resting upon it.[131] With the acceptance of IBC, itself the exhaustive culmination of commodity fetishism, as natural and eternal, it comes to seem banal and self-evident that commodified things, and not socially producing persons, automatically self-generate values. The world gets turned truly upside-down (*verkehrte und auf den Kopf*). IBC completes and universalizes this inversion. It gives birth to the wholly fetishized capitalist universe. And with capitalist production, exchange, and consumption exponentially expanded, intensified, and accelerated thanks to the fuel of financial capital, IBC and its ilk prove to be potent enhancers and reinforcers of commodity fetishism. Capitalist interest is indeed "the mother of every insane form" (*die Mutter aller verrückten Formen*).

§16. SHADES OF GREEN: LACAN AND CAPITALISM'S VEILS

The tenth and final session (June 16, 1971) of Lacan's *Seminar XVIII: Of a Discourse That Would Not Be a Semblance* (1971) contains a now well-known assertion. On that occasion, Lacan claims that Marx is responsible for inventing, albeit *avant la lettre*, the specifically psychoanalytic concept of the symptom.[132] In this context, Lacan promptly identifies Marx's analysis of money in connection with commodity fetishism as the site of this proto-Freudian innovation within the Marxian corpus.[133] Much of what follows below involves me unpacking all of this in light of IBC as per *Capital*, volume 3.

Of course, in psychoanalysis, all sorts of phenomena can count as symptoms in the Freudian sense: dreams, parapraxes, slips of the tongue, compulsive repetitions, apparently somatic ailments, etc. Yet Lacan, taking his lead from the first volume of *Das Kapital*, repeatedly focuses on fetishes as exemplary analytic symptoms. Several times, he posits an equivalency (or, at least, significant overlapping) of usage of the term "fetishism" between Marxism and psychoanalysis.[134] As early as *Seminar V*, Lacan zeroes in on "the fetishistic value of gold."[135] In *Seminar VI*, he identifies Marx's miser, the hoarder of gold, as the paradigmatic fetishist.[136] Likewise, in *Seminar XVI*, money is spoken of as the "enigmatic . . . fetish *par excellence*."[137]

At this same moment in the sixteenth seminar, Lacan makes a mistake in his discussion of money à la Marx (a mistake perhaps attributable to the influence of Georg Simmel's 1900 *The Philosophy of Money* on Lacan's understanding of monetary matters).[138] He contends that for Marx, money has no use value.[139] This is erroneous on two levels. First, if currency in its physical form (i.e., as metal, paper, etc.) is at issue, the tangible qualities of currency indeed possess use value(s). With metallic coins, one can scratch off lottery tickets, perform flips to decide between binary alternatives ("heads or tails?"), pry certain things open, and so on. And if one chooses to do so, one can write on bills, turn them into paper airplanes, light cigars with them, and the like. These are examples of uses that coins and bills possess by virtue of their character as particular kinds of material objects. Moreover, these use values are distinct from their roles in facilitating the exchange of other commodities. Hence, money as currency indeed has use values apart from exchange values.

Second, there is money as interest. One should recall that IBC is defined by Marx as money insofar as it possesses the potential to produce more money. In other words, IBC is money with the use value of giving rise to surplus value, with the rate of interest as the market price for this particular use value. Perhaps Lacan overlooks this second type of use value with which money (as capital) is endowed because of his apparent neglect of Marx's discussions of commodity fetishism and interest specifically in the third volume of *Capital*. Lacan's musings about commodity fetishism seem to be limited to references to the first volume alone.

I wish to overcome this limitation by extending the Lacanian treatment of Marxian commodity fetishism to cover this fetishism as it completes itself via IBC as per *Capital*, volume 3. Doing so promises to enrich an appreciation of the psychoanalytic mechanisms of repression (*Verdrängung*) and disavowal (*Verleugnung*) especially. But in order to attain these enrichments, a more detailed engagement with Lacan's account of fetishism is necessary.

Fetishism receives the greatest amount of Lacan's attention during the period of his teaching from the mid-1950s through the early 1960s. The fourth (*The Object Relation* [1956–1957]), fifth, and sixth seminars contain the majority of his comments on this topic. However, a handful of remarks on fetishism are scatted across subsequent years of *le Séminaire*.

First of all, Lacan repeatedly depicts fetishism as epitomizing the libidinal economics of human subjectivity in general. More precisely, Lacan associates fetishism with what is at the heart of his distinctive conception of desire (*désir*). In the same contexts during which he discusses fetishists and their fetishes, he emphasizes the essential, inherent perversity of human desire as such[140] (in Lacan's footsteps, Octave Mannoni, in his classic 1963 essay on fetishism, "Je sais bien, mais quand même . . . ," likewise anchors fetishism, with its mechanism of disavowal [*Verleugnung*],[141] in the ostensibly transhistorical makeup of Lacanian desire).[142] At these moments, Lacan also crowns fetishism "the perversion of all perversions"[143] and maintains that "all of desire's objects are fetishistic in character."[144] He portrays fetishism as "an especially fundamental example of the dynamics of desire."[145] Lacan likewise casts the fetish object as a "milestone of desire" (*borne miliaire du désir*).[146]

Very much in the spirit of the "return to Freud" of the 1950s, Lacan carefully grounds his own account of fetishism in Freud's writings on the topic. In the 1927 essay "Fetishism," Freud states the following apropos his central thesis having it that fetish objects are stand-ins for the absent feminine penis, ersatz things designed specifically to ward off castration anxiety:

> When now I announce that the fetish is a substitute for the penis, I shall certainly create disappointment; so I hasten to add that it is not a substitute for any chance penis, but for a particular and quite special penis [*eines bestimmten, ganz besonderen Penis*] that had been extremely important in early childhood but had later been lost. That is to say, it should normally have been given up, but the fetish is precisely designed to preserve it from extinction. To put it more plainly: the fetish is a substitute for the woman's (the mother's) penis.[147]

This "particular and quite special penis" is nothing other than the impossible, nonexistent maternal phallus, i.e., "the woman's (the mother's) penis." Lacan endorses Freud's core thesis concerning fetishism here.[148] And insofar as those sexed female by definition do not have penises, a feminine phallus, as precisely what fetish objects are disguised substitutes for, is akin to a square circle. Like a square circle, it is a fiction sustainable only in and through linguistic symbolizations.[149]

For Lacan, who appropriately focuses on Freud's "*bestimmten, ganz besonderen Penis*," the only sort of "castration" feminine subjects, the mother included, can undergo is of a symbolic sort. Why? As I explain elsewhere:

> In . . . the mid-1950s, Lacan introduces a tripartite schema of negatives on the basis of his register theory. More precisely, in recasting Freud's ideas with regard to castration, he distinguishes between "privation" (as Real, an incarnate nonpresence dwelling in material being in itself), "castration" (as Symbolic, a deficit created in reality by the interventions of sociolinguistic mediators), and "frustration" (as Imaginary, a representational confusion of Real privation and/or Symbolic castration as deprivations and obstacles gratuitously imposed from without—to the extent that the Imaginary misrecognizes the Real as the Symbolic and vice versa, frustration reacts to privation as castration and to castration as privation).[150]

188   THE SELF-CLEANING FETISH

I subsequently add:

> Biologically female human organisms, in the (material) Real, are not "missing" a penis or anything else; they simply are as they are. With regard to the dimension of the Lacanian Real pictured as the presupposed plenum of asubjective incarnate being, there are no absences or lacks. Instead, with respect to the matters at issue in the psychoanalytic castration complex, there are, from this angle, just vaginas and penises. The vagina is not the absence of a penis, since trying to situate these organs vis-à-vis each other in this way is, according to Lacan's register theory, a category mistake in which a comparison between proverbial apples and oranges is subreptionally transformed into a binary opposition between having and not having, one and zero, plus and minus, and so on.[151]

I continue:

> But, of course, Freud and Lacan both consider the committing of this category mistake, in which penises and vaginas go from being apples and oranges to becoming presences and absences, to be a near-inevitability during ontogenetic subject formation as taking shape within still-reigning phallocentric symbolic orders. In Lacan's rendering of the castration complex, the inscription of lacks in the Real by the Symbolic—it is only through symbolization that something can be said to be missing, strictly speaking—establishes the very distinction between privation and castration per se. As regards a biological female, privation would be the fact that having a vagina entails not having a penis (as the Spinozistic-Hegelian ontological principle has it, *omnis determinatio est negatio*, or "all determination is negation"). This privation is transubstantiated into castration proper if and only if such determination-as-negation is symbolized as itself a non-determination, namely, as an absence relative to a specific corresponding presence (in elementary formal-logical terms, when a difference between A and B is reinscribed as a contradiction between A and not-A). According to Lacan, "castration" is intrinsically Symbolic—for him, it is always "symbolic castration"—both for these reasons, as well as because the castration complex epitomizes the more general existential ordeal of the living human creature being subjected to the overriding and overwriting dictates of the big Other as symbolic order with its overdetermining significations.[152]

The theoretical-conceptual triad of privation-castration-frustration I gloss in these passages is presented by Lacan primarily in *Seminar IV*, which itself also contains his single most sustained set of reflections on fetishism. The missing maternal phallus central to both Freud's and Lacan's interpretations of fetish objects is the object of specifically symbolic castration as per Lacan and his trinity of privation, castration, and frustration.

Indeed, Lacan again and again denies that the phallus of the fetishist has to do with the Real or Imaginary penis (as the object of privation or frustration respectively).[153] Instead, the missing maternal phallus ultimately at stake in all instances of fetishism as per psychoanalysis is the one created and sustained ex nihilo by the signifiers involved with symbolic castration. This special phallus is Symbolic in (second) nature.[154] Accordingly, fetish objects are and have to do with the artificial and false (*factice*).[155] In one of Lacan's earliest pieces to appear in English, 1956's "Fetishism: The Symbolic, the Imaginary, and the Real" (coauthored with Wladimir Granoff and contemporaneous with Lacan's fourth seminar), the connection between fetishes and Symbolic signifiers is stressed throughout.[156]

Also in *Seminar IV*, in the section Jacques-Alain Miller entitles "The Fetish Object" (a section consisting of three consecutive sessions, January 30, February 6, and February 27, 1957), Lacan speaks of the symbolic order as giving rise to "the desire of the impossible" (*le désir de l'impossible*).[157] During this same seminar session (February 27, 1957), he relatedly asserts that fetishism, "the perversion of all perversions," has nothing(ness) as its object ("*l'objet est exactement rien*").[158] As I noted a moment ago, this same Lacan views fetishism as displaying the distilled essence of human *désir* tout court. Moreover, Lacanian desire consistently is linked to a libidinal dynamic involving absence, lack, nothing(ness), etc.

The fetishist's desire is governed by the missing maternal phallus. This desired thing is a contradictory, unreal (non)object sustained as a point of reference only in and through symbolization. Thus fetishism brings out in especially sharp relief the essence of desire in general as fixated upon signifier-marked impossibilities and inexistences. This explains both Lacan's association of the phallus and the fetish object with the Platonic *ágalma* in *Seminar VIII*[159] as well as his equation of the fetish with *objet petit a* as cause of desire in *Seminar X* (*Anxiety* [1962–1963]).[160]

In a fortuitous turn of phrase, the Lacan of the fourth seminar refers to the phallus as "*la monnaie majeure*" ("main currency").[161] This might very well be an intentional wording, given that the Lacan of this period soon proceeds to link his discussion of analytic fetishism with commodity fetishism à la Marx (as involving money, gold, and the like). At this juncture, though, I want to pause briefly in order to draw a comparison between the missing maternal phallus as per Lacan and Marx's account of interest in the third volume of *Das Kapital*.

190   THE SELF-CLEANING FETISH

Already in *Capital*, volume 1, in the second half of the first paragraph of "The Fetishism of the Commodity and Its Secret," Marx employs the example of a wooden table to bring out the weirdness of commodities, these apparently banal objects, within capitalism. He famously states:

> The form of wood, for instance, is altered if a table is made out of it. Nevertheless the table continues to be wood, an ordinary, sensuous thing [*ein ordinäres sinnliches Ding*]. But as soon as it emerges as a commodity, it changes into a thing which transcends sensuousness [*ein sinnlich übersinnliches Ding*]. It not only stands with its feet on the ground, but, in relation to all other commodities, it stands on its head [*auf den Kopf*], and evolves out of its wooden brain grotesque ideas, far more wonderful than if it were to begin dancing of its own free will.[162]

Arguably, the symbolized nonentity that is the absent feminine phallus underlying fetishism and its peculiar objects is of a degree of sense-transcending strangeness comparable to Marx's wooden table qua commodity (with the Marxian commodity here being "a sensible supersensible thing" [*ein sinnlich übersinnliches Ding*]).

What is more, one should remember that commodity fetishism, according to Marx, reaches its definitive apotheosis in the form of IBC. As IBC, money gives the impression of being uniquely capable of sustaining the dynamic of M-M′, namely, self-valorization as the production of surplus value ex nihilo. An object that seems to behave as a subject, an inert, lifeless product of human artifice that looks as though it spontaneously engages in an autoenhancing frenetic movement of self-multiplication—is this not at least as fantastical as maternal phalli? When functioning as IBC, money appears more than any other commodity (whether wooden tables or whatever else) "to begin dancing of its own free will." Interestingly, Norman O. Brown performs the Freudian gesture of tethering interest as money breeding money to childhood fantasies about feces—"Money is inorganic dead matter which has been made alive by inheriting the magic power which infantile narcissism attributes to the excremental product."[163] Brown soon adds that "money inherits the infantile magic of excrement and then is able to breed and have children."[164]

Before addressing Lacan's fashions of linking analytic and Marxian fetishisms, another facet of the Lacanian rendition of the fetish object is important for me to highlight. In the three sessions of *Seminar IV* entitled "The Fetish Object," Lacan brings to the fore the figure of the veil (*le voile*) or curtain (*le rideau*). The function of veiling is crucial to Lacan's speculations about fetishism.[165]

THE SELF-CLEANING FETISH   191

Lacan declares that "the curtain is . . . the idol of absence."[166] What he means by this is that the fetish object can be traced back to the last thing the young fetishist-to-be sees before this little person's vision confronts the maternal Other's lack of a phallus. This classic Freudian narrative explains, for instance, the prominence of shoe fetishism, since the mother's shoe is something seen by the small child's gaze ascending up her legs just before it alights upon her genital region. For Lacan, the fetish is "a substitute, a monument"[167]—"The fetish is a *Denkmal*."[168] That is to say, the fetish object memorializes for the fetishist the moment right before the crossing of the threshold into a registration of "castration" and/as sexual difference.[169]

During the fourth seminar, Lacan utilizes a reference to the medium of film so as to further concretize his linkage between the fetish and the curtain/veil. He describes the fetish object as arising from the sudden stoppage of a filmed sequence in which a frame immediately before the frames containing the scene of the missing maternal phallus is frozen in place. This frozen frame becomes the template for the subsequent fetish object(s). Moreover, with the freezing of the film at a moment preceding the scene of "castration," the frozen frame operates as a sort of veil covering the missing phallus. Similarly, since this same frame is part of a longer sequence, it is a metonymic fragment standing for the whole filmed episode that reaches its denouement in the confrontation with the maternal Other as deprived of the phallus.[170]

The fetish object, like a screen memory[171] as well as other types of analytic symptoms, simultaneously reveals and conceals that against which it serves as a defense. Analytic symptoms are repressions and, at the same time, returns of the repressed. As a stand-in, the fetish object conceals the maternal phallus for which it substitutes. As a monument, the fetish object reveals its repressed (or, rather, disavowed) origins, memorializing its roots for those with eyes to see and ears to hear.

Curtains and veils likewise both conceal and reveal. On the one hand, they cover over something hidden behind them. On the other hand, through this same covering, they suggest a number of possible presences or absences on their nether sides. Curtains and veils encourage those they confront to project various things into the indeterminate beyonds they shroud. Lacan's well-known recounting, in *Seminar XI*, of the trompe l'oeil painting contest between Zeuxis and Parrhasios nicely makes this point.[172] What is more, the curtain/veil serves to maintain a desire-sustaining distance between desire itself and its corresponding object.[173]

Much earlier here, I spent some time stressing the multiple connotations of the German adjective *äußerlichste* ("most superficial") in my reading of Marx's

IBC as fetishistic in *Capital*, volume 3. I proposed that a dialectics weaving together surfaces and depths as well as visibilities and invisibilities is suggested by Marx in his positing of a maximal superficiality in the fetishism of M-M'. Lacan's parsing of the analytic fetish object as a curtain/veil that simultaneously both obscures a beyond (as a kind of repression) and bears witness, like a monument or memorial, to what it obscures (as a sort of return of the repressed) arguably elucidates the type of superficiality at work in Marxian commodity fetishism as culminating in IBC. If the fetishist's object is an analytic symptom par excellence, then the place where Marx perhaps most strikingly anticipates the symptom in the analytic sense (an anticipation Lacan explicitly attributes to him) is in the treatment of interest in the third volume of *Das Kapital*.

IBC's M-M' is the fetishized seventh veil of capitalism. IBC, as the culmination of commodity fetishism, is the surface, or even the iceberg's tip, on which the revealing return of the repressed perversely coincides with the most concealing repression. On the revealing hand, M-M' renders visible the truth that capitalists accrue surplus value as something for nothing, without themselves contributing productive labor. Yet on the concealing hand, M-M' renders invisible the truth that labor, not capital, produces all values (Robinson seems blind to this truth when she remarks, "Whether we choose to say that capital is productive, or that capital is necessary to make labour productive, is not a matter of much importance").[174] IBC hides this truth behind its opposite, namely, the diametrically opposed false appearance according to which capital itself, as self-valorizing value, is the mother of all values.

In *Seminar V*, Lacan initiates a process of interweaving the Marxian and psychoanalytic theories of fetishism. Inspired by Marx, he holds up the example of gold as a paradigmatic avatar of human desire.[175] Gold historically embodies and epitomizes currency as the universal equivalent, namely, the one commodity exchangeable for all other commodities. In Lacan's terms, this makes gold, as the emblem of exchange value, a Symbolic facilitator of a *désir* sliding indefinitely from commodity to commodity. Gold-qua-money is the signifier of desire's inherent tendency to drift metonymically, restlessly, and ceaselessly from object to object.[176]

Soon after this, in *Seminar VI*, Lacan consequently insists that commodity fetishism is to be situated in his register of the Symbolic. He contends that Marx's version of fetishism depends upon the logic of the signifier as decoded by Lacanian psychoanalysis.[177] However, Lacan's conceptions of desire and Symbolic signifiers avowedly are meant to be transhistorical. In the spirit of Freudian metapsychology, Lacan is committed to a perspective according to which psychoanalysis can and does pinpoint psychical-subjective structures and dynamics common to all humans in all times and places. Moreover, Lacan even insists on the transhistorical status of core analytic concepts right when referencing Marx on money and commodity fetishism. Considering Marx's historicizing bent, this is rather perplexing.[178]

The question of just how much of a historicizer Marx is or is not is itself very tricky. On my reading of him (as developed elsewhere), he is not automatically and unqualifiedly opposed to hypothesizing transhistorical forces and factors. Indeed, certain components of his own historical materialism look as though they need to function as transcendental-type possibility conditions for history and its myriad phenomena.[179]

Yet at least when it comes to commodity fetishism, Marx almost certainly would be resistant to Lacan's gestures of wrapping it up with a desire purportedly inherent to humanity's *Gattungswesen*. Marx defines commodities such that they are objects peculiar to capitalism alone. Furthermore, although interest as money breeding money shows up in various historical modes of production, IBC as money breeding surplus value through lending to commercial/industrial (i.e., productive) capital (as M-C-M′) also is peculiar to capitalism alone. IBC is different from interest yielded by lending to nonproducing traders or consumers.

At the same time, Marx might be willing to acknowledge that the more general logic of interest as M-M′ (i.e., as operative in lending to consumers, merchants, and capitalists alike) goes from being a freak exception before capitalism (as portrayed by Aristotle,[180] for instance) to becoming the normalized rule under the reign of finance capital. Nonetheless, given the difference in kind between a consumerist desire oriented toward use values (as C-M-C′) and a properly capitalist desire oriented toward exchange/surplus values (as M-C-M′), the Lacanian move of annexing capitalistic commodity fetishism to desire as a universal, transhistorical category risks obscuring more than it illuminates.

Despite such dangers, Lacan's analytic meditations on commodity fetishism nevertheless also subtly enhance the sense in which, according to Marx, fetishism entails relations between persons showing up in the guise of relations between things.[181] To be more exact, Lacan links fetish objects, including Marxian commodities, to his notion of *le désir de l'Autre* (the desire of the Other). He proposes that the exchanged objects of commodity fetishism signify this desire.[182] Blending together Marx's and Lacan's wordings, this would be to say that fetishized commodity-objects are things substituting, memorializing, or standing in for Others and the subject's (fraught non)relationships with them. But what precisely does this mean? And, what are its implications for Marxism and/or psychoanalysis?

194 THE SELF-CLEANING FETISH

Beginning to answer these questions requires me invoking the title of this chapter, namely, the phrase "the self-cleaning fetish." This phrase might initially call to mind symptomatic compulsive hand washing. However, I am referring with this title instead to capitalist money as laundering itself. Although money is not really self-valorizing—it appears so only through capital's illusory eclipsing of the productivity of the labor power it exploits—it certainly looks to be self-laundering under capitalism.

In fact, at this juncture, three different modes of capitalistic money's self-laundering ought to be identified. First, there is the ideology of the level playing field of job markets wherein capital and labor meet and negotiate fair-and-square employment contracts. In particular, there is the myth of a day's wages for a day's work. This myth insidiously conflates the market value of the peculiar commodity that is labor power (i.e., "a day's wages" as the subsistence price of the production and reproduction of this labor power as the one commodity that can generate more exchange value than it itself costs)[183] with the market value of the other commodities produced by the application of this labor power (i.e., "a day's work" as real labor actually performed over the course of the working day at the behest of capital, with this real labor generally producing the "surplus" of more exchange value than the exchange value embodied in this labor's daily wages).[184] Obviously, this myth trades upon a false equivalence between the quantity of monetary remuneration for labor performed and the quantity of time spent in performing said labor. Money as wages thereby, within the frame of this fiction, conceals capitalism's structurally necessary exploitation of labor power in the guise of surplus unpaid labor as surplus value appropriated gratis by capital.

Second, there is, as I explained earlier, the difference between rate of surplus value and rate of profit. The rate of surplus value calculates this value in relation to variable capital only. By contrast, the rate of profit calculates surplus value in relation to total capital (i.e., variable plus constant capital). Hence, looking at surplus value as profit makes it seem as though capital is extracting much less from labor than it is in actuality. Worse still, the notion of profit tends to be ideologically packaged as "wages of superintendence" and/or "profit of enterprise," namely, income genuinely earned by capitalists performing specialized sorts of their own labor. The members of the bourgeoisie sweat too. They truly deserve just compensation.

Third, there are the illusions emanating from money as IBC. Such money capital is indeed the apex of commodity fetishism. It presents the fiction of a golden egg laying more golden eggs—and this without either goose or goose-rearing farmer. IBC is the divine miracle, the immaculate conception, of surplus value enhancing itself ex nihilo, without productive labor or any living subjective agency whatsoever.[185] M-M′ is akin to a thingly version of Baron Munchausen, money pulling itself up ever higher by nothing but its own hair. A person performing such a feat just once is fantastical enough. An inert object doing so ad infinitum is beyond belief. Yet interest fetishism is precisely belief in this fantastical thing, this incredible fiction. Such belief in the power of self-multiplying money launders (i.e., represses) acknowledgment that labor, not capital, is the sole and ultimate source of all use, exchange, and surplus values.

But even if one discovers and comes to see through all three of these self-laundering operations of capitalism's money, such insight alone is not enough. The Enlightenment article of faith having it that knowing the truth is itself already liberating fails to hold in Marxism and psychoanalysis, and especially in cases of both commodity and analytic fetishism. Freud's and Lacan's analyses of fetishism are particularly helpful in further elucidating and buttressing Marx's long-standing thesis according to which theoretical critique (i.e., the "weapon of criticism") is no substitute for corresponding practical action (i.e., the "criticism of weapons").[186]

Marx starts distinguishing himself from the Left Hegelian fellow travelers of his youth in concluding that purely intellectual attacks by themselves are insufficient for revolutionary change.[187] Psychoanalysis, particularly in relation to commodity fetishism as per the mature Marx, is of great assistance in reinforcing this feature of Marx's position. However, as will be seen, this assistance might be so great as to indicate that at a bigger-picture level, Marx was too sanguine about the nearness of capitalism's demise. In this manner, psychoanalysis might prove to be a dangerous, albeit crucial, supplement for (classical) Marxism.

One of the peculiarities of fetishism, according to psychoanalysis, is its distinctive defense mechanism. Freud identifies "disavowal" (*Verleugnung*) as fetishism's signature way of dealing with castration qua the absence of the maternal phallus.[188] Freudian *Verleugnung* entails a "divided attitude" (*zweispältige Einstellung*).[189] Mannoni famously encapsulates this divided attitude of the disavowing fetishist with the mantra "*Je sais bien, mais quand même...*"[190] The division is between the affirmation of castration (i.e., Freud's "*die Behauptung*"[191] and Mannoni's "I know full well") and its denial (i.e., Freud's *Verleugnung* and Mannoni's "but nonetheless..."). Lacan describes this cleavage of mindset as an ambivalence characteristic of the fetishist.[192] Freud himself even goes so far, in two texts from the end of his life (*An Outline of Psycho-Analysis*[193] and "Splitting of the Ego in the Process of Defense,"[194] both from 1938), as to connect disavowal as fetishistic *Verleugnung* with a "splitting of the ego"

(*Ichspaltung*) into irreconcilable portions.[195] Consistency definitely is not a hobgoblin of fetishistic minds.

The perversions in general are difficult to treat clinically. Since perverse subjects enjoy their symptoms, they tend not to seek out treatment of their own volition. If they present for an analysis (or for nonanalytic psychotherapy), often it is because they are being pushed into doing so either by law enforcement or a spouse threatening divorce. The prognosis for a reluctant, coerced analysand is never good.[196] Analysands tend to be sufficiently motivated to endure the hardships of the analytic process only if and when their symptoms become, on balance, more unsatisfactory than satisfactory, with their libidinal investments in these symptoms thereby being promisingly loosened and diminished. Only faltering pathologies and failing defenses promise therapeutic successes.

With fetishism in particular, as a species of the genus perversion, the difficulty for analysis is even greater still. Freud, near the end of his 1927 piece on the subject, notes of fetishisms with pronounced disavowal that "a fetish of this sort, doubly derived from contrary ideas, is of course especially durable [*Ein solcher Fetisch, aus Gegensätzen doppelt geknüpft, hält natürlich besonders gut*]."[197] The fetishist's divided attitude, with its "contrary ideas," enables the fetishist to defang and render ineffective the analyst's interpretations of his/her (but almost always his) perverse symptoms through a sort of intellectual acceptance of the repressed—with intellectual acceptance as a maneuver in which the return of the repressed redoubles the initial repression, rather than undoing it. As per Mannoni, to each analytic interpretation, the fetishistic analysand can (and usually does) respond with a version of "I know full well" (*Je sais bien*). Thereby, no interpretive bull's-eyes stick.

Then, there is the corresponding disavowal of this same knowledge (of castration, sexual difference, and the impossible, nonexistent feminine phallus)[198] in the style of the fetishist's immediately ensuing "but nonetheless... [*mais quand même*]." This negating "nonetheless" typically occurs not so much in (conscious) thoughts and words but, instead, is crystallized in the form of the fetish object itself[199] (and the enacted sexual behavior accompanying it, in which female genitalia are sidelined). The fetish object is a prosthetic believer. That is to say, it is as though this privileged thing does the believing in the feminine phallus for the fetishist.

The fetishistic subject thus is permitted to not believe that he really, unconsciously believes what is consciously "known full well" to be absurd, disgusting, disturbing, horrifying, incomprehensible, nonsensical, ridiculous, traumatic, etc. Through the fetish, belief is depsychologized and objectified, preserved in being ossified and held manipulably, manageably at arm's length. In this case, spirit really is a bone, with the fetishist's disavowed belief (spirit) rematerializing as the fetish object (bone). Even for professional analysts, it is remarkably challenging to disabuse people of beliefs they do not believe they have—although these people sometimes even literally are holding these beliefs in their hands while denying they retain them.[200]

The opening paragraph of "The Fetishism of the Commodity and Its Secret" indicates that the commodity fetishist too does not believe in the "metaphysical subtleties and theological niceties" materialized within both commodities and the commodity fetishist's externalized behavior toward them in society's marketplaces. As Marx comments in the first sentence of this most famous section of volume 1 of *Capital*, "A commodity appears at first sight to be an extremely obvious, trivial thing."[201] Convincing a commodity fetishist that he/she, in his/her efficacious public conduct, does not actually relate to commodities as "obvious" and "trivial" poses similar challenges to analyzing a sexual fetishist.

The same might hold for IBC, the capitalist commodity fetish par excellence. IBC's fetishist fetishizes the peculiar commodity that is money capital. Some of these interest fetishists perhaps know full well that money by itself does not really engender more money, but nonetheless . . . when they lend out their money, it tends to return to them in an amount larger than that initially lent.[202] Even if they personally do not believe in money breeding money, why would they stop loaning it if they keep receiving M′ from others in exchange for M? If others are fools enough to continue doing this, they too would be fools in turn were they to stop taking advantage of this persisting social fact.

The cynically enlightened financial capitalist safely can bank on others desiring money and believing in its seemingly magical powers to grow on its own despite its lifeless artificiality. Borrowing more language from Mannoni, this jaded rentier does not "believe in magic" but rather believes in "a magic of belief" (i.e., others' beliefs and, ultimately, the beliefs of a faceless, indeterminate Other).[203] The idle speculator conjures up his income from this very magic. Why cease enjoying others' symptoms? Why not live off of the easy, effortless con-artistry of capitalizing on "a magic of belief?" Why not make a career out of being a professional compulsive gambler playing with other people's money in casinos ranging from national stock markets to online day-trading websites?

Lacan, and Mannoni following him, furnishes valuable assistance here. The Lacanian approach to commodity fetishism brings into theoretical consideration the desires and beliefs of others.[204] In the case of Marx's commodity fetishist, one can imagine "curing" an individual commodity fetishist in a two-step process. First, he/she is somehow or other finally brought to recognize and admit that he/she in truth does indeed subscribe to a host of "metaphysical subtleties and theological niceties" apropos those objects that are commodities. Second, this commodity fetishist is then converted into being a thoroughgoing critic of these now-avowed beliefs, wholeheartedly denouncing them as ideological, illusory, insidious, and so on.

Yet even for such a "cured" commodity fetishist, if others around him/her still go on behaving in fashions conforming to commodity fetishism, then the surrounding socioeconomic system (i.e., the capitalistic symbolic order, capital as big Other) compels him/her likewise to perseverate in commodity-fetishistic behavior. He/she thus is not effectively cured after all. In general, one believes in money because one believes that others believe in money. As Andrew Feenberg aptly puts this, "money is money only insofar as we act as though it were money and it is the success of this sort of action that determines our conviction that money is in fact money."[205] Belief in money is a second- and third-hand belief, not a first-person one. Hence, if, for instance, a "cured" IBC fetishist remains convinced that others are convinced of the wondrous self-multiplying powers of money capital as M-M', then he/she is not even really cured of his/her fetishism in the first place.

What is more, the others to whom the disillusioned commodity fetishist relates hypothetically could themselves also, as individuals, be disabused of commodity fetishism too. But so long as each "cured" subject relates to the others as if these others are not cured, then commodity fetishism strangely persists as an effective socioeconomic reality to which nobody subjectively adheres in terms of first-person belief. Everyone's being cured is not enough. Everyone has to believe that everyone else has been cured too—and, even then . . . An anonymous Other, perhaps nowhere instantiated among society's subjects taken merely as an aggregate of individuals interrelating, is enough to sustain commodity fetishism. So long as "they believe," all singular subjects are free to take themselves to be disbelievers while continuing to produce and reproduce really existing commodity fetishism as an integral part of the external socioeconomic system of capitalism.[206]

Freud's 1927 underscoring of the "especially durable" (*hält . . . besonders gut*) quality of the fetish is worth noting again at this point. Bringing Lacan and Mannoni to bear on Marx makes this Freudian observation especially resonant with commodity fetishism as I have parsed it in the immediately preceding paragraphs. The durability of commodity fetishes, IBC included, now can be more profoundly appreciated.

Initially, commodity fetishists do not believe that they fetishize commodities ("For me, commodities are extremely obvious, trivial things"). If they come to realize and see through their (previously unconscious) beliefs in "metaphysical subtleties and theological niceties," they likely continue to believe that others continue to believe in such subtleties and niceties. In so doing, they compulsively reproduce their own commodity fetishism in what really counts, namely, their actions. Furthermore, if even these others also have self-consciously disinvested in the ideology of commodity fetishism, this still is insufficient to deactivate and dissolve the reality of commodity fetishism so long as each subject (mis)attributes investment in this fetishism to others (or to the spectral Other as a ghostly presence both everywhere and nowhere at once, a vague and impersonal They). Like the Freudian fetish, commodity fetishism is surprisingly stubborn.

When all is said and done, commodity fetishism as per Marx is grounded in and amounts to the objective (and not subjective) alienation in which, under capitalism, it truly is the case that persons and their social relations are governed by things and things' exchange relations.[207] Unless and until social control is (re) asserted over the palpably concrete invisible hand of commodities and their market interactions, commodity fetishism will persist uncured.[208] Minus the anticapitalistic, materialist criticism of weapons, no antifetishistic, idealist weapon of criticism will deal commodity fetishism the coup de grâce. As Marx puts this:

> The religious reflections of the real world [*Der* religiöse Widerschein *der wirkli-chen Welt*] can...vanish only when the practical relations of everyday life between man and man, and man and nature, generally present themselves to him in a transparent and rational form [*die Verhältnisse des praktischen Werkel-tagslebens den Menschen tagtäglich durchsichtig vernünftige Beziehungen zuein-ander und zur Natur darstellen*]. The veil is not removed [*streift nur ihren myst-ischen Nebelschleier ab*] from the countenance of the social life-process [*Gestalt des gesellschaftlichen Lebensprozesses*], i.e. the process of material production, until it becomes production by freely associated men [*frei vergesellschafteter Menschen*], and stands under their conscious and planned control. This, how-ever, requires that society possess a material foundation [*eine materielle Grund-lage*], or a series of material conditions of existence [*eine Reihe materieller Existenzbedingungen*], which in their turn are the natural and spontaneous product of a long and tormented historical development [*einer langen und qual-vollen Entwicklungsgeschichte*].[209]

The first sentence of this passage has deep roots in Marx's thinking, going back to some of his earliest writings (most notably, the opening paragraphs of his 1843/1844 essay "A Contribution to the Critique of Hegel's Philosophy of Right. Introduction").[210] My psychoanalytic reflections on commodity fetishism suggest that a qualification should be appended to these remarks from the first volume of *Capital*: Alas, the "social life-process [*Gestalt des gesellschaftlichen Lebensprozesses*], i.e. the process of material production" can survive and continue on, at least for a long while, after the removal of the veil (or, more in line with Marx's German here, the dissipation of the mystical mist [*mystischen Nebelschleier*], the ideological veil of fog).

As Žižek expresses this caveat, Marx's old formula for ideology, "They do not know what they are doing, but they are doing it nonetheless," needs to be counterbalanced by a new formula for ideology having it that "They know full well what they are doing, but they are doing it nonetheless"[211] (a reformulation foreshadowed by Marcuse).[212] The history of capitalism after Marx's death in 1883 and up through the present has rendered utterly implausible the Bible-borrowed Enlightenment confidence of "Know the truth, and the truth will set you free." Analytic sexual fetishism, more than any other psychopathological phenomenon, drives home the power of commodity fetishism, and the entire mode of production with which it is inseparably enmeshed, to endure even after its dirty secrets have been publicly aired.

Marx writes above of future social trajectories having to undergo "a long and tormented historical development" (*einer langen und qualvollen Entwicklungsgeschichte*) in order to bring about the dismantling of the capitalist mode of production (and, with it, of the materialized fetishism of commodities). The psychoanalytic perspective on fetishism does not (at least not necessarily) contradict the idea that such development might eventually come to pass. Perhaps, at some point on the road ahead, the calibration of satisfactions and dissatisfactions with the social symptoms that are commodity fetishes will tilt decisively in the direction of dissatisfaction for a critical mass of capitalism's subjects.[213]

But in the meantime, a twenty-first-century Lacano-Marxist reassessment of commodity fetishism forecasts an even longer, more tormented historical development ahead than Marx somewhat optimistically expected. As for the sexual fetishist's analyst, so too for the historical-materialist critic of commodity fetishists: Patience is a virtue. A new communist patience is urgently needed.[214]

4

The Triumph of Theological Economics

God Goes Underground

§17. GOD IS UNDEAD:
THE INVISIBLE HAND RISES FROM THE GRAVE

Lacan, during his deservedly celebrated eleventh seminar of 1964 on *The Four Fundamental Concepts of Psychoanalysis*, issues what I soon will interpret as a warning that Marxists especially should heed—"the true formula of atheism is not *God is dead* . . . the true formula of atheism is *God is unconscious.*"[1] One of Lacan's explicit points of reference at this very moment is Freud's *Totem and Taboo*. Specifically, Lacan has in mind the Freudian "primal father" of the primitive horde as the prehistorical prototype of history's subsequent paternal gods.[2]

For Freudian psychoanalysis à la Lacan, the deceased deity of *"God is dead"* would be, first and foremost, none other than the *Urvater* murdered by the rebellious band of brothers.[3] And as Freud famously observes in his 1913 exercise in speculative anthropology, "The dead father became stronger than the living one had been."[4] Via these analytic premises, Lacan arrives at his striking, counterintuitive conclusion: God is perhaps more potent and oppressive when dead rather than alive. Or maybe one could say that the withering away of the theological letter, at least sometimes, paradoxically results in an invigoration of the sectarian spirit. A specifically spiritual hangover might be the longest and worst of all.[5]

But by Lacan's reasoning, what directly connects *"God is dead"* with *"God is unconscious"*? Why is the former not, as it so often is taken to be, "the true formula of atheism"? Similarly, why, according to Lacan, might a God presumed to be dead be more formidable and influential than an ostensibly living deity? As I explain elsewhere:

The Lacanian lesson for aspiring atheists is not only that consciously mouthing the words "God is dead" is insufficient for ridding oneself of religiosity once and for all—intoning such a mantra, under the impression that it possesses the power to conjure away the spirits of theism, risks blinding one to the multifarious manners in which ghostly unconscious religious beliefs continue to enjoy a psychical afterlife in the aftermath of the supposed accession to atheism at the level of self-consciousness. In fact, if anything, to be a full-fledged atheist, one must, as Lacan indicates, be warily aware that "God is unconscious"—which, in psychoanalysis, is to be far from dead and gone. In other words, unless and until one is willing and able to accept that theological and quasi-theological residues will subsist in an unconscious that will continue to speak in oneself and despite oneself—this unconscious God does not die if and when consciousness declares the divine to be deceased and departed—one is likely to remain in the thrall of religiosity (even more so the less one believes oneself to believe). How many people, perceiving themselves decisively to have abandoned religion and everything associated with it long ago in their personal histories, discover on an analyst's couch just how persistent and pervasive in their present lives are the lingering spectral traces of a never-really-discarded-faith? Like the ghost of Freud's murdered *Urvater*, God can and does return in even more powerful guises in the wake of having been declared dead. Altering a line from the 1995 film *The Usual Suspects* . . . maybe the greatest trick God can play is convincing the world he does not exist.[6]

For Lacan, atheism means eternal vigilance regarding this (un)dead God.[7] A central feature of my line of argumentation in what follows is the straightforward application of this psychoanalytic cautionary insight apropos religiosity at the individual psychical level to the transindividual social level as dealt with by the historical-materialist critique of political economy. This application is made easier and defensible by virtue of religion itself being simultaneously a singularly personal and collectively social reality. One of my claims in the present chapter is that there is a crucial fashion in which Lacan's "*God is unconscious*" rings true for late capitalism's material base at least as much as for particular analysands' unconsciouses. Without appreciating this truth, historical materialism today risks underestimating the resilience and endurance of capitalism's economic infrastructure and its religious superstructures as interacting with each other in hitherto underappreciated ways I will delineate subsequently.

Indeed, Lacan, at the close of the 1973 written version of *Télévision*, speaks darkly of "the hand that draws only from Dad to worse [*ce qui ne parie que du père au pire*]."[8] My pivot to Marx and his critical assessments of capitalist economics below will suggest that the Smithian "invisible hand of the market" is not unrelated to this Lacanian appendage moving *"du père au pire."* This movement would be none other than that of the hand of the visible living God at the superstructural level of the religious (i.e., "Dad") turning into an invisible undead specter at the infrastructural level of the economic (i.e., "worse"). This religious-become-economic spirit, a pseudosecularizing sublimation of the theological, would be one (if not the) incarnation of God after the death of God, an unconscious revenant firmly gripping even the most self-consciously atheistic subjects (of course, Marx compares capital to the undead, specifically to vampires feeding off the living).[9] To paraphrase Marx's own paraphrase of William Shakespeare,[10] well grubbed, old God!

Returning to Freud again, the author of 1927's *The Future of an Illusion* appears to have forgotten his own earlier lesson about the dead father's fierce persistence in the forms of an earthly afterlife. Surrounded by such phenomena as the rapid rise of European fascism along with myriad stubborn "resistances to psychoanalysis," Freud succumbs to the false comforts of an all-too-traditional Enlightenment progress narrative about the eventual sociocultural victory of secular scientific reason. He imagines his irrational religious (if not also political) enemies as doomed to inevitable defeat.[11] Even the founder of psychoanalysis is far from immune to the everyday and not-so-everyday psychopathological mechanisms he discovers. How else is one to explain the later Freud managing, if only momentarily, to ignore his own career-long critical delineations of the limits of reason and corresponding confrontations with the psyche's incredible capacities for clinging to fantasies, sustaining contradictions, and denying the undeniable?

The title of Oskar Pfister's 1928 response to *The Future of an Illusion*, "The Illusion of a Future,"[12] is a fitting designation for an immanent critique of this particular Freud.[13] Pfister, a longtime friend and correspondent of Freud's, is justified precisely on Freudian grounds in challenging the Freud of 1927 by suggesting that the latter's "soft voice of the intellect" may not "gain a hearing" (*"die Stimme des Intellekts ist leise, aber sie ruht nicht, ehe sie sich Gehör geschafft hat"*),[14] perhaps ever. Contra Freud's faith that humanity shall by destiny come to know the Godless truth and be set free from religiosity by it, Pfister maintains that God will not be disappearing anytime soon.

Roughly the past century of social history up through the present appears to be a massive rebuke to the predictions of *The Future of an Illusion*. With this fact in view, Lacan, in an interview with Italian journalists given in Rome in 1974, speaks, *pace* Freud, of "the triumph of religion"[15] (the phrase Jacques-Alain Miller chooses as the title for this text). Indeed, the title of the present chapter is, in part, an allusion to this now well-known interview. Although, to the best of my knowledge, Lacan nowhere makes direct reference to Pfister, the former's "triumph of religion" cross-resonates with the latter's "illusion of a future."[16] With the further benefit of later-twentieth-century hindsight, Lacan cannot but enter into uncharacteristic overt disagreement with Freud. Throughout the 1970s, the later Lacan's prevailing attitude toward religiosity, sharply contrasting with Freud's 1927 (false) optimism about the supposedly fated victory of irreligious rationality, is one of resignation, of an exhausted, pessimistic anticipation of God's indefinite survival far off into the *à venir*.[17]

Until recently, it seemed that Europe, if nowhere else, was the notable exception to the rule of the past century's noncompliance with Enlightenment-style forecasts (ones sometimes endorsed by both Marx and Freud) of the fading away of religions. For a time, it looked as though, at least in certain quarters of the Continent, statistically measurable increases in secularization went hand in hand with the expansion and intensification of the technoscientific mediation of quotidian life. In "The Triumph of Religion," Lacan, again contradicting the author of *The Future of an Illusion*, puts forward an anti-Enlightenment prediction according to which the increasing saturation of the Real by the natural sciences and their technological offspring, rather than sustaining secularizing tendencies, will give a further boost to theologies, spiritualisms, and the like. By Lacan's lights, the more that technoscientific mediation reduces existence to meaningless mathematized materiality, the more tightly will human beings cling to religious supplements as apparent anchors of meaning within a sea of senselessness.[18]

But Lacan's antithesis to the Enlightenment conception of the zero-sum relation between the religious and scientific worldviews aside, the early twenty-first century has seen even Europe come to be blatantly at odds with Marx's and Freud's eighteenth-century-vintage visions of capitalism- and science-driven desacralization. Things religious prominently feature in the currently rolling tidal wave of right-wing populism sweeping across the Continent as well as other parts of the world—albeit not so much in terms of theological or spiritualist belief in the other-worldly but, instead, as all-too-this-worldly tribal insignias of us-versus-them cultural identity. One need only call to mind, to list just a few examples, the French Catholicism invoked by Marine Le Pen's Rassemblement National, the Western Christendom of Germany's Patriotische Europäer gegen die Islamisierung des Abendlandes (PEGIDA), Jarosław Kaczyński's Catholic Law and Justice Party in Poland, and the Hungarian Christianity upheld by Fidesz and Jobbik. Sadly, the corrupt wastrel brazenly breaking most, if not all, of the Ten Commandments purportedly holy and dear to his loyal Christian Evangelical supporters is nothing exceptional. As an aside, I admittedly have difficulty imagining that Donald Trump often asks himself, "What would Jesus do?"

§18. TRANSUBSTANTIATIONS: DESACRALIZATION AND THE AFTERLIFE OF THE SACRED

Of course, Marx intellectually comes of age on a Continent permeated with mixtures of reaction and religion—more precisely, in the context of the Protestant-underwritten conservative Prussian politics of Friedrich Wilhelm III, a politics wishing to turn back the clock of history to before 1789. Understandably, the Left Hegelian comrades of Marx's youth, constrained by political oppression and excruciatingly aware of Christianity's role in legitimizing it, indirectly condemn this politics by directly assaulting its religious buttresses. Throughout the 1830s, the young Marx and his fellow travelers invest much hope in the very German (especially Lutheran) notion that a spiritual reform is the key to a secular revolution. They believe that attacking the Christian religion with "the weapons of criticism" will render unnecessary any inconveniently bloody confrontation of the secular state with, as in next-door France, "the criticism of weapons."[19]

During the first half of the 1840s, as is well known, Marx becomes his own thinker in losing this faith in the critique of religion as the Alpha and Omega of radical leftism. Thanks to a combination of critical reflection on Hegel's political philosophy of the state as well as becoming acutely cognizant of the importance of economic dimensions primarily through encountering Engels,[20] Marx comes into his own by repudiating key aspects of Left Hegelianism. His signature gesture of rupture with Feuerbach et al. is to point out that forms of alienation analogous to Feuerbachian religious alienation are fully in force at the (supposedly) secular levels of politics and economics. Humanity, through its self-alienating self-objectifications, misrecognizes its own hands not only as those of God but also as those of the State and the Market. Disposing of just one pair of invisible appendages still leaves the others intact and operative, still pulling the strings of its human creators-become-puppets.

Hence Marx, by the mid-1840s, fatefully concludes that theoretically subverting religion is not enough by itself. It is no substitute for practically struggling against the institutions of economy and government. All of this is elegantly encapsulated in the opening pages of Marx's 1843/1844 introductory overview

206 ~❀ THE TRIUMPH OF THEOLOGICAL ECONOMICS

of his critique of Hegel's political philosophy.[21] Likewise, in the 1844 Paris *Economic and Philosophical Manuscripts*, Marx distinguishes atheism as "theoretical humanism" from communism as "practical humanism."[22] In 1844 and 1845, Marx and Engels, in their coauthored *The Holy Family, or Critique of Critical Criticism* as well as *The German Ideology*, relatedly indict the Left Hegelians for, with their Hegelianism, allegedly making history "march on its head." Such Hegelians, however much they criticize religion, fundamentally remain in thrall to religiosity's idealism, an idealism according to which material reality, with its profane practices of the stupid many, is ruled by mental spirit, with its sacred theories of the smart few.[23]

Just a handful of years later, the *Communist Manifesto* famously prophesies capitalism inadvertently bringing about the dissolution of religiosity (a prophecy Marx and Engels continue to believe in after 1848).[24] For this Marx and Engels, the bourgeoisie itself renders progressive leftist critics of religion largely redundant. Bourgeois capitalism already spontaneously critiques and erodes its spiritualist superstructural accompaniments, leaving irreligious theorists merely to dot some I's and cross some T's in its wake. This automatic, infrastructurally induced desacralization is part of why "the bourgeoisie, historically, has played a most revolutionary [*höchst revolutionäre*] part."[25] (Incidentally, Smith, in *The Wealth of Nations*, foreshadows the thesis of the *Communist Manifesto* according to which infrastructural development spontaneously sweeps away superstructural ideologies.)[26] Marx and Engels continue:

> The bourgeoisie, wherever it has got the upper hand [*Herrschaft*], has put an end to all feudal, patriarchal, idyllic relations. It has pitilessly torn asunder the motley feudal ties that bound man to his "natural superiors," and has left remaining no other nexus between man and man than naked self-interest, than callous "cash payment" [*bare Zahlung*]. It has drowned the most heavenly ecstasies of religious fervor [*die heiligen Schauer der frommen Schwärmerei*], of chivalrous enthusiasm [*Begeisterung*], of philistine sentimentalism, in the icy water of egotistical calculation [*eiskalten Wasser egotischer Berechnung*]. It has resolved personal worth into exchange value, and in place of the numberless indefeasible chartered freedoms, has set up that single, unconscionable freedom—free trade. In one word, for exploitation, veiled by religious and political illusions, it has substituted naked, shameless, direct, brutal exploitation.[27]

They soon add:

> The bourgeoisie cannot exist without constantly revolutionizing the instruments of production, and thereby the relations of production, and with them

the whole relations of society. Conservation of the old modes of production in unaltered form, was, on the contrary, the first condition of existence for all earlier industrial classes. Constant revolutionizing of production, uninterrupted disturbance of all social conditions, everlasting uncertainty and agitation distinguish the bourgeois epoch from all earlier ones. All fixed, fast-frozen relations, with their train of ancient and venerable prejudices and opinions, are swept away, all new-formed ones become antiquated before they can ossify. All that is solid [*Ständische und Stehende*] melts into air, all that is holy [*Heilige*] is profaned, and man is at last compelled to face with sober senses, his real condition of life, and his relations with his kind.[28]

It appears that subsequent history has been just as unkind to Marx and Engels's 1848 heralding and celebration of economically driven profanation as it has been to Freud's 1927 anticipation and endorsement of scientifically driven secularization. Enlightenment dreams of historical progress disappointingly have turned out to be just that. The Left Hegelians, for all their antireligiosity, never escaped from the confines of spiritualist idealism. Maybe Marx and Engels, for all their anticapitalism, failed to see that much of capitalism's frenetic, ever-intensifying activity is, ultimately, a case of *plus ça change*.[29] The revolutions of the bourgeoisie actually are essentially conservative—and this in line with Lacan's highlighting of the celestial sense of "revolution" (i.e., movement orbiting around the same old fixed point) as a barbed retort to the aspiring political revolutionaries of May '68.[30]

So, obviously, capitalism and religion, perhaps not unrelatedly, have proven to enjoy much longer leases on life than Marx, Engels, and Freud hoped and expected. Ironically for the Marx who indulges in progress narratives, part of what makes Marx's historical materialism so timely and relevant at present is the sad fact that the twenty-first century looks disturbingly like a regression to the Dickensian economic inequalities and bellicose ethnoreligious identitarianisms of the nineteenth and early twentieth centuries. Nowadays, even non-Marxist historians are observing with alarm and dismay that today's world looks an awful lot like the powder keg that eventually exploded in the First World War (with the ensuing Great Depression and Second World War). To rebut Marx-the-Enlightenment-optimist with a variation on this very Marx's own words, humanity keeps repeatedly confronting the same set of tasks it shows itself to be continually unable to solve.[31] A solution to the problems of capitalism, to capitalism itself as the problem, feels as far away as ever.

In addition to its forecasts of desacralization, the *Communist Manifesto*, as does much of the rest of Marx's corpus, also contains predictions according to which capitalism sooner or later will reach a peak-like developmental tipping point, a phase transition at which it will reduce itself to the ashes out of which will arise the phoenix of a socialism destined to grow into full-fledged communism. At least thus far, history since Marx's and Engels's deaths has refused to vindicate this prophecy too. A perverse recycling of the catastrophes of the first half of the twentieth century now seems a more likely prospect than global communist salvation. Of course, for roughly the past century, Marxists after Marx and Engels have kept themselves quite busy revising Marxism so as to account for the various ways in which post-1883 events have deviated markedly from Marx's sanguine nineteenth-century projections.

One of my core contentions in this chapter is that historical materialism has to be revised in response not only to the past century's economic and geopolitical contradictions of Marx's readings of his own century's tea leaves but also in response to Lacan's "triumph of religion." Indeed, a Marxist repetition of Lacan is in order here. Insofar as Marx subscribes to the same eighteenth-century secular rationalist progress narratives as the Freud of *The Future of an Illusion* (a subscription glaringly on display in the infamous preface to 1859's *A Contribution to the Critique of Political Economy*[32] in addition to the *Communist Manifesto*), the past one-hundred-plus years of social history obligates any intellectually honest Marxist to perform vis-à-vis Marx what the Lacan of 1974 performs vis-à-vis the Freud of 1927.

However, just as Lacan's critique of this Freud is immanent rather than external, so too with what I am proposing with respect to Marx: A critique of Marx's historical materialism can and should be a historical-materialist one (i.e., what Karl Korsch describes as *"the application of the materialist conception of history to the materialist conception of history itself"*).[33] What I might risk calling Freud's own psychoanalytic "critique of pure reason" provides some of the best means for problematizing his occasional embraces of Enlightenment rationalism (such as in *The Future of an Illusion*). Similarly, Marx's oeuvre is littered with resources permitting an immanent-critical challenging of his eighteenth-century-era faith in the inevitability of religiosity's progressive withering away.

In particular, Marx's texts from his youth onward are peppered with irreverent redeployments of religious (especially Judeo-Christian) language, symbolism, imagery, etc. These instances are far too numerous and frequent to be cited individually. Suffice it to say preliminarily that their functions vary. Occasionally, Marx appears merely to be amusing himself with provocative bits of playful impiety. More often, he comes across as underscoring his above-mentioned post-Feuerbachian thesis according to which there are structural isomorphisms between, on the one hand, religious phenomena and, on the other hand, political and economic ones. At their most serious, Marx's mobilizations of religious references seem to approach the crucial insight not only that an economy is always-already a political economy (i.e., economic infrastructures are shaped and sustained by political superstructures) but also that economies, at least sometimes, are religious economies too.[34]

Indeed, Marx, in his mature critique of political economy, implicitly acknowledges that the historical-materialist distinction between the infrastructural and the superstructural requires nuancing insofar as economic infrastructure is stabilized and perpetuated via political superstructures mediating it from within.[35] (Michel Foucault is simply wrong to accuse Marx and his historical materialism of failing to acknowledge complex social entanglements such as those between juridical and economic dimensions.)[36] Marx's wide-ranging discussions of capitalism and its history include myriad registrations of how such political superstructures as parliamentary legislation, legal regulations, judicial interventions, foreign aid, colonial enterprises, police actions, and military force have been and continue to be essential conditions for the very existence of capital and its ongoing processes of self-valorization. As the opening sentence of the preface to *A Contribution to the Critique of Political Economy* stipulates, a detailed treatment of the state was one of the planned but unwritten volumes of *Capital*—hence envisioned by Marx as an integral part of the critique of political economy.[37]

However, perhaps as a result of Marx's mid-1840s rupture with Feuerbach and the Left Hegelians, his unfulfilled plans for *Das Kapital*, while including a volume on political superstructure as indispensable for economic infrastructure, do not include one on religious superstructure as similarly indispensable. Yet at the same time, there are moments in the portions of the critique of political economy Marx did manage to write when, for instance, he beats Weber to the punch in recognizing and underscoring the pivotal role of Protestantism in the historical development of European capitalism.[38] Later, I will address the differences between Marx's and Weber's handlings of Protestant Christianity (and this in tandem with addressing the non-Marxist "theologies" of Carl Schmitt and Giorgio Agamben).

The most familiar moment in which Marx signals that political economy is also theological economy is the famous opening paragraph of part 1, chapter 1, section 4 of the first volume of *Capital*, namely, the celebrated section entitled "The Fetishism of the Commodity and Its Secret" (with "fetishism" here being a concept borrowed from the history of religions). Specifically, I have in mind this opening paragraph's first two sentences—"A commodity appears at first sight an extremely obvious [*selbstverständliches*], trivial thing. But its analysis brings out that it is a very strange thing [*ein sehr vertracktes Ding*], abounding in metaphysical subtleties [*metaphysischer Spitzfindigkeit*] and theological niceties [*theologischer Mucken*]."[39] As both Étienne Balibar and Žižek perspicaciously have brought out, these lines by Marx suggest a reversal of the standard idea of ideology critique: Instead of, as per the Left Hegelian critique of religion, trying to get people to see the this-worldly in place of the other-worldly, the Marxist critique of commodity fetishism inversely aims to reveal the other-worldly hiding in plain sight within the this-worldly.[40] And in line with Marx's notion of "real abstraction,"[41] the excessive nuances (*als metaphysischer Spitzfindigkeit*) and flea-crackers' molehills (*als theologischer Mucken*) of the metaphysics and theology dwelling within the capitalist economy, although abstract, are anything but unreal.

Balibar's and Žižek's valuable insights aside, I wish to propose taking Marx's uses of the words "fetishism" and "theological" in his critical analysis of the economic category of the commodity perhaps more literally than even Marx might intend. According to one reading, "The Fetishism of the Commodity and Its Secret" would be merely a striking exemplar of Marx's long-standing post-Feuerbachian procedure of drawing parallels between religious and economic forms of alienation.[42] An alternative reading would credit Marx with here recognizing an immanent theology internal to the economy, rather than a parallel between the religious and the economic as entirely separate and distinct superstructural and infrastructural dimensions respectively.[43]

I would go yet further and contend that the difference between these two readings of Marx on commodity fetishism reflect a tension actually internal to Marx's own thinking about the religious, the economic, and their relations. More precisely, I see the post-1845 historical-materialist Marx as, somewhat inconsistently, holding religion (as superstructural) and economy (as infrastructural) apart while also simultaneously appreciating the strange theology subsisting within the economy itself. Adequately theorizing the latter (i.e., the theologized and/or theologizing economy) would require further refining and dialecticizing (without eliminating altogether) the infrastructure-superstructure distinction of classical historical materialism (such as Marx presents it in, for instance, his [in]famous 1859 preface). It additionally would require much more than just identifying within infrastructural modes of production their specific relations of production as the Cartesian-style pineal glands connecting and interfacing infrastructures and corresponding superstructures (as does the Althusser of the manuscript *Sur la reproduction*).[44]

I also discern a related tension in Marx's body of work apropos the topic of religiosity. On the one hand, Marx repeatedly anticipates future social history as driven along by capitalism eventuating in increasing desacralization. As I already observed, in these instances he participates, like Freud, in Enlightenment rationalist teleological optimism about the predestined triumph of secularization. But on the other hand, Marx appears to detect, as I noted, that a subtly disguised supernaturalistic holiness of sorts inheres within capitalism and the real abstractions of its economic categories. That is to say, and putting together these two sides of Marx's religion-related reflections, a sacredness shelters within the infrastructural base that itself supposedly will bring about desacralization. Perhaps this tension helps partially explain why, throughout the course of capitalist history since 1883, religiosity has not withered away as Marx predicted.

Of course, the *Communist Manifesto* contains Marx's best-known predictions of secularization qua desacralization. So, in wording borrowed from this 1848 text's prognostications along these lines, "religious fervor" has not "drowned" in "the icy water of egotistical calculation." Instead, I maintain that it has infused itself into and colored this water. The "melting into air" of which the *Manifesto* speaks diffuses but does not destroy old religious solidity (and a toxin in particulate form can be much more dangerous than when left as a comparatively inert solid). *Pace* Marx and Engels, theology has undergone an *Aufhebung*-like sublation or sublimation but not an outright negation (on this point, history up through the present seems to have vindicated Hegel[45] and Feuerbach[46] instead). God has gone underground, but not in the sense of being finally interred for good. Admittedly, in a society in which anything can be purchased, everything indeed has a price. But in paying these prices, one does not buy one's freedom from religiosity in the bargain—quite the contrary.

Whereas Marx and Engels generally stick to a commonsensical opposition between the sacred and the profane, the recent history of the relationships between capital and religion calls for brokering a counterintuitive convergence of opposites. Specifically, a renewed contemporary Marxist historical materialism needs the seemingly oxymoronic category of desacralized religion at both the infrastructural and superstructural levels. Infrastructurally, desacralized religion would be religion's theological, metaphysical, supernaturalist, symbolic, etc. aspects as having migrated into and fused with the edifices and processes of the economic base, namely, desacralized religion as theological economics.[47] Superstructurally, desacralized religion would be the this-worldly institutional and practical remains of all-too-human profane sects, namely, desacralized religion as cultural identitarianism.

As early as 1843, the young Marx, already signaling his departure from the Left Hegelians, declares "the *criticism of religion*" in the German-speaking world "essentially completed" (*wesentlichen beendigt*).[48] However, I would argue that between the 1840s and now, the critique of various things religious has been doubly undone. First, there is the starkly obvious afterlife of religion defying

Marx's (and Freud's) Enlightenment rationalist predictions, albeit an afterlife in the forms of very earthly cultural-sectarian embodiments. Second, there is the less obvious theologization of the capitalist economy via the supernaturalist superstitions of religion not dissipating but, instead, migrating underground. These "metaphysical subtleties" and "theological niceties" have suffused themselves throughout and hidden themselves within the infrastructure. They thereby leave religious superstructures more and more free to take on their this-worldly political identitarian functions.

In the twenty-first century, religion is thoroughly distributed across both infrastructure and superstructure. A grubby, profane God stalks the earth wearing the two faces of belligerent culturalism and high-handed neoliberalism. In a topsy-turvy (*verkehrtes*)[49] inversion between the this-worldly and the other-worldly, contemporary humanity is now secular where it believes itself to be religious and religious where it believes itself to be secular. The enchanted and the disenchanted have traded places, with the apparently enchanted now being disenchanted and vice versa.

This detheologization of religion and related theologization of the economy have gone very far. Indeed, and counterfactually, even if humanity were to become thoroughly irreligious at the superstructural level of ideologies and institutions, even if Marx and Engels's (along with Freud's) secular Enlightenment dreams of a future total and complete desacralization eventuating in absolutely atheistic human societies were to be wholly realized—nonetheless, the death of religious theology would not automatically be tantamount to the death of economic theology. Hence, the criticism of superstructural religion Marx declared finished and fulfilled in 1843 needs to be reborn today as a new historical-materialist critique of religious economy. To refer again to the Marx of the 1844 *Manuscripts*, it no longer is enough for communism to be the practical humanism to atheism's theoretical humanism. Communism also has to come to stand for an infrastructural atheism, in addition to the superstructural atheisms disbelieving in the religious God and his political ersatz, the State. We are not yet economic atheists. We must become so.

§19. PROSPERITY AS ITS OWN GOSPEL: THE POSTULATES OF IMPURE ECONOMIC UNREASON

I feel compelled to confess that I never have found Kant's salvaging of Christian faith via his "postulates of pure practical reason" to be at all convincing as a robust defense of this religion (or of religion in general, for that matter). In fact, I am inclined to agree with Hegel's objections according to which, if anything, the Kantian manner of banking upon a heavenly God and an immortal soul, rather than reinforcing theology, discredits the deontological metaphysics of morals. Hegel concludes, against the Kant of the second *Critique* and related texts, that an ethics too good for this world is, in reality, not good enough.[50]

Although the Kantian postulates of pure practical reason arguably entail nothing favorable for either religion or ethics, they certainly do say something about the theological secretions of apparently rational-qua-nonreligious ethics. This lesson apropos ethics, according to which the superficially secular quietly exudes undercurrents of spiritualist and supernaturalist emissions, can and should be applied to economics too. Of course, the Germans have long been notorious for collapsing macro- into microeconomics and treating economics in its entirety as a mere branch of ethics, a notoriety at a high-water mark nowadays given the relatively recent reactions of Angela Merkel, Wolfgang Schäuble, and the German right to Greece and the wider European Union debt crisis of roughly the past decade. If only the likes of Yanis Varoufakis could be turned into good Swabian housewives, Europe's troubles would soon be over.

Under the reign of capital, prosperity becomes its own Gospel. The primarily Protestant cult of the prosperity Gospel is on the very cusp of explicitly blurting out core unacknowledged truths about both Christianity and capitalism—and this in the same way the figure of Jesus Christ is at the threshold of the Hegelian-Feuerbachian philosophical *Aufhebung* of theology. There are both macro- and microeconomic versions (as well as overlaps between them) of theologized economics (i.e., of prosperity as its own Gospel) in my sense.

For whole societies and nations (macro) as well as individual persons (micro), debt and its associated economic categories and subcategories undeniably have come to take on a range of functions historically linked by tradition to religions and their moralities. I would not feign to be able to do justice to the massive amount of important work that has been carried out regarding this topic, particularly in the past couple of decades (but going back to such authors as Marx, Nietzsche, and Weber). For the time being, I will limit myself to gesturing in passing at a few economic-theological phenomena familiar to a contemporary audience thanks to the global financial crisis triggering the Great Recession as well as the ongoing economic repercussions of the COVID-19 pandemic making the specter of debt loom larger than ever: the shadowy, rootless legions of foreign investors, bondholders, and international finance networks as forming an anonymous God acting with a vengeful invisible yet palpable hand; the "sins of the fathers" as national deficits, unfunded pensions liabilities, tax-starved social programs, and so on transmitted across the generations; austerity measures as the performance of penance and self-flagellation to appease the wrathful divine Market . . . and on and on.

In terms of the economic theology of everyday life (i.e., at the micro level), credit histories and their scores palpably represent the praise- or blameworthiness of one's financial soul, merits or demerits with all-too-real concrete consequences for one's future destiny. Quotidian survival within contemporary capitalism, for the steadily growing ranks of the vast majority of people, seems spontaneously to generate postulates of impure economic unreason corresponding to those of Kant's pure practical reason. Life is experienced as economically livable only by assuming these two postulates—and this exclusively for those fortunate enough to qualify as upper middle class by current capitalist standards. The unfortunate would be all those "left behind" as nonentities condemned to the many layers of hell on earth by global capitalism (with the "rapture" mythologies of America's white evangelical Christians being an ideological-religious inversion of economic reality, an inversion in which the decadent and perverse liberal elites of globalism are the ones "left behind").

On the one hand, one needs an immortal soul in order to: have enough time to pay off all the credit cards, student loans, medical bills, and mortgages; put away money for a university education that still will plunge one's own children into staggering debt themselves; save for a viable retirement in which one would not be reduced to eating canned dog food . . . On the other hand, one invests one's desperate hopes in an inscrutable but potentially merciful God to dispense economic grace in such fantasized guises as miraculously striking it rich quickly, getting a hot investment tip from a benevolent stranger, enjoying remarkable good luck in one's gambles on the marketplace, unexpectedly coming into a sizable inheritance, winning the lottery, having the government forgive one's student loans, etc. For ever more people, the prospect of a debt-free postemployment existence in modest, reasonable comfort increasingly looks like a continually receding heavenly afterlife that only divine intervention could deliver.

The logic of capitalist production and reproduction requires a volatile mixture of minimized taxation, maximized consumption, stagnant or declining wages, and privatized commons, among other factors. With consumer capitalism demanding in particular a combination of flat or falling workers' earnings with ever-more consumption on the part of these same workers, this capitalism's consumers are goaded into borrowing ever further and deeper against their abstractly extending futures, mortgaging their time remaining up to the hilt. In earlier historical stages of capitalist development visible to the likes of Marx and Weber, capital's subjects practiced deferring gratifications and self-deprivation at the behest of a superstructural paternal deity. In the later consumerist phases holding sway for well over half a century now, an infrastructural God-like authority commands the inverse, namely, sacrificing the future for the sake of the present, engaging in instant gratifications and (apparent) self-indulgence as offerings with which to feed the gods of capital.[51] Of course, with Freud and Lacan inhabiting these earlier and later forms of capitalism respectively, the differences between the Freudian and Lacanian superegos, with the former ordering renunciation and the latter dictating enjoyment (qua *jouissance*),[52] reflect these contrasting features of changing capitalist societies (although I would be skeptical of any attempt to reduce the distinction between Freud's and Lacan's superegos to nothing more than a mirroring of sociohistorical transformations).[53]

Furthermore, capital itself, with the quantifications of its mathematical mediations, is a ceaseless thrust of infinite striving irreducible to any of its particular incarnations. The quantitative infinitization of economic life involved with capitalism comes to exert tangible, direct influences transforming the libidinal-subjective lives of everyone from the lowest of the *Lumpenproletariat Pöbel* to the biggest of the big bourgeoisie. These transformations already are brought to the fore in exquisite detail by Marx's own analyses in his critique of political economy—which thus also already is a critique of capitalist libidinal economy.

These intersections between political and libidinal economies provide an opportunity for me to refer to another moment in Lacan's eleventh seminar, one complementing the 1964 moment with which I began this chapter (i.e., that concerning atheism and God as unconscious rather than dead). Near the very end of the concluding session of *Seminar XI*, Lacan invokes then-fresh European memories of the historical catastrophe of Adolf Hitler's Third Reich: "There is something profoundly masked in the critique of the history that we have experienced. This, re-enacting the most monstrous and supposedly superseded [*prétendues dépassées*] forms of the holocaust, is the drama of Nazism."[54] He continues: "I would hold that no meaning given to history, based on Hegeliano-Marxist premises, is capable of accounting for this resurgence—which only goes to show that the offering to obscure gods [*dieux obscurs*] of an object of sacrifice is something to which few subjects [*peu de sujets*] can resist succumbing, as if under some monstrous spell [*monstrueuse capture*]."[55] Lacan then proceeds to add:

> Ignorance, indifference, an averting of the eyes may explain beneath what veil this mystery still remains hidden. But for whoever is capable of turning a courageous gaze towards this phenomenon—and, once again, there are certainly few

who do not succumb to the fascination of the sacrifice in itself—the sacrifice signifies that, in the object of our desires [*l'objet de nos désirs*], we try to find evidence for the presence of the desire of this Other [*cet Autre*] that I call here *the dark God* [le Dieu obscur].[56]

I suspect that Lacan is challenging not just what he takes to be the Hegelian and/or Marxian fashion of historically accounting for Nazism but any strictly historical explanation for the Holocaust whatsoever. This suspicion is reinforced by the fact that Lacan's remarks mobilize the terminology of his ahistorical, (quasi-)transcendental metapsychology (for instance, such terms as "subject" [$], "object of desire" [*a*], and "Other" [A]).

Rather than getting myself bogged down in assessing the pros and cons of Lacan's antihistoricism generally and his ahistorical perspective on European antisemitism specifically, I wish to begin playing devil's advocate in favor of Marxist historical materialism in this context by responding to Lacan with a paraphrasing of Horkheimer: Whoever is prepared to talk about fascism should also be prepared to talk about capitalism. In line with this, I believe that transposing Lacan's remarks about *le Dieu obscur*, whatever their limitations and drawbacks, into the register of the historical-materialist critique of capitalist political economy is a worthwhile and productive move to make. Moreover, doing so in conjunction with mobilizing yet other moments both in the eleventh seminar and in additional portions of Lacan's oeuvre will enable me to advance further my reflections on the relations between the economic and the religious.

Given that Lacan's *dark God* surfaces at the end of the same annual seminar in which he speaks of God as both dead and unconscious, it is not much of a stretch for me to connect *le Dieu obscur* with *Dieu est mort*. In the second session of *Seminar XI*, Lacan, addressing Nietzsche's long shadow, comments: "The myth of the *God is dead*—which, personally, I feel much less sure about, as a myth of course, than most contemporary intellectuals, which is in no sense a declaration of theism, nor of faith in the resurrection—perhaps this myth is simply a shelter against the threat of castration [*l'abri trouvé contre la menace de la castration*]."[57] Just as an atheist who is also a consistent Marxist would have to believe in a far-from-dead (more specifically, an undead) God as a nonepiphenomenal real abstraction, so too does Lacan, although himself an analytic atheist, doubt that God is "dead" in the sense of lacking any living causal efficacy. That said, Lacan also indicates that he is concerned not so much with Nietzsche himself but, rather, with "most contemporary intellectuals."

The French existentialists of the mid-twentieth century are likely those "contemporary intellectuals" at the very forefront of Lacan's mind on this occasion.

Especially from a historical-materialist vantage point, it perhaps is no coincidence that an existentialism declaring the death of God surfaces and achieves popularity during the same decades in which capitalism is mutating into its consumerist modes. Indeed, the early Lacan, inspired precisely by none other than Horkheimer,[58] alludes to this mutation with his 1938 thesis about the twentieth-century "decline of the paternal *imago*,"[59] namely, the waning of the traditional prohibitory sociosymbolic authority epitomized by Judeo-Christianity's "God-the-Father." And as I noted a short while ago, the later Lacan's recasting of the superego as commanding enjoyment—this is instead of, as with a Freud encircled by an earlier phase of capitalism dominated by a Weberian-style Protestant ethic, the superego as ordering renunciation—is intended, in part, to reflect the rise of late-capitalist, postmodern indulgence and hedonism. But what do these observations have to do with "*God is unconscious*," "*the dark God*," and/or a theologized economics?

I can begin answering this question by clarifying what Lacan means when, in the previous quotation from the eleventh seminar, he characterizes "the myth of the *God is dead*" as "a shelter against the threat of castration." My sense is that two interrelated claims are being made through this characterization. First, declarations of God's death are superstructural-ideological expressions of consumerist capitalism's rejection of earlier industrial-capitalist "castration" in the forms of religiously reinforced self-renunciation, delayed gratification, and the like (as epitomized, again, in the spirit of European Protestantism particularly). This would be the declared death of the sort of God informing the Freudian superego that says "No!" to subjects' drives and desires. Informed by the other deity that is the version of Capital behind consumerism, the Lacanian superego instead insists on saying "Yes!" to a not-so-enjoyable enjoyment.

The second claim I discern in Lacan's above-quoted 1964 remarks about the dead divine Father and the menace of castration, closely related to the first claim, has to do with the psychoanalytic defensiveness implied by the word *l'abri*. This would be "shelter" in the sense of a bomb shelter, refuge, or protective cover. Thus, "*l'abri trouvé contre la menace de la castration*," given that this is a matter of shielding oneself against a threat, points to a defensiveness motivated by negative affect—specifically in this psychoanalytic context, castration anxiety. To be even more exact, "God is dead" serves as a magic formula repeatedly pronounced so as to conjure away defensively anxieties about the old Father of tradition exacting revenge and punishing consumerism's (apparent) transgressions.

But this anxious defensiveness is misdirected. That is to say, the subjects of consumerist late capitalism should not fear the traditional prohibitory God of sacred religious superstructure as he was so much as this God's transubstantiation into the nontraditional permissive God of profane economic infrastructure. Moreover, apropos the death of the former deity, one must recall Lacan's reversal of a famous line from Fyodor Dostoyevsky's *The Brothers Karamazov*: If God is dead, then nothing is permitted.[60] Lacan makes clear that his twist on Dostoyevsky is nothing other than a pointed reformulation of the lesson from Freud's *Totem and Taboo* according to which "the dead father became stronger than the living one had been"[61] (a lesson illustrated on a daily basis by the psychopathologies and symptoms so familiar within the analytic clinic of the neuroses). Or maybe one could propose that the Lacanian superego ordering *jouissance* is even more oppressive than the Freudian one dictating renunciation. But how does this translate into a historical-materialist examination of the shifting relations between the religious and the economic in the unfurling of capitalism up through the present?

The death of the superstructural-religious God consciously believed in—this is the ideological deity of the antireligious mantra "God is dead"—does not free people from subservience to an alienating external power. Instead, this (supposedly) dead God returns at the infrastructural-economic level. Moreover, like the Freudian *Urvater*, this undead authority is even stronger than before (i.e., when "alive"). As unconsciously (rather than consciously) believed in, God can grip subjects with an even firmer (invisible) hand. Those who do not believe that they believe do not struggle against a belief they cannot or will not acknowledge themselves as having. Even if, as still seems extremely improbable, all religions and associated superstitious beliefs were to vanish into thin air, leaving behind an ostensibly atheistic humanity, so long as a capitalism having absorbed elements of religiosity into its mode of production persists, God will continue to survive as, at a minimum, an unconscious postulate of impure economic unreason.

Along these same lines, the Lacanian "God is unconscious" and Lacan's dark/obscure God, both from *Seminar XI*, should be integrated into a renewed historical materialism capable of doing justice to what Lacan has in view with his "triumph of religion" (a triumph unforeseen by Marx and Freud alike). In historical-materialist terms, "God is unconscious" can be translated as "theology becomes economy." Likewise, and with this becoming-economic of the theological, *le Dieu obscur* would be Capital itself.

When Lacan, near the end of the eleventh seminar, speaks of the dark/obscure God, he does so in conjunction with the notion of sacrifice. As seen, he emphasizes the enthralling, compelling quality of the sacrificial vis-à-vis his *Dieu obscur*: "the offering to obscure gods [*dieux obscurs*] of an object of sacrifice is something to which few subjects [*peu de sujets*] can resist succumbing, as if under some monstrous spell [*monstrueuse capture*]," and "there are certainly few who do not succumb to the fascination of the sacrifice in itself." Capitalism, despite one of its most popular self-presentations and self-justifications, is not driven by selfishness, neither in its earlier industrial periods colored by religious asceticism (i.e., versions of capitalism familiar to both Marx and Weber) nor in its later consumerist periods colored by secular hedonism (i.e., versions of capitalism postdating both Marx and Weber). In fact, capitalist societies have proven (and continue to prove) themselves to be utterly abysmal, by myriad criteria, at serving the selfish interests of persons.[62]

Rather than servicing the "selfish" needs and wants of individuals, Capital functions as Lacan's dark God, extorting sacrifices from everyone in order to gratify its insatiable structural greed for self-valorization through the accumulation of ever-more surplus value in perpetuity. Even capitalists themselves qua the "bearers" (*Träger*) or "personifications" (*Personifikationen*) of Capital, as its individual agents or representatives, can remain capitalists only so long as they surrender their autonomy and idiosyncratic inclinations to the invisible hand and its guiding perpetual motion of M-C-M'. If any single capitalist misreads or ceases to obey the commands of the obscure Market, he/she is in danger of being swiftly and harshly punished by being stripped of the status of capitalist and pushed out of the loop, the charmed circle, of capital's circuit of autoenhancement. He/she thereby might end up joining the ranks of the masses continually forced to lay down their lives one hour at a time by offering up as daily sacrifices to Capital their unpaid labor time.

As the (il)logic of self-valorization ceaselessly and relentlessly strains in the direction of further self-valorization, with the blind automaticity of the psychoanalytic death drive, lakes of capital accumulate that even the most decadent, debauched bourgeois bon vivant would need an unbelievably long afterlife to get anywhere close to draining exclusively through private consumption. Meanwhile, the ranks of those with not enough or nothing whatsoever continue to swell, and the shadows of various imminent collective disasters loom larger and larger. To what end? Who, if anyone, gets off on all of this? Who is capitalism's subject-supposed-to-enjoy? What if the still-unfolding social history of capitalism ultimately is animated by a collective "succumbing" to the "monstrous spell" of Capital as a *Dieu obscur* demanding endless sacrifices that themselves are meaningless and self-destructive for this dark God's unfortunate servants? What if the only subject who truly enjoys capitalism is anonymous Capital itself as the idiotic, acephalous repetition of M-C-M', as a drive without a driver, so to speak?[63]

§20. OLD WINE IN NEW BOTTLES?:
ECONOMIC THEOLOGY VERSUS THEOLOGICAL ECONOMICS

In Lacan's self-described "dialectical materialism," signifiers can and do fall into signifieds.[64] This passage of the register of the Symbolic into the registers of the Imaginary and even the Real resonates with Marx's concept of *Realabstraktion*. But what is more, the updated permutation of historical materialism I am advocating in this chapter allows and accounts for instances in which it could be said that the superstructural falls into the infrastructural.

Marx registers one type of infusion of superstructure into infrastructure, namely, the fall of the political into the economic. For him, "political economy" is not just a name for the new intellectual discipline established during the eighteenth century by the French Physiocrats and the British liberals. This phrase also reflects the fact that the economy comes to rely upon mediation by politics, that modes of production are internally regulated by ideas, norms, values, etc. they absorb from the political strata of superstructure—and this instead of politics remaining entirely external to the economy as part of a superstructural transcendence.

However, whereas Marx explicitly acknowledges in multiple fashions economic infrastructure's assimilation of political superstructures, he evidently does not do the same with respect to religious superstructures. Although there are implicit indications of this in the guises of allusions, hints, rhetoric, and the like, Marx does not directly put forward the claim that specifically religious superstructures fall into the economic base. In other words, Marx's historical materialism, while centrally and manifestly involving a critique of political economy, only peripherally and latently develops a corresponding critique of theological economy.

As I announced earlier, one of my guiding intentions on this occasion is to repeat in relation to Marx the later Lacan's maneuver of reconciling Freud with the triumph of religion. My model of superstructures falling into infrastructures, inspired by a combination of Marx and Lacan, permits a contemporary historical-materialist rendition of religion's recent and ongoing persistence as contradicting the outlook of secular rationalism. In particular, I am focused on the survival of religions on the other side of the sociohistorical transition to globalized consumer capitalism from the mid-twentieth century up through today.

Capitalism's transition to mass-media consumerism would seem to involve epitomizations of the desacralizing tendencies of the bourgeoisie upon which Marx and Engels pin their Enlightenment hopes for eventual spontaneous secularization. Viewed through the lenses of Marx's nineteenth-century sensibilities, the repressive desublimations staged by consumerist capitalism, as spectacular and increasingly pornographic displays of hedonistic enjoyment, probably would look like glaring symptoms of a dynamic in which indeed "all that is holy is profaned." Contemporary religious fundamentalists, be they Christian, Jewish, Muslim, Buddhist, Hindu, etc., certainly see recent social trends in this way. But looks can be deceiving. And the fundamentalists' denunciations of globalized permissive societies should be seen as the expressions of Hegelian beautiful souls quietly complicit in the circumstances they loudly condemn.

As regards the social history of things religious, the mid-twentieth century through the present has involved a two-sided defiance of Enlightenment predictions of the withering away of religions. I earlier identified these two sides as those of the coin of "desacralized religion." On the side of superstructure, religious institutions and activities continue, well after Marx's death, to enjoy prominent roles in the lives of societies—albeit, as I contend, largely in the profane forms of cultural identitarianisms helping to fulfill the bleak prophecy of a Huntingtonian "clash of civilizations," the gratuitous barbaric alternative to any move beyond capitalism. On the side of infrastructure, one of my primary contentions here is that during the course of the transition to consumerist (late) capitalism with its postmodern permissiveness, religion also lives on covertly in economically disguised sublimations, in the economy itself as a peculiar supernatural realm with the real abstractions of its own theological metaphysics.

At this juncture, my proposals can be refined further through comparing and contrasting them with alternative views on the same set of issues put forward by a number of figures. These figures neatly divide into Marxist and non-Marxist groups. Among the Marxists, I primarily will address twentieth-century European ones. In the next section of this chapter, I will begin to reassess—this reassessment then will continue in the conclusion of this book—Western Marxism's general tendency to (over)emphasize the importance of the superstructural as a response to crudely reductive economisms (such as those espoused both by the Second International and by Stalinism's vulgarization of historical materialism). Special attention will be paid to Walter Benjamin's 1921 fragment "Capitalism as Religion," a piece obviously of direct relevance given my guiding concerns in this context.

However, I will begin in the present section by engaging with the non-Marxists. In terms of the relations between capitalism and religion, Weber, Schmitt, and Agamben constitute a trio arguing for the decisive and enduring sociohistorical significance of religious beliefs and practices, a significance arguably shaping (speciously) secular modernity and postmodernity too. Of course, Weber's 1905 *The Protestant Ethic and the "Spirit" of Capitalism* offers renowned pushback against what Marx's historical materialism too often is taken to be, namely, a simplistic economic determinism in which the infrastructural base causally controls everything superstructural.[65]

As I have pointed out a few times in the preceding, Marx already acknowledges the crucial parts played by Protestantism in the historical rise of capitalism as a socioeconomic system. To complicate matters further, although the Weber of *The Protestant Ethic and the "Spirit" of Capitalism* is a non-Marxist, he is not exactly an unambivalent anti-Marxist. His condemnation of "naive historical materialism"[66] leaves open the option of not condemning a non-naïve version. Moreover, Weber sees himself as balancing between the poles represented by historical materialists and their opponents, anticipating that each side will perceive him as too close to its adversary.[67] He also concedes that religion is far from everything and that one cannot deduce capitalism in toto from Protestantism alone.[68]

Nonetheless, Weber pits himself against even non-naïve Marxist historical materialism by affirming the operative existence of "purely" superstructural "constellations" (here politico-religious ones), "which not only do not fit into any economic 'law,' but fit into no economic scheme of any kind."[69] Simultaneously, this same Weber foreshadows and influences subsequent twentieth-century Western Marxisms, especially Frankfurt School critical theory. Such Marxisms strive, in a rejection of economism, to decouple historical materialism from any theoretical or practical privileging whatsoever of the infrastructural over the superstructural. Weber writes of "elective affinities" between the plethora of layers and strata of societies, with no structural hierarchy of levels obtaining between these multiple dimensions.[70] Such Western Marxist endeavors as the "progressive-regressive method" of the later Sartre's "critique of dialectical reason" with its "auxiliary disciplines" and the Gramsci-inspired poststructuralist theory of hegemony put forward by Ernesto Laclau and Chantal Mouffe, to take just two examples, are expressions of what could be described as a Weberianization of Marx's historical materialism (in a recently published 1978 manuscript, Althusser harshly criticizes Gramsci for allegedly neglecting and sidelining all things infrastructural).[71] I will take up the question of whether a Weberianized Marxism still can qualify as properly Marxist qua historical materialist when I shift from the non-Marxist trinity of Weber, Schmitt, and Agamben to those twentieth-century Marxists likewise reflecting on religious factors in social history.

If one has Marx, one does not need Weber in order to affirm the importance of politico-religious superstructure generally and Protestantism specifically for the historical development of capitalism. What is more, like Marx,

Weber does not live to witness the completed metamorphosis of modern industrial capitalist societies into their postmodern consumerist permutations. With respect to Marx and Weber alike, one of my contentions is that this mutation postdating their deaths requires revising both thinkers' conceptions of the religion-economy rapport.

Despite their many differences, Marx and Weber share in common a view of religion as separate from (although related to) the economy. For both, Protestantism is an external factor aiding and abetting but not merging into the secular capitalistic mode of production. By contrast, I maintain that as part of the transition to later consumerist capitalism, superstructural religion falls into infrastructural economy, with the latter thereby becoming directly theologized. After this fall, what remains of institutional religion at the superstructural level is thereby freed up from religion's ideologically crucial traditional functions of directly guaranteeing individuals' complicity with their socioeconomic milieus through its discipline and regulations (encoded theologically, ethico-morally, and even bodily). From at least a Marxist (if not a Weberian) perspective, it then could be said that institutional religions such as Protestantism come to play a more indirect role in maintaining the economic inequalities of capitalistic relations of production by facilitating the mistranslation and misrecognition of class struggle as noneconomic identitarian culture wars and clashes of civilizations. Postmodern religions, as primarily providing badges of this-worldly group belonging, help make it so that, to put this via a twist on Benjamin, revolutions fail by immediately turning into fascisms.

Before shifting my attention to Schmitt and, especially, Agamben, there is an additional observation I want to articulate as regards Weber. This is another manner of spelling out my thesis apropos "the triumph of religion" within consumer capitalism. To paraphrase *Hamlet* once again, capitalism doth make Protestants of us all. This is so even without membership in any Protestant Church (or even, hypothetically, in the absence of Protestantism specifically and/or institutional religion generally). The most vehement atheists in conscious superstructural terms, for whom "God is dead," continue to believe in "metaphysical subtleties" and "theological niceties" at the material infrastructural level insofar as they still participate through their socially efficacious conduct in the capitalist economy. This is all the more so in that these atheists do not believe that they believe. For them, "God is unconscious," as Lacan would put it.

I turn now to Schmitt, specifically his famous thesis, according to which, "All significant concepts of the modern theory of the state are secularized theological concepts."[72] In what follows, I am not concerned with those aspects of Schmitt's right-wing political philosophy of greatest relevance to Marxists, such as his critiques of liberal democracy and emphasis on the friend-enemy distinction as central to the very essence of politics. What is more, I am not so much interested in Schmitt on his own as on how his conception of political theology inspires a certain Agamben, namely, the author of 2007's *The Kingdom and the Glory: For a Theological Genealogy of Economy and Government*, with its outline of an economic theology.

Admittedly, this Agamben tries to establish a certain amount of distance between his economic theology and Schmittian political theology. In *The Kingdom and the Glory*, Schmitt's originally political Christian theology is opposed with an initially economic (prior to political) Christian theology instead[73] (although, as I will proceed to note momentarily, Schmittian political theology persists side by side with economic theology throughout Agamben's *Homo Sacer* saga). Later, Agamben asserts that reliance on Schmitt is not necessary in order to affirm the theological roots of recent and contemporary politics and economics.[74] Instead, he contends that even though Foucault himself did not arrive at an appreciation of economic theology as outlined in *The Kingdom and the Glory*, Foucault's historical methods can and do lead to this uncovering of the religious-theological origins of seemingly secular economics.[75]

Nonetheless, Agamben's profound debts to Schmitt's philosophy, including and especially his political theology, not only is on display throughout the larger *Homo Sacer* project as well as other portions of the Agambenian corpus— early on in *The Kingdom and the Glory*, Agamben plays off Schmitt against Weber to the favor of the former apropos the topic of modern secularization.[76] Schmitt and Agamben concur that secular modernity is pseudosecular, masking the continued conformity of its politics and/or economics to premodern theological templates. In *The Kingdom and the Glory*, Agamben goes so far as to deny that modern science seriously pushes back against religion[77] and to contend that secularization in its entirety is a process wholly internal to the Christian faith's divine economy.[78] Likewise, *The Kingdom and the Glory* concludes with a lengthy insistence to the effect that modern secular economics is pseudosecular.[79]

In terms of Agamben's Schmittianism, his theory of sovereignty, delineated in various portions of the *Homo Sacer* series, could be characterized as fusing Foucault's account of biopolitics with Schmitt's conception of the state of exception.[80] In line with this Schmitt-Foucault synthesis spelled out in other *Homo Sacer* volumes, *The Kingdom and the Glory* opens by identifying "two paradigms." Specifically, these are two purported historical offshoots of early Christianity: on the one hand, the transcendent sovereign power of political theology à la Schmitt (as associated with forms of absolutism); on the other hand, the immanent biopower of economic theology à la Foucault (as associated with forms of democracy).[81] Clearly, economic theology complements, rather than displaces, Schmittian political theology. The latter remains a component of *The Kingdom and the Glory*, in such guises as portrayals of politics as liturgy[82] and the suggested project of an "archaeology of glory."[83]

Agamben also takes some passing swipes at the Marxist tradition in the course of elaborating his economic theology. Left Hegelianisms generally are said by him simply to substitute a human economy for a divine one without fundamentally altering the structures and logics of the latter.[84] Likewise, Marx specifically is faulted for merely secularizing divine agency in the guise of human praxis.[85] However, like Lucio Colletti's Marx, Agamben, with his humanism of "man without content" as a de-essentialized openness, relies on Pico della Mirandola too.[86] That is to say, Marx's humanism of a self-denaturalized humanity making and remaking its very essence in and through its practices is much closer to Agamben's image of the human than the latter is willing and able to acknowledge. This unacknowledged proximity to Marx also can be seen in *The Kingdom and the Glory*.[87]

Alberto Toscano, in his article "Divine Management," concisely articulates a devastating, multipronged critique of Agamben's religiously oriented historical narratives in general and the economic theology of *The Kingdom and the Glory* in particular. I am largely in agreement with Toscano's historical-materialist rebuttals of the "theological genealogy" of Agambenian economic theology and the accompanying redeployment of political theology in the overarching framework of the *Homo Sacer* undertaking.[88] Nonetheless, after delineating the disagreements between Toscano and Agamben, I will situate my historical-materialist theological economics—I use the phrase "theological economics" so as to distinguish this from Agamben's "economic theology"—as a third position situated somewhere in between Toscano and Agamben, albeit closer to the historical materialism defended by the former. The differences between Toscano and Agamben will enable me better to clarify and sharpen what I am after in terms of a Marxist critique of economic theology.

As a historical materialist, Toscano understandably complains about the excessively Schmittian and Heideggerian aspects of Agamben's philosophical prism.[89] Agamben, siding with Schmitt contra Weber on secularization, assumes there to exist a substantial, uninterrupted continuity of the essence of the theological from antiquity to the allegedly pseudosecular present (however, Schmitt shares with Weber, among many others, a [problematic] critique of Marxist historical materialism as economically reductive).[90] The resemblances to Heidegger's grand narratives about "onto-theology" and "Western metaphysics" are obvious. Toscano adds a further immanent-critical inflection to this by pointing out that Agamben's investments in Schmitt and Heidegger lead him to betray the very Foucault whose historical methods Agamben claims to carry forward and utilize in his own pursuits[91] (Toscano also sketches a broader critique of Agamben's methodology and its "theory of signatures").[92] Foucault's archaeological and genealogical efforts work to bring about, among other things, a shattering of grand narratives and a confrontation with the discontinuities and disunities of a history pluralized into a nontotalizable ensemble of histories irreducible to one another.[93]

However, zeroing in on the Foucault with the greatest impact on Agamben's thinking, the one of the Collège de France seminars of the 1970s, a mixture of fidelities and deviations becomes apparent. On the one hand, Foucault, unlike Agamben, seems to recognize that the historical genesis of modern economies (initially in the forms of "mercantilism and cameralism") brought about major (superstructural) changes introducing discontinuities into the flow of history (specifically for Foucault, an unprecedented "art of government").[94] Likewise, Foucault argues that the emergence of "population" as an object of governance thanks to the rise of disciplines such as statistics and demographics during the seventeenth and eighteenth centuries creates a rupture between premodern economics (as concerned with the domestic sphere of the familial household qua *oikos*) and modern economics (now decoupled from the *oikos*, with the family unit itself being absorbed into the larger category-object of population).[95] This would entail, on Foucauldian grounds to which Agamben pledges loyalty, that Agamben's uses of the concept-term "economy" to establish an ostensible continuity of economic theology from antiquity to the present indefensibly conflates premodern and modern forms of economics.

On the other hand, this very same Foucault indulges in his own version of hypothesizing ancient theological origins for modern (and even postmodern) secular phenomena. Foucault's genealogy of the modern art of government (or "governmentality") identifies early Christian pastoralism ("pastoral power") as the premodern precursor of this modern art.[96] I offer here no verdict on whether this qualifies as an exceptional instance of Foucault overriding the usually prevailing rule of his aversion to relying upon deep and extended historical continuities. Suffice it for my present purposes to note that the content on the pastorate in Foucault's Collège de France lectures anticipates and is echoed by Agamben's economic theology. (Perhaps Foucault is closer to formulating an economic theology of his own than Agamben is willing or able to acknowledge.)

Toscano also bemoans "Agamben's banal Heideggerian prejudices about the place of labour and productivity in the Marxian critique of political economy."[97] For someone buying into a "fundamental ontology" in which an ineffable Being mysteriously discloses itself from time to time throughout the course of history through the pens of the canonical figures of Western philosophy, dismissing Marx's historical materialism as a regional ontic concern trapped within the confines of nihilistic techno-scientific enframing is easy enough. However, something this easy is likely to be of little worth. In this vein, Toscano also condemns "the poverty of trying to perpetuate the tired idea of Marx's thought as a 'secularisation' of some cloaked and damning theological content."[98] This indeed is Agamben's primary objection to Marxism. But consistent with Toscano, I think that Agamben, with his belief in the enduring and seamless continuity of the theological even within apparent secularization, seriously underestimates just how much significant discontinuity Marx's post-Feuerbachian bringing of heaven down to earth introduces into the history (or histories) at stake.

As Toscano observes, Agamben's *Homo Sacer* edifice basically ignores capitalism as a specific sociohistorical formation.[99] What is worse, although *The Kingdom and the Glory* focuses on the economics (as also purportedly theological) of antiquity, Toscano perspicuously notes its silence regarding Aristotle's chrematistics as distinct from the ancient conception of *oikonomia*.[100] This is telling in that the Aristotelian treatment of certain merchants' "love of money" qua exchange value, distinct from the economics of use values, foreshadows key aspects of capitalism as the first and only economic system in social history in which production is not driven by the category of use value.[101] Given Agamben's Left Heideggerianism and his consequent neglect of anything along the lines of a historical-materialist critique of capitalist political economy, Toscano judges that "it does not suffice to combine political theology with economic theology to overcome the shortcomings of Agamben's work as a tool for politically thinking the present."[102] As I note above, Agamben, throughout the volumes of *Homo Sacer*, already combines Schmitt's political theology with his own economic theology. As per Toscano's critical analyses, what Agamben's Left Heideggerian combination of political and economic theologies leaves out is nothing other than political economy. Agamben replaces both *Homo economicus* and *Homo faber* with *Homo sacer*, namely, economics and labor with theology.

Because Agamben lets the theological overshadow and dominate the economic in his analyses, Toscano writes with emphasis of "Agamben's *theological* genealogy."[103] Toscano thereby signals that Agamben not only erroneously makes history march on its (superstructural-religious) head—he also commits

228 THE TRIUMPH OF THEOLOGICAL ECONOMICS

the same mistake vis-à-vis religion that according to Marx from the early 1840s onward, traditional political philosophy commits vis-à-vis the state.[104] In both cases, superstructure is presented as governing infrastructure, rather than, as per historical materialism, vice versa.

On Toscano's assessment, Agamben promotes a reductive idealism in which historical details vanish into the monochromatically dark night of a single theological History-with-a-capital-H, amounting to a mirror-image inversion of the very crudest pseudo-Marxist reductive materialism (i.e., an economism collapsing all social history into the predictably lawful workings of infrastructure alone).[105] Looking at how far Agamben has bent the stick toward idealism, Toscano considers it preferable to risk bending the stick back in the direction of a more classical historical materialism affirming the primacy of infrastructure over superstructure.[106] Here I very much side with Toscano. Although neither of us advocates a reductive economism, I would go so far as to say that the stick needs bending back toward the infrastructural in response not only to non-Marxists like Agamben but also to Western Marxists overemphasizing the superstructural through obsessive preoccupations with cultural ideology critique above all else (resulting in a neglect of the critique of political economy so central for Marx).

Toscano concludes "Divine Management" by underscoring the material limitations posing obstacles in relation to Agamben's vision of a spiritual salvation of humanity *à venir*. Toscano posits that "a certain economy still functions as a constraint that no amount of genealogy or archaeology could redeem us from."[107] He adds: "The preoccupation with real needs and material constraints, as well as with the resistances of nature, means that some form of 'economic' thinking, of governing and ordering and distributing resources, is inescapable outside of the purely religious horizon of redemption."[108]

I again concur with Toscano. However, in addition to Toscano's historical-materialist contestation of Agamben's messianic speculations regarding the future, I perceive a need for further Marxist critical labors with respect to the past as it relates to Agambenian archaeology/genealogy. Through these labors, I will be able to specify my above-mentioned positioning in between Toscano's historical materialism and Agamben's Schmittian-Heideggerian idealism (albeit with my position being much closer to that of Toscano).

Despite my overall agreement with Toscano's withering assault on *The Kingdom and the Glory*, I am convinced that a few "rational kernels" nonetheless remain to be salvaged out of the "mystical shell" of Agamben's theological rendition of history. In a 2012 interview covering some of what is involved in economic theology, Agamben utters a line, one serving as this interview's title, stating that "God did not die; he was transformed into money."[109] Obviously, my notion of a process of religious superstructure falling into economic infrastructure (specifically in the transition from the industrial capitalism analyzed by both Marx and Weber to the consumer capitalism arising after their deaths) resonates with this now-familiar Agambenian one-liner. Moreover, there is a cross-resonance between Agamben's Heideggerian assertion that (pseudo)secular liberal democracies cannot think the thought of economic theology (with the latter as democracy's "unthought")[110] and my Lacanian thesis according to which "God is unconscious" within later consumer capitalism.

But there are a number of crucial differences between Agamben's economic theology and my theologized economics (the latter being more in line with the historical materialism defended by Toscano). I can start by claiming that not only, as per Agamben, has God been "transformed into money"—God also has been simultaneously transformed into a culture-warrior Goliath, an anthropological champion representing such identitarian forces as nationalism, racism, sectarianism, etc. For me, there are two distinct but interrelated levels to the phenomenon of desacralized religion as per an updated historical materialism, namely, an infrastructural dimension (i.e., Agamben's God-transformed-into-money and my theologized economics) and a superstructural dimension (i.e., my God-transformed-into-identity). God is now Janus-faced, wearing an identitarian face in addition to a monetary one. If the old God was tragic, this new, two-faced God is farcical (or, perhaps, tragicomic).

Again pushing off Agamben's economic theology, I would maintain that not only did God get transformed into money (as well as identity)—he was born out of money too, as it were. By this I mean to call to mind a core tenet of historical materialism regarding the past, a tenet fundamentally at odds with the Agambenian picture of history generally and economic history specifically. In *The Kingdom and the Glory*, Agamben describes theology and economics as equiprimordial. He insists on an original Ur-fusion of the theological and the economic and argues that early Christians are the first instantiations of the figure of *Homo economicus*.[111] But for historical materialism, even if the geneses of economic infrastructure and religious superstructure coincide chronologically, even if they are equiprimordial in terms of linear temporal order, they are not equal in terms of their social-ontological weight vis-à-vis each other. One is more appearance than the other. Moreover, the bulk of Agamben's historical reflections suggest that between theology and economics, the primordiality is not really equi-, that theology is the first among equals.

Either way, whether theology is equal to or surpasses economics in its historical primacy for Agamben, Agamben's genealogy of economic theology is at odds with historical materialism and its critique of political economy (the later, bio-political Foucault pointedly rejects historical materialism's prioritization of economic forces and factors and claims this materialist orientation to be undermined by a biopower it purportedly fails to think).[112] In fact, with all three non-Marxists I have dealt with here (i.e., Weber, Schmitt, and Agamben), religion's idealist, supernaturalistic image of itself as eternal, as driving history rather than being driven by it, looks to have contaminated their thinking. For Weber, the Protestantism making possible capitalism, if it is to be explained historically, is to be situated within specifically religious-ideational (rather than economic-material) history. For Schmitt and Agamben, politics and economics derive from theology and not the other way around (as Schmitt states, "the economic postulates of free trade and commerce are, for an examination within the realm of the history of ideas, only derivatives of a metaphysical core").[113]

To put this in the language of *The German Ideology*, these non-Marxists, as idealists, proceed "from heaven to earth," whereas historical materialism follows the opposed movement "from earth to heaven."[114] Hence, and to refer back to Agamben's above-glossed aphorism, the sequence "God → money" should be expanded into "money → God → money." That is to say, "God" qua the superstructure of religion/theology cannot be, according to historical materialism, an absolute, *unhintergehbar* beginning ex nihilo. The "heavenly" superstructure that falls into "earthly" infrastructure (i.e., the God that gets transformed into money) itself arose out of infrastructure at an earlier historical stage. The theological is not immaculately conceived in an asocial vacuum.

§21. INTERMITTENT DETERMINISM: ECONOMY, RELIGION, AND ANOTHER FORM OF UNEVEN DEVELOPMENT

The same differences between me (along with Toscano) and Agamben as a non-Marxist leftist already are bones of contention between Marx and a leftist contemporary of his, namely, Pierre-Joseph Proudhon. Marx's 1847 *The Poverty of Philosophy*, an assault on Proudhon's *The System of Economic Contradictions, or The Philosophy of Poverty*, involves him deploying and justifying, against Proudhon, some of the load-bearing axioms of historical materialism. For instance, Marx comments:

> M. Proudhon the economist understands very well that men make cloth, linen or silk materials in definite relations of production. But what he has not

THE TRIUMPH OF THEOLOGICAL ECONOMICS ❧ 231

understood is that these definite social relations are just as much produced by men as linen, flax, etc. Social relations are closely bound up with productive forces. In acquiring new productive forces men change their mode of production; and in changing their mode of production, in changing the way of earning their living, they change all their social relations. The handmill gives you society with the feudal lord; the steam-mill, society with the industrial capitalist.[115]

Marx immediately adds, "The same men who establish their social relations in conformity with their material productivity, produce also principles, ideas and categories, in conformity with their social relations."[116] This Marx, as will be seen momentarily, also shows up in such texts as *The German Ideology* and *A Contribution to the Critique of Political Economy*. However, he has come to be rejected not only by non/anti-Marxists but even by many self-professed Marxists terrified of being accused of lapsing into vulgar reductive economism. But before I weigh in on this rejection, this Marx deserves a further hearing.

Another passage from *The Poverty of Philosophy* merits appreciation in this same vein. Therein, Marx declares:

> Each principle has had its own century in which to manifest itself. The principle of authority, for example, had the eleventh century, just as the principle of individualism had the eighteenth century. In logical sequence, it was the century that belonged to the principle, and not the principle that that belonged to the century. In other words it was the principle that made the history, and not the history that made the principle. When, consequently, in order to save principles as much as to save history, we ask ourselves why a particular principle was manifested in the eleventh or in the eighteenth century rather than in any other, we are necessarily forced to examine minutely what men were like in the eleventh century, what they were like in the eighteenth, what were their respective needs, their productive forces, their mode of production, the raw materials of their production—in short, what were the relations between man and man which resulted from all these conditions of existence. To get to the bottom of all these questions—what is this but to draw up the real, profane history [*l'histoire réelle, profane*] of men in every century and to present these men as both the authors and the actors of their own drama? But the moment you present men as the actors and authors of their own history, you arrive—by a detour—at the real starting point, because you have abandoned those eternal principles of which you spoke at the outset.[117]

THE TRIUMPH OF THEOLOGICAL ECONOMICS

This passage expresses what would be the most fundamental historical-materialist objection to theological (pseudo)histories along the lines of Schmittian political or Agambenian economic theologies. Behind any and every theology lies "profane history."

Yet this Marx, whose more economistic emphasis might raise the specter of crude socioeconomic determinism for some, is no straightforward determinist. Subjects write the very scripts they also play out (as "the authors and the actors of their own drama/history"). At a minimum, this entails a rather sophisticated dialectical compatibilism apropos the issue of freedom versus determinism. This compatibilism also is suggested at the outset of *The Eighteenth Brumaire of Louis Bonaparte*: "Men make their own history, but not of their own free will; not under circumstances they themselves have chosen but under the given and inherited circumstances with which they are directly confronted."[118]

What Marx insists upon in 1847 reflects what he and Engels already stipulated regarding "The Essence of the Materialist Conception of History" in 1845's *The German Ideology*. They maintain:

> The phantoms formed in the brains of men [*die Nebelbildungen im Gehirn der Menschen*] are also, necessarily, sublimates of their material life-process, which is empirically verifiable [*empirisch konstatierbaren*] and bound to material premises. Morality, religion, metaphysics, and all the rest of ideology as well as the forms of consciousness corresponding to these, thus no longer retain the semblance of independence. They have no history, no development; but men, developing their material production and their material intercourse, alter, along with this their actual world [*Wirklichkeit*], also their thinking and the products of their thinking. It is not consciousness that determines life, but life that determines consciousness.[119]

Apropos Weber, Schmitt, and Agamben, among others, the last line of this quotation could be reworded to claim that "it is not theology that determines economics, but economics that determines theology" (at least "in the last instance," to invoke an Engels to whom I will return shortly). Of course, Althusser takes up the idea of ideology having "no history" in his celebrated article "Ideology and Ideological State Apparatuses," although he disparages "the positivist and historicist" materialism of *The German Ideology*.[120] I will come back to Althusser soon. For the moment, suffice it to say that I seek to reactivate some of what is here rubbished as "positivism" and "historicism."

The passages I have quoted from *The German Ideology* and *The Poverty of Philosophy* foreshadow the 1859 preface to *A Contribution to the Critique of*

Political Economy. This preface's most (in)famous stretch echoes these passages.[121] This stretch has come to be repudiated even by most Western Marxists. Both here and elsewhere,[122] I myself take critical distance from it, particularly its teleological-necessitarian optimism about further progressive historical change in the near-term future.

During the twentieth century, Western Marxists, faced with the twin vulgarities of Second International and Stalinist economisms and inspired by such non-Western points of reference as Lenin's antieconomistic theory of the "weakest link"[123] and Mao's account of contradiction,[124] develop strong allergies to those moments in Marx's thinking I highlight in the immediately preceding. In response to deterministic materialisms not only within Marxism itself (in the form of economism) but also in non-Marxist social sciences seeking to conform with an industrial capitalist picture of scientificity à la mechanistic natural science, Lukács, Gramsci, the Frankfurt School, and many others see fit to pull historical materialism very far in the direction of antieconomism specifically and antireductionism generally. The result is what I earlier characterized as the Weberianization of Marxism, namely, the elevation of superstructure to a crucial (if not leading) role and correlative downgrading of the importance of infrastructure. In this twentieth-century revision of Marx's ideas, the economy becomes (once again) just one among myriad factors propelling history along. For such Marxists, the militant materialism Marx espouses in the 1859 preface and elsewhere becomes a source of shame and discomfort to be quickly dismissed (or even to be blamed on Engels's purportedly malign influence).

Anyone wishing to defend this Marx disavowed by many of his own descendants might be tempted to temper his emphases on the infrastructural with certain qualifications. Such caveats might include two claims: First, the new paradigm of historical materialism had to bend the stick of history away from traditional historians' privileging of the superstructural (especially of politics, states, and "great men" as the agents of historical movements), and second, in the context both of heated polemics with Proudhon and Feuerbach (in *The Poverty of Philosophy* and *The German Ideology* respectively) as well as accessible introductory presentations (the 1859 preface), Marx opts in favor of elegant (over)simplifications for the sake of concision, clarity, and attention-grabbing forcefulness. Marx's economism might be largely a calculated, self-conscious exaggeration. Such qualifications are not entirely without validity.

Nevertheless, instead of falling back on these sorts of apologetics excusing the more economically minded Marx, I wish to plead for the timeliness and urgency in the twenty-first century of the infrastructural focus of Marx's historical-materialist critique of political economy. When one's chief adversaries

234   THE TRIUMPH OF THEOLOGICAL ECONOMICS

are reductive economists and mechanistic naturalists (such as was the case for early-to-mid-twentieth-century Marxists on the European Continent), it at least is understandable to err in the direction of stressing the significance of super-structural configurations and processes. But when one's chief adversaries are, instead, cultural idealists and identitarians on both sides of the left-right political divide—this arguably is the case today—then insisting on the primacy of non-economic phenomena in the manner of the Western Marxists of the previous century is much worse than just outdated; it plays into the social-theoretic assumptions of adversaries. As the young Lukács warned just over a century ago, "Marxist orthodoxy is no guardian of traditions, it is the eternally vigilant prophet proclaiming the relation between the tasks of the immediate present and the totality of the historical process."[125]

Such antidogmatic orthodoxy is indeed characteristic of historical-dialectical materialism. It demands that any proper Marxist be tactically nimble in response to "the tasks of the immediate present" and correspondingly prepared to jettison "traditions" (including ones internal to Marxism, such as twentieth-century critical theory) and ready and willing to recalibrate theoretical as well as practical weightings of priorities. In the current circumstances, superstructural identity categories (minus infrastructural class identities) reign supreme both practically and theoretically across the political spectrum. Simultaneously and ironically, the era of global capitalism, culminating in today's new Belle Époque, continues to intensify further the direct influences of flows of capital on struggles widely ranging from the micro to the macro. Nowadays, Marxists desperately need to draw attention to the economic bases of much of contemporary national and international politics. Joining in the present culturalist choruses singing the praises of any and every identity except class ones is a huge mistake. Critique of ideology should complement, not replace, critique of political economy.

Furthermore, even during the twentieth century, the Marxist champions of superstructure over infrastructure were guilty of helping reinforce a crude false dilemma. They tended, with varying degrees of explicitness, to put forward an all-or-nothing forced choice between either reductive, deterministic economism or complete revocation of infrastructure's prioritization in relation to superstructure. Under these constraints, one has to choose between either Karl Kautsky and Edouard Bernstein or Weber. This dilemma should have been denounced as false last century. But whereas it was at least a forgivable deviation in the virtuous fight with economistic thinking then, it now is an indefensible vice when the danger is under-, rather than over-, estimating the power of economics.

But without simply reactivating vulgar economism, what is the alternative? I propose that one option is what I will call here a historical-materialist doctrine of "intermittent determinism." Obviously, the determinism in question would be economic. The core idea is quite straightforward: Rather than infrastructure being either always or never the dominant factor in societies and their histories, as per reductive economism and its opponents respectively, infrastructure sometimes plays this commanding role. In other words, the infrastructural intermittently determines the superstructural.

Yet I immediately must append a crucial nuance to the simple alternative of "sometimes" for either "always" or "never." Even when the economy is not, as during periods of acute economic crises or overt class struggles, directly determining the more-than-economic strata of social structure, it still, as classical Marxism insists, continues to exert a steady gravitational pull on the full ensemble of society's interlinked components. Superstructural mediations modulate but do not eliminate this constant tug. Capital is inflected, not vetoed, by its more-than-economic contextualizations.[126]

Relatedly, a continuous indirect determinism corresponds to intermittent direct determinism. Recourse to the above-mentioned Mao will enable me to elucidate what I have in mind at this point. In the terms of 1937's "On Contradiction," intermittent direct determinism would be when an economic contradiction is the "primary contradiction" in relation to other social contradictions. Correlatively, continuous indirect determinism would be when a noneconomic contradiction is the primary one. But why associate the primacy of a noneconomic contradiction with any economic determinism whatsoever, however indirect?

Staying with Mao's language, even when the primary contradiction itself is not immediately economic, the ability of a noneconomic contradiction to be primary is, so to speak, on loan from the economy. In other words, superstructural forces and factors can play the leading roles in social history only if and when infrastructure does not override (or, I might dare say, does not trump) them, that is, when the economy permits more-than-economic variables to exert themselves apart from it. Superstructure serves in a dominant role at infrastructure's pleasure. Therefore, the distinction between intermittent direct determinism and continuous indirect determinism is comparable to the difference between short- and long-leash control respectively. At least so long as Capital remains in charge, an economic leash, however long, will remain fastened in place.

This theory of intermittent determinism calls for a revisitation of Engels's notorious qualification, in his October 27, 1890, letter to Conrad Schmidt, concerning the economy being determinative "in the last instance."[127] I consider there to be two senses in which this caveat is meaningful and defensible. First, at the synchronic level, infrastructure tends on balance to exert greater influence over superstructure than vice versa. Second, at the diachronic level, broader arcs of social history, despite containing within themselves detailed zigs and zags testifying to superstructural influences, exhibit larger general trajectories bearing witness to the sway of modes of production. Although Engels seems unaware of this fact, Hegel, with his often misunderstood or unappreciated fashion of distinguishing between "actuality" (*Wirklichkeit*) versus "existence" (*Existenz*) and "being-there" (*Dasein*),[128] foreshadows Engels's infamous qualifier. Hegelian *Wirklichkeit* arguably functions like the Engelsian "last instance," albeit, of course, *avant la lettre*.[129]

One of Althusser's better-known one-liners is his pronouncement that "the lonely hour of the 'last instance' never comes" (*l'heure solitaire de la «dernière instance» ne sonne jamais*)[130] (in 1975, Althusser evinces overt, unambiguous sympathy for the notion of the "last instance" in relation to Marx's conception of history,[131] a sympathy also hinted at in earlier of his texts too.)[132] However, against this Althusser of the mid-1960s (and perhaps, albeit differently, against Engels too), my account of intermittent determinism indicates that this hour, although never arriving once and for all in the guise of a single event of historical reckoning, periodically reoccurs at regular but unpredictable intervals. The bell keeps tolling again and again, at least as frequently as every recurring economic downturn.

Interestingly, the classical Althusser of 1965's *For Marx* and *Reading Capital* foreshadows some of what I am after with intermittent determinism as a way beyond the sterile impasse between economism and antieconomism. In his essay "On the Materialist Dialectic: On the Unevenness of Origins," he faults vulgar economism for conflating "the determinant-contradiction-in-the-last-instance" with "the *role* of the dominant contradiction."[133] For this Althusser, "the determinant-contradiction-in-the-last-instance" is economic. More precisely, it is the foundational tension between the forces of production and the relations of production, a tension situated at the very heart of the economy according to the mature Marx's version of historical materialism. "On the Materialist Dialectic" suggests that this contradictory aspect of the infrastructure then conditions which other contradictions, often superstructural ones (for example, conflicts involving not only class but race, gender, nationality, religion, etc.), secondarily become the prominent foci of potential or actual social dynamics and clashes.[134] In connection with this Althusser, André Glucksmann remarks, "The strategically dominant instance in a social structure will rarely be the economy, although it is the relations of production that govern the *mise en scène* and apparition of the different principal roles."[135] Or, as Robin Blackburn and Gareth Stedman Jones put it, "*the determinant selects the dominant*"[136] (with the determinant as economic and the dominant as usually more-than-economic).

One upshot of this is that the social "dominance" (or, one might say, "hegemony") of more-than-economic forces and factors arguably is on loan from the economy.[137] As Balibar, in his contribution to *Reading Capital*, succinctly puts this Althusserian point, "*the economy is determinant in that it determines which of the instances of the social structure occupies the determinant place.*"[138] Norman Geras explains this thus:

> To dispel the apparent paradox of an economy determinant in the last instance, but not necessarily always dominant, determination in the last instance is defined as follows: the economy determines for the non-economic elements their respective degrees of autonomy/dependence in relation to itself and to one another, thus their differential degrees of specific effectivity. It can determine itself as dominant or non-dominant at any particular time, and in the latter case it determines which of the other elements is to be dominant.[139]

Admittedly, more-than-economic instances/elements can and do play leading parts in shaping social struggles and histories. But even when economic instances/elements do not assume the dominant role, only they can permit other instances/elements to do so instead. Or, to risk a Hegelian-style formulation, the distinction between economic and more-than-economic determination is a distinction internal to economic determination itself.

Having noted this classic Althusserian precedent, one of the merits of intermittent determinism is that it makes antieconomistic Marxist talk about the "relative autonomy" of superstructure more than a hollow phrase masking an utter abandonment of historical materialism under the cover of such terminology as "hegemony," "historical bloc," "real abstractions," "chains of equivalence," and so on. To be crystal clear, I do not reject this family of concepts sharing in common a project of further refining and enriching historical-materialist accounts of superstructure. On the contrary—I too am staunchly committed to a nonreductive materialism. But I am at least as committed to the "materialism" part as to the "nonreductive" one.

Therefore, what I want to resist is the tendency of antireductive projects, as a danger inherent within them, to cross points of no return in relation to the materialism of historical materialism. Rescues of things superstructural from economism too easily tip over into outright refusals to accord even a qualified privilege to the economy. What is more, the heroic adversaries of economic reductionism frequently persist in laying claim to the titles of "Marxism" and "historical materialism" even after they have thrown away the core commitments of Marx's own works distinguishing his approach from non-Marxist social theories (such as Weberianism, Foucauldianism, etc.).[140]

By way of concluding, I come now to Benjamin's 1921 fragment "Kapitalismus als Religion." This suggestive, compact snippet of text, as its title alone already announces, could not be more relevant to my endeavors. I have striven in the preceding to construct a revised historical-materialist account of the relation between economic infrastructure and religious superstructure as an alternative both to non-Marxist politico-economic theologies as well as to excessively anti-economistic Marxist social theories. Benjamin is a figure standing smack dab in the middle of the intellectual and chronological crossroads with which the present chapter is preoccupied. And this is especially the case with the author of "Capitalism as Religion."

Benjamin opens his 1921 fragment by observing that "one can behold in capitalism a religion, that is to say, capitalism essentially serves to satisfy the same worries, anguish, and disquiet formerly answered by so-called religion."[141] He promptly differentiates this observation from the Weberian perspective on Protestantism vis-à-vis capitalism by describing the latter as "not only a religiously conditioned construction, as Weber thought, but as an essentially religious phenomenon."[142] Later, near the end of this fragment, Benjamin adds to this the thesis that Christianity morphed into (rather than persisted in externally regulating) capitalism—"Christianity in the time of the Reformation did not encourage the emergence of capitalism, but rather changed itself into capitalism."[143] From the side of infrastructure, this same "emergence"/"change" amounts to the economy reaching a point at which "it could draw from Christianity enough mythical elements in order to constitute its own myth."[144] I construe capitalism's "own myth" à la Benjamin to be what I delineate above as the infrastructural side of desacralized religion, with its postulates of impure economic unreason.

Benjamin and I obviously differ as regards historical timing. Benjamin goes back to the sixteenth century and posits that Christianity becomes capitalistic as soon as it becomes Protestant, that Protestantism itself is the fall of Christian religious superstructure into capitalist economic infrastructure. Although not mutually exclusive in relation to this Benjaminian thesis, my focus is on a more recent mutation of the religion-economy relationship transpiring over the course of the twentieth century in conjunction with the shift from industrial to consumer capitalism.

In terms of historical chronology, Benjamin also would appear to differ from Agamben, given the latter's claim that early Christianity, long before both capitalism and Protestantism, was always-already an economic theology. Yet "Capitalism as Religion" also sounds a more Agambenian note in its concluding paragraph. Therein, Benjamin proposes, "It contributes to the knowledge of capitalism as a religion to imagine that the original paganism certainly and most proximately grasped religion not as a 'higher' 'moral' interest, but as the most immediately practical."[145] Both Benjamin and Agamben propose that religion originally is also economic, although the former says this apropos paganism and the latter apropos Christianity. It may be asked whether Benjamin's commitment to historical materialism means that unlike Agamben, he conceives of the economic part of the original economy-religion couplet as the more determinative factor of the two.

That noted, I want now to turn attention to some of the details of Benjamin's comparison of capitalism with religion. One of the first things in this vein stressed by Benjamin is that "capitalism is a pure religious cult, perhaps the most extreme there ever was. Within it everything only has meaning in direct relation to the cult: it knows no special dogma, no theology."[146] From the standpoint of capitalism, all things, no matter who or what they are, count exclusively as potential or actual sources of yet-more surplus value. Just like the fervent religious mystic who sees nothing but God everywhere, the devoted, fanatical capitalist perceives everything under the sun as the possibility or reality of the further self-valorization of Capital. And in its purely quantitative infinitude and universality, inevitably globalizing Capital is indifferent to and cuts across any and all finite, particular qualities, namely, "special dogmas" or "theologies" differentiating local cultural formations from one another. For global capitalism too, "There is neither Jew nor Greek, slave nor free, male nor female . . ."

Benjamin immediately proceeds to write of "the permanent duration of the cult."[147] He maintains that "capitalism is the celebration of the cult *sans rêve et sans merci*. Here there is no 'weekday,' no day that would not be a holiday in the awful sense of exhibiting all sacred pomp—the extreme exertion of worship"[148] (with "*rêve*" [dream] likely being a mistake in place of "*trêve*" [truce]).[149] What is being described here is the permanent carnivalesque frenzy, the perpetual socioeconomic churn, of capitalist life as governed by the repetitive cycle of production, distribution, exchange, and consumption. Under the ceaseless pressure of capital's drive for ever-greater accumulation of surplus value, not only does capital universalize itself spatially, traversing different cultures and civilizations around the globe—it also universalizes itself temporally, with the relentless acceleration of capital's reproduction/turnover time dictating that everyone dance madly everyday to the tune of M-C-M'. No days are not extravagant celebrations of Capital ("all sacred pomp—the extreme exertion of worship"), whether in the manner of production and/or consumption. Every day is a feast day or, at least, frantic preparation for one. With the advent of full-fledged consumerist capitalism, in which Capital wishes that everyone would shop as if Christmas were right around the corner of each and every day, Benjamin's prescient description of the never-ending holiday of Capital becomes even more painfully accurate. If only Benjamin had lived to see the American suburban shopping mall of the second half of the twentieth century, not to mention the always-open-for-business virtual marketplace, this dream for insomniac consumers and entrepreneurs alike that is the never-closed internet, the worldwide web of flows of capital.

A third cardinal feature of capitalism-as-religion highlighted by Benjamin has to do with the twin phenomena of blame and guilt.[150] As in various religions, so too in the capitalist cult—accusation and culpability feature prominently in it. Members of all classes within capitalism are made to feel guilty in the face of failures to live up to multiple injunctions: workers who do not toil hard and save enough, consumers who spend too much or too little but never the proper amount, capitalists who do not invest enough and do not maximize their profits. Capitalism's superego (or even capitalism-as-superego), whether commanding self-renunciations out of its Freudian mouth or self-indulgences out of its Lacanian mouth, is never satisfied. Its subjects experience themselves as always lacking and inadequate in relation to its injunctions. Capital continually finds its bearers, personifications, and victims to be wanting.

Benjamin, in this 1921 fragment, proceeds to address psychoanalysis on the heels of foregrounding the accusation-culpability dynamic essential to capitalism. Well aware of the significance of the affect of guilt within the analytic clinic of the neuroses, he arrives at the judgment that "Freudian theory also belongs to the priestly rule of this cult. It is thoroughly capitalistic in thought."[151] Needless to say, I disagree with Benjamin on this point. His very own Frankfurt School peers and heirs, such as Marcuse, help reveal the ways in which Freud's framework provides powerful means of critiquing capitalism from various angles. If, as per Benjamin, analysis is an outgrowth of capitalism, it arguably is a dialectical one, namely, another symptom of capitalism's autoundermining dynamics, its spontaneous self-criticism.

Also in the context of discussing capitalistic blame and guilt in "Kapitalismus als Religion," Benjamin contends, "God's transcendence has fallen, but he is not dead. He is drawn into the fate of man [*Gottes Tranzsendenz ist gefallen. Aber er ist nicht tot, er ist ins Menschenschicksal einbezogen*]."[152] This "fall" is that

THE TRIUMPH OF THEOLOGICAL ECONOMICS   241

of (pseudo)transcendent religious superstructure into the rushing currents of social history as per historical materialism (i.e., "the fate of man" [*Menschenschicksal*] as the vicissitudes of humanity). My sympathetic variant on Benjamin's contention specifies that in being swept up and absorbed into the immanence of the this-worldly, God acquires not one profane (after)life but two: both that of cultural-identitarian avatar (qua superstructural desacralized religion) as well as that of theologized economics (qua infrastructural desacralized religion). The divine continues to live on, living parallel lives, within today's combustible combinations of clashing civilizations and globalized capital.

I will close by proposing that my reappraisal of classical historical materialism in light of the changing economy-religion rapport over roughly the past century indicates the effective existence of another form of uneven development. In line with historical materialism as per Marx, I maintain (contra the likes of Schmitt and Agamben) that economic infrastructure indeed originally generates religious superstructure. But I add to this, picking up on both Marx's employments of theological language as well as his registrations of the political mediation of the economic, that this thus-generated religious superstructure can and does return to (by falling into) economic infrastructure. In other words, economy comes to be not only politicized but theologized too.

With respect to the general conceptual parameters of historical materialism as a theoretical apparatus, I have outlined a movement from infrastructure to (religious) superstructure and back again. But how does this represent a new species of the genus "uneven development"? Rather than there being a smooth, steady evolution of infrastructure and superstructure in lockstep with each other, a religious superstructure produced out of an older mode of production belatedly seeps into and contaminates a newer mode of production. In the historical sequence of concern to me on this occasion, elements of a Christianity arising well before the surfacing of consumer capitalism nevertheless come to permeate this same later infrastructural constellation.

One could say that this process of an older superstructure collapsing into a newer infrastructure puts the brakes on the latter's tendency, posited by Marx especially apropos capitalism, to break with the historical past. In Marx's own words, "The tradition of the dead generations weighs like a nightmare on the minds of the living [*wie ein Alp auf dem Gehirne der Lebenden*]."[153] The heavy, invisible hand of an undead God slows, even if it does not stop, what would otherwise be the revolutionary self-liquidating kinetics of capitalist social history.

For the historical past to be broken with for good, as the "nightmare" of (un)dead prior "generations," this past has to die twice: first, through superstructural desacralization, in which the ghosts of established idealist traditions are exorcized, and second, through infrastructural desacralization, in which the economic return of these revenants after the preceding exorcism is combated and undone. At present, we could be described, in Lacan's language, as inhabiting a stretch of history "between two deaths"[154]—specifically, between the already-transpired death of the old superstructural God and the yet-to-transpire death of the new infrastructural one. In the absence of a still-unrealized economic atheism to match Enlightenment secularism, God remains, as it were, unconscious, enjoying a subterranean afterlife.

This particular variety of uneven development and the two deaths it seems to require for revolutionary transformations might help explain both capitalism and religion outlasting Marx's premature predictions of their imminent disappearances. Yet as with most truly great thinkers, Marx is his own best critic. The young Marx of the early 1840s remarks that "history is thorough and passes through many stages while bearing an ancient form to its grave [*Die Geschichte ist gründlich und macht viele Phasen durch, wenn sie eine alte Gestalt zu Grabe trägt*]."[155] But what if "an ancient form" (*eine alte Gestalt*) rises up from its grave?

Maybe the Marx hoping and expecting the impending withering away of both capitalism and, with it, religiosity underestimated just how thorough (*gründlich*) history would continue to be apropos these interlinked infrastructural and superstructural arrangements, undercounting the number (and type) of stages (*Phasen*) it must pass through. Or, put differently, perhaps Marx did not consistently count on the spectral staying power of certain sociohistorical phenomena, on the need to kill and bury some of these things twice over before finally being done with them. Nevertheless, I desperately hope that Marx is right about the ultimate mortality of capitalism, even if he was wrong about the nearness of its irreversible demise.

Conclusion

Real Reduction: It's the Stupid Economy!

One of Lenin's best-known philosophical pronouncements is to be found in his *Philosophical Notebooks*. Specifically, in his "Conspectus of Hegel's Book *Lectures on the History of Philosophy*," Lenin famously remarks, "Intelligent idealism is closer to intelligent materialism than stupid materialism."[1] For roughly the past century, Marxists of (or inspired by) the European West have treated this Leninist one-liner as a green light for a number of idealistic maneuvers vis-à-vis classical Marxism, including playing off a social-constructivist historical materialism against a naturalistic dialectical materialism to the detriment of the latter, heavily qualifying or jettisoning altogether traditional Marxism's emphasis on the centrality of economic matters, and making superstructures as or more socially decisive than infrastructures. Some even have applied the just-quoted remark from Lenin's *Philosophical Notebooks* to Lenin himself, splitting Lenin between the allegedly "stupid materialism" of 1908's *Materialism and Empirio-Criticism* and a supposed materialism made more intelligent through a heavy infusion of Hegelian idealism's dialectics as per Hegel's *Science of Logic* in particular.[2]

I have covered much of this ground at length in my 2019 book *Prolegomena to Any Future Materialism*, volume 2, *A Weak Nature Alone*.[3] In that prior context, I focus on Western Marxism's general hostility, starting with the young Lukács of 1923's *History and Class Consciousness*, to anything along the lines of Engelsian *Naturdialektik*. This hostility amounts to a wholesale repudiation of dialectical materialism insofar as this materialism brings with it a naturalism informed by the natural sciences.

However, alongside the Lukács-initiated tendency to pit historical against dialectical materialism, Western Marxism also exhibits a similar tendency to play off a nonreductive, antieconomistic historical materialism against a reductive, economistic historical materialism. The economically reductive inclinations of the Second International and Stalinism alike understandably inspire reactions against these inclinations in various European Marxists sensitive to both theoretical complexities and historical details problematizing ham-fisted gestures of grounding everything under the sun directly in infrastructural modes of production.[4] But with the dual tendencies to reject both the dialectics of nature as well as economic reductionism being hallmark features of Western Marxism from the early Lukács onward, this family of twentieth-century European Marxist orientations effectively sidelines two fields at the heart of Marx's and Engels's concerns: economics (as per historical materialism) and science (as per dialectical materialism).

In the second volume of my *Prolegomena to Any Future Materialism*, I argue against Western Marxism's anti-Engelsian opposition to a naturalistic dialectical materialism. Complementing this, I now will push back in this conclusion against what I take to be the excesses of Western Marxism's antieconomistic program. In my view, a twenty-first-century revitalization of Marxism requires restoring, in line with the spirit of its founders, both science and economics to central places within a materialism that is both historical (à la Marx) and dialectical (à la Engels). Moreover, insofar as various permutations of Marxism-with-psychoanalysis thus far have been dominated by the superstructure-obsessed Western Marxist tradition, my efforts throughout the present book at remarrying Marxism and psychoanalysis along more infrastructural lines call for some critical pushback specifically against the antieconomism influencing, often implicitly, established Freudo- and Lacano-Marxisms via their reliance on the Western Marxists. This conclusion provides precisely such pushback.

The Lukács of *History and Class Consciousness* lays the foundations of what Maurice Merleau-Ponty, in 1955's *Adventures of the Dialectic*, subsequently baptizes "Western Marxism."[5] However, the implications of this work of Lukács for the issue of economism (i.e., economic reductionism) in historical materialism are open to divergent interpretations. In what follows, I soon will proceed to argue that the consequences of *History and Class Consciousness*, with its core concept of "reification" (*Verdinglichung*), as regards the status of the economy for societies and their histories indeed are profoundly and importantly equivocal. As I also will contend, this equivocality, once brought to light, presents difficulties for those vehemently antieconomistic Western Marxisms departing from Lukács's 1923 masterpiece.

CONCLUSION   245

However, two of the young Lukács's contemporaries, the Karl Korsch of 1923's *Marxism and Philosophy* and the Antonio Gramsci of the *Prison Notebooks*, provide much more univocal expressions of the antieconomism that becomes a recurrent feature of twentieth-century Western Marxism. Korsch's *Marxism and Philosophy* is associated with Lukacs's *History and Class Consciousness* not only because these two books appeared in the same year and were by authors who had a working relationship with each other but also and primarily because both texts were lumped together and jointly condemned as idealist deviations by the Bolshevik authorities (via Grigory Zinoviev's denunciations of these two publications at the Fifth Congress of the Communist International in 1924). Korsch himself expresses basic solidarity with the early Lukács.[6]

Starting with Korsch and Gramsci in the 1920s and 1930s, one of Western Marxism's distinguishing features comes to be its critique of vulgar mechanistic versions of historical materialism. Such versions drastically simplify Marxist social theory by turning it into a doctrine according to which a given infrastructure (i.e., a specific society's mode of production as its economic base) causally determines corresponding features of an accompanying superstructure (i.e., a specific society's more-than-economic political, civic, cultural, educational, religious, intellectual, etc. institutions, customs, beliefs, rituals, norms, values, and so on). According to this impoverished rendition of historical materialism, one can interpret any and all superstructural features as effects directly expressing immediately underlying infrastructural factors. For example, within a capitalist society, every single more-than-economic phenomenon (whether political, cultural, etc.) would be, from this unsophisticated perspective, an outgrowth of the economic means and/or relations of production characteristic of an industrial mode of production. Likewise, the march of social history would be explicable as a predictable movement obeying efficient causal laws ostensibly established by historical materialism as a science of history resembling such other sciences as physics.

The problems with the crude economistic rendition of historical materialism are both numerous and, at least with the benefit of hindsight, obvious. Rendering everything superstructural an epiphenomenal effect of one and only one infrastructural base inevitably requires fabricating ever more reductive narratives as just-so stories about the powers of a mode of production to keep all of the components of society on very short leashes. Furthermore, the striking fashions in which the first half of the twentieth century defies classical nineteenth-century Marxism's predictions about the subsequent course of social history force the more intellectually honest Marxists of the opening decades of the twentieth century to rework historical materialism in light of the surprising events and developments they witness.

One could say that for the economic determinism of economistic Marxism, infrastructure is the only really important dimension of both societies and social history. An essential feature of Western Marxism from its birth in the 1920s onward is its adamant antieconomism.[7] A key motto of this tradition would be "Superstructure matters!" Accordingly, in the chapter of *Adventures of the Dialectic* in which Merleau-Ponty coins the label "Western Marxism," he characterizes this thus-labeled tradition as one emphasizing, against reductive and mechanistic economism, such superstructural factors as consciousness, ideology, etc.[8] Perry Anderson likewise explains:

> Western Marxism as a whole, when it proceeded beyond questions of method to matters of substance, came to concentrate overwhelmingly on study of superstructures. Moreover, the specific superstructural orders with which it showed the most constant and close concern were those ranking "highest" in the hierarchy of distance from the economic infrastructure, in Engels's phrase. In other words, it was not the State or Law which provided the typical objects of its research. It was culture that held the central focus of its attention.[9]

On a subsequent occasion, he adds, "the major exponents of Western Marxism … typically pioneered studies of *cultural* processes—in the higher ranges of the superstructures—as if in glittering compensation for their neglect of the structures and infrastructures of politics and economics."[10] I believe the fundamental accuracy of Anderson's summary will be largely substantiated by my ensuing analyses here starting with Korsch (not to mention its being substantiated by Theodor Adorno's almost exclusive, and quite snobbish, fixation on European high culture). Indeed, for Lukács, Korsch, Gramsci, and Ernst Bloch, with these four being the founding fathers of Western Marxism, more-than-economic constellations and experiences come to receive the sustained attention they were deprived of by economism.[11] As will be seen in a moment, both Korsch and Gramsci appear to go so far as to render superstructure as (if not more) important as infrastructure.

In *Marxism and Philosophy*, Korsch presents himself as a defender of true Marxist orthodoxy against its vulgarizations in the vein of the economic determinism of so-called scientific socialism. In so doing, he stresses the dialectical side of Marxian materialism. Korsch contends that "it is essential for modern dialectical materialism to grasp philosophies and other ideological systems in theory as realities [*Wirklichkeiten*], and to treat them in practice as

CONCLUSION   247

such."[12] He soon asserts, speaking of Marx and Engels, that "they always treated ideologies—including philosophy—[*alle Ideologien und also auch die Philosophie*] as concrete realities [*reale Wirklichkeiten*] and not as empty fantasies [*leere Hirngespinste*]."[13]

Two things should be borne in mind apropos Korsch's remarks. First, he does not employ the phrase "dialectical materialism" in its standard sense as designating the extension of the models of historical materialism, developed through analyses of societies and social history, to cover pre- and nonhuman realities (first and foremost, objective nature as per the natural sciences). Instead, by "dialectical materialism," Korsch means historical materialism insofar as it opposes itself to reductive materialisms—with "dialectical" here signaling a sharp contrast with "mechanical." That is to say, he is not endorsing Engels's "dialectics of nature" by using this phrase so closely associated with Engelsian *Naturdialektik*.

Second, one should note that Korsch refers especially to "ideologies" and/as "philosophies." I believe that he is deliberately referring to those superstructural phenomena appearing to be at the greatest remove from the infrastructural mode of production. From the standpoint of economism as vulgarly mechanistic materialism, such high-altitude cultural and ideational constructs would be nothing more than shadowy epiphenomena merely reflecting through a glass darkly the causal influences flowing from the economic base's means and relations of production. Hence, Korsch's stress on ideologies and philosophies as "concrete realities," as nonepiphenomenal real abstractions endowed with their own causal efficacy, combats the epiphenomenalism of economism regarding matters superstructural.

Korsch soon proceeds to maintain that for Marxism's two founders, dialectics in the sense of antireductionism outweighs even materialism itself in theoretical importance. He states: "It is essential to take it as a constant starting point that Marx and Engels were dialecticians before they were materialists. The sense of their materialism is distorted in a disastrous and irreparable manner if one forgets that Marxist materialism was dialectical from the very beginning."[14] Later in the same paragraph, Korsch goes on to say: "No really dialectical materialist conception of history (certainly not that of Marx and Engels) could cease to regard philosophical ideology, or ideology in general, as a material component of general socio-historical reality—that is, a real part which had to be grasped in materialist theory and overthrown by materialist practice [*ein theoretisch-materialistisch in seiner Wirklichkeit zu begreifender und praktisch-materialistisch in seiner Wirklichkeit umzuwälzender*]."[15]

This second passage can be viewed as an early anticipation of Althusser's notion of the "materiality of ideology"[16] (a notion arguably courting the danger of broadening the meaning of "matter" to such an extent that anything and everything whatsoever somehow or other counts as "material," with such a broadening threatening the specificity and precision of Marxist materialism).[17] That said, the first passage seems to suggest that Marx's and Engels's most fundamental, overriding theoretical allegiance is to "dialectics" and not materialism. This 1923 suggestion by Korsch is pregnant with implications for subsequent figures and orientations in Western Marxism.

By 1930, Korsch, while trying to defend *Marxism and Philosophy*, registers the fact that his 1923 text's valorization of things superstructural was well received by non-Marxists, with this valorization seeming to encourage bourgeois appropriations of a historical materialism now purged of its inconvenient stresses on economy, class, and the like.[18] By 1938, in his study *Karl Marx*, he becomes implicitly quite self-critical of his 1923 position. This later Korsch, although still just as critical of crude economism as in *Marxism and Philosophy*,[19] cautions that too extreme an antieconomistic valorization of superstructures and social totalities harmfully dilutes historical materialism's emphasis on material modes of production (i.e., the infrastructural economic base).[20] Warning apropos then-recent developments in European Marxism (to which *Marxism and Philosophy* contributed in no small measure), the Korsch of 1938 speaks of "the younger generation of Marxists who, under the cover of an attack on a too simple and 'vulgar' interpretation of Marx's materialism, really aimed at depriving the new doctrine of its revolutionary implications in order to make it acceptable to the bourgeoisie."[21]

Having noted Korsch's post-1923 hesitations and changes of mind, the Korsch of *Marxism and Philosophy* also appeals to Marx's 1845 "Theses on Feuerbach," especially the first of these eleven theses.[22] Thesis 1 famously declares:

> The chief defect of all hitherto existing materialism [that of Feuerbach's included] is that the thing [*der Gegenstand*], reality [*die Wirklichkeit*], sensuousness [*Sinnlichkeit*], is conceived only in the form of the object or of contemplation [*Objekts oder der Anschauung*], but not as sensuous human activity [*sinnlich menschliche Tätigkeit*], practice [*Praxis*], not subjectively [*subjektiv*]. Hence, in contradistinction to materialism, the active side was developed abstractly by idealism—which, of course, does not know real, sensuous activity as such. Feuerbach wants sensuous objects, really distinct from the thought objects, but he does not conceive human activity itself as objective activity. Hence, in *Das Wesen des Christentums*, he regards the theoretical attitude as the only genuinely human attitude, while practice is conceived and fixed only

CONCLUSION ❧ 249

in its dirty-juridical manifestation. Hence he does not grasp the significance of "revolutionary," of "practical-critical," activity.[23]

On Korsch's reading, Marx's opposition here to "all hitherto existing materialism (that of Feuerbach's included)" (i.e., "contemplative" materialism) arguably is more important than his repudiation of idealism in myriad guises. The latter at least enjoys the virtue of including within itself a not-reduced-away (conscious) subjectivity as the "active side" of "human activity" qua praxis.[24] Korsch claims that these stipulations in the "Theses on Feuerbach" hold for Marx's and Engels's later theoretical endeavors too.[25]

Korsch also argues for the practical-political significance of Marx's theoretical-philosophical break with and advance over nondialectical materialisms. At this same moment in *Marxism and Philosophy*, he begins his argument by situating "vulgar-marxism" (i.e., economistic historical materialism) on the side of the Feuerbachian contemplative materialism surpassed by Marx starting in 1845. Korsch asserts:

> A theoretical method which was content in good Feuerbachian fashion to reduce all ideological representations to their material and earthly kernel would be abstract and undialectical. A revolutionary practice confined to direct action against the terrestrial kernel of nebulous religious ideas, and unconcerned with overthrowing and superseding these ideologies themselves, would be no less so. When vulgar-marxism adopts this abstract and negative attitude to the reality of ideologies, it makes exactly the same mistake as those proletarian theoreticians, past and present, who use the Marxist thesis of the economic determination of legal relations, state forms and political actions, to argue that the proletariat can and should confine itself to direct economic action alone.[26]

Consequently, he deems this vulgar Marxist position "theoretically inadequate and practically dangerous."[27] Theoretically, for this Korsch, the Feuerbachian procedure of tracing heaven (as theology à la Feuerbach) back to earth (as anthropology à la Feuerbach) must be complemented by the distinctively Marxian move of showing how and why this heaven (as more-than-economic superstructure) arises out of this earth (as economic infrastructure). On this point, Korsch appeals specifically to the fourth of the "Theses on Feuerbach" and to a particular passage in the first volume of *Capital*.[28]

Practically, crude Marxist materialism, for this same Korsch, would erroneously and even perhaps disastrously restrict militant political activity to directly economic struggles. Thereby, those various other sites of status quo–destabilizing volatility not centered on industrial hourly wage laborers striking just outside the factory gates presumably would be neglected as irrelevant distractions by the economism of vulgar Marxism. Before Korsch's 1923 *Marxism and Philosophy*, Lenin's turn-of-the-century *What Is to Be Done?* already warns against such a narrow practical-political focus. Rebuking the same economistic tendencies later targeted by Korsch, this Lenin urges revolutionary agents to be ready, willing, and able to seize upon the opportunities for the furtherance of their aims furnished by social struggles involving groups other than the proletariat and issues other than those immediately bound up with laboring.[29] One or more of these other, more-than-economic struggles may indeed end up presenting revolutionaries with the "weakest link" in the chains of social struggle, which, if grasped, will provide the leverage enabling the revolution to be advanced successfully.[30]

In fact, this Korsch stands between, before him, the Lenin of *What Is to Be Done?* and, after him, the Gramsci of the *Prison Notebooks*. In advance of the theory of hegemony and the concept of the ideological "war of position" spelled out in the *Prison Notebooks*[31]—I will turn to Gramsci shortly—*Marxism and Philosophy* urges Marxist revolutionaries to attend to superstructural factors (political, legal, theological, philosophical, etc.) as at least as integral for the prospects of their political projects as anything strictly economic. For both Korsch and Gramsci, revolutionaries ignore superstructure at their peril.

Also anticipating Gramsci (specifically, the Gramscian theory of intellectuals),[32] Korsch underscores that higher-order intellectual strata and phenomena of social superstructure warrant much more serious consideration than they are given by "vulgar Marxists." He declares:

> Even today most Marxist theoreticians conceive of the efficacy of so-called intellectual phenomena [*geistigen Tatsachen*] in a purely negative, abstract and undialectical sense, when they should analyse this domain of social reality [*diesen Teil der gesellschaftlichen Gesamtwirklichkeit*] with the materialist and scientific method moulded by Marx and Engels. Intellectual life should be conceived in union with social and political life, and social being and becoming (in the widest sense, as economics, politics, or law) should be studied in union with social consciousness in its many different manifestations, as a real yet also ideal [or "ideological"] component of the historical process in general [*gesellschaftlichen Gesamtwirklichkeit*]. Instead, all consciousness is approached with totally abstract and basically metaphysical dualism, and declared to be a reflection of the one really concrete and material developmental process, on which it is

CONCLUSION   251

completely dependent (even if relatively independent, still dependent in the last instance).[33]

Korsch soon adds in this same vein:

> Many vulgar-marxists to this day have never, even in theory, admitted that intellectual life [*geistigen Lebensprozesses*] and forms of social consciousness [*gesellschaftlichen Bewußtseinsformen*] are comparable realities. Quoting certain statements by Marx and especially Engels they simply explain away the *intellectual (ideological) structures of society* as a mere *pseudo-reality* [*Schein-wirklichkeit*] which only exists in the minds of ideologues—as error, imagination, and illusion, devoid of a genuine object. At any rate, this is supposed to be true for all the so-called "higher" ideologies.[34]

Once again, Korsch wishes to highlight that even those strata of superstructure seemingly at the furthest remove from infrastructure are not immaterial, neither in the sense of being unreal vis-à-vis the real material ground of society nor in the sense of lacking import, weight, etc. These superstructural strata would be "higher" formations, such as philosophy and similar theoretical domains (presumably including the Marxist political theory grasped in and for itself by a proletarian class consciousness eventually to emerge), whose "height" distances them from the down-to-earth lowliness of the economic base.

By Korsch's lights, even if one uncritically accepts the spatial metaphors of base, height, and the like accompanying talk of the infrastructure-superstructure distinction, the most elevated tiers of superstructure still are capable of, as it were, action at a distance. They can and do enjoy ontological heft and possess powers to effect real material changes in the world. Such "'higher' ideologies" include, for Korsch, economics itself as an intellectual discipline devoted to studying the infrastructural base and closely connected matters.[35] And in line with Korsch's argument about the nonepiphenomenal status of such "ideologies," it indeed seems to be the case that economics has influenced and continues to influence the actual workings of economies.

Korsch's employment of the phrase "last instance" at the end of the first of the two block quotations immediately above is an obvious reference to Engels. *Marxism and Philosophy* evinces an ambivalence toward Marx's key collaborator.[36] Although sometimes positive about Engels,[37] Korsch, in the above-quoted deployment of the Engelsian "last instance," appears to argue that even a heavily qualified privileging of the economy, one ceding to the more-than-economic a great deal of "relative autonomy," is still too economistic qua economically deterministic. In the context of this same passage, Korsch also, with his use of the word "union," tellingly looks as though he is moving in the direction of merging infrastructures and superstructures into each other as coequal dimensions of social totalities. This unifying move, in which the economy loses the distinctive priority granted it by more traditional forms of historical materialism, arguably is realized in the Gramscian concept of the "historical bloc" (about which I will say more below). *Marxism and Philosophy* clearly foreshadows this concept from the *Prison Notebooks*.[38] Furthermore, this sets the stage for the eventual emergence out of Western Marxism, occurring later in the twentieth century, of a post-Marxism whose antieconomism goes to the extreme of pointedly refusing to privilege economic factors in any way whatsoever (subsequently in what follows, I will take up the case of Ernesto Laclau as epitomizing such post-Marxism).

Also in the two preceding block quotations from *Marxism and Philosophy*, Korsch objects to the infamous "reflection theory" as it features within certain strains of Marxism. But he does not focus so much on the notorious Engelsian-Leninist epistemological version of this as regards issues of realism, truth, and verification primarily in connection with the empirical, experimental natural sciences of modernity. Instead, Korsch, with his overriding concern to develop a nonreductive historical materialism as a counterweight to economism, argues against the notion that superstructure is nothing more than a "reflection" of infrastructure, namely, "a mere *pseudo-reality* which only exists in the minds of ideologues—as error, imagination, and illusion." Superstructure, for him, is not epiphenomenal, not a causally inefficacious and superficial shining.

What is more, Korsch accuses this economistic reflection-theoretic version of Marxist materialism of being "undialectical" and relying on a "totally abstract and basically metaphysical dualism." Later in *Marxism and Philosophy*, he further specifies that vulgar Marxists' reflection dualism is itself a result of such vulgarizers' uncritically remaining in thrall to the crude spontaneous metaphysics of commonsensical "naïve realism."[39] Korsch is suggesting that vulgar Marxism, although purporting to be thoroughly monistic in terms of its fundamental materialist ontology, actually betrays this purported monism by dualistically splitting off an ostensibly ideal, immaterial superstructure from a real, material infrastructure. This gesture of splitting thereby generates the dualism of two worlds, even though one of these worlds is deemed to be fictitious, illusory, and the like.

Korsch indeed is onto something here. As with any reductionism or eliminativism (such as those seeking to reduce or eliminate mind in favor of matter

CONCLUSION ❧ 253

alone), so too with economism: Insofar as the appearances to be reduced or eliminated are acknowledged by their reducers or eliminators (however implicitly and/or grudgingly) as not utter nothingness, they must be separated from the reducers' and eliminators' plane of reality and quarantined within another plane, namely, that of unreality. The result is an intended monism compelled to posit two planes, namely, an actual dualism (whether of matter and mind, substance and attributes/modes, or infrastructure and superstructure).

Finally, Korsch, in line with the very title of his 1923 intervention, understandably sees fit to mention Marx's oft-cited eleventh thesis from the "Theses on Feuerbach." On Korsch's construal, this famous declaration by Marx is not a call to throw out philosophy altogether, as it so often is taken to be.[40] Rather, philosophies, as superstructural-but-nonepiphenomenal "'higher' ideologies," have roles to play in shaping consciousnesses, including the class consciousness of the revolutionary proletariat—and, in shaping the latter, a role to play in catalyzing and nudging concrete economic and political practices. For this Korsch, Gramsci's choice of the phrase "philosophy of praxis" as a synonym for "historical materialism" is not just a result of the need for an imprisoned Gramsci to escape the attention of his captors' censors. In Korsch's eyes, historical materialism itself indeed is a philosophy, albeit a peculiar one drastically different from all philosophies hitherto (i.e., before Marx).

The concluding pages of *Marxism and Philosophy* involve Korsch summarizing the content of his text. His manner of closing this 1923 contribution emphasizes the importance and urgency of Marxists giving superstructure its due.[41] Both this emphasis itself and Korsch's fashion of articulating it resonate powerfully with Gramsci's writings of only a few years later.[42] I turn now to these.

As with Korsch circa 1923, so too with Gramsci: The foregrounding of the ineliminable centrality of superstructural factors to social history constitutes a red thread for Gramsci's thinking. Like *Marxism and Philosophy*, the *Prison Notebooks* contain vehement insistences on the nonepiphenomenal reality of superstructures for Marx and all sound-minded true Marxists.[43] In a statement resonating with some of Korsch's assertions, Gramsci, gesturing at Marx,[44] maintains: "If humans become conscious of their task on the terrain of superstructures, it means that there is a necessary and vital connection between structure and superstructures, just as there is between the skin and the skeleton in the human body. It would be silly to say that a person stands erect on his skin rather than his skeleton, and yet this does not mean that the skin is merely an appearance and an illusion."[45] In terms of Marx's supposedly anti-Hegelian "history does not march on its head," this Gramsci would make a similar observation. He would observe that although it might be silly to say that a person walks on his head (as superstructure) rather than his feet (as [infra]structure), this does not mean that the head is merely an appearance and an illusion. The head still plays a non-negligible role in the activity of walking (as social history).

As I noted earlier, Korsch utilizes the phrase "dialectical materialism" not in an Engelsian sense (i.e., as bound up with Engels's dialectics of nature) but as a synonym for "historical materialism." What makes historical materialism dialectical for the author of *Marxism and Philosophy* is the dialectic of back-and-forth influences flowing both ways between the infrastructural and superstructural strata of societies. Gramsci likewise hypothesizes the existence of reciprocal interactions between the economic and the more-than-economic.[46] Along these same lines, he refers to Marx's "Theses on Feuerbach" and asks of this Marx, "Did he not mean to say that the superstructure reacts dialectically to the structure and modifies it?"[47] With Korsch and Gramsci quietly in the background, István Mészáros subsequently describes the reciprocity between infrastructures and superstructures such as to make glaringly visible this reciprocity's antieconomistic implications—"if economics is the 'ultimate determinant,' it is also a 'determined determinant': it does not exist outside the always concrete, historically changing complex of concrete mediations, including the most 'spiritual' ones."[48]

Gramsci goes even further. He not only asserts the dialectical qua reciprocal character of the infrastructure-superstructure relationship. He also argues for the autonomy of at least certain components and dynamics of superstructural historical processes.[49] For instance, within such more-than-economic institutions as church and state, certain developments may indeed be directly or indirectly triggered by economic forces. But there also will be, for example, theological and political developments determined by intrachurch and intrastate factors independent of the mode of production contemporaneous with these developments.

Although Gramsci's rendition of Marxist historical materialism as the philosophy of praxis indeed has recourse to the distinction between infrastructure and superstructure, he seems to problematize this very distinction at certain moments in the *Prison Notebooks*. At one point, he highlights how this distinction breaks down in cases of entities that can be simultaneously infrastructural and superstructural. The paradigmatic instance of such a breakdown occurs, for Gramsci, in the linked realities of science and technology (interestingly and, given Gramsci's anti-Stalinism, ironically, for Stalin too the sciences and mathematics, as well as natural languages, likewise defy classification as either infrastructural or superstructural).[50] Scientific *savoir* and technological *savoir-faire* play multiple dual roles, often at the same time, across both the economic and more-than-economic layers of social orders.[51] This is even more evident in today's capitalism. The cozy relations between university science departments, government funding agencies, the military-industrial complex, and private-sector business interests readily reveal that science and technology, at least within capitalist societies, straddle lines between economic, academic, and political frameworks.

However, Gramsci's problematization of historical materialism's infrastructure-superstructure distinction is most on display in the concept of "historical bloc" he sketches in the *Prison Notebooks*. Defining this concept, he states, "The structure and superstructures form a 'historical bloc.' In other words, the complex and discordant ensemble of the superstructures reflects the ensemble of the social relations of production."[52] In one sense, the phrase "historical bloc" simply designates the totality formed by the combination of the infrastructural with the superstructural tiers of society. This echoes Lukács's vehement insistence on the paramount importance of the category of totality, as social totality, for Marxism.[53]

But, in this just-quoted statement, Gramsci at least looks as though, by contrast with Korsch, he endorses the idea that superstructures are reflections of infrastructures. Yet at the end of this same fragment in the *Prison Notebooks*, he promptly invokes again "the necessary reciprocity between structure and superstructures (a reciprocity that is, precisely, the real dialectical process)."[54] With this invocation, Gramsci seems abruptly to swing away from the superstructural being a secondary afterimage of the infrastructural to (re)emphasizing that, in a historical bloc, the superstructural enjoys at least rough parity in influence with (and back upon) the infrastructure.

Elsewhere in the *Prison Notebooks*, Gramsci employs some musings specifically about ideologies to motivate and buttress the concept of the historical bloc. He writes:

Recall the assertion frequently made by Marx about the "solidity of popular beliefs" being a necessary element of a specific situation. He says, more or less: "when this mode of thinking acquires the force of popular beliefs," etc.... Marx also stated that a popular conviction often has as much energy as a material force, or something similar, and it is very important. The analysis of these statements, in my view, lends support to the concept of "historical bloc" in which in fact the material forces are the content and ideologies are the form. This distinction between form and content is just heuristic because material forces would be historically inconceivable without form and ideologies would be individual fantasies without material forces.[55]

Gramsci likely is thinking of the following assertion from Marx's 1843/1844 "A Contribution to the Critique of Hegel's Philosophy of Right. Introduction"— "theory also becomes a material force once it has gripped the masses."[56] Of course, set within the larger theoretical framework of historical materialism, the (superstructural-ideological) "theory" spoken of in this assertion would have to be seen as, first, originally arising from an infrastructural mode of production and, second, able both to "grip the masses" and to become a socially efficacious "material force" thanks at least in part to economic factors. As Marx and Engels go on to warn in 1845's *The Holy Family*, "*Ideas* can never lead beyond an old world order but only beyond the ideas of the old world order. Ideas *cannot carry out anything* at all. In order to carry out ideas men are needed who can exert practical force."[57] Whether the Gramscian concept of historical bloc can and does preserve these two just-mentioned historical-materialist qualifications to the line from the early Marx's critique of Hegel's *Elements of the Philosophy of Right* Gramsci has in mind is an open question, one that will be at stake below. For now, suffice it to say that Gramsci's historical bloc, by contrast with more traditional Marxian historical materialism's assigning of greater weight to matters economic, favors an Aristotelian hylomorphism of equiprimordial infrastructural matter and superstructural form.

Tellingly, Gramsci talks about Marx's "effort to go beyond the traditional conceptions of 'idealism' and 'materialism.'"[58] He promptly underscores, "As for this expression 'historical materialism,' greater stress is placed on the second word, whereas it should be placed on the first: Marx is fundamentally a 'historicist,' etc."[59] Gramsci reiterates these claims several times elsewhere in the *Prison Notebooks*.[60] They put him at odds with that strain of Marxism which, starting with Engels, situates Marxist theory within an ongoing zero-sum struggle between idealism and materialism, a struggle allegedly forming the oft-obscured central fault line of the entire history of philosophy from antiquity through the present.

All too frequently, rhetoric about leaving behind an entrenched philosophical opposition, such as that between idealism and materialism, masks a surreptitious retention and continued privileging of one side of the old opposition purportedly transcended. Put differently, one can "go beyond" an antagonism like that of idealism-versus-materialism in a number of fashions, including doing so in ways that amount to a failure actually to surpass the antagonism in question insofar as one of its terms is still favored and carried forward. In this vein, a number of features of Gramsci's theorizing already in view at this juncture lead one to wonder whether a historicist idealism elevating superstructural thinking over infrastructural being, with a correlative downplaying of the material economic base, is being advanced in the *Prison Notebooks*.

CONCLUSION   257

The subsequent history of Western Marxism indicates that even if it was not Gramsci's own original intention antimaterialistically to ditch outright Marxism's emphasis on the economy, he inspired many who indeed went on to drag radical leftism down such idealistic paths. Already in the 1920s, Western Marxism's founders were in danger of helping dissolve historical materialism into a theoretically eclectic cultural studies discursive ethos with no real connection to materialism—with this danger arguably realizing itself in the ensuing decades. Symptomatically, the figure of Gramsci has been fetishized to the point of his being treated as a secular saint among post-Marxists and their fellow travelers in today's theoretical humanities. As Anderson observes, "No Marxist thinker after the classical epoch is so generally respected in the West as Antonio Gramsci."[61] For such venerators of the author of the *Prison Notebooks*, what is most worthy of veneration is precisely the Gramsci who "frees" leftism from such supposed evils as economic reductionism, "class essentialism," and the like. In so doing, this Gramsci, or, at least, part of his legacy, brings historical materialism into proximity with certain bourgeois traditions of sociohistorical theory (as represented by thinkers such as Weber and Benedetto Croce).[62]

As regards suspicions of surreptitious idealism, Gramsci even has approving words for Henri Bergson at one moment in the *Prison Notebooks*. Specifically, he praises Bergson's critique of "new materialistic theology"[63] (especially as the "dogmatism" of "positivist materialism"). And as Gramsci's intensive and extensive opposition to economism makes abundantly evident, one version of this "new materialistic theology" is, for him, Marxist materialism put forward as a positivistic science of history built on the foundations of a critique of political economy. Here Gramsci prefers the company of Bergson the romantic idealist to the likes of Engels, Lenin, Nicolai Bukharin, and their "economistic" ilk[64] (whether representatives of the Second International, German Social Democracy, Bolshevism, or Stalinism—a set of strange bedfellows also opposed by Korsch).[65] Relatedly, Martin Jay portrays the young Lukács's 1923 theory of reification as influenced by *Lebensphilosophie* and Bergson.[66] Andrew Arato and Paul Breines similarly cast *History and Class Consciousness* as an idealist and romantic work.[67]

Just as Gramsci applauds Bergson's rejection of "materialistic theology," he correspondingly laments certain historical materialists' "theologistic" prioritization of infrastructure (à la positivism/scientism as "theologism"). In Gramsci's prison correspondence, he remarks, "many so-called theoreticians of historical materialism might have fallen into a philosophical position similar to medieval theologism and might have made of 'economic structure' a sort of 'unknown god.'"[68] In another letter, he comments: "In the philosophy of praxis structure is

CONCLUSION

like a hidden god . . . might be true if the philosophy of praxis were a speculative philosophy and not an absolute historicism, really and not just in words freed from all transcendental and theological residues."[69] Gramsci essentially distinguishes between a false historical materialism (as a "speculative philosophy" with the "transcendental and theological residues" of its "hidden god") and a true historical materialism (as "the philosophy of praxis" qua "absolute historicism"). There looks to be an implicit immanent critique of economically minded Marxists operative here: If Marxists are really to be the atheists they proclaim themselves to be as a feature of their Marxism, then they must disavow and abandon not only the gods of all religions but also their pseudosecular substitute god, namely, the economy as an all-determining infrastructural base.

But in forwarding this immanent critique, does Gramsci not forget that the young Marx begins coming into his own in part by discerning in the secular spheres of the political and the economic the same sort of alienation Feuerbach confines to the sphere of the religious alone? For instance, in making "fetishism" central to the functioning of capitalist socioeconomic orders, does the mature Marx not signal that at least under capitalism, it actually is the case that the economy does indeed function like a "hidden god"? If this is so, then would not the Gramscian philosopher of praxis, in refusing to have any truck with this divine-type power, forgo truly knowing the reality of the capitalism it seeks to criticize and surpass? Would not this seeking likely prove futile, given its willful ignorance of the economy's centrality for capitalism? Along these lines, Lucio Colletti observes that "Gramsci had not really mastered Marxist economic theory."[70]

At various points in the *Prison Notebooks*, Gramsci nuances his critique of economism. He calls for careful navigation between the Scylla of mechanistic economism (in which social history is run by anonymous, transindividual structures) and the Charybdis of voluntarist ideologism (in which social history is dictated by the thoughts and actions of so-called great men).[71] He opposes purely economic accounts of social history,[72] although this is not at all tantamount to excluding economic elements from analyses of historical sequences. The economism Gramsci's philosophy of praxis, with its theory of hegemony, opposes is a "mechanistic" and "fatalistic" worldview.[73] By implication, a nonmechanistic and nonfatalistic incorporation of economic considerations into historical materialism would not be objectionable.

At the same time, Gramsci urges that historical materialism needs to include "ethico-political" (i.e., superstructurally driven) history within its (re)constructions, in addition to infrastructurally driven history.[74] Similarly, he draws a connection between Engels's "in the last instance" qualification of the economy's

CONCLUSION ❧ 259

deterministic influence and Marx's 1859 assertion that, as Gramsci paraphrases him, "it is on the terrain of ideologies that men 'become conscious' of the conflict between form and content in the world of production."[75] For Gramsci, making this connection supports his theory of hegemony and, with it, his concept of the war of position, namely, a gradual soft-power campaign for hearts and minds via intellectual (i.e., cultural, educational, and ideological) means—and this by contrast with the war of maneuver as an abrupt hard-power struggle involving revolutionary violence with its force of arms.

Gramsci's contentions in these veins urge Marxist philosophers of praxis, at least in the West, to concentrate their political efforts on superstructure rather than infrastructure. This urging runs contrary to the dictates of economistic (pseudo-)Marxism (as John Merrington observes, antieconomism arguably is the ultimate guiding thread of Gramsci's meditations in prison).[76] And Gramsci adds to the list of theoretical and practical problems with economism a warning that this vulgarization of historical materialism threatens to derail Marxists' cultural war of position, to doom their efforts to make historical materialism hegemonic among wider swaths of intellectuals (themselves key to winning hegemony for Marxism among a critical mass of the population). This is because, as Gramsci explains, the crudeness of "historical economism," masquerading as historical materialism, is likely to be repellent to "intelligent persons."[77] Such "primitive infantilism"[78] at the level of theory hence poses real dangers at the level of practice too.

Another notable critical point made by Gramsci contra economism has to do with the topic of political errors. He explains:

> A particular political act may have been an error of calculation on the part of the leaders of the dominant classes, an error that historical development corrects and moves beyond through the governmental parliamentary "crises" of the ruling classes. Mechanical historical materialism does not take the possibility of error into account; it assumes that every political act is determined directly by the structure and is therefore the reflection of a real and permanent (in the sense of secured) modification of the structure. The principle of "error" is complex: it could consist in an individual impulse stemming from a mistaken calculation, or it could also be the manifestation of the attempts (which may fail) of specific groups or cliques to attain hegemony within the leading group.[79]

Economism's flat monism renders it incapable of accounting for how any subject, as reduced to being nothing more or other than a mere bearer/personification of a class identity/position, could make mistakes in the sense of behaving in fashions that fail to reflect and advance the interests of the class of which he/she is a member. Yet such blunders can, have, and do occur. Gramsci suggests that accounting for them requires considering elements and facets beyond just the infrastructural mode of production with its relations of production as simplified into a conflict between two internally unified and homogeneous classes. Errors indicate that subjects, whether they intend to or not, are able to think and act in ways irreducible to exclusively economic determination.

Gramsci also brings up a self-contradiction in economism's stance apropos human mindedness, like-mindedness, and agency, with these seeming to be not immediately economic and largely bound up with superstructural phenomena. He observes, "The attitude of economism toward political will, action, and initiative is, to say the least, strange: as if these were not themselves an expression, and even the effective expression of the economy."[80] That is to say, if economistic vulgar Marxists really do believe in their own crudely reductive theoretical framework, then they should find nothing troubling or threatening when other sorts of Marxists appeal to consciousness, volition, and the like, since these cannot be anything other than yet more expressions of the all-determining infrastructural base. Nevertheless, economistic critiques of Lenin's vanguardism by reformist Western leftists and of Lukács's focus on class consciousness by the Soviets exhibit the performative contradiction pointed out by Gramsci. Through such critiques, the economistically minded simultaneously display a confidence in everything being reducible to economics and a fear that consciousness, etc. might not be so reducible.

However, Gramsci's just-quoted critical observation about economism harbors an attention-worthy ambiguity—an ambiguity, I will argue, already contained in Lukács's *History and Class Consciousness* and affecting the entire subsequent history of Western Marxism up through the present. Is Gramsci limiting himself to making explicit an inconsistency in economistic Marxists' positions only in order to reject entirely their emphases on the economy? Or, by saying that "political will, action, and initiative" are "themselves an expression, and even the effective expression of the economy," is Gramsci granting, in however qualified a manner, that such subjective superstructural factors are, in fact, somehow or other still ultimately rooted in infrastructural grounds when all is said and done (for example, "in the last instance")? Does Gramsci rescind entirely any prioritization of economics in historical materialism? Or does he preserve some sort of privilege for it notwithstanding his repudiations of economic reductionism?

A particular remark by Gramsci about his concept of hegemony offers a clue in response to the preceding questions. At one moment in the *Prison Notebooks*, he claims that "hegemony is political but also and above all economic, it has its material base in the decisive function exercised by the hegemonic group in the decisive core of economic activity."[81] With this remark, it would seem that despite his fierce antieconomism, he does not entirely reject classical historical materialism's uneven weighting of sociohistorical influences in favor of infrastructures over superstructures.

For someone like Laclau (whom I will address at greater length later), those moments in the *Prison Notebooks* when Gramsci appears to retain some degree of priority for the economy are backsliding betrayals of his own original theoretical breakthroughs. From Laclau's post-Marxist perspective, such moments are lingering residues of old Marxist dogma (i.e., class essentialism, etc.) to be left by the historical wayside. The Laclauian account of hegemony, deeply indebted to Gramsci in particular, utilizes the Gramscian substitution of the totality of the historical bloc in place of the historical-materialist duality of infrastructure and superstructure precisely so as to deny economics any special role whatsoever in leftist sociopolitical theory.[82]

Whereas Laclau and his ilk fault Gramsci for still being too economistic despite his antieconomism, Althusser indicts him for not being economistic enough. For many with at least a passing familiarity with Althusser, this Althusserian indictment likely comes as quite a surprise. This is because Althusser's single best-known text probably is the 1970 essay "Ideology and Ideological State Apparatuses: Notes Towards an Investigation." This essay, with its distinction between repressive state apparatuses ruling by coercion and ideological state apparatuses ruling by consent, obviously is inspired by Gramsci's treatment of superstructure as fundamentally divided between the state, with its hard power, and civil society, with its soft power.[83] And the longer manuscript from which it was extracted, *On the Reproduction of Capitalism*, offers qualified yet explicit praise for Gramsci.[84]

Yet in a recently published 1978 manuscript entitled *Que faire?*, Althusser lays out a set of scathing criticisms of the author of the *Prison Notebooks*. By Althusser's lights, Gramsci's philosophy of praxis is so "original" that it loses any connection with Marx and historical materialism.[85] One could say that, for Althusser, Gramsci goes so far with his antieconomism that he leaves behind Marxism to become the first post-Marxist *avant la lettre*. Less harshly and more ambivalently, Colletti similarly remarks, "The very deficiency of Gramsci's economic formation allowed him to be a more original and important Marxist than he might otherwise have been, if he had possessed a more orthodox training."[86]

In *Que faire?*, Althusser depicts Gramsci as excessively preoccupied with combating the Bolshevik and Stalinist versions of economism.[87] Gramsci's repeated attacks on Bukharin's 1921 *Historical Materialism: A System of Sociology* are symptomatic of this. Althusser objects to the use in the *Prison Notebooks* of a critique of this Bukharin, with Bukharin's rendition of the infrastructure-superstructure distinction, to justify a wholesale jettisoning of this distinction.[88] Being forced to choose between either Bukharin's mechanistic version of the infrastructure-superstructure pair or no version of it whatsoever would be a false dilemma.

Althusser's criticisms of Gramsci in *Que faire?* all concern the status (or lack thereof) of Marxism's economic base in Gramsci's reworking of historical materialism as the philosophy of praxis. This Althusser portrays the philosophy of praxis as at odds with historical materialism, given the former's alleged erasure of infrastructure.[89] But exactly how, if at all, does Gramsci theoretically erase infrastructure?

According to Althusser in 1978, Gramsci's historical bloc renders the economic base conceptually ungraspable by merging it with the superstructure (i.e., erasing the very difference between the infrastructural and the superstructural). Through this Gramscian merger, Marx's mode of production disappears beneath the muddied waters of a both-and/neither-nor economic/more-than-economic social totality.[90] Similarly, Gramsci's recourse to the vague and sometimes even ambiguous phrase "civil society" leaves the topic of the economy in the blank of a silence.[91]

Although Gramsci wishes to focus attention on superstructures, his blurring or dissipation of the infrastructure-superstructure distinction, so Althusser claims, undermines his ability to maintain this focus.[92] It is as though Gramsci is trying to hold onto with one hand something he tries to throw away with the other. But, assuming he can (partially) retain the superstructural in its distinctness, Althusser charges that he begins, but only begins, to think superstructures' influences on infrastructures—and not vice versa, given Gramsci's deliberate downplaying of infrastructural influences in the guise of his rubbishing of economism qua economic determinism.[93]

Relatedly, Althusser contends that Gramsci's fixation on superstructures and his recasting of societies as historical blocs cause him to regress from an explanatory theory of history (i.e., historical materialism) to a merely descriptive (but not explanatory) "empiricism" (i.e., the philosophy of praxis).[94] In other words, for this Althusser, Gramsci problematically absorbs the "science" of historical materialism into the "philosophy" (or ideology) of "historicism"[95] (and, with reference to Gramsci's "absolute historicism," Althusser writes, " 'absolute' historicism . . . is philosophically *unthinkable*"[96] by virtue of trying to be simultaneously historical and ahistorical qua universal).[97] Put differently, Althusser's

CONCLUSION &~ 263

critical contention is that whereas Marxism explains how and why social history unfolds in the fashions and tempos in which it does—historical materialism does so precisely on the basis of the infrastructure-superstructure theoretical schema—Gramscianism contents itself with merely describing what it observes by way of the concatenations of empirical historical facts. It cannot and does not get back behind these concatenations to understand and conceptualize the logic(s) structuring them.

As seen, Gramsci himself affirms, albeit with his own caveats, Engels's notion of the economy as "determinative in the last instance." However, *Que faire?* invokes this same Engels contra the Gramscian philosophy of praxis.[98] Moreover, against Gramsci's historical bloc, Althusser declares, "Every society has a base, if not it is in the void. Every demonstration should master the base of what it talks about by thought, if not it is in the void."[99] Althusser leaves the *Prison Notebooks* drifting about in a groundless state, unable to provide firm foundations and clear orientations for the Marxist tradition. Yet Gramsci goes on to become one of the leading lights of Western Marxism during much of the rest of the twentieth century. Today, he enjoys the status of a canonized intellectual hero and saintly political martyr of the radical left.

So exactly how fair and accurate are Althusser's 1978 criticisms of Gramsci? A short while ago, I concluded my selective unpacking of Gramsci's carceral writings by noting a possible basic ambiguity in how he positions himself vis-à-vis the centrality or noncentrality of the economy. It looks as though he wavers between revoking any special status for infrastructures and holding onto some sort of qualified privilege for economic forces and factors. Hence, in *Que faire?*, Althusser is only partly justified in his critique of Gramsci. However, this critique gains in legitimacy when one takes into consideration the fate of Gramsci's ideas in post-Gramscian Western Marxism. Subsequent Western Marxists and post-Marxists recurrently appeal to Gramsci, particularly his theory of hegemony, when downplaying or sidelining political economy. Similarly, insofar as Gramsci's corpus is appealed to by more centrist leftists preferring reform to revolution, Anderson is not without justification when he observes apropos Gramsci, "Against his own intention, formal conclusions can be drawn from his work that lead away from revolutionary socialism."[100]

Furthermore, Gramsci's hesitation and wavering as regards the status of the economy in his philosophy of praxis arguably is foreshadowed in the young Lukács's *History and Class Consciousness*, itself the founding document of the Western Marxist tradition. An oscillation between traditional historical materialism (as prioritizing infrastructure) and antieconomism (as deemphasizing infrastructure) already is exhibited by what is perhaps the best-known feature of this 1923 book, namely, its account of "reification" (*Verdinglichung*). The celebrated chapter of *History and Class Consciousness* on "Reification and the Consciousness of the Proletariat" contains a section entitled "The Antinomies of Bourgeois Thought." Similarly, Anderson speaks of "The Antinomies of Antonio Gramsci." Apropos Lukács's and Gramsci's inconsistent vacillations vis-à-vis matters economic, one also could zero in on reification as crystallizing an "antinomy of Georg Lukács" and, following him, one shaping much of the rest of Western Marxism.

Lukács's 1967 "Preface to the New Edition" of *History and Class Consciousness*, in line with his post-1924 self-critical turn, contains a disavowal of his youthful notion of reification. Lukács indicts reification circa 1923 for ending up connoting any and every subjective process of (self-)objectification, thereby failing to remain precise enough to be specific to capitalism in particular,[101] despite the early Lukács's attempts to remain focused on capitalism in its sociohistorical uniqueness.[102] (Joseph Gabel's book *False Consciousness: An Essay on Reification*, originally published in French in 1962, epitomizes the problems the later Lukács identifies with his early conception of reification—with Gabel decoupling this conception from anything economic so as to incorporate it into a vague and sweeping ahistorical perspective blending together Bergsonism with an existential-psychiatric *Daseinsanalyse*.)[103] However, Lukács's self-critique of reification does not bring out the antinomic tension within this renowned Lukácsian concept that I intend to illuminate below. The closest the self-critical Lukács of 1967 comes to what I soon will be addressing is when he acknowledges the influence of Weber on his early readings of Marx.[104]

Turning now to "Reification and the Consciousness of the Proletariat," Lukács opens this pivotal chapter of *History and Class Consciousness* with a paragraph that contains the following claims: "The problem of commodities must not be considered in isolation or even regarded as the central problem in economics, but as the central, structural problem of capitalist society in all its aspects. Only in this case can the structure of commodity-relations be made to yield a model of all the objective forms of bourgeois society together with all the subjective forms corresponding to them."[105] Lukács deliberately chooses to begin where Marx himself begins.[106] That is to say, the first chapter of the first volume of *Capital* is devoted to the topic of the commodity. Marx's critique of political economy starts with the commodity as the condensed nucleus of the entire capitalist socioeconomic formation. All of *Das Kapital* unfolds and blossoms forth out of this initial germinal seed.

Moreover, Lukács's theory of reification as per *History and Class Consciousness* makes especially clear that the famous final section of chapter 1 of *Capital*, volume 1—this is the section entitled "The Fetishism of the Commodity and Its Secret"—provides the key to demystifying and comprehending how the commodity form not only anchors capitalist infrastructure but comes to color the layers and expanses of superstructure. Thanks particularly to commodity fetishism, what happens in the capitalist economy does not stay in the economy. It seeps into every nook and cranny of the social edifice, including the highest and most intimate spheres of more-than-economic life.[107]

Lukács even redefines "commodity" in its technical Marxist sense such that it includes within its very "essence" this centrifugal force moving toward social universalization, this drive to colonize all sectors of the capitalist lifeworld as a "totality."[108] He states:

> The commodity can only be understood in its undistorted essence when it becomes the universal category of society as a whole. Only in this context does the reification produced by commodity relations assume decisive importance both for the objective evolution of society and for the stance adopted by men towards it. Only then does the commodity become crucial for the subjugation of men's consciousness to the forms in which this reification finds expression and for their attempts to comprehend the process or to rebel against its disastrous effects and liberate themselves from servitude to the "second nature" so created.[109]

With Marx, what renders the category of the commodity specific to capitalism (as distinct from the category of the good or the ware as not specific to capitalism) is that the commodity is a use value bearing an exchange value, with this exchange value in turn containing within itself a quota of surplus value (and everything the category of surplus value, as peculiar to capitalism, brings with it). What Lukács adds to this, inspired by Marx (particularly Marx's account of commodity fetishism), is another essential facet to the capitalist commodity, namely, its allegedly inherent tendency to remake everything in its own image, to stamp its form upon all social structures, dynamics, and agents without exception, including subjects, objects, relationships, and happenings well outside the confines of the economic base (as Korsch puts it, *"The commodity is a born leveller"*).[110] This Lukácsian addition to the Marxian conception of the commodity presupposes both the economically reductive thrust of capitalism in general as well as the compulsion to privatize in particular intrinsic to the very logic of capital.

As "Reification and the Consciousness of the Proletariat" proceeds, Lukács further enriches his characterizations of *Verdinglichung*. Reification is described by him in multiple ways: as both objective (i.e., being reified) and subjective (i.e., feeling reified),[111] as dehumanizing,[112] and as induced and embodied by industrial mechanization as well as by irrationally rationalistic technocratic bureaucratization.[113] The modern factory is identified as the condensed microcosmic epitome of the Weberian "iron cage" of capitalist society as a whole.[114] Capitalism's commodity-centered mode of production produces not only commodities as economic units but also more-than-economic social relations, be they legal, political, religious, intellectual, or whatever else, modeled on commodities and these things' market-mediated interactions.[115] As Colletti notes along these same lines, "under capitalism all important social relations become exchange relations."[116]

Even the individual's inner "soul," as his/her "total personality" and "the whole consciousness of man," is said by Lukács to fall victim to capitalist reification.[117] Echoing Bergson and anticipating the Heidegger of 1927's *Being and Time*, "Reification and the Consciousness of the Proletariat" narrates how, under the influence of developments such as Taylorism, workers' subjective phenomenal experiences of temporality, both inside and outside the workplace, are flattened out into the anonymous spatial uniformity of carefully managed schedules and calendars.[118] With time being money in capital's ceaseless pursuit of ever-more surplus value for itself, capital has no time for modes of temporality other than its own clocks, deadlines, and turnover rates. The impoverishment suffered by laborers' senses of temporal flows under such industrial regimes is not confined to working hours on the factory floor. The 24/7 rhythms and routines of all life come under the sway of capitalistic cadences. Everyone marches and dances to capital's beat around the clock.[119]

Many aspects of the young Lukács's account of reification clearly resonate with non-Marxist (or even, in the case of Heidegger, anti-Marxist) critical assessments of capitalism in its modern techno-scientific, industrial guises. In particular, there is a strong Weberian streak running through the texts of the early Lukács, with Weber having been a significant influence on his initial readings of Marx by his own admission.[120] Arato and Breines refer to the youthful Lukács's "Marx-Weber synthesis of social theory."[121] Speaking of this synthesis, they claim that "one of the young Lukács's signal and most infamous contributions is that he brought this current of social and cultural theory into Marxism"[122] (thereby helping pave the way for the Frankfurt School especially).[123] Gareth Stedman Jones, referring to *History and Class Consciousness* with its Weberian aspects in view,[124] relatedly remarks, "It represents the first major irruption of the romantic anti-scientific tradition of bourgeois thought into Marxist theory,"[125] adding apropos this 1923 book that "its original hope, and ambition, is to

CONCLUSION ☙ 267

arrange a marriage between romantic anti-scientific *Lebensphilosophie* and historical materialism."[126] Andrew Feenberg likewise sees the author of *History and Class Consciousness* as profoundly Weberian.[127] Göran Therborn and Merrington also underscore the young Lukács's Weberianism[128] (with Therborn additionally associating the Korsch of *Marxism and Philosophy* with this Weberianizing tendency coloring the origins of Western Marxism).[129]

Axel Honneth too highlights Weber's impact on this Lukács with his theory of *Verdinglichung*.[130] Relatedly, in the course of Honneth's post-Marxist reassessment of the most celebrated concept from *History and Class Consciousness*, he highlights a tension between Lukács's Marxian (i.e., economic) and Weberian (i.e., noneconomic) explanations for reification.[131] True to Frankfurt School form, Honneth favors the Weberian over the Marxian side of the early Lukács.

Honneth repudiates exclusively or primarily economy-based accounts for the genesis and persistence of *Verdinglichung*.[132] In so doing, he jettisons anything resembling traditional historical materialism, more or less completely leaving behind Marx and his legacy. Honneth replaces this abandoned framework with his "recognition-theoretic" story about human beings' thingification of one another and themselves.

Already in "Reification and the Consciousness of the Proletariat," Lukács associates the decoupling of accounts of reifications from economics with the capitalist-bourgeois perspective.[133] Indeed, the second and third generations of the Frankfurt School have achieved academic institutional success arguably through following the formula of repackaging the bland center-left bourgeois liberal bromides of a moderately progressive idealism in the technical jargon of a theoretical eclecticism pasting together a motley set of non-Marxist frameworks and notions. All of this then benefits from being accompanied by a faint whiff of leftist radicalism thanks only to lingering fumes from the early history of the Frankfurt School and its associates.

Well before Honneth, other commentators on *History and Class Consciousness* alight upon a tension between the economic/infrastructural and more-than-economic/superstructural dimensions of the young Lukács's meditations. Although the early Lukács indeed is the grandfather of a Western Marxist orientation foregrounding the importance of superstructure, more economistic notes and implications remain throughout his 1923 book. As Russell Jacoby observes, "Lukács defined capitalism by its reductionism, an insatiable market subordinating all to profit and money."[134] Indeed, one of the fundamental upshots of "Reification and the Consciousness of the Proletariat" is that, through reification, capitalism reduces everything without exception to the forms and relations characteristic of commodities.[135] As Arato expresses this, "No sphere of life escapes the world of capitalist alienation."[136] Nothing is exempt from, or at least should be exempt from, commodification.[137]

On the basis of capitalism's own inherent economically reductive tendencies as emphasized by Lukácsian reification, Arato and Breines draw the conclusion that "historical materialism turns out to be an ideology of the capitalist epoch, a function of the age in which the autonomous economy reduces everything to its laws."[138] Is this to say that historical materialism ought to be rejected because its deliberate theoretical reductionism (as privileging of the infrastructural over the superstructural, all other things being equal) ideationally reflects the automatic practical reductionism of its actual object of investigation, namely, really existing capitalism in and of itself? If so, one should pause to register the strangeness of this rejection: A theory is being rubbished as "ideology" not because it deviates from and distorts the target of its inquiry but precisely because it tarries with and accurately renders this target.

Along lines similar to Arato and Breines, Timothy Bewes also worries about the economic reductionism implied by classical Lukácsian *Verdinglichung*. In a study devoted to this topic, Bewes comments that "the *concept* of reification, as Lukács discovered very quickly, is itself reifying."[139] However, one might ask in response: Is it (only) the concept of reification that is reifying? Or, is it (also) the facts on the ground thus conceptualized that already are reified in and of themselves? If capitalist societies indeed are thoroughly reified and reifying, then is it not fitting for historical-materialist theory somehow or other to mirror in its concepts the spontaneous economic reductionism of the very being of capitalism *an sich*? A refusal by the critical theorist of capitalism to reflect this reductionism, in the name of antieconomism and/or intellectual sophistication, risks amounting to mere wishful thinking vainly (or even dangerously) denying the really reductive nature of capitalist reality in all its brute, stupid crudity. Relatedly, I would suggest that at least in some sociohistorical contexts, it is better to risk a reduction than a relativism or a reaction.

What I have been calling "the antinomy of Georg Lukács" (as "the antinomy of reification") is closest to being made explicit in and through Feenberg's interpretive vacillations apropos *History and Class Consciousness*. On the one hand, Feenberg emphasizes the early Lukács's fashions of resisting economism, economic determinism, and the like.[140] Admittedly, "Reification and the Consciousness of the Proletariat" utilizes Marx's conception of commodity fetishism so as to shift Marxists' attention away from an obsessive focus on infrastructure alone and toward superstructure, specifically, the superstructural reverberations and consequences of capitalist commodification. Do not Lukács's explorations of

CONCLUSION &ᵃ 269

the mental, phenomenological, political, psychological, and even romantic dimensions of life under capital-induced reifications distance him from the more mechanistic and scientistic "vulgar Marxists" of both certain German-speaking as well as Soviet trends?

On the other hand, Feenberg is aware that the shift of attention to more-than-economic phenomena in "Reification and the Consciousness of the Proletariat" nonetheless remains tied to a more classically Marxist thesis according to which these phenomena are profoundly conditioned by directly economic elements. He admits that Lukács stays faithful to Marx by stressing "the overriding influence of the economy on all sectors of capitalist society."[141] Feenberg then frets that "if commodity-relations cause objects and subjects to take a reified form, then Lukács would appear to have lapsed into crude economic determinism."[142] Hence, taking Feenberg's various just-cited remarks together, *History and Class Consciousness* should be seen as crystallizing within its pages an antagonism between economistic and antieconomistic leanings.

Like the Lenin of *The State and Revolution*, the Lukács of *History and Class Consciousness* emphasizes that the prioritization of economics is not, by itself, the distinctive hallmark characteristic of Marxism.[143] But as emphasized by the very concept of reification, this same Lukács underscores that capitalism is distinguished by, among other of its features, its bringing about a "total economic penetration of society"[144]—and this despite his contemporaneous polemics against the "mechanistic fatalism" of vulgar economism.[145] The later Lukács's self-critical preface to the 1967 edition of *History and Class Consciousness* more or less inadvertently owns up to what I have been identifying as the antinomy of reification subsisting at the heart of this 1923 book.[146]

Relatedly, in the same 1967 preface, the mature Lukács portrays his early *chef-d'oeuvre* as organized around a false dilemma between the extremes of either economic reductionism or subjectivistic voluntarism.[147] Indeed, Arato deserves credit for portraying *History and Class Consciousness*, especially its chapter on reification, as plagued by a permutation of the third of Kant's "Antinomies of Pure Reason." This Kantian hangover shows up in the young Lukács's writing as an unresolved contradiction between infrastructural determinism and superstructural freedom (the latter being the self-determination of revolutionary class consciousness).[148]

Subsequent generations of Western Marxists are inheritors of the inconsistencies around issues of the place and importance of economics I have traced above in relation to the first generation of this tradition. As seen, Gramsci, Korsch, and Lukács (along with Bloch),[149] the founding figures of Western Marxism, evince pronounced ambivalences vis-à-vis the privileged status of the economy (as infrastructural base) in classical historical materialism. The Frankfurt School, starting with its original members, carries forward and intensifies the antieconomistic emphasis on the significance of more-than-economic social superstructures already integral to the likes of Gramsci, Korsch, and the early Lukács.[150]

Despite the founders of Western Marxism and the founders of the Frankfurt School (i.e., the first and second generations of Western Marxists, respectively) sharing an antieconomistic outlook, the reasons for their common preoccupation with superstructural variables differ. One could argue that in the climate of the early 1920s especially, the shift of European Marxists' attention toward noneconomic dimensions of societies and social developments reflects in part an intellectual-theoretical digestion of lessons imparted by the experiences of the Bolshevik Revolution. As such, the antieconomism of the first Western Marxists is bound up with an optimism regarding the revolutionary path forward in the near-term future.

By marked contrast with the optimistic atmosphere of the years immediately following the 1917 victory of Lenin and his comrades in Russia—this atmosphere surrounds Gramsci, Korsch, and the young Lukács—the Frankfurt School is founded in the midst of sociohistorical circumstances severely depressing for any leftist. The Bolshevik Revolution degenerates into Stalinist state terror. Europe endures the triumph of virulently racist fascism. Mass-scale industrial genocide is carried out within the heart of the Continent. An age of humanity in imminent danger of extinguishing itself dawns with the blinding light of the atom bombs dropped on Hiroshima and Nagasaki. And capitalism stubbornly keeps refusing to wither away or implode, despite undergoing numerous crises both economic and more-than-economic. Starting in the 1930s particularly, the hopes of earlier generations of Marxists appear to get dashed to pieces by the rolling catastrophes of the mercilessly unfolding twentieth century.

Understandably, the setbacks and disasters of the middle decades of the twentieth century lead to a pervasive pessimism coloring the thinking of the first generation of the Frankfurt School.[151] Numerous scholars of Western Marxism and critical theory concur that more than anything else, the Frankfurt School with its pessimism is a product of defeat.[152] These defeats are nothing other than those I enumerated in the preceding paragraph.

The same scholars who highlight the defeat-induced pessimism of the Frankfurt School's founders also tend to see these critical theorists' overriding focus on scrutinizing cultural and ideological phenomena, and their corresponding neglect of the critique of political economy, as consequences of this pessimism. With twentieth-century capitalism defying traditional Marxism's

CONCLUSION   271

nineteenth-century predictions of its impending demise—and, after surviving
the Great Depression and two world wars, Western capitalism appears as though
it emerges stronger than ever, bolstered by a new mass consumerism—Western
Marxists become discouraged about looking to economics as a key site for radical leftism's hopes and struggles. For instance, speaking of the pessimism-
inducing set of defeats as an "impasse," Anderson observes: "The consequence
of this impasse was to be the studied silence of Western Marxism in those areas
most crucial to the classical traditions of historical materialism: scrutiny of the
economic laws of motion of capitalism as a mode of production, analysis of
the political machinery of the bourgeois state, strategy of the class struggle necessary to overthrow it."[153] Jacoby likewise comments, "In Europe the defeats of
the revolutions reinforced the domination of orthodoxy and branded Western
Marxism: Making only occasional forays into political economy and tactics,
Western Marxism retreated to aesthetics, philosophy, and psychoanalysis."[154]

Even as sympathetic an interlocutor of the Frankfurt School as Martin Jay
concedes that their retreat from historical materialism's stress on economic components in the structures and dynamics of societies goes so far as to render them
"para-Marxists."[155] More Weberian than Marxian, the core members of the
Frankfurt School follow their Western Marxist predecessors in deprioritizing
any economic base through a revised historical materialism in which superstructures act upon and are at least as socially influential as infrastructures.[156] Jay also
characterizes the Frankfurt School's main founding figures as wary and igno-
rant of economics because of their pronounced fear of any form of "economic
determinism."[157]

I will not be analyzing here each of the major first-generation figures of the
Frankfurt School. Obviously, someone like Adorno, with his highbrow cultural
elitism and dark air of withdrawn resignation, epitomizes the sort of Western
Marxist tendencies I am critically examining in the present context. Indeed,
Adorno more than anyone else prompts the older Lukács to dismiss the mem-
bers of the Frankfurt School as the comfortable residents of the well-appointed
Schopenhauerian "Grand Hotel Abyss."[158]

However, my focus on the intersection between Marxism and psychoanalysis
justifies selectively highlighting Marcuse's positioning along the lines I have
been following in the immediately preceding. Marcuse, as the author of *Eros
and Civilization* in particular, is the leading representative of the Frankfurt
School's brand of Freudo-Marxism. As such, his oscillations apropos the
infrastructure-superstructure rapport are worth registering now.

Of course, the turn to psychoanalysis by certain twentieth-century Marxists, such as Marcuse, is motivated at least in part by the need to qualify or

supplement traditional historical materialism (the older Sartre has something similar in mind when he puts forward psychoanalysis as an "auxiliary discipline" offering valuable assistance to Marxism).[159] This need is caused by the twentieth century defying many of the predictions made by Marx and Engels in the nineteenth century. Freudo-Marxism involves the conviction that, particularly so as to account for capitalism surviving various crises and disasters without mass-scale revolutionary upheaval on its native soil, the infrastructure-focused classical critique of political economy requires buttressing by psychoanalytic metapsychology.

Perhaps the analytically illuminated workings of persons' intrapsychical libidinal economies will reveal why those living under capitalism's exploitative yoke continue not to revolt against their oppressive burdens. Maybe such non- or more-than-economic variables as (unconscious) desires, drives, fantasies, fetishes, perversions, and the like will lead to success in explaining the nonmaterialization of the revolutionary overthrow of capitalism where a historical materialism unaided by Freudian metapsychology would fail. It might take a psychoanalyst's ear to discern why and how superstructural phenomena such as ideologies, religions, and worldviews falsely naturalizing, eternalizing, and rationalizing the capitalist status quo stubbornly retain a firm grip on individuals' hearts and minds, hopes and dreams.

Thus, Frankfurt School Freudo-Marxism can be contextualized as bound up with the broader Western Marxist project, going back to Lukács, Gramsci, et al., to recast historical materialism by making superstructures as or more important for societies and their histories as infrastructures. However, Marcuse, like the early Lukács before him, evinces ambivalence about this recasting of traditional Marxism's appreciation of economics. As with what I above label Lukács's "antinomy of reification," so too with Marcuse's reflections on the infrastructure-superstructure distinction: Marcuse likewise oscillates between upholding the centrality of the economy for society as a whole and contesting this same centrality.

Two propositions from 1964's *One-Dimensional Man*, placed side by side, bring out the tension coloring Marcuse's relation with Western Marxist antieconomism. In this famous book, Marcuse at one point indicates that an economically reductive treatment of capitalist society is not a theoretical shortcoming of any such treatment of capitalism, classical historical materialism included. Rather, this rightly reflects the really economically reductive character of capitalism in and of itself as a concrete sociohistorical reality. The theoretical abstractions of traditional Marxism are not just theoretical—they (also) are real abstractions constitutive of capitalism *an sich*. Referring to the reduction to the economic as

CONCLUSION · 273

"hypostatization," this Marcuse writes, "this hypostatization takes place in reality, *is* the reality, and the analysis can overcome it only by recognizing it and by comprehending its scope and its causes."[160]

Yet later in the very same book, Marcuse seems to deny the reality of such hypostatization. He does so in the context of addressing the concept of reification, with this Lukácsian concept being more or less synonymous with what Marcuse has in mind when referring to hypostatization. He bluntly states that "reification is an illusion."[161] This statement occurs in a context in which reification (and along with it, commodification and commodity fetishism) is being depicted as a matter of mere false consciousness, of erroneous ideological articles of faith confined to the inner lives of subjects. And it looks to be at odds with Marcuse's just-noted insistence, earlier in *One-Dimensional Man*, on the objective social reality of hypostatization over and above any subjective mental contents. This insistence suggests that reification is anything but a private illusion qua subjective false belief, being instead a public reality qua objective true fact. Again, capitalism in itself really is a spontaneously economically reductive system.

The same economy-related wobbles can be seen a year after *One-Dimensional Man* in a collection of Marcuse's essays entitled *Negations*. In fact, two consecutive pages of the essay entitled "The Concept of Essence," originally published in 1936, exhibit the tensions I have been tracking here. On the one hand, Marcuse acknowledges the objective reality under capitalism of economic reductionism, asserting, "In the current historical period, the economy as the fundamental level has become 'essential' in such a way that all other levels have become its 'manifestations' [*Erscheinungsform*]."[162] The German *Erscheinungsform*, thanks to the connotations of *Schein*, *erscheinen*, and *Erscheinung*, suggests illusion and sham. At least within capitalist societies, more-than-economic phenomena really are reduced to being nothing more than *Erscheinungen* of economic determinants. Elsewhere in *Negations* (specifically, the 1937 essay "Philosophy and Critical Theory"), Marcuse reaffirms the primacy of the economy in capitalist social formations.[163]

However, this very same Marcuse also seems to resist or reject reducing the superstructural, even under capitalism, to being nothing more than the shining/seeming (*erscheinen*) of the infrastructural. In "The Concept of Essence," in the paragraph immediately following the paragraph containing the just-quoted remark about *Erscheinungsform*, he claims, "To the extent that individuals and groups base their actions and thoughts on immediate appearances, the latter are, of course, not 'mere' appearances but themselves factors essential to the functioning of the process and to the maintenance of its organization."[164] Arato and

274　CONCLUSION

Breines bring out the young-Lukácsian background likely informing Marcuse's thinking here:

> The world of commodity exchange, according to Lukács, constitutes a "second nature" of appearances, of the phenomena of reification. Although *illusion* [*Schein*] has a systematic place in this world, it is not merely a world of illusions. The appearances [*Erscheinungen*] do take on the form of illusion when, for instance, they appear to be historically unchangeable. But as appearances, they are the historically necessary forms of existence in which their likewise historical "inner core," their essence, is manifest. This essence is identical to the substratum of the historical action of men in a given social framework which is, in turn, the foundation of the concrete totality to be synthesized.[165]

Indeed, the chapter on reification in *History and Class Consciousness* contains the observation that "the reified world appears ... quite definitively ... as the only possible world, the only conceptually accessible, comprehensive world vouchsafed to us humans."[166] According to this line of thought, what makes reified/reifying illusions illusory in the sense of misleading is not so much their (admittedly distorted/distorting) reflection of actual reality but, rather, their refusal to reflect the possibility that things could be otherwise than as they presently are. Such ideologically refracted *Erscheinungen* partly reveal in addition to partly conceal—as Althusser puts it, ideology as dishonestly concealing "illusion" is also at the same time honestly revealing "allusion" to ideology's real material conditions[167]—the socioeconomic status quo. But through the false naturalization typical of the ideological, they attempt to conceal completely the feasible existence of really possible alternatives to this status quo.

Clearly, both Lukács and Marcuse repudiate any sort of strongly reductive or outright epiphenomenalist version of economistic historical materialism. They eschew any vulgar (pseudo-)Marxism having it that superstructural phenomena are mere appearances qua sterile illusions, inefficacious shadows cast by infrastructural machinery as the only real causal power in social history. In the (in)famous 1859 preface to *A Contribution to the Critique of Political Economy*, Marx, referring to conflict between infrastructure and superstructure as driving revolutionary social change,[168] writes of "ideological forms in which men become conscious of this conflict and fight it out."[169] Although this preface ends up encouraging crude economic determinisms among a good number of Marx's heirs (i.e., the mechanistic versions of historical materialism common to the Second International, Stalinism, etc.), the likes of Lukács, Marcuse, and Althusser are able to argue that even here Marx, at his most seemingly economistic, acknowledges the non-negligible causal efficacy, the nonepiphenomenal social-ontological status, of more-than-economic (i.e., superstructural, ideological) ideas, representations, etc.

With the just-quoted Lukács (circa 1923) and Marcuse (circa both 1936–1937 and 1964–1965), given their talk of appearances (als Erscheinungen) and essences, another figure besides Marx looms large in the background: Hegel. I have no doubts that Lukács and Marcuse both are relying heavily on Hegel's *Logik*, especially its discussion of the appearance-essence relationship in "The Doctrine of Essence"[170] (with their writings on Hegel revealing their intimate familiarity with the Logic generally and "The Doctrine of Essence" specifically).[171] Without me reconstructing this stretch of Hegelian Logic, suffice it for now to say that Hegel's dialectical-speculative treatment of the category of appearance (*Erscheinung*) indeed lends substantial philosophical support to Lukács's and Marcuse's notion that superstructural appearances are as essential to sociohistorical dynamics as infrastructural essences themselves. And with Marcuse being a Freudian in addition to a Hegelian Marxist, these superstructural appearances would have to include the partly idiosyncratic ideational materials of individuals' psyches (such as cathexes, complexes, delusions, dreams, fantasies, hallucinations, identifications, and so on).

Yet although the Marx appealed to by the likes of the young Lukács and Marcuse acknowledges the importance of the superstructural, this same Marx also stresses the comparatively greater importance of the infrastructural. Marx's economistically minded successors are not without reasons for finding in, for instance, the preface to 1859's *A Contribution to the Critique of Political Economy* ample support for their insistences on the primacy of the economic base in shaping societies and their histories.[172] Both the founders of Western Marxism as well as the first generation of the Frankfurt School intermittently register the power of the economy to colonize and remake everything under the sun in its own image. They are especially prone to admit this when confronting capitalism as a specific socioeconomic system tending in and of itself to leave nothing economically untouched and unquantified. Nonetheless, these twentieth-century inheritors of Marx's legacy look to be unwilling or unable consistently to hold onto and further develop historical materialism's infrastructure-focused critique of political economy while simultaneously elevating the standing and significance of superstructural phenomena.

Marcuse and other Western Marxists turning to psychoanalysis as a supplement to historical materialism do so as part of the larger project of raising the status of superstructural factors in the face of vulgar Marxists' economistic preoccupations with infrastructural modes and means of production. However, what such Freudo-Marxists (and even many later Lacano-Marxists) neglect are those facets of psychoanalysis offering the opportunity to help explain not various things defying reduction to the economic but, on the contrary, those aspects of the psychical apparatus rendering it susceptible, even receptive, to capitalism and capitalism's inherent tendency to reduce everything without exception to the economic. That is to say, Western Marxist marriages between Marxism and psychoanalysis from the mid-twentieth century through today, blinded by the vehemence of Western Marxist antieconomism, have ignored more or less completely how Freudian and Lacanian metapsychologies promise to illuminate the fashions in which libidinal economies come to be overwritten by political economies, especially under capitalist conditions. Indeed, throughout much of this book, I have sought to illuminate precisely this.

I will return to the matter of psychoanalysis and reductionism shortly. For now, I need to add a few more details apropos economism. This is because Western Marxism's antieconomistic obsession with the superstructural arguably is responsible for its failure to appreciate the ways in which psychoanalysis might assist in comprehending how capitalism really does reduce its subjects to being nothing (or barely anything) more than bearers or personifications of economic categories. Freudian and Lacanian analysis is not only of value in constructing nonreductive permutations of Marxist materialism. It also has a thus-far un- or underappreciated capacity to aid in accounting for the spontaneously reductive tendencies and consequences of capitalism in particular. Likewise, and as per twentieth-century Western Marxisms as doctrines of defeat, psychoanalysis not only can be utilized in understanding leftism's failures over the course of the past century-plus (failures arguably not foreseen by classical nineteenth-century historical materialism unaided by a yet-to-be-invented analysis). Psychoanalysis correspondingly also can be employed in comprehending capitalism's successes, particularly its conquest and subjugation of psychical life, its hijacking and redirection of singular psyches' drives, desires, and fantasies.

There is a straight line from Western Marxism's antieconomistic valorization of superstructures to the recent and contemporary left's more or less complete abandonment of class struggle and the critique of political economy. This abandonment is prepared for and encouraged (however inadvertently or not) by the (over)emphasis on superstructure initially championed by Lukács, Korsch, and Gramsci and advanced by their various Western Marxist successors. Particularly in the German- and French-speaking contexts of the second half of the twentieth century, as well as an English-speaking world influenced by these Continental European contexts, a general form of post-Marxism congeals in which the "post-" signifies more a leaving behind than a carrying forward. A Marxism

CONCLUSION   277

purged of its stress on matters economic easily leads to a leftist jettisoning of any sort of historical materialism in favor of exclusive concerns with ideology critique as well as the politics of all identities save for class ones. To call what remains even "post-Marxism" is still misleading, insofar as, minus materialist analyses of political economies, nothing recognizably Marxist remains in these brands of today's leftism. And as Colletti justifiably remarks in a well-known interview, "The only way in which Marxism can be revived is if . . . books like Hilferding's *Finance Capital* and Luxemburg's *Accumulation of Capital*—or even Lenin's *Imperialism*, which was a popular brochure—are once again written."[173]

Capitalism in particular makes it such that economic categories, including class identities, are in general more socially efficacious and influential, on balance, than noneconomic ones. And admittedly, Marxists in the vein of, for example, Lenin and Mao are concerned reflectively to conceptualize and actively to mobilize the complex networks of various more-than-economic social dimensions with which modes of production, classes, and the like are always-already intricately intertwined in actual sociohistorical configurations. This is not just an issue of theoretical correctness in terms of an accurate rendition of the tangled complexities of really existing societies. It also is a matter of practical potency, since agents of economically based struggles will need to establish alliances, coalitions, common fronts, etc. with other agents representative of noneconomic identities in order to have a chance to make real gains. Even many more economistically minded revolutionary Marxists likely would be prone to concede that forms of organizing and intervening involving a "left-populist" approach (whether as Lenin's "weakest link," Mao's "primary and secondary contradictions," Gramsci's "hegemony" and "war of position," or whatever else along these lines) are, at a minimum, tactically shrewd.

However, insofar as what could be called today's left populism is associated with identity politics, intersectionality, and the like, this sort of populism has proven to be tantamount to a surrender on the front of class struggle. This can be seen, for instance, in the case of a leading theorist of left populism, namely, the post-Marxist Laclau (whose last significant book-length intervention before he died in 2014 was 2005's *On Populist Reason*). Already in 1985's *Hegemony and Socialist Strategy*, Laclau and his coauthor Chantal Mouffe, despite relying heavily upon Gramsci for their own account of hegemony, complain about the residues of a more traditional Marxist privileging of economic variables in the *Prison Notebooks* despite Gramsci's antieconomistic emphases on superstructural social dimensions. Incidentally, what Laclau sees as a vice in Gramsci I view as a virtue. That said, Laclau's subsequent conception of populism continues in this same vein, with him insisting that even under capitalism, class identities should enjoy no priority or privileging in leftist theory and practice.[174]

However, if one were to ask Laclau whether really existing capitalism is centered on the all-consuming pursuit of surplus value ad infinitum, I have great difficulty believing that he would answer with anything other than a "Yes," however this affirmation might be qualified. It is hard for me to envision that Laclau, even in his post-Marxism, would deny that capital's circuit of M-C-M' remains a central influence upon ongoing social production and reproduction. At least, I imagine that Laclau would not deny this without deploying a swarm of caveats in a state of palpable embarrassment. What self-respecting leftist of whatever stripe would or could deny with an unashamed straight face that profit-, rent-, and interest-seeking are dominant social motivations in capitalism?

But as soon as one grants the centrality of the economic category of surplus value to capitalism, there are unavoidable consequences. Marx's critique of political economy and the capitalist mode of production it reflects are both systems. As systematic, capitalism and its historical-materialist theorization consist of networks of tightly interconnected categories, moments, structures, and dynamics.

Thus, one cannot easily cherry-pick from Marx's critique of political economy. For example, as soon as one grants the validity of the category of surplus value, this category automatically brings with it other categories such as the bourgeois and proletarian classes, commodities and commodified labor power, and so on.[175] Therefore, the above-imagined hypothetical Laclau, as soon as he concedes the existence of a capitalism organized around surplus value, would immediately have his post-Marxist antieconomism problematized by implications and arguments challenging this antieconomism. He would have to face once again a more traditional historical materialism and its claims about infrastructural and class determinants of modern (and postmodern) sociopolitical life.

I would propose bluntly confronting not only Laclau but all non- and post-Marxist left populists with the pointed question: Is capitalism a socioeconomic system grounded on the incessant striving after surplus value in all its forms (profit, rent, interest, etc.)? And to those leftists who would respond with yeses but still would gripe about the economic essentialism of the historical-materialist critique of political economy, I would respond in turn: But capitalism itself is economically essentialist.

The twentieth-century Western Marxist tradition out of which things like Laclau's post-Marxism emerge involves emphasizing more-than-economic superstructure as of equal or greater importance by comparison with economic

CONCLUSION   279

infrastructure. The implicit and explicit developments of Marx's notion of real abstractions by thinkers such as Korsch and Sohn-Rethel[176] are part of this anti-economistic refocusing on the superstructural. I by no means refuse to recognize the power and usefulness of the Marxian concept of real abstraction.

Nonetheless, I would propose that the concept of real abstraction, especially as symptomatic of Western Marxism's wandering away from economics, urgently needs supplementation by a counterbalancing concept, namely, what I would label "real reduction" (a concept pulling Marxism back toward a resumption of the critique of political economy). In 2004, the comedian Rob Corddry, playing a reporter addressing the challenges of covering George W. Bush's Iraq War in a "fair and balanced" fashion, mused on Jon Stewart's *The Daily Show*, "How does one report the facts in an unbiased way when the facts themselves are biased? . . . Facts in Iraq have an anti-Bush agenda." Obviously, this comedic bit suggests the falsity of the commonplace conflation of the neutral (or nonpartisan) and the objective, thereby indirectly lending further credence to the Marxist idea of the inherent partisanship of truth (particularly in class-riven societies).

Moreover, Corddry's words can be paraphrased so as to make a crucial point I mean to capture with the notion of real reduction: How does one theorize social reality in a nonreductive way when this reality itself is reductive? Capitalist reality has an economically reductive agenda. If historical materialism is economically reductive and/or class essentialist—many non- and post-Marxist leftists, including some left populists, repeatedly accuse it of such alleged sins—this arguably is not a deficiency in its thinking but a reflection of the very being of what it thinks accurately.

There is no merit in social theorizing staying scrupulously antireductive and antiessentialist when the societies it surveys are themselves reductive and essentialist. Relatedly, my phrase "real reduction" means that reductions are not exclusively negative false features of ideal-subjective thinking for us but also, at least sometimes, positive true features of real-objective being in itself (just as the Marxist phrase "real abstraction" means the same for abstractions). Realities, and not only theories, can be reductive. In addition to the truth sometimes being partisan as per certain Marxists, the truth sometimes is stupid (i.e., reductive, essentialist, etc.) too, as per Lacan (with his motif of "the stupidity of truth [*la connerie de la vérité*]").[177] Relatedly, being smarter than reality is itself a special form of stupidity. So long as social reality itself is reductive, historical materialism must be reductive too. Such materialism must be stupidly smart (i.e., intelligently calibrating itself to the manifest idiocy of its object of inquiry, namely, capitalism) and not smartly stupid (i.e., too clever by far for an anything-but-clever real).

280   CONCLUSION

With the concept of real reduction in view, I would go so far as to plead for a reversal of the standard sense of the distinction between historical and dialectical materialisms along the lines of that between the antireductive and the reductive respectively. I have critically scrutinized the Western Marxist rejection of Engelsian and Soviet dialectical materialism, with its "dialectics of nature," purportedly in the name of historical materialism properly understood elsewhere.[178] So I will not rehearse all those details here.

For now, I will limit myself to pointing out that Western Marxism, with its participation in an antinaturalism common to much of Continental European philosophy and theory throughout roughly the past two centuries, tends to dismiss *Naturdialektik* within both classical and non-Western Marxisms on the basis of a specific assumption. This is the assumption having it that nature qua the explanatory jurisdiction of the empirical, experimental natural sciences is, in this nature's *an sich* asubjective being, a really reductive reality devoid of anything dialectical whatsoever. For the typical Western Marxist opponent of dialectical materialism with its dialectics of nature, the physical universe minus humanity (i.e., nature as nonhuman objectivity) is more or less accurately reflected by the reductionistic (i.e., atomistic, deterministic, mechanistic, etc.) sciences of nature.

Starting with the young Lukács's critique of Engelsian *Naturdialektik*,[179] Western Marxists relatedly maintain that human social history, by sharp contrast with nonhuman nature, is really in and of itself non/antireductive. That is to say, they claim that the historical development of humanity's myriad societies, ostensibly unlike nature and its processes, indeed does exhibit movements and mutations best captured by the configurations and kinetics of a speculative dialectics indebted to both Hegel and Marx. From this Western Marxist perspective, historical materialism takes as its object a human history whose multilevel richness calls for dialectical sophistication, while so-called dialectical materialism takes as its object a nonhuman nature whose one-dimensional poverty calls for setting aside dialectical finesse in favor of plodding reduction. Western Marxism divides intellectual labor such that there is antireductive historical materialism (with Western Marxism also rejecting economism's nonnatural yet reductive treatment of social history) and (appropriately) reductive natural science, with nothing left in between. The option of a nonreductive naturalistic materialism represented by Engelsian *Naturdialektik* is excluded as at best superfluous and at worst both false as well as dangerous.[180]

In the second volume of my *Prolegomena to Any Future Materialism*, I argue against the Western Marxist notion of nature as spontaneously reductive, of the physical universe as a flat expanse of dumb matter in nothing more than

CONCLUSION   281

efficient-causal motion. From both within and well beyond the Marxist tradition, various resources can be appealed to as offering challenges to this notion of nature (including work on such topics as emergentism, downward causation, plasticity, epigenetics, phase transitions, tipping points, punctuated equilibrium, etc.). There are many good reasons for seriously doubting or even outright rejecting the association of the natural with the reductive, an association profoundly informing the Western Marxists.[181]

Here, I clearly am arguing against Western Marxism's correlative association of the historical with the nonreductive. In this vein, I would go so far as to contend that Western Marxists are antireductive where they should be reductive and reductive where they should be antireductive. At least for precommunist social history thus far (i.e., Marx's "history hitherto") as the target object of historical materialism, this history shows itself as actually reducing (or, at least, constantly trying to reduce) human beings to the status of compliant bearers or personifications of roles dictated by given modes, means, and relations of production (as together constituting the infrastructure, the economic base, of given societies). This reduction is not ideal as a mere artifact of the economically minded theoretical observer of social history. Instead, it is real as an overwhelmingly powerful tendency inherent to the spontaneous dynamics of the historical unfoldings of class-based societies throughout history so far.

Nevertheless, the picture of human beings as really reduced by social history hitherto to their class roles in relations of production—this would be an upshot of a historical materialism acknowledging the economistic tendencies inherent to class-based societies as really (not just ideally) reductive—is made possible by, at least in part, the plasticity of humanity's *Gattungswesen* as conceptualized through dialectical-materialist philosophical anthropology.[182] That is to say, the openness of humans' first natures to being formed and reformed by societies' second natures, as per an antireductive dialectical materialism, enables these same humans to be reduced to being nothing more than the bearers/personifications of economic class roles, as per a reductive historical materialism. My way of combining dialectical and historical materialisms is based on the proposition that the rigid reductiveness of the societies of history hitherto as analyzed by the historical-materialist critique of political economy depends upon the receptive malleability of human nature as thereby able to be subjected to such reductiveness.[183]

However, acknowledging the above is not at all tantamount to endorsing eternally deterministic and inflexibly mechanistic versions of simplified classical Marxism. These would be the sort of "crude" or "vulgar" permutations of historical materialism associated with both the Second International and

Stalinism, permutations understandably repudiated by the majority of twentieth-century Western Marxists starting with Lukács, Gramsci, et al. in the 1920s and 1930s. Invoking the economically reductive alienating objectification to which sellers of labor power always-already automatically are subjected under capitalism, Shlomo Avineri remarks, "When the worker comprehends that under capitalist production he is degraded to the status of a mere object, of a commodity, he ceases to be a commodity, an object, and becomes a subject."[184] In a Marxist twist on Freud's "*Wo Es war, soll Ich werden*," the liberated "I" (*Ich*) of the class-conscious subject (really, a "we" [*Wir*] more than an "I") comes to be precisely in and through the worker's recognition of his/her necessary socioeconomic subjugation within the capitalist system (as "It" [*Es*]).

Only through realizing just how thoroughly commodified I am can I have a chance to decommodify myself. Correlatively, Bertell Ollman warns, "Man is most completely a class determined being when he least believes himself to be one."[185] Resonating with the Hegelian-Engelsian notion of freedom as "known necessity,"[186] pushing back against economic reductionism is enabled by nothing other than admitting and confronting the full extent of such reductionism (rather than, as with the wishful thinking of Western Marxism's antieconomism, essentially pretending in theory that this reductionism does not exist in practice). In relation to the above-mentioned antireductive philosophical anthropology of dialectical materialism, this anthropology's rendition of human nature, of humanity's "species-being" (*Gattungswesen*) as per Feuerbach's and Marx's use of this term, indicates this nature's susceptibility to the reductive worst, the antireductive best, and everything in between. When this nature is reduced, it always still can be unreduced, and vice versa.

In other words, registering how socially determined I am by an economically reductive class society (such as present-day capitalist America, for instance) does not or, at least, should not result in capitulation to defeatist resignation or paralyzing fatalism. Thanks to a theoretical perspective combining an antireductive dialectical materialism with a reductive historical materialism, one can, as is crucial to do, face up to just how determined and reduced one is within the social status quo while nevertheless knowing that the same material conditions of possibility for this determination and reduction (i.e., the underdetermined plasticity of human nature)[187] are double-edged swords that also, however unlikely the prospect might be, can slice in the directions of freedom and flourishing. To quote Avineri again, "The determination of man by his economic circumstances means his determination by his own historical products."[188] In coming to recognize how thoroughly we have determined (i.e., alienated, objectified, reduced, reified, etc.) ourselves, we simultaneously also come to recognize how free we

CONCLUSION   283

remain to undo this same determination. In fact, we can realize this potential freedom exclusively in the wake of thoroughly registering our actual lack of freedom.

At this juncture, a point about reductionism in the writings of Marx himself, especially his mature texts on political economy, ought to be noted. Any standard conception of reductionism in general (whether physical, biological, economic, etc.) tends to associate it with a process moving from the higher to the lower. To reduce in the explanatory sense is to account for a given phenomenon by getting beneath it, by digging under surface appearances so as to ground those appearances on the basis of something (or things) more elementary, fine-grained, fundamental, primitive, and the like. From this perspective, the economic reductionism at stake in debates both inside and outside Marxist circles from Marx's and Engels's lifetimes through the present presumably would involve boiling down the multifaceted complexities of everything more-than-economic to the workings of the economy alone as the underlying material bedrock, the "base," of societies and their histories. Purportedly, economically focused species of historical materialism simply collapse the entirety of the heights of superstructure into the depths of infrastructure.

Yet are Marx and, along with him, the more sophisticated practitioners of the Marxist critique of political economy really guilty of indulging in reductionism, specifically in the guise of an economism explaining away everything extraeconomic as mere secondary effects, epiphenomena, shadows, etc. of the economy in its primacy? Žižek, in his 2017 book *Incontinence of the Void*, argues against this by maintaining that Marx actually is concerned with the bottom-up genesis of the higher (such as the superstructural) out of the lower (such as the infrastructural), rather than, as with the just-characterized standard notion of reduction, the reverse movement of proceeding from the higher to the lower. After quoting a passage on the genesis of the value form located in the first chapter of volume 1 of Marx's *Capital*,[189] Žižek observes: "Marx is at his most antireductionist here: the task of a dialectical theory is not to reduce a phenomenon to its material base but the exact opposite, to inquire into how this phenomenon arose out of the antinomies of its base; it is not to bring out the content hidden by deceiving form, but to inquire into why this content articulated itself in this form."[190] One way to depict Žižek's insight is to say that the mature Marx's economism, including as articulated in such (in)famous places as the preface to 1859's *A Contribution to the Critique of Political Economy*, is a dialectical emergentism (tracing an upward ontological movement in being from the lower to the higher) rather than an analytical reductionism (tracing a downward epistemological movement in thinking from the higher to the lower). Instead of breaking down the more-than-economic into the economic, Marx's materialism, with its dialectical (i.e., antireductive) sensibilities, seeks to show how the economic must build up out of itself more-than-economic constellations that come to achieve some degree of autonomy, self-sufficiency, and downward causal power vis-à-vis their economic origins.

Adding to this a further Lacanian inflection likely congenial to Žižek, I would contend that for classical Marxist historical materialism properly comprehended, both infrastructures and superstructures are "not all" (*pas tout*). As for the infrastructural, and as Žižek's observation reminds readers, Marx's economic base, as a mode of production consisting of interrelated means and relations of production, is itself riven from within by negativities associated with class antagonisms (i.e., what Žižek refers to as "the antinomies of its base"). Of course, Marxian superstructures, especially in the guises of ideologies and states, arise and function in part so as to stabilize conflict-ridden infrastructures, to tame and domesticate potentially destabilizing class struggles. In this sense, the economic base is "not all" insofar as it is not an "all" qua harmonious, homogeneous, and unified sphere free of tensions and strife.

Furthermore, superstructure too is *pas tout*, albeit in a different sense. In *Seminar XX*, Lacan relies on a quasi-formalized logic of the "not all" (as a negated universal quantifier [$\sim\forall x$]) specifically to depict feminine sexuality in his "formulas of sexuation."[191] Without getting bogged down in explaining the details of this, suffice it for my present purposes to note that for this Lacan, those subjects sexed as feminine neither escape unscathed from the symbolic castration of a phallocentric big Other (i.e., a masculinist symbolic order) nor are reducible in their subjectivity to this marking of their being by "castrating" sociosymbolic mediation. Each feminine subject is *pas tout* in the sense of not all of her subjectivity being reducible to a phallic economy by which she is partly defined nonetheless.

What holds for feminine subjectivity à la Lacan's psychoanalytic theory of sexual difference likewise holds for superstructure à la Marx's historical-materialist critique of political economy. Although superstructural phenomena are far from fully reducible to infrastructural grounds, no part of superstructure ever remains entirely unmarked and uninfluenced by the economy. On the one hand, "not all" of any given piece of superstructure is reducible to infrastructure. On the other hand, no piece of superstructure is ever entirely free from the gravitational tug of infrastructure.

That said, and to move toward a close to this conclusion, chapter 48 ("The Trinity Formula") of the third volume of *Capital* contains a well-known comment by Marx about scientificity (including the "science" [*Wissenschaft*] of historical materialism and its critique of political economy). Therein, he states, "all science would be superfluous if the form of appearance of things directly coincided with their essence [*alle Wissenschaft wäre überflüssig, wenn die Erscheinungsform und das Wesen der Dinge unmittelbar zusammenfielen*]."[192] Obviously, Marx intentionally is echoing some of the central features of "The Doctrine of Essence" from Hegel's *Logik*, particularly its manner of distinguishing between appearance (*Erscheinung*) and essence (*Wesen*).

As regards scientificity, Marx's just-quoted remark suggests that a scientific approach, whether that of Newtonian physics, political economy, or historical materialism, involves proceeding from manifest, visible surface (as appearance) to latent, invisible depth (as essence). This movement similarly can be depicted as a trajectory from the stupid thoughtlessness of pre/nonscientific superficiality (mindlessly caught up with appearances) to the intelligent thoughtfulness of scientific profundity (considerately taking up the essences behind the appearances). This Marx exhibits not only a Hegelian influence but also influences flowing from the Scottish Enlightenment (especially Smith's and Ricardo's efforts to discover the invisible deep laws of the economy undergirding the visible surface turbulence of quotidian marketplaces).

But taking into consideration other core features of Marx's historical-materialist critique of political economy, there is an additional psychoanalytically motivated step to be taken in the Marxian scientific procedure as moving from the surfaces of stupid appearances (as registered by pre/nonscientific experience) to the depths of intelligent essences (as comprehended by properly scientific thought). This additional step is one from intelligent depth to this depth's even deeper ultimate and stupid core. If, as a Marx inspired by Hegel, Smith, and Ricardo has it, stupidity is associated with surface and intelligence is associated with depth, this further Lacanian step brings one face to face with an "extimate" stupidity. Such extimacy, as per Lacan's neologism-concept *extimité* (i.e., inner foreignness or intimate externality), would be a nucleus within the deepest essential core of an existent where what initially appears to be confined (as inessential) to the superficial outer layers of the object of scientific investigation in question returns (as essential) in the guise of the very heart at the innermost center of the scientifically investigated object.[193] Of course, such a reversal between the paired positions of the essential and the inessential is typical of the dialectical dynamics already foregrounded by the Hegel of the *Wesenslogik*.

Marx seems to limit a scientific approach to a two-step (i.e., stupid surface appearance → intelligent deep essence), rather than a three-step (i.e., stupid surface appearance → intelligent deep essence → stupid and even more central *Ur*-essence), process. However, much of Marx's work testifies to an awareness on his part of what I am gesturing at by using a combination of Lacan's conceptions of stupidity and extimacy to characterize capitalism as both real (in its objective being) and ideal (as an object of [scientific] theorizing, of subjective thinking). Lacan, with the Marxist tradition in view, points out with respect to capitalism that "there is but this that makes the system function. It's surplus-value [*Il n'y a que ça qui fait fonctionner le système. C'est la plus-value*]."[194] Similarly, when Lacan compares the economy to the primary processes of the unconscious—the latter follow the structured but senseless logic of ideational representations (as Freudian *Vorstellungen* or Lacanian signifiers) in their meaningless acoustic and/or graphic materiality—one implication is that the economy's logic also is stupid and devoid of meaning, sense, and the like.[195]

One fairly could maintain that Marx's discovery of the capitalist economic category of surplus value is itself the load-bearing central pillar of the entire edifice of his mature critique of political economy. And this centrality of surplus value to both capitalism and the Marxist critique of it is expressed in Marx's fundamental formula for the logic of capital: M-C-M′ (with surplus-value as the "′" at the end, in fact as the *telos*, of this short formula). When all is said and done, capitalism invariably is about nothing other or more than the idiotic repetitious looping through of the sequence "money → commodities → more money." What could be more stupid than the automatic, knee-jerk pursuit, ad infinitum and ad nauseam, of the accumulation of ever-more meaningless quantitative units, all else be damned? Capitalism, regardless of its combined infrastructural and superstructural complexity, really does ultimately boil down to a senseless cycle easily encapsulated by a rudimentary formalization: M-C-M′. This fundamentally simplistic three-step dance truly does govern the overall cadence of life under capitalism.

A more recent distillation of capitalism's essential stupidity is provided, albeit inadvertently, by one of its deservedly most notorious rationalizers and apologists: the University of Chicago economist Milton Friedman, the intellectual champion of the neoliberalism that has reigned disastrously for the past forty or so years of global capitalist social history. What I have in mind is a Marxian-Lacanian reading of Friedman's statement having it that "the business of business is business." Is this not an unintentional confession to the effect that capitalism actually does turn over the entirety of social existence lock, stock, and barrel to a mindless mechanical dynamic callously heedless of the costs, both economic and more-than-economic, it inflicts on everyone and everything else?

Yet despite (or, perhaps, even because of) capitalism's foundational stupidity, it has proven to be much more resilient and stubbornly persistent than Marx and many Marxists anticipated. Indeed, I have attempted throughout much of

CONCLUSION   287

this book to synthesize Marxian and psychoanalytic insights precisely so as to help explain this resilience and persistence. A contemporary critic of capitalism informed by this synthesis must admit, once again paraphrasing Brecht, that it is the stupid thing that is hard to undo. In the meantime, such a critic, while waiting for the undoing of capitalism, must rest content with this cold comfort: Perhaps the single most damning judgment one can pass on a society is noting that its truth can be printed on a T-shirt.

Notes

PREFACE. SELF-DESTRUCTIVE SELFISHNESS: DEVOURING ITS OWN CHILDREN

1. Adam Smith, *The Wealth of Nations*, books 1–3, ed. Andrew Skinner (New York: Penguin, 1986), 119.
2. Anthony Shorrocks, James Davies, and Rodrigo Lluberas, *Global Wealth Report 2020*, Credit Suisse Research Institute, October 2020, https://inequality.org/facts/global-inequality/.
3. Karl Marx and Friedrich Engels, *The Communist Manifesto*, trans. Samuel Moore, in *Karl Marx: Selected Writings*, ed. David McLellan (Oxford: Oxford University Press, 1977), 222.
4. Alain Badiou, *Je vous sais si nombreux...* (Paris: Fayard, 2017), 12–13, 15–17, 35, 49, 55; Alain Badiou, *Petrograd, Shanghai: Les deux révolutions du XXe siècle* (Paris: La Fabrique éditions, 2018), 18–19, 31–33; Alain Badiou, "Les quatre principes du marxisme," in Alain Badiou, Étienne Balibar, Jacques Bidet, Michael Löwy, and Lucien Sève, *Avec Marx, philosophie et politique*, ed. Alexis Cukier and Isabelle Garo (Paris: La Dispute, 2019), 35–37; Alain Badiou, "Néolithique, capitalisme et communisme," in *Les possibles matins de la politique: Interventions, 2016–2020* (Paris: Fayard, 2021), 13–21.
5. Paul A. Baran and Paul M. Sweezy, *Monopoly Capital: An Essay on the American Economic and Social Order* (New York: Monthly Review Press, 1966), 285, 289.

INTRODUCTION. INFRASTRUCTURAL ANALYSIS: REMARRYING MARXISM AND PSYCHOANALYSIS

1. Adrian Johnston, "Humanity, That Sickness: Louis Althusser and the Helplessness of Psychoanalysis," *Crisis and Critique* 2, no. 2, special issue: *"Reading Capital* and *For Marx*: 50 Years Later,"* ed. Frank Ruda and Agon Hamza (2015): 217–61.
2. Adrian Johnston, "'A Mass of Fools and Knaves': Psychoanalysis and the World's Many Asininities," in *Psychoanalytic Reflections on Stupidity and Stupor*, ed. Cindy Zeiher (Lanham, MD: Rowman & Littlefield, 2023).

1. THE CONFLICTED POLITICAL ANIMAL: THE PSYCHOANALYTIC BODY AND THE BODY POLITIC

1. Bruce Brown, *Marx, Freud, and the Critique of Everyday Life: Toward a Permanent Cultural Revolution* (New York: Monthly Review Press, 1973), 63.

2. Russell Jacoby, *Social Amnesia: A Critique of Conformist Psychology from Adler to Laing* (Boston: Beacon, 1975), 25.

3. Thomas Hobbes, *The Citizen: Philosophical Rudiments Concerning Government and Society*, in *Man and Citizen*, ed. Bernard Gert (New York: Anchor, 1972), 89–90; *SE* 21:111–12; Guy Lardreau and Christian Jambet, *L'ange. Pour une cynégétique du semblant* (Paris: Grasset, 1976), 26, 28; Elmar Waibl, *Gesellschaft und Kultur bei Hobbes und Freud* (Vienna: Löcker, 1980), 19, 27, 35, 40, 63, 78–79, 81; Jean Roy, *Hobbes and Freud*, trans. Thomas G. Osler (Toronto: Canadian Philosophical Monographs, 1984), vii, 17.

4. *SE* 21:113.

5. Antonio Gramsci, "Letter to Julca Schucht, December 30, 1929," in *Letters from Prison*, ed. Frank Rosengarten, trans. Raymond Rosenthal (New York: Columbia University Press, 1994), 1:302.

6. *SE* 21:113.

7. *GW* 14:472–73; *SE* 21:113.

8. *GW* 14:473; *SE* 21:113.

9. *SE* 21:113.

10. *SE* 21:113–14.

11. *SE* 21:115.

12. *SE* 21:143.

13. *GW* 14:504; *SE* 21:143.

14. *SE* 21:143.

15. *SXVII* [Fr.], 102; *SXVII*, 90.

16. *SXVII*, 92, 206–7; Jacques Lacan, "Acte de fondation," in *Autres écrits*, ed. Jacques-Alain Miller (Paris: Éditions du Seuil, 2001), 237; Jacques Lacan, "Radiophonie," in *Autres écrits*, 424; Jacques Lacan, "Television," trans. Denis Hollier, Rosalind Krauss, and Annette Michelson, in *Television/A Challenge to the Psychoanalytic Establishment*, ed. Joan Copjec (New York: Norton, 1990), 30–31.

17. *SXXIII*, 117.

18. Jacques Lacan, "Du discours psychanalytique," in *Lacan in Italia, 1953–1978* (Milan: La Salamandra, 1978), 46.

19. *SVI* [Fr.], 486–87; *SVI*, 412.

20. *SXXI*, 3/19/74.

21. *SXIII*, 1/12/66; *SXVI*, 17, 240; *SXVII*, 206.

22. *SE* 22:180, 208, 211–12.

23. *SE* 22:67, 178–79.

24. *GW* 15:73–74; *SE* 22:67.

25. *GW* 14:501–5; *SE* 21:141–44.

26. Friedrich Engels, "Letter to Conrad Schmidt, October 27, 1890," https://www.marxists.org /archive/marx/works/1890/letters/90_10_27.htm.

27. A. R. Luria, "Psychoanalysis as a System of Monistic Psychology," *Soviet Psychology* 16, no. 2 (1977): 41.

28. Jacoby, *Social Amnesia*, 84.

29. Brown, *Marx, Freud, and the Critique of Everyday Life*, 58–59; Reuben Osborn, *Marxism and Psychoanalysis* (New York: Farrar, Straus and Giroux, 1974), 85, 98–100.

I. THE CONFLICTED POLITICAL ANIMAL   291

30. Bertell Ollman, *Alienation: Marx's Conception of Man in Capitalist Society* (Cambridge: Cambridge University Press, 1971), 241–43.

31. Karl Marx, *Karl-Marx-Ausgabe: Werke-Schriften-Briefe, Band IV: Ökonomische Schriften, erster Band*, ed. Hans-Joachim Lieber, *Das Kapital: Kritik der politischen Ökonomie, erster Band* (Darmstadt: Wissenschaftliche Buchgesellschaft, 1962), 147–48; Karl Marx, *Capital: A Critique of Political Economy, Volume One*, trans. Ben Fowkes (New York: Penguin, 1976), 254–55; Karl Marx, *Theories of Surplus-Value, Part One: Volume IV of Capital*, ed. S. Ryazanskaya, trans. Emile Burns (Moscow: Progress Publishers, 1963), 282, 389; Karl Marx, *Theories of Surplus-Value, Part Three: Volume IV of Capital*, ed. S. W. Ryazanskaya and Richard Dixon, trans. Jack Cohen and S. W. Ryazanskaya (Moscow: Progress Publishers, 1971), 296.

32. *SXX*, 3, 7–8.

33. *SE* 4:318; *SE* 5:596; *SE* 14:186; *SE* 22:73–74.

34. *SE* 14:187.

35. *SE* 22:73.

36. *SE* 21:142–43.

37. *SE* 22:61–62, 163–64.

38. *SE* 19:167.

39. Karl Marx, *Grundrisse: Foundations of the Critique of Political Economy (Rough Draft)*, trans. Martin Nicolaus (New York: Penguin, 1973), 232; Karl Marx, *A Contribution to the Critique of Political Economy*, ed. Maurice Dobb, trans. S. W. Ryazanskaya (New York: International, 1970), 130; Marx, *Theories of Surplus-Value, Part Three*, 448.

40. *GW* 15:194–95; *SE* 22:179–80.

41. *SE* 22:176–77.

42. *SE* 22:158–82.

43. Karl Marx, "Letter to Mikhailovsky," in *Karl Marx: Selected Writings*, ed. David McLellan (Oxford: Oxford University Press, 1977), 572.

44. Karl Marx, "Letter to Vera Sassoulitch," in *Karl Marx*, 576–80; Karl Marx, "Preface to the Russian Edition of the *Communist Manifesto*," in *Karl Marx*, 583–84; Karl Marx, "Letters 1863–1881: Marx to Kugelmann, 17 Apr. 1871," in *Karl Marx*, 593.

45. Karl Marx and Friedrich Engels, *The Communist Manifesto*, in *Karl Marx*, 222.

46. Jacoby, *Social Amnesia*, xviii.

47. Herbert Marcuse, "Repressive Tolerance," in Robert Paul Wolff, Barrington Moore Jr., and Herbert Marcuse, *A Critique of Pure Tolerance* (Boston: Beacon, 1969), 81–123; Martin Jay, *The Dialectical Imagination: A History of the Frankfurt School and the Institute of Social Research, 1923–1950* (Boston: Little, Brown, 1973), 97.

48. Herbert Marcuse, *Eros and Civilization: A Philosophical Inquiry Into Freud* (Boston: Beacon, 1974), 99–101, 224–25; Herbert Marcuse, *One-Dimensional Man: Studies in the Ideology of Advanced Industrial Society* (Boston: Beacon, 1964), 72; Herbert Marcuse, *An Essay on Liberation* (Boston: Beacon, 1969), 9; Herbert Marcuse, "Progress and Freud's Theory of Instincts," in *Five Lectures: Psychoanalysis, Politics, and Utopia*, trans. Jeremy J. Shapiro and Shierry M. Weber (Boston: Beacon, 1970), 38–39; Herbert Marcuse, "The Obsolescence of the Freudian Concept of Man," in *Five Lectures*, 57–58; Herbert Marcuse, *Counterrevolution and Revolt* (Boston: Beacon, 1972), 59–60, 76, 80, 113; Marcuse, "Repressive Tolerance," 114–15; Paul A. Robinson, *The Freudian Left: Wilhelm Reich, Geza Roheim, Herbert Marcuse* (New York: Harper & Row, 1969), 240; Brown, *Marx, Freud, and the Critique of Everyday Life*, 153, 159–63, 165; Martin Jay, "Irony and Dialectics: *One-Dimensional Man* and 1968," in *Splinters in Your Eye: Frankfurt School Provocations* (London: Verso, 2020), 140.

49. Marcuse, "Repressive Tolerance," 85.

50. Marcuse, "Repressive Tolerance," 98.

51. Louis Althusser, "Marxism and Humanism," in *For Marx*, trans. Ben Brewster (London: Verso, 2005), 232–36; Louis Althusser, *On the Reproduction of Capitalism: Ideology and Ideological State Apparatuses*, trans. G. M. Goshgarian (London: Verso, 2014), 84; Louis Althusser, *Que faire?*, ed. G. M. Goshgarian (Paris: Presses Universitaires de France, 2018), 32–33.

52. Marx, *A Contribution to the Critique of Political Economy*, 21.

53. Antonio Gramsci, *Prison Notebooks, Volume Two*, ed. and trans. Joseph A. Buttigieg (New York: Columbia University Press, 1996), Fourth Notebook, §15 (157–58), §38 (184).

54. *SXXI*, 2/12/74.

55. *SIX*, 6/6/62; *SXIII*, 5/25/66; *SXX*, 42, 126–27.

56. *SIX*, 6/6/62; *SXIII*, 5/25/66; *SXX*, 43.

57. *SXX* [Fr.], 33, 114; *SXX*, 32, 126–27.

58. *SXXIV*, 12/14/76.

59. *SXX* [Fr.], 111; *SXX*, 123.

60. *SXX* [Fr.], 37; *SXX*, 36.

61. Jacques Lacan, "La troisième," *Lettres de l'École freudienne* 16 (1975): 184.

62. *SXX* [Fr.], 32; *SXX*, 30.

63. *SXX* [Fr.], 32; *SXX*, 30.

64. Wilhelm Reich, *Dialectical Materialism and Psychoanalysis* (London: Socialist Reproduction, 1972), 14.

65. *SXX* [Fr.], 32; *SXX*, 30.

66. Walter Benjamin, "Theses on the Philosophy of History," in *Illuminations: Essays and Reflections*, ed. Hannah Arendt, trans. Harry Zohn (New York: Schocken, 1969), 253–64.

67. Bernard Sichère, "Du ghetto symbolique à l'action révolutionnaire," in *Marxisme-léninisme et psychanalyse* (Paris: François Maspero, 1975), 73.

68. *SXVII*, 12–13; *SXIX*, 30, 131–33, 205; *SXX*, 17, 30, 54; *SXXI*, 12/11/73, 1/15/74, 4/9/74, 5/21/74.

69. *SXIX*, 131.

70. Karl Marx and Friedrich Engels, *The German Ideology* (Amherst, MA: Prometheus, 1998), 42.

71. Adrian Johnston, *Irrepressible Truth: On Lacan's 'The Freudian Thing'* (Basingstoke: Palgrave, 2017), 230–31.

72. *Seminar XVII*, 180; *SXIX*, 100; Lacan, "Radiophonie," 426; Adrian Johnston, "Misfelt Feelings: Unconscious Affect Between Psychoanalysis, Neuroscience, and Philosophy," in Adrian Johnston and Catherine Malabou, *Self and Emotional Life: Philosophy, Psychoanalysis, and Neuroscience* (New York: Columbia University Press, 2013), 82, 153–62; Adrian Johnston, *Adventures in Transcendental Materialism: Dialogues with Contemporary Thinkers* (Edinburgh: Edinburgh University Press, 2014), 209–10.

73. *SE* 22:160–61; *SXIX*, 198–99.

74. *SXX*, 31.

75. Adrian Johnston, *A New German Idealism: Hegel, Žižek, and Dialectical Materialism* (New York: Columbia University Press, 2018), 40–41.

76. *SXX* [Fr.], 33; *SXX*, 31.

77. *SXX* [Fr.], 33; *SXX*, 31.

78. Martin Heidegger, "Letter on Humanism," trans. Frank A. Capuzzi and J. Glenn Gray, in *Basic Writings*, ed. David Farrell Krell (New York: HarperCollins, 1993), 217.

79. *SXX* [Fr.], 53; *SXX*, 56.

80. Jacques Lacan, "Mis en question du psychanalyste," in *Lacan redivivus*, ed. Jacques-Alain Miller and Christiane Alberti (Paris: Navarin, 2021), 94.

81. *GW* 15:193–94; *SE* 22:178–79.

82. Max Weber, *The Protestant Ethic and the "Spirit" of Capitalism*, in *The Protestant Ethic and the "Spirit" of Capitalism and Other Writings*, ed. and trans. Peter Baehr and Gordon C. Wells (New

York: Penguin, 2002), 13–14, 19, 26, 197; Max Weber, "Remarks on the Foregoing 'Reply' (1908) (Weber's second rejoinder to H. Karl Fischer)," in *The Protestant Ethic and the "Spirit" of Capitalism and Other Writings*, 233–34, 241–42; Max Weber, "Rebuttal of the Critique of the 'Spirit' of Capitalism (1910) (Weber's first rejoinder to Felix Rachfahl)," in *The Protestant Ethic and the "Spirit" of Capitalism and Other Writings*, 262.

83. Gramsci, *Prison Notebooks, Volume Two*, Fourth Notebook, §38 (185).

84. Karl Marx, *Economic and Philosophical Manuscripts*, in *Early Writings*, trans. Rodney Livingstone and Gregor Benton (New York: Penguin, 1992), 328–29; Marx, *Capital, Volume One*, 284; Friedrich Engels, *Ludwig Feuerbach and the Outcome of Classical German Philosophy*, ed. C. P. Dutt (New York: International, 1941), 48–49, 52–53.

85. Ollman, *Alienation*, 9.

86. *SE* 18:42–43, 50, 52, 60–61, 91–92, 258–59; *SE* 19:40–47, 56, 159–60, 163–64, 218, 239; *SE* 20:57, 122, 265; *SE* 21:108, 210; *SE* 22:103–4; *SE* 23:148–51, 197–98, 242–43, 246–47.

87. *GW* 13:289; *SE* 19:59.

88. *SE* 21:122.

89. *GW* 14:481; *SE* 21:122.

90. Osborn, *Marxism and Psychoanalysis*, 26.

91. *GW* 14:506; *SE* 21:145.

92. Jürgen Habermas, *Knowledge and Human Interests*, trans. Jeremy J. Shapiro (Boston: Beacon, 1971), 283–85.

93. Russell Jacoby, *The Repression of Psychoanalysis: Otto Fenichel and the Political Freudians* (New York: Basic Books, 1983), 104; Peter Gay, *Freud: A Life for Our Time* (New York: Norton, 1988), 546–50; Joel Whitebook, *Perversion and Utopia: A Study in Psychoanalysis and Critical Theory* (Cambridge, MA: MIT Press, 1995), 97; Jean-Marie Vaysse, *L'inconscient des modernes. Essai sur l'origine métaphysique de la psychanalyse* (Paris: Gallimard, 1999), 446–47.

94. Jay, *The Dialectical Imagination*, 105.

95. Edwin R. Wallace, *Freud and Anthropology: A History and Reappraisal* (New York: International Universities Press, 1983), 54.

96. José Brunner, *Freud and the Politics of Psychoanalysis* (London: Transaction, 2001), 75–76.

97. Philip Rieff, *Freud: The Mind of the Moralist* (Chicago: University of Chicago Press, 1979), 221–22.

98. Paul Ricoeur, *Freud and Philosophy: An Essay on Interpretation*, trans. Denis Savage (New Haven, CT: Yale University Press, 1970), 211; Whitebook, *Perversion and Utopia*, 21–22.

99. *SE* 13:140–61; Rieff, *Freud*, 222–23.

100. Roy, *Hobbes and Freud*, viii, 59–60.

101. Jean-Jacques Rousseau, *Discourse on the Origin and Foundations of Inequality Among Men (Second Discourse)*, in *The First and Second Discourses*, ed. Roger D. Masters, trans. Roger D. Masters and Judith R. Masters (New York: Saint Martin's, 1964), 128–31; Louis Althusser, *Psychoanalysis and the Human Sciences*, trans. Steven Rendall (New York: Columbia University Press, 2016), 60–63.

102. Marcuse, *Eros and Civilization*, 147.

103. *SXX*, 90–91; *SXXII*, 4/15/75.

104. Immanuel Kant, "Idee zu einer allgemeinen Geschichte in weltbürgerlicher Absicht," in *Werkausgabe XI: Schriften zur Anthropologie, Geschichtsphilosophie, Politik und Pädagogik 1*, ed. Wilhelm Weischedel (Frankfurt am Main: Suhrkamp, 1977), 37; Immanuel Kant, "Idea for a Universal History with a Cosmopolitan Intent," in *Perpetual Peace and Other Essays on Politics, History, and Morals*, trans. Ted Humphrey (Indianapolis, IN: Hackett, 1983), 31–32.

105. Kant, "Idee zu einer allgemeinen Geschichte in weltbürgerlicher Absicht," 37–38; Kant, "Idea for a Universal History with a Cosmopolitan Intent," 32.

294   I. THE CONFLICTED POLITICAL ANIMAL

106. Lucio Colletti, "Mandeville, Rousseau and Smith," in *From Rousseau to Lenin: Studies in Ideology and Society*, trans. John Merrington and Judith White (New York: Monthly Review Press, 1972), 206–7.

107. Plato, *Protagoras*, trans. Stanley Lombardo and Karen Bell, in *Plato: Complete Works*, ed. John M. Cooper (Indianapolis, IN: Hackett, 1997), ll. 320d–322a (756–757).

108. Giovanni Pico della Mirandola, "On the Dignity of Man," in *On the Dignity of Man*, trans. Charles Glenn Wallis, Paul J. W. Miller, and Douglas Carmichael (Indianapolis, IN: Hackett, 1998), 4–7, 10–11.

109. Baron Paul Henri Thiry d'Holbach, *Good Sense*, trans. Anna Knoop (Amherst, NY: Prometheus, 2004), 47.

110. Adrian Johnston, *Prolegomena to Any Future Materialism*, vol. 2: *A Weak Nature Alone* (Evanston, IN: Northwestern University Press, 2019), vii, 148, 246–47.

111. Kant, "Idee zu einer allgemeinen Geschichte in weltbürgerlicher Absicht," 36–37; Kant, "Idea for a Universal History with a Cosmopolitan Intent," 31.

112. d'Holbach, *Good Sense*, 47.

113. Adrian Johnston, "Humanity, That Sickness: Louis Althusser and the Helplessness of Psychoanalysis," *Crisis and Critique* 2, no. 2, special issue: "*Reading Capital* and *For Marx*: 50 Years Later," ed. Frank Ruda and Agon Hamza (2015): 217–61.

114. *SE* 1:318; *SE* 20:154–55, 167; *SE* 21:17–19, 30.

115. Sigmund Freud, *Entwurf einer Psychologie*, in *Aus den Anfängen der Psychoanalyse, 1887–1902*, ed. Marie Bonaparte, Anna Freud, and Ernst Kris (Frankfurt am Main: S. Fischer, 1975), 326; *SE* 1:318.

116. *GW* 14:186–87; *SE* 20:154–55.

117. *GW* 14:352; *SE* 21:30.

118. Jean Laplanche and Jean-Bertrand Pontalis, *The Language of Psycho-Analysis*, trans. Donald Nicholson-Smith (New York: Norton, 1973), 431.

119. Herbert Marcuse, "Freedom and Freud's Theory of Instincts," in *Five Lectures*, 7.

120. *GW* 15:115; *SE* 22:107.

121. *GW* 16:23; *SE* 22:212.

122. *GW* 15:196–97; *SE* 22:180–81.

123. Paul A. Baran and Paul M. Sweezy, *Monopoly Capital: An Essay on the American Economic and Social Order* (New York: Monthly Review Press, 1966), 4–6.

124. Marx and Engels, *The Communist Manifesto*, 223–24.

125. Gilles Dostaler and Bernard Maris, *Capitalisme et pulsion de mort* (Paris: Fayard, 2010), 9, 21.

126. Joseph A. Schumpeter, *Capitalism, Socialism, and Democracy* (New York: Harper & Row, 1975), 209.

127. Theodor W. Adorno, "Sociology and Psychology, Part I," trans. Irving N. Wohlfarth, *New Left Review* 46 (November/December 1967): 68.

128. Jay, *The Dialectical Imagination*, 86.

129. Wilhelm Reich, *Reich Speaks of Freud: Wilhelm Reich Discusses His Work and His Relationship with Sigmund Freud*, ed. Mary Higgins and Chester M. Raphael, trans. Therese Pol (New York: Farrar Straus and Giroux, 1967), 42–44; Robinson, *The Freudian Left*, 31–32, 36–37; Brown, *Marx, Freud, and the Critique of Everyday Life*, 66; Jacoby, *The Repression of Psychoanalysis*, 80.

130. Martin A. Miller, *Freud and the Bolsheviks: Psychoanalysis in Imperial Russia and the Soviet Union* (New Haven, CT: Yale University Press, 1998), 96–97.

131. Lev Vygotsky and Alexander Luria, "Introduction to the Russian Translation of Freud's *Beyond the Pleasure Principle*," in *The Vygotsky Reader*, ed. René van der Veer and Jaan Valsiner (Oxford: Blackwell, 1994), 11.

132. Luria, "Psychoanalysis as a System of Monistic Psychology," 8.

1. THE CONFLICTED POLITICAL ANIMAL

133. Luria, "Psychoanalysis as a System of Monistic Psychology," 8–10, 13; Johnston, *Prolegomena to Any Future Materialism*, 2:73–136.
134. L. S. Vygotsky, "Problems of Method," in *Mind in Society: The Development of Higher Psychological Processes*, ed. Michael Cole, Vera John-Steiner, Sylvia Scribner, and Ellen Souberman (Cambridge, MA: Harvard University Press, 1978), 64–65.
135. Vygotsky, "Problems of Method," 73.
136. Louis Althusser, "Freud and Lacan," in *Writings on Psychoanalysis: Freud and Lacan*, trans. Jeffrey Mehlman (New York: Columbia University Press, 1996), 32.
137. Louis Althusser, "The Discovery of Dr. Freud," in *Writings on Psychoanalysis*, 103; Johnston, *Prolegomena to Any Future Materialism*, 2:137–53.
138. Althusser, "The Discovery of Dr. Freud," 107.
139. Osborn, *Marxism and Psychoanalysis*, 112; Johnston, "Humanity, That Sickness," 217–61.
140. Louis Althusser, "Three Notes on the Theory of Discourses," in *The Humanist Controversy and Other Writings*, ed. François Matheron, trans. G. M. Goshgarian (London: Verso, 2003), 38–41, 43.
141. Althusser, "Three Notes on the Theory of Discourses," 63–67.
142. Althusser, "Three Notes on the Theory of Discourses," 67.
143. Althusser, "Three Notes on the Theory of Discourses," 53–63, 71–73.
144. Luria, "Psychoanalysis as a System of Monistic Psychology," 14.
145. Reich, *Dialectical Materialism and Psychoanalysis*, 14–15, 43.
146. Luria, "Psychoanalysis as a System of Monistic Psychology," 10.
147. Luria, "Psychoanalysis as a System of Monistic Psychology," 35.
148. Luria, "Psychoanalysis as a System of Monistic Psychology," 14–15, 19–20, 22, 24, 34, 37.
149. Luria, "Psychoanalysis as a System of Monistic Psychology," 15–17, 36–37, 39–40.
150. Reich, *Dialectical Materialism and Psychoanalysis*, 18–19; Jacoby, *Social Amnesia*, 90.
151. Vygotsky, "Problems of Method," 60.
152. Vygotsky, "Problems of Method," 60–61.
153. Luria, "Psychoanalysis as a System of Monistic Psychology," 18.
154. Luria, "Psychoanalysis as a System of Monistic Psychology," 19.
155. Luria, "Psychoanalysis as a System of Monistic Psychology," 19.
156. Johnston, "Humanity, That Sickness," 217–61.
157. Lev Vygotsky, "The Problem of the Cultural Development of the Child," in *The Vygotsky Reader*, 59.
158. Luria, "Psychoanalysis as a System of Monistic Psychology," 20.
159. Mark Solms and Oliver Turnbull, *The Brain and the Inner World: An Introduction to the Neuroscience of Subjective Experience* (New York: Other Press, 2002), 56–57; Antonio Damasio, *Looking for Spinoza: Joy, Sorrow, and the Feeling Brain* (New York: Harcourt, 2003), 12, 133, 209.
160. Karen Kaplan-Solms and Mark Solms, *Clinical Studies in Neuro-Psychoanalysis: Introduction to a Depth Neuropsychology* (London: Karnac, 2002), 26–43.
161. A. M. Deborin, "Spinoza's World-View," in *Spinoza in Soviet Philosophy*, ed. and trans. George L. Kline (London: Routledge & Kegan Paul, 1952), 90–91, 102, 108–13; I. K. Luppol, "The Historical Significance of Spinoza's Philosophy," in *Spinoza in Soviet Philosophy*, 175; Johnston, *Adventures in Transcendental Materialism*, 23–49; Johnston, *Prolegomena to Any Future Materialism*, 2:73–136.
162. *SE* 7:147–48; *SE* 14:118, 120–23.
163. Luria, "Psychoanalysis as a System of Monistic Psychology," 22.
164. Luria, "Psychoanalysis as a System of Monistic Psychology," 24.
165. Luria, "Psychoanalysis as a System of Monistic Psychology," 24–25.
166. Luria, "Psychoanalysis as a System of Monistic Psychology," 24–25, 28–29, 39–40.

167. *SE* 14:174–75; *SE* 19:191; *SE* 20:32; *SE* 23:97, 144–45.

168. Kaplan-Solms and Solms, *Clinical Studies in Neuro-Psychoanalysis*, 17–25, 43, 54–55, 60, 250–51, 260, 276.

169. *SE* 18:60; Vygotsky and Luria, "Introduction to the Russian Translation of Freud's *Beyond the Pleasure Principle*," 13.

170. Luria, "Psychoanalysis as a System of Monistic Psychology," 27.

171. *SE* 18:40–53; Vygotsky and Luria, "Introduction to the Russian Translation of Freud's *Beyond the Pleasure Principle*," 14.

172. Luria, "Psychoanalysis as a System of Monistic Psychology," 27–29.

173. Luria, "Psychoanalysis as a System of Monistic Psychology," 30–34.

174. Luria, "Psychoanalysis as a System of Monistic Psychology," 34–35.

175. Luria, "Psychoanalysis as a System of Monistic Psychology," 35.

176. Luria, "Psychoanalysis as a System of Monistic Psychology," 45.

177. Osborn, *Marxism and Psychoanalysis*, 154.

178. L. S. Vygotsky, *Thought and Language*, ed. and trans. Eugenia Hanfmann and Gertrude Vakar (Cambridge, MA: MIT Press, 1962), 21.

179. Reich, *Dialectical Materialism and Psychoanalysis*, 25, 27, 38–39.

180. Vygotsky and Luria, "Introduction to the Russian Translation of Freud's *Beyond the Pleasure Principle*," 16.

181. Vygotsky and Luria, "Introduction to the Russian Translation of Freud's *Beyond the Pleasure Principle*," 16–17.

182. Vygotsky and Luria, "Introduction to the Russian Translation of Freud's *Beyond the Pleasure Principle*," 17.

183. Reich, *Dialectical Materialism and Psychoanalysis*, 30, 41–42; Otto Fenichel, "Psychoanalysis as the Nucleus of a Future Dialectical-Materialist Psychology," ed. Suzette H. Annin and Hanna Fenichel, trans. Olga Barsis, *American Imago* 24, no. 4 (Winter 1967): 297–98.

184. Wilhelm Reich, "Psychoanalysis in the Soviet Union," in *Sex-Pol: Essays, 1929–1934*, ed. Lee Baxandall, trans. Anna Bostock, Tom DuBose, and Lee Baxandall (New York: Vintage, 1972), 82.

185. Bertell Ollman, "The Marxism of Wilhelm Reich: The Social Function of Sexual Repression," in *The Unknown Dimension: European Marxism Since Lenin*, ed. Dick Howard and Karl E. Klare (New York: Basic Books, 1972), 219–20.

186. Marcuse, *Eros and Civilization*, 55–58; Robinson, *The Freudian Left*, 197.

187. Marcuse, *Eros and Civilization*, 5.

188. Marcuse, *Eros and Civilization*, 16.

189. Theodor W. Adorno, *Negative Dialectics*, trans. E. B. Ashton (New York: Continuum, 1973), 351.

190. Jacoby, *Social Amnesia*, 79.

191. Reich, *Dialectical Materialism and Psychoanalysis*, 15–16, 55; Fenichel, "Psychoanalysis as the Nucleus of a Future Dialectical-Materialist Psychology," 301; Robinson, *The Freudian Left*, 19, 43–45.

192. Vygotsky, *Thought and Language*, 10.

193. *SXII*, 12/9/64; *SXIII*, 4/20/66.

194. Vygotsky, "The Problem of the Cultural Development of the Child," 63–64.

195. Friedrich Engels, "The Part Played by Labour in the Transition from Ape to Man," in *Dialectics of Nature*, trans. and ed. Clemens Dutt (New York: International, 1940), 279–96.

196. L. S. Vygotsky, "Internalization of Higher Psychological Functions," in *Mind in Society*, 54; Vygotsky, *Thought and Language*, 48–49.

197. Alexander Luria, "The Problem of the Cultural Behaviour of the Child," in *The Vygotsky Reader*, 46.

198. Robinson, *The Freudian Left*, 41.

I. THE CONFLICTED POLITICAL ANIMAL ❧ 297

199. Reich, *Dialectical Materialism and Psychoanalysis*, 24–25; Robinson, *The Freudian Left*, 33.

200. *SE* 21:86–92, 94–97, 129; Marcuse, *Eros and Civilization*, 4–5, 17.

201. Marcuse, *Eros and Civilization*, 34–37, 40, 44–45, 87–88.

202. Habermas, *Knowledge and Human Interests*, 275–76, 280.

203. *SE* 21:101, 139.

204. Marcuse, *Eros and Civilization*, 134.

205. Marx, *Economic and Philosophical Manuscripts*, 327–31; Marx, *Grundrisse*, 470, 611.

206. Marcuse, *Eros and Civilization*, 213–14, 223–24.

207. Marcuse, *Eros and Civilization*, 47, 154.

208. Marcuse, *Eros and Civilization*, 46–48, 157, 245; Baran and Sweezy, *Monopoly Capital*, 355–56.

209. Marcuse, *Eros and Civilization*, 191.

210. Marcuse, *Eros and Civilization*, 231.

211. Marcuse, *Eros and Civilization*, 35–37, 40, 44–45, 87–88.

212. Karl Marx, *Capital: A Critique of Political Economy, Volume Three*, trans. David Fernbach (New York: Penguin, 1981), 958–59; Marcuse, *Eros and Civilization*, 152–53, 194–95.

213. Marx, *Economic and Philosophical Manuscripts*, 322–34; Herbert Marcuse, "New Sources on the Foundation of Historical Materialism," in *Heideggerian Marxism*, ed. Richard Wolin and John Abromeit (Lincoln: University of Nebraska Press, 2005), 89–93, 96–97, 104–7; Herbert Marcuse, "On the Philosophical Foundations of the Concept of Labor in Economics," in *Heideggerian Marxism*, 139, 149.

214. Georg Lukács, "Reification and the Consciousness of the Proletariat," in *History and Class Consciousness: Studies in Marxist Dialectics*, trans. Rodney Livingstone (Cambridge, MA: MIT Press, 1971), 89–90.

215. Marcuse, *Eros and Civilization*, 201; Robinson, *The Freudian Left*, 207–8.

216. Göran Therborn, "The Frankfurt School," in *Western Marxism: A Critical Reader*, ed. New Left Review (London: Verso, 1977), 100.

217. Adrian Johnston, *Time Driven: Metapsychology and the Splitting of the Drive* (Evanston, IL: Northwestern University Press, 2005), xxxiv, 154–55, 244–45, 253–55; Adrian Johnston, "A Blast from the Future: Freud, Lacan, Marcuse, and Snapping the Threads of the Past," in *Umbr(a): Utopia*, ed. Ryan Anthony Hatch (Buffalo: Center for the Study of Psychoanalysis and Culture, State University of New York at Buffalo, 2008), 67–84.

218. Johnston, *Time Driven*, xxix–xxx, 5–57, 218–19, 315–16.

219. Johnston, *Time Driven*, xxvii–xxxviii, 218–332, 343–47.

220. Robinson, *The Freudian Left*, 202–3.

221. *GW* 14:504; *SE* 21:143.

222. *SXX*, 111–12; Johnston, *Time Driven*, xxiv, xxxiv–xxxv, 239–41, 243, 248, 250, 282–83, 285–87, 297–98, 318, 324–25, 327, 329–30, 336–37, 339.

223. Jacques Lacan, "Science and Truth," in *Écrits: The First Complete Edition in English*, trans. Bruce Fink (New York: Norton, 2006), 738.

224. Lacan, "Radiophonie," 424; Lacan, "Television," 32–33, 46.

225. Reich, *Dialectical Materialism and Psychoanalysis*, 20–21, 56; Fenichel, "Psychoanalysis as the Nucleus of a Future Dialectical-Materialist Psychology," 294–96, 311; Marcuse, *Eros and Civilization*, 132–33.

226. Luria, "Psychoanalysis as a System of Monistic Psychology," 22, 24–25; Vygotsky and Luria, "Introduction to the Russian Translation of Freud's *Beyond the Pleasure Principle*," 14; Reich, *Dialectical Materialism and Psychoanalysis*, 21–21; Fenichel, "Psychoanalysis as the Nucleus of a Future Dialectical-Materialist Psychology," 295–96, 302, 306; Marcuse, *Eros and Civilization*, 11–12, 21, 31.

227. *SXVIII*, 164.

228. Osborn, *Marxism and Psychoanalysis*, 74.

229. Frederic Jameson, "An American Utopia," in *An American Utopia: Dual Power and the Universal Army*, ed. Slavoj Žižek (New York: Verso, 2016), 73–74.

230. Jameson, "An American Utopia," 74.

231. Jameson, "An American Utopia," 75.

232. *SE* 14:93–97, 100–2; *SE* 16:428–29; *SE* 19:28; *SE* 22:64–66.

233. *SE* 18:108–10, 112–14, 116, 129–33.

234. *SE* 1:318, 331.

235. Jameson, "An American Utopia," 64, 79.

236. Shlomo Avineri, *The Social and Political Thought of Karl Marx* (Cambridge: Cambridge University Press, 1968), 223–24.

237. Alexandre Kojève, *Introduction to the Reading of Hegel: Lectures on the Phenomenology of Spirit*, ed. Raymond Queneau and Allan Bloom, trans. James H. Nichols, Jr. (Ithaca, NY: Cornell University Press, 1980), 65, 102, 159, 215, 259.

238. *SXVI*, 32; *SXVII*, 81, 98.

239. *SXVI*, 32.

240. *SXVII* [Fr.], 93; *SXVII*, 81.

241. *SXVII*, 98.

242. *SE* 5:561; *SE* 15:226.

243. *SXVII* [Fr.], 111; *SXVII*, 98.

244. *SXVII* [Fr.], 111–12; *SXVII*, 98.

245. Osborn, *Marxism and Psychoanalysis*, 147–48.

246. Althusser, *On the Reproduction of Capitalism*, 181; Louis Althusser, "L'idéologie (extrait de Théorie marxiste et Parti comministe)," in *Socialisme idéologique et socialisme scientifique, et autres écrits*, ed. G. M. Goshgarian (Paris: Presses Universitaires de France, 2022), 177–78; Louis Althusser, "Lettre aux camarades du Comité Central du Parti communiste français," in *Socialisme idéologique et socialisme scientifique, et autres écrits*, 209.

247. Adrian Johnston, "The Late Innate: Jean Laplanche, Jaak Panksepp, and the Distinction Between Sexual Drives and Instincts," in *Inheritance in Psychoanalysis*, ed. Joel Goldbach and James A. Godley (Albany: State University of New York Press, 2018), 57–84.

248. *SXVIII*, 21.

249. *SXVIII*, 21.

250. Jacques Lacan, "The Subversion of the Subject and the Dialectic of Desire in the Freudian Unconscious," in *Écrits*, 696.

251. Johnston, *Time Driven*, xix–xxiv, 184–341.

252. Samo Tomšič, *The Capitalist Unconscious: Marx and Lacan* (London: Verso, 2015), 108–9.

253. Marx, *Grundrisse*, 105.

254. *SXVII* [Fr.], 105; *SXVII*, 92.

255. *SXIV*, 415.

256. Benjamin Y. Fong, *Death and Mastery: Psychoanalytic Drive Theory and the Subject of Late Capitalism* (New York: Columbia University Press, 2016), 2–3.

257. *SXIV*, 255–56.

258. *SXVI*, 29–30.

259. Élisabeth Roudinesco, *Jacques Lacan & Co.: A History of Psychoanalysis in France, 1925–1985*, trans. Jeffrey Mehlman (Chicago: University of Chicago Press, 1990), 384.

260. Élisabeth Roudinesco, *Jacques Lacan: Outline of a Life, History of a System of Thought*, trans. Barbara Bray (New York: Columbia University Press, 1997), 307.

261. Lucien Sebag, *Marxisme et structuralisme* (Paris: Payot, 1964), 223–64.

I. THE CONFLICTED POLITICAL ANIMAL   299

262. Louis Althusser, "The Object of *Capital*," in Louis Althusser, Étienne Balibar, Roger Establet, Pierre Macherey, and Jacques Rancière, *Reading Capital: The Complete Edition*, trans. Ben Brewster and David Fernbach (London: Verso, 2015), 255, 334, 341–43.

263. Althusser, "The Object of *Capital*," 254, 343; Louis Althusser, "Contradiction and Overdetermination: Notes for an Investigation," in *For Marx*, 87–128; Louis Althusser, "On the Materialist Dialectic: On the Unevenness of Origins," in *For Marx*, 204–6, 209–10, 213–14, 216–17; Althusser, "Marxism and Humanism," 233–34.

264. Johnston, "Humanity, That Sickness," 217–61.

265. *SXIV*, 273.

266. *SXIV*, 292.

267. Johnston, *Time Driven*, xix–xxiv.

268. *SXIV*, 306–10.

269. Johnston, *Time Driven*, xxiv, xxxiv–xxxv, 184–341.

270. *SVII*, 150, 152.

271. Lacan, "Du discours psychanalytique," 49.

272. Tony Smith, *The Logic of Marx's Capital: Replies to Hegelian Criticisms* (Albany: State University of New York, 1990), 161.

273. Jacques Lacan, "Mon enseignement, sa nature et ses fins," in *Mon enseignement*, ed. Jacques-Alain Miller (Paris: Éditions du Seuil, 2005), 82–83; Jacques Lacan, "My Teaching, Its Nature and Its Ends," in *My Teaching*, ed. Jacques-Alain Miller, trans. David Macey (London: Verso, 2008), 64.

274. Lacan, "Mon enseignement, sa nature et ses fins," 83; Lacan, "My Teaching, Its Nature and Its Ends," 64.

275. Johnston, *Prolegomena to Any Future Materialism*, 2:xix–xx, 117–18, 132–34, 187, 200, 207–21.

276. *SE* 1:243, 273; *SE* 4:200; *SE* 5:403; *SE* 9:168, 173–74; *SE* 11:106; *SE* 12:187–90, 196–97; *SE* 17:72–74, 76, 82, 127–28, 130–32; Osborn, *Marxism and Psychoanalysis*, 15.

277. Dominique Laporte, *History of Shit*, trans. Nadia Benabid and Rodolphe el-Khoury (Cambridge, MA: MIT Press, 2000), 40.

278. Marx and Engels, *The Communist Manifesto*, 231.

279. Karl Marx, *Wage-Labour and Capital*, in *Wage-Labour and Capital/Value, Price and Profit* (New York: International Publishers, 1976), 48.

280. Richard Boothby, *Freud as Philosopher: Metapsychology After Lacan* (New York: Routledge, 2001), 249.

281. Althusser, *On the Reproduction of Capitalism*, 20–21, 52, 140, 148–49, 246–47.

282. Weber, *The Protestant Ethic and the "Spirit" of Capitalism*, 19–20, 28, 73, 80.

283. Slavoj Žižek, *The Plague of Fantasies* (London: Verso, 1997), 4.

284. Žižek, *The Plague of Fantasies*, 4–5.

285. Žižek, *The Plague of Fantasies*, 5.

286. V. I. Lenin, "The Three Sources and Three Component Parts of Marxism," in *The Lenin Anthology*, ed. Robert C. Tucker (New York: Norton, 1975), 640–44.

287. *SE* 8:170–71, 204; *SE* 11:233–34; *SE* 21:161–66.

288. Althusser, *On the Reproduction of Capitalism*, 76–77, 172–73, 175, 184–87; Althusser, *Que faire?*, 33–34, 93–94, 110; Louis Althusser, *How to Be a Marxist in Philosophy*, ed. and trans. G. M. Goshgarian (London: Bloomsbury, 2017), 124–25.

289. Gramsci, *Prison Notebooks, Volume Two*, Notebook 3 (1930), §49 (52–53).

290. Karl Marx and Friedrich Engels, *Die deutsche Ideologie* (Berlin: Dietz, 1953), 22–23.

291. Laporte, *History of Shit*, 37.

292. *SVII*, 139; *SXI*, 268; *SXVI*, 224–25, 249.

300 · I. THE CONFLICTED POLITICAL ANIMAL

293. V. I. Lenin, "The Importance of Gold Now and After the Complete Victory of Socialism," in *The Lenin Anthology*, 515.

294. Althusser, *On the Reproduction of Capitalism*, 186; Louis Althusser, "Ideology and Ideological State Apparatuses (Notes Towards an Investigation)," in *On the Reproduction of Capitalism*, 260.

2. FROM CLOSED NEED TO INFINITE GREED: MARXIAN DRIVES

1. Galileo Galilei, "The Assayer," in *Discoveries and Opinions of Galileo*, trans. Stillman Drake (New York: Anchor, 1957), 274–78; Alexandre Koyré, *From the Closed World to the Infinite Universe* (New York: Harper Torchbooks, 1958), 99, 278.

2. Koyré, *From the Closed World to the Infinite Universe*, 4–5, 14, 16–17, 24, 29–30, 32–35, 40–43, 60–61, 63–65, 67, 69, 96, 112, 188, 275–76.

3. Koyré, *From the Closed World to the Infinite Universe*, 72, 84, 161.

4. Adrian Johnston, *Prolegomena to Any Future Materialism*, vol. 1: *The Outcome of Contemporary French Philosophy* (Evanston, IL: Northwestern University Press, 2013), 6, 146–47; Adrian Johnston, *Adventures in Transcendental Materialism: Dialogues with Contemporary Thinkers* (Edinburgh: Edinburgh University Press, 2014), 73, 254–55; Adrian Johnston, *Prolegomena to Any Future Materialism*, vol. 2: *A Weak Nature Alone* (Evanston, IL: Northwestern University Press, 2019), 140–41, 187–88.

5. Jürgen Habermas, *Knowledge and Human Interests*, trans. Jeremy J. Shapiro (Boston: Beacon, 1971), 282.

6. Jacques Lacan, "The Function and Field of Speech and Language in Psychoanalysis," in *Écrits: The First Complete Edition in English*, trans. Bruce Fink (New York: Norton, 2006), 235–39; Jacques Lacan, "Variations on the Standard Treatment," in *Écrits*, 299–300; Jacques Lacan, "On an Ex Post Facto Syllabary," in *Écrits*, 608; Jacques Lacan, "Position of the Unconscious," in *Écrits*, 712; Jacques Lacan, "Science and Truth," in *Écrits*, 726–28; *SII*, 298–99; *SIII*, 238; *SXI*, 47, 231; *SXIII*, 12/8/65; *SXX*, 81–82; Samo Tomšič, *The Capitalist Unconscious: Marx and Lacan* (London: Verso, 2015), 73, 183–84, 238.

7. *SXII*, 2/3/65; *SXIV*, 199.

8. Adrian Johnston, *Time Driven: Metapsychology and the Splitting of the Drive* (Evanston, IL: Northwestern University Press, 2005), 61–71; Johnston, *Prolegomena to Any Future Materialism*, 1:6, 40, 42, 58; Johnston, *Adventures in Transcendental Materialism*, 73, 254–55.

9. Jean-Claude Milner, *L'œuvre claire. Lacan, la science, la philosophie* (Paris: Éditions du Seuil, 1995), 39–42, 47–48, 50–51, 64–69, 81–82, 85–87, 89–90, 92–95, 97–111, 136–37; Jean-Claude Milner, *Le périple structural. Figures et paradigme* (Paris: Éditions du Seuil, 2002), 147–48, 174, 186, 188–89, 192–96, 198–99, 220–22.

10. *SXII*, 6/9/65.

11. *SE* 16:284–85; *SE* 17:140–41; *SE* 19:221; *SE* 22:158–82.

12. Bertell Ollman, *Alienation: Marx's Conception of Man in Capitalist Society* (Cambridge: Cambridge University Press, 1971), 183.

13. Johnston, *Prolegomena to Any Future Materialism*, 2:73–95.

14. Aristotle, *Politics*, trans. C. D. C. Reeve (Indianapolis, IN: Hackett, 1998), ll. 1257a–1258a (15–18); Patrick Avrane, *Petite psychanalyse de l'argent* (Paris: Presses Universitaires de France, 2015), 60, 68.

15. Georg Lukács, "Reification and the Consciousness of the Proletariat," in *History and Class Consciousness: Studies in Marxist Dialectics*, trans. by Rodney Livingstone (Cambridge, MA: MIT Press, 1971), 83–110.

16. *SVII*, 225–26.
17. Pierre Martin, *Argent et psychanalyse* (Paris: Navarin, 1984), 185.
18. Wilhelm Reich, *Dialectical Materialism and Psychoanalysis* (London: Socialist Reproduction, 1972), 15–16, 31, 56; Wilhelm Reich, "Psychoanalysis in the Soviet Union," in *Sex-Pol: Essays, 1929–1934*, ed. Lee Baxandall, trans. Anna Bostock, Tom DuBose, and Lee Baxandall (New York: Vintage, 1972), 78–79.
19. Otto Fenichel, "Psychoanalysis as the Nucleus of a Future Dialectical-Materialist Psychology," ed. Suzette H. Annin and Hanna Fenichel, trans. Olga Barsis, *American Imago* 24, no. 4 (Winter 1967): 290–91.
20. Fenichel, "Psychoanalysis as the Nucleus of a Future Dialectical-Materialist Psychology," 306.
21. Reich, *Dialectical Materialism and Psychoanalysis*, 20–21; Fenichel, "Psychoanalysis as the Nucleus of a Future Dialectical-Materialist Psychology," 311.
22. Reich, *Dialectical Materialism and Psychoanalysis*, 40; Fenichel, "Psychoanalysis as the Nucleus of a Future Dialectical-Materialist Psychology," 297–298, 311.
23. Russell Jacoby, *The Repression of Psychoanalysis: Otto Fenichel and the Political Freudians* (New York: Basic Books, 1983), 83–86.
24. Fenichel, "Psychoanalysis as the Nucleus of a Future Dialectical-Materialist Psychology," 295.
25. Fenichel, "Psychoanalysis as the Nucleus of a Future Dialectical-Materialist Psychology," 295–96.
26. Fenichel, "Psychoanalysis as the Nucleus of a Future Dialectical-Materialist Psychology," 303–4.
27. Herbert Marcuse, *Eros and Civilization: A Philosophical Inquiry Into Freud* (Boston: Beacon, 1974), 55.
28. Adrian Johnston, "Humanity, That Sickness: Louis Althusser and the Helplessness of Psychoanalysis," *Crisis and Critique* 2, no. 2, special issue: *"Reading Capital* and *For Marx*: 50 Years Later," ed. Frank Ruda and Agon Hamza (2015): 217–61.
29. Habermas, *Knowledge and Human Interests*, 282–83.
30. Ernest Mandel, *Marxist Economic Theory*, trans. Brian Pearce (New York: Monthly Review Press, 1970), 2:669.
31. Fenichel, "Psychoanalysis as the Nucleus of a Future Dialectical-Materialist Psychology," 297.
32. Otto Fenichel, "The Drive to Amass Wealth," *Psychoanalytic Quarterly* 7 (1938): 72–73, 93–95.
33. Sandor Ferenczi, "The Ontogenesis of the Interest in Money," in *First Contributions to Psycho-Analysis*, trans. Ernest Jones (New York: Routledge, 1994), 326, 328, 331; Fenichel, "The Drive to Amass Wealth," 82–83.
34. Lacan, "The Function and Field of Speech and Language in Psychoanalysis," 260.
35. Lacan, "The Function and Field of Speech and Language in Psychoanalysis," 266; Adrian Johnston, *Irrepressible Truth: On Lacan's 'The Freudian Thing'* (Basingstoke: Palgrave, 2017), 93–107.
36. Lacan, "Variations on the Standard Treatment," 280–85.
37. *SVIII*, 255.
38. *SXV*, 3/27/68.
39. Jacques Lacan, *Télévision* (Paris: Éditions du Seuil, 1973), 51–52; Jacques Lacan, "Television," trans. Denis Hollier, Rosalind Krauss, and Annette Michelson, in *Television/A Challenge to the Psychoanalytic Establishment*, ed. Joan Copjec (New York: Norton, 1990), 29–31.
40. Lacan, "The Function and Field of Speech and Language in Psychoanalysis," 215–16; Jacques Lacan, "Mis en question du psychanalyste," in *Lacan redivivus*, ed. Jacques-Alain Miller and Christiane Alberti (Paris: Navarin, 2021), 65; *SXV*, 11/29/67.
41. Jacoby, *The Repression of Psychoanalysis*, 6–7, 32, 36.
42. Lacan, "The Function and Field of Speech and Language in Psychoanalysis," 279–80; Jacques Lacan, "The Instance of the Letter in the Unconscious, or Reason Since Freud," in *Écrits*, 433; *SI*, 16–17, 53, 110–12, 285.

43. *SXI*, 11.

44. *SXI*, 182.

45. *SXV*, 11/29/67.

46. Johnston, *Adventures in Transcendental Materialism*, 65–107.

47. Johnston, *Adventures in Transcendental Materialism*, 65–107.

48. Jacques Lacan, "Introduction à l'édition allemande d'un premier volume des Écrits," in *Autres écrits*, ed. Jacques-Alain Miller (Paris: Éditions du Seuil, 2001), 555.

49. Russell Jacoby, *Social Amnesia: A Critique of Conformist Psychology from Adler to Laing* (Boston: Beacon, 1975), 123–24; Jacoby, *The Repression of Psychoanalysis*, 17, 23–24, 105–11, 125, 142, 153–54, 157–58.

50. Marcuse, *Eros and Civilization*, 5–8, 238–74.

51. Paul A. Robinson, *The Freudian Left: Wilhelm Reich, Geza Roheim, Herbert Marcuse* (New York: Harper & Row, 1969), 37–38, 42–43.

52. Martin Jay, *The Dialectical Imagination: A History of the Frankfurt School and the Institute of Social Research, 1923–1950* (Boston: Little, Brown, 1973), 343; Johnston, *Irrepressible Truth*, xx–xxi, 4–6, 63–64, 76–78, 98–99, 191, 195–96, 221, 229–30, 235–36.

53. Jacques Lacan, "The Mirror Stage as Formative of the *I* Function as Revealed in Psychoanalytic Experience," in *Écrits*, 78–79; Robinson, *The Freudian Left*, 23.

54. Max Horkheimer, "Authority and the Family," in *Critical Theory: Selected Essays*, trans. Matthew J. O'Connell et al. (New York: Continuum, 1982), 47–128.

55. Jacques Lacan, "Les complexes familiaux dans la formation de l'individu: Essai d'analyse d'une fonction en psychologie," in *Autres écrits*, 56–61.

56. Martin Jay, "'In Psychoanalysis Nothing Is True but the Exaggerations': Freud and the Frankfurt School," in *Splinters in Your Eye: Frankfurt School Provocations* (London: Verso, 2020), 58.

57. Marcuse, *Eros and Civilization*, 96; Robinson, *The Freudian Left*, 211.

58. Juan Pablo Lucchelli, *Lacan: De Wallon à Kojève* (Paris: Éditions Michèle, 2017), 85–86.

59. Max Horkheimer and Theodor W. Adorno, *Dialectic of Enlightenment: Philosophical Fragments*, ed. Gunzelin Schmid Noerr, trans. Edmund Jephcott (Stanford, CA: Stanford University Press, 2002), 63–93; Jacques Lacan, "Kant with Sade," in *Écrits*, 645–68.

60. Lucchelli, *Lacan*, 192–93, 199, 201–2.

61. Dany Nobus, *The Law of Desire: On Lacan's 'Kant with Sade'* (Basingstoke: Palgrave Macmillan, 2017), xxviii–xxix, xxxi–xxxii, 6, 15.

62. Slavoj Žižek, *Incontinence of the Void: Economico-Philosophical Spandrels* (Cambridge, MA: MIT Press, 2017), 302.

63. Johnston, *Adventures in Transcendental Materialism*, 65–107.

64. Johnston, *Time Driven*, xxxiii–xxxiv, 242–255; Adrian Johnston, "A Blast from the Future: Freud, Lacan, Marcuse, and Snapping the Threads of the Past," in *Umbr(a): Utopia*, ed. Ryan Anthony Hatch (Buffalo: Center for the Study of Psychoanalysis and Culture, State University of New York at Buffalo, 2008), 67–84.

65. Karl Marx, *Grundrisse: Foundations of the Critique of Political Economy (Rough Draft)*, trans. Martin Nicolaus (New York: Penguin, 1973), 111.

66. Marx, *Grundrisse*, 105.

67. Ronald L. Meek, *Studies in the Labor Theory of Value*, 2nd ed. (New York: Monthly Review Press, 1956), 20; Ollman, *Alienation*, 174, 179.

68. Johnston, *Time Driven*, 9, 22, 48, 53, 78, 135, 141, 143, 147–48, 154, 217, 231, 325, 345, 375.

69. Karl Marx, *Grundrisse der Kritik der politischen Ökonomie (Rohentwurf)* (Frankfurt: Europäische Verlaganstalt, 1967), 13–14; Marx, *Grundrisse*, 92.

70. Fenichel, "Psychoanalysis as the Nucleus of a Future Dialectical-Materialist Psychology," 302.

71. Fenichel, "The Drive to Amass Wealth," 70–71.

72. Bernard Sichère, "Du ghetto symbolique à l'action révolutionnaire," in *Marxisme-léninisme et psychanalyse* (Paris: François Maspero, 1975), 74.
73. Marx, *Grundrisse* [Gr.], 312–13; Marx, *Grundrisse*, 408–9.
74. James F. Becker, *Marxian Political Economy: An Outline* (Cambridge: Cambridge University Press, 1977), 234–35, 245, 247, 260, 270–71.
75. Herbert Marcuse, "Industrialization and Capitalism in the Work of Max Weber," in *Negations: Essays in Critical Theory*, trans. Jeremy J. Shapiro (Boston: Beacon, 1968), 206–7.
76. Harry Braverman, *Labor and Monopoly Capital: The Degradation of Work in the Twentieth Century* (New York: Monthly Review Press, 1974), 302; Moishe Postone, *Time, Labor, and Social Domination: A Reinterpretation of Marx's Critical Theory* (Cambridge: Cambridge University Press, 1993), 331; David Harvey, *A Companion to Marx's Capital* (London: Verso, 2010), 89–90.
77. Herbert Marcuse, *One-Dimensional Man: Studies in the Ideology of Advanced Industrial Society* (Boston: Beacon, 1964), 246; Ollman, *Alienation*, 147; G. A. Cohen, *Karl Marx's Theory of History: A Defense* (Princeton, NJ: Princeton University Press, 1978), 298, 300, 302–3, 306, 320; David Harvey, *Marx, Capital, and the Madness of Economic Reason* (London: Profile, 2017), 198.
78. G. W. F. Hegel, *Grundlinien der Philosophie des Rechts oder Naturrecht und Staatswissenschaft im Grundrisse: Mit Hegels eigenhändigen Notizen und den mündlichen Zusätzen, Werke in zwanzig Bänden*, 7, ed. Eva Moldenhauer and Karl Markus Michel (Frankfurt am Main: Suhrkamp, 1970), §191 (349); G. W. F. Hegel, *Elements of the Philosophy of Right*, ed. Allen W. Wood, trans. H. B. Nisbet (Cambridge: Cambridge University Press, 1991), §191 (229).
79. Adam Smith, *The Wealth of Nations, Books I–III*, ed. Andrew Skinner (New York: Penguin, 1986), 109–26.
80. G. W. F. Hegel, *System of Ethical Life*, in *System of Ethical Life and First Philosophy of Spirit*, trans. H. S. Harris and T. M. Knox (Albany: State University of New York Press, 1979), 103–7, 124, 154; G. W. F. Hegel, *First Philosophy of Spirit*, in *System of Ethical Life and First Philosophy of Spirit*, 247–49; Hegel, *Elements of the Philosophy of Right*, §188–89 (226–28), §192 (229–30), §198–99 (232–33), §229–30 (259–60).
81. Hegel, *Elements of the Philosophy of Right*, §190–91 (228–29), §195 (231).
82. Tony Smith, *The Logic of Marx's Capital: Replies to Hegelian Criticisms* (Albany: State University of New York, 1990), 229.
83. Karl Marx, *Karl-Marx-Ausgabe: Werke-Schriften-Briefe, Band V: Ökonomische Schriften, zweiter Band*, ed. Hans-Joachim Lieber, *Das Kapital: Kritik der politischen Ökonomie, dritter Band, drittes Buch, Der Gesamtprozess der kapitalistichen Produktion, Kapitel I-XV* (Darmstadt: Wissenschaftliche Buchgesellschaft, 1963), 811; Karl Marx, *Capital: A Critique of Political Economy, Volume Three*, trans. David Fernbach (New York: Penguin, 1981), 290.
84. Friedrich Engels, *The Condition of the Working Class in England*, ed. David McLellan, trans. Florence Kelley-Wischnewetsky (Oxford: Oxford University Press, 1993), 95.
85. Smith, *The Wealth of Nations, Books I–III*, 269.
86. Lucien Sebag, *Marxisme et structuralisme* (Paris: Payot, 1964), 167.
87. Herbert Marcuse, *An Essay on Liberation* (Boston: Beacon, 1969), 10–11, 16–17; Herbert Marcuse, *Counterrevolution and Revolt* (Boston: Beacon, 1972), 66; Bruce Brown, *Marx, Freud, and the Critique of Everyday Life: Toward a Permanent Cultural Revolution* (New York: Monthly Review Press, 1973), 159; Jacoby, *Social Amnesia*, 65.
88. Habermas, *Knowledge and Human Interests*, 239, 345.
89. Marx, *Grundrisse*, 413; Rosa Luxemburg, *The Accumulation of Capital*, trans. Agnes Schwarzschild (New York: Routledge, 2003), 10–12; Ernest Mandel, *Late Capitalism*, trans. Joris De Bres (London: Verso, 1978), 27; Postone, *Time, Labor, and Social Domination*, 267, 269–70, 353, 383; Harvey, *A Companion to Marx's Capital*, 73–74, 139, 162, 323; David Harvey, *A Companion to Marx's Capital, Volume Two* (London: Verso, 2013), 213–14, 218, 235–36, 319, 326–27.

304   　　　2. FROM CLOSED NEED TO INFINITE GREED

90. Karl Marx, *A Contribution to the Critique of Political Economy*, ed. Maurice Dobb, trans. S. W. Ryazanskaya (New York: International, 1970), 132.

91. Marx, *Grundrisse* [Gr.], 133–34; Marx, *Grundrisse*, 222–23.

92. Marx, *Capital, Volume Three*, 609; Thomas Presskorn-Thygesen and Ole Bjerg, "The Falling Rate of Enjoyment: Consumer Capitalism and Compulsive Buying Disorder," *Ephemera: Theory and Politics in Organization* 14, no. 2 (2014); 199.

93. Marx, *Grundrisse* [Gr.], 134; Marx, *Grundrisse*, 223.

94. Karl Marx, *Karl-Marx-Ausgabe: Werke-Schriften-Briefe, Band IV: Ökonomische Schriften, erster Band*, ed. Hans-Joachim Lieber, *Das Kapital: Kritik der politischen Ökonomie, erster Band* (Darmstadt: Wissenschaftliche Buchgesellschaft, 1962), 120; Karl Marx, *Capital: A Critique of Political Economy, Volume One*, trans. Ben Fowkes (New York: Penguin, 1976), 229.

95. Karl Marx, *Theories of Surplus-Value, Part One: Volume IV of Capital*, ed. S. Ryazanskaya, trans. Emile Burns (Moscow: Progress Publishers, 1963), 283.

96. Engels, *The Condition of the Working Class in England*, 159, 175, 220, 226.

97. Friedrich Engels, *Die Lage der arbeitenden Klasse in England, nach eigner Anschauung und authentischen Quellen* (Stuttgart: Dietz, 1892), 152.

98. Engels, *Die Lage der arbeitenden Klasse in England*, 169, 216, 221.

99. Engels, *The Condition of the Working Class in England*, 181, 254.

100. Engels, *Die Lage der arbeitenden Klasse in England*, 175, 250.

101. Marx, *Das Kapital, erster Band*, 122; Marx, *Capital, Volume One*, 230–31.

102. Marx, *Das Kapital, erster Band*, 706, 733; Marx, *Capital, Volume One*, 741, 763.

103. Karl Marx, *Karl-Marx-Ausgabe: Werke-Schriften-Briefe, Band VI: Ökonomische Schriften, dritter Band*, ed. Hans-Joachim Lieber, *Das Kapital: Kritik der politischen Ökonomie, dritter Band, drittes Buch*, ed. Hans-Joachim Lieber and Benedikt Kautsky (Darmstadt: Wissenschaftliche Buchgesellschaft, 1964), 880; Marx, *Capital, Volume Three*, 352–53.

104. Karl Marx, *Theories of Surplus-Value, Part Three: Volume IV of Capital*, ed. S. W. Ryazanskaya and Richard Dixon, trans. Jack Cohen and S. W. Ryazanskaya (Moscow: Progress Publishers, 1971), 48–49.

105. David Ricardo, *The Principles of Political Economy and Taxation* (New York: Dover, 2004), 179, 181.

106. Jean Laplanche, *Problématiques III. La sublimation* (Paris: Presses Universitaires de France, 1980), 65–66; Jean Laplanche, "The Drive and Its Source-Object: Its Fate in the Transference," trans. Leslie Hill, in *Essays on Otherness* (New York: Routledge, 1999), 120; Johnston, *Time Driven*, 113, 137–39, 195, 359; Ilana Reiss-Schimmel, *La psychanalyse et l'argent* (Paris: Éditions Odile Jacob, 1993), 78.

107. Johnston, *Prolegomena to Any Future Materialism*, 2:73–183.

108. Marx, *A Contribution to the Critique of Political Economy*, 123–24; Marx, *Theories of Surplus-Value, Part One*, 374; Marx, *Theories of Surplus-Value, Part Three*, 253.

109. Christian Barrère, *Crise du système de crédit et capitalisme monopoliste d'état* (Paris: Economica, 1977), 36; Postone, *Time, Labor, and Social Domination*, 268.

110. Marx, *Capital, Volume Three*, 1020.

111. Marx, *Capital, Volume One*, 163–77.

112. Saul A. Kripke, *Naming and Necessity* (Cambridge, MA: Harvard University Press, 1972), 116–19, 123–27, 134–40, 142–43, 157.

113. Marx, *Grundrisse*, 262–63; Suzanne de Brunhoff, *Marx on Money*, 2nd ed., trans. Maurice J. Goldbloom (New York: Verso, 2015), 39; Michael Heinrich, *An Introduction to the Three Volumes of Karl Marx's Capital*, trans. Alexander Locascio (New York: Monthly Review Press, 2012), 85.

114. Marx, *Grundrisse* [Gr.], 144–45; Marx, *Grundrisse*, 233–34.

2. FROM CLOSED NEED TO INFINITE GREED 305

115. Saul A. Kripke, *Wittgenstein on Rules and Private Language: An Elementary Exposition* (Cambridge, MA: Harvard University Press, 1982), 79, 89, 109–10.
116. Harvey, *A Companion to Marx's Capital*, 257.
117. Brunhoff, *Marx on Money*, 40; Smith, *The Logic of Marx's Capital*, 231.
118. Adrian Johnston, "Capitalism's Implants: A Hegelian Theory of Failed Revolutions," *Crisis and Critique* 8, no. 2, special issue: "The Two-Hundredth Anniversary of Hegel's Philosophy of Right," ed. Agon Hamza and Frank Ruda (2021): 122–81.
119. Harvey, *A Companion to Marx's Capital*, 258; Frederic Jameson, *Representing Capital: A Commentary on Volume One* (London: Verso, 2011), 41.
120. Fenichel, "The Drive to Amass Wealth," 78.
121. Thomas Picketty, *Capital in the Twenty-First Century*, trans. Arthur Goldhammer (Cambridge, MA: Harvard University Press, 2014), 636.
122. Karl Marx, "On the Question of Free Trade," in *The Poverty of Philosophy* (Moscow: Foreign Languages Publishing House, 1956), 207–24.
123. Joseph Schumpeter, *Capitalism, Socialism, and Democracy* (New York: Harper & Row, 1975), 59, 81–86, 89, 104–5, 130, 134, 139, 142–46, 151–53, 156–57, 161–62.
124. Walter Benjamin, "Theories of German Fascism," in *Selected Writings*, vol. 2, part 1, *1927–1930*, ed. Michael W. Jennings, Howard Eiland, and Gary Smith, trans. Rodney Livingstone et al. (Cambridge, MA: Harvard University Press, 1999), 321.
125. Rosa Luxemburg, "The Junius Pamphlet: The Crisis of German Social Democracy," 1915, https://www.marxists.org/archive/luxemburg/1915/junius/.
126. Karl Marx, "Pauperism and Free Trade—The Approaching Commercial Crisis: Published November 1, 1852," in *Dispatches for the New York Tribune: Selected Journalism of Karl Marx*, ed. James Ledbetter (New York: Penguin, 2007), 163.
127. Schumpeter, *Capitalism, Socialism, and Democracy*, 144–45.
128. G. W. F. Hegel, *Lectures on Natural Right and Political Science: The First Philosophy of Right, Heidelberg 1817–1818, with Additions from the Lectures of 1818–1819*, trans. J. Michael Stewart and Peter C. Hodgson (Berkeley: University of California Press, 1995), §164 (306–8); Hegel, *Elements of the Philosophy of Right*, §345 (373–74); G. W. F. Hegel, *The Philosophy of History*, trans. J. Sibree (New York: Dover, 1956), 21.
129. Marx, *The Poverty of Philosophy*, 121.
130. Marx, *The Poverty of Philosophy*, 61, 68, 109, 120–23, 125–26, 173–74.
131. André Amar, "Essai psychanalytique sur l'argent," in *Psychanalyse de l'argent*, ed. Ernest Borneman, trans. Daniel Guérineau (Paris: Presses Universitaires de France, 1978), 375.
132. Karl Marx, *Theories of Surplus-Value, Part Two: Volume IV of Capital*, ed. S. Ryazanskaya, trans. Emile Burns (Moscow: Progress Publishers, 1968), 492; Anthony Brewer, *A Guide to Marx's Capital* (Cambridge: Cambridge University Press, 1984), 35; Serge Viderman, *De l'argent en psychanalyse et au-delà* (Paris: Presses Universitaires de France, 1992), 40–41; Michel Aglietta, "Monnaie, liquidité, confiance," in Michel Aglietta et al., *L'argent et la psychanalyse. Économie, dette et désir* (Paris: Éditions Campagne Première, 2017), 21, 24.
133. Harvey, *A Companion to Marx's Capital, Volume Two*, 172, 176.
134. Heinrich, *An Introduction to the Three Volumes of Karl Marx's Capital*, 123.
135. Harvey, *Marx, Capital, and the Madness of Economic Reason*, 21.
136. Harvey, *Marx, Capital, and the Madness of Economic Reason*, 173.
137. Marx, *Grundrisse* [Gr.], 181; Marx, *Grundrisse*, 270.
138. Marx, *Grundrisse* [Gr.], 231; Marx, *Grundrisse*, 325.
139. Marx, *Grundrisse* [Gr.], 240; Marx, *Grundrisse*, 334–35.
140. Marx, *Grundrisse* [Gr.], 247; Marx, *Grundrisse*, 341.
141. Marx, *A Contribution to the Critique of Political Economy*, 132.

142. Marx, *Das Kapital, erster Band*, 122; Marx, *Capital, Volume One*, 230.

143. Marx, *Das Kapital, erster Band*, 148; Marx, *Capital, Volume One*, 254.

144. Marx, *Das Kapital, erster Band*, 288; Marx, *Capital, Volume One*, 377.

145. Marx, *Capital, Volume One*, 252–53; Paul M. Sweezy, *The Theory of Capitalist Development: Principles of Marxian Political Economy*, 2nd ed. (New York: Monthly Review Press, 1956), 143; Braverman, *Labor and Monopoly Capital*, 206; Barrère, *Crise du système de crédit et capitalisme monopoliste d'état*, 29; Duncan Foley, *Understanding Capital: Marx's Economic Theory* (Cambridge, MA: Harvard University Press, 1986), 33–34; Heinrich, *An Introduction to the Three Volumes of Karl Marx's Capital*, 87, 104; Žižek, *Incontinence of the Void*, 153.

146. Marx, *Das Kapital, erster Band*, 149; Marx, *Capital, Volume One*, 255.

147. Marx, *Das Kapital, erster Band*, 150; Marx, *Capital, Volume One*, 256.

148. Tony Smith, "Hegel, Marx, and the Comprehension of Capitalism," in *Marx's Capital and Hegel's Logic: A Reexamination*, ed. Fred Mosley and Tony Smith (Chicago: Haymarket, 2015), 23.

149. Marx, *Capital, Volume One*, 255.

150. *SXI* [Fr.], 165; *SXI*, 181.

151. *SXI* [Fr.], 167; *SXI*, 184.

152. Marx, *Das Kapital, erster Band*, 287; Marx, *Capital, Volume One*, 375.

153. Henryk Grossmann, *The Law of Accumulation and Breakdown of the Capitalist System: Being Also a Theory of Crises*, trans. Jairus Banaji (London: Pluto, 1992), 126.

154. Marx, *Theories of Surplus-Value, Part One*, 282, 389; Marx, *Theories of Surplus-Value, Part Three*, 296; Sweezy, *The Theory of Capitalist Development*, 80; Braverman, *Labor and Monopoly Capital*, 301.

155. Marx, *Das Kapital, erster Band*, 147–48; Marx, *Capital, Volume One*, 254–55.

156. Marx, *Das Kapital, erster Band*, 704–5; Marx, *Capital, Volume One*, 739.

157. Kojin Karatani, *Transcritique: On Kant and Marx*, trans. Sabu Kohso (Cambridge, MA: MIT Press, 2003), 209–10.

158. Schumpeter, *Capitalism, Socialism, and Democracy*, 10–11, 30, 265; Shlomo Avineri, *The Social and Political Thought of Karl Marx* (Cambridge: Cambridge University Press, 1968), 110, 157; Postone, *Time, Labor, and Social Domination*, 267.

159. Roman Rosdolsky, *The Making of Marx's 'Capital'*, trans. Pete Burgess (London: Pluto, 1977), 156.

160. Max Weber, *The Protestant Ethic and the "Spirit" of Capitalism*, in *The Protestant Ethic and the "Spirit" of Capitalism and Other Writings*, ed. and trans. Peter Baehr and Gordon C. Wells (New York: Penguin, 2002), 13–14, 19, 26, 197; Max Weber, "Remarks on the Foregoing 'Reply' (1908) (Weber's second rejoinder to H. Karl Fischer)," in *The Protestant Ethic and the "Spirit" of Capitalism and Other Writings*, 233–34, 241–42; Max Weber, "Rebuttal of the Critique of the 'Spirit' of Capitalism, (1910) (Weber's first rejoinder to Felix Rachfahl)," in *The Protestant Ethic and the "Spirit" of Capitalism and Other Writings*, 262.

161. Weber, *The Protestant Ethic and the "Spirit" of Capitalism*, 122, 199–200; Weber, "Rebuttal of the Critique of the 'Spirit' of Capitalism," 258, 272; Max Weber, "Appendix II: Prefatory Remarks to Collected Essays in the Sociology of Religion," in *The Protestant Ethic and the "Spirit" of Capitalism and Other Writings*, 366.

162. Weber, *The Protestant Ethic and the "Spirit" of Capitalism*, 116–17, 122, 198, 200–1; Weber, "Remarks on the Foregoing 'Reply,'" 241; Harvey, *A Companion to Marx's Capital, Volume Two*, 234.

163. Marx, *Grundrisse* [Gr.], 231; Marx, *Grundrisse*, 325.

164. Marx, *Grundrisse* [Gr.], 143; Marx, *Grundrisse*, 232.

165. Karl Marx, *Zur Kritik der politischen Ökonomie*, 1859, http://www.mlwerke.de/me/me13/me13_003.htm; Marx, *A Contribution to the Critique of Political Economy*, 129.

166. Marx, *A Contribution to the Critique of Political Economy*, 130.

167. Marx, *Theories of Surplus-Value, Part Three*, 448.
168. Viderman, *De l'argent en psychanalyse et au-delà*, 106.
169. Marx, *Das Kapital, erster Band*, 122; Marx, *Capital, Volume One*, 231.
170. Marx, *Theories of Surplus-Value, Part One*, 282, 326.
171. Avrane, *Petite psychanalyse de l'argent*, 11.
172. *SXVI*, 284–85.
173. Marx, *Theories of Surplus-Value, Part One*, 370.
174. Marx, *Zur Kritik der politischen Ökonomie*; Marx, *A Contribution to the Critique of Political Economy*, 54.
175. Sweezy, *The Theory of Capitalist Development*, 139.
176. Marx, *Theories of Surplus-Value, Part Two*, 483; Cohen, *Karl Marx's Theory of History*, 302–3.
177. Avrane, *Petite psychanalyse de l'argent*, 59.
178. Marx, *Theories of Surplus-Value, Part Three*, 120; Michał Kalecki, *Theory of Economic Dynamics: An Essay on Long-Run Changes in Capitalist Economy* (New York: Monthly Review Press, 1968), 91–92, 94–95; Ollman, *Alienation*, 155; Smith, *The Logic of Marx's Capital*, 241.
179. Marx, *Das Kapital, erster Band*, 707; Marx, *Capital, Volume One*, 741.
180. Marx, *Theories of Surplus-Value, Part One*, 282.
181. Karl Marx, *Karl-Marx-Ausgabe: Werke-Schriften-Briefe, Band V, Das Kapital: Kritik der politischen Ökonomie, zweites Buch, Der Zirkulationsprozess des Kapitals*, ed. Hans-Joachim Lieber (Darmstadt: Wissenschaftliche Buchgesellschaft, 1963), 112–13; Karl Marx, *Capital: A Critique of Political Economy, Volume Two*, trans. David Fernbach (New York: Penguin, 1978), 199.
182. Weber, "Appendix II: Prefatory Remarks to *Collected Essays in the Sociology of Religion*," 359.
183. *SXVI*, 109.
184. Marx, *Das Kapital, dritter Band, drittes Buch*, 879; Marx, *Capital, Volume Three*, 351–52.
185. Marx, *Zur Kritik der politischen Ökonomie*; Marx, *A Contribution to the Critique of Political Economy*, 134.
186. Marx, *Theories of Surplus-Value, Part One*, 270; Marx, *Theories of Surplus-Value, Part Three*, 54–55.
187. Marx, *Theories of Surplus-Value, Part Two*, 495, 502–3, 509, 534, 547, 552; Joan Robinson, *An Essay on Marxian Economics*, 2nd ed. (London: Macmillan, 1966), 29, 49; David Harvey, *The Limits to Capital* (London: Verso, 2006), 29; Silvia Lippi, "Introduction: Marx à Cerisy," in *Marx, Lacan. L'acte révolutionnaire et l'acte analytique*, ed. Sylvia Lippi and Patrick Landman (Toulouse: Érès, 2013), 18; Jean-Jacques Rassial, "Intérêt et désir: Marx et Lacan," in *Marx, Lacan*, 204–5.
188. Weber, *The Protestant Ethic and the "Spirit" of Capitalism*, 12, 19–20, 23–24, 28, 115–16; Max Weber, "A Final Rebuttal of Rachfahl's Critique of the 'Spirit of Capitalism' (1910)," in *The Protestant Ethic and the "Spirit" of Capitalism and Other Writings*, 293–94; Weber, "Appendix II: Prefatory Remarks to *Collected Essays in the Sociology of Religion*," 359; Luxemburg, *The Accumulation of Capital*, 264, 407; Norman O. Brown, *Life Against Death: The Psychoanalytical Meaning of History*, 2nd ed. (Hanover, NH: University Press of New England, 1985), 303; Becker, *Marxian Political Economy*, 185, 302; Heinrich, *An Introduction to the Three Volumes of Karl Marx's Capital*, 15–16; Harvey, *A Companion to Marx's Capital, Volume Two*, 80–81.
189. Marx, *Theories of Surplus-Value, Part One*, 282–83.
190. Meek, *Studies in the Labor Theory of Value*, 58; Paul A. Baran and Paul M. Sweezy, *Monopoly Capital: An Essay on the American Economic and Social Order* (New York: Monthly Review Press, 1966), 44.
191. Sweezy, *The Theory of Capitalist Development*, 339.
192. Rosdolsky, *The Making of Marx's 'Capital,'* 155, 187; Gilles Dostaler and Bernard Maris, *Capitalisme et pulsion de mort* (Paris: Fayard, 2010), 69.

193. Postone, *Time, Labor, and Social Domination*, 342; Smith, "Hegel, Marx and the Comprehension of Capitalism," 20–21.

194. Braverman, *Labor and Monopoly Capital*, 265–66.

195. Byung-Chul Han, *Capitalism and the Death Drive*, trans. Daniel Steuer (Cambridge: Polity, 2021), 104, 106.

196. Sweezy, *The Theory of Capitalist Development*, 228–29.

197. Marx, *Theories of Surplus-Value, Part One*, 270; Karatani, *Transcritique*, 211, 215; Jameson, *Representing Capital*, 41, 64.

198. Karatani, *Transcritique*, 205.

199. Sebag, *Marxisme et structuralisme*, 67.

200. *SVII*, 110; *SXX*, 112; Jacques Lacan, "The Subversion of the Subject and the Dialectic of Desire in the Freudian Unconscious," in *Écrits*, 680; Lacan, "Television," 24; Johnston, *Time Driven*, 206–7, 214.

201. Karl Marx and Friedrich Engels, *The Communist Manifesto*, trans. Samuel Moore, in *Karl Marx: Selected Writings*, ed. David McLellan (Oxford: Oxford University Press, 1977), 223.

202. *SXVI*, 285.

203. Jacques Lacan, "Radiophonie," in *Autres écrits*, 435.

204. Karl Marx, *Economic and Philosophical Manuscripts*, in *Early Writings*, trans. Rodney Livingstone and Gregor Benton (New York: Penguin, 1992), 375–79; Agnes Heller, *The Theory of Need in Marx* (London: Allison & Busby, 1976), 52; Viderman, *De l'argent en psychanalyse et au-delà*, 119; Reiss-Schimmel, *La psychanalyse et l'argent*, 75, 78, 247–48, 265–66.

205. Marx and Engels, *The Communist Manifesto*, 222–24.

206. Ollman, *Alienation*, 77–78.

207. Marx, *A Contribution to the Critique of Political Economy*, 20–21; Marx, *Grundrisse*, 496.

208. Karl Marx, *Der achtzehnte Brumaire des Louis Bonaparte*, in *Karl-Marx-Ausgabe: Werke-Schriften-Briefe, Band III: Politische Schriften, erster Band*, ed. Hans-Joachim Lieber (Darmstadt: Wissenschaftliche Buchgesellschaft, 1960), 271; Karl Marx, *The Eighteenth Brumaire of Louis Bonaparte*, trans. Ben Fowkes, in *Surveys from Exile: Political Writings*, ed. David Fernbach (Harmondsworth: Penguin, 1973), 2:146.

209. Jean-Paul Sartre, *Search for a Method*, trans. Hazel E. Barnes (New York: Vintage, 1968), 41, 60–65.

210. Tomšič, *The Capitalist Unconscious*, 123.

211. Marx, *Grundrisse*, 222–23.

212. Tomšič, *The Capitalist Unconscious*, 123–24.

213. Smith, *The Wealth of Nations, Books I–III*, 269.

214. Reiss-Schimmel, *La psychanalyse et l'argent*, 267; Tomšič, *The Capitalist Unconscious*, 138.

215. G. W. F. Hegel, *Science of Logic*, trans. A. V. Miller (London: George Allen & Unwin, 1969), 336, 369–70; G. W. F. Hegel, *The Encyclopedia Logic: Part I of the Encyclopedia of the Philosophical Sciences with the Zusätze*, trans. T. F. Geraets, W. A. Suchting, and H. S. Harris (Indianapolis, IN: Hackett, 1991), §108 (171); G. W. F. Hegel, *Lectures on Logic: Berlin, 1831*, trans. Clark Butler (Bloomington: Indiana University Press, 2008), §109 (125–26).

216. Tomšič, *The Capitalist Unconscious*, 124.

217. Marx, *Grundrisse*, 92.

218. *SXI*, 169, 176, 178–80; Johnston, *Time Driven*, 20, 168, 191–92, 203, 215, 372–74.

219. Tomšič, *The Capitalist Unconscious*, 124–25.

220. Johnston, *Prolegomena to Any Future Materialism*, 2:73–95.

221. Marx, *Grundrisse* [Gr.], 133–34; Marx, *Grundrisse*, 222–23.

222. Mandel, *Late Capitalism*, 25.

223. Grossmann, *The Law of Accumulation and Breakdown of the Capitalist System*, 61.

2. FROM CLOSED NEED TO INFINITE GREED 309

224. John Maynard Keynes, *The General Theory of Employment, Interest, and Money* (New York: Harcourt, Brace & World, 1962), 159.
225. Tomšič, *The Capitalist Unconscious*, 231.
226. Tomšič, *The Capitalist Unconscious*, 231.
227. Tomšič, *The Capitalist Unconscious*, 233.
228. Tomšič, *The Capitalist Unconscious*, 234.
229. Tomšič, *The Capitalist Unconscious*, 233.
230. Tomšič, *The Capitalist Unconscious*, 231–32, 235, 237–38.
231. Tomšič, *The Capitalist Unconscious*, 238.
232. *SVII*, 139; *SXI*, 268; *SXVI*, 224–25, 249.
233. Marx, *A Contribution to the Critique of Political Economy*, 21.
234. *SE* 14:75, 90; *SE* 19:30, 46.
235. Johnston, *Irrepressible Truth*, 135–50.
236. *SV*, 72–73.
237. *SVI*, 106–7.
238. *SXVI*, 172; Jacques Lacan, "Acte de fondation," in *Autres écrits*, 237.
239. Jacques Lacan, "Presentation on Psychical Causality," in *Écrits*, 157; *SVII*, 206.
240. *SXVII* [Fr.], 81; *SXVII*, 71.
241. *SXIV*, 199.
242. *SXVI*, 209.
243. *SVI*, 313; *SXVI*, 21.
244. *SXVI*, 285.
245. Johnston, *Adventures in Transcendental Materialism*, 65–107; Adrian Johnston, "Lacan's Endgame: Philosophy, Science, and Religion in the Final Seminars," *Crisis and Critique* 6, no. 1, special issue: "Lacan: Psychoanalysis, Philosophy, Politics," ed. Agon Hamza and Frank Ruda (2019): 156–87.
246. *SXXV*, 12/20/77; Jacques Lacan, "L'étourdit," in *Autres écrits*, 494.
247. Karl Marx, *Critique of Hegel's Doctrine of the State*, in *Early Writings*, 161; Marx, *Grundrisse*, 85, 88, 100–2, 104–5, 142–46, 157, 164, 331, 449–50, 831–32; Marx, *A Contribution to the Critique of Political Economy*, 30–31, 49; Marx, *Capital, Volume One*, 739, 909; Marx, *Capital, Volume Two*, 185; Marx, *Capital, Volume Three*, 275, 596–97, 603; Ernest Mandel, *The Formation of the Economic Thought of Karl Marx: 1843 to Capital*, trans. Brian Pearce (New York: Monthly Review Press, 1971), 47; Heinrich, *An Introduction to the Three Volumes of Karl Marx's Capital*, 49.
248. *SXIV*, 265–67; *SXVI*, 16–18, 30, 64–65.
249. Jacques Lacan, "Subversion du sujet et dialectique du désir dans l'inconscient freudien," in *Écrits* (Paris: Éditions du Seuil, 1966), 827; Lacan, "The Subversion of the Subject and the Dialectic of Desire in the Freudian Unconscious," 700.
250. Martin, *Argent et psychanalyse*, 36, 118, 139–40; Alain Vanier, "Some Remarks on the Symptom and the Social Link: Lacan with Marx," trans. John Monahan, *JPCS: Journal for the Psychoanalysis of Culture and Society* 6, no. 1 (2001): 43; Pierre Bruno, *Lacan, passeur de Marx. L'invention du symptôme* (Toulouse: Érès, 2010), 321–22.
251. Lacan, "Radiophonie," 435.
252. *SXVII*, 79; Jacques Lacan, "Discours à l'École freudienne de Paris," in *Autres écrits*, 278; Lacan, "Radiophonie," 435; Jacques Lacan, "Postface au Séminaire XI," in *Autres écrits*, 505; Jacques Lacan, "Un homme et une femme," *Bulletin de l'Association freudienne* 54 (September 1993): 14; Lacan, "Du discours psychanalytique," in *Lacan in Italia, 1953–1978* (Milan: La Salamandra, 1978), 46, 49, 51; Lacan, "La troisième," 189, 199–200; Jacques Lacan, "Journées d'étude des cartels de l'École freudienne: Séance de cloture," *Lettres de l'École freudienne* 18 (1976): 268.

253. *SXVI*, 16–18, 29–30, 64–65, 172; *SXVII*, 107–8; Slavoj Žižek, *The Sublime Object of Ideology* (London: Verso, 1989), 50–53; Lippi, "Introduction," 18–19; André Michels, "Travail, aliénation, valeur: Lacan avec Marx," in *Marx, Lacan*, 183.

254. Pierre Bruno, "Portrait de Lacan par Marx," in *Marx, Lacan*, 157–59.

255. Lacan, "Radiophonie," 434.

256. *SXVI*, 103; Jacques Lacan, "D'une réforme dans son trou," *Pas-tout Lacan*, http://ecole-lacanienne .net/wp-content/uploads/2016/04/1969-02-03.pdf; Jacques Lacan, "Jacques Lacan à l'École belge de psychanalyse," *Quarto* 5 (1981): 11, 20; Amar, "Essai psychanalytique sur l'argent," 374–75.

257. Vanier, "Some Remarks on the Symptom and the Social Link," 43.

258. *SXVIII*, 49–50.

259. *SXVI*, 45–46; Jacques Lacan, "Responses to Students of Philosophy Concerning the Object of Psychoanalysis," trans. Jeffrey Mehlman, in *Television/A Challenge to the Psychoanalytic Establishment*, 111.

260. Jacques Lacan, "En guise de conclusion," *Lettres de l'École freudienne* 8 (1971): 211–12.

261. *SXVII*, 79; Michels, "Travail, aliénation, valeur," 181; Martin Bakero Carrasco, "Symptôme et capitalisme: Excès et nécessité dans la production du sujet et la culture," in *Marx, Lacan*, 243.

262. Dostaler and Maris, *Capitalisme et pulsion de mort*, 112.

263. *SXVII* [Fr.], 93; *SXVII*, 81; Marcel Drach, "Les deux fétichismes de l'argent," in *Marx, Lacan*, 268.

264. *SXVI*, 333; *SXIX*, 39–40; Presskorn-Thygesen and Bjerg, "The Falling Rate of Enjoyment," 206, 216.

265. Lacan, "Radiophonie," 434.

266. Mandel, *Late Capitalism*, 505.

267. *SXVI*, 29.

268. Han, *Capitalism and the Death Drive*, 122.

269. *SXVII* [Fr.], 19; *SXVII*, 20.

270. *SXVII* [Fr.], 19; *SXVII*, 20.

271. Louis Althusser, "The Object of *Capital*," in Louis Althusser, Étienne Balibar, Roger Establet, Pierre Macherey, and Jacques Rancière, *Reading Capital: The Complete Edition*, trans. Ben Brewster and David Fernbach (London: Verso, 2015), 224–25, 228–30, 237–38, 273; Ollman, *Alienation*, 168–69.

272. Ollman, *Alienation*, 196.

273. Meek, *Studies in the Labor Theory of Value*, 184; Michio Morishima, *Marx's Economics: A Dual Theory of Value and Growth* (Cambridge: Cambridge University Press, 1973), 6.

274. *SXVII*, 20.

275. Lacan, "Television," 30.

276. *SXVII*, 107.

277. *SXVIII*, 49–50, 164–65; *SXIX*, 1/6/72.

278. *SIII*, 132–33.

279. Aristotle, *Nicomachean Ethics*, trans. Terrence Irwin (Indianapolis, IN: Hackett, 1999), book I, 1095b (4), book IX, 1170b (150).

280. G. W. F. Hegel, *Phenomenology of Spirit*, trans. A. V. Miller (Oxford: Oxford University Press, 1977), 111–19.

281. *SXVII*, 107.

282. *SXVII* [Fr.], 123; *SXVII*, 107–8.

283. Adrian Johnston, "Misfelt Feelings: Unconscious Affect Between Psychoanalysis, Neuroscience, and Philosophy," in Adrian Johnston and Catherine Malabou, *Self and Emotional Life: Philosophy, Psychoanalysis, and Neuroscience* (New York: Columbia University Press, 2013), 158–61.

284. Theodor W. Adorno, "Sociology and Psychology, Part I," trans. Irving N. Wohlfarth, *New Left Review* 46 (November/December 1967): 73–74.

285. *SXXII*, 4/8/75.

286. *SXVII* [Fr.], 84; *SXVII*, 73.

287. Martin, *Argent et psychanalyse*, 145; Vanier, "Some Remarks on the Symptom and the Social Link," 44.

288. Marx, *Grundrisse* [Gr.], 133–34; Marx, *Grundrisse*, 222–23.

289. *SXVII* [Fr.], 207; *SXVII*, 177.

290. *SXIII*, 4/20/66.

291. Marx, *Grundrisse*, 405.

292. Lacan, "Radiophonie," 424.

293. Smith, *The Wealth of Nations, Books I–III*, 358–59, 512; Adam Smith, *The Wealth of Nations, Books IV–V*, ed. Andrew Skinner (New York: Penguin, 1999), 297–98, 302–4.

294. Herbert Marcuse, "On Hedonism," in *Negations*, 185, 188, 192.

3. THE SELF-CLEANING FETISH: REPRESSION UNDER THE SHADOW OF FICTITIOUS CAPITAL

1. Paul Ricoeur, "Consciousness and the Unconscious," trans. Willis Domingo, in *The Conflict of Interpretations: Essays in Hermeneutics*, ed. Don Ihde (London: Continuum, 2004), 97; Paul Ricoeur, "Psychoanalysis and the Movement of Contemporary Culture," trans. Willis Domingo, in *The Conflict of Interpretations*, 143–47.

2. Otto Fenichel, "Psychoanalysis as the Nucleus of a Future Dialectical-Materialist Psychology," ed. Suzette H. Annin and Hanna Fenichel, trans. Olga Barsis, *American Imago* 24, no. 4 (Winter 1967): 302; Otto Fenichel, "The Drive to Amass Wealth," *Psychoanalytic Quarterly* 7 (1938): 74, 94; Herbert Marcuse, *Eros and Civilization: A Philosophical Inquiry Into Freud* (Boston: Beacon, 1974), 11–12.

3. Wilhelm Reich, *Dialectical Materialism and Psychoanalysis* (London: Socialist Reproduction, 1972), 25, 27, 30, 38–42; Fenichel, "Psychoanalysis as the Nucleus of a Future Dialectical-Materialist Psychology," 297, 302–4, 309; Fenichel, "The Drive to Amass Wealth," 70–71; Marcuse, *Eros and Civilization*, xxvii–xxviii, 5–6, 16, 34–37, 40, 44–45, 87–88, 132–33.

4. *SE* 12:131–33.

5. *SE* 1:243, 273; *SE* 4:200; *SE* 5:403; *SE* 9:168, 173–74; *SE* 11:106; *SE* 12:187–90, 196–97; *SE* 17:72–74, 76, 82, 127–28, 130–32.

6. Sandor Ferenczi, "The Ontogenesis of the Interest in Money," in *First Contributions to Psycho-Analysis*, trans. Ernest Jones (New York: Routledge, 1994), 320–21, 327; Sandor Ferenczi, "«Pecunia—olet» (L'argent—a une odeur)," in *Psychanalyse de l'argent*, ed. Ernest Borneman, trans. Daniel Guérineau (Paris: Presses Universitaires de France, 1978), 106–9; Bernhard Dattner, "Or et excrément," in *Psychanalyse de l'argent*, 91–93; Isador H. Coriat, "Remarques sur les traits de caractère anaux de l'instinct capitaliste," in *Psychanalyse de l'argent*, 103–5; Isador H. Coriat, "Traits de caractère analérotiques chez Shylock," in *Psychanalyse de l'argent*, 115–20; Fenichel, "The Drive to Amass Wealth," 72, 75, 81–82, 94–95; Norman O. Brown, *Life Against Death: The Psychoanalytical Meaning of History*, 2nd ed. (Hanover, NH: University Press of New England, 1985), 288, 292–93; David V. Forrest, "Further Developmental Stages of the Interest in Money," *American Journal of Psychoanalysis* 50, no. 4 (1990): 320, 332–33; Patrick Avrane, *Petite psychanalyse de l'argent* (Paris: Presses Universitaires de France, 2015), 19, 232.

7. Jacques Lacan, "Seminar on 'The Purloined Letter,'" in *Écrits: The First Complete Edition in English*, trans. Bruce Fink (New York: Norton, 2006), 27.

8. Frederic Jameson, "An American Utopia," in *An American Utopia: Dual Power and the Universal Army*, ed. Slavoj Žižek (New York: Verso, 2016), 91.

312   3. THE SELF-CLEANING FETISH

9. *SI*, 191; *SIII*, 46, 60; *SXIV*, 82.

10. Karl Marx, *Capital: A Critique of Political Economy, Volume One*, trans. Ben Fowkes (New York: Penguin, 1976), 163–64.

11. David Harvey, *Marx, Capital, and the Madness of Economic Reason* (London: Profile, 2017), 66, 69, 84–85.

12. Karl Marx, *Karl-Marx-Ausgabe: Werke-Schriften-Briefe, Band IV: Ökonomische Schriften, erster Band*, ed. Hans-Joachim Lieber, *Das Kapital: Kritik der politischen Ökonomie, erster Band* (Darmstadt: Wissenschaftliche Buchgesellschaft, 1962), 52; Marx, *Capital, Volume One*, 168–69.

13. Karl Marx, *Grundrisse: Foundations of the Critique of Political Economy (Rough Draft)*, trans. Martin Nicolaus (New York: Penguin, 1973), 100–2, 105, 107; Marx, *Capital, Volume One*, 102–3.

14. Karl Marx and Friedrich Engels, *Die deutsche Ideologie* (Berlin: Dietz, 1953), 22; Karl Marx and Friedrich Engels, *The German Ideology* (Amherst, MA: Prometheus, 1998), 42.

15. Adam Smith, *The Wealth of Nations, Books I–III*, ed. Andrew Skinner (New York: Penguin, 1986), 291, 294, 334; David Ricardo, *The Principles of Political Economy and Taxation* (New York: Dover, 2004), 5–7, 17–18, 23–24, 48, 189.

16. Marx, *Das Kapital, erster Band*, 48; Marx, *Capital, Volume One*, 165.

17. Marx, *Das Kapital, erster Band*, 51; Marx, *Capital, Volume One*, 167–68.

18. Marx, *Capital, Volume One*, 187.

19. Marx, *Grundrisse*, 156–58, 163–65, 239–40; Marx, *Capital, Volume One*, 165–66.

20. Bertell Ollman, *Alienation: Marx's Conception of Man in Capitalist Society* (Cambridge: Cambridge University Press, 1971), 224.

21. Ben Fine and Alfredo Saad-Filho, *Marx's Capital*, 6th ed. (London: Pluto, 2016), 26; Duncan K. Foley, *Understanding Capital: Marx's Economic Theory* (Cambridge: Harvard University Press, 1986), 29.

22. Karl Marx, *Critique of Hegel's Doctrine of the State*, in *Early Writings*, trans. Rodney Livingstone and Gregor Benton (New York: Penguin, 1992), 62–63, 80, 87–90, 167, 184; Karl Marx, "A Contribution to the Critique of Hegel's Philosophy of Right. Introduction," in *Early Writings*, 243–45; Karl Marx, "Excerpts from James Mill's *Elements of Political Economy*," in *Early Writings*, 260–61; Karl Marx, *Economic and Philosophical Manuscripts*, in *Early Writings*, 322–34, 342.

23. Marx, *Critique of Hegel's Doctrine of the State*, 161; Marx, *Grundrisse*, 85, 88, 100–2, 104–5, 142–46, 157, 164, 331, 449–50, 831–32; Marx, *Capital, Volume One*, 739, 909; Karl Marx, *Capital: A Critique of Political Economy, Volume Two*, trans. David Fernbach (New York: Penguin, 1978), 185; Karl Marx, *Capital: A Critique of Political Economy, Volume Three*, trans. David Fernbach (New York: Penguin, 1981), 275, 596–97, 603; Herbert Marcuse, "The Concept of Essence," in *Negations: Essays in Critical Theory*, trans. Jeremy J. Shapiro (Boston: Beacon, 1968), 71; Moishe Postone, *Time, Labor, and Social Domination: A Reinterpretation of Marx's Critical Theory* (Cambridge: Cambridge University Press, 1993), 215.

24. Shlomo Avineri, *The Social and Political Thought of Karl Marx* (Cambridge: Cambridge University Press, 1968), 179; Fine and Saad-Filho, *Marx's Capital*, 23–25; G. A. Cohen, *Karl Marx's Theory of History: A Defense* (Princeton, NJ: Princeton University Press, 1978), 331; Anthony Brewer, *A Guide to Marx's Capital* (Cambridge: Cambridge University Press, 1984), 27.

25. Marx, "A Contribution to the Critique of Hegel's Philosophy of Right. Introduction," 244.

26. Postone, *Time, Labor, and Social Domination*, 6, 62; Ricardo Bellofiore, "Lost in Translation? Once Again on the Marx-Hegel Connection," in *Marx's Capital and Hegel's Logic: A Reexamination*, ed. Fred Mosley and Tony Smith (Chicago: Haymarket, 2015), 177–78, 187.

27. I. I. Rubin, *Essays on Marx's Theory of Value*, trans. Miloš Samardžija and Fredy Perlman (Detroit: Black & Red, 1972), 59.

3. THE SELF-CLEANING FETISH 313

28. Karl Marx, *Zur Kritik der politischen Ökonomie*, 1859, http://www.mlwerke.de/me/me13/me13 _003.htm; Karl Marx, *A Contribution to the Critique of Political Economy*, ed. Maurice Dobb, trans. S. W. Ryazanskaya (New York: International Publishers, 1970), 49.

29. Frederic Jameson, *Representing Capital: A Commentary on Volume One* (London: Verso, 2011), 44.

30. Karl Marx, "Zur Kritik der Hegelschen Rechtsphilosophie. Einleitung," in *Karl-Marx-Ausgabe: Werke-Schriften-Briefe, Band I: Frühe Schriften, erster Band*, ed. Hans-Joachim Lieber and Peter Furth (Darmstadt: Wissenschaftliche Buchgesellschaft, 1962), 488; Marx, "A Contribution to the Critique of Hegel's Philosophy of Right. Introduction," 244; Lucio Colletti, "Marxism: Science or Revolution," in *From Rousseau to Lenin: Studies in Ideology and Society*, trans. John Merrington and Judith White (New York: Monthly Review Press, 1972), 232–33.

31. Fine and Saad-Filho, *Marx's Capital*, 4.

32. Michael Heinrich, *An Introduction to the Three Volumes of Karl Marx's Capital*, trans. Alexander Locascio (New York: Monthly Review Press, 2012), 73–75, 78.

33. Marx, *Das Kapital, erster Band*, 50; Marx, *Capital, Volume One*, 167.

34. Ollman, *Alienation*, 245; Cohen, *Karl Marx's Theory of History*, 330–31.

35. Heinrich, *An Introduction to the Three Volumes of Karl Marx's Capital*, 156.

36. Marx, *Das Kapital, erster Band*, 74; Marx, *Capital, Volume One*, 187.

37. Fine and Saad-Filho, *Marx's Capital*, 130; Brewer, *A Guide to Marx's Capital*, 157.

38. Michio Morishima, *Marx's Economics: A Dual Theory of Value and Growth* (Cambridge: Cambridge University Press, 1973), 45, 86.

39. Marx, *Grundrisse*, 767; Marx, *Capital, Volume Three*, 267, 400; Karl Marx, *Theories of Surplus-Value, Part Three: Volume IV of Capital*, ed. S. W. Ryazanskaya and Richard Dixon, trans. Jack Cohen and S. W. Ryazanskaya (Moscow: Progress Publishers, 1971), 459; Roman Rosdolsky, *The Making of Marx's 'Capital,'* trans. Pete Burgess (London: Pluto, 1977), 369–70; Brewer, *A Guide to Marx's Capital*, 129; Foley, *Understanding Capital*, 91–92, 104; David Harvey, *A Companion to Marx's Capital* (London: Verso, 2010), 131; Patrick Murray, "The Secret of Capital's Self-Valorization 'Laid Bare': How Hegel Helped Marx to Overturn Ricardo's Theory of Profit," in *Marx's Capital and Hegel's Logic*, 189–90; Mario L. Robles-Báez, "Dialectics of Labour and Value-Form in Marx's *Capital*: A Reconstruction," in *Marx's Capital and Hegel's Logic*, 306.

40. Harvey, *A Companion to Marx's Capital*, 55.

41. Joan Robinson, *An Essay on Marxian Economics*, 2nd ed. (London: Macmillan, 1966), 16.

42. Rudolf Hilferding, *Finance Capital: A Study of the Latest Phase of Capitalist Development*, ed. Tom Bottomore, trans. Morris Watnick and Sam Gordon (London: Routledge & Kegan Paul, 1981), 150.

43. Hilferding, *Finance Capital*, 149–50.

44. Karl Marx, *Karl-Marx-Ausgabe: Werke-Schriften-Briefe, Band VI: Ökonomische Schriften, dritter Band*, ed. Hans-Joachim Lieber, *Das Kapital: Kritik der politischen Ökonomie, dritter Band, drittes Buch*, ed. Hans-Joachim Lieber and Benedikt Kautsky (Darmstadt: Wissenschaftliche Buchgesellschaft, 1964), 146; Marx, *Capital, Volume Three*, 506.

45. Marx, *Das Kapital, dritter Band, drittes Buch*, 145–146; Marx, *Capital, Volume Three*, 506.

46. Marx, *Capital, Volume Three*, 503–4; Ollman, *Alienation*, 199.

47. Marx, *Capital, Volume One*, 254–55; Karl Marx, *Theories of Surplus-Value, Part One: Volume IV of Capital*, ed. S. Ryazanskaya, trans. Emile Burns (Moscow: Progress Publishers, 1963), 270, 282, 389; Marx, *Theories of Surplus-Value, Part Three*, 296.

48. Marx, *Theories of Surplus-Value, Part One*, 108, 408; Marx, *Theories of Surplus-Value, Part Three*, 492.

49. Smith, *The Wealth of Nations, Books I–III*, 151–52.

50. Marx, *Capital, Volume Three*, 506, 968; David Harvey, *The Limits to Capital* (London: Verso, 2006), 258; David Harvey, *A Companion to Marx's Capital, Volume Two* (London: Verso, 2013), 200.

51. Marx, *Capital, Volume Three*, 506.

52. Rubin, *Essays on Marx's Theory of Value*, 21; Suzanne de Brunhoff, *Marx on Money*, 2nd ed., trans. Maurice J. Goldbloom (New York: Verso, 2015), 86; Christian Barrère, *Crise du système de crédit et capitalisme monopoliste d'état* (Paris: Economica, 1977), 27; Ben Fine and Laurence Harris, *Rereading Capital* (New York: Columbia University Press, 1979), 87; Harvey, *The Limits to Capital*, 72, 272; Harvey, *A Companion to Marx's Capital, Volume Two*, 175; Harvey, *Marx, Capital, and the Madness of Economic Reason*, 18–20, 22–23.

53. Friedrich Engels, "Outlines of a Critique of Political Economy," in *The Young Hegelians: An Anthology*, ed. Lawrence S. Stepelevich (Amherst, MA: Humanity Books, 1999), 289.

54. Cohen, *Karl Marx's Theory of History*, 124.

55. Marx, *Capital, Volume Three*, 459–60, 464–65, 473.

56. Marx, *Capital, Volume Three*, 517; John Maynard Keynes, *The General Theory of Employment, Interest, and Money* (New York: Harcourt, Brace & World, 1962), 369; James F. Becker, *Marxian Political Economy: An Outline* (Cambridge: Cambridge University Press, 1977), 107; Harvey, *Marx, Capital, and the Madness of Economic Reason*, 39, 42.

57. Harvey, *The Limits to Capital*, 72; Harvey, *A Companion to Marx's Capital, Volume Two*, 171, 183; Fine and Saad-Filho, *Marx's Capital*, 126; Brewer, *A Guide to Marx's Capital*, 156; Heinrich, *An Introduction to the Three Volumes of Karl Marx's Capital*, 156.

58. Marx, *Das Kapital, dritter Band, drittes Buch*, 156; Marx, *Capital, Volume Three*, 515.

59. Karl Marx, *Theorien über den Mehrwert, dritter Band*, ed. Karl Kautsky (Stuttgart: Dietz, 1910), 522; Marx, *Theories of Surplus-Value, Part Three*, 453.

60. Foley, *Understanding Capital*, 109.

61. Marx, *Das Kapital, dritter Band, drittes Buch*, 667; Marx, *Capital, Volume Three*, 955.

62. Rudolf Hilferding, *Das Finanzkapital: Eine Studie über die jüngste Entwicklung des Kapitalismus* (Berlin: Dietz, 1947), 296; Hilferding, *Finance Capital*, 235.

63. Mark Meaney, "Capital Breeds: Interest-Bearing Capital as Purely Abstract Form," in *Marx's Capital and Hegel's Logic*, 47, 49.

64. Enrique Dussel, *Towards an Unknown Marx: A Commentary on the Manuscripts of 1861–63*, ed. Fred Mosley, trans. Yolanda Angulo (New York: Routledge, 2001), 137.

65. Dussel, *Towards an Unknown Marx*, 134–36.

66. Heinrich, *An Introduction to the Three Volumes of Karl Marx's Capital*, 159.

67. Brewer, *A Guide to Marx's Capital*, 159.

68. Foley, *Understanding Capital*, 112.

69. Harvey, *A Companion to Marx's Capital, Volume Two*, 176; Harvey, *Marx, Capital, and the Madness of Economic Reason*, 174.

70. Marx, *Das Kapital, dritter Band, drittes Buch*, 157; Marx, *Capital, Volume Three*, 515–16.

71. Marx, *Theorien über den Mehrwert, dritter Band*, 524; Marx, *Theories of Surplus-Value, Part Three*, 453.

72. Marx, *Capital, Volume Three*, 517; Harvey, *A Companion to Marx's Capital, Volume Two*, 185.

73. Marx, *Das Kapital, dritter Band, drittes Buch*, 249; Marx, *Capital, Volume Three*, 596.

74. Marx, *Capital, Volume Three*, 609.

75. Brewer, *A Guide to Marx's Capital*, 51.

76. Marx, *Das Kapital, dritter Band, drittes Buch*, 158; Marx, *Capital, Volume Three*, 517.

77. Marx, *Capital, Volume Three*, 516–17, 523–24.

78. Marx, *Das Kapital, dritter Band, drittes Buch*, 683; Marx, *Capital, Volume Three*, 968.

79. Marx, *Das Kapital, dritter Band, drittes Buch*, 249; Marx, *Capital, Volume Three*, 596.

3. THE SELF-CLEANING FETISH ❦ 315

80. Hilferding, *Das Finanzkapital*, 345; Hilferding, *Finance Capital*, 277.

81. Harvey, *A Companion to Marx's Capital, Volume Two*, 242–43.

82. Marx, "Excerpts from James Mill's *Elements of Political Economy*," 265.

83. Barrère, *Crise du système de crédit et capitalisme monopoliste d'état*, 102.

84. Heinrich, *An Introduction to the Three Volumes of Karl Marx's Capital*, 159, 165.

85. Hilferding, *Finance Capital*, 208.

86. Foley, *Understanding Capital*, 112.

87. Heinrich, *An Introduction to the Three Volumes of Karl Marx's Capital*, 156.

88. Heinrich, *An Introduction to the Three Volumes of Karl Marx's Capital*, 156.

89. Henryk Grossmann, *The Law of Accumulation and Breakdown of the Capitalist System: Being Also a Theory of Crises*, trans. Jairus Banaji (London: Pluto, 1992), 86–87.

90. Marx, *Capital, Volume Three*, 486.

91. Marx, *Capital, Volume Three*, 486; Brunhoff, *Marx on Money*, 90.

92. Marx, *Capital, Volume Three*, 500–1.

93. Smith, *The Wealth of Nations, Books I–III*, 453.

94. Ernest Mandel, *Late Capitalism*, trans. Joris De Bres (London: Verso, 1978), 189.

95. Brunhoff, *Marx on Money*, 98.

96. Marx, *Capital, Volume Three*, 501.

97. Heinrich, *An Introduction to the Three Volumes of Karl Marx's Capital*, 157–58.

98. Cohen, *Karl Marx's Theory of History*, 117–19, 123–24; Mandel, *Late Capitalism*, 502–3; Harvey, *A Companion to Marx's Capital*, 41, 46–47; Harvey, *A Companion to Marx's Capital, Volume Two*, 243; Harvey, *Marx, Capital, and the Madness of Economic Reason*, 54.

99. Marx, *Capital, Volume Three*, 501.

100. Marx, *A Contribution to the Critique of Political Economy*, 200; Harvey, *A Companion to Marx's Capital, Volume Two*, 389.

101. Rubin, *Essays on Marx's Theory of Value*, 32–33; Tony Smith, *The Logic of Marx's Capital: Replies to Hegelian Criticisms* (Albany: State University of New York, 1990), 191.

102. Hilferding, *Finance Capital*, 99–100; Brunhoff, *Marx on Money*, 75–76; Fine and Saad-Filho, *Marx's Capital*, 50–51, 127–28; Brewer, *A Guide to Marx's Capital*, 90; Harvey, *A Companion to Marx's Capital, Volume Two*, 50–51.

103. Brewer, *A Guide to Marx's Capital*, 156.

104. Becker, *Marxian Political Economy*, 287.

105. Marx, *Capital, Volume Three*, 645–51, 704–5, 709; Harvey, *The Limits to Capital*, 296–97; Harvey, *A Companion to Marx's Capital, Volume Two*, 292.

106. Grossmann, *The Law of Accumulation and Breakdown of the Capitalist System*, 91; Harvey, *A Companion to Marx's Capital, Volume Two*, 176.

107. Barrère, *Crise du système de crédit et capitalisme monopoliste d'état*, 28.

108. Ollman, *Alienation*, 200; Heinrich, *An Introduction to the Three Volumes of Karl Marx's Capital*, 143.

109. Marx, *Das Kapital, dritter Band, drittes Buch*, 158; Marx, *Capital, Volume Three*, 516.

110. Marx, *Capital, Volume One*, 163–64.

111. Marx, *Das Kapital, erster Band*, 62; Marx, *Capital, Volume One*, 177.

112. Marx, *Theories of Surplus-Value, Part Three*, 130.

113. G. W. F. Hegel, "The Science of Laws, Morals and Religion [For the Lower Class]," in *The Philosophical Propaedeutic*, ed. Michael George and Andrew Vincent, trans. A. V. Miller (Oxford: Blackwell, 1986), §15 (28).

114. Heinrich, *An Introduction to the Three Volumes of Karl Marx's Capital*, 111, 190.

115. Tony Smith, "Hegel, Marx, and the Comprehension of Capitalism," in *Marx's Capital and Hegel's Logic*, 39–40.

116. Marx, *Das Kapital, dritter Band, drittes Buch*, 258; Marx, *Capital, Volume Three*, 603.

117. Marx, *Capital, Volume One*, 167–68.

118. Marx, *Das Kapital, dritter Band, drittes Buch*, 684; Marx, *Capital, Volume Three*, 968–69.

119. Marx, *Capital, Volume One*, 167–68; Postone, *Time, Labor, and Social Domination*, 136, 151–52; Heinrich, *An Introduction to the Three Volumes of Karl Marx's Capital*, 184–85, 198; Harvey, *A Companion to Marx's Capital, Volume Two*, 70; *SXVII*, 14–15.

120. Russell Jacoby, *Social Amnesia: A Critique of Conformist Psychology from Adler to Laing* (Boston: Beacon, 1975), 68.

121. Ronald L. Meek, *Studies in the Labor Theory of Value*, 2nd ed. (New York: Monthly Review Press, 1956), xii–xiii; Brewer, *A Guide to Marx's Capital*, 181; Harvey, *A Companion to Marx's Capital, Volume Two*, 203.

122. Heinrich, *An Introduction to the Three Volumes of Karl Marx's Capital*, 159, 165.

123. Harvey, *Marx, Capital, and the Madness of Economic Reason*, 204.

124. Robinson, *An Essay on Marxian Economics*, 69.

125. *SE* 3:303–22; Adrian Johnston, *Time Driven: Metapsychology and the Splitting of the Drive* (Evanston, IL: Northwestern University Press, 2005), xxx, 8–10, 21–22, 219, 345.

126. *SE* 1:356; *SE* 4:204–5; Jean Laplanche and Jean-Bertrand Pontalis, *The Language of Psycho-Analysis*, trans. Donald Nicholson-Smith (New York: Norton, 1973), 111–14; Johnston, *Time Driven*, xxx, 9–10, 18–19, 22, 57, 119, 141, 218–19, 226–27, 316, 345–46.

127. *SIV*, 149–50.

128. Marx, *Grundrisse*, 105.

129. *SE* 3:322.

130. Marx, *Das Kapital, erster Band*, 46; Marx, *Capital, Volume One*, 163.

131. Marx, *Das Kapital, erster Band*, 425; Marx, *Capital, Volume One*, 494.

132. *SXVIII*, 164.

133. *SXVIII*, 164–65.

134. *SVI*, 478; *SXIV*, 269.

135. *SV*, 62.

136. *SVI*, 312–13.

137. *SXVI*, 285.

138. Georg Simmel, *The Philosophy of Money*, trans. Tom Bottomore and David Frisby (London: Routledge & Kegan Paul, 1978), 152–53; *SVII*, 158; *SXVI*, 211.

139. *SXVI*, 285.

140. *SIV*, 157–158; *SV*, 68.

141. *GW* 14:316; *SE* 21:156.

142. Octave Mannoni, "I Know Well, but All the Same . . . ," trans. G. M. Goshgarian, in *Perversion and the Social Relation*, ed. Molly Anne Rothenberg, Dennis A. Foster, and Slavoj Žižek (Durham, NC: Duke University Press, 2003), 80–81.

143. *SIV*, 186.

144. *SVI*, 312.

145. *SIV*, 157.

146. *SIV* [Fr.], 381; *SIV*, 372.

147. *GW* 14:312; *SE* 21:152.

148. *SV*, 210, 263, 329.

149. Adrian Johnston, "Non-Existence and Sexual Identity: Some Brief Remarks on Meinong and Lacan," *Lacanian Ink* 3 (Fall/Winter 2002), http://www.lacan.com/nonexistf.htm.

150. Adrian Johnston, *Prolegomena to Any Future Materialism*, vol. 2: *A Weak Nature Alone* (Evanston, IL: Northwestern University Press, 2019), 204.

3. THE SELF-CLEANING FETISH   ❧   317

151. Johnston, *Prolegomena to Any Future Materialism*, 2:218–19.
152. Johnston, *Prolegomena to Any Future Materialism*, 2:219.
153. *SIV*, 144–145, 162, 168.
154. *SIV*, 144–45, 150; *SV*, 212–13.
155. *SIV* [Fr.], 170; *SIV*, 162.
156. Jacques Lacan and Wladimir Granoff, "Fetishism: The Symbolic, the Imaginary, and the Real," in *Perversions: Psychodynamics and Therapy*, ed. Sandor Lorand and Michael Balint (New York: Gramercy, 1956), 265–76.
157. *SIV* [Fr.], 183; *SIV*, 175.
158. *SIV* [Fr.], 194; *SIV*, 186.
159. *SVIII*, 140–41.
160. *SX*, 102–3.
161. *SIV* [Fr.], 159; *SIV*, 151; Avrane, *Petite psychanalyse de l'argent*, 33.
162. Marx, *Das Kapital, erster Band*, 46; Marx, *Capital, Volume One*, 163–64.
163. Brown, *Life Against Death*, 279.
164. Brown, *Life Against Death*, 279.
165. *SIV*, 147–48; Guy Rosolato, "Étude des perversions sexuelles à partir du fétichisme," in Piera Aulagnier-Spairani, Jean Clavreul, François Perrier, Guy Rosolato, and Jean-Paul Valabrega, *Le désir et la perversion* (Paris: Éditions du Seuil, 1967), 20–21.
166. *SIV*, 147.
167. *SIV* [Fr.], 156.
168. *SIV*, 148.
169. Mannoni, "I Know Well, but All the Same . . . ," 70.
170. *SIV*, 149, 157–58, 186.
171. *SIV*, 149–50.
172. *SXI*, 103, 111–12.
173. *SVI*, 439.
174. Robinson, *An Essay on Marxian Economics*, 18.
175. *SV*, 62.
176. *SV*, 62.
177. *SVI*, 313.
178. *SVI*, 312–13.
179. Adrian Johnston, "Meta-Transcendentalism and Error-First Ontology: The Cases of Gilbert Simondon and Catherine Malabou," in *New Realism and Contemporary Philosophy*, ed. Gregor Kroupa and Jure Simoniti (London: Bloomsbury, 2020), 171–75.
180. Aristotle, *Politics*, trans. C. D. C. Reeve (Indianapolis, IN: Hackett, 1998), ll. 1257a–1258a (15–18).
181. Marx, *Theories of Surplus-Value, Part Three*, 514.
182. *SVI*, 478–79.
183. Ollman, *Alienation*, 173.
184. Brewer, *A Guide to Marx's Capital*, 63; Foley, *Understanding Capital*, 34, 40, 46–47; Murray, "The Secret of Capital's Self-Valorization 'Laid Bare,'" 206.
185. Marx, *Theories of Surplus-Value, Part Three*, 494; Postone, *Time, Labor, and Social Domination*, 136; Meaney, "Capital Breeds," 47, 49.
186. Marx, "A Contribution to the Critique of Hegel's Philosophy of Right. Introduction," 251.
187. Marx, "A Contribution to the Critique of Hegel's Philosophy of Right. Introduction," 243–45; Marx, *Economic and Philosophical Manuscripts*, 395; Karl Marx, "Theses on Feuerbach," trans. S. Ryazanskaya, in *Karl Marx: Selected Writings*, ed. David McLellan (Oxford: Oxford University

318 ✦ 3. THE SELF-CLEANING FETISH

Press, 1977), 156–58; Karl Marx and Friedrich Engels, *The Holy Family, or Critique of Critical Criticism: Against Bruno Bauer, and Company*, trans. Richard Dixon and Clemens Dutt (Moscow: Progress Publishers, 1975), 66–67, 103, 105, 118, 148.

188. *GW* 14:316; *SE* 21:156; Rosolato, "Étude des perversions sexuelles à partir du fétichisme," 10–11.

189. *GW* 14:316; *SE* 21:156.

190. Mannoni, "I Know Well, but All the Same . . . ," 70–71.

191. *GW* 14:316; *SE* 21:156.

192. *SIV*, 158.

193. *GW* 17:133; *SE* 23:202–3.

194. *SE* 23:275–78.

195. Rosolato, "Étude des perversions sexuelles à partir du fétichisme," 15, 18, 20.

196. Adrian Johnston, *Badiou, Žižek, and Political Transformations: The Cadence of Change* (Evanston, IL: Northwestern University Press, 2009), 101–2.

197. *GW* 14:316; *SE* 21:157.

198. Rosolato, "Étude des perversions sexuelles à partir du fétichisme," 9–11, 18.

199. Mannoni, "I Know Well, but All the Same . . . ," 70–71.

200. Mannoni, "I Know Well, but All the Same . . . ," 90; Johnston, *Badiou, Žižek, and Political Transformations*, 117–18.

201. Marx, *Capital, Volume One*, 163.

202. Harvey, *A Companion to Marx's Capital*, 90–91.

203. Mannoni, "I Know Well, but All the Same . . . ," 88.

204. Avrane, *Petite psychanalyse de l'argent*, 25–26; Patrick Avrane, "La valeur du petit caillou," in Michel Aglietta et al., *L'argent et la psychanalyse. Économie, dette et désir* (Paris: Éditions Campagne Première, 2017), 170.

205. Andrew Feenberg, *The Philosophy of Praxis: Marx, Lukács, and the Frankfurt School* (London: Verso, 2014), 65.

206. Mannoni, "I Know Well, but All the Same . . . ," 77–78, 91; Johnston, *Badiou, Žižek, and Political Transformations*, 88.

207. Meek, *Studies in the Labor Theory of Value*, 62.

208. Foley, *Understanding Capital*, 29–30.

209. Marx, *Das Kapital, erster Band*, 57; Marx, *Capital, Volume One*, 173.

210. Marx, "A Contribution to the Critique of Hegel's Philosophy of Right. Introduction," 243–45.

211. Slavoj Žižek, *The Sublime Object of Ideology* (London: Verso, 1989), 29, 33.

212. Herbert Marcuse, *One-Dimensional Man: Studies in the Ideology of Advanced Industrial Society* (Boston: Beacon, 1964), 103; Herbert Marcuse, "Aggressiveness in Advanced Industrial Society," in *Negations*, 253.

213. *SXVI*, 354.

214. Johnston, *Badiou, Žižek, and Political Transformations*, 35–36, 53.

4. THE TRIUMPH OF THEOLOGICAL ECONOMICS: GOD GOES UNDERGROUND

1. *SXI*, 59.

2. *SE* 13:147–49, 154.

3. *SVII*, 126–27, 142–43, 177, 179–81.

4. *SE* 13:143.

5. Adrian Johnston, *Adventures in Transcendental Materialism: Dialogues with Contemporary Thinkers* (Edinburgh: Edinburgh University Press, 2014), 219–20.
6. Johnston, *Adventures in Transcendental Materialism*, 219–20.
7. François Balmès, *Dieu, le sexe et la vérité* (Ramonville Saint-Agne: Érès, 2007), 13–15, 169–70.
8. Jacques Lacan, *Télévision* (Paris: Éditions du Seuil, 1973), 72; Jacques Lacan, "Television," trans. Denis Hollier, Rosalind Krauss, and Annette Michelson, in *Television/A Challenge to the Psychoanalytic Establishment*, ed. Joan Copjec (New York: Norton, 1990), 46.
9. Karl Marx, *The Eighteenth Brumaire of Louis Bonaparte*, trans. Ben Fowkes, in *Surveys from Exile: Political Writings*, ed. David Fernbach (Harmondsworth: Penguin, 1973), 2:242; Karl Marx, *Grundrisse: Foundations of the Critique of Political Economy (Rough Draft)*, trans. Martin Nicolaus (New York: Penguin, 1973), 646; Karl Marx, *Capital: A Critique of Political Economy, Volume One*, trans. Ben Fowkes (New York: Penguin, 1976), 342, 367, 415–16; Karl Marx, "Inaugural Address of the International Working Men's Association," in *The First International and After: Political Writings, Volume 3*, ed. David Fernbach (Harmondsworth: Penguin, 1974), 79; Karl Marx, *The Civil War in France*, in *The First International and After*, 215.
10. Marx, *The Eighteenth Brumaire of Louis Bonaparte*, 2:237.
11. SE 21:38, 49–50, 53–56; Adrian Johnston, "A Blast from the Future: Freud, Lacan, Marcuse, and Snapping the Threads of the Past," in *Umbr(a): Utopia*, ed. Ryan Anthony Hatch (Buffalo: Center for the Study of Psychoanalysis and Culture, State University of New York at Buffalo, 2008), 67–68.
12. Oskar Pfister, "The Illusion of a Future: A Friendly Disagreement with Prof. Sigmund Freud," ed. Paul Roazen, trans. Susan Abrams, *International Journal of Psycho-Analysis* 74, no. 3 (1993): 557–79.
13. Johnston, *Adventures in Transcendental Materialism*, 187–88.
14. GW 14:377; SE 21:53.
15. Jacques Lacan, "The Triumph of Religion," in *The Triumph of Religion, Preceded by Discourse to Catholics*, trans. Bruce Fink (Cambridge: Polity, 2013), 64.
16. Johnston, *Adventures in Transcendental Materialism*, 187–88.
17. Johnston, "A Blast from the Future," 67–68; Adrian Johnston, "Lacan's Endgame: Philosophy, Science, and Religion in the Final Seminars," *Crisis and Critique* 6, no. 1, special issue: "Lacan: Psychoanalysis, Philosophy, Politics," ed. Agon Hamza and Frank Ruda (2019): 156–87.
18. Lacan, "The Triumph of Religion," 56, 67, 71–72; SXXIV, 5/17/77; Adrian Johnston, *Prolegomena to Any Future Materialism*, vol. 1: *The Outcome of Contemporary French Philosophy* (Evanston, IL: Northwestern University Press, 2013), xiii, 32–33, 37, 175–76.
19. Karl Marx, "A Contribution to the Critique of Hegel's Philosophy of Right. Introduction," in *Early Writings*, trans. Rodney Livingstone and Gregor Benton (New York: Penguin, 1992), 251.
20. Ronald L. Meek, *Studies in the Labor Theory of Value*, 2nd ed. (New York: Monthly Review Press, 1956), 135, 140.
21. Marx, "A Contribution to the Critique of Hegel's Philosophy of Right. Introduction," 243–45.
22. Karl Marx, *Economic and Philosophical Manuscripts*, in *Early Writings*, 349, 357–58, 395.
23. Karl Marx and Friedrich Engels, *The Holy Family, or Critique of Critical Criticism: Against Bruno Bauer, and Company*, trans. Richard Dixon and Clemens Dutt (Moscow: Progress Publishers, 1975), 103, 118, 238–39; Karl Marx and Friedrich Engels, *The German Ideology* (Amherst, MA: Prometheus, 1998), 33–36, 42–43.
24. Marx, *Grundrisse*, 110, 838–39, 865; Marx, *Capital, Volume One*, 172–73, 990; Friedrich Engels, *Anti-Dühring: Herr Eugen Dühring's Revolution in Science*, 2nd ed. (Moscow: Foreign Languages Publishing House, 1959), 435–37, 476; Friedrich Engels, *Socialism: Utopian and Scientific*, trans. Edward Aveling (New York: International, 1975), 28.

320 ❧ 4. THE TRIUMPH OF THEOLOGICAL ECONOMICS

25. Karl Marx and Friedrich Engels, *Manifest der kommunistischen Partei*, 1848, https://www
.marxists.org/deutsch/archiv/marx-engels/1848/manifest/index.htm; Karl Marx and Friedrich
Engels, *The Communist Manifesto*, trans. Samuel Moore, in *Karl Marx: Selected Writings*, ed.
David McLellan (Oxford: Oxford University Press, 1977), 223.

26. Adam Smith, *The Wealth of Nations, Books IV–V*, ed. Andrew Skinner (New York: Penguin,
1999), 391–93.

27. Marx and Engels, *Manifest der kommunistischen Partei*; Marx and Engels, *The Communist Manifesto*, 223.

28. Marx and Engels, *Manifest der kommunistischen Partei*; Marx and Engels, *The Communist Manifesto*, 224.

29. Karl Marx, *The Poverty of Philosophy* (Moscow: Foreign Languages Publishing House, 1956), 150.

30. *SXVI*, 238; *SXVII*, 55, 87, 207.

31. Karl Marx, *A Contribution to the Critique of Political Economy*, ed. Maurice Dobb, trans. S. W.
Ryazanskaya (New York: International, 1970), 21.

32. Marx, *A Contribution to the Critique of Political Economy*, 20–22.

33. Karl Korsch, "The Present State of the Problem of 'Marxism and Philosophy'—An Anti-
Critique," in *Marxism and Philosophy*, trans. Fred Halliday (New York: New Left Books,
1970), 102.

34. Kojin Karatani, *Transcritique: On Kant and Marx*, trans. Sabu Kohso (Cambridge, MA: MIT
Press, 2003), 203.

35. Karl Marx, *Value, Price and Profit*, in *Wage-Labour and Capital/Value, Price and Profit* (New
York: International Publishers, 1976), 57–59, 61–62; Marx, *Grundrisse*, 88, 95, 570–71, 573; Marx,
Capital, Volume One, 382, 408–9; Karl Marx, *Capital: A Critique of Political Economy, Volume
Three*, trans. David Fernbach (New York: Penguin, 1981), 998–99.

36. Michel Foucault, *The Birth of Biopolitics: Lectures at the Collège de France, 1978–1979*, ed. Michel
Senellart, trans. Graham Burchell (Basingstoke: Palgrave Macmillan, 2008), 162–67.

37. Marx, *A Contribution to the Critique of Political Economy*, 19.

38. Marx, *Grundrisse*, 232; Marx, *A Contribution to the Critique of Political Economy*, 130; Bertell Ollman, *Alienation: Marx's Conception of Man in Capitalist Society* (Cambridge: Cambridge University Press, 1971), 222–23; Roman Rosdolsky, *The Making of Marx's 'Capital,'* trans. Pete Burgess
(London: Pluto, 1977), 156; Bruce Brown, *Marx, Freud, and the Critique of Everyday Life: Toward
a Permanent Cultural Revolution* (New York: Monthly Review Press, 1973), 87–88; David Harvey, *A Companion to Marx's Capital* (London: Verso, 2010), 45.

39. Karl Marx, *Karl-Marx-Ausgabe: Werke-Schriften-Briefe, Band IV: Ökonomische Schriften, erster
Band*, ed. Hans-Joachim Lieber, *Das Kapital: Kritik der politischen Ökonomie, erster Band*
(Darmstadt: Wissenschaftliche Buchgesellschaft, 1962), 46; Marx, *Capital, Volume One*, 163.

40. Étienne Balibar, *The Philosophy of Marx*, trans. Chris Turner (London: Verso, 2007), 36, 47, 60;
Slavoj Žižek, *The Parallax View* (Cambridge, MA: MIT Press, 2006), 351–52; Slavoj Žižek, *Dispari-
ties* (London: Bloomsbury, 2016), 125–26, 277; Slavoj Žižek, *Incontinence of the Void: Economico-
Philosophical Spandrels* (Cambridge, MA: MIT Press, 2017), 184.

41. Karl Marx, *Critique of Hegel's Doctrine of the State*, in *Early Writings*, 161; Marx, *Grundrisse*, 85,
88, 100–2, 104–5, 142–46, 157, 164, 331, 449–50, 831–32; Marx, *Capital, Volume One*, 739, 909;
Karl Marx, *Capital: A Critique of Political Economy, Volume Two*, trans. David Fernbach (New
York: Penguin, 1978), 185; Marx, *Capital, Volume Three*, 275, 596–97, 603; Ernest Mandel, *The
Formation of the Economic Thought of Karl Marx: 1843 to Capital*, trans. Brian Pearce (New York:
Monthly Review Press, 1971), 47.

42. Shlomo Avineri, *The Social and Political Thought of Karl Marx* (Cambridge: Cambridge University Press, 1968), 38–40, 102, 123.

43. Karatani, *Transcritique*, 209–10, 212.

4. THE TRIUMPH OF THEOLOGICAL ECONOMICS   321

44. Louis Althusser, *On the Reproduction of Capitalism: Ideology and Ideological State Apparatuses*, trans. G. M. Goshgarian (London: Verso, 2014), 20–21, 52, 140, 148–49, 246–47.

45. G. W. F. Hegel, *System of Ethical Life*, in *System of Ethical Life and First Philosophy of Spirit*, trans. H. S. Harris and T. M. Knox (Albany: State University of New York Press, 1979), 143–45, 166–67; G. W. F. Hegel, *First Philosophy of Spirit (Part III of the System of Speculative Philosophy 1803/4)*, in *System of Ethical Life and First Philosophy of Spirit*, 211; G. W. F. Hegel, *Phenomenology of Spirit*, trans. A. V. Miller (Oxford: Oxford University Press, 1977), 329–49; G. W. F. Hegel, *Elements of the Philosophy of Right*, ed. Allen W. Wood, trans. H. B. Nisbet (Cambridge: Cambridge University Press, 1991), §258 (279); G. W. F. Hegel, *The Philosophy of History*, trans. J. Sibree (New York: Dover, 1956), 422–23; G. W. F. Hegel, *Lectures on the Philosophy of Religion, One-Volume Edition: The Lectures of 1827*, ed. Peter C. Hodgson, trans. R. F. Brown, P. C. Hodgson, J. M. Stewart, and H. S. Harris (Berkeley: University of California Press, 1988), 484–85; G. W. F. Hegel, *Lectures on the Philosophy of Religion*, vol. 3: *The Consummate Religion*, ed. Peter C. Hodgson, trans. R. F. Brown, P. C. Hodgson, J. M. Stewart, and H. S. Harris (Berkeley: University of California Press, 1985), 373–74; G. W. F. Hegel, "The Relationship of Religion to the State (1831)," in *Political Writings*, ed. Laurence Dickey and H. B. Nisbet, trans. H. B. Nisbet (Cambridge: Cambridge University Press, 1999), 226.

46. Ludwig Feuerbach, "Preliminary Theses on the Reform of Philosophy," in *The Fiery Brook: Selected Writings*, trans. Zawar Hanfi (London: Verso, 2012), 172–73; Ludwig Feuerbach, "Fragments Concerning the Characteristics of My Philosophical Development," in *The Fiery Brook*, 273.

47. André Amar, "Essai psychanalytique sur l'argent," in *Psychanalyse de l'argent*, ed. Ernest Borneman, trans. Daniel Guérineau (Paris: Presses Universitaires de France, 1978), 376.

48. Karl Marx, "Zur Kritik der Hegelschen Rechtsphilosophie. Einleitung," in *Karl-Marx-Ausgabe: Werke-Schriften-Briefe, Band I: Frühe Schriften, erster Band*, ed. Hans-Joachim Lieber and Peter Furth (Darmstadt: Wissenschaftliche Buchgesellschaft, 1962), 488; Karl Marx, "A Contribution to the Critique of Hegel's Philosophy of Right. Introduction," in *Early Writings*, 243.

49. G. W. F. Hegel, *Phänomenologie des Geistes, Werke in zwanzig Bänden, 3*, ed. Eva Moldenhauer and Karl Markus Michel (Frankfurt am Main: Suhrkamp, 1970), 118–19; Hegel, *Phenomenology of Spirit*, 89.

50. G. W. F. Hegel, "Hegel to Schelling: Bern, April 16, 1795," in *Hegel: The Letters*, trans. Clark Butler and Christiane Seiler (Bloomington: Indiana University Press, 1984), 35–36; G. W. F. Hegel, *The Spirit of Christianity and Its Fate*, in *Early Theological Writings*, trans. T. M. Knox (Philadelphia: University of Pennsylvania Press, 1975), 211–15, 244; Hegel, *Phenomenology of Spirit*, 365–83; G. W. F. Hegel, *Science of Logic*, trans. A. V. Miller (London: George Allen & Unwin, 1969), 131–36, 139–54; G. W. F. Hegel, *The Encyclopedia Logic: Part I of the Encyclopedia of the Philosophical Sciences with the Zusätze*, trans. T. F. Geraets, W. A. Suchting, and H. S. Harris (Indianapolis, IN: Hackett, 1991), §93–95 (149–51); G. W. F. Hegel, *Lectures on the History of Philosophy*, trans. E. S. Haldane and Frances H. Simson (New York: Humanities Press, 1955), 3:461–64.

51. Brown, *Marx, Freud, and the Critique of Everyday Life*, 154, 158–59; Byung-Chul Han, *Capitalism and the Death Drive*, trans. Daniel Steuer (Cambridge: Polity, 2021), 17.

52. *SXX*, 3, 7–8.

53. Adrian Johnston, *Time Driven: Metapsychology and the Splitting of the Drive* (Evanston, IL: Northwestern University Press, 2005), xxxvi–xxxviii, 293–99, 331, 335–37.

54. *SXI* [Fr.], 246; *SXI*, 274–75.

55. *SXI* [Fr.], 246–47; *SXI*, 275.

56. *SXI* [Fr.], 247; *SXI*, 275.

57. *SXI* [Fr.], 29; *SXI*, 27.

322   ◆   4. THE TRIUMPH OF THEOLOGICAL ECONOMICS

58. Juan Pablo Lucchelli, *Lacan: De Wallon à Kojève* (Paris: Éditions Michèle, 2017), 81–90.

59. Jacques Lacan, "Les complexes familiaux dans la formation de l'individu: Essai d'analyse d'une fonction en psychologie," in *Autres écrits*, ed. Jacques-Alain Miller (Paris: Éditions du Seuil, 2001), 56–61.

60. Jacques Lacan, "A Theoretical Introduction to the Functions of Psychoanalysis in Criminology," in *Écrits: The First Complete Edition in English*, trans. Bruce Fink (New York: Norton, 2006), 106–7; *SV*, 470; *SXVII*, 119–20; Johnston, *Time Driven*, 286; Johnston, *Adventures in Transcendental Materialism*, 219–20; François Balmès, *Le nom, la loi, la voix* (Ramonville Saint-Agne: Érès, 1997), 94.

61. Jacques Lacan, "Discourse to Catholics," in *The Triumph of Religion, Preceded by Discourse to Catholics*, 24–25.

62. Thomas Presskorn-Thygesen and Ole Bjerg, "The Falling Rate of Enjoyment: Consumer Capitalism and Compulsive Buying Disorder," *Ephemera: Theory and Politics in Organization* 14, no. 2 (2014): 198.

63. G. W. F. Hegel, *Philosophy of Mind: Part Three of the Encyclopedia of the Philosophical Sciences*, trans. A. V. Miller (Oxford: Oxford University Press, 1971), §577 (314–15).

64. *SIII*, 305; Johnston, *Adventures in Transcendental Materialism*, 65–107.

65. Max Weber, *The Protestant Ethic and the "Spirit" of Capitalism*, in *The Protestant Ethic and the "Spirit" of Capitalism and Other Writings*, ed. and trans. Peter Baehr and Gordon C. Wells (New York: Penguin, 2002), 26.

66. Weber, *The Protestant Ethic and the "Spirit" of Capitalism*, 13–14.

67. Max Weber, "Remarks on the Foregoing 'Reply,' (1908) (Weber's second rejoinder to H. Karl Fischer)," in *The Protestant Ethic and the "Spirit" of Capitalism and Other Writings*, 241–242; Max Weber, "Rebuttal of the Critique of the 'Spirit' of Capitalism (1910) (Weber's first rejoinder to Felix Rachfahl)," in *The Protestant Ethic and the "Spirit" of Capitalism and Other Writings*, 275; Max Weber, "A Final Rebuttal of Rachfahl's Critique of the 'Spirit of Capitalism' (1910)," in *The Protestant Ethic and the "Spirit" of Capitalism and Other Writings*, 285.

68. Weber, "Rebuttal of the Critique of the 'Spirit' of Capitalism," 262.

69. Weber, *The Protestant Ethic and the "Spirit" of Capitalism*, 36.

70. Weber, *The Protestant Ethic and the "Spirit" of Capitalism*, 36.

71. Louis Althusser, *Que faire?*, ed. G. M. Goshgarian (Paris: Presses Universitaires de France, 2018), 59–62, 67, 88, 102–3, 124–27.

72. Carl Schmitt, *Political Theology: Four Chapters on the Concept of Sovereignty*, trans. George Schwab (Cambridge, MA: MIT Press, 1985), 36.

73. Giorgio Agamben, *The Kingdom and the Glory: For a Theological Genealogy of Economy and Government (Homo Sacer II, 2)*, trans. Lorenzo Chiesa with Matteo Mandarini (Stanford, CA: Stanford University Press, 2011), 66.

74. Agamben, *The Kingdom and the Glory*, 229–30.

75. Agamben, *The Kingdom and the Glory*, 110–13.

76. Agamben, *The Kingdom and the Glory*, 3–4.

77. Agamben, *The Kingdom and the Glory*, 122–23.

78. Agamben, *The Kingdom and the Glory*, 4.

79. Agamben, *The Kingdom and the Glory*, 281–87.

80. Giorgio Agamben, *Homo Sacer: Sovereign Power and Bare Life*, trans. Daniel Heller-Roazen (Stanford, CA: Stanford University Press, 1998), 15, 17–19, 24–25, 32, 35, 37, 39–40, 83–84; Giorgio Agamben, *State of Exception*, trans. Kevin Attell (Chicago: University of Chicago Press, 2005), 1, 4–6, 16, 24, 26, 31, 35, 69–70.

81. Agamben, *The Kingdom and the Glory*, 1, 142–143, 230, 277.

82. Agamben, *The Kingdom and the Glory*, 167, 174, 188, 193–94.

4. THE TRIUMPH OF THEOLOGICAL ECONOMICS 323

83. Agamben, *The Kingdom and the Glory*, 168.

84. Agamben, *The Kingdom and the Glory*, 46.

85. Agamben, *The Kingdom and the Glory*, 91.

86. Giovanni Pico della Mirandola, "On the Dignity of Man," in *On the Dignity of Man*, trans. Charles Glenn Wallis, Paul J. W. Miller, and Douglas Carmichael (Indianapolis, IN: Hackett, 1998), 4–5; Lucio Colletti, *Marxism and Hegel*, trans. Lawrence Garner (London: Verso, 1979), 234, 238–41, 243–46; Giorgio Agamben, *The Man Without Content*, trans. Georgia Albert (Stanford, CA: Stanford University Press, 1999), 65–72; Giorgio Agamben, *The Open: Man and Animal*, trans. Kevin Attell (Stanford, CA: Stanford University Press, 2004), 16, 21–22, 26, 29–30; Johnston, *Adventures in Transcendental Materialism*, 159–60.

87. Agamben, *The Kingdom and the Glory*, 245–46, 250–51.

88. Alberto Toscano, "Divine Management: Critical Remarks on Giorgio Agamben's *The Kingdom and the Glory*," *Angelaki: Journal of the Theoretical Humanities* 16, no. 3 (September 2011): 127, 133.

89. Toscano, "Divine Management, "128."

90. Schmitt, *Political Theology*, 43–44.

91. Giorgio Agamben, *The Signature of All Things: On Method*, trans. Luca D'Isanto with Kevin Attell (New York: Zone, 2009), 82–83; Toscano, "Divine Management," 128–29, 135.

92. Agamben, *The Signature of All Things*, 33–80; Toscano, "Divine Management," 127–28.

93. Michel Foucault, *"Society Must Be Defended": Lectures at the Collège de France, 1975–1976*, ed. Mauro Bertani and Alessandro Fontana, trans. David Macey (New York: Picador, 2003), 6, 8–9; Foucault, *The Birth of Biopolitics*, 2–3.

94. Michel Foucault, *Security, Territory, Population: Lectures at the Collège de France, 1977–1978*, ed. Michel Senellart, trans. Graham Burchell (New York: Picador, 2007), 101, 337–39; Foucault, *The Birth of Biopolitics*, 10, 18–19, 21–22, 282, 295.

95. Foucault, *Security, Territory, Population*, 104–6, 273–74, 278, 315.

96. Foucault, *Security, Territory, Population*, 129, 150, 154–56, 165, 179, 184.

97. Toscano, "Divine Management," 132.

98. Toscano, "Divine Management," 132.

99. Toscano, "Divine Management," 130–32.

100. Toscano, "Divine Management," 130–32.

101. Aristotle, *Politics*, trans. C. D. C. Reeve (Indianapolis, IN: Hackett, 1998), ll. 1257a–1258a (15–18).

102. Toscano, "Divine Management," 132.

103. Toscano, "Divine Management," 129.

104. Marx, *Critique of Hegel's Doctrine of the State*, 87–88, 184, 189.

105. Toscano, "Divine Management," 128.

106. Toscano, "Divine Management," 128.

107. Toscano, "Divine Management," 133.

108. Toscano, "Divine Management," 134.

109. Giorgio Agamben, "'God Didn't Die, He Was Transformed Into Money': An Interview with Giorgio Agamben [with Peppe Savà]," libcom.org, 2014, https://libcom.org/library/god-didnt-die-he-was-transformed-money-interview-giorgio-agamben-peppe-savà.

110. Agamben, *The Kingdom and the Glory*, 276.

111. Agamben, *The Kingdom and the Glory*, 3, 24–25.

112. Foucault, *"Society Must Be Defended,"* 13–14, 261–62.

113. Schmitt, *Political Theology*, 62.

114. Marx and Engels, *The German Ideology*, 42.

115. Marx, *The Poverty of Philosophy*, 109.

116. Marx, *The Poverty of Philosophy*, 109.

324 **4. THE TRIUMPH OF THEOLOGICAL ECONOMICS**

117. Karl Marx, *Misère de la philosophie: Réponse à la Philosophie de la misère de Proudhon*, 1847, https://www.marxists.org/francais/marx/works/1847/06/misere.pdf; Marx, *The Poverty of Philosophy*, 115.

118. Marx, *The Eighteenth Brumaire of Louis Bonaparte*, 2:146.

119. Karl Marx and Friedrich Engels, *Die deutsche Ideologie* (Berlin: Dietz, 1953), 23; Marx and Engels, *The German Ideology*, 42.

120. Louis Althusser, "Ideology and Ideological State Apparatuses (Notes Towards an Investigation)," in *On the Reproduction of Capitalism: Ideology and Ideological State Apparatuses*, trans. G. M. Goshgarian (London: Verso, 2014), 253–55.

121. Marx, *A Contribution to the Critique of Political Economy*, 20–22.

122. Adrian Johnston, *A New German Idealism: Hegel, Žižek, and Dialectical Materialism* (New York: Columbia University Press, 2018), 125.

123. V. I. Lenin, *What Is to Be Done?: Burning Questions of Our Movement*, ed. Victor J. Jerome, trans. Joe Fineberg and George Hanna (New York: International, 1969), 68–71, 79, 82, 84–85, 87–88, 90, 159.

124. Mao Tse-Tung, "On Contradiction," in *On Practice and Contradiction*, ed. Slavoj Žižek (London: Verso, 2007), 67–102.

125. Georg Lukács, "What Is Orthodox Marxism?," in *History and Class Consciousness: Studies in Marxist Dialectics*, trans. Rodney Livingstone (Cambridge, MA: MIT Press, 1971), 24.

126. G. A. Cohen, *Karl Marx's Theory of History: A Defense* (Princeton, NJ: Princeton University Press, 1978), 138.

127. Friedrich Engels, "Letter to Conrad Schmidt, October 27, 1890," https://www.marxists.org/archive/marx/works/1890/letters/90_10_27.htm.

128. G. W. F. Hegel, *Grundlinien der Philosophie des Rechts oder Naturrecht und Staatswissenschaft im Grundrisse: Mit Hegels eigenhändigen Notizen und den mündlichen Zusätzen, Werke in zwanzig Bänden, 7*, ed. Eva Moldenhauer and Karl Markus Michel (Frankfurt am Main: Suhrkamp, 1970), 24; Hegel, *Elements of the Philosophy of Right*, 20.

129. Johnston, *A New German Idealism*, 81–90, 98–102.

130. Louis Althusser, "Contradiction et surdétermination (Notes pour une recherche)," in *Pour Marx* (Paris: Éditions La Découverte, 2005), 113; Louis Althusser, "Contradiction and Overdetermination: Notes for an Investigation," in *For Marx*, trans. Ben Brewster (London: Verso, 2005), 113.

131. Louis Althusser, "À propos de Marx et l'histoire," in *Écrits sur l'histoire (1963–1986)*, ed. G. M. Goshgarian (Paris: Presses Universitaires de France, 2018), 262–63.

132. Louis Althusser, *Montesquieu: Politics and History*, in *Politics and History: Montesquieu, Rousseau, Marx*, trans. Ben Brewster (London: Verso, 2007), 53; Louis Althusser, *Socialisme idéologique et socialisme scientifique*, in *Socialisme idéologique et socialisme scientifique, et autres écrits*, ed. G. M. Goshgarian (Paris: Presses Universitaires de France, 2022), 133–35; Louis Althusser, "L'idéologie (extrait de Théorie marxiste et Parti comministe)," in *Socialisme idéologique et socialisme scientifique, et autres écrits*, 167; Louis Althusser, "Sur la Révolution culturelle chinoise," in *Socialisme idéologique et socialisme scientifique, et autres écrits*, 297, 301; Louis Althusser, "Sur l'idéologie (Fragment inédit de «Sur la Révolution culturelle chinoise»)," in *Socialisme idéologique et socialisme scientifique, et autres écrits*, 317.

133. Louis Althusser, "On the Materialist Dialectic: On the Unevenness of Origins," in *For Marx*, 213.

134. Robin Blackburn and Gareth Stedman Jones, "Louis Althusser and the Struggle for Marxism," in *The Unknown Dimension: European Marxism Since Lenin*, ed. Dick Howard and Karl E. Klare (New York: Basic Books, 1972), 370, 379–80.

135. André Glucksmann, "A Ventriloquist Structuralism," in *Western Marxism: A Critical Reader*, ed. New Left Review (London: Verso, 1978), 293.

136. Blackburn and Stedman Jones, "Louis Althusser and the Struggle for Marxism," 379.

137. Althusser, *Socialisme idéologique et socialisme scientifique*, 135, 137–38, 142–43; Althusser, "Sur la Révolution culturelle chinoise," 298–99.

138. Étienne Balibar, "On the Basic Concepts of Historical Materialism," in *Reading Capital: The Complete Edition*, trans. Ben Brewster and David Fernbach (London: Verso, 2015), 385.

139. Norman Geras, "Althusser's Marxism: An Assessment," in *Western Marxism*, 251–52.

140. Louis Althusser, "Livre sur l'impérialisme (extraits)," in *Écrits sur l'histoire (1963–1986)*, 154.

141. Walter Benjamin, "Capitalism as Religion," trans. Chad Kautzer, in *The Frankfurt School on Religion: Key Writings by the Major Thinkers*, ed. Eduardo Mendieta (New York: Routledge, 2004), 259.

142. Benjamin, "Capitalism as Religion," 259.

143. Benjamin, "Capitalism as Religion," 261.

144. Benjamin, "Capitalism as Religion," 261.

145. Benjamin, "Capitalism as Religion," 261.

146. Benjamin, "Capitalism as Religion," 259.

147. Benjamin, "Capitalism as Religion," 259.

148. Benjamin, "Capitalism as Religion," 259.

149. Benjamin, "Capitalism as Religion," 262.

150. Benjamin, "Capitalism as Religion," 259–60.

151. Benjamin, "Capitalism as Religion," 260.

152. Walter Benjamin, "Kapitalismus als Religion," in *Gesammelte Schriften, Band VI: Fragmente vermischten Inhalts, autobiographische Schriften*, ed. Hermann Schweppenhäuser and Rolf Tiedemann (Frankfurt am Main: Suhrkamp, 1985), 101; Benjamin, "Capitalism as Religion," 261.

153. Karl Marx, *Der achtzehnte Brumaire des Louis Bonaparte*, in *Karl-Marx-Ausgabe: Werke-Schriften-Briefe, Band III: Politische Schriften, erster Band*, ed. Hans-Joachim Lieber (Darmstadt: Wissenschaftliche Buchgesellschaft, 1960), 271; Marx, *The Eighteenth Brumaire of Louis Bonaparte*, 2:146.

154. *SVII*, 320; *SVIII*, 97–98.

155. Marx, "Zur Kritik der Hegelschen Rechtsphilosophie. Einleitung," 493; Marx, "A Contribution to the Critique of Hegel's Philosophy of Right. Introduction," 247.

CONCLUSION. REAL REDUCTION: IT'S THE STUPID ECONOMY!

1. V. I. Lenin, "Conspectus of Hegel's Book *Lectures on the History of Philosophy*," in *Collected Works*, vol. 38: *Philosophical Notebooks*, ed. Stewart Smith, trans. Clemence Dutt (Moscow: Progress Publishers, 1976), 274.

2. Maurice Merleau-Ponty, *Adventures of the Dialectic*, trans. Joseph Bien (Evanston, IL: Northwestern University Press, 1973), 59–65, 67; Gustav A. Wetter, *Dialectical Materialism: A Historical and Systematic Survey of Philosophy in the Soviet Union*, trans. Peter Heath (New York: Frederick A. Praeger, 1958), 130–31; David Joravsky, *Soviet Marxism and Natural Science: 1917–1932* (London: Routledge & Kegan Paul, 1961), 20; Henri Lefebvre, "Les paradoxes d'Althusser," in *L'idéologie structuraliste* (Paris: Éditions Anthropos, 1971), 229; Michael Löwy, "De la Grande Logique de Hegel à la gare finlandaise de Petrograd," in *Dialectique et révolution: Essais de sociologie et d'histoire du marxisme* (Paris: Éditions Anthropos, 1973), 132–33, 139–40, 142; Michael Löwy, "Notes historiques sur le marxisme russe," in *Dialectique et révolution*, 151, 153–54; Raya Dunayevskaya, *Philosophy and Revolution: From Hegel to Sartre, and from Marx to Mao* (New York: Dell, 1973), 95–120, 204; Raya Dunayevskaya, *The Power of Negativity: Selected Writings on*

the *Dialectic in Hegel and Marx*, ed. Peter Hudis and Kevin B. Anderson (Lanham: Lexington, 2002), 50, 69, 105, 167, 214–15, 217, 251; Guy Planty-Bonjour, *Hegel et la pensée philosophique en Russie, 1830–1917* (The Hague: Martinus Nijhoff, 1974), 317; Stathis Kouvelakis, "Lenin as Reader of Hegel: Hypotheses for a Reading of Lenin's Notebooks on Hegel's *The Science of Logic*," in *Lenin Reloaded: Toward a Politics of Truth*, ed. Sebastian Budgen, Stathis Kouvelakis, and Slavoj Žižek (Durham, NC: Duke University Press, 2007), 173–75, 187–89; Kevin Anderson, *Lenin, Hegel, and Western Marxism: A Critical Study* (Urbana: University of Illinois Press, 1995), 4, 14, 23, 40, 42, 58–60, 64–65, 78–81, 95, 102–3, 174–75; Kevin B. Anderson, "The Rediscovery and Persistence of the Dialectic in Philosophy and in World Politics," in *Lenin Reloaded*, 125–27.

3. Adrian Johnston, *Prolegomena to Any Future Materialism*, vol. 2: *A Weak Nature Alone* (Evanston, IL: Northwestern University Press, 2019), 73–183.

4. Bruce Brown, *Marx, Freud, and the Critique of Everyday Life: Toward a Permanent Cultural Revolution* (New York: Monthly Review Press, 1973), 14–16.

5. Merleau-Ponty, *Adventures of the Dialectic*, 30–58.

6. Karl Korsch, "The Present State of the Problem of 'Marxism and Philosophy'—An Anti-Critique," in *Marxism and Philosophy*, trans. Fred Halliday (New York: New Left Books, 1970), 101–2.

7. Karl E. Klare, "The Critique of Everyday Life, the New Left, and the Unrecognizable Marxism," in *The Unknown Dimension: European Marxism Since Lenin*, ed. Dick Howard and Karl E. Klare (New York: Basic Books, 1972), 7–8, 10; Brown, *Marx, Freud, and the Critique of Everyday Life*, 127–28.

8. Merleau-Ponty, *Adventures of the Dialectic*, 41–42.

9. Perry Anderson, *Considerations on Western Marxism* (London: New Left Books, 1976), 75–76.

10. Perry Anderson, *In the Tracks of Historical Materialism: The Wellek Library Lectures* (London: Verso, 1983), 17.

11. Mihály Vajda, "Karl Korsch's 'Marxism and Philosophy,'" in *The Unknown Dimension*, 132.

12. Karl Korsch, *Marxismus und Philosophie*, ed. Erich Gerlach (Frankfurt am Main: Europäische Verlagsanstalt, 1966), 112; Karl Korsch, *Marxism and Philosophy*, 72.

13. Korsch, *Marxismus und Philosophie*, 113; Korsch, *Marxism and Philosophy*, 73.

14. Korsch, *Marxism and Philosophy*, 76–77.

15. Korsch, *Marxismus und Philosophie*, 117; Korsch, *Marxism and Philosophy*, 77.

16. Louis Althusser, *On the Reproduction of Capitalism: Ideology and Ideological State Apparatuses*, trans. G. M. Goshgarian (London: Verso, 2014), 76–77, 172–73, 175, 184–87; Louis Althusser, *Que faire?*, ed. G. M. Goshgarian (Paris: Presses Universitaires de France, 2018), 33–34, 93–94, 110; Louis Althusser, *How to Be a Marxist in Philosophy*, ed. and trans. G. M. Goshgarian (London: Bloomsbury, 2017), 124–25.

17. Bernard Sichère, "Le faux matérialisme «tel quel»," in *Marxisme-léninisme et psychanalyse* (Paris: François Maspero, 1975), 111–12.

18. Korsch, "The Present State of the Problem of 'Marxism and Philosophy,'" 99.

19. Karl Korsch, *Karl Marx* (Chicago: Haymarket, 2017), 158.

20. Korsch, *Karl Marx*, 160–64.

21. Korsch, *Karl Marx*, 163.

22. Korsch, *Marxism and Philosophy*, 78.

23. Karl Marx, "Thesen über Feuerbach," in *Karl Marx-Friedrich Engels Werke, Band 3, 1845–1846* (Berlin: Dietz, 1981), 5; Karl Marx, "Theses on Feuerbach," trans. S. Ryazanskaya, in *Karl Marx: Selected Writings*, ed. David McLellan (Oxford: Oxford University Press, 1977), 156.

24. Vajda, "Karl Korsch's 'Marxism and Philosophy,'" 135.

25. Korsch, *Marxism and Philosophy*, 78–80.

26. Korsch, *Marxism and Philosophy*, 79.

CONCLUSION ❧ 327

27. Korsch, *Marxism and Philosophy*, 80.

28. Marx, "Theses on Feuerbach," 157; Karl Marx, *Capital: A Critique of Political Economy, Volume One*, trans. Ben Fowkes (New York: Penguin, 1976), 494; Korsch, *Marxism and Philosophy*, 78–80.

29. V. I. Lenin, *What Is to Be Done?: Burning Questions of Our Movement*, ed. Victor J. Jerome, trans. Joe Fineberg and George Hanna (New York: International, 1969), 58–59, 62, 68–71, 79, 84–85, 88.

30. Lenin, *What Is to Be Done?*, 159; Georg Lukács, *Lenin: A Study on the Unity of His Thought*, trans. Nicholas Jacobs (London: Verso, 2009), 81–82.

31. Antonio Gramsci, *Prison Notebooks*, vol. 1, ed. and trans. Joseph A. Buttigieg (New York: Columbia University Press, 1992), Notebook 1 (1929–1930): First Notebook, §133–§134 (217–20), Notebook 2 (1929–1933): Miscellaneous I, §149 (360); Antonio Gramsci, *Prison Notebooks*, vol. 2, ed. and trans. Joseph A. Buttigieg (New York: Columbia University Press, 1996), Notebook 4 (1930–1932), §38 (179–80); Antonio Gramsci, *Prison Notebooks*, vol. 3, ed. and trans. Joseph A. Buttigieg (New York: Columbia University Press, 2007), Notebook 6 (1930–1932), §138 (109), §155 (117), Notebook 7 (1930–1931), §10 (161–63), §16 (168–69), Notebook 8 (1930–1932), §169 (330), §191 (345); Antonio Gramsci, "Letter to Tatiana Schucht, September 7, 1931," in *Letters from Prison*, ed. Frank Rosengarten, trans. Raymond Rosenthal (New York: Columbia University Press, 1994), 2:67; Antonio Gramsci, "Letter to Tatiana Schucht, May 2, 1932," in *Letters from Prison*, 2:169; Antonio Gramsci, "Letter to Tatiana Schucht, May 9, 1932," in *Letters from Prison*, 2:171–72.

32. Gramsci, *Prison Notebooks*, First Notebook, §46 (1:152–53); Gramsci, *Prison Notebooks*, Notebook 4 (1930–1932), §49 (2:199–210); Gramsci, *Prison Notebooks*, Notebook 7 (1930–1031), §62 (3:201), Notebook 8 (1930–1932), §169 (3:331); Gramsci, "Letter to Tatiana Schucht, September 7, 1931," 67.

33. Korsch, *Marxismus und Philosophie*, 120–21; Korsch, *Marxism and Philosophy*, 81.

34. Korsch, *Marxismus und Philosophie*, 121–22; Korsch, *Marxism and Philosophy*, 82.

35. Korsch, *Marxism and Philosophy*, 83.

36. Korsch, *Marxism and Philosophy*, 81–82.

37. Korsch, *Marxism and Philosophy*, 78–79, 92.

38. Korsch, *Marxism and Philosophy*, 88–89.

39. Korsch, *Marxism and Philosophy*, 86–87.

40. Korsch, *Marxism and Philosophy*, 94–95.

41. Korsch, *Marxism and Philosophy*, 95–97.

42. Vajda, "Karl Korsch's 'Marxism and Philosophy,'" 136.

43. Gramsci, *Prison Notebooks*, Notebook 4 (1930–1932), §15 (2:157–58); Gramsci, *Prison Notebooks*, Notebook 8 (1930–1932), §234 (3:377).

44. Karl Marx, *A Contribution to the Critique of Political Economy*, ed. Maurice Dobb, trans. S. W. Ryazanskaya (New York: International Publishers, 1970), 21.

45. Gramsci, *Prison Notebooks*, Notebook 4 (1930–1932), §15 (2:157).

46. Gramsci, *Prison Notebooks*, Notebook 4 (1930–1932), §39 (2:188).

47. Gramsci, *Prison Notebooks*, Notebook 7 (1930–1931), §1 (3:157).

48. István Mészáros, *Marx's Theory of Alienation* (New York: Harper & Row, 1970), 115.

49. Gramsci, *Prison Notebooks*, Notebook 7 (1930–1931), §24 (3:174–75), Notebook 8 (1930–1932), §196 (3:347–48).

50. J. V. Stalin, "Concerning Marxism in Linguistics," in *Marxism and Problems of Linguistics* (Peking: Foreign Languages Press, 1972), 5–9, 25; J. V. Stalin, "Concerning Certain Problems of Linguistics," in *Marxism and Problems of Linguistics*, 33–35; Ethan Pollock, *Stalin and the Soviet Science Wars* (Princeton, NJ: Princeton University Press, 2006), 56–57, 59, 104–35.

51. Gramsci, *Prison Notebooks*, Notebook 4 (1930–1932), §12 (2:153–54).

52. Gramsci, *Prison Notebooks*, Notebook 8 (1930–1932), §182 (3:340).

53. Georg Lukács, "What Is Orthodox Marxism?," in *History and Class Consciousness: Studies in Marxist Dialectics*, trans. Rodney Livingstone (Cambridge, MA: MIT Press, 1971), 6, 8, 10, 13; Georg Lukács, "The Marxism of Rosa Luxemburg," in *History and Class Consciousness*, 34; Georg Lukács, "Class Consciousness," in *History and Class Consciousness*, 55, 57–58, 74; Georg Lukács, "Reification and the Consciousness of the Proletariat," in *History and Class Consciousness*, 100; Georg Lukács, "The Changing Function of Historical Materialism," in *History and Class Consciousness*, 249; Lukács, *Lenin*, 17–18; Lucien Sebag, *Marxisme et structuralisme* (Paris: Payot, 1964), 57; Klare, "The Critique of Everyday Life, the New Left, and the Unrecognizable Marxism," 9–10; David Gross, "Ernst Bloch: The Dialectics of Hope," in *The Unknown Dimension*, 124.

54. Gramsci, *Prison Notebooks*, Notebook 8 (1930–1932), §182 (3:340).

55. Gramsci, *Prison Notebooks*, Notebook 7 (1930–1931), §21 (3:171–72).

56. Karl Marx, "A Contribution to the Critique of Hegel's Philosophy of Right. Introduction," in *Early Writings*, trans. Rodney Livingstone and Gregor Benton (New York: Penguin, 1992), 251.

57. Karl Marx and Friedrich Engels, *The Holy Family, or Critique of Critical Criticism: Against Bruno Bauer, and Company*, trans. Richard Dixon and Clemens Dutt (Moscow: Progress Publishers, 1975), 148.

58. Gramsci, *Prison Notebooks*, Notebook 4 (1930–1932), §11 (2:153).

59. Gramsci, *Prison Notebooks*, Notebook 4 (1930–1932), §11 (2:153).

60. Gramsci, *Prison Notebooks*, Notebook 4 (1930–1932), §37 (2:176–77); Gramsci, *Prison Notebooks*, Notebook 7 (1930–1931), §29 (3:178–79).

61. Perry Anderson, *The Antinomies of Antonio Gramsci: With a New Preface* (London: Verso, 2017), 29.

62. Lucio Colletti, "A Political and Philosophical Interview [with Perry Anderson]," in *Western Marxism: A Critical Reader*, ed. New Left Review (London: Verso, 1978), 317, 346; Anderson, *The Antinomies of Antonio Gramsci*, 99–100; Anderson, *In the Tracks of Historical Materialism*, 16.

63. Gramsci, *Prison Notebooks*, Notebook 1 (1929–1930): First Notebook, §78 (1:183).

64. Antonio Gramsci, "Letter to Tatiana Schucht, April 18, 1932," in *Letters from Prison*, 2:164.

65. Korsch, "The Present State of the Problem of 'Marxism and Philosophy,'" 99–102.

66. Martin Jay, *Marxism and Totality: The Adventure of a Concept from Lukács to Habermas* (Berkeley: University of California Press, 1984), 454.

67. Andrew Arato and Paul Breines, *The Young Lukács and the Origins of Western Marxism* (New York: Continuum, 1979), 6, 76, 133–34, 196.

68. Antonio Gramsci, "Letter to Tatiana Schucht, December 1, 1930," in *Letters from Prison*, 1:365.

69. Gramsci, "Letter to Tatiana Schucht, May 9, 1932," 171.

70. Colletti, "A Political and Philosophical Interview," 346.

71. Gramsci, *Prison Notebooks*, Notebook 4 (1930–1932), §38 (2:177–78).

72. Gramsci, *Prison Notebooks*, Notebook 4 (1930–1932), §38 (2:179–80).

73. Gramsci, "Letter to Tatiana Schucht, May 2, 1932," 169.

74. Gramsci, "Letter to Tatiana Schucht, May 9, 1932," 171–72.

75. Marx, *A Contribution to the Critique of Political Economy*, 21; Gramsci, *Prison Notebooks*, Notebook 4 (1930–1932), §38 (2:184).

76. John Merrington, "Theory and Practice in Gramsci's Marxism," in *Western Marxism*, 142–44.

77. Gramsci, *Prison Notebooks*, Notebook 4 (1930–1932), §38 (2:186).

78. Gramsci, *Prison Notebooks*, Notebook 7 (1930–1931), §24 (3:173).

79. Gramsci, *Prison Notebooks*, Notebook 7 (1930–1931), §24 (3:174).

80. Gramsci, *Prison Notebooks*, Notebook 4 (1930–1932), §38 (2:183).

81. Gramsci, *Prison Notebooks*, Notebook 4 (1930–1932), §38 (2:183).

82. Ernesto Laclau, *On Populist Reason* (London: Verso, 2005), 248–49.

CONCLUSION   329

83. Louis Althusser, "Ideology and Ideological State Apparatuses (Notes Towards an Investigation)," in *On the Reproduction of Capitalism*, 232–72.

84. Althusser, *On the Reproduction of Capitalism*, 242, 244.

85. Althusser, *Que faire?*, 88.

86. Colletti, "A Political and Philosophical Interview," 347.

87. Althusser, *Que faire?*, 61–62.

88. Althusser, *Que faire?*, 60–61.

89. Althusser, *Que faire?*, 59–60.

90. Althusser, *Que faire?*, 67.

91. Althusser, *Que faire?*, 102–3, 124–25.

92. Althusser, *Que faire?*, 60.

93. Althusser, *Que faire?*, 61.

94. Althusser, *Que faire?*, 62, 67.

95. Althusser, *Que faire?*, 57, 81–82, 85.

96. Althusser, *Que faire?*, 70.

97. Adrian Johnston, "Meta-Transcendentalism and Error-First Ontology: The Cases of Gilbert Simondon and Catherine Malabou," in *New Realism and Contemporary Philosophy*, ed. Gregor Kroupa and Jure Simoniti (London: Bloomsbury, 2020), 171–75.

98. Althusser, *Que faire?*, 126–27.

99. Althusser, *Que faire?*, 126.

100. Anderson, *The Antinomies of Antonio Gramsci*, 135.

101. Georg Lukács, "Preface to the New Edition (1967)," in *History and Class Consciousness*, xxiv, xxxvi; Shlomo Avineri, *The Social and Political Thought of Karl Marx* (Cambridge: Cambridge University Press, 1968), 96–97; Rüdiger Dannemann, *Das Prinzip Verdinglichung: Studie zur Philosophie Georg Lukács'* (Frankfurt am Main: Sendler, 1987), 53.

102. Lukács, "Reification and the Consciousness of the Proletariat," 84–85.

103. Joseph Gabel, *False Consciousness: An Essay on Reification*, trans. Margaret A. Thompson (New York: Harper Torchbooks, 1978), 84–85, 89, 103.

104. Lukács, "Preface to the New Edition (1967)," ix.

105. Lukács, "Reification and the Consciousness of the Proletariat," 83.

106. Lukács, "Reification and the Consciousness of the Proletariat," 83–84.

107. Andrew Arato, "Georg Lukács: The Search for a Revolutionary Subject," in *The Unknown Dimension*, 95–97; Dannemann, *Das Prinzip Verdinglichung*, 40–43, 102.

108. Brown, *Marx, Freud, and the Critique of Everyday Life*, 13.

109. Lukács, "Reification and the Consciousness of the Proletariat," 86.

110. Korsch, *Karl Marx*, 109.

111. Lukács, "Reification and the Consciousness of the Proletariat," 87.

112. Lukács, "Reification and the Consciousness of the Proletariat," 92.

113. Lukács, "Reification and the Consciousness of the Proletariat," 88–89, 98–99, 102–3.

114. Lukács, "Reification and the Consciousness of the Proletariat," 90–91.

115. Gillian Rose, *Hegel Contra Sociology* (London: Verso, 2009), 30; Dannemann, *Das Prinzip Verdinglichung*, 55.

116. Lucio Colletti, "Bernstein and the Marxism of the Second International," in *From Rousseau to Lenin: Studies in Ideology and Society*, trans. John Merrington and Judith White (New York: Monthly Review Press, 1972), 94.

117. Lukács, "Reification and the Consciousness of the Proletariat," 88, 100.

118. Lukács, "Reification and the Consciousness of the Proletariat," 90.

119. Byung-Chul Han, *Capitalism and the Death Drive*, trans. Daniel Steuer (Cambridge: Polity, 2021), 76–77.

330 CONCLUSION

120. Lukács, "Preface to the New Edition (1967)," ix; Lukács, "Reification and the Consciousness of the Proletariat," 95–96; Georg Lukács, "Towards a Methodology of the Problem of Organization," in *History and Class Consciousness*, 318; Arato, "Georg Lukács," 91–92, 98; Rose, *Hegel Contra Sociology*, 31; Anderson, *In the Tracks of Historical Materialism*, 16; Dannemann, *Das Prinzip Verdinglichung*, 18, 22, 48, 79–83, 89–90, 92–93, 175; Frederic Jameson, *Representing Capital: A Commentary on Volume One* (London: Verso, 2011), 28.

121. Arato and Breines, *The Young Lukács and the Origins of Western Marxism*, 155.

122. Arato and Breines, *The Young Lukács and the Origins of Western Marxism*, 211.

123. Jeremy J. Shapiro, "The Dialectic of Theory and Practice in the Age of Technological Rationality: Herbert Marcuse and Jürgen Habermas," in *The Unknown Dimension*, 277–78; Gareth Stedman Jones, "The Marxism of the Early Lukács," in *Western Marxism*, 57; Göran Therborn, "The Frankfurt School," in *Western Marxism*, 97–99, 104; Andrew Feenberg, *The Philosophy of Praxis: Marx, Lukács, and the Frankfurt School* (London: Verso, 2014), 167.

124. Jones, "The Marxism of the Early Lukács," 13, 32.

125. Jones, "The Marxism of the Early Lukács," 33.

126. Jones, "The Marxism of the Early Lukács," 48.

127. Feenberg, *The Philosophy of Praxis*, 72–73.

128. Therborn, "The Frankfurt School," 93; Merrington, "Theory and Practice in Gramsci's Marxism," 144–45.

129. Therborn, "The Frankfurt School," 92.

130. Axel Honneth, "Reification and Recognition: A New Look at an Old Idea," trans. Joseph Ganahl, in *Reification: A New Look at an Old Idea*, ed. Martin Jay (Oxford: Oxford University Press, 2008), 17.

131. Honneth, "Reification and Recognition," 23.

132. Honneth, "Reification and Recognition," 23–24, 27–28, 58, 75–80; Axel Honneth, "Rejoinder," trans. Joseph Ganahl, in *Reification*, 157.

133. Lukács, "Reification and the Consciousness of the Proletariat," 95.

134. Russell Jacoby, *Dialectic of Defeat: Contours of Western Marxism* (Cambridge: Cambridge University Press, 1981), 85.

135. Brown, *Marx, Freud, and the Critique of Everyday Life*, 18.

136. Arato, "Georg Lukács," 90.

137. Han, *Capitalism and the Death Drive*, 21, 61.

138. Arato and Breines, *The Young Lukács and the Origins of Western Marxism*, 89.

139. Timothy Bewes, *Reification, or The Anxiety of Late Capitalism* (London: Verso, 2002), 253.

140. Feenberg, *The Philosophy of Praxis*, 67, 72–73.

141. Feenberg, *The Philosophy of Praxis*, 66–67.

142. Feenberg, *The Philosophy of Praxis*, 73.

143. V. I. Lenin, *The State and Revolution: The Marxist Theory of the State and the Tasks of the Proletariat in the Revolution*, in *Lenin: Selected Works, One-Volume Edition* (New York: International, 1971), 287; Lukács, "The Marxism of Rosa Luxemburg," 27.

144. Lukács, "Class Consciousness," 62.

145. Lukács, "Towards a Methodology of the Problem of Organization," 305–6.

146. Lukács, "Preface to the New Edition (1967)," xvii–xviii.

147. Lukács, "Preface to the New Edition (1967)," xxxiii.

148. Arato, "Georg Lukács," 88–90, 101.

149. Jay, *Marxism and Totality*, 180.

150. Martin Jay, *The Dialectical Imagination: A History of the Frankfurt School and the Institute of Social Research, 1923–1950* (Boston: Little, Brown, 1973), 21; Feenberg, *The Philosophy of Praxis*, 167.

CONCLUSION 331

151. Anderson, *Considerations on Western Marxism*, 88–89; Anderson, *In the Tracks of Historical Materialism*, 17.

152. Anderson, *Considerations on Western Marxism*, 42–45, 48, 99; Anderson, *In the Tracks of Historical Materialism*, 15–16; Therborn, "The Frankfurt School," 118–19; Colletti, "A Political and Philosophical Interview [with Perry Anderson]," 349; Jacoby, *Dialectic of Defeat*, 103, 115.

153. Anderson, *Considerations on Western Marxism*, 44–45.

154. Jacoby, *Dialectic of Defeat*, 103.

155. Jay, *The Dialectical Imagination*, 173–74.

156. Jay, *The Dialectical Imagination*, 125; James F. Becker, *Marxian Political Economy: An Outline* (Cambridge: Cambridge University Press, 1977), 282.

157. Jay, *The Dialectical Imagination*, 152.

158. Georg Lukács, *The Destruction of Reason*, trans. Peter Palmer (Atlantic Highlands, NJ: Humanities Press, 1981), 243; Georg Lukács, *The Theory of the Novel: A Historico-Philosophical Essay on the Forms of Great Epic Literature*, trans. Anna Bostock (Cambridge, MA: MIT Press, 1971), 22.

159. Jean-Paul Sartre, *Search for a Method*, trans. Hazel E. Barnes (New York: Vintage, 1968), 60–65, 83–84.

160. Herbert Marcuse, *One-Dimensional Man: Studies in the Ideology of Advanced Industrial Society* (Boston: Beacon, 1964), 191.

161. Marcuse, *One-Dimensional Man*, 256.

162. Herbert Marcuse, "The Concept of Essence," in *Negations: Essays in Critical Theory*, trans. Jeremy J. Shapiro (Boston: Beacon, 1968), 70.

163. Herbert Marcuse, "Philosophy and Critical Theory," in *Negations*, 134–35, 144–45.

164. Marcuse, "The Concept of Essence," 71.

165. Arato and Breines, *The Young Lukács and the Origins of Western Marxism*, 114.

166. Lukács, "Reification and the Consciousness of the Proletariat," 110.

167. Althusser, *On the Reproduction of Capitalism*, 181; Althusser, "Ideology and Ideological State Apparatuses," 256.

168. Marx, *A Contribution to the Critique of Political Economy*, 20–22.

169. Marx, *A Contribution to the Critique of Political Economy*, 21.

170. G. W. F. Hegel, *Science of Logic*, trans. A. V. Miller (London: George Allen & Unwin, 1969), 391, 395–99, 479, 499, 503–4, 507; G. W. F. Hegel, *The Encyclopedia Logic: Part I of the Encyclopedia of the Philosophical Sciences with the Zusätze*, trans. T. F. Geraets, W. A. Suchting, and H. S. Harris (Indianapolis, IN: Hackett, 1991), §112 (175–76, 178), §131 (199–201); G. W. F. Hegel, *Lectures on Logic: Berlin, 1831*, trans. Clark Butler (Bloomington: Indiana University Press, 2008), §112 (129), §131 (147–48).

171. Georg Lukács, *The Ontology of Social Being 1: Hegel's False and His Genuine Ontology*, trans. David Fernbach (London: Merlin Press, 1978), 79, 95–96, 99; Herbert Marcuse, *Hegel's Ontology and the Theory of Historicity*, trans. Seyla Benhabib (Cambridge, MA: MIT Press, 1987), 73, 79, 84; Herbert Marcuse, *Reason and Revolution: Hegel and the Rise of Social Theory*, 2nd ed. (New York: Routledge, 2000), 142–43, 148–49.

172. Agnes Heller, *The Theory of Need in Marx* (London: Allison & Busby, 1976), 76.

173. Colletti, "A Political and Philosophical Interview [with Perry Anderson]," 350.

174. Ernesto Laclau and Chantal Mouffe, *Hegemony and Socialist Strategy: Towards a Radical Democratic Politics*, 2nd ed. (London: Verso, 2001), viii–x, 12, 21, 28, 31, 36–37, 40–41, 50–51, 53, 58, 75–77, 85–87, 133–34, 137–43, 174–76, 191–92; Laclau, *On Populist Reason*, 71, 115–16, 150, 183, 225–26, 230, 248–50.

175. Bertell Ollman, *Alienation: Marx's Conception of Man in Capitalist Society* (Cambridge: Cambridge University Press, 1971), 182.

176. Alfred Sohn-Rethel, *Intellectual and Manual Labour: A Critique of Epistemology*, trans. Martin Sohn-Rethel (London: Macmillan, 1978), 6–8, 17, 20–21, 28–29, 57, 60–61, 74, 77–78.

177. Adrian Johnston, "'A Mass of Fools and Knaves': Psychoanalysis and the World's Many Asininities," in *Psychoanalytic Reflections on Stupidity and Stupor*, ed. Cindy Zeiher (Lanham, MD: Rowman & Littlefield, 2023), forthcoming.

178. Johnston, *Prolegomena to Any Future Materialism*, 2:73–183.

179. Lukács, "What Is Orthodox Marxism?," 24.

180. Lucio Colletti, "From Hegel to Marcuse," in *From Rousseau to Lenin*, 132, 134–35; Anderson, *Considerations on Western Marxism*, 56, 59–61; Jacoby, *Dialectic of Defeat*, 38–39, 100; Jay, *Marxism and Totality*, 115–16.

181. Johnston, *Prolegomena to Any Future Materialism*, 2:73–183.

182. Johnston, *Prolegomena to Any Future Materialism*, 2:73–183.

183. Adrian Johnston, "Humanity, That Sickness: Louis Althusser and the Helplessness of Psychoanalysis," *Crisis and Critique* 2, no. 2, special issue: "*Reading Capital* and *For Marx*: 50 Years Later," ed. Frank Ruda and Agon Hamza (2015): 217–61.

184. Avineri, *The Social and Political Thought of Karl Marx*, 148.

185. Ollman, *Alienation*, 211.

186. G. W. F. Hegel, *Die Philosophie des Geistes: Enzyklopädie der philosophischen Wissenschaften III, Werke in zwanzig Bänden, 10*, ed. Eva Moldenhauer and Karl Markus Michel (Frankfurt am Main: Suhrkamp, 1970), 190; Hegel, *Science of Logic*, 725; Hegel, *The Encyclopedia Logic*, §147 (222), §158 (233); G. W. F. Hegel, *Philosophy of Nature: Part Two of the Encyclopedia of the Philosophical Sciences*, trans. A. V. Miller (Oxford: Oxford University Press, 1970), §245 (5); G. W. F. Hegel, *Philosophy of History*, trans. J. Sibree (New York: Dover, 1956), 27; Friedrich Engels, *Anti-Dühring: Herr Eugen Dühring's Revolution in Science*, 2nd ed. (Moscow: Foreign Languages Publishing House, 1959), 157; Adrian Johnston, *A New German Idealism: Hegel, Žižek, and Dialectical Materialism* (New York: Columbia University Press, 2018), 95–102.

187. Johnston, "Humanity, That Sickness," 217–61.

188. Avineri, *The Social and Political Thought of Karl Marx*, 230.

189. Marx, *Capital, Volume One*, 173–74.

190. Slavoj Žižek, *Incontinence of the Void: Economico-Philosophical Spandrels* (Cambridge: MIT Press, 2017), 184.

191. *SXX*, 7, 73–89.

192. Karl Marx, *Karl-Marx-Ausgabe: Werke-Schriften-Briefe, Band V: Ökonomische Schriften, zweiter Band*, ed. Hans-Joachim Lieber, *Das Kapital: Kritik der politischen Ökonomie, dritter Band, drittes Buch, Der Gesamtprozess der kapitalistichen Produktion, Kapitel I-XV* (Darmstadt: Wissenschaftliche Buchgesellschaft, 1963), 668; Karl Marx, *Capital: A Critique of Political Economy, Volume Three*, trans. David Fernbach (New York: Penguin, 1981), 956.

193. Johnston, "'A Mass of Fools and Knaves.'"

194. Jacques Lacan, "Du discours psychanalytique," in *Lacan in Italia, 1953–1978* (Milan: La Salamandra, 1978), 49.

195. *SXIV*, 292.

Bibliography

All citations of works by Sigmund Freud are references to his *Gesammelte Werke* (German) or *Standard Edition* (English). These are abbreviated as *GW* or *SE*, followed by the volume number and the page number (*GW/SE #:#*). The abbreviation system for Jacques Lacan's seminars is a little more complicated. All seminars are abbreviated *S*, followed by the Roman numeral of the volume number. For those seminars available in English (seminars 1, 2, 3, 4, 5, 6, 7, 8, 10, 11, 17, 19, 20, and 23), I simply give the page numbers of the volumes as published by Norton and, more recently, Polity (e.g., Lacan *SXI*, 256). In a few instances, I refer to the original French editions of these translated seminars; when I do so, I indicate this in brackets as [Fr.]. For those seminars published in French in book form but not translated into English (seminars 14, 16, and 18), the listed page numbers refer to the French editions published by Éditions du Seuil (e.g., Lacan *SXVI*, 52). As for the rest of the seminars, the dates of the seminar sessions (month/day/year) are listed in place of page numbers (e.g., Lacan *SXV*, 12/6/67). Also, in instances when I am citing at the same time both a French or German text in the original and its English translation and there might be confusion about which is the original and which the translation, I put [Fr.] or [Gr.] next to the French or German original respectively (for example, *Grundrisse* [Gr.]).

Adorno, Theodor W. "Sociology and Psychology, Part I." Trans. Irving N. Wohlfarth. *New Left Review* 46 (November–December 1967): 67–80.
——. *Negative Dialectics*. Trans. E. B. Ashton. New York: Continuum, 1973.
Agamben, Giorgio. "'God Didn't Die, He Was Transformed Into Money': An Interview with Giorgio Agamben." With Peppe Savà. *Libcom.org*, 2014, https://libcom.org/library/god-didnt-die-he-was -transformed-money-interview-giorgio-agamben-peppe-savà.
——. *Homo Sacer: Sovereign Power and Bare Life*. Trans. Daniel Heller-Roazen. Stanford, CA: Stanford University Press, 1998.
——. *The Kingdom and the Glory: For a Theological Genealogy of Economy and Government (Homo Sacer II, 2)*. Trans. Lorenzo Chiesa with Matteo Mandarini. Stanford, CA: Stanford University Press, 2011.
——. *The Man Without Content*. Trans. Georgia Albert. Stanford, CA: Stanford University Press, 1999.
——. *The Open: Man and Animal*. Trans. Kevin Attell. Stanford, CA: Stanford University Press, 2004.
——. *The Signature of All Things: On Method*. Trans. Luca D'Isanto with Kevin Attell. New York: Zone, 2009.
——. *State of Exception*. Trans. Kevin Attell. Chicago: University of Chicago Press, 2005.

BIBLIOGRAPHY

Aglietta, Michel. "Monnaie, liquidité, confiance." In Michel Aglietta et al., *L'argent et la psychanalyse. Économie, dette et désir*, 13–31. Paris: Éditions Campagne Première, 2017.

Althusser, Louis. "À propos de Marx et l'histoire." In *Écrits sur l'histoire (1963–1986)*, ed. G. M. Goshgarian, 261–78. Paris: Presses Universitaires de France, 2018.

——. "Contradiction and Overdetermination: Notes for an Investigation." In *For Marx*, trans. Ben Brewster, 87–128. London: Verso, 2005.

——. "Contradiction et surdétermination (Notes pour une recherche)." In *Pour Marx*, 85–128. Paris: Éditions La Découverte, 2005.

——. "The Discovery of Dr. Freud." In *Writings on Psychoanalysis: Freud and Lacan*, trans. Jeffrey Mehlman, 85–105. New York: Columbia University Press, 1996.

——. "Freud and Lacan." In *Writings on Psychoanalysis: Freud and Lacan*, trans. Jeffrey Mehlman, 7–31. New York: Columbia University Press, 1996.

——. *How to Be a Marxist in Philosophy*. Ed. and trans. G. M. Goshgarian. London: Bloomsbury, 2017.

——. "Ideology and Ideological State Apparatuses (Notes Towards an Investigation)." In *On the Reproduction of Capitalism: Ideology and Ideological State Apparatuses*, trans. G. M. Goshgarian, 232–72. London: Verso, 2014.

——. "Lettre aux camarades du Comité Central du Parti communiste français." In *Socialisme idéologique et socialisme scientifique, et autres écrits*, ed. G. M. Goshgarian, 199–239. Paris: Presses Universitaires de France, 2022.

——. "L'idéologie (extrait de Théorie marxiste et Parti comministe)." In *Socialisme idéologique et socialisme scientifique, et autres écrits*, ed. G. M. Goshgarian, 159–81. Paris: Presses Universitaires de France, 2022.

——. "Livre sur l'impérialisme (extraits)." In *Écrits sur l'histoire (1963–1986)*, ed. G. M. Goshgarian, 103–260. Paris: Presses Universitaires de France, 2018.

——. "Marxism and Humanism." In *For Marx*, trans. Ben Brewster, 219–47. London: Verso, 2005.

——. *Montesquieu: Politics and History*. In *Politics and History: Montesquieu, Rousseau, Marx*, trans. Ben Brewster, 9–109. London: Verso, 2007.

——. "The Object of *Capital*." In Louis Althusser, Étienne Balibar, Roger Establet, Pierre Macherey, and Jacques Rancière, *Reading Capital: The Complete Edition*, trans. Ben Brewster and David Fernbach, 215–355. London: Verso, 2015.

——. *Psychoanalysis and the Human Sciences*. Trans. Steven Rendall. New York: Columbia University Press, 2016.

——. "On the Materialist Dialectic: On the Unevenness of Origins." In *For Marx*, trans. Ben Brewster, 161–218. London: Verso, 2005.

——. *On the Reproduction of Capitalism: Ideology and Ideological State Apparatuses*. Trans. G. M. Goshgarian. London: Verso, 2014.

——. *Que faire?*. Ed. G. M. Goshgarian. Paris: Presses Universitaires de France, 2018.

——. *Socialisme idéologique et socialisme scientifique*. In *Socialisme idéologique et socialisme scientifique, et autres écrits*, ed. G. M. Goshgarian, 55–158. Paris: Presses Universitaires de France, 2022.

——. "Sur la Révolution culturelle chinoise." In *Socialisme idéologique et socialisme scientifique, et autres écrits*, ed. G. M. Goshgarian, 277–312. Paris: Presses Universitaires de France, 2022.

——. "Sur l'idéologie (fragment inédit de 'Sur la Révolution culturelle chinoise.')." In *Socialisme idéologique et socialisme scientifique, et autres écrits*, ed. G. M. Goshgarian, 313–23. Paris: Presses Universitaires de France, 2022.

——. "Three Notes on the Theory of Discourses." In *The Humanist Controversy and Other Writings*, ed. François Matheron, trans. G. M. Goshgarian, 33–84. London: Verso, 2003.

Amar, André. "Essai psychanalytique sur l'argent." In *Psychanalyse de l'argent*, ed. Ernest Borneman, trans. Daniel Guérineau, 366–79. Paris: Presses Universitaires de France, 1978.

Anderson, Kevin. *Lenin, Hegel, and Western Marxism: A Critical Study*. Urbana: University of Illinois Press, 1995.

BIBLIOGRAPHY

——. "The Rediscovery and Persistence of the Dialectic in Philosophy and in World Politics." In *Lenin Reloaded: Toward a Politics of Truth*, ed. Sebastian Budgen, Stathis Kouvelakis, and Slavoj Žižek, 120–47. Durham, NC: Duke University Press, 2007.

Anderson, Perry. *The Antinomies of Antonio Gramsci: With a New Preface*. London: Verso, 2017.

——. *Considerations on Western Marxism*. London: New Left Books, 1976.

——. *In the Tracks of Historical Materialism: The Wellek Library Lectures*. London: Verso, 1983.

Arato, Andrew. "Georg Lukács: The Search for a Revolutionary Subject." In *The Unknown Dimension: European Marxism Since Lenin*, ed. Dick Howard and Karl E. Klare, 81–106. New York: Basic Books, 1972.

Arato, Andrew, and Paul Breines. *The Young Lukács and the Origins of Western Marxism*. New York: Continuum, 1979.

Aristotle. *Nicomachean Ethics*. Trans. Terrence Irwin. Indianapolis, IN: Hackett, 1999.

——. *Politics*. Translated by C. D. C. Reeve. Indianapolis, IN: Hackett, 1998.

Avineri, Shlomo. *The Social and Political Thought of Karl Marx*. Cambridge: Cambridge University Press, 1968.

Avrane, Patrick. "La valeur du petit caillou." In Michel Aglietta et al., *L'argent et la psychanalyse. Économie, dette et désir*, 165–75. Paris: Éditions Campagne Première, 2017.

——. *Petite psychanalyse de l'argent*. Paris: Presses Universitaires de France, 2015.

Badiou, Alain. *Je vous sais si nombreux . . . .* Paris: Fayard, 2017.

——. "Les quatre principes du marxisme." In Alain Badiou, Étienne Balibar, Jacques Bidet, Michael Löwy, and Lucien Sève, *Avec Marx, philosophie et politique*, ed. Alexis Cukier and Isabelle Garo, 31–38. Paris: La Dispute, 2019.

——. "Néolithique, capitalisme et communisme." In *Les possibles matins de la politique: Interventions, 2016–2020*, 13–21. Paris: Fayard, 2021.

——. *Petrograd, Shanghai: Les deux révolutions du XXe siècle*. Paris: La Fabrique éditions, 2018.

Balibar, Étienne. "On the Basic Concepts of Historical Materialism." In *Reading Capital: The Complete Edition*, trans. Ben Brewster and David Fernbach, 357–480. London: Verso, 2015.

——. *The Philosophy of Marx*. Trans. Chris Turner. London: Verso, 2007.

Balmès, François. *Dieu, le sexe et la vérité*. Ramonville Saint-Agne: Érès, 2007.

——. *Le nom, la loi, la voix*. Ramonville Saint-Agne: Érès, 1997.

Baran, Paul A., and Paul M. Sweezy. *Monopoly Capital: An Essay on the American Economic and Social Order*. New York: Monthly Review Press, 1966.

Barrère, Christian. *Crise du système de crédit et capitalisme monopoliste d'état*. Paris: Economica, 1977.

Becker, James F. *Marxian Political Economy: An Outline*. Cambridge: Cambridge University Press, 1977.

Bellofiore, Ricardo. "Lost in Translation? Once Again on the Marx-Hegel Connection." In *Marx's Capital and Hegel's Logic: A Reexamination*, ed. Fred Mosley and Tony Smith, 164–88. Chicago: Haymarket, 2015.

Benjamin, Walter. "Capitalism as Religion." Trans. Chad Kautzer. In *The Frankfurt School on Religion: Key Writings by the Major Thinkers*, ed. Eduardo Mendieta, 259–62. New York: Routledge, 2004.

——. "Kapitalismus als Religion." In *Gesammelte Schriften, Band VI: Fragmente vermischten Inhalts, autobiographische Schriften*, ed. Hermann Schweppenhäuser and Rolf Tiedemann, 100–3. Frankfurt: Suhrkamp, 1985.

——. "Theories of German Fascism." In *Selected Writings*, vol. 2, part 1: *1927–1930*, ed. Michael W. Jennings, Howard Eiland, and Gary Smith, trans. Rodney Livingstone et al., 312–21. Cambridge, MA: Harvard University Press, 1999.

——. "Theses on the Philosophy of History." In *Illuminations: Essays and Reflections*, ed. Hannah Arendt, trans. Harry Zohn, 253–64. New York: Schocken, 1969.

Bewes, Timothy. *Reification, or The Anxiety of Late Capitalism*. London: Verso, 2002.

336 BIBLIOGRAPHY

Blackburn, Robin, and Gareth Stedman Jones. "Louis Althusser and the Struggle for Marxism." In *The Unknown Dimension: European Marxism Since Lenin*, ed. Dick Howard and Karl E. Klare, 365–87. New York: Basic Books, 1972.

Boothby, Richard. *Freud as Philosopher: Metapsychology After Lacan*. New York: Routledge, 2001.

Braverman, Harry. *Labor and Monopoly Capital: The Degradation of Work in the Twentieth Century*. New York: Monthly Review Press, 1974.

Brewer, Anthony. *A Guide to Marx's Capital*. Cambridge: Cambridge University Press, 1984.

Brown, Bruce. *Marx, Freud, and the Critique of Everyday Life: Toward a Permanent Cultural Revolution*. New York: Monthly Review Press, 1973.

Brown, Norman O. *Life Against Death: The Psychoanalytical Meaning of History*. 2nd ed. Hanover, NH: University Press of New England, 1985.

Brunhoff, Suzanne de. *Marx on Money*. 2nd ed. Trans. Maurice J. Goldbloom. New York: Verso, 2015.

Brunner, José. *Freud and the Politics of Psychoanalysis*. London: Transaction, 2001.

Bruno, Pierre. *Lacan, passeur de Marx. L'invention du symptôme*. Toulouse: Érès, 2010.

——. "Portrait de Lacan par Marx." In *Marx, Lacan. L'acte révolutionnaire et l'acte analytique*, ed. Sylvia Lippi and Patrick Landman, 151–60. Toulouse: Érès, 2013.

Carrasco, Martin Bakero. "Symptôme et capitalisme. Excès et nécessité dans la production du sujet et la culture." In *Marx, Lacan. L'acte révolutionnaire et l'acte analytique*, ed. Sylvia Lippi and Patrick Landman, 241–54. Toulouse: Érès, 2013.

Cohen, G. A. *Karl Marx's Theory of History: A Defense*. Princeton, NJ: Princeton University Press, 1978.

Colletti, Lucio. "Bernstein and the Marxism of the Second International." In *From Rousseau to Lenin: Studies in Ideology and Society*, trans. John Merrington and Judith White, 45–108. New York: Monthly Review Press, 1972.

——. "From Hegel to Marcuse." In *From Rousseau to Lenin: Studies in Ideology and Society*, trans. John Merrington and Judith White, 111–40. New York: Monthly Review Press, 1972.

——. "Mandeville, Rousseau, and Smith." In *From Rousseau to Lenin: Studies in Ideology and Society*, trans. John Merrington and Judith White, 195–216. New York: Monthly Review Press, 1972.

——. *Marxism and Hegel*. Trans. Lawrence Garner. London: Verso, 1979.

——. "Marxism: Science or Revolution." In *From Rousseau to Lenin: Studies in Ideology and Society*, trans. John Merrington and Judith White, 229–36. New York: Monthly Review Press, 1972.

——. "A Political and Philosophical Interview [with Perry Anderson]." In *Western Marxism: A Critical Reader*, ed. *New Left Review*, 315–50. London: Verso, 1978.

Coriat, Isador H. "Remarques sur les traits de caractère anaux de l'instinct capitaliste." In *Psychanalyse de l'argent*, ed. Ernest Borneman, trans. Daniel Guérineau, 103–5. Paris: Presses Universitaires de France, 1978.

——. "Traits de caractère analérotiques chez Shylock." In *Psychanalyse de l'argent*, ed. Ernest Borneman, trans. Daniel Guérineau, 115–20. Paris: Presses Universitaires de France, 1978.

Damasio, Antonio. *Looking for Spinoza: Joy, Sorrow, and the Feeling Brain*. New York: Harcourt, 2003.

Dannemann, Rüdiger. *Das Prinzip Verdinglichung: Studie zur Philosophie Georg Lukács'*. Frankfurt am Main: Sendler, 1987.

Dattner, Bernhard. "Or et excrément." In *Psychanalyse de l'argent*, ed. Ernest Borneman, trans. Daniel Guérineau, 91–93. Paris: Presses Universitaires de France, 1978.

Deborin, A.M. "Spinoza's World-View." In *Spinoza in Soviet Philosophy*, ed. and trans. George L. Kline, 90–119. London: Routledge & Kegan Paul, 1952.

D'Holbach, Baron Paul Henri Thiry. *Good Sense*. Trans. Anna Knoop. Amherst, NY: Prometheus, 2004.

Dostaler, Gilles, and Bernard Maris. *Capitalisme et pulsion de mort*. Paris: Fayard, 2010.

Drach, Marcel. "Les deux fétichismes de l'argent." In *Marx, Lacan. L'acte révolutionnaire et l'acte analytique*, ed. Sylvia Lippi and Patrick Landman, 257–75. Toulouse: Érès, 2013.

BIBLIOGRAPHY   337

Dunayevskaya, Raya. *Philosophy and Revolution: From Hegel to Sartre, and from Marx to Mao.* New York: Dell, 1973.

——. *The Power of Negativity: Selected Writings on the Dialectic in Hegel and Marx.* Ed. Peter Hudis and Kevin B. Anderson. Lanham, MD: Lexington, 2002.

Dussel, Enrique. *Towards an Unknown Marx: A Commentary on the Manuscripts of 1861–63.* Ed. Fred Mosley. Trans. Yolanda Angulo. New York: Routledge, 2001.

Engels, Friedrich. *Anti-Dühring: Herr Eugen Dühring's Revolution in Science.* 2nd ed. Moscow: Foreign Languages Publishing House, 1959.

——. *The Condition of the Working Class in England.* Ed. David McLellan. Trans. Florence Kelley-Wischnewetsky. Oxford: Oxford University Press, 1993.

——. *Die Lage der arbeitenden Klasse in England, nach eigner Anschauung und authentischen Quellen.* Stuttgart: Dietz, 1892.

——. "Letter to Conrad Schmidt, October 27, 1890." https://www.marxists.org/ archive/marx/ works/1890/letters/90_10_27.htm.

——. *Ludwig Feuerbach and the Outcome of Classical German Philosophy.* Ed. C. P. Dutt. New York: International, 1941.

——. "Outlines of a Critique of Political Economy." In *The Young Hegelians: An Anthology,* ed. Lawrence S. Stepelevich, 278–302. Amherst, MA: Humanity, 1999.

——. "The Part Played by Labour in the Transition from Ape to Man." In *Dialectics of Nature,* trans. and ed. Clemens Dutt, 279–96. New York: International, 1940.

——. *Socialism: Utopian and Scientific.* Trans. Edward Aveling. New York: International, 1975.

Feenberg, Andrew. *The Philosophy of Praxis: Marx, Lukács, and the Frankfurt School.* London: Verso, 2014.

Fenichel, Otto. "The Drive to Amass Wealth." *Psychoanalytic Quarterly* 7 (1938): 69–95.

——. "Psychoanalysis as the Nucleus of a Future Dialectical-Materialist Psychology." Ed. Suzette H. Annin and Hanna Fenichel. Trans. Olga Barsis. *American Imago* 24, no. 4 (Winter 1967): 290–311.

Ferenczi, Sandor. "The Ontogenesis of the Interest in Money." In *First Contributions to Psycho-Analysis,* trans. Ernest Jones, 319–31. New York: Routledge, 1994.

——. "«Pecunia—olet» (L'argent—a une odeur)." In *Psychanalyse de l'argent,* ed. Ernest Borneman, trans. Daniel Guérineau, 106–9. Paris: Presses Universitaires de France, 1978.

Feuerbach, Ludwig. "Fragments Concerning the Characteristics of My Philosophical Development." In *The Fiery Brook: Selected Writings,* trans. Zawar Hanfi, 265–96. London: Verso, 2012.

——. "Preliminary Theses on the Reform of Philosophy." In *The Fiery Brook: Selected Writings,* trans. Zawar Hanfi, 153–73. London: Verso, 2012.

Fine, Ben, and Laurence Harris. *Rereading Capital.* New York: Columbia University Press, 1979.

Fine, Ben, and Alfredo Saad-Filho. *Marx's Capital.* 6th ed. London: Pluto, 2016.

Foley, Duncan K. *Understanding Capital: Marx's Economic Theory.* Cambridge, MA: Harvard University Press, 1986.

Fong, Benjamin Y. *Death and Mastery: Psychoanalytic Drive Theory and the Subject of Late Capitalism.* New York: Columbia University Press, 2016.

Forrest, David V. "Further Developmental Stages of the Interest in Money." *American Journal of Psychoanalysis* 50, no. 4 (1990): 319–35.

Foucault, Michel. *The Birth of Biopolitics: Lectures at the Collège de France, 1978–1979.* Ed. Michel Senellart. Trans. Graham Burchell. Basingstoke: Palgrave Macmillan, 2008.

——. *Security, Territory, Population: Lectures at the Collège de France, 1977–1978.* Ed. Michel Senellart. Trans. Graham Burchell. New York: Picador, 2007.

——. *"Society Must Be Defended": Lectures at the Collège de France, 1975–1976.* Ed. Mauro Bertani and Alessandro Fontana. Trans. David Macey. New York: Picador, 2003.

338 BIBLIOGRAPHY

Freud, Sigmund. *Entwurf einer Psychologie*. In *Aus den Anfängen der Psychoanalyse, 1887–1902*, ed. Marie Bonaparte, Anna Freud, and Ernst Kris, 371–466. Frankfurt am Main: S. Fischer, 1975.

Freud, Sigmund. *Gesammelte Werke*. Ed. E. Bibring, W. Hoffer, E. Kris, and O. Isakower. Frankfurt: S. Fischer, 1952.

——. *Abriss der Psychoanalyse. GW* 17:63–138.

——. "Fetischismus." *GW* 14:309–17.

——. *Hemmung, Symptom und Angst. GW* 14:111–205.

——. *Das Ich und das Es. GW* 13:235–89.

——. *Neue Folge der Vorlesungen zur Einführung in die Psychoanalyse. GW* 15.

——. *Das Unbehagen in der Kultur. GW* 14:419–506.

——. "Warum Krieg?" *GW* 16:11–27.

——. *Die Zukunft einer Illusion. GW* 14:323–80.

Freud, Sigmund. *The Standard Edition of the Complete Psychological Works of Sigmund Freud*. 24 vols. Ed. and trans. James Strachey, in collaboration with Anna Freud, assisted by Alix Strachey and Alan Tyson. London: Hogarth Press and the Institute of Psycho-Analysis, 1953–1974.

——. "Analysis Terminable and Interminable." *SE* 23:209–53.

——. *An Autobiographical Study. SE* 20:1–74.

——. *Beyond the Pleasure Principle. SE* 18:1–64.

——. "Character and Anal Erotism." *SE* 9:167–75.

——. *Civilization and Its Discontents. SE* 21:57–145.

——. "A Difficulty in the Path of Psycho-Analysis." *SE* 17:135–44.

——. "Dreams in Folklore (Freud and Oppenheim)." *SE* 12:175–203.

——. "The Economic Problem of Masochism." *SE* 19:155–72.

——. *The Ego and the Id. SE* 19:1–66.

——. "Two Encyclopedia Articles: (B) The Libido Theory." *SE* 18:255–59.

——. "Extracts from the Fliess Papers." *SE* 1:173–280.

——. *From the History of an Infantile Neurosis. SE* 17:1–123.

——. "Fetishism." *SE* 21:147–57.

——. *The Future of an Illusion. SE* 21:1–56.

——. "The Goethe Prize: Address Delivered in the Goethe House at Frankfurt." *SE* 21:208–12.

——. *Group Psychology and the Analysis of the Ego. SE* 18:65–143.

——. "Humour." *SE* 21:159–66.

——. *Inhibitions, Symptoms and Anxiety. SE* 20:75–172.

——. "Instincts and Their Vicissitudes." *SE* 14:109–40.

——. *The Interpretation of Dreams. SE* 4–5.

——. *Introductory Lectures on Psycho-Analysis. SE* 15–16.

——. *Jokes and Their Relation to the Unconscious. SE* 8.

——. "Leonardo Da Vinci and a Memory of His Childhood." *SE* 11:57–137.

——. *Moses and Monotheism. SE* 23:1–137.

——. "Negation." *SE* 19:233–39.

——. *New Introductory Lectures on Psycho-Analysis. SE* 22:1–182.

——. "On Beginning the Treatment (Further Recommendations on the Technique of Psycho-Analysis I)." *SE* 12:121–44.

——. "On Narcissism: An Introduction." *SE* 14:67–102.

——. "On Transformations of Instinct as Exemplified in Anal Erotism." *SE* 17:125–33.

——. *An Outline of Psycho-Analysis. SE* 23:139–207.

——. "Project for a Scientific Psychology." *SE* 1:281–387.

——. "Psycho-Analysis." *SE* 20:259–70.

——. "The Resistances to Psycho-Analysis." *SE* 19:211–24.

——. "Screen Memories." *SE* 3:299–322.

BIBLIOGRAPHY   339

——. "A Short Account of Psycho-Analysis." *SE* 19:189–209.

——. "Shorter Writings: Letter to Dr. Friedrich S. Krauss on *Anthropophyteia*." *SE* 11:233–35.

——. "Splitting of the Ego in the Process of Defense." *SE* 23:271–78.

——. *Three Essays on the Theory of Sexuality. SE* 7:123–245.

——. *Totem and Taboo. SE* 13:1–161.

——. "The Unconscious." *SE* 14:159–204.

——. "Why War?" *SE* 22:195–215.

Gabel, Joseph. *False Consciousness: An Essay on Reification*. Trans. Margaret A. Thompson. New York: Harper Torchbooks, 1978.

Galilei, Galileo. "The Assayer." In *Discoveries and Opinions of Galileo*, trans. Stillman Drake, 229–80. New York: Anchor, 1957.

Gay, Peter. *Freud: A Life for Our Time*. New York: Norton, 1988.

Geras, Norman. "Althusser's Marxism: An Assessment." In *Western Marxism: A Critical Reader*, ed. *New Left Review*, 232–72. London: Verso, 1978.

Glucksmann, André. "A Ventriloquist Structuralism." In *Western Marxism: A Critical Reader*, ed. *New Left Review*, 282–314. London: Verso, 1978.

Gramsci, Antonio. *Prison Notebooks*. 3 vols. Ed. and trans. Joseph A. Buttigieg. New York: Columbia University Press, 1992, 1996, 2007.

——. "Letter to Julca Schucht, December 30, 1929." In *Letters from Prison*, ed. Frank Rosengarten, trans. Raymond Rosenthal, 1:300–3. New York: Columbia University Press, 1994.

——. "Letter to Tatiana Schucht, April 18, 1932." In *Letters from Prison*, ed. Frank Rosengarten, trans. Raymond Rosenthal, 2:162–65. New York: Columbia University Press, 1994.

——. "Letter to Tatiana Schucht, December 1, 1930." In *Letters from Prison*, ed. Frank Rosengarten, trans. Raymond Rosenthal, 1:363–66. New York: Columbia University Press, 1994.

——. "Letter to Tatiana Schucht, May 2, 1932." In *Letters from Prison*, ed. Frank Rosengarten, trans. Raymond Rosenthal, 2:167–70. New York: Columbia University Press, 1994.

——. "Letter to Tatiana Schucht, May 9, 1932." In *Letters from Prison*, ed. Frank Rosengarten, trans. Raymond Rosenthal, 2:170–73. New York: Columbia University Press, 1994.

——. "Letter to Tatiana Schucht, September 7, 1931." In *Letters from Prison*, ed. Frank Rosengarten, trans. Raymond Rosenthal, 2:65–68. New York: Columbia University Press, 1994.

Gross, David. "Ernst Bloch: The Dialectics of Hope." In *The Unknown Dimension: European Marxism Since Lenin*, ed. Dick Howard and Karl E. Klare, 107–30. New York: Basic Books, 1972.

Grossmann, Henryk. *The Law of Accumulation and Breakdown of the Capitalist System: Being Also a Theory of Crises*. Trans. Jairus Banaji. London: Pluto, 1992.

Habermas, Jürgen. *Knowledge and Human Interests*. Trans. Jeremy J. Shapiro. Boston: Beacon, 1971.

Han, Byung-Chul. *Capitalism and the Death Drive*. Trans. Daniel Steuer. Cambridge: Polity, 2021.

Harvey, David. *A Companion to Marx's Capital*. London: Verso, 2010.

——. *A Companion to Marx's Capital, Volume Two*. London: Verso, 2013.

——. *The Limits to Capital*. London: Verso, 2006.

——. *Marx, Capital, and the Madness of Economic Reason*. London: Profile, 2017.

Hegel, G. W. F. *Elements of the Philosophy of Right*. Ed. Allen W. Wood. Trans. H. B. Nisbet. Cambridge: Cambridge University Press, 1991.

——. *The Encyclopedia Logic: Part I of the Encyclopedia of the Philosophical Sciences with the Zusätze*. Trans. T. F. Geraets, W. A. Suchting, and H. S. Harris. Indianapolis, IN: Hackett, 1991.

——. *First Philosophy of Spirit (Part III of the System of Speculative Philosophy 1803/4)*. In *System of Ethical Life and First Philosophy of Spirit*, trans. H. S. Harris and T. M. Knox, 187–250. Albany: State University of New York Press, 1979.

——. *Grundlinien der Philosophie des Rechts oder Naturrecht und Staatswissenschaft im Grundrisse: Mit Hegels eigenhändigen Notizen und den mündlichen Zusätzen, Werke in zwanzig Bänden, 7*. Ed. Eva Moldenhauer and Karl Markus Michel. Frankfurt am Main: Suhrkamp, 1970.

——. "Hegel to Schelling: Bern, April 16, 1795." In *Hegel: The Letters*, trans. Clark Butler and Christiane Seiler, 35–36. Bloomington: Indiana University Press, 1984.

——. *Lectures on the History of Philosophy*, vol. 3. Trans. E. S. Haldane and Frances H. Simson. New York: Humanities Press, 1955.

——. *Lectures on Logic: Berlin, 1831*. Trans. Clark Butler. Bloomington: Indiana University Press, 2008.

——. *Lectures on Natural Right and Political Science: The First Philosophy of Right, Heidelberg 1817–1818, with Additions from the Lectures of 1818–1819*. Trans. J. Michael Stewart and Peter C. Hodgson. Berkeley: University of California Press, 1995.

——. *Lectures on the Philosophy of Religion, One-Volume Edition: The Lectures of 1827*. Ed. Peter C. Hodgson. Trans. R. F. Brown, P. C. Hodgson, J. M. Stewart, and H. S. Harris. Berkeley: University of California Press, 1988.

——. *Lectures on the Philosophy of Religion*. Vol. 3: *The Consummate Religion*. Ed. Peter C. Hodgson. Trans. R. F. Brown, P. C. Hodgson, J. M. Stewart, and H. S. Harris. Berkeley: University of California Press, 1985.

——. *Phänomenologie des Geistes, Werke in zwanzig Bänden, 3*. Ed. Eva Moldenhauer and Karl Markus Michel. Frankfurt am Main: Suhrkamp, 1970.

——. *Phenomenology of Spirit*. Trans. A. V. Miller. Oxford: Oxford University Press, 1977.

——. *Die Philosophie des Geistes: Enzyklopädie der philosophischen Wissenschaften III, Werke in zwanzig Bänden, 10*. Ed. Eva Moldenhauer and Karl Markus Michel. Frankfurt am Main: Suhrkamp, 1970.

——. *Philosophy of History*. Trans. J. Sibree. New York: Dover, 1956.

——. *Philosophy of Mind: Part Three of the Encyclopedia of the Philosophical Sciences*. Trans. A. V. Miller. Oxford: Oxford University Press, 1971.

——. *Philosophy of Nature: Part Two of the Encyclopedia of the Philosophical Sciences*. Trans. A. V. Miller. Oxford: Oxford University Press, 1970.

——. "The Relationship of Religion to the State (1831)." In *Political Writings*, ed. Laurence Dickey and H. B. Nisbet, trans. H. B. Nisbet, 225–33. Cambridge: Cambridge University Press, 1999.

——. "The Science of Laws, Morals and Religion [for the Lower Class]." In *The Philosophical Propaedeutic*, ed. Michael George and Andrew Vincent, trans. A. V. Miller, 1–54. Oxford: Blackwell, 1986.

——. *Science of Logic*. Trans. A. V. Miller. London: George Allen & Unwin, 1969.

——. *The Spirit of Christianity and Its Fate*. In *Early Theological Writings*, trans. T. M. Knox, 182–301. Philadelphia: University of Pennsylvania Press, 1975.

——. *System of Ethical Life*. In *System of Ethical Life and First Philosophy of Spirit*, trans. H. S. Harris and T. M. Knox, 97–177. Albany: State University of New York Press, 1979.

Heidegger, Martin. "Letter on Humanism." Trans. Frank A. Capuzzi and J. Glenn Gray. In *Basic Writings*, ed. David Farrell Krell, 217–65. New York: HarperCollins, 1993.

Heinrich, Michael. *An Introduction to the Three Volumes of Karl Marx's Capital*. Trans. Alexander Locascio. New York: Monthly Review Press, 2012.

Heller, Agnes. *The Theory of Need in Marx*. London: Allison & Busby, 1976.

Hilferding, Rudolf. *Finance Capital: A Study of the Latest Phase of Capitalist Development*. Ed. Tom Bottomore. Trans. Morris Watnick and Sam Gordon. London: Routledge & Kegan Paul, 1981.

——. *Das Finanzkapital: Eine Studie über die jüngste Entwicklung des Kapitalismus*. Berlin: Dietz, 1947.

Hobbes, Thomas. *The Citizen: Philosophical Rudiments Concerning Government and Society*. In *Man and Citizen*, ed. Bernard Gert, 87–386. New York: Anchor, 1972.

Honneth, Axel. "Reification and Recognition: A New Look at an Old Idea." Trans. Joseph Ganahl. In *Reification: A New Look at an Old Idea*, ed. Martin Jay, 15–94. Oxford: Oxford University Press, 2008.

——. "Rejoinder." Trans. Joseph Ganahl. In *Reification: A New Look at an Old Idea*, ed. Martin Jay, 145–59. Oxford: Oxford University Press, 2008.

BIBLIOGRAPHY

Horkheimer, Max. "Authority and the Family." In *Critical Theory: Selected Essays*, trans. Matthew J. O'Connell et al., 47–128. New York: Continuum, 1982.

Jacoby, Russell. *Dialectic of Defeat: Contours of Western Marxism*. Cambridge: Cambridge University Press, 1981.

——. *The Repression of Psychoanalysis: Otto Fenichel and the Political Freudians*. New York: Basic Books, 1983.

——. *Social Amnesia: A Critique of Conformist Psychology from Adler to Laing*. Boston: Beacon, 1975.

Jameson, Frederic. "An American Utopia." In *An American Utopia: Dual Power and the Universal Army*, ed. Slavoj Žižek, 1–96. New York: Verso, 2016.

——. *Representing Capital: A Commentary on Volume One*. London: Verso, 2011.

Jay, Martin. *The Dialectical Imagination: A History of the Frankfurt School and the Institute of Social Research, 1923–1950*. Boston: Little, Brown, 1973.

——. "'In Psychoanalysis Nothing Is True but the Exaggerations': Freud and the Frankfurt School." In *Splinters in Your Eye: Frankfurt School Provocations*, 48–65. London: Verso, 2020.

——. "Irony and Dialectics: *One-Dimensional Man* and 1968." In *Splinters in Your Eye: Frankfurt School Provocations*, 133–50. London: Verso, 2020.

——. *Marxism and Totality: The Adventure of a Concept from Lukács to Habermas*. Berkeley: University of California Press, 1984.

Johnston, Adrian. *Adventures in Transcendental Materialism: Dialogues with Contemporary Thinkers*. Edinburgh: Edinburgh University Press, 2014.

——. *Badiou, Žižek, and Political Transformations: The Cadence of Change*. Evanston, IL: Northwestern University Press, 2009.

——. "A Blast from the Future: Freud, Lacan, Marcuse, and Snapping the Threads of the Past." In *Umbr(a): Utopia*, ed. Ryan Anthony Hatch, 67–84. Buffalo: Center for the Study of Psychoanalysis and Culture, State University of New York at Buffalo, 2008.

——. "Capitalism's Implants: A Hegelian Theory of Failed Revolutions." *Crisis and Critique* 8, no. 2, special issue: "The Two- Hundredth Anniversary of Hegel's *Philosophy of Right*," ed. Agon Hamza and Frank Ruda (2021): 122–81.

——. "Humanity, That Sickness: Louis Althusser and the Helplessness of Psychoanalysis." *Crisis and Critique* 2, no. 2, special issue: "*Reading Capital* and *For Marx*: 50 Years Later," ed. Frank Ruda and Agon Hamza (2015): 217–61.

——. *Irrepressible Truth: On Lacan's 'The Freudian Thing.'* Basingstoke: Palgrave, 2017.

——. "Lacan's Endgame: Philosophy, Science, and Religion in the Final Seminars." *Crisis and Critique* 6, no. 1, special issue: "Lacan: Psychoanalysis, Philosophy, Politics," ed. Agon Hamza and Frank Ruda (2019): 156–87.

——. "The Late Innate: Jean Laplanche, Jaak Panksepp, and the Distinction Between Sexual Drives and Instincts." In *Inheritance in Psychoanalysis*, ed. Joel Goldbach and James A. Godley, 57–84. Albany: State University of New York Press, 2018.

——. "'A Mass of Fools and Knaves': Psychoanalysis and the World's Many Asininities." In *Psychoanalytic Reflections on Stupidity and Stupor*, ed. Cindy Zeiher. Lanham, MD: Rowman & Littlefield, 2023.

——. "Meta-Transcendentalism and Error-First Ontology: The Cases of Gilbert Simondon and Catherine Malabou." In *New Realism and Contemporary Philosophy*, ed. Gregor Kroupa and Jure Simoniti, 145–78. London: Bloomsbury, 2020.

——. "Misfelt Feelings: Unconscious Affect Between Psychoanalysis, Neuroscience, and Philosophy." In Adrian Johnston and Catherine Malabou, *Self and Emotional Life: Philosophy, Psychoanalysis, and Neuroscience*, 73–210. New York: Columbia University Press, 2013.

——. *A New German Idealism: Hegel, Žižek, and Dialectical Materialism*. New York: Columbia University Press, 2018.

——. "Non-Existence and Sexual Identity: Some Brief Remarks on Meinong and Lacan." *Lacanian Ink* 3 (Fall/Winter 2002): http://www.lacan.com/ nonexistf.htm.

——. *Prolegomena to Any Future Materialism*. Vol. 1: *The Outcome of Contemporary French Philosophy*. Evanston, IL: Northwestern University Press, 2013.

——. *Prolegomena to Any Future Materialism*. Vol. 2: *A Weak Nature Alone*. Evanston, IL: Northwestern University Press, 2019.

——. *Time Driven: Metapsychology and the Splitting of the Drive*. Evanston, IL: Northwestern University Press, 2005.

Joravsky, David. *Soviet Marxism and Natural Science: 1917–1932*. London: Routledge & Kegan Paul, 1961.

Kalecki, Michał. *Theory of Economic Dynamics: An Essay on Long-Run Changes in Capitalist Economy*. New York: Monthly Review Press, 1968.

Kant, Immanuel. "Idea for a Universal History with a Cosmopolitan Intent." In *Perpetual Peace and Other Essays on Politics, History, and Morals*, trans. Ted Humphrey, 29–40. Indianapolis, IN: Hackett, 1983.

——. "*Idee zu einer allgemeinen Geschichte in weltbürgerlicher Absicht*." In *Werkausgabe XI: Schriften zur Anthropologie, Geschichtsphilosophie, Politik und Pädagogik 1*, ed. Wilhelm Weischedel, 31–50. Frankfurt am Main: Suhrkamp, 1977.

Kaplan-Solms, Karen, and Mark Solms. *Clinical Studies in Neuro-Psychoanalysis: Introduction to a Depth Neuropsychology*. London: Karnac, 2002.

Karatani, Kojin. *Transcritique: On Kant and Marx*. Trans. Sabu Kohso. Cambridge, MA: MIT Press, 2003.

Keynes, John Maynard. *The General Theory of Employment, Interest, and Money*. New York: Harcourt, Brace & World, 1962.

Klare, Karl E. "The Critique of Everyday Life, the New Left, and the Unrecognizable Marxism." In *The Unknown Dimension: European Marxism Since Lenin*, ed. Dick Howard and Karl E. Klare, 3–33. New York: Basic Books, 1972.

Kojève, Alexandre. *Introduction to the Reading of Hegel: Lectures on the Phenomenology of Spirit*. Ed. Raymond Queneau and Allan Bloom. Trans. James H. Nichols Jr. Ithaca, NY: Cornell University Press, 1980.

Korsch, Karl. *Karl Marx*. Chicago: Haymarket, 2017.

——. *Marxism and Philosophy*. Trans. Fred Halliday. New York: New Left Books, 1970.

——. *Marxismus und Philosophie*. Ed. Erich Gerlach. Frankfurt am Main: Europäische Verlagsanstalt, 1966.

——. "The Present State of the Problem of 'Marxism and Philosophy'—An Anti-Critique." In *Marxism and Philosophy*, trans. Fred Halliday, 98–144. New York: New Left Books, 1970.

Kouvelakis, Stathis. "Lenin as Reader of Hegel: Hypotheses for a Reading of Lenin's Notebooks on Hegel's *The Science of Logic*." In *Lenin Reloaded: Toward a Politics of Truth*, ed. Sebastian Budgen, Stathis Kouvelakis, and Slavoj Žižek, 164–204. Durham, NC: Duke University Press, 2007.

Koyré, Alexandre. *From the Closed World to the Infinite Universe*. New York: Harper Torchbooks, 1958.

Kripke, Saul A. *Naming and Necessity*. Cambridge, MA: Harvard University Press, 1972.

——. *Wittgenstein on Rules and Private Language: An Elementary Exposition*. Cambridge, MA: Harvard University Press, 1982.

Lacan, Jacques. "Acte de fondation." In *Autres écrits*, ed. Jacques-Alain Miller, 229–41. Paris: Éditions du Seuil, 2001.

——. "Les complexes familiaux dans la formation de l'individu. Essai d'analyse d'une fonction en psychologie." In *Autres écrits*, ed. Jacques-Alain Miller, 23–84. Paris: Éditions du Seuil, 2001.

——. "Discours à l'École freudienne de Paris." In *Autres écrits*, ed. Jacques-Alain Miller, 261–81. Paris: Éditions du Seuil, 2001.

BIBLIOGRAPHY   343

——. "Discourse to Catholics." In *The Triumph of Religion, Preceded by Discourse to Catholics*, trans. Bruce Fink, 1–52. Cambridge: Polity, 2013.

——. "D'une réforme dans son trou." *Pas-tout Lacan*, 1969. http://ecole-lacanienne.net/wp- content /uploads/2016/04/1969-02-03.pdf.

——. "Du discours psychanalytique." In *Lacan in Italia, 1953–1978*, 32–55. Milan: La Salamandra, 1978.

——. "En guise de conclusion." *Lettres de l'École freudienne* 8 (1971): 205–17.

——. "L'étourdit." In *Autres écrits*, ed. Jacques-Alain Miller, 449–95. Paris: Éditions du Seuil, 2001.

——. "The Function and Field of Speech and Language in Psychoanalysis." In *Écrits: The First Complete Edition in English*, trans. Bruce Fink, 197–268. New York: Norton, 2006.

——. "Un homme et une femme." *Bulletin de l'Association freudienne* 54 (September 1993): 13–21.

——. "The Instance of the Letter in the Unconscious, or Reason Since Freud." In *Écrits: The First Complete Edition in English*, trans. Bruce Fink, 412–41. New York: Norton, 2006.

——. "Introduction à l'édition allemande d'un premier volume des *Écrits*." In *Autres écrits*, ed. Jacques-Alain Miller, 553–59. Paris: Éditions du Seuil, 2001.

——. "Jacques Lacan à l'École belge de psychanalyse." *Quarto* 5 (1981): 4–22.

——. "Journées d'étude des cartels de l'École freudienne: Séance de cloture." *Lettres de l'École freudienne* 18 (1976): 263–70.

——. "The Mirror Stage as Formative of the I Function as Revealed in Psychoanalytic Experience." In *Écrits: The First Complete Edition in English*, trans. Bruce Fink, 75–81. New York: Norton, 2006.

——. "Mis en question du psychanalyste." In *Lacan Redivivus*, ed. Jacques-Alain Miller and Christiane Alberti, 36–102. Paris: Navarin, 2021.

——. "Mon enseignement, sa nature et ses fins." In *Mon enseignement*, ed. Jacques-Alain Miller, 75–112. Paris: Éditions du Seuil, 2005.

——. "My Teaching, Its Nature and Its Ends." In *My Teaching*, ed. Jacques-Alain Miller, trans. David Macey, 57–89. London: Verso, 2008.

——. "On an Ex Post Facto Syllabary." In *Écrits: The First Complete Edition in English*, trans. Bruce Fink, 602–9. New York: Norton, 2006.

——. "Position of the Unconscious." In *Écrits: The First Complete Edition in English*, trans. Bruce Fink, 703–21. New York: Norton, 2006.

——. "Postface au Séminaire XI." In *Autres écrits*, ed. Jacques-Alain Miller, 503–7. Paris: Éditions du Seuil, 2001.

——. "Presentation on Psychical Causality." In *Écrits: The First Complete Edition in English*, trans. Bruce Fink, 123–58. New York: Norton, 2006.

——. "Radiophonie." In *Autres écrits*, ed. Jacques-Alain Miller, 403–47. Paris: Éditions du Seuil, 2001.

——. "Responses to Students of Philosophy Concerning the Object of Psychoanalysis." Trans. Jeffrey Mehlman. In *Television/A Challenge to the Psychoanalytic Establishment*, ed. Joan Copjec, 107–14. New York: Norton, 1990.

——. "Science and Truth." In *Écrits: The First Complete Edition in English*, trans. Bruce Fink, 726–45. New York: Norton, 2006.

——. "Seminar on 'The Purloined Letter.'" In *Écrits: The First Complete Edition in English*, trans. Bruce Fink, 6–48. New York: Norton, 2006.

——. "Subversion du sujet et dialectique du désir dans l'inconscient freudien." In *Écrits*, 793–827. Paris: Éditions du Seuil, 1966.

——. "The Subversion of the Subject and the Dialectic of Desire in the Freudian Unconscious." In *Écrits: The First Complete Edition in English*, trans. Bruce Fink, 671–702. New York: Norton, 2006.

——. "Television." Trans. Denis Hollier, Rosalind Krauss, and Annette Michelson. In *Television/A Challenge to the Psychoanalytic Establishment*, ed. Joan Copjec, 1–46. New York: Norton, 1990.

——. *Télévision*. Paris: Éditions du Seuil, 1973.

——. "A Theoretical Introduction to the Functions of Psychoanalysis in Criminology." In *Écrits: The First Complete Edition in English*, trans. Bruce Fink, 102–22. New York: Norton, 2006.

——. "The Triumph of Religion." In *The Triumph of Religion, Preceded by Discourse to Catholics*, trans. Bruce Fink, 53–85. Cambridge: Polity, 2013.

——. "La troisième." *Lettres de l'École freudienne* 16 (1975): 177–203.

——. "Variations on the Standard Treatment." In *Écrits: The First Complete Edition in English*, trans. Bruce Fink, 269–302. New York: Norton, 2006.

Lacan, Jacques. The Seminars:

——. *The Seminar of Jacques Lacan, Book I: Freud's Papers on Technique, 1953–1954*. Ed. Jacques-Alain Miller. Trans. John Forrester. New York: Norton, 1988.

——. *The Seminar of Jacques Lacan, Book II: The Ego in Freud's Theory and in the Technique of Psychoanalysis, 1954–1955*. Ed. Jacques-Alain Miller. Trans. Sylvana Tomaselli. New York: Norton, 1988.

——. *The Seminar of Jacques Lacan, Book III: The Psychoses, 1955–1956*. Ed. Jacques- Alain Miller. Trans. Russell Grigg. New York: Norton, 1993.

——. *Le séminaire de Jacques Lacan, Livre IV: La relation d'objet, 1956–1957*. Ed. Jacques- Alan Miller. Paris: Éditions du Seuil, 1994.

——. *The Seminar of Jacques Lacan, Book IV: The Object Relation, 1956–1957*. Ed. Jacques-Alain Miller. Trans. A. R. Price. Cambridge: Polity, 2020.

——. *The Seminar of Jacques Lacan, Book V: Formations of the Unconscious, 1957–1958*. Ed. Jacques-Alain Miller. Trans. Russell Grigg. Cambridge: Polity, 2017.

——. *Le séminaire de Jacques Lacan, Livre VI: Le désir et son interprétation, 1958–1959*. Ed. Jacques-Alain Miller. Paris: Éditions de la Martinière, 2013.

——. *The Seminar of Jacques Lacan, Book VI: Desire and Its Interpretation, 1958–1959*. Ed. Jacques-Alain Miller. Trans. Bruce Fink. Cambridge: Polity, 2019.

——. *The Seminar of Jacques Lacan, Book VII: The Ethics of Psychoanalysis, 1959–1960*. Ed. Jacques-Alain Miller. Trans. Dennis Porter. New York: Norton, 1992.

——. *The Seminar of Jacques Lacan, Book VIII: Transference, 1960–1961*. Ed. Jacques- Alain Miller. Trans. Bruce Fink. Cambridge: Polity, 2015.

——. *Le séminaire de Jacques Lacan, Livre IX: L'identification, 1961–1962*. Unpublished typescript.

——. *The Seminar of Jacques Lacan, Book X: Anxiety, 1962–1963*. Ed. Jacques-Alain Miller. Trans. A. R. Price. Cambridge: Polity, 2014.

——. *Le séminaire de Jacques Lacan, Livre XI: Les quatre concepts fondamentaux de la psychanalyse, 1964*. Ed. Jacques-Alain Miller. Paris: Éditions du Seuil, 1973.

——. *The Seminar of Jacques Lacan, Book XI: The Four Fundamental Concepts of Psychoanalysis, 1964*. Ed. Jacques-Alain Miller. Trans. Alan Sheridan. New York: Norton, 1977.

——. *Le séminaire de Jacques Lacan, Livre XII: Problèmes cruciaux pour la psychanalyse, 1964–1965*. Unpublished typescript.

——. *Le séminaire de Jacques Lacan, Livre XIII: L'objet de la psychanalyse, 1965–1966*. Unpublished typescript.

——. *Le séminaire de Jacques Lacan, Livre XIV: La logique du fantasme, 1966–1967*. Ed. Jacques-Alain Miller. Paris: Éditions du Seuil, 2023.

——. *Le séminaire de Jacques Lacan, Livre XV: L'acte psychanalytique, 1967–1968*. Unpublished typescript.

——. *Le séminaire de Jacques Lacan, Livre XVI: D'un Autre à l'autre, 1968–1969*. Ed. Jacques-Alain Miller. Paris: Éditions du Seuil, 2006.

——. *Le séminaire de Jacques Lacan, Livre XVII: L'envers de la psychanalyse, 1969–1970*. Ed. Jacques-Alain Miller. Paris: Éditions du Seuil, 1991.

——. *The Seminar of Jacques Lacan, Book XVII: The Other Side of Psychoanalysis, 1969–1970*. Ed. Jacques- Alain Miller. Trans. Russell Grigg. New York: Norton, 2007.

BIBLIOGRAPHY

——. *Le séminaire de Jacques Lacan, Livre XVIII: D'un discours qui ne serait pas du semblant, 1971*. Ed. Jacques-Alain Miller. Paris: Éditions du Seuil, 2006.

——. *The Seminar of Jacques Lacan, Book XIX: . . . or Worse, 1971–1972*. Ed. Jacques-Alain Miller. Trans. A. R. Price. Cambridge: Polity, 2018.

——. *Le séminaire de Jacques Lacan, Livre XIX: Le savoir du psychanalyste, 1971–1972*. Unpublished typescript.

——. *Le séminaire de Jacques Lacan, Livre XX: Encore, 1972–1973*. Ed. Jacques-Alain Miller. Paris: Éditions du Seuil, 1975.

——. *The Seminar of Jacques Lacan, Book XX: Encore, 1972–1973*. Ed. Jacques-Alain Miller. Trans. Bruce Fink. New York: Norton, 1998.

——. *Le séminaire de Jacques Lacan, Livre XXI: Les non-dupes errent, 1973–1974*. Unpublished typescript.

——. *Le séminaire de Jacques Lacan, Livre XXII: R.S.I., 1974–1975*. Unpublished typescript.

——. *The Seminar of Jacques Lacan, Book XXIII: The Sinthome, 1975–1976*. Ed. Jacques-Alain Miller. Trans. A. R. Price. Cambridge: Polity, 2016.

——. *Le séminaire de Jacques Lacan, Livre XXIV: L'insu que sait de l'une-bévue, s'aile à mourre, 1976–1977*. Unpublished typescript.

——. *Le séminaire de Jacques Lacan, Livre XXV: Le moment de conclure, 1977–1978*. Unpublished typescript.

Lacan, Jacques, and Wladimir Granoff. "Fetishism: The Symbolic, the Imaginary, and the Real." In *Perversions: Psychodynamics and Therapy*, ed. Sandor Lorand and Michael Balint, 265–76. New York: Gramercy, 1956.

Laclau, Ernesto. *On Populist Reason*. London: Verso, 2005.

Laclau, Ernesto, and Chantal Mouffe. *Hegemony and Socialist Strategy: Towards a Radical Democratic Politics*. 2nd ed. London: Verso, 2001.

Laplanche, Jean. "The Drive and Its Source-Object: Its Fate in the Transference." Trans. Leslie Hill. In *Essays on Otherness*, 117–32. New York: Routledge, 1999.

——. *Problématiques III: La sublimation*. Paris: Presses Universitaires de France, 1980.

Laplanche, Jean, and Jean-Bertrand Pontalis. *The Language of Psycho-Analysis*. Trans. Donald Nicholson-Smith. New York: Norton, 1973.

Laporte, Dominique. *History of Shit*. Trans. Nadia Benabid and Rodolphe el-Khoury. Cambridge, MA: MIT Press, 2000.

Lardreau, Guy, and Christian Jambet. *L'ange. Pour une cynégétique du semblant*. Paris: Grasset, 1976.

Lefebvre, Henri. "Les paradoxes d'Althusser." In *L'idéologie structuraliste*, 191–251. Paris: Éditions Anthropos, 1971.

Lenin, V. I. "Conspectus of Hegel's Book *Lectures on the History of Philosophy*." In *Collected Works*, vol. 38: *Philosophical Notebooks*, ed. Stewart Smith, trans. Clemence Dutt, 243–302. Moscow: Progress Publishers, 1976.

——. "The Importance of Gold Now and After the Complete Victory of Socialism." In *The Lenin Anthology*, ed. Robert C. Tucker, 511–17. New York: Norton, 1975.

——. *The State and Revolution: The Marxist Theory of the State and the Tasks of the Proletariat in the Revolution*. In *Lenin: Selected Works, One-Volume Edition*, 264–351. New York: International Publishers, 1971.

——. "The Three Sources and Three Component Parts of Marxism." In *The Lenin Anthology*, ed. Robert C. Tucker, 640–44. New York: Norton, 1975.

——. *What Is to Be Done? Burning Questions of Our Movement*. Ed. Victor J. Jerome. Trans. Joe Fineberg and George Hanna. New York: International Publishers, 1969.

Lippi, Silvia. "Introduction: Marx à Cerisy." In *Marx, Lacan. L'acte révolutionnaire et l'acte analytique*, ed. Sylvia Lippi and Patrick Landman, 9–21. Toulouse: Érès, 2013.

BIBLIOGRAPHY

Löwy, Michael. "De la Grande Logique de Hegel à la gare finlandaise de Petrograd." In *Dialectique et révolution. Essais de sociologie et d'histoire du marxisme*, 129–50. Paris: Éditions Anthropos, 1973.
——. "Notes historiques sur le marxisme russe." In *Dialectique et révolution. Essais de sociologie et d'histoire du marxisme*, 151–60. Paris: Éditions Anthropos, 1973.
Lucchelli, Juan Pablo. *Lacan. De Wallon à Kojève*. Paris: Éditions Michèle, 2017.
Lukács, Georg. "The Changing Function of Historical Materialism." In *History and Class Consciousness: Studies in Marxist Dialectics*, trans. Rodney Livingstone, 223–55. Cambridge, MA: MIT Press, 1971.
——. "Class Consciousness." In *History and Class Consciousness: Studies in Marxist Dialectics*, trans. Rodney Livingstone, 46–82. Cambridge, MA: MIT Press, 1971.
——. *The Destruction of Reason*. Trans. Peter Palmer. Atlantic Highlands, NJ: Humanities Press, 1981.
——. *Lenin: A Study on the Unity of His Thought*. Trans. Nicholas Jacobs. London: Verso, 2009.
——. "The Marxism of Rosa Luxemburg." In *History and Class Consciousness: Studies in Marxist Dialectics*, trans. Rodney Livingstone, 27–45. Cambridge, MA: MIT Press, 1971.
——. *The Ontology of Social Being 1: Hegel's False and His Genuine Ontology*. Trans. David Fernbach. London: Merlin.
——. "Preface to the New Edition (1967)." In *History and Class Consciousness: Studies in Marxist Dialectics*, trans. Rodney Livingstone, ix–xxxix. Cambridge, MA: MIT Press, 1971.
——. "Reification and the Consciousness of the Proletariat." In *History and Class Consciousness: Studies in Marxist Dialectics*, trans. Rodney Livingstone, 83–222. Cambridge, MA: MIT Press, 1971.
——. *The Theory of the Novel: A Historico-Philosophical Essay on the Forms of Great Epic Literature*. Trans. Anna Bostock. Cambridge, MA: MIT Press, 1971.
——. "Towards a Methodology of the Problem of Organization." In *History and Class Consciousness: Studies in Marxist Dialectics*, trans. Rodney Livingstone, 295–342. Cambridge, MA: MIT Press, 1971.
——. "What Is Orthodox Marxism?" In *History and Class Consciousness: Studies in Marxist Dialectics*, trans. Rodney Livingstone, 1–26. Cambridge, MA: MIT Press, 1971.
Luppol, I. K. "The Historical Significance of Spinoza's Philosophy." In *Spinoza in Soviet Philosophy*, ed. and trans. George L. Kline, 162–76. London: Routledge & Kegan Paul, 1952.
Luria, A. R. "The Problem of the Cultural Behaviour of the Child." In *The Vygotsky Reader*, ed. René van der Veer and Jaan Valsiner, 46–56. Oxford: Blackwell, 1994.
——. "Psychoanalysis as a System of Monistic Psychology." *Soviet Psychology* 16, no. 2 (1977): 7–45.
Luxemburg, Rosa. *The Accumulation of Capital*. Trans. Agnes Schwarzschild. New York: Routledge, 2003.
——. "The Junius Pamphlet: The Crisis of German Social Democracy." 1915. Marxists.org, https://www.marxists.org/archive/luxemburg/1915/junius/.
Mandel, Ernest. *The Formation of the Economic Thought of Karl Marx: 1843 to Capital*. Trans. Brian Pearce. New York: Monthly Review Press, 1971.
——. *Late Capitalism*. Trans. Joris De Bres. London: Verso, 1978.
——. *Marxist Economic Theory*. Vol. 2. Trans. Brian Pearce. New York: Monthly Review Press, 1970.
Mannoni, Octave. "I Know Well, but All the Same . . ." Trans. G. M. Goshgarian. In *Perversion and the Social Relation*, ed. Molly Anne Rothenberg, Dennis A. Foster, and Slavoj Žižek, 68–92. Durham, NC: Duke University Press, 2003.
Mao Tse-Tung. "On Contradiction." In *On Practice and Contradiction*, ed. Slavoj Žižek, 67–102. London: Verso, 2007.
Marcuse, Herbert. "Aggressiveness in Advanced Industrial Society." In *Negations: Essays in Critical Theory*, trans. Jeremy J. Shapiro, 248–68. Boston: Beacon, 1968.
——. "The Concept of Essence." In *Negations: Essays in Critical Theory*, trans. Jeremy J. Shapiro, 43–87. Boston: Beacon, 1968.
——. *Counterrevolution and Revolt*. Boston: Beacon, 1972.
——. *Eros and Civilization: A Philosophical Inquiry Into Freud*. Boston: Beacon, 1974.

BIBLIOGRAPHY ❧ 347

——. *An Essay on Liberation*. Boston: Beacon, 1969.

——. "Freedom and Freud's Theory of Instincts." In *Five Lectures: Psychoanalysis, Politics, and Utopia*, trans. Jeremy J. Shapiro and Shierry M. Weber, 1–27. Boston: Beacon, 1970.

——. "On Hedonism." In *Negations: Essays in Critical Theory*, trans. Jeremy J. Shapiro, 159–200. Boston: Beacon, 1968.

——. *Hegel's Ontology and the Theory of Historicity*. Trans. Seyla Benhabib. Cambridge, MA: MIT Press, 1987.

——. "Industrialization and Capitalism in the Work of Max Weber." In *Negations: Essays in Critical Theory*, trans. Jeremy J. Shapiro, 201–26. Boston: Beacon, 1968.

——. "New Sources on the Foundation of Historical Materialism." In *Heideggerian Marxism*, ed. Richard Wolin and John Abromeit, 86–121. Lincoln: University of Nebraska Press, 2005.

——. "The Obsolescence of the Freudian Concept of Man." In *Five Lectures: Psychoanalysis, Politics, and Utopia*, trans. Jeremy J. Shapiro and Shierry M. Weber, 44–61. Boston: Beacon, 1970.

——. "On the Philosophical Foundations of the Concept of Labor in Economics." In *Heideggerian Marxism*, ed. Richard Wolin and John Abromeit, 122–50. Lincoln: University of Nebraska Press, 2005.

——. *One-Dimensional Man: Studies in the Ideology of Advanced Industrial Society*. Boston: Beacon, 1964.

——. "Philosophy and Critical Theory." In *Negations: Essays in Critical Theory*, trans. Jeremy J. Shapiro, 134–58. Boston: Beacon, 1968.

——. "Progress and Freud's Theory of Instincts." In *Five Lectures: Psychoanalysis, Politics, and Utopia*, trans. Jeremy J. Shapiro and Shierry M. Weber, 28–43. Boston: Beacon, 1970.

——. *Reason and Revolution: Hegel and the Rise of Social Theory*. 2nd ed. New York: Routledge, 2000.

——. "Repressive Tolerance." In Robert Paul Wolff, Barrington Moore Jr., and Herbert Marcuse, *A Critique of Pure Tolerance*, 81–123. Boston: Beacon, 1969.

Martin, Pierre. *Argent et psychanalyse*. Paris: Navarin, 1984.

Marx, Karl. *Capital: A Critique of Political Economy*. Vol. 1. Trans. Ben Fowkes. New York: Penguin, 1976.

——. *Capital: A Critique of Political Economy*. Vol. 2. Trans. David Fernbach. New York: Penguin, 1978.

——. *Capital: A Critique of Political Economy*. Vol. 3. Trans. David Fernbach. New York: Penguin, 1981.

——. *The Civil War in France*. In *The First International and After: Political Writings, Volume 3*, ed. David Fernbach, 187–236. Harmondsworth: Penguin, 1974.

——. "A Contribution to the Critique of Hegel's Philosophy of Right. Introduction." In *Early Writings*, trans. Rodney Livingstone and Gregor Benton, 243–57. New York: Penguin, 1992.

——. *A Contribution to the Critique of Political Economy*. Ed. Maurice Dobb. Trans. S. W. Ryazanskaya. New York: International, 1970.

——. *Critique of Hegel's Doctrine of the State*. In *Early Writings*, trans. Rodney Livingstone and Gregor Benton, 57–198. New York: Penguin, 1992.

——. *Economic and Philosophical Manuscripts*. In *Early Writings*, trans. Rodney Livingstone and Gregor Benton, 279–400. New York: Penguin, 1992.

——. *The Eighteenth Brumaire of Louis Bonaparte*. Trans. Ben Fowkes. In *Surveys from Exile: Political Writings, Volume 2*, ed. David Fernbach, 143–249. Harmondsworth: Penguin, 1973.

——. "Excerpts from James Mill's *Elements of Political Economy*." In *Early Writings*, trans. Rodney Livingstone and Gregor Benton, 259–78. New York: Penguin, 1992.

——. *Grundrisse der Kritik der politischen Ökonomie (Rohentwurf)*. Frankfurt: Europäische Verlagsanstalt, 1967.

——. *Grundrisse: Foundations of the Critique of Political Economy (Rough Draft)*. Trans. Martin Nicolaus. New York: Penguin, 1973.

——. "Inaugural Address of the International Working Men's Association." In *The First International and After: Political Writings, Volume 3*, ed. David Fernbach, 73–81. Harmondsworth: Penguin, 1974.

——. *Karl-Marx-Ausgabe: Werke-Schriften-Briefe, Band III: Politische Schriften, erster Band.* Ed. Hans-Joachim Lieber. *Der achtzehnte Brumaire des Louis Bonaparte*, 268–387. Darmstadt: Wissenschaftliche Buchgesellschaft, 1960.

——. *Karl-Marx-Ausgabe: Werke-Schriften-Briefe, Band IV: Ökonomische Schriften, erster Band.* Ed. Hans-Joachim Lieber. *Das Kapital: Kritik der politischen Ökonomie, erster Band.* Darmstadt: Wissenschaftliche Buchgesellschaft, 1962.

——. *Karl-Marx-Ausgabe: Werke-Schriften-Briefe, Band V, Das Kapital: Kritik der politischen Ökonomie, zweites Buch, Der Zirkulationsprozess des Kapitals.* Ed. Hans-Joachim Lieber, 1–607. Darmstadt: Wissenschaftliche Buchgesellschaft, 1963.

——. *Karl-Marx-Ausgabe: Werke-Schriften-Briefe, Band V: Ökonomische Schriften, zweiter Band.* Ed. Hans-Joachim Lieber. *Das Kapital: Kritik der politischen Ökonomie, dritter Band, drittes Buch, Der Gesamtprozess der kapitalistichen Produktion, Kapitel I–XV*, 609–908. Darmstadt: Wissenschaftliche Buchgesellschaft, 1963.

——. *Karl-Marx-Ausgabe: Werke-Schriften-Briefe, Band VI: Ökonomische Schriften, dritter Band.* Ed. Hans-Joachim Lieber. *Das Kapital: Kritik der politischen Ökonomie, dritter Band, drittes Buch.* Ed. Hans-Joachim Lieber and Benedikt Kautsky. Darmstadt: Wissenschaftliche Buchgesellschaft, 1964.

——. "Letter to Mikhailovsky." In *Karl Marx: Selected Writings*, ed. David McLellan, 571–72. Oxford: Oxford University Press, 1977.

——. "Letter to Vera Sassoulitch." In *Karl Marx: Selected Writings*, ed. David McLellan, 576–80. Oxford: Oxford University Press, 1977.

——. "Letters 1863–1881: Marx to Kugelmann, 17 Apr. 1871." In *Karl Marx: Selected Writings*, ed. David McLellan, 593. Oxford: Oxford University Press, 1977.

——. *Misère de la philosophie. Réponse à la philosophie de la misère de Proudhon.* 1847. https://www.marxists.org/francais/marx/works/1847/06/misere.pdf.

——. "On the Question of Free Trade." In *The Poverty of Philosophy*, 207–24. Moscow: Foreign Languages Publishing House, 1956.

——. "Pauperism and Free Trade—the Approaching Commercial Crisis: Published November 1, 1852." In *Dispatches for the New York Tribune: Selected Journalism of Karl Marx*, ed. James Ledbetter, 161–63. New York: Penguin, 2007.

——. *The Poverty of Philosophy.* Moscow: Foreign Languages Publishing House, 1956.

——. "Preface to the Russian Edition of the Communist Manifesto." In *Karl Marx: Selected Writings*, ed. David McLellan, 583–84. Oxford: Oxford University Press, 1977.

——. *Theorien über den Mehrwert, dritter Band.* Ed. Karl Kautsky. Stuttgart: Dietz, 1910.

——. *Theories of Surplus-Value, Part One: Volume IV of Capital.* Ed. S. Ryazanskaya. Trans. Emile Burns. Moscow: Progress Publishers, 1963.

——. *Theories of Surplus-Value, Part Two: Volume IV of Capital.* Ed. S. Ryazanskaya. Trans. Emile Burns. Moscow: Progress Publishers, 1968.

——. *Theories of Surplus-Value, Part Three: Volume IV of Capital.* Ed. S. W. Ryazanskaya and Richard Dixon. Trans. Jack Cohen and S. W. Ryazanskaya. Moscow: Progress Publishers, 1971.

——. "Thesen über Feuerbach." In *Karl Marx-Friedrich Engels Werke, Band 3, 1845–1846*, 5–7. Berlin: Dietz, 1981.

——. "Theses on Feuerbach." Trans. by S. Ryazanskaya. In *Karl Marx: Selected Writings*, ed. David McLellan, 156–58. Oxford: Oxford University Press, 1977.

——. *Value, Price and Profit.* In *Wage-Labour and Capital/Value, Price and Profit*, 49–110. New York: International Publishers, 1976.

——. *Wage-Labour and Capital.* In *Wage-Labour and Capital/Value, Price and Profit*, 1–48. New York: International Publishers, 1976.

——. "Zur Kritik der Hegelschen Rechtsphilosophie. Einleiting." In *Karl-Marx-Ausgabe: Werke-Schriften-Briefe, Band I: Frühe Schriften, erster Band*, ed. Hans-Joachim Lieber and Peter Furth, 488–505. Darmstadt: Wissenschaftliche Buchgesellschaft, 1962.

——. *Zur Kritik der politischen Ökonomie*. 1859. http://www.mlwerke.de/me/me13/ me13_003.htm.

Marx, Karl, and Friedrich Engels. *The Communist Manifesto*. Trans. Samuel Moore. In *Karl Marx: Selected Writings*, ed. David McLellan, 221–47. Oxford: Oxford University Press, 1977.

——. *Die deutsche Ideologie*. Berlin: Dietz, 1953.

——. *The German Ideology*. Amherst, MA: Prometheus, 1998.

——. *The Holy Family, or Critique of Critical Criticism: Against Bruno Bauer, and Company*. Trans. Richard Dixon and Clemens Dutt. Moscow: Progress Publishers, 1975.

——. *Manifest der kommunistischen Partei*. 1848. https://www.marxists.org/deutsch/archiv/marx-engels /1848/manifest/index.htm.

Meaney, Mark. "Capital Breeds: Interest-Bearing Capital as Purely Abstract Form." In *Marx's Capital and Hegel's Logic: A Reexamination*, ed. Fred Mosley and Tony Smith, 41–63. Chicago: Haymarket, 2015.

Meek, Ronald L. *Studies in the Labor Theory of Value*. 2nd ed. New York: Monthly Review Press, 1956.

Merleau-Ponty, Maurice. *Adventures of the Dialectic*. Trans. Joseph Bien. Evanston, IL: Northwestern University Press, 1973.

Merrington, John. "Theory and Practice in Gramsci's Marxism." In *Western Marxism: A Critical Reader*, ed. *New Left Review*, 140–75. London: Verso, 1978.

Mészáros, István. *Marx's Theory of Alienation*. New York: Harper & Row, 1970.

Michels, André. "Travail, aliénation, valeur: Lacan avec Marx." In *Marx, Lacan. L'acte révolutionnaire et l'acte analytique*, ed. Sylvia Lippi and Patrick Landman, 167–89. Toulouse: Érès, 2013.

Miller, Martin A. *Freud and the Bolsheviks: Psychoanalysis in Imperial Russia and the Soviet Union*. New Haven, CT: Yale University Press, 1998.

Milner, Jean-Claude. *L'œuvre claire. Lacan, la science, la philosophie*. Paris: Éditions du Seuil, 1995.

——. *Le périple structural. Figures et paradigme*. Paris: Éditions du Seuil, 2002.

Morishima, Michio. *Marx's Economics: A Dual Theory of Value and Growth*. Cambridge: Cambridge University Press, 1973.

Murray, Patrick. "The Secret of Capital's Self-Valorization 'Laid Bare': How Hegel Helped Marx to Overturn Ricardo's Theory of Profit." In *Marx's Capital and Hegel's Logic: A Reexamination*, ed. Fred Mosley and Tony Smith, 189–213. Chicago: Haymarket, 2015.

Nobus, Dany. *The Law of Desire: On Lacan's 'Kant with Sade.'* Basingstoke: Palgrave Macmillan, 2017.

Ollman, Bertell. *Alienation: Marx's Conception of Man in Capitalist Society*. Cambridge: Cambridge University Press, 1971.

——. "The Marxism of Wilhelm Reich: The Social Function of Sexual Repression." In *The Unknown Dimension: European Marxism Since Lenin*, ed. Dick Howard and Karl E. Klare, 197–224. New York: Basic Books, 1972.

Osborn, Reuben. *Marxism and Psychoanalysis*. New York: Farrar, Straus and Giroux, 1974.

Pfister, Oskar. "The Illusion of a Future: A Friendly Disagreement with Prof. Sigmund Freud." Ed. Paul Roazen. Trans. Susan Abrams. *International Journal of Psycho-Analysis* 74 , no. 3 (1993): 557–79.

Pico della Mirandola, Giovanni. "On the Dignity of Man." In *On the Dignity of Man*, trans. Charles Glenn Wallis, Paul J. W. Miller, and Douglas Carmichael, 1–34. Indianapolis, IN: Hackett, 1998.

Piketty, Thomas. *Capital in the Twenty-First Century*. Trans. Arthur Goldhammer. Cambridge, MA: Harvard University Press, 2014.

Planty-Bonjour, Guy. *Hegel et la pensée philosophique en Russie, 1830–1917*. The Hague: Martinus Nijhoff, 1974.

Plato. *Protagoras*. Trans. Stanley Lombardo and Karen Bell. In *Plato: Complete Works*, ed. John M. Cooper, 746–90. Indianapolis, IN: Hackett, 1997.

Pollock, Ethan. *Stalin and the Soviet Science Wars*. Princeton, NJ: Princeton University Press, 2006.

Postone, Moishe. *Time, Labor, and Social Domination: A Reinterpretation of Marx's Critical Theory*. Cambridge: Cambridge University Press, 1993.

Presskorn-Thygesen, Thomas, and Ole Bjerg. "The Falling Rate of Enjoyment: Consumer Capitalism and Compulsive Buying Disorder." *Ephemera: Theory and Politics in Organization* 14, no. 2 (2014): 197–220.

Rassial, Jean-Jacques. "Intérêt et désir: Marx et Lacan." In *Marx, Lacan. L'acte révolutionnaire et l'acte analytique*, ed. Sylvia Lippi and Patrick Landman, 193–209. Toulouse: Érès, 2013.

Reich, Wilhelm. *Dialectical Materialism and Psychoanalysis*. London: Socialist Reproduction, 1972.

——. "Psychoanalysis in the Soviet Union." In *Sex-Pol: Essays, 1929–1934*, ed. Lee Baxandall, trans. Anna Bostock, Tom DuBose, and Lee Baxandall, 75–88. New York: Vintage, 1972.

——. *Reich Speaks of Freud: Wilhelm Reich Discusses His Work and His Relationship with Sigmund Freud*. Ed. Mary Higgins and Chester M. Raphael. Trans. Therese Pol. New York: Farrar, Straus and Giroux, 1967.

Reiss-Schimmel, Ilana. *La psychanalyse et l'argent*. Paris: Éditions Odile Jacob, 1993.

Ricardo, David. *The Principles of Political Economy and Taxation*. New York: Dover, 2004.

Ricoeur, Paul. "Consciousness and the Unconscious." Trans. Willis Domingo. In *The Conflict of Interpretations: Essays in Hermeneutics*, ed. Don Ihde, 97–118. London: Continuum, 2004.

——. *Freud and Philosophy: An Essay on Interpretation*. Trans. Denis Savage. New Haven, CT: Yale University Press, 1970.

——. "Psychoanalysis and the Movement of Contemporary Culture." Trans. Willis Domingo. In *The Conflict of Interpretations: Essays in Hermeneutics*, ed. Don Ihde, 119–56. London: Continuum, 2004.

Rieff, Philip. *Freud: The Mind of the Moralist*. Chicago: University of Chicago Press, 1979.

Robinson, Joan. *An Essay on Marxian Economics*. 2nd ed. London: Macmillan, 1966.

Robinson, Paul A. *The Freudian Left: Wilhelm Reich, Geza Roheim, Herbert Marcuse*. New York: Harper & Row, 1969.

Robles-Báez, Mario L. "Dialectics of Labour and Value-Form in Marx's Capital: A Reconstruction." In *Marx's Capital and Hegel's Logic: A Reexamination*, ed. Fred Mosley and Tony Smith, 292–317. Chicago: Haymarket, 2015.

Rosdolsky, Roman. *The Making of Marx's 'Capital.'* Trans. Pete Burgess. London: Pluto, 1977.

Rose, Gillian. *Hegel Contra Sociology*. London: Verso, 2009.

Rosolato, Guy. "Étude des perversions sexuelles à partir du fétichisme." In Piera Aulagnier- Spairani, Jean Clavreul, François Perrier, Guy Rosolato, and Jean-Paul Valabrega, *Le désir et la perversion*, 7–52. Paris: Éditions du Seuil, 1967.

Roudinesco, Élisabeth. *Jacques Lacan & Co.: A History of Psychoanalysis in France, 1925–1985*. Trans. Jeffrey Mehlman. Chicago: University of Chicago Press, 1990.

——. *Jacques Lacan: Outline of a Life, History of a System of Thought*. Trans. Barbara Bray. New York: Columbia University Press, 1997.

Rousseau, Jean-Jacques. *Discourse on the Origin and Foundations of Inequality Among Men (Second Discourse)*. In *The First and Second Discourses*, ed. Roger D. Masters, trans. Roger D. Masters and Judith R. Masters, 77–228. New York: Saint Martin's, 1964.

Roy, Jean. *Hobbes and Freud*. Trans. Thomas G. Osler. Toronto: Canadian Philosophical Monographs, 1984.

Rubin, I. I. *Essays on Marx's Theory of Value*. Trans. Miloš Samardžija and Fredy Perlman. Detroit: Black & Red, 1972.

Sartre, Jean-Paul. *Search for a Method*. Trans. Hazel E. Barnes. New York: Vintage, 1968.

Schmitt, Carl. *Political Theology: Four Chapters on the Concept of Sovereignty*. Trans. George Schwab. Cambridge, MA: MIT Press, 1985.

Schumpeter, Joseph A. *Capitalism, Socialism, and Democracy*. New York: Harper & Row, 1975.

Sebag, Lucien. *Marxisme et structuralisme*. Paris: Payot, 1964.

Shapiro, Jeremy J. "The Dialectic of Theory and Practice in the Age of Technological Rationality: Herbert Marcuse and Jürgen Habermas." In *The Unknown Dimension: European Marxism Since Lenin*, ed. Dick Howard and Karl E. Klare, 276–303. New York: Basic Books, 1972.

Shorrocks, Anthony, James Davies, and Rodrigo Lluberas. *Global Wealth Report 2020*. Credit Suisse Research Institute. October 2020. https://inequality.org/facts/global-inequality/.

Sichère, Bernard. "Du ghetto symbolique à l'action révolutionnaire." In *Marxisme-léninisme et psychanalyse*, 43–79. Paris: François Maspero, 1975.

——. "Le faux matérialisme «tel quel»." In *Marxisme-léninisme et psychanalyse*, 111–62. Paris: François Maspero, 1975.

Simmel, Georg. *The Philosophy of Money*. Trans. Tom Bottomore and David Frisby. London: Routledge & Kegan Paul, 1978.

Smith, Adam. *The Wealth of Nations*. Books I–III. Ed. Andrew Skinner. New York: Penguin, 1986.

——. *The Wealth of Nations*. Books IV–V. Ed. Andrew Skinner. New York: Penguin, 1999.

Smith, Tony. "Hegel, Marx, and the Comprehension of Capitalism." In *Marx's Capital and Hegel's Logic: A Reexamination*, ed. Fred Mosley and Tony Smith, 17–40. Chicago: Haymarket, 2015.

——. *The Logic of Marx's Capital: Replies to Hegelian Criticisms*. Albany: State University of New York, 1990.

Solms, Mark, and Oliver Turnbull. *The Brain and the Inner World: An Introduction to the Neuroscience of Subjective Experience*. New York: Other Press, 2002.

Stalin, J. V. "Concerning Certain Problems of Linguistics." In *Marxism and Problems of Linguistics*, 33–40. Peking: Foreign Languages Press, 1972.

——. "Concerning Marxism in Linguistics." In *Marxism and Problems of Linguistics*, 3–32. Peking: Foreign Languages Press, 1972.

Stedman Jones, Gareth. "The Marxism of the Early Lukács." In *Western Marxism: A Critical Reader*, ed. *New Left Review*, 11–60. London: Verso, 1978.

Sweezy, Paul M. *The Theory of Capitalist Development: Principles of Marxian Political Economy*. 2nd ed. New York: Monthly Review Press, 1956.

Therborn, Göran. "The Frankfurt School." In *Western Marxism: A Critical Reader*, ed. *New Left Review*, 83–139. London: Verso, 1977.

Tomšič, Samo. *The Capitalist Unconscious: Marx and Lacan*. London: Verso, 2015.

Toscano, Alberto. "Divine Management: Critical Remarks on Giorgio Agamben's *The Kingdom and the Glory*." *Angelaki: Journal of the Theoretical Humanities* 16, no. 3 (September 2011): 125–36.

Vajda, Mihály. "Karl Korsch's 'Marxism and Philosophy.'" In *The Unknown Dimension: European Marxism Since Lenin*, ed. Dick Howard and Karl E. Klare, 131–46. New York: Basic Books, 1972.

Vanier, Alain. "Some Remarks on the Symptom and the Social Link: Lacan with Marx." Trans. John Monahan. *JPCS: Journal for the Psychoanalysis of Culture and Society* 6, no. 1 (2001): 40–45.

Vaysse, Jean-Marie. *L'inconscient des modernes. Essai sur l'origine métaphysique de la psychanalyse*. Paris: Gallimard, 1999.

Viderman, Serge. *De l'argent en psychanalyse et au-delà*. Paris: Presses Universitaires de France, 1992.

Vygotsky, L. S. "Internalization of Higher Psychological Functions." In *Mind in Society: The Development of Higher Psychological Processes*, ed. Michael Cole, Vera John-Steiner, Sylvia Scribner, and Ellen Souberman, 52–57. Cambridge, MA: Harvard University Press, 1978.

——. "Problems of Method." In *Mind in Society: The Development of Higher Psychological Processes*, ed. Michael Cole, Vera John-Steiner, Sylvia Scribner, and Ellen Souberman, 58–75. Cambridge, MA: Harvard University Press, 1978.

——. "The Problem of the Cultural Development of the Child." In *The Vygotsky Reader*, ed. René van der Veer and Jaan Valsiner, 57–72. Oxford: Blackwell, 1994.

——. *Thought and Language*. Ed. and trans. Eugenia Hanfmann and Gertrude Vakar. Cambridge, MA: MIT Press, 1962.

Vygotsky, Lev, and Alexander Luria. "Introduction to the Russian Translation of Freud's *Beyond the Pleasure Principle*." In *The Vygotsky Reader*, ed. René van der Veer and Jaan Valsiner, 10–18. Oxford: Blackwell, 1994.

Waibl, Elmar. *Gesellschaft und Kultur bei Hobbes und Freud*. Vienna: Löcker, 1980.

Wallace, Edwin R. *Freud and Anthropology: A History and Reappraisal*. New York: International Universities Press, 1983.

Weber, Max. "Appendix II: Prefatory Remarks to *Collected Essays in the Sociology of Religion*." In *The Protestant Ethic and the "Spirit" of Capitalism and Other Writings*, ed. and trans. Peter Baehr and Gordon C. Wells, 356–72. New York: Penguin, 2002.

——. "A Final Rebuttal of Rachfahl's Critique of the 'Spirit of Capitalism' (1910)." In *The Protestant Ethic and the "Spirit" of Capitalism and Other Writings*, ed. and trans. Peter Baehr and Gordon C. Wells, 282–339. New York: Penguin, 2002.

——. *The Protestant Ethic and the "Spirit" of Capitalism*. In *The Protestant Ethic and the "Spirit" of Capitalism and Other Writings*, ed. and trans. Peter Baehr and Gordon C. Wells, 1–202. New York: Penguin, 2002.

——. "Rebuttal of the Critique of the 'Spirit' of Capitalism (1910) (Weber's first rejoinder to Felix Rachfahl)." In *The Protestant Ethic and the "Spirit" of Capitalism and Other Writings*, ed. and trans. Peter Baehr and Gordon C. Wells, 244–81. New York: Penguin, 2002.

——. "Remarks on the Foregoing 'Reply' (1908) (Weber's second rejoinder to H. Karl Fischer)." In *The Protestant Ethic and the "Spirit" of Capitalism and Other Writings*, ed. and trans. Peter Baehr and Gordon C. Wells, 232–43. New York: Penguin, 2002.

Wetter, Gustav A. *Dialectical Materialism: A Historical and Systematic Survey of Philosophy in the Soviet Union*. Trans. Peter Heath. New York: Frederick A. Praeger, 1958.

Whitebook, Joel. *Perversion and Utopia: A Study in Psychoanalysis and Critical Theory*. Cambridge, MA: MIT Press, 1995.

Žižek, Slavoj. *Disparities*. London: Bloomsbury, 2016.

——. *Incontinence of the Void: Economico-Philosophical Spandrels*. Cambridge, MA: MIT Press, 2017.

——. *The Parallax View*. Cambridge, MA: MIT Press, 2006.

——. *The Plague of Fantasies*. London: Verso, 1997.

——. *The Sublime Object of Ideology*. London: Verso, 1989.

Index

absolute historicism, 258, 262

abstract hedonism, 106, 108, 123

accumulation: consumption and, 93, 181; expenditure and, 107

Accumulation of Capital (Luxemburg), 277

addiction (*Sucht*), 106

Adorno, Theodor, 59, 97, 271

Adventures of the Dialectic (Merleau-Ponty), 244, 246

Agamben, Giorgio, 221–30, 232, 239, 241

aggression: death drive and, 10, 12, 13, 21, 32–33, 35, 42, 45; with Freud and Marxism, 29–49; private property and, 11

alienation: capitalism and, 61, 199; labor and, 62; Marx and, xvii; religion and, 164, 258

Althusser, Louis, 22–23, 36, 83; *Hilflosigkeit* and, 94; ideology and, 73, 86, 274; "Ideology and Ideological State Apparatuses," 232, 261; influences on, 91; *For Marx*, 236; Marxism and, 78; "materiality of ideology" and, 86, 247–48; "On the Materialist Dialectic," 236; *Que faire?*, 261–63; *Reading Capital*, 151, 236, 237; *On the Reproduction of Capitalism*, 261; "Three Notes on the Theory of Discourses," 51

ambivalence, 269, 272; communism and, 29–49; Lacan and, 36, 68, 195; primal, 35

"American Utopia, An" (Jameson), 68–69

analytic fetishism, 189, 195

Anderson, Perry, 246, 257, 263, 264, 271

anticapitalists, xi–xii, 199

Anti-Dühring (Engels), 50

antieconomism, 3, 233, 236, 244, 261, 268, 278; historical materialism and, xvi, 263–64; Western Marxism and, 6, 31, 245–46, 252, 270, 272, 276, 282. *See also* economism

Antigone (Sophocles), 79

"Antinomies of Antonio Gramsci, The" (Anderson), 264

"Antinomies of Bourgeois Thought, The" (Lukács), 264

"Antinomies of Pure Reason" (Kant), 269

antireductive, 52, 93, 237, 279–82, 284

antisemitism, 216

Anxiety (1962–1963). See Seminar X

"Anxiety and Instinctual Life" (Freud), 42

apes, human anatomy and, 75, 98–99, 184

Arato, Andrew, 257, 266, 268, 269, 273–74

Aristotle, 8, 39, 68, 99, 256; with merchants as money hoarders, 92, 227; regression and, 153

atheism, 201–2, 206, 212, 215, 242

atom bombs, 270

Aufsichtslohns (wages of superintendence), 167–69, 194

auri sacra fames (greed for gold), 105, 106, 130

äußerlichste ("most superficial"), 171, 191–92

austerity measures, 120, 214

Authoritarian Personality, The (Frankfurt School), 60

"Authority and the Family" (Horkheimer), 97

Avineri, Shlomo, 282

axis of alteration, drive and, 64

axis of iteration, drive and, 64

354 ⬤ INDEX

Bacon, Francis, 90
Badiou, Alain, xiv
Balibar, Étienne, 210, 237
banking, 175–76, 182
bearers (*Träger*), 49, 124, 154, 219
Bedürfnis. See need
Being: "The Doctrine of Being," 140; language and, 28; ontology and, 29; *parlêtre*, 24, 148; "species-being," 198, 281, 282
Being and Time (Heidegger), 266
Belle Époque, xiv, 234
Benjamin, Walter, 119, 221, 223, 238–41
Bereicherung (enrichment), 106, 130, 132
Bergson, Henri, 257, 266
Bernstein, Edouard, 234
Bersani, Leo, 83
Berufsmensch ("man of the calling"), 83
Bewes, Timothy, 268
Beyond the Pleasure Principle (Freud), 10, 32, 39, 50, 58, 59
Bible, the, 17
big Other, 69, 78, 116, 120, 122, 148, 188, 284
billionaires, 115–16, 156
Blackburn, Robin, 237
Bloch, Ernst, 2, 246
body politic, xi, 83. *See also* psychoanalytic body, body politic and
Boesky, Ivan, xii
Bolshevik Revolution (October 1917), 9, 12, 44, 47, 270
Bolsheviks, 11, 17, 23, 43–44, 47, 50, 65, 88
Bolshevism, 3, 10–12, 16–17, 23, 29, 43–44, 257; Marxism and, 21; socialism, communism and, 9, 45
Boothby, Richard, 83
borne miliaire du désir (milestone of desire), 187
bourgeois: "The Antinomies of Bourgeois Thought," 264; science, 49, 58; Stalinism and persecution of, 11
Brecht, Bertolt, 5, 161, 287
Breines, Paul, 257, 266, 268, 274
Brewer, Anthony, 173
Brothers Karamazov, The (Dostoyevsky), 218
Brown, Norman O., 190
Brunhoff, Suzanne de, 112
Brunner, José, 35
Bukharin, Nicolai, 257, 262
Bush, George W., 279

Capital. See Das Kapital
Capital in the Twenty-First Century (Picketty), 117
capitalism: alienation and, 61, 199; Christianity and, 238; consumers and, 15, 110, 114, 131, 217, 221, 223, 240; consumption and, 128–31, 133, 136; creative destruction of, 118, 120; economic analyses of, xiv; *Economist* on, 119–20; failure of, xv; fictitious capital with commodities, interest and, 161–69; Freud and, 215, 217, 240; greed, xviii, xix, 107, 114, 123, 131–32, 138; *Grundrisse* and, 123–27, 130; headless subject and, 122–37; IBC and, 161–62, 168; *jouissance* and, 80; *Das Kapital* and, 123, 125, 127–29; labor and, 61; Lacan and, 185–200; *Late Capitalism*, 150; narcissistic animal and, 144–46; neoliberal, xiii; Protestantism and, 90, 209, 217, 222, 230, 238–39; *The Protestant Ethic and the "Spirit" of Capitalism*, 125–26, 221–22; *On the Reproduction of Capitalism*, 261; sacred pomp of, 239; selfishness and, xxi, 112–22; selflessness of, 129, 147, 153; with socialism/communism, 46; social reality of, 101; superego of, 240; veiling of, 190–92, 199–200
"Capitalism as Religion" (Benjamin), 221, 238–41
capitalist economics, 47, 184, 238, 286; Freud and, 72; Lacano-Marxism and, 137–57; (neo) liberalism and, 121; natural science and, 131
capitalist-entrepreneur relationship, 72–73, 75
capitalist mode of production, 20, 48–49, 75, 146, 184, 200; interest and, 176–78, 183; M-C-M' and, 7; monopolies within, xiv; political economy and, 278; profit and, 182; Protestantism and, 223; selfishness and, xvi, xvii; surplus value and, 80, 130
capitalists: fetishism of, 181; with M-C-M', 109, 123–24, 128; misers and, 125–27; money as "narcissistic supply" for, 116; with surplus value, 114–15, 157, 286; virtues of, 127, 128
Capitalist Unconscious, The (Tomšič), 75, 137, 143
capital of libido, 72, 74
castration, 148, 153–55, 187–89, 191, 195–96, 216–17, 284
Catholicism, 17, 204
Catholic Law and Justice Party, Poland, 204
children, 41, 47, 59, 73–74, 136, 190, 214
Christensen, Clayton, 118
Christianity, 224, 240–41; capitalism and, 238; as economic theology, 239; *The Essence of*

INDEX

Christianity, 164; Kant and, 212–13; Protestantism, 16, 83, 90, 125–26, 205, 209, 213, 217, 221–23, 230, 238–39; supporters, 204–5

Civilization and Its Discontents (Freud), 10–13, 32; with Eros and death drive, 33; on fate of humanity, 34; superego in, 14

civilizations, 10, 30, 33, 239; clash of, 221, 223, 241; discontent in, 13, 71. *See also Eros and Civilization*

class, 11, 26, 47, 73, 82, 107; conflict, 22, 152, 236, 284; consciousness, 20, 159, 251, 253, 260, 282; essentialism, 257, 279; identity, 15, 259, 277, 278; societies, xiv, 19, 20, 22, 281, 282; struggle, 223, 235, 271, 276, 277, 284. *See also History and Class Consciousness*

C-M-C', 109–11

Cohen, G. A., 169

Colletti, Lucio, 36, 225, 266, 277

commodities: exchange value and, 172, 174, 180, 181; "The Fetishism of the Commodity and Its Secret," 108–9, 161–66, 179, 182, 190, 197, 209–10, 265; fictitious capital with capitalism, interest and, 161–69; Lukács on, 264–65, 274; money and, 108. *See also* M-C-M'

commodity fetishism, 5, 89, 113, 115, 134, 160, 268; as alienating illusion, 163; consumption and, 109–10; "The Fetishism of the Commodity and Its Secret," 108–9, 161–66, 179, 182, 190, 197, 209–10, 265; greed and, 123–24; IBC and, 164, 169–75, 179, 181, 183–86, 190, 192, 194; Lacan, capitalism and, 185–86, 189–90, 192–95, 197–200; miser with, 110–12, 127; psychoanalysis and, 195; twin hedonisms of, 105–12, 130, 149

communism, 10, 50, 89, 144, 206, 208, 212; ambivalence and, 29–49; inhumanity or, xxi; liberalism with capitalism and, 112–22; superego and, 16. *See also* socialism/communism

Communist Manifesto, The (Marx and Engels), 47, 134, 206–8, 211

conception du monde. See worldview

"Concept of Essence, The" (Marcuse), 273

Condition of the Working Class, The (Engels), 107

consumers: capitalism and, 15, 110, 114, 131, 217, 221, 223, 240; with C-M-C', 109; credit, 178, 184; God and, 215; interest with, 178

consumption, 82, 117, 150, 180, 185, 214; accumulation and, 93, 181; capitalism and, 128–31, 133, 136; commodity fetishism and, 109–10; conspicuous, 111, 115; cycle of, 239; M-C-M' and, xviii, 4, 113, 240; private, xx, 114, 116, 219; production and, 99–104

"Contribution to the Critique of Hegel's Philosophy of Right, A" (Marx), 256

Contribution to the Critique of Political Economy, A (Marx), 231, 283; capitalist greed and, 123; on class conflict, 22; commodity fetishism and, 164–66; historical materialism and, 145; on hoarders of money, 126, 129; preface to, 22, 145, 208, 209, 232–33, 274, 275

"Copernican revolution," 92, 143

Corddry, Rob, 279

Corporation, The (documentary film), 132–33

COVID-19 pandemic, 213

credit, 110, 131, 175, 214; debt and, xx; merchant and consumer, 178, 184; system, 182

Credit Suisse Global Wealth Report (2020), xiii

"cultural superego" (*das Kultur-Über-Ich*), 14, 15, 16

Daily Show, The (TV show), 279

dark God (*le Dieu obscur*), 4, 216–19

Das Kapital (*Capital*) (Marx), 92, 99, 249, 264, 283; capitalism and, 123, 125, 127–29; credit system in, 182; "The Fetishism of the Commodity and Its Secret," 108–9, 161–66, 179, 182, 190, 197, 209–10, 265; greed and, 106, 107; IBC in, 169–71, 175, 181; M-C-M' in, 173; need in, 104; "Postface to the Second Edition," 162; scientificity and, 284–85

dead father, 201, 203, 218

death drive (*Todestrieb*): aggression and, 10, 12, 13, 21, 32–33, 35, 42, 45; destructiveness of, 42; Eros and, 33, 39, 42, 56; greed and, 132

debt, xx, 110, 120, 213, 214

defeat, doctrines of, 270–71, 276

deregulation, xiv

desacralization: afterlife of sacred and, 205–12; infrastructural, 242; of religion, 211, 221, 229, 238; science and, 204; superstructural, 241

Descartes, René, 130

désir (desire), 13, 74, 148, 192; *de l'Autre*, 193; *de l'enfance*, 72–73; *de l'impossible*, 189; drive (*pulsion*) and, 138, 139–40, 143; fetishism and, 186–87; with *jouissance* and *objet petit a*, 4; milestone of, 187

Desire and Its Interpretation (1958–1959).
  See Seminar VI
destructiveness, 10, 42, 43, 127
dialectical materialism, 24, 94, 97, 234, 243–44;
  antireductive, 281, 282; historical and, 1, 67,
  247, 254, 280; Korsch and, 246, 247, 254;
  Lacan and, 220; Marxism with Freud and,
  49–68
Dialectical Materialism and Psychoanalysis
  (Reich), 59–60, 93, 95–96
Dialectic of Enlightenment (Horkheimer and
  Adorno), 97
dialectics of nature, 244, 247, 280
Dialectics of Nature (Engels), 50, 243, 247, 280
disavowal (*Verleugnung*), 186, 195–96
"discontent in civilization," 13, 71
"disruptive innovation," 118
"Divine Management" (Toscano), 225, 228
"Doctrine of Being, The" (Hegel), 140
"Doctrine of Essence, The" (Hegel), 275, 285
Dostoyevsky, Fyodor, 218
Douglas, Michael, xii
dream (*rêve*), 13, 24, 159, 185, 239; *Interpretation of*
  Dreams, 75; production, 72, 73; theory, 72, 76;
  utopian, 66
drives (*Triebe*), 9, 91; axes of iteration and
  alteration, 64; Luria on, 54–55; of Marxism,
  49–68; plastic structure, 104–5; *pulsion*,
  139–40, 143; "source-object" of, 107. *See also*
  Marxian drives
drive (*Trieb*) theory, 3, 64, 99, 133, 138, 142;
  Freudian, 4, 55–56, 67, 97, 135; Marx and,
  100–102, 106, 107, 113, 123, 134, 135, 140, 141, 155;
  psychoanalytic, xix, 4, 41, 54, 67, 91, 92, 100
"Drive to Amass Wealth, The" (Fenichel), 94
Dussel, Enrique, 171–72

Economic and Philosophical Manuscripts (Marx),
  206, 212
economic essentialism, xvi, 278
economics: capitalist, 47, 72, 121, 131, 137–57, 184,
  238, 286; inequality, 207, 223; science and,
  244; superstructure, 13, 249, 267, 278. *See also*
  theological economics
economic theology, 212, 214; Christianity as, 239;
  theological economics versus, 220–30
economism, 234, 237, 253, 257, 260, 262, 283;
  antieconomism and, xvi, 3, 6, 31, 233, 236,
  244–46, 252, 261, 263–64, 268, 270, 272, 276,

278, 282; criticism of, 258; reductive, 7, 31, 228,
  231, 235; rejection of, 222; vulgar, 177, 235–36,
  248, 250, 259, 269
Economist (magazine), 117–21
economy: libidinal, 98–105, 158–61; religion and,
  6; with religion and uneven development,
  230–42; theologization of, 212. *See also*
  political economy; theological economics
ego, 33, 61, 63–64, 146–47, 196; *Group Psychology*
  and the Analysis of the Ego, 69; id and, 39, 41;
  imago-Gestalt and, 29; psychology, 95, 96;
  superego and, 16, 69
Ego and the Id, The (Freud), 16, 33
Eighteenth Brumaire of Louis Bonaparte, The
  (Marx), 136, 232
Einstein, Albert, 13
Elements of the Philosophy of Right (Hegel),
  103, 256
Encore (1972–1973). See Seminar XX
Engels, Friedrich, 31, 257, 263; *Anti-Dühring*, 50;
  The Condition of the Working Class, 107;
  Dialectics of Nature, 50, 243, 247, 280; Hegel
  and, 236; *Ludwig Feuerbach and the Outcome*
  of Classical German Philosophy, 50; Marx and,
  47, 87, 134–35, 163, 205–8, 211, 212, 220,
  230–33, 244, 247–49, 251, 256, 272, 283;
  "money-greed" and, 107; "The Part Played by
  Labour in the Transition from Ape to Man,"
  59; Schmidt and, 14, 235–36
England, with France and Germany, 84–85, 87
enjoyment. *See Genuss; jouissance*
Enlightenment, 5, 6, 21–22, 121, 203, 207–8, 210,
  212, 220–21, 242; anti-, 204; *Dialectic of*
  Enlightenment, 97; Scottish, 285; truth and,
  195, 200
enrichment (*Bereicherung*), 106, 130, 132
Eros, 41, 43, 57; death drive and, 33, 39, 42, 56;
  Freud and, 32, 33, 40, 45, 70
Eros and Civilization (Marcuse), 34–36, 58–60,
  64–65, 271; on time and sex, 63; on work and
  play, 61–62
Essence of Christianity, The (Feuerbach), 164
Ethics of Psychoanalysis, The (1959–1960).
  See Seminar VII
être ("to be"), 28–29
European Union, debt crisis, 213
exchange value, 86, 109, 127, 129, 133, 147, 192, 206;
  commodities and, 172, 174, 180, 181; money
  with use and, 179–80, 185–86; social, 111, 163,

165, 180, 181; surplus and, 48–49, 92, 103, 108, 113, 138, 141–42, 172, 177, 194; use and, 110–12, 115, 170, 178, 179, 181, 186, 227, 276

excrement (shit), 81–89, 190

expenditure, accumulation and, 107

exploitation, 22, 105, 144, 206; labor and, 128, 152, 166, 168, 174, 177, 194, 282; profit and, 167

"extimate" stupidity, 285–86

Fable of the Bees, The (Mandeville), xii

fascism, 60, 119, 158, 203, 216, 223, 270

father: dead, 201, 203, 218; primal, 35, 201; *Urvater*, 35, 40, 201–2, 218. *See also* God

Feenberg, Andrew, 198, 267, 268–69

feminine penis, 187–89

Fenichel, Otto, 1, 3, 9, 50, 137; Freudo-Marxism and, 93–94; with infrastructure and superstructure, 67; Lacan on, 95–96; on money, 116; "Psychoanalysis as the Nucleus of a Future Dialectical-Materialist Psychology," 60, 93, 95–96

Ferenczi, Sandor, 94–95, 159

fetishism: analytic, 189, 195; desire and, 186–87; as "especially durable," 196, 198; Freud on, 187, 195–96, 198; psychoanalysis and, 195–96; shoe, 191. *See also* commodity fetishism

"Fetishism" (Freud), 187

"Fetishism" (Lacan and Granoff), 189

"fetishism of capital," 181

"Fetishism of the Commodity and Its Secret, The." *See Das Kapital*

Feuerbach, Ludwig, 52, 164, 205, 209, 233; with alienation and religion, 258; Marx on, 248–49, 253, 254

fictitious capital: with commodities, interest and capitalism, 161–69; IBC and commodity fetishism, 169–75; with Lacan and capitalism, 185–200; with political and libidinal economy, 158–61; retroactivity of fetishistic interest and, 175–85

Fidesz, Hungary, 204

film, with frozen frame, 191

Finance Capital (Hilferding), 167, 176, 277

Foley, Duncan, 173, 176

Forbes (magazine), 115–16, 117, 156

For Marx (Althusser), 236

Formations of the Unconscious (1957–1958). See Seminar V

Foucault, Michel, 224–25, 226

Four Fundamental Concepts of Psychoanalysis, The (1964). See Seminar XI

France, 1, 205; with Germany and England, 84–85, 87; Rassemblement National, 204

Frankfurt School, 50, 96, 97, 222, 233, 240; *The Authoritarian Personality*, 60; with defeat-induced pessimism, 270; Freudo-Marxism, 1, 271, 272; second and third generations of, 267; Western Marxism and, 270–71, 272, 275

"free love" ethos, 11

Freud (Rieff), 35

Freud, Sigmund: "Anxiety and Instinctual Life," 42; capitalism and, 215, 217, 240; capitalist economics and, 72; capitalist-entrepreneur relationship and, 72–73, 75; *Civilization and Its Discontents*, 10–14, 32–34; "Copernican revolution" and, 92, 143; desacralization and, 207–8, 210–12; with drives between historical materialism and psychoanalysis, 90–97; drive theory and, 4, 55–56, 67, 97, 135; *The Ego and the Id*, 16, 33; Eros and, 32, 33, 40, 45, 70; "Fetishism," 187; on fetishism, 187, 195–96, 198; *The Future of an Illusion*, 40, 203, 204, 208; God and, 201–4; *Group Psychology and the Analysis of the Ego*, 69; human nature and, 31–32, 34–35, 40, 44, 45; *Inhibitions, Symptoms and Anxiety*, 39, 40; *Interpretation of Dreams*, 75; *Jokes and Their Relation to the Unconscious*, 85; with Marx and partisanship of truth, 8–23; with Marxism and aggression, 29–49; Marxism with dialectical materialism and, 49–68; on money, 160; *Beyond the Pleasure Principle*, 10, 32, 39, 50, 58, 59; "Project for a Scientific Psychology," 39–40, 69; psychoanalysis as cult of, 18, 20; "The Question of a *Weltanschauung*," 17–18, 29–32, 43–45; religion and, 220; with scientific and technological advances, 5; scientificity and, 22; "Screen Memories," 184; superego and, 13–14, 15, 31; *Totem and Taboo*, 35, 201, 218; "Why War," 13, 42, 48; with *"Wo Es war, soll Ich werden,"* 282. *See also New Introductory Lectures on Psycho-Analysis*

Freud and the Bolsheviks (M. A. Miller), 50

Freudo-Lacano-Marxism, 97, 135

Freudo-Marxism, 2, 9, 76, 134–35, 137, 158, 159; Frankfurt School, 1, 271, 272; with historical materialism and psychoanalysis, 90–97; Marcuse and, 35, 60, 63, 66

Friedman, Milton, 286

Friedrich Wilhelm III (King of Prussia), 205

*From an Other to the other (1968–1969). See
Seminar XVI*

From the Closed World to the Infinite Universe
(Koyré), 90–91, 122, 131

"Function and Field of Speech and Language in
Psychoanalysis, The" (Lacan), 95

fundamentalists, religious, 221

fundamental ontology, 27–28, 227

Future of an Illusion, The (Freud), 40, 203,
204, 208

Galileo Galilei, 90, 91, 131

Gattungswesen ("species-being"), 193, 281, 282

Genuss (enjoyment), 103, 106, 126–27, 132, 133

Geras, Norman, 237

German Ideology, The (Marx and Engels), 87, 163,
206, 230–33

Germany: with France and England, 84–85, 87;
Greece and, 213; PEGIDA, 204

gesellschaftliche Hieroglyphe ("social
hieroglyphic"), 165

"ghost walking," 182

Gilded Age, xiv

Gini coefficient, xv–xvi

global wealth, xiii

Glucksmann, André, 236–37

God, 24, 53, 66, 181, 211, 212, 239; consumers and,
215; dark, 4, 216–19; with economic grace, 214;
hidden, 258; invisible hand of, 122, 201–5, 213,
241; transformed into money, 229, 230; as
undead, 201–5, 240

"God is dead," 201–2, 216–18, 223

"God is unconscious," 201–2, 217–18, 223, 229, 242

Good Sense (Holbach), 37–38

Gordon Gekko (fictional character), xii

Gospel, prosperity as, 213

Gramsci, Antonio, 2, 10, 31, 233, 264;
antieconomism and, 261; criticism of, 262–63;
historical bloc and, 252, 255–56, 261–63;
historical materialism and, 254–63; with
infrastructure-superstructure distinction,
253–55; "philosophy of praxis" and, 3, 253–54,
257–58, 261–63; on political errors, 259–60;
Prison Notebooks, 245, 250, 252–58, 260–63,
277; Western Marxism and, 245, 246, 263,
269, 276, 282

Granoff, Wladimir, 189

Great Depression, 158, 271

Great Recession, 213

Greece, 213

greed: capitalist, xviii, xix, 107, 114, 123, 131–32,
138; commodity fetishism and, 123–24; death
drive and, 132; money and, 105–6, 107; need
and, 105–6, 108, 122

greed for gold (*auri sacra fames*), 105, 106, 130

Group Psychology and the Analysis of the Ego
(Freud), 69

Grundrisse (Marx), 92; capitalism and, 123–27,
130; greed and, 107, 138; with human anatomy
and apes, 98–99, 184; on need and greed,
105–6; production and consumption in,
99–103; surplus value and production in,
101–2

gulags, xi, 12

Habermas, Jürgen, 94, 104

hainamoration (hate-love), 36

Hamlet (Shakespeare), 223

Han, Byung-Chul, 132

Harvey, David, 126, 173

hate-love (*hainamoration*), 36

"haunted" ("*Spuk treiben*"), 182

hedonism: abstract, 106, 108, 123; capitalists and,
124; miserliness and, 106

Hegel, G. W. F., 8, 39, 54; "The Doctrine of
Being," 140; "The Doctrine of Essence," 275,
285; *Elements of the Philosophy of Right*, 103,
256; Engels and, 236; Germany-France-
England triad and, 84–85; influence of, 275;
Logik, 28, 140, 162, 176, 243, 275, 285; with
"Lordship and Bondage" dialectic, 152–54;
Marx and, 68, 87, 103, 121, 145–46, 172, 195,
205–6, 256, 280; natural sciences and, 93;
nature and, 113; *Phenomenology of Spirit*, 71,
152–53

Hegemony and Socialist Strategy (Laclau and
Mouffe), 277

Heidegger, Martin, 27–28, 62, 225–29, 266

Heine, Heinrich, 27

Heinrich, Michael, 173, 176, 181, 183

helplessness (*Hilflosigkeit*), 38–41, 53, 69, 73–75,
81, 94

Hilferding, Rudolf, 167, 171, 175–76, 277

Hilflosigkeit (helplessness), 38–41, 53, 69, 73–75,
81, 94

historical bloc, 237, 252, 255–56, 261–63

INDEX · 359

historical materialism, 2–3, 13–14, 16–18, 21–22, 86–87; antieconomism and, xvi, 263–64; dialectical and, 1, 67, 247, 254, 280; drives between psychoanalysis and, 90–97; economic theology and, 229–30; false and true, 258; Gramsci and, 254–63; Marx on, 145; psychoanalysis and, 51, 61; rejection of, 268; Weber and, 222; Western Marxism and, 245–46, 257

Historical Materialism (Bukharin), 262

History and Class Consciousness (Lukács), 243–45, 257, 260, 263–69, 274

Hitler, Adolf, 215

Hobbes, Thomas, 8, 10, 35–36, 70, 113

Holbach, Paul-Henri Thiry d', 36, 37–38

Holy Family, or Critique of Critical Criticism, The (Marx and Engels), 206, 256

Homer, 98, 99

homo homini lupus, 10, 35

homophony, 27–28, 150

Homo Sacer (Agamben), 224–25, 227

Homo sapiens, xv, xxii, 40, 75

Honneth, Axel, 267

honte (shame), 27, 81, 233

hontologie, 27

Horkheimer, Max, 97, 216, 217

human anatomy, apes and, 75, 98–99, 184

human beings: with destructiveness, 10; fate of, 34; as lone wolf, 8, 10; narcissism of, 143–44; "speaking being" and, 24; as *zoon politikon*, 8, 38–39

human nature, xi, xvii, 12–13, 59, 113, 125, 282; Aristotelian picture of, 8; Freud and, 31–32, 34–35, 40, 44, 45; Kant and, 36; malleability of, 104, 281; Marcuse and, 65, 104; Marx and, 10; non-, 280; transubstantiation of, 65

Hungary, 204

IBC. *See* interest-bearing capital

id, 16, 33, 39, 41, 61, 63–64, 94

"Idea for a Universal History with a Cosmopolitan Intent" (Kant), 36–37, 38

ideology: as allusion and illusion, 73, 274; *The German Ideology*, 87, 163, 206, 230–33; Korsch and, 247; "materiality of," 86, 247–48; science and, 22–23; theory of, 21, 86; *Weltanschauung* and, 21

"Ideology and Ideological State Apparatuses" (Althusser), 232, 261

Iliad (Homer), 98, 99

"Illusion of a Future, The" (Pfister), 203

Imaginary, 22–23, 187, 189, 220

imago, paternal, 97, 217

imago-Gestalt, 29

Imperialism (Lenin), 277

incest, 74–75, 79

Incontinence of the Void (Žižek), 283

industrial capitalists, xiv, 130, 168–69, 177, 217, 223, 231, 233

inequality, 11, 70, 144; economic, 207, 223; material, xiii, xv, 12, 47; wealth, xiii, xiv, xv, xxi, 32

infinitude, xix, 112, 123–24, 127, 131–32, 239

infrastructure: economic, 6, 83, 202, 209, 218, 220, 229, 238, 241, 246, 249, 267, 279; superstructure and, 6, 13–14, 67, 83, 86, 93–94, 137, 154, 202, 209–10, 212, 220, 228–30, 233–36, 238, 241, 243, 245, 251–55, 259, 261–63, 268, 271–72, 274, 283–84

Inhibitions, Symptoms and Anxiety (Freud), 39, 40

inhumanity, xx, xxi

interest: capitalist mode of production and, 176–78, 183; fictitious capital with capitalism, commodities and, 161–69; with merchants and consumers, 178; money as, 186

interest-bearing capital (IBC): capitalism and, 161–62, 168; commodity fetishism and, 164, 169–75, 179, 181, 183–86, 190, 192, 194; defined, 170; M-C-M′ and, 170–74, 177–79; retroactivity of fetishistic interest and, 176–79, 181–85

intermittent determinism, 235–37

International Psychoanalytic Association (IPA), 95, 96

Interpretation of Dreams (Freud), 75

invisible hand, of God, 122, 201–5, 213, 241

invisible hand of the market, xx, xxi, 120, 122, 199, 203, 219

IPA (International Psychoanalytic Association), 95, 96

Iraq War, 279

Islam, 17

Jacoby, Russell, 9, 19, 52, 59, 267, 271

Jameson, Fredric, 68–71

Jay, Martin, 257, 271

Jesus Christ, 213

Jobbik, Hungary, 204

360   INDEX

Johnston, Adrian, 63, 64, 243–44, 280–81
Jokes and Their Relation to the Unconscious
    (Freud), 85
jouissance (enjoyment), 4, 70, 133, 142, 218;
    capitalism and, 80; expected and obtained,
    65–66, 79; *Genuss* and, 126–27, 132; M-C-M′
    and, 77; *plus-de-jouir* and surplus, 73–74, 76,
    80, 148–50, 153, 155–56; surplus, 72–74, 76, 80,
    148–57; value, 78, 79–80
journalism, 19, 117–21, 279
Jung, Carl, 69
"Junius Pamphlet" (Luxemburg), 119

Kaczyński, Jarosław, 204
Kant, Immanuel, 16, 27, 97; "Antinomies of Pure
    Reason," 269; Christianity and, 212–13; "Idea
    for a Universal History with a Cosmopolitan
    Intent," 36–37, 38; "unsocial sociability" and,
    36, 38, 70
"Kant with Sade" (Lacan), 97
Karl Marx (Korsch), 248
Kautsky, Karl, 234
Kingdom and the Glory, The (Agamben), 224, 225,
    227, 229
Kojève, Alexandre, 71
Koran, 17
Korsch, Karl, 2, 31, 255, 257, 270, 279; dialectical
    materialism and, 246, 247, 254; historical
    materialism and, 253, 254; *Marxism and
    Philosophy*, 245–46, 248–54, 267; "reflection
    theory" and, 252; superstructure and, 250–52;
    Western Marxism and, 245, 246, 269, 276
Koyré, Alexandre, 90–91, 122, 131
Kulaks, 11
Kultur-Über-Ich, das ("cultural superego"),
    14, 15, 16

labor: alienation and, 62; capitalism and, 61;
    division of, 103; exploitation and, 128, 152, 166,
    168, 174, 177, 194, 282; necessary, 68, 151; "The
    Part Played by Labour in the Transition from
    Ape to Man," 59; surplus, 62, 151, 168; surplus
    value and, 151, 166, 172, 175, 192; time, 62, 65,
    168, 219; unpaid, 151, 168, 172, 177, 194, 219;
    wages of workers, 151, 177, 182, 194, 250; work
    and play, 61–62
Lacan, Jacques, 1, 3, 9, 12, 15, 51, 65, 67;
    ambivalence and, 36, 68, 195; capitalism and,
    185–200; capitalist economics with Marxism

and, 137–57; castration and, 188–89;
    desacralization and, 207, 208; *désir* and, 4, 13,
    72–74, 138–40, 143, 148, 186–87, 189, 192–93;
    dialectical materialism and, 220; "Fetishism,"
    189; on fetishism and desire, 186–87;
    Freudo-Marxism and, 90–97; "The Function
    and Field of Speech and Language in
    Psychoanalysis," 95; God and, 4, 201–4,
    216–19, 223, 229, 242; influences on, 91; "Kant
    with Sade," 97; language and, 136; with
    Marxism and psychoanalysis, 68–89; on
    money, 160; nature and, 36; Nazism and, 215,
    216; with *objet petit a*, 4, 74, 76, 149–50, 189;
    political economy and, 71, 80–81;
    "Radiophonie," 152, 156; on Reich and
    Fenichel, 95–96; "Science and Truth," 66;
    "Seminar on 'The Purloined Letter,'" 160;
    with stupidity of truth, 279; "The Subversion
    of the Subject and the Dialectic of Desire in
    the Freudian Unconscious," 148; *Télévision*,
    202; "The Triumph of Religion," 204;
    Weltanschauung question and, 23–29. *See also*
    specific seminars
Lacano-Marxism, 1, 2, 76, 96, 132, 134, 244; with
    capitalist economics and Marxian drives,
    137–57; Freudo-Lacano-Marxism, 97, 135
Laclau, Ernesto, 3, 222, 261, 277–78
L'acte psychanalytique (1967–1968).
    See Seminar XV
language: Being and, 28; "The Function and Field
    of Speech and Language in Psychoanalysis,"
    95; Lacan and, 136; *Thought and Language*,
    57, 59
Laplanche, Jean, 107
Laporte, Dominique, 81–82, 87
Late Capitalism (Mandel), 150
Lebensphilosophie, 257, 267
le Dieu obscur (dark God), 4, 216–19
left populism, 277–78
Lenin, V. I., 1, 3, 44, 233, 257; Bolshevik
    Revolution and, 270; criticism of, 260;
    Imperialism, 277; on intelligent idealism and
    materialism, 243; *Materialism and Empirio-
    Criticism*, 243; *Philosophical Notebooks*, 243;
    in *Pravda*, 88–89; *The State and Revolution*,
    269; "The Three Sources and Three
    Component Parts of Marxism," 85; *What Is to
    Be Done?*, 250
Le Pen, Marine, 204

Les non-dupes errent (1973–1974).
    See Seminar XXI
"Letter on Humanism" (Heidegger), 28
Lévi-Strauss, Claude, 77
liberalism: with capitalism and communism,
    112–22; journalism and, 119–21; neoliberalism,
    xii, xiii–xiv, 117–18, 120–21, 145, 212, 286;
    selfishness and, 114, 119
liberating intolerance, 19
libidinal economy: fictitious capital with
    political and, 158–61; of modern social
    history, 98–105
Liebesbedürfnis (need to be loved), 30, 32, 34,
    39–41, 45
*L'insu que sait de l'une-bévue, s'aile à mourre
    (1976–1977). See Seminar XXIV*
Lire le Capital (Althusser), 151
Logic of Fantasy, The (1966–1967).
    See Seminar XIV
Logik (Science of Logic) (Hegel), 28, 140, 162, 176,
    243, 275, 285
lone wolf, 8, 10, 36
"Lordship and Bondage" dialectic, Hegel with,
    152–54
love: "free," 11; hate-love, 36; *Liebesbedürfnis*, 30,
    32, 34, 39–41, 45. *See also* Eros
Lucchelli, Juan Pablo, 97
*Ludwig Feuerbach and the Outcome of Classical
    German Philosophy* (Engels), 50
Lukács, Georg, 2, 31, 62–63, 233–34; "The
    Antinomies of Bourgeois Thought," 264;
    antinomy of reification and, 268, 269, 272; on
    commodities, 264–65, 274; Hegel and, 275;
    History and Class Consciousness, 243–45, 257,
    260, 263–69, 274; reification and, 257;
    "Reification and the Consciousness of the
    Proletariat," 264–69; Western Marxism and,
    245, 246, 269, 276, 282
Luria, Alexander Romanovich, 1, 3, 9, 50–57,
    59, 66
Lustprinzip. See pleasure principle
Luxemburg, Rosa, 119, 277

magic, money and, 166, 177, 181, 190, 197
maître, with master and *m'être*, 28–29,
    152, 154
Mandel, Ernest, 94, 149–50, 176
Mandeville, Bernard, xii, 36
Mannoni, Octave, 195–98

"man of the calling" (*Berufsmensch*), 83
Mao Tse-Tung, 233, 235, 277
Marcuse, Herbert, 3, 9, 19–20, 41, 97, 274; "The
    Concept of Essence," 273; ego psychology
    and, 96; *Eros and Civilization*, 34–36, 58–65,
    271; with Freud and dialectical materialism,
    50, 58–59, 60–65; Freudo-Marxism and, 35,
    60, 63, 66; Hegel and, 275; *Hilflosigkeit* and,
    94; human nature and, 65, 104; with
    infrastructure and superstructure, 67;
    Negations, 273; *One-Dimensional Man*,
    272–73
Marx, Karl, 3, 31, 214, 221, 225, 227, 238; alienation
    and, xvii; atheism and, 206; commodity
    fetishism and, 199–200; "A Contribution to
    the Critique of Hegel's Philosophy of Right.
    Introduction," 256; desacralization and,
    205–12; drive theory and, 100–102, 106, 107,
    113, 123, 134, 135, 140, 141, 155; with economic
    analyses of capitalism, xiv; *Economic and
    Philosophical Manuscripts*, 206, 212; *The
    Eighteenth Brumaire of Louis Bonaparte*, 136,
    232; Engels and, 47, 87, 134–35, 163, 205–8,
    211, 212, 220, 230–33, 244, 247–49, 251, 256,
    272, 283; with Freud and partisanship of
    truth, 8–23; God and, 201–4; Hegel and, 68,
    87, 103, 121, 145–46, 172, 195, 205–6, 256, 280;
    human nature and, 10; influence of, 265;
    liberalism and, 112–22; with libidinal
    economy of modern social history, 98–105;
    For Marx, 236; M-C-M′ and, xviii–xix, xxi;
    money and, 185–86; "On the Question of Free
    Trade," 118; political economy and, 215, 220,
    264; *The Poverty of Philosophy*, 121, 147,
    230–32; religion and, 6, 21, 241, 242; *Theories
    of Surplus-Value*, 107, 126, 128, 130, 171,
    173–74, 180–81; "Theses on Feuerbach,"
    248–49, 253, 254; Weber and, 222–23; with
    wooden table example, 190. *See also
    Contribution to the Critique of Political
    Economy, A; Das Kapital; Grundrisse;
    Western Marxism*
Marxian drives: capitalism and headless subject,
    122–37; commodity fetishism and, 105–12;
    between historical materialism and
    psychoanalysis, 90–97; Lacano-Marxism and
    capitalist economics, 137–57; liberalism and,
    112–22; libidinal economy of modern social
    history and, 98–105

362 INDEX

Marxism: Bolshevism and, 21; capitalist economics with Lacan and, 137–57; with Freud and aggression, 29–49; with Freud and dialectical materialism, 49–68; Freudo-Lacano-Marxism, 97, 135; Freudo-Marxism, 1, 2, 9, 90–97; Lacan on, 26, 27; psychoanalysis and, 1, 3, 8, 9, 29, 50, 67, 68–89, 137; religion and, 21; Stalinism and, 120; "The Three Sources and Three Component Parts of Marxism," 85. *See also* Lacano-Marxism; Western Marxism

Marxism and Philosophy (Korsch), 245–46, 248–54, 267

Marxisme et structuralisme (Sebag), 77–78

Mass Psychology of Fascism, The (Reich), 60

master, with *maître* and *m'être*, 28–29, 152, 154

material inequality, xv, 12, 47

Materialism and Empirio-Criticism (Lenin), 243

"materialistic theology," 257

"materiality of ideology," 86, 247–48

maternal phallus, 187, 189, 191, 195

mathematics, 139, 167, 215; nature and, 90, 122; science and, 19, 20

M-C-M' (money-commodity–more money), xxi, 48–49, 62, 110–11, 116–17, 132, 154–55, 167, 278; capitalists with, 109, 123–24, 128; consumption and, xviii, 4, 113, 240; as endless loop, xix, 7, 77, 82–83, 115, 123, 133, 219, 286; IBC and, 170–74, 177–79; invisible hand guiding, 219; *jouissance* and, 77; with shitty political economy, 83; surplus value and, 150, 166

"meat market," 76

merchants: credit, 178, 184; interest with, 178; as money hoarders, 92, 227

Merkel, Angela, 213

Merleau-Ponty, Maurice, 2, 244, 246

Merrington, John, 267

Messianism, 26, 27

Mészáros, István, 254

m'être, with *maître* and master, 28–29, 152, 154

Mikhailovsky, Nikolay, 18

milestone of desire (*borne miliaire du désir*), 187

Miller, Jacques-Alain, 189

Miller, Judith, 77

Miller, Martin A., 50

Milner, Jean-Claude, 91, 143–44

miserliness, hedonism and, 106

misers: with capitalism and headless subject, 122–37; capitalists and, 125–28; with commodity fetishism, 110–12, 127; as fetishist, 185

modernity: natural sciences and, 90, 252; premodernity and, 90, 92, 144, 156, 224, 226; science, 21, 26, 90–91, 131, 143–44, 224

money: C-M-C' and, 109–11; commodity and, 108; with exchange and use value, 179–80, 185–86; Freud and Lacan on, 160; God transformed into, 229, 230; gold and, 192; greed and, 105–6, 107; hoarders of, 92, 126, 129, 227; as interest, 186; laundering, 5, 161–69, 194–95; magic and, 166, 177, 181, 190, 197; Marx and, 185–86; in material and social form, 112, 115; as "narcissistic supply" for capitalists, 116; as wages, 109, 194. *See also* fictitious capital; interest-bearing capital

money-commodity–more money. *See* M-C-M'

"most superficial" (*äußerlichste*), 171, 191–92

"mother of every insane form, the" (*die Mutter aller verrückten Formen*), 175, 185

Mouffe, Chantal, 222, 277

Mutter aller verrückten Formen, die ("the mother of every insane form"), 175, 185

Nachträglichkeit/après-coup, 137, 183

narcissism, 122, 147, 190; of human beings, 143–44; selfishness and, 116, 145, 146

narcissistic animal, capitalism and, 144–46

"narcissistic supply," money as, 116

natural sciences, 18–19, 24–25, 31, 37, 130, 144, 204, 233, 243; capitalist economics and, 131; empirical and experimental, 252, 280; Hegel and, 93; Marx on, 102; modernity and, 90, 252

Naturdialektik, 243, 247, 280

nature: dialectics of, 244, 247, 280; *Dialectics of Nature*, 50; Hegel and, 113; Kant on, 36–37, 38; mathematics and, 90, 122; psychoanalysis and, 24; as reductive, 280–81; "state of," 8, 10, 36, 38–39, 46; worldview and, 23. *See also* human nature

Nazism, 96, 215, 216

need (*Bedürfnis*): elasticity of, 104; greed and, 105–6, 108, 122; production and, 100–102; system of, 103

need to be loved (*Liebesbedürfnis*), 30, 32, 34, 39–41, 45

Negations (Marcuse), 273

INDEX   ❦   363

neofeudalism, xiv
neoliberalism, xii, xiii–xiv, 117–18, 120–21, 145, 212, 286
(neo)liberal globalization, journalism and, 117–18, 120
New Introductory Lectures on Psycho-Analysis (Freud), 13–16, 23, 34; "Anxiety and Instinctual Life," 42; "The Question of a *Weltanschauung*," 17–18, 29–32, 43–45
"New Man," xi, 13, 66
Nietzsche, Friedrich, 216
"noble savage," 10
Nobus, Dany, 97

objectivity, 7, 19–20, 62, 165
Object of Psychoanalysis, The (1965–1966). See Seminar XIII
Object Relation, The (1956–1957). See Seminar IV
object relations, 93, 137
objet petit a, 4, 74, 76, 149–50, 189
October Revolution. *See* Bolshevik Revolution
Oedipus at Colonus (Sophocles), 79
Oedipus complex, 16, 69, 78–79, 152
Oedipus Rex (Sophocles), 78–79
Of a Discourse That Would Not Be a Semblance (1971). See Seminar XVIII
Ollman, Bertell, 282
One-Dimensional Man (Marcuse), 272–73
"On the Materialist Dialectic" (Althusser), 236
"On the Question of Free Trade" (Marx), 118
On the Reproduction of Capitalism (Althusser), 261
"Ontogenesis of the Interest in Money, The" (Ferenczi), 94–95
ontological difference, 27–28
ontology: Being and, 29; fundamental, 27–28, 227
Other, the, 68–71, 193
Other Side of Psychoanalysis, The (1969–1970). See Seminar XVII

parlêtre (speaking being), 24, 148
Parrhasios, 191
"Part Played by Labour in the Transition from Ape to Man, The" (Engels), 59
Patriotische Europäer gegen die Islamisierung des Abendlandes (PEGIDA), 204
penis, 187–89
Pfister, Oskar, 203–4
phallus, 154, 187, 189–91, 195–96
Phenomenology of Spirit (Hegel), 71, 152–53

Philosophical Notebooks (Lenin), 243
philosophy: "Contribution to the Critique of Hegel's Philosophy of Right, A. Introduction," 256; *Elements of the Philosophy of Right*, 103, 256; *Ludwig Feuerbach and the Outcome of Classical German Philosophy*, 50; *Marxism and Philosophy*, 245–46, 248–54, 267; *The Poverty of Philosophy*, 121, 147, 230–32; of praxis, 3, 253–54, 257–58, 261–63; *The System of Economic Contradictions, or The Philosophy of Poverty*, 230
Picketty, Thomas, 117
Pico della Mirandola, Giovanni, 36, 225
pineal gland, 67, 83, 88, 94, 210
Plato, 36, 189
Plautus, 10
play, work and, 61–62
pleasure, time and, 64–65
pleasure principle (*Lustprinzip*), 4, 32, 41–42, 45, 57, 61–64
plus-de-jouir (surplus *jouissance*), 73–74, 76, 80, 148–50, 153, 155–56
Poe, Edgar Allan, 169
Poland, 204
political economy, 22, 26, 31, 45; capitalist mode of production and, 278; fictitious capital with libidinal and, 158–61; Marx and, 215, 220, 264; with Marxism and psychoanalysis, 68–89; *The Principles of Political Economy and Taxation*, 107; shit and, 83. *See also Contribution to the Critique of Political Economy, A*
political errors, 259–60
political journalism, 19
political superstructure, 209, 220, 222
Poverty of Philosophy, The (Marx), 121, 147, 230–32
Pravda (newspaper), 88–89
premodernity, 90, 92, 144, 156, 224, 226
primal ambivalence, 35
primal father, 35, 201
primal horde, 35
Principles of Political Economy and Taxation, The (Ricardo), 107
Prison Notebooks (Gramsci), 245, 250, 252–58, 260–63, 277
private property (*Privateigentum*), 10, 11, 22, 47, 49, 146
"Problem of the Cultural Behaviour of the Child, The" (Luria), 59

364   INDEX

procapitalists, xi–xii, xix, 113, 117, 121
production: consumption and, 99–104; dream, 72;
     need and, 100–102; surplus value and, 101–2,
     129. *See also* capitalist mode of production
profit: capitalist mode of production and, 182;
     exploitation and, 167; surplus value and, 166,
     176–77, 194
profit of enterprise (*Unternehmergewinns*),
     167–69, 179, 194
"Project for a Scientific Psychology" (Freud),
     39–40, 69
Prolegomena to Any Future Materialism,
     volume 2, *A Weak Nature Alone* (Johnston),
     243–44, 280–81
prosperity, as Gospel, 213
*Protestant Ethic and the "Spirit" of Capitalism,
     The* (Weber), 125–26, 221–22
Protestantism, 16, 125–26, 205, 221; capitalism
     and, 90, 209, 217, 222, 230, 238–39; capitalist
     mode of production and, 223; "man of the
     calling," 83; with prosperity as Gospel, 213
Proudhon, Pierre-Joseph, 121, 147, 230–31, 233
psychoanalysis: commodity fetishism and, 195; as
     cult of Freud, 18, 20; *Dialectical Materialism
     and Psychoanalysis*, 59–60, 93, 95–96; drives
     between historical materialism and, 90–97;
     drive theory, xix, 4, 41, 54, 67, 91, 92, 100; *The
     Ethics of Psychoanalysis [1959–1960]*, 79;
     fetishism and, 195–96; *The Four Fundamental
     Concepts of Psychoanalysis [1964]*, 124, 141–42,
     191, 201, 215–18; "The Function and Field of
     Speech and Language in Psychoanalysis," 95;
     historical materialism and, 51, 61; IPA, 95, 96;
     Marxism and, 1, 3, 8, 9, 29, 50, 67, 68–89, 137;
     nature and, 24; *The Object of Psychoanalysis
     [1965–1966]*, 78, 156; *The Other Side of
     Psychoanalysis [1969–1970]*, 71, 72, 75, 149, 150,
     152–56; symptoms in, 67, 185
"Psychoanalysis as a System of Monistic
     Psychology" (Luria), 50–57
"Psychoanalysis as the Nucleus of a Future
     Dialectical-Materialist Psychology"
     (Fenichel), 60, 93, 95–96
"Psychoanalysis in the Soviet Union" (Reich), 58
psychoanalytic body, body politic and: with
     Freud, Marxism and aggression, 29–49; Lacan
     and *Weltanschauung* question, 23–29; with
     Marx, Freud and partisanship of truth, 8–23;
     with Marxism, Freud and dialectical

materialism, 49–68; political economy with
     Marxism and psychoanalysis, 68–89
Psychoanalytic Theory of Neurosis, The (Fenichel), 95
psychology: ego, 95, 96; *The Mass Psychology of
     Fascism*, 60; "Project for a Scientific
     Psychology," 39–40, 69; "Psychoanalysis as a
     System of Monistic Psychology," 50–57;
     "Psychoanalysis as the Nucleus of a Future
     Dialectical-Materialist Psychology," 60, 93,
     95–96; as science, 31
Psychoses, The (1955–1956). See Seminar III
pulsion, désir and, 139–40, 143
"Purloined Letter, The" (Poe), 169

Que faire? (Althusser), 261–63
Quelle-Objekt ("source-object") of drive, 107
"Question of a *Weltanschauung*, The" (Freud),
     17–18, 29–32, 43–45

"radical democracy," 3
"Radiophonie" (Lacan), 152, 156
Reading Capital (Althusser), 236, 237
Realabstraktion, 220
reality principle, 41, 57, 58, 60–61, 63–64
real reduction, 279–80
rectum, surplus value as, 83
reductionism: antireductive and, 52, 93, 237,
     279–82, 284; nature and, 280–81; real,
     279–80; social reality and, 279
"reflection theory," 252
Reich, Wilhelm, 1, 3, 9, 26, 50, 52, 137; *Dialectical
     Materialism and Psychoanalysis*, 59–60, 93,
     95–96; with ego as "character armor," 96;
     Freudo-Marxism and, 93–96; with
     infrastructure and superstructure, 67; Lacan
     on, 95–96; *The Mass Psychology of Fascism*,
     60; "Psychoanalysis in the Soviet Union," 58
reification (*Verdinglichung*), 244, 257, 264–67;
     antinomy of, 268, 269, 272; as illusion, 273
"Reification and the Consciousness of the
     Proletariat" (Lukács), 264–69
religion: alienation and, 164, 258; atheism and,
     201–2, 206, 212, 215, 242; "Capitalism as
     Religion," 221, 238–41; desacralized, 211, 221,
     229, 238; detheologization of, 212; economy
     and, 6; economy with uneven development
     and, 230–42; Freud and, 220;
     fundamentalists, 221; Marx and, 6, 21, 241,
     242; postulates of impure economic unreason

and, 238; with prosperity as Gospel, 213; sacred and, 17, 217, 239; science and, 5, 17, 18, 21, 204; superstructure, 6, 202, 209, 212, 217, 220–22, 229–30, 238, 241; "triumph of religion," 6, 203–4, 208, 218, 220, 223; Weber and, 223; worldviews and, 26. *See also* God

rentiers, xiv, xx, 178, 197

repression, 60, 169, 186; analytic symptoms and, 191; surplus, 62, 65

repressive desublimation, 20, 63, 65, 221

"repressive progress," 20

"repressive tolerance," 19

rêve. See dream

Ricardo, David, 107, 151

Ricoeur, Paul, 159

Rieff, Philip, 35, 39

Robber Barons, xiv

Robinson, Joan, 166–67, 183

Rosdolsky, Roman, 126

Roudinesco, Élisabeth, 77

Rousseau, Jean-Jacques, 10, 36

R.S.I. (1974–1975). See Seminar XXII

Russia, 9, 10, 11, 43–44, 50, 58, 270

sacred, 17, 205–12, 217, 239

Sartre, Jean-Paul, 137

Sassoulitch, Vera, 18

Schäuble, Wolfgang, 213

Schmidt, Conrad, 14, 235–36

Schmitt, Carl, 221–28, 230, 232

Schumpeter, Joseph, 118

science: bourgeois, 49, 58; desacralization and, 204; economics and, 244; ideology and, 22–23; mathematics and, 19, 20; modern, 21, 26, 90–91, 131, 143–44, 224; psychology as, 31; religion and, 5, 17, 18, 21, 204; technology and, 5, 48, 254–55; *Weltanschauung* and, 21–24, 26, 143; worldview and, 27. *See also* natural sciences

Science, bourgeois, 49, 58

"Science and Truth" (Lacan), 66

Science of Logic. See Logik

scientificity, 17, 22, 51–52, 233, 284–85

Scottish Enlightenment, 285

screen memories, 183, 191

"Screen Memories" (Freud), 184

Sebag, Lucien, 77–78

Second International, 31, 233, 244, 257, 281

Selbsterhaltungstrieb (self-preservative instinct), 30, 32, 34, 41, 45

"self-cleaning fetish, the," 194

self-destructiveness, 42, 43

selfishness: capitalism and, xxi, 112–22; capitalist mode of production and, xvi, xvii; liberalism and, 114, 119; narcissism and, 116, 145, 146; transubstantiation of, xii

selflessness: of capitalism, 129, 147, 153; socialism/communism and, xxi

self-preservative instinct (*Selbsterhaltungstrieb*), 30, 32, 34, 41, 45

Seminar III (*The Psychoses [1955–1956]*) (Lacan), 152

Seminar IV (*The Object Relation [1956–1957]*) (Lacan), 186, 188–91

"Seminar on 'The Purloined Letter'" (Lacan), 160

Seminar V (*Formations of the Unconscious [1957–1958]*) (Lacan), 147, 185, 186, 192

Seminar VI (*Desire and Its Interpretation [1958–1959]*) (Lacan), 13, 147, 185, 186, 192

Seminar VII (*The Ethics of Psychoanalysis [1959–1960]*) (Lacan), 79

Seminar VIII (*Transference [1960–1961]*) (Lacan), 95, 189

Seminar X (*Anxiety [1962–1963]*) (Lacan), 189

Seminar XI (*The Four Fundamental Concepts of Psychoanalysis [1964]*) (Lacan), 124, 141–42, 191, 201, 215–18

Seminar XIII (*The Object of Psychoanalysis [1965–1966]*) (Lacan), 78, 156

Seminar XIV (*The Logic of Fantasy [1966–1967]*) (Lacan), 75–80

Seminar XV (*L'acte psychanalytique [1967–1968]*) (Lacan), 95

Seminar XVI (*From an Other to the other [1968–1969]*) (Lacan), 71–72, 77, 150, 185

Seminar XVII (*The Other Side of Psychoanalysis [1969–1970]*) (Lacan), 71, 72, 75, 149, 150, 152–56

Seminar XVIII (*Of a Discourse That Would Not Be a Semblance [1971]*) (Lacan), 74, 185

Seminar XX (*Encore [1972–1973]*) (Lacan), 24–28, 284

Seminar XXI (*Les non-dupes errent [1973–1974]*) (Lacan), 13

Seminar XXII (*R.S.I. [1974–1975]*) (Lacan), 154

Seminar XXIV (*L'insu que sait de l'une-bévue, s'aile à mourre [1976–1977]*) (Lacan), 24

sex, 34, 47, 63, 95

"sexo-leftism," 95

sexuality, 41, 95, 284

Shakespeare, William, 203, 223

shame (*honte*), 27, 81, 233

shit (excrement), 81–89, 190

shoe fetishism, 191

Slovene School, 97, 132

Smith, Adam, xi–xii, 103–4, 139, 144, 151, 157

social exchange value, 111, 163, 165, 180, 181

"social hieroglyphic" (*gesellschaftliche Hieroglyphe*), 165

social history, libidinal economy of modern, 98–105

socialism/communism, 6, 8, 11, 32, 41, 44, 65, 71; Bolshevism and, 9, 45; capitalism with, 46; selflessness and, xxi

social reality, 174, 202, 250, 273; of capitalism, 101; external, 41, 61; reductive, 279

social superstructure, 27, 250, 270

social theory, 19, 245, 266

Socrates, 99

Sohn-Rethel, Alfred, 279

Solms, Mark, 56

Sophocles, 78–79

"source-object" (*Quelle-Objekt*) of drive, 107

Soviet Union, 1, 13, 43, 50, 58

speaking being (*parlêtre*), 24, 148

"species-being" (*Gattungswesen*), 193, 281, 282

Spinoza, Baruch, 53–55

"*Spuk treiben*" ("haunted"), 182

Stalin, J. V., 12, 254

Stalinism, 16, 31, 49–50, 221, 244, 257, 282; anti-, 254; bourgeois and, 11; Marxism and, 120

State and Revolution, The (Lenin), 269

"state of nature," 8, 10, 36, 38–39, 46

Stedman Jones, Gareth, 237, 266–67

Stewart, Jon, 279

Stone, Oliver, xii

Strachey, James, 45

string theory, 24–25

stupidity: Brecht and, 287; "extimate," 285–86; of truth, 279

sublimation, 48, 132, 134, 142, 203, 211, 221

"subsequent burden of guilt," 35

"Subversion of the Subject and the Dialectic of Desire in the Freudian Unconscious, The" (Lacan), 148

Sucht (addiction), 106

superego, 30, 69, 102, 217, 240; cultural, 14, 15, 16; Freud and, 13–14, 15, 31

superstructure, 22, 87, 237, 244, 246, 248, 265, 276; economic, 13, 249, 267, 278;

infrastructure and, 6, 13–14, 67, 83, 86, 93–94, 137, 154, 202, 209–10, 212, 220, 228–30, 233–36, 238, 241, 243, 245, 251–55, 259, 261–63, 268, 271–72, 274, 283–84; Korsch and, 250–52; political, 209, 220, 222; religious, 6, 202, 209, 212, 217, 220–22, 229–30, 238, 241; social, 27, 250, 270

surplus *jouissance* (*plus-de-jouir*), 73–74, 76, 80, 148–50, 153, 155–56

surplus labor, 62, 151, 168

surplus repression, 62, 65

surplus value: capitalist mode of production, 80, 130; capitalists with, 114–15, 157, 286; exchange and, 48–49, 92, 103, 108, 113, 138, 141–42, 172, 177, 194; *jouissance* and, 80; labor and, 151, 166, 172, 175, 192; M-C-M' and, 150, 166; production and, 101–2, 129; profit and, 166, 176–77, 194; profit of enterprise and, 167–69, 179, 194; quantitative-become-qualitative, 176–77; as rectum, 83; rents, xiv; *Theories of Surplus-Value*, 107, 126, 128, 130, 173–74, 180–81; wages of superintendence and, 167–69, 194

symbolic castration, 154, 187–89, 284

symptoms, 4, 39, 40, 130, 169, 196–97; analytic, 191–92; of commodity fetishism, 109–10, 200; in psychoanalysis, 67, 185

System of Economic Contradictions, or The Philosophy of Poverty, The (Proudhon), 230

technology, 5, 17, 48, 119, 254–55

Télévision (Lacan), 202

teloi, xv, 110, 139, 142

Ten Commandments, 204–5

terror, xi, 12, 270

theological economics: desacralization and afterlife of sacred, 205–12; economic theology versus, 220–30; economy, religion and uneven development, 230–42; with God as undead, 201–5; intermittent determinism and, 235–37; postulates of impure economic unreason and, 212–19

Theories of Surplus-Value (Marx), 107, 126, 128, 130, 171, 173–74, 180–81

Therborn, Göran, 267

"Theses on Feuerbach" (Marx), 248–49, 253, 254

Thought and Language (Vygotsky), 57, 59

"Three Notes on the Theory of Discourses" (Althusser), 51

"Three Sources and Three Component Parts of Marxism, The" (Lenin), 85

time: labor, 62, 65, 168, 219; pleasure and, 64–65; sex and, 63

Time Driven (Johnston), 63, 64

timeless, unconscious as, 63

"to be" (*être*), 28–29

Todestrieb. See death drive

toilets, European, 84–87

Tomšič, Samo, 75–76, 137–46

Too Much and Never Enough (M. Trump), xx

Toscano, Alberto, 225–26, 227–28

Totem and Taboo (Freud), 35, 201, 218

Träger (bearers), 49, 124, 154, 219

Träger (vehicle), 13, 15

Transference (1960–1961). See Seminar VIII

transubstantiation, xii, 65, 205–12, 218, 229

Triebe. See drives

Triebtheorie, 107, 131, 135, 143

Trieb theory. *See* drive theory

trillionaires, xiv

"triumph of religion," 6, 203–4, 208, 218, 220, 223

"Triumph of Religion, The" (Lacan), 204

trompe l'oeil painting contest, 191

Trump, Donald, 205

Trump, Mary, xx

truth: Enlightenment and, 195, 200; knowledge and, 19; "Science and Truth," 66; stupidity of, 279

truth, partisanship of: with conflation of neutral and objective, 279; Marx, Freud and, 8–23

unconscious: *The Capitalist Unconscious*, 75, 137, 143; "God is unconscious," 201–2, 217–18, 223, 229, 242; id and, 64; ideology and, 86; *Jokes and Their Relation to the Unconscious*, 85; "The Subversion of the Subject and the Dialectic of Desire in the Freudian Unconscious," 148; as timeless, 63

unpaid labor, 151, 168, 172, 177, 194, 219

"unsocial sociability," 36, 38, 70

Unternehmergewinns (profit of enterprise), 167–69, 179, 194

Urvater (primal father), 35, 40, 201–2, 218

use value: exchange and, 110–12, 115, 170, 178, 179, 181, 186, 227, 276; money with exchange and, 179–80, 185–86

vagina, 188

Varoufakis, Yanis, 213

vehicle (*Träger*), 13, 15

veiling, of capitalism, 190–92, 199–200

Verdinglichung. See reification

Verleugnung (disavowal), 186, 195–96

Vygotsky, Lev, 1, 3, 9, 50–53, 56–59, 66

wages: declining, 104, 214; money as, 109, 194; of workers, 151, 177, 182, 194, 250

wages of superintendence (*Aufsichtslohns*), 167–69, 194

Wallace, Edwin R., 35

Wall Street (film), xii

wealth: billionaires and, 115–16, 156; distribution, 12; "The Drive to Amass Wealth," 94; gaps, xiv, xv; global, xiii; inequality, xiii, xiv, xv, xxi, 32; mania for, 106, 108, 111–12

Wealth of Nations, The (Smith), xii, 103

Weber, Max, 16, 83, 129, 153, 156, 224–25, 229–30, 232–34, 238, 271; with capitalism and religion, 221; historical materialism and, 222; influence of, 264, 266, 267; Marx and, 222–23; with Protestant Christianity, 209; *The Protestant Ethic and the "Spirit" of Capitalism*, 125–26, 221–22; religion and, 223

Weltanschauung, 16; ideology and, 21; Lacan and question of, 23–29; "The Question of a *Weltanschauung*," 17–18, 29–32, 43–45; scientific, 21–24, 26, 143

Western Marxism, 2, 263; antieconomism and, 6, 31, 245–46, 252, 270, 272, 276, 282; as antireductive, 281; defeat and, 271, 276; Frankfurt School and, 270–71, 272, 275; historical materialism and, 245–46, 257; superstructure and, 246

What Is to Be Done? (Lenin), 250

"Why War" (Freud), 13, 42, 48

"*Wo Es war, soll Ich werden*," Freud with, 282

wooden table example, Marx with, 190

Wordsworth, William, 47

work, play and, 61–62

workers, wages of, 151, 177, 182, 194, 250

worldview (*conception du monde*), 10, 16–18, 21, 23–27, 29, 204, 258, 272

World War I, xiv, 119, 207, 271

World War II, 271

Zeuxis, 191

Žižek, Slavoj, 1, 24, 83–88, 132, 200, 210, 283–84

zoon politikon, 8, 36, 38–39, 59, 68, 70

Printed in the USA
CPSIA information can be obtained
at www.ICGtesting.com
JSHW021522270624
65510JS00001B/5